Fractional-Order Systems and Its Applications in Engineering

Fractional-Order Systems and Its Applications in Engineering

Editors

Hassen Fourati
Abdellatif Ben Makhlouf
Omar Naifar

MDPI

Basel • Beijing • Wuhan • Barcelona • Belgrade • Novi Sad • Cluj • Manchester

Editors
Hassen Fourati
Department of Automatic
Control - GIPSA-Lab
Université Grenoble Alpes
Grenoble
France

Abdellatif Ben Makhlouf
Department of Mathematics
Sfax University
Sfax
Tunisia

Omar Naifar
Control and Energy
Management Laboratory
National School of Engineering
Sfax University
Sfax
Tunisia

Editorial Office
MDPI
St. Alban-Anlage 66
4052 Basel, Switzerland

This is a reprint of articles from the Special Issue published online in the open access journal *Symmetry* (ISSN 2073-8994) (available at: www.mdpi.com/journal/symmetry/special_issues/YHI2O8I993).

For citation purposes, cite each article independently as indicated on the article page online and as indicated below:

Lastname, A.A.; Lastname, B.B. Article Title. *Journal Name* **Year**, *Volume Number*, Page Range.

ISBN 978-3-7258-0820-5 (Hbk)
ISBN 978-3-7258-0819-9 (PDF)
doi.org/10.3390/books978-3-7258-0819-9

Contents

About the Editors

Hassen Fourati

Hassen Fourati, PhD, is currently an associate professor of the electrical engineering and computer science at the University of Grenoble Alpes, Grenoble, France, and a member of the Dynamics and Control of Networks Team (DANCE), affiliated with the Pôle Automatique et Diagnostic (PAD) of the GIPSA-Lab. In 2006, hearned his bachelor of engineering degree in electrical engineering at the National Engineering School of Sfax (ENIS), Tunisia; in 2007, he earned his master's degree in automated systems and control at the University of Claude Bernard (UCBL), Lyon, France; and, in 2010, he earned his PhD degree in automatic control at the University of Strasbourg, France. His research interests include nonlinear filtering, estimation and multisensor fusion with applications in navigation, motion analysis, mobility and traffic management. He has published several research papers in scientific journals, international conferences, book chapters and books. He can be reached at hassen.fourati@gipsa-lab.fr.

Abdellatif Ben Makhlouf

Dr. Abdellatif Ben Makhlouf obtained his bachelor's and master's degrees from the Department of Mathematics at University of Sfax, Tunisia, and a Ph.D. in Mathematics in 2015 from University of Sfax, Tunisia. Currently, he is an Associate Professor of Mathematics at University of Sfax, Tunisia. His current research interests include Fractional Differential Equations, Ordinary Differential Equations, Stochastic Differential Equations, Control Theory and Stability Theory.

Omar Naifar

Dr. Omar Naifar completed his Master's degree in Computer Science from the Faculty of Sciences of Sfax at the University of Sfax, Tunisia, in 2010; his Master's project in Automatic and Industrial Computing at the National School of Engineering of Sfax in 2012; his PhD degree in Electrical Engineering in 2015; and his HdR degree in Electrical Engineering at the same institute in 2021. He is a member of the Control and Energy Management Laboratory (CEM-Lab) at the Department of Electrical Engineering of the National School of Engineers of Sfax. Currently, he is an associate professor of electrical engineering at the Higher Institute of Applied Sciences and Technology of Kairouan. He is also an Associate Editor of the international journal *Asian Journal of Control*—Wiley, indexed by the Web of Science Clarivate database. His research interests include robust nonlinear control (higher-order sliding mode, backstepping, and adaptive control), theoretical aspects of nonlinear observer design, control and fault diagnosis, and fractional order control systems.

Preface

As data systems become more effective, more and more mathematical approaches have been applied to real-world applications to achieve exceptional outcomes. Fractional approaches (such as fractional calculus, fractional Fourier analysis, and the linear canonical transform) are gaining importance in the area of mathematics and are gaining attention from the community of applied mathematicians. The theory and method of fractional domain analysis may further define the dynamic process of signal translation from time domains to frequency domains, creating a new avenue for non-stationary signal analyses and treatment studies. In technical domains such as the radar, communications, and sonar domains, fractional approaches are preferable to traditional integral methods because they offer novel concepts, procedures, and ideas. Due to the unpredictability of the sent signal in actual engineering systems and the effect of different disturbances and noises on the transmission process, despite the numerous benefits of these new fractional approaches, a few critical issues still need to be resolved. Simultaneously, fraction theory is confronted with several practical limits in engineering, such as sampling and filtering in the sphere of multidimensional signals. This Special Issue focuses on the current successes and potential difficulties of fractional techniques in engineering theory and applications.

Hassen Fourati, Abdellatif Ben Makhlouf, and Omar Naifar
Editors

symmetry MDPI

Article

A Dynamic Behavior Analysis of a Rolling Mill's Main Drive System with Fractional Derivative and Stochastic Disturbance

Guobo Wang [1,2] and Lifeng Ma [1,2,*]

1 School of Mechanical Engineering, Taiyuan University of Science and Technology, Taiyuan 030024, China; wgb0506@tyust.edu.cn
2 Shanxi Provincial Key Laboratory of Metallurgical Device Design Theory and Technology, Taiyuan 030024, China
* Correspondence: mlf_zgtyust@163.com

Abstract: Taking the random factors into account, a fractional main drive system of a rolling mill with Gaussian white noise is developed. First, the potential deterministic bifurcation is investigated by a linearized stability analysis. The results indicate that the fractional order changes the system from a stable point to a limit cycle with symmetric phase trajectories. Then, the stochastic response is obtained with the aid of the equivalent transformation of the fractional derivative and stochastic averaging methods. It is found that the joint stationary probability density function appears to have symmetric distribution. Finally, the influence of the fractional order and noise intensity on system dynamics behavior is discussed. The study is beneficial to understand the intrinsic mechanisms of vibration abatement.

Keywords: rolling mill system; bifurcation; fractional derivative; stochastic response; noise

Citation: Wang, G.; Ma, L. A Dynamic Behavior Analysis of a Rolling Mill's Main Drive System with Fractional Derivative and Stochastic Disturbance. *Symmetry* **2023**, *15*, 1509. https://doi.org/10.3390/sym15081509

Academic Editors: Hassen Fourati, Abdellatif Ben Makhlouf and Omar Naifar

Received: 29 June 2023
Revised: 22 July 2023
Accepted: 28 July 2023
Published: 31 July 2023

1. Introduction

The rolling mill system is a kind of complex system which combines mechanical, electrical, hydraulic and multiple nonlinear factors. For the convenience of analysis, researchers often highly abstract the system into a 'mass spring' system [1,2]. Yarita, I. et al. [3] are the first scholars to study the vibration problem of rolling mills. They analyzed the influence of process parameters and emulsion properties on vibration. Tlusty, J. et al. [4] propose that the vertical vibration of a rolling mill is a self-excited vibration caused by a negative damping effect when the phase difference between the rear tension fluctuation and rolling force fluctuation is 90°. In subsequent studies [5], the results all showed that the vibration of the rolling mills was caused by the dynamic change in the rolling mill's structure and the interaction of the rolling process, which caused the self-excited vibration. Therefore, the research focus was shifted to the theoretical modeling of the rolling mill structure and rolling process.

In rolling mill production, torsional vibration problems of complex rolling mill systems are inevitable [6,7]. For example, in the case of a sudden load (such as steel biting, steel throwing, etc.) [8,9] or a roll slipping, the static and stable state of the roller's connecting shaft torque is changed, resulting in a torsional vibration phenomenon of rolling mills. Therefore, it is very important and necessary to study the dynamics and responses of rolling mill systems [10,11].

In the past decades, fractional systems have attracted much attention and have been extensively studied in many scientific and engineering fields [12–14], such as bioengineering [15,16], automatic control [17], signal processing [18,19], quantum evolutionary complex systems [20], etc. Fractional systems have many better properties than integer-order differential systems. Because of this, some works have studied the effects of fractional order derivatives on the dynamic properties of rolling mill systems [21,22]. In 2014, Zhang [11] studied the dynamic properties of a class of rolling mill systems, and mainly analyzed the

Hopf analysis properties of the system. However, the influence of the fractional derivative on the dynamics of the system was ignored. Wang [23] analyzed the Hopf bifurcation control for the main drive delay system of rolling mills. However, the study did not consider the impact of noise on the system.

In addition, random factors are ubiquitous and non-negligible [24–29]. Actually, there are lots of random factors in rolling mill systems and rolling process [30,31]. However, there was little literature concerning the effect of stochastic excitations on the dynamics of the rolling mill system. Based on the above analysis, different from the previous studies on rolling mill systems, this paper considers the stochastic response of rolling mill systems. With the aid of the equivalent transformation of a fractional derivative and the stochastic averaging method, the effect of noise and the fractional derivative on the dynamics of the concerned system is indicated. Our results also provide a new perspective to studies on dynamical analysis of rolling mill systems. We end this part by highlighting the novelties and contributions of this work as follows:

- The fractional derivative and random factor are simultaneously introduced to the rolling mill's main drive system;
- Combining the equivalent transformation of the fractional derivative with the stochastic averaging method, we obtain the stochastic response of the proposed system;
- The influence of fractional derivative and noise intensity on system dynamics behavior is revealed.

The structure of this study is underscored as follows. In Section 2, the model of a rolling mill system with fractional damping and noise is designed. Simplification and an approximate analytical solution of the rolling mill model are presented in Section 3. In Section 4, deterministic bifurcation of the fractional rolling mill system is studied theoretically and numerically. Subsequently, the stochastic response of rolling mill system is investigated with varied fractional order and noise intensity in Section 5. In Section 6, we conclude this paper.

2. The Rolling Mill's Main Drive System with Fractional Damping and Noise

In this work, the rolling mill's main drive system closely follows Ref. [11] and the dimensionless equation is given below in (1).

$$\ddot{\theta}(t) + \omega^2\theta(t) + k_1\dot{\theta}(t) + k_2\dot{\theta}^2(t) + k_3\dot{\theta}^3(t) = 0. \tag{1}$$

where θ stands for roll angle, and k_1, k_2, k_3 ω are system parameters. The specific meaning of the parameters can be seen in Ref. [11].

As the rolling mill's main drive system (1), there has been almost no consideration of the viscoelastic properties of the damping term and external disturbance of the system. To make the model more general, we adopt a model with fractional derivatives and external disturbance, and its kinetic equation is as follows:

$$\ddot{\theta}(t) + \omega^2\theta(t) + k_1\dot{\theta}(t) + k_2\dot{\theta}^2(t) + k_3\dot{\theta}^3(t) + D^\alpha\theta(t) = \xi(t), \tag{2}$$

where k_1, k_2, k_3 are constants.

The fractional order term is used to model the viscoelasticity of stick-slip friction between rolls and rolled parts and Gaussian white noise is adopted to represent the external stochastic disturbance.

$D^\alpha\eta$ represents the fractional derivative within the Captuo's definition:

$$D^\alpha\theta(t) = \frac{1}{\Gamma(1-\alpha)}\int_0^t (t-\tau)^{-\alpha}\dot{\theta}(t)d\tau, 0 < \alpha \le 1, \tag{3}$$

and $\xi(t)$ represents the Gaussian white noise satisfying the following statistical characteristics:

$$\langle\xi(t)\rangle = 0, \langle\xi(t)\xi(t+h)\rangle = 2d\delta(h). \tag{4}$$

3. Equivalent Model and Theoretical Analysis

In consideration of $0 < \alpha \leq 1$, the term associated with the fractional derivative can be considered to contribute to both the damped term and the stiffness term [32,33].

$$D^{\alpha}\theta \approx \omega^{\alpha-1}\sin\frac{\alpha\pi}{2}\dot{\theta} + \omega^{\alpha}\cos\frac{\alpha\pi}{2}\theta. \tag{5}$$

Substituting (5) into (2):

$$\ddot{\theta}(t) + \omega_0^2\theta(t) + \left(k_1 + \omega^{\alpha-1}\sin\frac{\alpha\pi}{2}\right)\dot{\theta}(t) + k_2\dot{\theta}^2(t) + k_3\dot{\theta}^3(t) = \xi(t), \tag{6}$$

where the dot represents the derivative with respect to t.

$$\omega_0^2 = \omega^2 + \omega^{\alpha}\cos\frac{\alpha\pi}{2}.$$

The new variables transformation is introduced as follows:

$$\begin{aligned} \theta(t) &= a(t)\cos\phi, \\ \phi &= \omega_0 t + \varphi(t). \end{aligned} \tag{7}$$

To take the first derivative of (7), we have

$$\dot{\theta} = \dot{a}\cos\phi - a\omega_0\sin\phi - a\dot{\varphi}\sin\phi. \tag{8}$$

Under the assumption that damping and excitation terms are small, $a(t)$ and $\varphi(t)$ are two slowly varying processes, i.e., the amplitude and the phase will be slowly varying with respect to time. Equation (8) can be simplified as follows:

$$\dot{\theta}(t) = -a(t)\omega_0\sin\phi. \tag{9}$$

Then the potential energy $U(\theta)$ and the total energy H of the system are as follows:

$$\begin{aligned} U(\theta) &= \textstyle\int_0^{\theta}\omega_0^2 x dx = \frac{1}{2}\omega_0^2\theta^2, \\ H &= U(\theta) + \tfrac{1}{2}\dot{\theta}^2. \end{aligned} \tag{10}$$

By aid of (7) and (9), (6) can be rearranged as an equation within variables a and φ,

$$\begin{cases} \dot{a} = \frac{\sin\phi}{\omega_0}[f - \xi(t)], \\ \dot{\varphi} = \frac{\cos\phi}{a\omega_0}[f - \xi(t)], \end{cases} \tag{11}$$

where

$$f = -(k_1 + \omega^{\alpha-1}\sin\frac{\alpha\pi}{2})a\omega_0\sin\phi + k_2a^2\omega_0^2\sin^2\phi - k_3a^3\omega_0^3\sin^3\phi.$$

To derive the stochastic equations for $a(t)$ and $\varphi(t)$, we take the average of Equation (11) over one period base on the method of stochastic averaging [34,35].

$$\begin{cases} da = (F_1 + \frac{d}{2a\omega_0^2})dt + \sqrt{\frac{d}{\omega_0^2}}dW_0(t), \\ d\varphi = F_2 dt + \frac{1}{a}\sqrt{\frac{d}{\omega_0^2}}dW_1(t)\ , \end{cases} \tag{12}$$

where

$$\begin{aligned} F_1 &= \tfrac{1}{2\pi}\textstyle\int_0^{2\pi}\frac{f}{\omega_0}\sin\varphi d\varphi, \\ F_2 &= \tfrac{1}{2\pi}\textstyle\int_0^{2\pi}\frac{f}{a\omega_0}\cos\varphi d\varphi\ . \end{aligned}$$

The amplitude $a(t)$ and phase $\varphi(t)$ are decoupled to independent variables. Then, we can derive the first derivative moment and second derivative moment of amplitude $a(t)$ as follows:

$$\begin{aligned} \bar{a}_1 &= -\tfrac{1}{2}(k_1 + \omega^{\alpha-1}\sin\tfrac{\alpha\pi}{2})a - \tfrac{3}{8}k_3\omega_0^2 a^3 + \tfrac{d}{2a\omega_0^2}, \\ \bar{b}_{11} &= \tfrac{d}{\omega_0^2}. \end{aligned} \quad (13)$$

Then, the Fokker–Planck–Kolmogorov (FPK) equation of the transition probability density function complies with the following equation:

$$\frac{\partial p(a,t)}{\partial t} = -\frac{\partial}{\partial a}[\bar{a}_1 p(a,t)] + \frac{1}{2}\frac{\partial}{\partial a^2}[\bar{b}_{11} p(a,t)] .$$

Letting $\frac{\partial p(a,t)}{\partial t} = 0$, one ultimately derives the expression of the stationary density in (14).

$$P(a) = Na\exp\left[\frac{\omega_0^2}{2d}(k_1 + \omega^{\alpha-1}\sin\frac{\alpha\pi}{2})a^2 - \frac{3\omega_0^4}{16d}k_3 a^4\right], \quad (14)$$

where N is normalization constant,

$$N = 1\bigg/\int_0^{+\infty} a\exp\left[\frac{\omega_0^2}{2d}(k_1 + \omega^{\alpha-1}sin\frac{\alpha\pi}{2})a^2 - \frac{3\omega_0^4}{16d}k_3 a^4\right]da.$$

Meanwhile, the total energy $H = U(a) = \frac{1}{2}\omega_0^2 a^2$, the stationary PDF of the total energy H can be obtained as follows:

$$P(H) = P(a)\left|\frac{da}{dH}\right| = \frac{P(a)}{\omega_0^2 a}. \quad (15)$$

Then the joint PDF of the displacement θ and velocity $\dot{\theta}$ is as follows:

$$\begin{aligned} P(\theta,\dot{\theta}) &= \tfrac{P(H)}{T(H)}\Big|_{H=\frac{1}{2}\omega^2\theta^2+\frac{1}{2}\dot{\theta}^2} \\ &= N\exp\left[\tfrac{\omega_0^2}{2d}(k_1 + \omega^{\alpha-1}\sin\tfrac{\alpha\pi}{2})(\theta^2 + \tfrac{\theta^2}{\omega_0^2}) - \tfrac{3\omega_0^4}{16d}k_3(\theta^2 + \tfrac{\theta^2}{\omega_0^2})^2\right]. \end{aligned} \quad (16)$$

In the above equation, $H = \frac{1}{2}\omega^2\theta^2 + \frac{1}{2}\dot{\theta}^2$, $T(H) = \frac{2\pi}{\omega_0}$, N is normalization constant,

$$N = 1\bigg/\int_{-\infty}^{+\infty}\int_{-\infty}^{+\infty} \exp\left[\frac{\omega_0^2}{2d}(k_1 + \omega^{\alpha-1}sin\frac{\alpha\pi}{2})(\theta^2 + \frac{\dot{\theta}^2}{\omega_0^2}) - \frac{3\omega_0^4}{16d}k_3(\theta^2 + \frac{\dot{\theta}^2}{\omega_0^2})^2\right]d\theta d\dot{\theta}.$$

4. Deterministic Case

In this section, we will investigate the potential bifurcation phenomenon of the rolling mill's main drive system without stochastic disturbance ($d = 0$). Then, (6) reduces to the following equation:

$$\ddot{\theta}(t) + \omega_0\theta(t) + \left(k_1 + \omega^{\alpha-1}\sin\frac{\alpha\pi}{2}\right)\dot{\theta}(t) + k_2\dot{\theta}^2(t) + k_3\dot{\theta}^3(t) = 0. \quad (17)$$

The eigenvalues of the Jacobian can be obtained in virtue of linearizing Equation (11) at $(\theta,\dot{\theta}) = (0,0)$

$$\lambda_{12} = \frac{1}{2}\left[-(k_1 + \omega^{\alpha-1}\sin\frac{\alpha\pi}{2}) \pm \sqrt{(k_1 + \omega^{\alpha-1}\sin\frac{\alpha\pi}{2})^2 - 4\omega_0^2}\right], \quad (18)$$

which yields the Hopf bifurcation condition as follows:

$$k_1 + \omega^{\alpha-1} \sin \frac{\alpha\pi}{2} = 0. \quad (19)$$

Next, the details of the bifurcation with the variation in the fractional order α will be explored. The parameters $k_2 = 0.01,\ k_3 = 0.05$ are fixed. The bifurcation diagram in parameter plane $k_1 - \alpha$ can be found and is shown in Figure 1 based on Equation (19).

Figure 1 shows that the red curve (the edge of the Hopf bifurcation) divides the parametric space into two regions. Subsequently, we fix $k_1 = -0.95$ and investigate the bifurcation on the fractional order q that vary along the horizontal dotted line in Figure 1. When $\alpha < 0.797$, the rolling mill's main drive system yields a stable limit cycle. When $\alpha > 0.797$, one yields a stable steady state.

The phase diagrams with fractional order of 0.7, 0.75, 0.85 are depicted in Figure 2. The time history diagram with fractional orders of 0.7, 0.75, 0.85 are depicted in Figure 3. In Figures 2 and 3, the same representative initial condition $I_1 = (\theta, \dot{\theta}) = (0.1, 0), I_2 = (\theta, \dot{\theta}) = (1, 0)$ are selected. A scrutiny of Figures 2 and 3 indicates that the phase diagram the rolling mill's main drive system changes from a limit cycle to a stable steady state along with the increase in the fractional order. This confirms the validity of our research results.

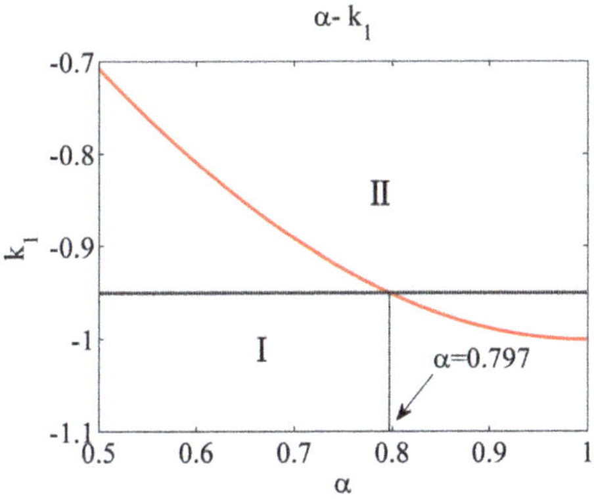

Figure 1. Bifurcation diagram of the deterministic system for $k_2 = 0.01,\ k_3 = 0.05$; The red curve denotes the edge of the Hopf bifurcation.

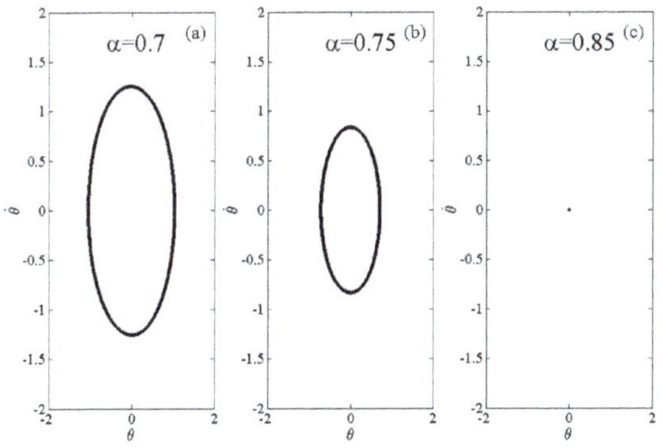

Figure 2. Phase planes of the deterministic system for different fractional order: (**a**) $\alpha = 0.7$, the system yields a large limit cycle; (**b**) $\alpha = 0.75$, the system yields a small limit cycle; (**c**) $\alpha = 0.85$, the system yields a stable steady state.

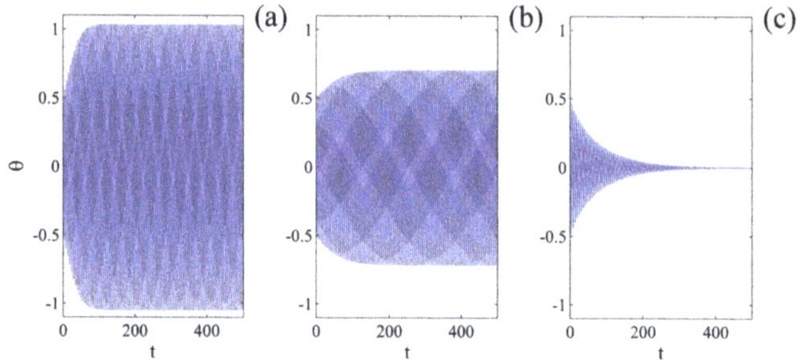

Figure 3. The time history diagram of θ in the deterministic system: (**a**) $\alpha = 0.7$; (**b**) $\alpha = 0.75$; (**c**) $\alpha = 0.85$.

5. Stochastic Case

As is well known, noise is omnipresent in many dynamics systems. Therefore, it is important to study the response of the the rolling mill's main drive system in the presence of noise. Subsequently, the effect of noise intensity and fractional order will be investigated in the rolling mill's main drive system. The parameters $k_1 = -0.95,\ k_2 = 0.01, k_3 = 0.05$ are fixed.

5.1. *Effect of Noise Intensity*

The effects of noise intensity d on the rolling mill's main drive system will be studied in this part. The theoretical results and numerical results of the stationary probability density function (PDF) $P(a)$ and joint stationary probability density function $P(\theta, \dot{\theta})$ are obtained and shown in Figures 4 and 5.

As can be seen from Figure 4, the stationary PDF $P(a)$ for different noise intensity showed a unimodal shape. Firstly, for noise intensity $d = 0.02$, the peak of the stationary PDF $P(a)$ corresponds to a smaller amplitude (see curve 1). For noise intensity $d = 0.06$, the amplitude corresponding to the peak of the stationary PDF becomes larger(see curve 2). With the noise intensity further increase ($d = 0.12$), the amplitude corresponding to the peak of the PDF still increases further (see curve 3). This implies that the system response is concentrated near a certain amplitude in the presence of noise and increases gradually with the monotonically increasing of noise intensity.

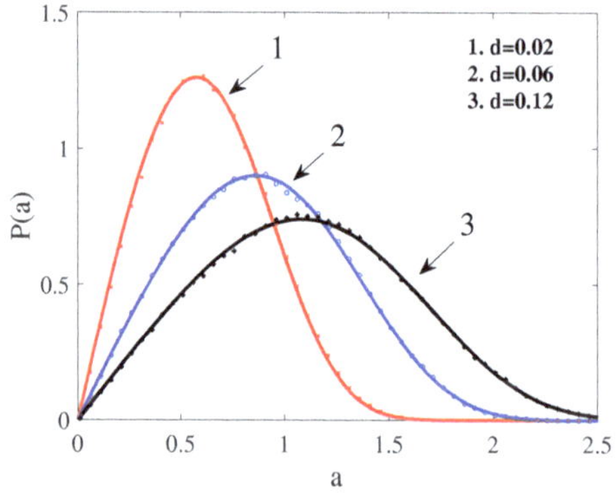

Figure 4. The stationary probability density function $P(a)$ of the amplitude for different noise intensity d with $k_1 = -0.95,\ k_2 = 0.01,\ k_3 = 0.05,\ \alpha = 0.9$. The lines denote the analytical results, whereas dots represent the numerical results.

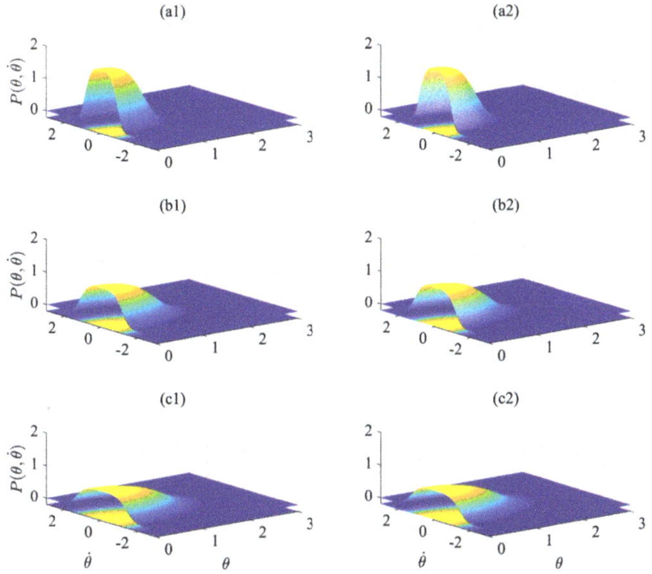

Figure 5. The joint stationary probability density function $P(\theta, \dot{\theta})$ with different noise intensity d. The the left side of the figure represent the analytic results and the right side denotes the numerical results. (**a1**, **a2**) $d = 0.002$, (**b1**, **b2**) $d = 0.06$, (**c1**, **c2**) $d = 0.12$.

5.2. Effect of Fractional Order

The effects of fractional order on the rolling mill's main drive system have been studied in this subsection. The theoretical results and numerical results of the stationary PDF $P(a)$ and joint stationary PDF $P(\theta, \dot{\theta})$ are obtained and shown Figures 6 and 7.

It reflects that both the stationary PDF $P(a)$ for different noise intensities showed a unimodal shape in Figure 6. Firstly, for fractional order $\alpha = 0.6$, the peak of the stationary PDF $P(a)$ corresponds to a larger amplitude (see curve 1). For fractional order $\alpha = 0.7$, the amplitude corresponding to the peak of the stationary PDF $P(a)$ becomes smaller (see curve 2). With the fractional order further increasing ($\alpha = 0.95$, see curve 3), the amplitude corresponding to the peak of the stationary PDF $P(a)$ still decreases further. This implies that the system response is concentrated near a certain amplitude in the presence of noise and decreases gradually with the monotonically increasing of fractional order.

To conclude, all of the above results mirror that noise intensity and fractional order can modulate the amplitude corresponding to the peak of the stationary PDF's left shift or right shift. The evolution of the response with the monotonic increasing of noise intensity and fractional order indicate that the noise intensity is conducive to modulate a larger amplitude. In contrast, the fractional order is conducive to induce a small amplitude.

It is worth pointing out that the response of the rolling mill's main drive system for different fractional orders yields a limit cycle or a stable fixed point in the absence of noise. Nevertheless, both the stationary probability density functions $P(a)$ for different system parameters (noise intensity and fractional order) showed a unimodal shape in the presence of noise. The theoretical and numerical results of the stationary probability density function $P(a)$ and joint stationary probability density function $P(\theta, \dot{\theta})$ verify the validity of the conclusion.

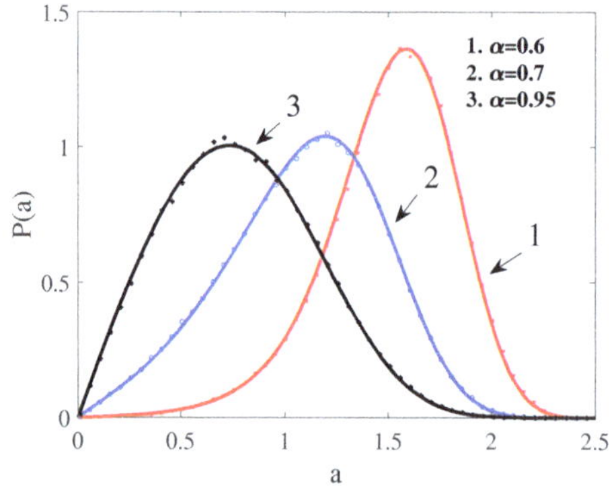

Figure 6. The stationary probability density function $P(a)$ of the amplitude for different fractional order α with $k_1 = -0.95$, $k_2 = 0.01, k_3 = 0.05$, $d = 0.04$. The lines denote the analytical results, whereas dots represent the numerical results.

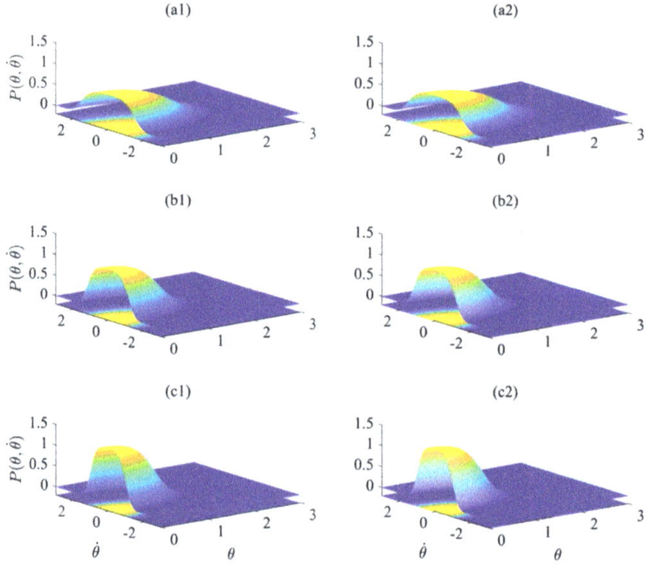

Figure 7. The joint stationary probability density function $P(\theta, \dot{\theta})$ with distinct values of α. The left side of the figure represent the analytic results and the right side denotes the numerical results. (**a1**, **a2**) $\alpha = 0.6$, (**b1**, **b2**) $\alpha = 0.7$, (**c1**, **c2**) $\alpha = 0.95$.

6. Conclusions and Discussion

In a summary, the rolling mill's main drive system with a fractional order derivative and stochastic disturbance was considered. The dynamics of the rolling mill's main drive system was investigated both in the absence and in the presence of stochastic disturbance.

For the absence of stochastic disturbance, the deterministic bifurcations induced by fractional order were explored based on the linearization method and a numerical simulation for the rolling mill's main drive system. The results indicated that fractional order can change the system from a stable point to a limit cycle.

For the presence of stochastic disturbance, the response of the rolling mill's main drive system was investigated with varying the fractional order and noise intensity. The evolution of the response with the monotonic increase in noise intensity and fractional order implied that the noise intensity was conducive to modulate a larger amplitude. In contrast, the fractional order was conducive to induce a small amplitude. Therefore, it provides an efficient strategy to control the system so that the amplitude of the vibration was small enough when the vibration occurs, which is going to be our later work.

In this paper, the rolling mill's main drive system with fractional order and stochastic disturbance is considered and the dynamic response is investigated both in the absence and presence of stochastic disturbance. We mainly focused on the impact of Gaussian white noise and fractional order on the dynamic behavior of the system. The impact of other types of noise and time delays on the dynamic behavior of the system is also a problem that needs further research.

Author Contributions: Formal analysis, G.W.; methodology, G.W.; writing—original draft preparation, G.W.; writing—review and editing, G.W. and L.M.; supervision, L.M. All authors have read and agreed to the published version of the manuscript.

Funding: This work is supported by the National Natural Science Foundation of China (Grant No. U1910213).

Institutional Review Board Statement: Not applicable.

Informed Consent Statement: Not applicable.

Data Availability Statement: Not applicable.

Conflicts of Interest: The authors declare no conflict of interest.

References

1. Mao, D.H.; Zhang, Y.F.; Nie, Z.H.; Liu, Q.H.; Zhong, J. Effects of ultrasonic treatment on structure of roll casting aluminum strip. *J. Cent. South Univ. Technol.* **2007**, *14*, 363–369. [CrossRef]
2. He, J.; Yu, S.; Zhong, J. Modeling for driving systems of four-high rolling mill. *Trans. Nonferrous Met. Soc. China* **2002**, *12*, 88–92.
3. Yarita, K.; Furukawa, K.; Seino, Y.; Takimoto, T.; Nakazato, Y.; Nakagawa, K. An analysis of chattering in cold rolling for ultrathin gauge steel strip. *Trans. Iron Steel Inst. Jpn.* **1978**, *18*, 1–10. [CrossRef]
4. Tlusty, J.; Chandra, G.; Critchley, S.; Paton, D. Chatter in cold rolling. *Cirp Ann.* **1982**, *31*, 195–199. [CrossRef]
5. Chefneux, L.; Fischbach, J.P.; Gouzou, J. Study and industrial control of chatter in cold rolling. *Iron Steel Eng.* **1984**, *61*, 17–26.
6. Dhaouadi, R.; Kubo, K.; Tobise, M. Two-degree-offreedom robust speed controller for high-performance rolling mill drives. *IEEE Trans. Ind. Appl.* **1993**, *29*, 919–926. [CrossRef]
7. Wang, Z.; Wang, D. Dynamic characteristics of a rolling mill drive system with backlash in rolling slippage. *J. Mater. Process. Technol.* **2000**, *97*, 69–73. [CrossRef]
8. Kashay, A.M. Torque Amplification and Vibration Investigation Project. *Iron Steel Eng.* **1973**, *50*, 55–70.
9. Klamka, J. Torque amplification and torsional vibration in large reversing mill drive. *Iron Steel Eng.* **1969**, *5*, 54–66.
10. Ding, Q.; Cooper, J.E.; Leung, A.Y.T. Hopf bifurcation analysis of a rotor/seal system. *J. Sound Vib.* **2002**, *252*, 817–833. [CrossRef]
11. Zhang, R.; Yang, P.; Cui, C. Hopf bifurcation for nonlinear delay system of rolling mill main drive. *J. Vib. Meas. Diagn.* **2014**, *234*, 909–914.
12. Mainardi, F. *Fractional Calculus and Waves in Linear Viscoelasticity: An Introduction to Mathematical Models*; World Scientific: Singapore, 2010.
13. Caponetto, R. *Fractional Order Systems: Modeling and Control Applications*; World Scientific: Singapore, 2010.
14. Monje, C.A.; Chen, Y.; Vinagre, B.M.; Xue, D.; Feliu-Batlle, V. *Fractional-Order Systems and Controls: Fundamentals and Applications*; Springer Science & Business Media: Berlin/Heidelberg, Germany, 2010.
15. Carpinteri, A.; Mainardi, F. *Fractals and Fractional Calculus in Continuum Mechanics*; Springer: Berlin/Heidelberg, Germany, 2014; p. 378.
16. Rossikhin, Y.A.; Shitikova, M.V. Application of fractional calculus for dynamic problems of solid mechanics: Novel trends and recent results. *Appl. Mech. Rev.* **2010**, *63*, 010801. [CrossRef]
17. Agrawal, O.P. A general formulation and solution scheme for fractional optimal control problems. *Nonl. Dyn.* **2004**, *38*, 323–337. [CrossRef]
18. Ozaktas, H.M.; Kutay, M.A. *2001 European Control Conference (ECC)*; IEEE: Piscataway, NJ, USA, 2001; pp. 1477–1483.
19. Das, S.; Pan, I. *Fractional Order Signal Processing: Introductory Concepts and Applications*; Springer Science & Business Media: Berlin/Heidelberg, Germany, 2011.
20. Kusnezov, D.; Bulgac, A.; Do Dang, G. Quantum levy processes and fractional kinetics. *Phys. Rev. Lett.* **1999**, *82*, 1136. [CrossRef]
21. Rossikhin, Y.A.; Shitikova, M.V. Analysis of damped vibrations of linear viscoelastic plates with damping modeled with fractional derivatives. *Signal Process.* **2006**, *86*, 2703–2711. [CrossRef]

22. Xie, J.; Zheng, Y.; Ren, Z.; Wang, T.; Shen, G. Numerical vibration displacement solutions of fractional drawing self-excited vibration model based on fractional Legendre functions. *Complexity* **2019**, *2019*, 9234586. [CrossRef]
23. Wang, J.; Ma, L.; Wang, Y. Hopf bifurcation control for the main drive delay system of rolling mill. *Adv. Differ. Equ.* **2020**, *2020*, 211. [CrossRef]
24. Duan, J.Q. *An Introduction to Stochastic Dynamics*; Cambridge University Press: Cambridge, UK, 2015.
25. Liu, J.K.; Xu, W. An averaging result for impulsive fractional neutral stochastic differential equations. *Appl. Math. Lett.* **2021**, *114*, 106892. [CrossRef]
26. Liu, J.K.; Wei, W.; Xu, W. An averaging principle for stochastic fractional differential equations driven by fBm involving impulses. *Fractal Fract.* **2022**, *6*, 256. [CrossRef]
27. Zakharova, A.; Vadivasova, T.; Anishchenko, V.; Koseska, A.; Kurths, J. Stochastic bifurcations and coherencelike resonance in a self-sustained bistable noisy oscillator. *Phys. Rev. E* **2010**, *81*, 011106. [CrossRef]
28. Jin, C.; Sun, Z.K.; Xu, W. Stochastic bifurcations and its regulation in a Rijke tube model. *Chaos Soliton Fract* **2022**, *154*, 111650. [CrossRef]
29. Liu, J.; Wei, W.; Wang, J.; Xu, W. Limit behavior of the solution of Caputo-Hadamard fractional stochastic differential equations. *Appl. Math. Lett.* **2023**, *140*, 108586. [CrossRef]
30. Xu, B.Y.; Wang, X.D.; Liu, Y.L.; Feng, H.C. Strip Rolling Mill Random Vibration Analysis Based on Pseudo-Excitation Method. *Appl. Mech. Mater.* **2012**, *143*, 250–254. [CrossRef]
31. Xu, B.Y.; Liu, Y.L.; Wang, X.D.; Dong, F. Stochastic Excitation Model of Strip Rolling Mill. *Appl. Mech. Mater.* **2011**, *216*, 378–382. [CrossRef]
32. Shen, Y.J.; Wei, P.; Yang, S.P. Primary resonance of fractional-order van der Pol oscillator. *Nonlinear Dyn.* **2014**, *77*, 1629–1642. [CrossRef]
33. Yang, Y.; Xu, W.; Gu, X.D. Stochastic response of a class of self-excited systems with Caputo-type fractional derivative driven by Gaussian white noise. *Chaos Soliton Fract* **2015**, *77*, 190–204. [CrossRef]
34. Zhu, W.Q.; Lin, Y.K. Stochastic averaging of energy envelope. *J. Eng. Mech.* **1991**, *117*, 1890–1905. [CrossRef]
35. Gu, X.; Zhu, W. A stochastic averaging method for analyzing vibro-impact systems under Gaussian white noise excitations. *J. Sound. Vib.* **2014**, *333*, 2632–2642. [CrossRef]

Disclaimer/Publisher's Note: The statements, opinions and data contained in all publications are solely those of the individual author(s) and contributor(s) and not of MDPI and/or the editor(s). MDPI and/or the editor(s) disclaim responsibility for any injury to people or property resulting from any ideas, methods, instructions or products referred to in the content.

Article

A Fractional-Order Density-Dependent Mathematical Model to Find the Better Strain of *Wolbachia*

Dianavinnarasi Joseph [1], Raja Ramachandran [2,3], Jehad Alzabut [4,5,*], Sayooj Aby Jose [6,7] and Hasib Khan [4,8]

[1] Centre for Nonlinear Systems, Chennai Institute of Technology, Chennai 600069, India
[2] Ramanujan Centre for Higher Mathematics, Alagappa University, Karaikudi 630004, India
[3] Department of Computer Science and Mathematics, Lebanese American University, Beirut 1102-2801, Lebanon
[4] Department of Mathematics and Sciences, Prince Sultan University, Riyadh 11586, Saudi Arabia
[5] Department of Industrial Engineering, OSTIM Technical University, Ankara 06374, Turkey
[6] Department of Mathematics, Alagappa University, Karaikudi 630004, India
[7] School of Mathematics & Statistics, Mahatma Gandhi University, Kottayam 686560, India
[8] Department of Mathematics, Shaheed Benazir Bhutto University Sheringal Dir Upper, Khyber Pakhtunkhwa 18000, Pakistan
* Correspondence: jalzabut@psu.edu.sa

Abstract: The primary objective of the current study was to create a mathematical model utilizing fractional-order calculus for the purpose of analyzing the symmetrical characteristics of *Wolbachia* dissemination among *Aedes aegypti* mosquitoes. We investigated various strains of *Wolbachia* to determine the most sustainable one through predicting their dynamics. *Wolbachia* is an effective tool for controlling mosquito-borne diseases, and several strains have been tested in laboratories and released into outbreak locations. This study aimed to determine the symmetrical features of the most efficient strain from a mathematical perspective. This was accomplished by integrating a density-dependent death rate and the rate of cytoplasmic incompatibility (CI) into the model to examine the spread of *Wolbachia* and non-*Wolbachia* mosquitoes. The fractional-order mathematical model developed here is physically meaningful and was assessed for equilibrium points in the presence and absence of disease. Eight equilibrium points were determined, and their local and global stability were determined using the Routh–Hurwitz criterion and linear matrix inequality theory. The basic reproduction number was calculated using the next-generation matrix method. The research also involved conducting numerical simulations to evaluate the behavior of the basic reproduction number for different equilibrium points and identify the optimal CI value for reducing disease spread.

Keywords: fractional-order model; wAlbB strain; density-dependent death; CI; *Wolbachia* spread symmetry

1. Introduction

In the realm of biology, it is quite common to observe the prevalence of symmetrical characteristics in various organisms. Mathematical biology is a vast area of research that will provide insight into most relevant real-world biological problems. The most important symmetrical property, i.e., the structure of disease spread among a particular species or among more than one species can be studied through mathematical models. Our study mainly concentrated on finding a biological control to suppress mosquito-borne diseases via mathematical tools. The mosquito leads the world's deadliest animals list by causing more than 0.7 million deaths per annum. Recent data show that annually, 390 million cases of mosquito-borne diseases are recorded. It is estimated that 0.5 million people face severe dengue illness; among them, nearly 3% of people die [1,2]. Mosquito-borne diseases include

DENV, yellow fever virus, Zika virus, West Nile virus, Japanese encephalitis, Chikungunya, etc. Dengue is the most common and life-threatening disease among mosquito-borne diseases [3,4]. The primary vector is *Aedes aegypti*, and the secondary vector is *Aedes albopictus* [5]. If a virus-carrying mosquito bites an uninfected human, that human will become infectious after the latent period (2–4 days). If an uninfected mosquito bites an infected human, then the mosquito will become infectious [6,7].

There is no effective vaccination strategy against dengue due to its four variants (DENV-1, DENV-2, DENV-3, DENV-4). The reason is the invented vaccinations are able to control only one of the variants each. This leads to the fact that there may be a chance of getting a severe infection from other virus variants. The preventive measures are using bed nets, insecticides, repellents, medical intervention, etc. Regardless, these methods are not sustainable, and nowadays mosquitoes are not reacting to insecticides [8,9]. In [10], the authors studied the effectiveness of implementing vaccination against various mosquito-borne diseases. We can thus find a novel and long-lasting strategy to manage illnesses spread by mosquitoes.

Currently, the research focuses on the intervention strategies, such as genetic modifications, the release of sterile mosquitoes, and the release of *Wolbachia*-infected mosquitoes [11]. Currently, the most promising way to control mosquito-borne diseases is releasing the endosymbiotic bacterium called *Wolbachia* into the dengue outbreak areas [12,13]. *Wolbachia* controls the spread of the virus among mosquitoes and the human population in two ways: population suppression and virus blocking. When a *Wolbachia*-infected mosquito bites a virus-infected human, it may become infectious, but there is no possibility for virus transmission from that mosquito to an uninfected human. This bacterium stops the virus's replication and blocks the virus inside the salivary gland. The article [14] studies the important properties of the pathogen blocking of *Wolbachia* in the *Aedes aegypti* population. This property of *Wolbachia* is called virus blocking. The *Wolbachia* bacterium induces cytoplasmic incompatibility in mosquito populations [14]. That is,

- When a *Wolbachia*-infected male mosquito mates with the wild female, the produced eggs will not hatch (CI).
- When a *Wolbachia*-infected female mates with a wild male, then the produced offspring will have *Wolbachia* infection (CI rescue).

Due to the effective properties of *Wolbachia*, this bacterium could provide mosquito-borne disease control methods [15]. More mathematical models are being developed to study the release strategies, such as male release [16], female release [17,18], the constant release strategy, the adaptive release strategy, and the crude adaptive release strategy [19].

Mathematical modeling is an effective tool for understanding and analyzing and may be used to find an optimal way to control the situation [20–23]. The research listed below shows how fractional mathematical models can be used to investigate and manage mosquito-borne diseases through *Wolbachia* intervention. These models could shed light on how to create efficient prevention plans for diseases, including dengue fever, the Zika virus, and chikungunya. In [18], for the propagation of *Wolbachia* in mosquito populations, the authors suggested a fractional-order differential equation model. They demonstrated that the model accurately predicts the phenomena of *Wolbachia*-induced cytoplasmic incompatibility, and they used numerical simulations to illustrate how efficient *Wolbachia* is as a preventative measure. In [24], the authors explore the use of fractional calculus models in understanding the complex dynamics of biological tissues. The authors proposed a model that incorporates both fractional-order derivatives and spatial diffusion and investigated its behavior using numerical simulations. In [25], the authors presented a study on a variable-order fractional version of the Benjamin–Bona–Mahony–Burger equation. The authors employed a pseudo-spectral method to numerically investigate the equation and obtain accurate solutions. The study is important for understanding the behavior of variable-order fractional differential equations, which have applications in various areas of science and engineering. In [26,27], the authors proposed a hybrid collocation method for solving multi-term, time-fractional partial differential equations and presented numerical solutions of variable-order, time-fractional (1+1)- and (1+2)-dimensional advection-dispersion and diffusion models. Throughout history, researchers have done research to eradicate mosquito-borne diseases in various aspects. For example, in [28–35], the interaction between wild mosquitoes and sterile mosquitoes (genetically modified male mosquitoes, when a wild female mosquito mates with a sterile male mosquito, the eggs produced will not hatch) is modeled in several situations, such as two-stage life cycles, incomplete sterility and a density-dependent model. The authors of [36], analyzed the interaction model at various release strategies. In [37], the authors of developed a three-compartmental model by dividing wild mosquito populations into aquatic and adult stages as two compartments and released genetically modified mosquitoes (sterile male mosquitoes) as a third compartment. The method used in the sterile insect release technique was utilized to model the interaction between *Wolbachia*-infected mosquitoes and wild mosquitoes, including the human population in [38–42]. The effects of using vaccination incorporated with a *Wolbachia* releasing strategy was studied in [43,44]. How the stochastic environment affects the *Wolbachia* transmission dynamics, and an impulsive release strategy using integer and fractional-order models, were studied in [18,45], respectively. Researchers modeled the transmission dynamics as different compartmental models considering only adults (females and males) in the aquatic stage; females and males (common groups containing both *Wolbachia* and wild); wild aquatic and *Wolbachia* aquatic wild females and males; *Wolbachia*-infected females and males; etc., with the continuous time model [46] and the discrete time model [47]. Larvae as one compartment and adult as another compartment were considered, and impulsive release of sterile mosquitoes was studied in [48].

In nature, there exist more *Wolbachia* strains, such as *wMel*—partial CI or none (native host: *Drosophila melanogaster*); *wMelPop*—partial CI or none (*Drosophila melanogaster*); *wAu*—no CI, (*Drosophila simulans*); *wMelCS*—low or none (*Drosophila melanogaster*); *wInn*—male killing, no CI (*Drosophila innubila*); *wPip*—high CI (*Culex pipiens*); and *wAlbB*—high CI (*Aedes albopictus*) [49].

Motivated by the existing literature, our main aim was to find the answer to, 'What is the best strain of *Wolbachia* to control mosquito-borne diseases?' Secondly, we studied whether when we release laboratory-reared mosquitoes into the wild mosquito population, there will exist some decay in both mosquitoes population due to the competition developed by density.

Main contributions of this article are listed as follows:

- The failure of integer order systems to accurately predict certain phenomena is a widely recognized issue, and thus, the use of fractional-order systems is a natural extension in many fields. This article presents a novel 10-compartmental, fractional-order, density dependent mathematical model. Then, we checked the model's eligibility by performing various mathematical analyses.
- A new parameter describing the CI mechanism in both the mosquito population and controlling the disease spread by reducing the population size of wild mosquitoes is introduced. Owing to this parameter's inclusion, we are able to find the better strain in the sense of having perfect CI.
- In the existing literature, vaccination strategies are included while developing a model. However, we neglected the vaccination strategy because there exists a licensed vaccination called Dengvaxia (CYD-TDV), and five more are in trials. Regardless, WHO recommends these vaccines to people who have a history of dengue infection. Although there are four different stereotypes of dengue virus (DENV-1, DENV-2, DENV-3, DENV-4), the invented vaccinations are not able to control all four DENVs. They provide immunity against one and do not provide immunity against the other three. For this reason, there is a chance of having severe dengue infection by the remaining three variants. This aspect of vaccination is considered seriously and neglected in the vaccination strategy from the disease-controlling process.
- Our proposed model shows that when there is the existence of *Wolbachia*-infected mosquitoes, there is a notable change in the spread of disease. We derived the basic

reproduction number of the disease and analyzed it at possible equilibrium points. The derived numerical results show that our releasing strategy is physically meaningful, and at some point, it works as a better strategy to control mosquito-borne diseases.
- Dynamical analysis of the proposed model is depicted as a time-series plot by numerically solving our model.

This article is structured as follows: The detailed methodology is presented in Section 2. Preliminaries take place in Section 3, and complete information about the development of integer and fractional-order models is presented in Section 4. Section 5 is about some properties of the proposed fractional-order model. Analysis of the model in terms of basic reproduction number, disease free equilibria, endemic equilibria, and their local and global stabilities is presented in Section 6. In Section 7, the sensitivity of the parameters is discussed. Numerical simulations are presented in Section 8, and the results are concluded in Section 9.

2. Methodology

(i) First we propose a fractional-order mathematical model using Caputo fractional derivative to expose the interaction dynamics of *Wolbachia*-infected, *Wolbachia*-uninfected mosquitoes and humans. Moreover, the influences of imperfect maternal transmission and density-dependent death rates are considered in mosquito populations.
(ii) To find the basic reproduction number, we used a next-generation method [50].
(iii) The local stability of four cases of the disease-free equilibrium and three cases of endemic equilibrium are analyzed by finding determinants and traces of the corresponding Jacobian matrix (Routh–Hurwitz criterion).
(iv) The global stability of the developed model is derived from linear matrix inequality theory and Lyapunov theory.
(v) Numerical simulations to prove the effectiveness of the parameters used in the model formulations and to show how the system dynamics are influenced by various *Wolbachia* strains.

3. Preliminaries

Definition 1. *(Caputo derivative) [51] M. Caputo in [52] derived a certain solution for a fractional-order differential equation as*

$$ {}_b^cD_t^\alpha g(t) = \frac{1}{\Gamma(\alpha-m)}\int_b^t \frac{g^{(n)}(s)\,\mathrm{d}s}{(t-s)^{\alpha+1-m}}, \quad m-1<\alpha<m. $$

For $\alpha \to m$, the Caputo derivative becomes a conventional m^{th} derivative of $g(t)$. Here, the operator ${}_b^cD_t^\alpha g(t)$ represents a fractional operator with an initial condition b, independent variable t, fractional-order α and c denoting that it is Caputo-sense.

Lemma 1 ([51]). *The following equation denotes the fractional differential equation in a Caputo sense:*

$$ \begin{aligned} {}_a^cD_t^\alpha x(t) &= f(t,x(t)) \\ x(t_0) &= x_0 \end{aligned} $$

The above equation is said to have an equilibrium point or fixed point x^* if it satisfies $f(t,x^*)=0$.

Lemma 2 ([53]). *A_1, A_2 and A_3 are $n\times n$ matrices with $A_1 = A_1^\top > 0$ and $A_2 = A_2^\top > 0$. Then,*

$$ A_1 + A_3^\top A_2^{-1} A_3 < 0 $$

if and only if

$$\begin{bmatrix} A_1 & A_3^\top \\ A_3 & -A_2 \end{bmatrix} < 0$$

or

$$\begin{bmatrix} -A_2 & A_3 \\ A_3^\top & A_1 \end{bmatrix} < 0.$$

Lemma 3 ([54]).

$$\Phi^\top(t)\Theta F(\Phi(t)) \leq \frac{1}{2\sigma}\Phi^\top(t)(\Theta\Theta^\top)\Phi(t) + \frac{\sigma}{2}F^\top(\Phi(t))F(\Phi(t))$$

where $\sigma > 0$ be scalar, $\Phi, F(\Phi(t)) \in \mathbb{R}^n$ and Θ is a matrix.

Definition 2. *(Laplace transformation) The Laplace transformation of the function which is defined in the sense of a Caputo derivative is as follows:*

$$\mathfrak{L}\{{}_a^c D_t^\alpha G(t), r\} = r^\alpha G(r) - \sum_{j=0}^{n-1} r^{\alpha-j-1} G^{(j)}(0),$$

where $\alpha \in (n-1, n)$ and n is a natural number.

The Mittag–Leffler function is shown by

$$E_{a,b} = \sum_{j=0}^{\infty} \frac{g^j}{\Gamma(aj+b)}$$

and the Laplace transform is

$$\mathfrak{L}\left[t^b E_{a,b}(\pm a t^a)\right] = \frac{u^{a-b}}{u^a \mp a}$$

4. Model Formulation

The present section is devoted to developing a mathematical model as close as possible to a real-life situation to analyze the symmetrical features. To ensure this, the density-dependent death rate with a fitness cost and the effectiveness of CI are incorporated. Through the developed model, we tried to find the answers to the following questions:

- How does the release of *Wolbachia*-mosquitoes affect the wild mosquito population in the sense of reducing the lifespan, occupying the habitats, male feminization, and CI?
- What is the best *Wolbachia* strain to be used in the real world?
- How CI will influence the disease-spread dynamics?

Before developing a physically meaningful mathematical model, a few hypotheses are necessary.

(H1) The three populations in the model are:

M_i *Wolbachia*-infected mosquitoes (both laboratory-reared and offspring having *Wolbachia* after CI rescue).

M_u Non-*Wolbachia* mosquitoes (both local and offspring produced by weak CI).

H Human population.

In contrast to mosquitoes, which are believed to have a variable population size, humans have a steady population size. as, in contrast to a single human generation, mosquitoes have many generations over that period.

(H2) People of all ages and all genders make up the human population.

(H3) The host population is monolithically intermingled. This implies that all individuals, irrespective of age, genetic development, sociocultural context, or geographic region, have almost the same pathogenic traits.
(H4) Only mature females were taken into account for modeling. As they require a blood meal to warm and develop the eggs before they can lay eggs, only sexually active female mosquitoes will engage with people.
(H5) Mosquitoes are divided into six groups representing the state variables: aquatic stage (eggs, larvae, pupae) of *Wolbachia* as M_i and non-*Wolbachia* as M_u. Adult female mosquitoes are divided into four groups: *Wolbachia*-infected and susceptible to virus—$M_{i,s}$; *Wolbachia*-infectious (virus)—$M_{i,i}$; non-*Wolbachia*-infected and susceptible to virus—$M_{u,s}$; and non-*Wolbachia*-infected (virus)—$M_{u,i}$. The human population is divided into four compartments as susceptible S_h, infectious I_h, hospitalized H_h, and recovered R_h. In both populations, we neglected the latent period (exposed) because the time span of latency is much smaller compared with the total life span of the human population and the mosquito population. Additionally, we assumed that $S_h + I_h + H_h + R_h = T_h(Constant)$ and $M_{i,s} + M_{i,i} + M_{u,s} + M_{u,i} = T_{m_i} + T_{m_u} = T_m$ (function of time).
(H6) All newborns are susceptible to the virus; there is no vertical transmission of the disease or heredity in the human population or mosquitoes.
(H7) However, in the case of *Wolbachia* spread. there is vertical transmission and heredity in mosquitoes. Notably, there is no horizontal transmission of *Wolbachia* between mosquito and human population.
(H8) A mosquito acquires an infection when it bites an infected individual, and a person who has been bitten by an infected mosquito contracts the infection as well. Male mosquitoes do not participate in this activity, since they solely feed on nectar.
(H9) There is a chance to generate a density-dependent concurrence for food, habitats, etc., when we intentionally introduce *Wolbachia*-infected mosquitoes as eggs in the form of 'Zancu KIT' and adult mosquitoes via drones, transportation, and manual release into mosquito-borne disease epidemic areas. This fact causes both *Wolbachia* and non-*Wolbachia* mosquitoes to die in a density-dependent manner.
(H10) The parameter c_y denotes the cytoplasmic incompatibility (CI) induced by *Wolbachia*. This CI will serve as a main component in reducing the population size of mosquitoes. As CI is the process that makes the males feminized and reduce the possibility of producing viable progeny. There exist many *Wolbachia* strains, such as $wPop$, $wMel$, $wAlbA$, $wAlbB$, wAu and $wAuWpip$. Among these strains, the superinfected strain $wAlbB$ has the highest CI [55].

4.1. Integer-Order Model

Motivated by [38], we have developed a *Wolbachia*, non-*Wolbachia* and human population interaction model to study symmetrical features:

Wolbachia mosquitoes:

$$\begin{cases} \frac{\mathrm{d}M_i}{\mathrm{d}t} &= \Lambda_1 + r_m\eta M_i - \lambda_{i_a}M_i - \lambda_{d_i}[M_i + M_u]M_i - t_w M_i \\ \frac{\mathrm{d}M_{i,s}}{\mathrm{d}t} &= t_w T_{m_i} - \frac{\alpha_i\rho_{m_h}I_h}{T_h}M_{i,s} - \lambda_{m_i}M_{i,s} \\ \frac{\mathrm{d}M_{i,i}}{\mathrm{d}t} &= \frac{\alpha_i\rho_{m_h}I_h}{T_h}M_{i,s} - \lambda_{m_i}T_m M_{i,i} \end{cases}$$

Non-*Wolbachia* mosquitoes:

$$\begin{cases} \frac{\mathrm{d}M_u}{\mathrm{d}t} &= \Lambda_2 + r_m(1-\eta)M_i - \lambda_{u_a}M_u - \lambda_{d_u}[M_i + M_u]M_i - t_w M_u \\ &\quad + r_m(1-c_y)M_u\frac{M_i}{M_i+M_u} - r_m M_u\frac{M_u}{M_i+M_u} \\ \frac{\mathrm{d}M_{u,s}}{\mathrm{d}t} &= t_w\left(1 - \frac{T_{m_i}}{T_m}\right)T_{m_u} - \frac{\alpha_u\rho_{m_h}I_h}{T_h}M_{u,s} - \lambda_{m_u}M_{u,s} \\ \frac{\mathrm{d}M_{u,i}}{\mathrm{d}t} &= \frac{\alpha_u\rho_{m_h}I_h}{T_h}M_{u,s} - \lambda_{m_u}T_m M_{u,i} \end{cases}$$

Human:

$$
\begin{cases}
\frac{\mathrm{d}\,S_h}{\mathrm{d}\,t} &= r_h - \frac{\alpha_i \rho_{m_i} M_{i,i}}{T_h} S_h - \frac{\alpha_u \rho_{m_u} M_{u,i}}{T_h} S_h - \lambda_h S_h \\
\frac{\mathrm{d}\,I_h}{\mathrm{d}\,t} &= \frac{\alpha_i \rho_{m_i} M_{i,i}}{T_h} S_h + \frac{\alpha_u \rho_{m_u} M_{u,i}}{T_h} S_h - \eta_h I_h - \gamma_{h_1} I_h - \lambda_h I_h \\
\frac{\mathrm{d}\,H_h}{\mathrm{d}\,t} &= \eta_h I_h - \gamma_{h_2} H_h - \lambda_h H_h \\
\frac{\mathrm{d}\,R_h}{\mathrm{d}\,t} &= \gamma_{h_1} I_h + \gamma_{h_2} H_h - \lambda_h R_h,
\end{cases}
\tag{1}
$$

where the initial conditions are $M_i \geq 0$, $M_u \geq 0$, $M_{i,s} \geq 0$, $M_{i,i} \geq 0$, $M_{u,s} \geq 0$, $M_{u,i} \geq 0$, $S_h \geq 0$, $I_h \geq 0$, $H_h \geq 0$, and $R_h \geq 0$. Additionally, the populations are represented as $T_h : [0,\infty) \to \mathbb{R}$ and $T_m : [0,\infty) \to \mathbb{R}$ and each $M_{i,s}, M_{i,i}, M_{u,s}, M_{u,i}, S_h, I_h, H_h, R_h : [0,\infty) \to \mathbb{R}$. For instance, refer Figure 1 to understand the structure of the model (1). The descriptions of variables and parameters are listed in Tables 1 and 2. In this work, all the parameters are assumed to be positive. The terms $r_m\eta$ and $r_m(1-\eta)$ are the rates at which adult mosquitoes emerge with the possibility of having and not having *Wolbachia*. $\frac{\alpha_i \rho_{m_h}}{T_h}$ is the rate at which *Wolbachia* mosquitoes become infectious after taking a blood meal from infected human, and $\frac{\alpha_u \rho_{m_h}}{T_h}$ is the rate at which non-*Wolbachia* mosquitoes become infectious after taking a blood meal from infected human. The term $\frac{\alpha_i \rho_{m_i}}{T_h} + \frac{\alpha_u \rho_{m_u}}{T_h}$ is the rate at which a susceptible human becomes infectious after getting bitten by a infected *Wolbachia* and non-*Wolbachia* mosquitoes. $t_w T_{m_i}$ is the emergence rate of *Wolbachia*-infected mosquitoes from M_i, $M_{i,s}$ and $M_{i,i}$ compartments (including hereditary). Finally, $t_w\left(1 - \frac{T_{m_i}}{T_m}\right) T_{m_u}$ is the term representing the emergence rate of non-*Wolbachia* mosquitoes from M_u, $M_{u,s}$ and $M_{u,i}$ compartments, i.e., a lack of CI.

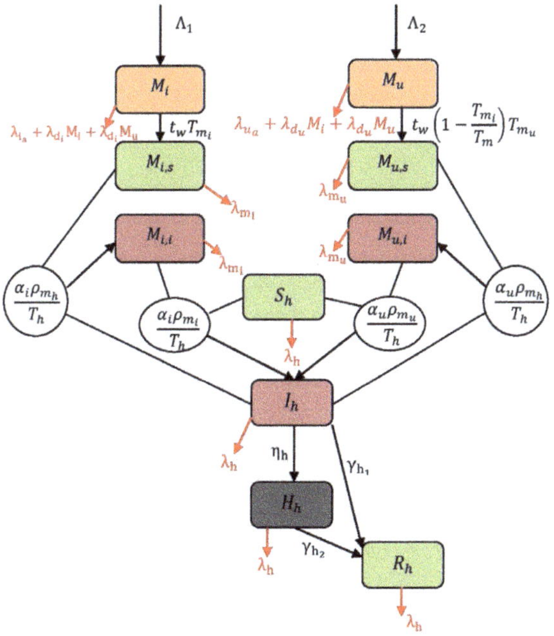

Figure 1. Flow map of virus spread dynamics.

Table 1. Descriptions of variables.

Variables	Description
M_i	The number of *Wolbachia*-infected mosquitoes at time 't'
$M_{i,s}$	The number of *Wolbachia*-infected mosquitoes susceptible
	to Dengue virus at a time 't'
$M_{i,i}$	The number of *Wolbachia*-infected mosquitoes infected by
	Dengue virus at time 't'
M_u	The number of non-*Wolbachia* mosquitoes at time 't'
$M_{u,s}$	The number of non-*Wolbachia* mosquitoes susceptible to
	Dengue virus at time 't'
$M_{u,i}$	The number of non-*Wolbachia* mosquitoes infected by
	Dengue virus at time 't'
S_h	The number of the susceptible human population at a time 't'
I_h	The number of the infectious human population at a time 't'
H_h	The number of hospitalized human population at a time 't'
R_h	The number of recovered human population at a time 't'

Table 2. Descriptions of parameters.

Parameters	Description	Values	Unit	Source
t_w	Reproduction rate of mosquitoes	1.25	1/day	[38]
Λ_2	Reproduction rate of wild mosquitoes	1.25	1/day	[38]
Λ_1	Reproduction rate of *Wolbachia* mosquitoes	$0.95 \times \Lambda_2$	1/day	[56]
r_m	Reproduction rate of mated female mosquitoes	0.4	1/day	[39]
η	fraction of produced offspring having *Wolbachia* infection	$(0,1)$	NA	[39]
$r_m(1-\eta)$	Fraction of produced offspring not having *Wolbachia* infection	$0.9 \times (1-\eta)$	NA	[39]
λ_{i_a}	Natural death rate of *Wolbachia* aquatic mosquitoes	1/14	1/day	[39]
λ_{d_i}	Density-dependent death rate of *Wolbachia* aquatic mosquitoes		1/day	
λ_{u_a}	Natural death rate of non-*Wolbachia* aquatic mosquitoes	1/14	1/day	[57]
λ_{d_u}	Density dependent death rate of non-*Wolbachia* aquatic mosquitoes		1/day	
t_w	Maturation rate of aquatic stage mosquitoes from which adult mosquitoes emerge	0.1	1/day	[57]
α_u	The average bitting rate of non-*Wolbachia* mosquitoes	0.63	1/day	[58]
α_i	Average bitting rate of *Wolbachia* mosquitoes	$0.95 \times \alpha_u$	1/day	[59]
ρ_{m_h}	Probability virus transmission from infected human to *Wolbachia* and non-*Wolbachia* mosquitoes	0.2614	NA	[39]
ρ_{m_i}	Virus transmission probability from infected *Wolbachia* mosquitoes to susceptible human	$0.5 \times \rho_{m_h}$	NA	[60]
ρ_{m_u}	Virus transmission probability from infected non-*Wolbachia* mosquitoes to susceptible human	0.2614	NA	[39]
λ_{m_u}	Mortality rate of non-*Wolbachia* adult mosquitoes	1/14	1/day	[57]
λ_{m_i}	Mortality rate of *Wolbachia* adult mosquitoes	$1.1 \times \lambda_{m_u}$	1/day	[56,61]
r_h	Birth rate of human	0.000012	1/day	[62]
λ_h	Natural death rate of human population	0.000012	1/day	[62]
η_h	Hospitalization rate of identified infected human	0.0904	1/day	[63]
γ_{h_1}	The rate of natural recovery of infected human due to immunity	0.0154	1/day	[63]
γ_{h_2}	The rate of recovery due to hospitalization	0.0840	1/day	[63]

4.2. Factional-Order Model—Caputo Sense

System (1) in terms of the integral form is followed by substituting the value of the kernel as a power-law correlation function. After applying the Caputo fractional derivative of order $\alpha - 1$, we obtain

$$
\begin{aligned}
{}^{c}_{a}D_t^{\alpha-1}\left[\frac{\mathrm{d}\,M_i}{\mathrm{d}\,t}\right] &= {}^{c}_{a}D_t^{\alpha-1}I_t^{\alpha-1}\left[\Lambda_1 + r_m\eta M_i - \lambda_{i_a}M_i - \lambda_{d_i}[M_i+M_u]M_i - t_w M_i\right]\\
{}^{c}_{a}D_t^{\alpha-1}\left[\frac{\mathrm{d}\,M_{i,s}}{\mathrm{d}\,t}\right] &= {}^{c}_{a}D_t^{\alpha-1}I_t^{\alpha-1}\left[t_w T_{m_i} - \frac{\alpha_i\rho_{m_h}I_h}{T_h}M_{i,s} - \lambda_{m_i}T_m M_{i,s}\right]\\
{}^{c}_{a}D_t^{\alpha-1}\left[\frac{\mathrm{d}\,M_{i,i}}{\mathrm{d}\,t}\right] &= {}^{c}_{a}D_t^{\alpha-1}I_t^{\alpha-1}\left[\frac{\alpha_i\rho_{m_h}I_h}{T_h}M_{i,s} - \lambda_{m_i}T_m M_{i,i}\right]\\
{}^{c}_{a}D_t^{\alpha-1}\left[\frac{\mathrm{d}\,M_u}{\mathrm{d}\,t}\right] &= {}^{c}_{a}D_t^{\alpha-1}I_t^{\alpha-1}\left[\Lambda_2 + r_m(1-\eta)M_i - \lambda_{u_a}M_u - \lambda_{d_u}[M_i+M_u]M_i - t_w M_u\right.\\
&\quad \left. + r_m(1-c_y)M_u\frac{M_i}{M_i+M_u} - r_m M_u\frac{M_u}{M_i+M_u}\right]\\
{}^{c}_{a}D_t^{\alpha-1}\left[\frac{\mathrm{d}\,M_{u,s}}{\mathrm{d}\,t}\right] &= {}^{c}_{a}D_t^{\alpha-1}I_t^{\alpha-1}\left[t_w\left(1-\frac{T_{m_i}}{T_m}\right)T_{m_u} - \frac{\alpha_u\rho_{m_h}I_h}{T_h}M_{u,s} - \lambda_{m_u}T_m M_{u,s}\right]\\
{}^{c}_{a}D_t^{\alpha-1}\left[\frac{\mathrm{d}\,M_{u,i}}{\mathrm{d}\,t}\right] &= {}^{c}_{a}D_t^{\alpha-1}I_t^{\alpha-1}\left[\frac{\alpha_u\rho_{m_h}I_h}{T_h}M_{u,s} - \lambda_{m_u}T_m M_{u,i}\right]\\
{}^{c}_{a}D_t^{\alpha-1}\left[\frac{\mathrm{d}\,S_h}{\mathrm{d}\,t}\right] &= {}^{c}_{a}D_t^{\alpha-1}I_t^{\alpha-1}\left[r_h - \frac{\alpha_i\rho_{m_i}M_{i,i}}{T_h}S_h - \frac{\alpha_u\rho_{m_u}M_{u,i}}{T_h}S_h - \lambda_h S_h\right]\\
{}^{c}_{a}D_t^{\alpha-1}\left[\frac{\mathrm{d}\,I_h}{\mathrm{d}\,t}\right] &= {}^{c}_{a}D_t^{\alpha-1}I_t^{\alpha-1}\left[\frac{\alpha_i\rho_{m_i}M_{i,i}}{T_h}S_h + \frac{\alpha_u\rho_{m_u}M_{u,i}}{T_h}S_h - \eta_h I_h - \gamma_{h_1}I_h - \lambda_h I_h\right]\\
{}^{c}_{a}D_t^{\alpha-1}\left[\frac{\mathrm{d}\,H_h}{\mathrm{d}\,t}\right] &= {}^{c}_{a}D_t^{\alpha-1}I_t^{\alpha-1}\left[\eta_h I_h - \gamma_{h_2}H_h - \lambda_h H_h\right]\\
{}^{c}_{a}D_t^{\alpha-1}\left[\frac{\mathrm{d}\,R_h}{\mathrm{d}\,t}\right] &= {}^{c}_{a}D_t^{\alpha-1}I_t^{\alpha-1}\left[\gamma_{h_1}I_h + \gamma_{h_2}H_h - \lambda_h R_h\right]
\end{aligned}
$$

Then, the Caputo-sense fractional-order model for virus transmission dynamics is as follows:

$$
\begin{aligned}
{}^{c}_{a}D_t^{\alpha}M_i &= \Lambda_1 + r_m\eta M_i - \lambda_{i_a}M_i - \lambda_{d_i}[M_i+M_u]M_i - t_w M_i\\
{}^{c}_{a}D_t^{\alpha}M_{i,s} &= t_w T_{m_i} - \frac{\alpha_i\rho_{m_h}I_h}{T_h}M_{i,s} - \lambda_{m_i}T_m M_{i,s}\\
{}^{c}_{a}D_t^{\alpha}M_{i,i} &= \frac{\alpha_i\rho_{m_h}I_h}{T_h}M_{i,s} - \lambda_{m_i}T_m M_{i,i}\\
{}^{c}_{a}D_t^{\alpha}M_u &= \Lambda_2 + r_m(1-\eta)M_i - \lambda_{u_a}M_u - \lambda_{d_u}[M_i+M_u]M_i - t_w M_u\\
&\quad + r_m(1-c_y)M_u\frac{M_i}{M_i+M_u} - r_m M_u\frac{M_u}{M_i+M_u}\\
{}^{c}_{a}D_t^{\alpha}M_{u,s} &= t_w\left(1-\frac{T_{m_i}}{T_m}\right)T_{m_u} - \frac{\alpha_u\rho_{m_h}I_h}{T_h}M_{u,s} - \lambda_{m_u}T_m M_{u,s}\\
{}^{c}_{a}D_t^{\alpha}M_{u,i} &= \frac{\alpha_u\rho_{m_h}I_h}{T_h}M_{u,s} - \lambda_{m_u}T_m M_{u,i}\\
{}^{c}_{a}D_t^{\alpha}S_h &= r_h - \frac{\alpha_i\rho_{m_i}M_{i,i}}{T_h}S_h - \frac{\alpha_u\rho_{m_u}M_{u,i}}{T_h}S_h - \lambda_h S_h\\
{}^{c}_{a}D_t^{\alpha}I_h &= \frac{\alpha_i\rho_{m_i}M_{i,i}}{T_h}S_h + \frac{\alpha_u\rho_{m_u}M_{u,i}}{T_h}S_h - \eta_h I_h - \gamma_{h_1}I_h - \lambda_h I_h\\
{}^{c}_{a}D_t^{\alpha}H_h &= \eta_h I_h - \gamma_{h_2}H_h - \lambda_h H_h\\
{}^{c}_{a}D_t^{\alpha}R_h &= \gamma_{h_1}I_h + \gamma_{h_2}H_h - \lambda_h R_h
\end{aligned}
\tag{2}
$$

with initial conditions $M_u(0) = M_u^0 \geq 0$, $M_i(0) = M_i^0 \geq 0$, $M_{u,s}(0) = M_{u,s}^0 \geq 0$, $M_{u,i}(0) = M_{u,i}^0 \geq 0$, $M_{i,s}(0) = M_{i,s}^0 \geq 0$, $M_{i,i}(0) = M_{i,i}^0 \geq 0$, $S_h(0) = S_h^0 \geq 0$, $I_h(0) = I_h^0 \geq 0$, $H_h(0) = H_h^0 \geq 0$ and $R_h(0) = S_h^0 \geq 0$.

The total human population is $T_h = S_h + I_h + H_h + R_h$. The mosquito population is $T_m = M_i + M_u$ and the total adult female mosquito populations are $T_{m_i} = M_{i,s} + M_{i,i}$ and $T_{m_u} = M_{u,s} + M_{u,i}$.

5. Fundamental Properties

In this section, some fundamental properties of solutions of the proposed model are analyzed for boundedness and positivity.

5.1. Positivity of the Solution

In a feasible domain, the dynamics of viruses propagation according to the Caputo fractional model (1) are investigated. Let us consider $R \subset R_+^2 \times R_+^2 \times R_+^2 \times R_+^4$ such that

$$\begin{aligned} R \;=\; & \Big\{T_m = (M_i, M_u) \in R_+^2, T_{m_i} = (M_{i,s}, M_{i,i}) \in R_+^2, T_{m_u} = (M_{u,s}, M_{u,i}) \in R_+^2, \\ & T_h = (S_h, I_h, H_h, R_h) \in R_+^4\Big\} \end{aligned}$$

Theorem 1. *For every positive initial condition, the solution of* (2) *remains positive for all $t > 0$ in R.*

Proof. After summing the components of the human population in a model (2), we obtain a total human population as follows:

$$ {}_a^C D_t^\alpha T_h = {}_a^C D_t^\alpha S_h + {}_a^C D_t^\alpha I_h + {}_a^C D_t^\alpha H_h + {}_a^C D_t^\alpha R_h $$

and we have

$$\begin{aligned} {}_a^C D_t^\alpha T_h &= r_h - \lambda_h T_h \\ {}_a^C D_t^\alpha T_h + \lambda_h T_h &= r_h \end{aligned}$$

Let us take Laplace's transformation for the above equation as

$$ T_h(u) = \frac{r_h}{u(u^\alpha + \lambda_h)} + T_h(0)\frac{u^{\alpha-1}}{u^\alpha + \lambda_h} $$

Now, using inverse Laplace's transformation,

$$ T_h(t) = T_h(0)\underbrace{E_{\alpha,1}(\lambda_h t^\alpha)}_{Positive} + \underbrace{r_h t^\alpha E_{\alpha,\alpha+1}(\lambda_h t^\alpha)}_{Positive} $$

Therefore, if the initial condition $T_h(0) \geq 0$, then the solution $T_h > 0$.

As a result, the model's solution in R with the non-negative criteria continues to be in R. Therefore, all of the solution $\mathbb{R}_+^4$ is drawn to the region R, which is positively invariant.

For *Wolbachia*-infected mosquitoes,

$$\begin{aligned} {}_a^C D_t^\alpha T_{m_i} &= {}_a^C D_t^\alpha M_{i,s} + {}_a^C D_t^\alpha M_{i,i} \\ &= t_m T_{m_i} - \lambda_{m_i} T_{m_i^2} \\ &= [t_w - \lambda_{m_i} T_{m_i}] T_{m_i} \\ &\leq t_w - \lambda_{m_i} T_{m_i} \\ {}_a^C D_t^\alpha T_{m_i} + \lambda_{m_i} T_{m_i} &\leq t_w. \end{aligned}$$

By using Laplace and inverse Laplace transforms,

$$\begin{aligned}
{}_a^cD_t^\alpha T_{m_i} + \lambda_{m_i} T_{m_i} &\leq t_w \\
T_{m_i}(u) &\leq \frac{t_m}{u(u^\alpha + \lambda_{m_i})} + T_{m_i}(0)\frac{u^{\alpha-1}}{u^\alpha + \lambda_{m_i}} \\
T_{m_i}(u) &\leq T_{m_i}(0)\underbrace{E_{\alpha,1}(t_w t^\alpha)}_{Positive} + \underbrace{\lambda_{m_i} t^\alpha E_{\alpha,\alpha+1}(\lambda_{m_i} t^\alpha)}_{Positive}
\end{aligned}$$

Therefore, if the initial condition $T_{m_i}(0) \geq 0$, then the solution $T_{m_i} > 0$. Similarly, for the solutions of non-*Wolbachia* compartments,

$$\begin{aligned}
{}_a^cD_t^\alpha T_{m_u} &= {}_a^cD_t^\alpha M_{u,s} + {}_a^cD_t^\alpha M_{u,i} \\
&= t_m T_{m_u} - \lambda_{m_u} T_{m_u^2} \\
&= [t_w - \lambda_{m_u} T_{m_u}] T_{m_u} \\
&\leq t_w - \lambda_{m_u} T_{m_u} \\
{}_a^cD_t^\alpha T_{m_u} + \lambda_{m_u} T_{m_u} &\leq t_w.
\end{aligned}$$

By using Laplace and inverse Laplace transforms,

$$\begin{aligned}
{}_a^cD_t^\alpha T_{m_i} + \lambda_{m_i} T_{m_i} &\leq t_w \\
T_{m_i}(u) &\leq \frac{t_m}{u(u^\alpha + \lambda_{m_i})} + T_{m_i}(0)\frac{u^{\alpha-1}}{u^\alpha + \lambda_{m_i}} \\
T_{m_i}(u) &\leq T_{m_u}(0)\underbrace{E_{\alpha,1}(t_w t^\alpha)}_{Positive} + \underbrace{\lambda_{m_u} t^\alpha E_{\alpha,\alpha+1}(\lambda_{m_u} t^\alpha)}_{Positive}
\end{aligned}$$

Therefore, if the initial condition $T_{m_u}(0) \geq 0$, then the solution $T_{m_u} > 0$. □

5.2. Positive Invariant Region

Now, let us discuss the system solution's positive aspects.

Proposition 1. *The solution of the model* (2) *is non-negative and bounded for all positive initial conditions for $t > 0$.*

Proof. It is necessary to demonstrate that every hyper-plane enclosing the positive orthant has a vector field point in order to demonstrate that the model's solution is non-negative $\mathbb{R}^2_+, \mathbb{R}^2_+, \mathbb{R}^2_+, \mathbb{R}^4_+$. From system (2), we have

$$\begin{aligned}
{}_a^cD_t^\alpha M_i|_{M_i=0} &= \Lambda_1 > 0 \\
{}_a^cD_t^\alpha M_{i,s}|_{M_{i,s}=0} &= t_w T_{m_i} \geq 0 \\
{}_a^cD_t^\alpha M_{i,i}|_{M_{i,i}=0} &= \frac{\alpha_i \rho_{m_h} I_h}{T_h} M_{i,s} \geq 0.
\end{aligned}$$

Now, ${}_a^cD_t^\alpha M_u|_{M_u=0} = \Lambda_2 + r_m(1-\eta)M_i - \lambda_{d_u} M_i^2 \geq 0$, if the density-dependent death rate of wild mosquitoes will be less than or equal to the sum of the reproduction rate of wild mosquitoes and the rate at which fraction of wild mosquitoes produced due to the imperfect maternal transmission. That is, if the following inequality holds

$$\Lambda_2 + r_m(1-\eta) \geq \lambda_{d_u} M_i$$

then ${}_a^cD_t^\alpha M_u|_{M_u=0} = \Lambda_2 + r_m(1-\eta) - \lambda_{d_u} M_i \geq 0$.

The negative sign on the left-hand side will not affect the positivity of the system. As η denotes the probability of having *Wolbachia*. It takes the values between $[0,1]$. This implies that the value of $(1-\eta)$ is always greater than equal to 0.

$$\begin{aligned}
{}^{C}_{a}D^{\alpha}_{t}M_{u,s}|_{M_{u,s}=0} &= t_w T_{m_u} \geq 0 \\
{}^{C}_{a}D^{\alpha}_{t}M_{u,i}|_{M_{u,i}=0} &= \frac{\alpha_u \rho_{m_h} I_h}{T_h} M_{u,s} \geq 0 \\
{}^{C}_{a}D^{\alpha}_{t}S_h|_{S_h=0} &= r_h > 0 \\
{}^{C}_{a}D^{\alpha}_{t}I_h|_{I_h=0} &= \frac{\alpha_i \rho_{m_i} M_{i,i}}{T_h} + \frac{\alpha_u \rho_{m_u} M_{u,i}}{T_h} \geq 0 \\
{}^{C}_{a}D^{\alpha}_{t}C_h|_{H_h=0} &= \eta_h I_h \geq 0 \\
{}^{C}_{a}D^{\alpha}_{t}R_h|_{R_h=0} &= \gamma_{h_1} I_h + \gamma_{h_2} H_h \geq 0
\end{aligned}$$

The solution of the system will remain in $\mathbb{R}^2_+$, $\mathbb{R}^2_+$, $\mathbb{R}^2_+$ and $\mathbb{R}^4_+$. □

6. Analysis of the Model

This section is devoted to examining the model for various characteristics, such as basic reproduction number, local stability (Routh–Hurwitz criterion) and global stability (Lyapunov and LMI theories).

6.1. Basis Reproduction Number

In the proposed model (2), the infected compartments are $M_{i,i}$, $M_{u,i}$ and I_h. Let us denote $y = (M_{i,i}, M_{u,i}, I_h)^\top$. Then, we have

$$\frac{dy}{dt} = \mathfrak{F} - \mathfrak{V},$$

where

$$\mathfrak{F} = \begin{pmatrix} \frac{\alpha_i \rho_{m_h} I_h^*}{T_h} M_{i,s}^* \\ \frac{\alpha_u \rho_{m_h} I_h^*}{T_h} M_{u,s}^* \\ \frac{\alpha_i \rho_{m_i} M_{i,i}^*}{T_h} S_h^* + \frac{\alpha_u \rho_{m_u} M_{u,i}^*}{T_h} S_h^* \end{pmatrix}$$

$$\mathfrak{V} = \begin{pmatrix} \lambda_{m_i} M_{i,i}^* \\ \lambda_{m_u} M_{u,i}^* \\ \eta_h I_h^* + \gamma_{h_i} I_h^* + \lambda_h I_h^* \end{pmatrix}$$

From this, we can derive F and V as

$$F = \begin{pmatrix} 0 & 0 & \frac{\alpha_i M_{is}^* \rho_{m_h}}{T_h} \\ 0 & 0 & \frac{\alpha_u M_{us}^* \rho_{m_h}}{T_h} \\ \frac{\alpha_i S_h^* \rho_{m_i}}{T_h} & \frac{\alpha_u S_h^* \rho_{m_u}}{T_h} & 0 \end{pmatrix}; V = \begin{pmatrix} \lambda_{m_i} & 0 & 0 \\ 0 & \lambda_{m_u} & 0 \\ 0 & 0 & \eta_h + \gamma_{h_1} + \lambda_h \end{pmatrix};$$

The basic reproduction number (R_0) is the spectral radius of the matrix (FV^{-1}). Here,

$$V^{-1} = \begin{bmatrix} \frac{1}{\lambda_{m_i}} & 0 & 0 \\ 0 & \frac{1}{\lambda_{mu}} & 0 \\ 0 & 0 & \frac{1}{k_1} \end{bmatrix}$$

Let us consider $K_1 = \eta_h + \gamma_{h_1} + \lambda_h$. Now,

$$FV^{-1} = \begin{bmatrix} 0 & 0 & \frac{\alpha_i \rho_{m_h} M^*_{i_s}}{k_1 T_h} \\ 0 & 0 & \frac{\alpha_u \rho_{m_h} M^*_{u_s}}{k_1 T_h} \\ \frac{S^*_h \alpha_i \rho_{m_i}}{T_h \lambda_{m_i}} & \frac{S^*_h \alpha_u \rho_{m_u}}{T_h \lambda_{m_u}} & 0 \end{bmatrix}.$$

Eigenvalues of FV^{-1} are $\Bigg\{0, -\frac{\sqrt{S^*_h}\sqrt{\rho_{m_h}}\sqrt{\alpha_i^2 \rho_{m_i} M^*_{i_s} \lambda_{m_u} + \alpha_u^2 \lambda_{m_i} \rho_{m_u} M^*_{u_s}}}{\sqrt{k_1} T_h \sqrt{\lambda_{m_i}} \sqrt{\lambda_{m_u}}},$
$\frac{\sqrt{S^*_h}\sqrt{\rho_{m_h}}\sqrt{\alpha_i^2 \rho_{m_i} M_{i_s} \lambda_{m_u} + \alpha_u^2 \lambda_{m_i} \rho_{m_u} M^*_{u_s}}}{\sqrt{k_1} T_h \sqrt{\lambda_{m_i}} \sqrt{\lambda_{m_u}}}\Bigg\}.$

The basic reproduction number R_0 is the spectral radius of FV^{-1}.
That is,

$$R_0 = \frac{1}{T_h}\sqrt{\frac{S^*_h \rho_{m_h}\left(\alpha_i^2 \rho_{m_i} M^*_{i_s} \lambda_{m_u} + \alpha_u^2 \lambda_{m_i} \rho_{m_u} M^*_{u_s}\right)}{k_1 \lambda_{m_i} \lambda_{m_u}}} \quad (3)$$

To find the equilibrium point of the fractional model (2), we equate the left-hand side to zero. That is, ${}^C_a D^\alpha_t M_{i,s} = {}^C_a D^\alpha_t M_{i,i} = {}^C_a D^\alpha_t M_{u,s} = {}^C_a D^\alpha_t M_{u,i} = {}^C_a D^\alpha_t S_h = {}^C_a D^\alpha_t I_h = {}^C_a D^\alpha_t C_h = {}^C_a D^\alpha_t R_h = 0$.

6.1.1. Disease-Free Equilibrium:

The case where there is no disease spread among all three populations is called the disease-free equilibrium. That is, $M^*_{i,i} = 0$, $M^*_{u,i} = 0$, $I^*_h = 0$, $C^*_h = 0$ and $R^*_h = 0$. Then, the model transformed as:

$$\begin{aligned} {}^C_a D^\alpha_t M_{i,s} &= t_w M_{i,s} - \lambda_{m_i}(M_{i,s} + M_{u,s})M_{i,s} \\ {}^C_a D^\alpha_t M_{u,s} &= t_w\left(1 - \frac{M_{i,s}}{M_{i,s} + M_{u,s}}\right)M_{u,s} - \lambda_{m_u}(M_{i,s} + M_{u,s})M_{u,s} \\ {}^C_a D^\alpha_t S_h &= r_h - \frac{\alpha_i \rho_{m_i} M_{i,i}}{T_h} S_h - \frac{\alpha_u \rho_{m_u} M_{u,i}}{T_h} S_h - \lambda_h S_h, \end{aligned} \quad (4)$$

since $T_m = M_{i,s} + M_{i,i} + M_{u,s} + M_{u,i}$, $T_{m_i} = M_{i,s} + M_{i,i}$ and $T_{m_u} = M_{u,s} + M_{u,i}$. Then, the corresponding disease-free equilibrium point is

$$^j\Sigma_0 = \left(M^*_{i,s}, 0, M^*_{u,s}, 0, S^*_h, 0, 0, 0\right), j = 1, 2, 3, 4.$$

To find the equilibrium points, equate the right-hand sides to zero.

$$r_h - \frac{\alpha_i \rho_{m_i} M^*_{i,i}}{T_h} S^*_h - \frac{\alpha_u \rho_{m_u} M^*_{u,i}}{T_h} S^*_h - \lambda_h S^*_h = 0.$$

Here, $M^*_{i,i} = M^*_{u,i} = 0$. This implies that

$$\begin{aligned} r_h - \lambda_h S^*_h &= 0 \\ S^*_h &= \frac{r_h}{\lambda_h}. \end{aligned} \quad (5)$$

when we analyze the disease-free equilibrium for mosquito species, there are four possible cases that exist. They are classified and analyzed as follows:

Annihilation of both wild and *Wolbachia* mosquitoes: If both mosquitoes are completely destructed, then the possible equilibrium point is

$$^{1}\Sigma_0 = \left(0,0,0,0,\frac{r_h}{\lambda_h},0,0,0\right).$$

Annihilation of Wild mosquito only: The equilibrium point when there is a successful replacement of wild mosquitoes by *Wolbachia*-infected mosquitoes is derived as

$$^{2}\Sigma_0 = \left(\frac{t_w}{\lambda_{m_i}},0,0,0,\frac{r_h}{\lambda_h},0,0,0\right).$$

Annihilation of *Wolbachia*-infected mosquitoes only: If the rate of an imperfect maternal transmission increases, then after some period, the sustainability of *Wolbachia* will be reduced to zero. For this zero *Wolbachia*-mosquitoes case, the equilibrium point is

$$^{3}\Sigma_0 = \left(0,0,\frac{t_w}{\lambda_{m_u}},0,\frac{r_h}{\lambda_h},0,0,0\right).$$

Co-existence of all wild and *Wolbachia*-infected mosquitoes with humans: An equilibrium point when all populations co-exist in a common environment is derived as

$$^{4}\Sigma_0 = \left(\frac{T_{m_i}t_w}{\lambda_{m_i}P_1T_{m_u}},0,\frac{t_w}{P_1^2\lambda_{m_u}},0,\frac{r_h}{\lambda_h},0,0,0\right).$$

where $P_1 = \frac{T_{ml}}{T_{mu}}$.

6.1.2. Endemic Equilibrium

There are two cases of endemic equilibrium corresponding to $^{2}\Sigma_0$ and $^{3}\Sigma_0$, as follows.

Successful replacement of wild mosquitoes by *Wolbachia*-infected mosquitoes: $^{2}\Sigma_1 = \left(M_{i,s}^*, M_{i,i}^*, 0, 0, S_h^*, I_h^*, H_h^*, R_h^*\right)$.

Annihilation of *Wolbachia*-infected mosquitoes: $^{3}\Sigma_1 = \left(0,0,M_{u,s}^*, M_{u,i}^*, S_h^*, I_h^*, H_h^*, R_h^*\right)$.

Now, take the following two cases.

1. **Successful replacement of wild mosquitoes by *Wolbachia*-infected mosquitoes:** That is, $M_{u,s}^* = M_{u,i}^* = 0$. Then, the model (2) is reduced as follows:

$$\begin{aligned}
{}_a^cD_t^\alpha M_{i,s} &= t_wT_{m_i} - \frac{\alpha_i\rho_{m_h}I_hM_{i,s}}{T_h} - \lambda_{m_i}T_{m_i}M_{i,s}\\
{}_a^cD_t^\alpha M_{i,i} &= \frac{\alpha_i\rho_{m_h}I_hM_{i,s}}{T_h} - \lambda_{m_i}T_{m_i}M_{i,i}\\
{}_a^cD_t^\alpha S_h &= r_h - \frac{\alpha_i\rho_{m_i}M_{i,i}}{T_h}S_h - \lambda_hS_h
\end{aligned}$$

$$\begin{aligned}
{}_a^cD_t^\alpha I_h &= \frac{\alpha_i\rho_{m_i}M_{i,i}}{T_h}S_h - \eta_hI_h - \gamma_{h_1}I_h - \lambda_hI_h\\
{}_a^cD_t^\alpha H_h &= \eta_hI_h - \gamma_{h_2}H_h - \lambda_hH_h \qquad (6)\\
{}_a^cD_t^\alpha R_h &= \gamma_{h_1}I_h + \gamma_{h_2}H_h - \lambda_hR_h
\end{aligned}$$

By adding the first two equations and adding the last four equations, we obtain

$$\begin{aligned} {}_{a}^{c}D_{t}^{\alpha}T_{m_i} &= t_w T_{m_i} - \lambda_{m_i} T_{m_i}^2 \\ {}_{a}^{c}D_{t}^{\alpha}T_h &= r_h - \lambda_h T_h. \end{aligned}$$

By solving for ${}_{a}^{c}D_{t}^{\alpha}T_{m_i} = 0 = {}_{a}^{c}D_{t}^{\alpha}T_h$, we obtain $T_{m_i}^* = \frac{t_w}{\lambda_{m_i}}$ and $T_h^* = \frac{r_h}{\lambda_h}$.
Let us equate the RHS of each equation in (6) to zero. After some manipulations, we obtain the following equilibrium point (${}^{5}\Sigma_0$):

$$\begin{aligned} M_{i,s}^* &= \frac{r_h t_w^2}{\lambda_{m_i}\left(I_h^* \lambda_h \alpha_i \rho_{m_h} + r_h t_w\right)}; \\ M_{i,i}^* &= \frac{I_h^* t_w \alpha_i \lambda_h \rho_{m_h}}{\lambda_{m_i}\left(r_h t_w + I_h^* \alpha_i \lambda_h \rho_{m_h}\right)}; \\ S_h^* &= \frac{r_h^2 \lambda_{m_i}\left(I_h^* \lambda_h \alpha_i \rho_{m_h} + r_h t_w\right)}{I_h^* \lambda_h^2 r_h \alpha_i \rho_{m_h} \lambda_{m_i} + I_h^* \lambda_h^2 \alpha_i^2 t_w \rho_{m_h} \rho_{m_i} + \lambda_h r_h^2 t_w \lambda_{m_i}}; \\ I_h^* &= \frac{r_h t_w\left(\lambda_h \alpha_i^2 \rho_{m_h} \rho_{m_i} - k_1 r_h \lambda_{m_i}\right)}{k_1 \lambda_h \alpha_i \rho_{m_h}\left(r_h \lambda_{m_i} + \alpha_i t_w \rho_{m_i}\right)} \\ H_h^* &= \frac{I_h^* \eta_h}{\gamma_{h_2} + \lambda_h}; \\ R_h^* &= \frac{I_h^*\left(\gamma_{h_1}\left(\gamma_{h_2} + \lambda_h\right) + \gamma_{h_2}\eta_h\right)}{\lambda_h\left(\gamma_{h_2} + \lambda_h\right)}; \end{aligned}$$

2. **Annihilation of *Wolbachia*-infected mosquitoes:**
That is, $M_{i,s}^* = M_{i,i}^* = 0$. Then, the model (2) is reduced as follows:

$$\begin{aligned} {}_{a}^{c}D_{t}^{\alpha}M_{u,s} &= t_w T_m - \frac{\alpha_u \rho_{m_h} I_h}{T_h} M_{u,s} - \lambda_{m_u} T_m M_{u,s} \\ {}_{a}^{c}D_{t}^{\alpha}M_{u,i} &= \frac{\alpha_u \rho_{m_h} I_h}{T_h} M_{u,s} - \lambda_{m_u} T_{m_u} M_{u,i} \qquad (7) \\ {}_{a}^{c}D_{t}^{\alpha}S_h &= r_h - \frac{\alpha_u \rho_{m_u} M_{u,i}}{T_h} S_h - \lambda_h S_h \\ {}_{a}^{c}D_{t}^{\alpha}I_h &= \frac{\alpha_u \rho_{m_u} M_{u,i}}{T_h} S_h - \eta_h I_h - \gamma_{h_1} I_h - \lambda_h I_h \\ {}_{a}^{c}D_{t}^{\alpha}H_h &= \eta_h I_h - \gamma_{h_2} H_h - \lambda_h H_h \\ {}_{a}^{c}D_{t}^{\alpha}R_h &= \gamma_{h_1} I_h + \gamma_{h_2} H_h - \lambda_h R_h \qquad (8) \end{aligned}$$

Adding the first two equations, and adding the last four equations, we obtain

$$\begin{aligned} {}_{a}^{c}D_{t}^{\alpha}T_{m_u} &= t_w T_{m_u} - \lambda_{m_u} T_{m_u}^2 \\ {}_{a}^{c}D_{t}^{\alpha}T_h &= r_h - \lambda_h T_h. \end{aligned}$$

By solving for ${}_{a}^{c}D_{t}^{\alpha}T_{m_u} = 0 = {}_{a}^{c}D_{t}^{\alpha}T_h$, we obtain $T_{m_u}^* = \frac{t_w}{\lambda_{m_u}}$ and $T_h^* = \frac{r_h}{\lambda_h}$.

Let us equate the RHS of each equation in (7) to zero. After some manipulations, we obtain the following equilibrium point ($^6\Sigma_0$).

$$\begin{aligned}
M^*_{u,s} &= \frac{r_h t_w^2}{\lambda_{m_u}\left(I_h^*\lambda_h\alpha_u\rho_{m_h} + r_h T_{m_u}\lambda_{m_u}\right)};\\
M^*_{u,i} &= \frac{I_h^*\lambda_h t_w^2\alpha_u\rho_{m_h}}{T_{m_u}\lambda_{m_u}^2\left(I_h^*\lambda_h\alpha_u\rho_{m_h} + r_h T_{m_u}\lambda_{m_u}\right)};\\
S_h^* &= \frac{r_h^2 T_{m_u}\lambda_{m_u}^2\left(I_h^*\lambda_h\alpha_u\rho_{m_h} + r_h T_{m_u}\lambda_{m_u}\right)}{\lambda_h\left(r_h T_{m_u}\lambda_{m_u}^2\left(I_h^*\lambda_h\alpha_u\rho_{m_h} + r_h T_{m_u}\lambda_{m_u}\right) + I_h^*\lambda_h t_w^2\alpha_u^2\rho_{m_h}\rho_{m_u}\right)};\\
I_h^* &= \frac{r_h\left(\lambda_h t_w^2\alpha_u^2\rho_{m_h}\rho_{m_u} - k_1 r_h T_{m_u}^2\lambda_{m_u}^3\right)}{k_1\lambda_h\alpha_u\rho_{m_h}\left(r_h T_{m_u}\lambda_{m_u}^2 + t_w^2\alpha_u\rho_{m_u}\right)};\\
H_h^* &= \frac{I_h^*\eta_h}{\gamma_{h_2} + \lambda_h};\\
R_h^* &= \frac{I_h^*\left(\gamma_{h_2}\eta_h + \gamma_{h_1}\left(\gamma_{h_2} + \lambda_h\right)\right)}{\lambda_h\left(\gamma_{h_2} + \lambda_h\right)};
\end{aligned}$$

6.1.3. Basis Reproduction Number at Disease-Free Equilibrium

There are four possible cases of equilibrium points, as we derived above.

(i) $^1\Sigma_0 = \left(0,0,0,0,\frac{r_h}{\lambda_h},0,0,0\right)$.

(ii) $^2\Sigma_0 = \left(\frac{t_w}{\lambda_{m_i}},0,0,0,\frac{r_h}{\lambda_h},0,0,0\right)$.

(iii) $^3\Sigma_0 = \left(0,0,\frac{t_w}{\lambda_{mu}},0,\frac{r_h}{\lambda_h},0,0,0\right)$.

(iv) $^4\Sigma_0 = \left(\frac{T_{m_i}t_w}{\lambda_{m_i}P_1T_{m_u}},0,\frac{t_w}{P_1^2\lambda_{mu}},0,\frac{r_h}{\lambda_h},0,0,0\right)$..

For an equilibrium point $^1\Sigma_0$, the basic reproduction number is $^1R_0 = 0$. There is no disease spread. For an equilibrium point $^2\Sigma_0$, the basic reproduction number is $^1R_0 = 0$. Since it is the disease-free, the equilibrium value is $T_h = S_h^*$. In this case,

$$\mathfrak{F} = \begin{pmatrix} \frac{\alpha_i\rho_{m_h}I_h^*}{S_h^*}M^*_{i,s} \\ \frac{\alpha_u\rho_{m_h}I_h^*}{S_h^*}M^*_{u,s} \\ \frac{\alpha_i\rho_{m_i}M^*_{i,i}}{S_h^*}S_h^* + \frac{\alpha_u\rho_{mu}M^*_{u,i}}{S_h^*}S_h^* \end{pmatrix}$$

$$\mathfrak{V} = \begin{pmatrix} \lambda_{m_i}M^*_{i,i} \\ \lambda_{m_u}M^*_{u,i} \\ \eta_h I_h^* + \gamma_{h_i}I_h^* + \lambda_h I_h^* \end{pmatrix}$$

From this, we can derive F and V as

$$F = \begin{pmatrix} 0 & 0 & \frac{\alpha_i M^*_{is}\rho_{m_h}}{S_h^*} \\ 0 & 0 & \frac{\alpha_u M^*_{us}\rho_{m_h}}{S_h^*} \\ \alpha_i\rho_{m_i} & \alpha_u S_h^*\rho_{m_u} & 0 \end{pmatrix}; V = \begin{pmatrix} \lambda_{m_i} & 0 & 0 \\ 0 & \lambda_{m_u} & 0 \\ 0 & 0 & k_1 \end{pmatrix};$$

The basic reproduction number ($^2R_0$) is the spectral radius of the matrix (FV^{-1}). Here,

$$V^{-1} = \begin{bmatrix} \frac{1}{\lambda_{m_i}} & 0 & 0 \\ 0 & \frac{1}{\lambda_{mu}} & 0 \\ 0 & 0 & \frac{1}{k_1} \end{bmatrix}$$

Here,

$$FV^{-1} = \begin{bmatrix} 0 & 0 & \frac{\alpha_i \rho_{m_h} M_{i_S}}{k_1 S_h^*} \\ 0 & 0 & \frac{\alpha_u \rho_{m_h} M_{u_S}}{k_1 S_h^*} \\ \frac{\alpha_i \rho_{m_i}}{\lambda_{m_i}} & \frac{\alpha_u \rho_{mu}}{\lambda_{mu}} & 0 \end{bmatrix}$$

$$^2R_0 = \sqrt{\frac{\lambda_h \alpha_i^2 t_w \rho_{m_h} \rho_{m_i}}{k_1 r_h \lambda_{m_i}^2}}.$$

In Figure 2, we can observe that the value of the basic reproduction number $^2R_0$ at an equilibrium point $^2\Sigma_0$ is less than one. There is no disease spread when only *Wolbachia* mosquitoes exist. Next, for the equilibrium point $^3\Sigma_0$, the basic reproduction number is

$$^3R_0 = spectral\ radius\ (FV^{-1}|_{^3\Sigma_0}).$$

That is,

$$^3R_0 = \sqrt{\frac{\lambda_h t_w \alpha_u^2 \rho_{m_h} \rho_{m_u}}{k_1 r_h \lambda_{m_u}^2}}.$$

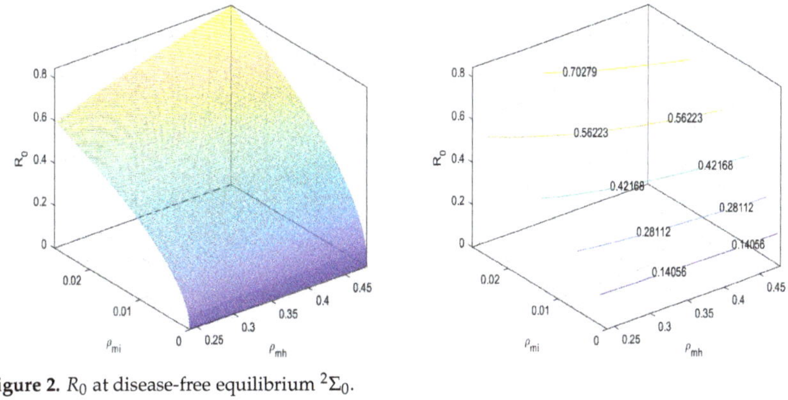

Figure 2. R_0 at disease-free equilibrium $^2\Sigma_0$.

In Figure 3, we can observe that the values the basic reproduction number $^3R_0$ at an equilibrium point $^3\Sigma_0$ is less than one.

Similarly, for an equilibrium point $^4\Sigma_0$, the basic reproduction number is

$$^4R_0 = spectral\ radius\ (FV^{-1}|_{^4\Sigma_0}).$$

That is,

$$^4R_0 = \sqrt{\frac{\lambda_h t_w \rho_{m_h} \left(\alpha_i^2 \rho_{m_i} (\lambda_{m_i} - \lambda_{m_u}) + \alpha_u^2 \lambda_{m_i} \rho_{m_u}\right)}{k_1 r_h \lambda_{m_i}^3}}.$$

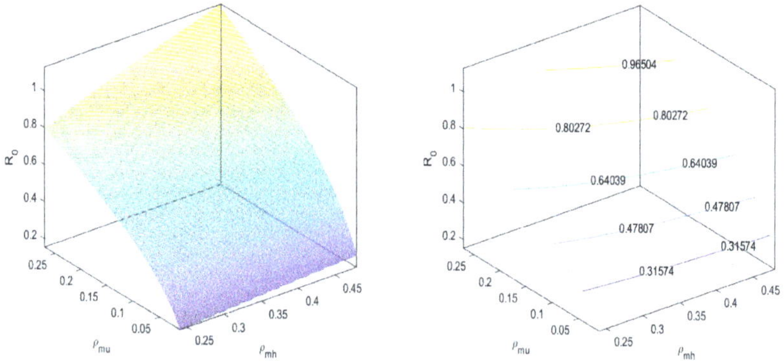

Figure 3. R_0 at disease-free equilibrium ${}^3\Sigma_0$.

In Figure 4, we can observe that the value of the basic reproduction number ${}^4R_0$ at an equilibrium point ${}^4\Sigma_0$ is near to one. That is, when there are both *Wolbachia* and non-*Wolbachia* mosquitoes, then the disease spread is controlled by increasing the release of *Wolbachia*-infected mosquitoes. We can maintain the spread under the threshold.

That is, for disease-free equilibrium in all four cases, $R_0 < 1$.

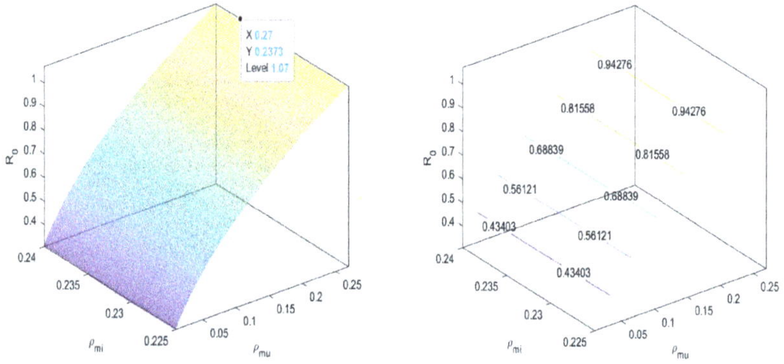

Figure 4. R_0 at disease-free equilibrium ${}^4\Sigma_0$.

6.1.4. Local Stability

Theorem 2. *The disease-free equilibrium points ${}^i\Sigma_0$ are locally asymptotically stable if the corresponding basic reproduction number ${}^iR_0 < 1$ for $i = 2, 3$. Otherwise, the system is unstable.*

The Jacobian for system (2) is

$$J = \begin{pmatrix} -J_{11} & 0 & 0 & 0 & 0 & -J_{16} & 0 & 0 \\ J_{21} & -J_{22} & 0 & 0 & 0 & J_{26} & 0 & 0 \\ 0 & 0 & -J_{33} & 0 & 0 & -J_{36} & 0 & 0 \\ 0 & 0 & J_{43} & -J_{44} & 0 & J_{46} & 0 & 0 \\ 0 & -J_{52} & 0 & -J_{54} & -J_{55} & 0 & 0 & 0 \\ 0 & J_{62} & 0 & J_{64} & J_{65} & -J_{66} & 0 & 0 \\ 0 & 0 & 0 & 0 & 0 & J_{76} & -J_{77} & 0 \\ 0 & 0 & 0 & 0 & 0 & J_{86} & J_{87} & -J_{88} \end{pmatrix},$$

where $J_{11} = \frac{I_h \alpha_i \rho_{m_h}}{T_h} - T_m \lambda_{m_i}$; $J_{16} = \frac{M_{i,s} \alpha_i \rho_{m_h}}{T_h}$; $J_{21} = \frac{I_h \alpha_i \rho_{m_h}}{T_h}$; $J_{22} = T_m \lambda_{m_i}$; $J_{26} = \frac{M_{i,s} \alpha_i \rho_{m_h}}{T_h}$; $J_{33} = \frac{I_h \alpha_u \rho_{m_h}}{T_h} - T_m \lambda_{m_u}$; $J_{36} = \frac{M_{u,s} \alpha_u \rho_{m_h}}{T_h}$; $J_{43} = \frac{I_h \alpha_u \rho_{m_h}}{T_h}$; $J_{44} = T_m \lambda_{m_u}$; $J_{46} = \frac{M_{u,s} \alpha_u \rho_{m_h}}{T_h}$;

$J_{52} = \frac{S_h \alpha_i \rho_{m_i}}{T_h}$; $J_{54} = \frac{S_h \alpha_u \rho_{mu}}{T_h}$; $J_{55} = \frac{M_{i,i} \alpha_i \rho_{m_i}}{T_h} - \lambda_h - \frac{M_{u,i} \alpha_u \rho_{mu}}{T_h}$; $J_{62} = \frac{S_h \alpha_i \rho_{m_i}}{T_h}$; $J_{64} = \frac{S_h \alpha_u \rho_{mu}}{T_h}$; $J_{65} = \frac{M_{i,i} \alpha_i \rho_{m_i}}{T_h} + \frac{M_{u,i} \alpha_u \rho_{mu}}{T_h}$; $J_{66} = k_1$; $J_{76} = \eta_h$; $J_{77} = \gamma_{h_2} + \lambda_h$; $J_{86} = \gamma_{h_1}$; $J_{87} = \gamma_{h_2}$; $J_{88} = \lambda_h$.

(i) **The Jacobian at disease-free equilibrium $^2\Sigma_0$:**

$$J_{3_{\Sigma_0}} = \begin{pmatrix} -t_w & 0 & 0 & 0 & 0 & -\frac{\lambda_h \alpha_i t_w \rho_{m_h}}{r_h \lambda_{m_i}} & 0 & 0 \\ 0 & -t_w & 0 & 0 & 0 & \frac{\lambda_h \alpha_i t_w \rho_{m_h}}{r_h \lambda_{m_i}} & 0 & 0 \\ 0 & 0 & -\frac{t_w \lambda_{mu}}{\lambda_{m_i}} & 0 & 0 & 0 & 0 & 0 \\ 0 & 0 & 0 & -\frac{t_w \lambda_{mu}}{\lambda_{m_i}} & 0 & 0 & 0 & 0 \\ 0 & -\alpha_i \rho_{m_i} & 0 & -\alpha_u \rho_{m_u} & -\lambda_h & 0 & 0 & 0 \\ 0 & \alpha_i \rho_{m_i} & 0 & \alpha_u \rho_{m_u} & 0 & \theta_{77} & 0 & 0 \\ 0 & 0 & 0 & 0 & 0 & \eta_h & -\gamma_{h_2} - \lambda_h & 0 \\ 0 & 0 & 0 & 0 & 0 & \gamma_{h_1} & \gamma_{h_2} & -\lambda_h \end{pmatrix}$$

where $-\gamma_{h_1} - \eta_h - \lambda_h$.

Here, $|J_{2_{\Sigma_0}}| = \frac{\lambda_h^2 t_w^4 (\gamma_{h_2} + \lambda_h) \lambda_{mu}^2 (k_1 r_h \lambda_{m_i} - \lambda_h \alpha_i^2 \rho_{m_h} \rho_{m_i})}{r_h \lambda_{m_i}^3} > 0$ if $(1 - {}^2R_0) > 0$ (i.e.,) ${}^2R_0 < 1$ and the trace of $J_{2_{\Sigma_0}} = -\left(\gamma_{h_2} + 3\lambda_h + \frac{2 t_w \lambda_{mu}}{\lambda_{m_i}} + k_1 + 2t_w\right) < 0$. Hence, by Routh Hurwitz's theorem, our system at disease-free equilibrium point $^2\Sigma_0$ is locally asymptotically stable when ${}^2R_0 < 1$.

(ii) **The Jacobian at disease-free equilibrium $^3\Sigma_0$:**

$$J_{3_{\Sigma_0}} = \begin{pmatrix} -\frac{t_w \lambda_{m_i}}{\lambda_{mu}} & 0 & 0 & 0 & 0 & 0 & 0 & 0 \\ 0 & -\frac{t_w \lambda_{m_i}}{\lambda_{mu}} & 0 & 0 & 0 & 0 & 0 & 0 \\ 0 & 0 & -t_w & 0 & 0 & -\frac{\lambda_h t_w \alpha_u \rho_{m_h}}{r_h \lambda_{mu}} & 0 & 0 \\ 0 & 0 & 0 & -t_w & 0 & \frac{\lambda_h t_w \alpha_u \rho_{m_h}}{r_h \lambda_{mu}} & 0 & 0 \\ 0 & -\alpha_i \rho_{m_i} & 0 & -\alpha_u \rho_{m_u} & -\lambda_h & 0 & 0 & 0 \\ 0 & \alpha_i \rho_{m_i} & 0 & \alpha_u \rho_{m_u} & 0 & -k_1 & 0 & 0 \\ 0 & 0 & 0 & 0 & 0 & \eta_h & -\gamma_{h_2} - \lambda_h & 0 \\ 0 & 0 & 0 & 0 & 0 & \gamma_{h_1} & \gamma_{h_2} & -\lambda_h \end{pmatrix}$$

Here, $|J_{3_{\Sigma_0}}| = \frac{\lambda_h^2 t_w^4 (\gamma_{h_2} + \lambda_h) \lambda_{m_i}^2 \left(1 - \frac{\lambda_h \alpha_u^2 \rho_{m_h} \rho_{mu}}{k_1 r_h \lambda_{mu}}\right)}{r_h \lambda_{mu}^3} > 0$ if $(1 - {}^3R_0) > 0$ (i.e.,) ${}^3R_0 < 1$ and the trace of $J_{3_{\Sigma_0}} = -\left(\gamma_{h_2} + 3\lambda_h + \frac{2 t_w \lambda_{m_i}}{\lambda_{mu}} + k_1 + 2t_w\right) < 0$. Hence, by Routh Hurwitz's theorem, our system at disease-free equilibrium point $^3\Sigma_0$ is locally asymptotically stable when ${}^3R_0 < 1$.

6.1.5. Global Stability: LMI Approach

In this section, the global stability of the developed model is studied via the linearization process. For this, the following assumptions are made for model (2):

$$\Psi = \begin{bmatrix} M_{i,s} - M_{i,s}^* \\ M_{i,i} - M_{i,i}^* \\ M_{u,s} - M_{u,s}^* \\ M_{u,i} - M_{u,i}^* \\ S_h - S_h^* \\ I_h - I_h^* \\ H_h - H_h^* \\ R_h - R_h^* \end{bmatrix}$$

Let us introduce the vector $\Psi = [M_{i,s}, M_{i,i}, M_{u,s}, M_{u,i}, S_h, I_h, H_h, R_h]^\top$.
Similarly, ${}_a^c D_t^\alpha \Psi = [{}_a^c D_t^\alpha M_{i,s}, {}_a^c D_t^\alpha M_{i,i}, {}_a^c D_t^\alpha M_{u,s}, {}_a^c D_t^\alpha M_{u,i}, {}_a^c D_t^\alpha S_h, {}_a^c D_t^\alpha I_h, {}_a^c D_t^\alpha H_h, {}_a^c D_t^\alpha R_h]^\top$.
The linearized system is derived as

$$\begin{aligned} {}_a^c D_t^\alpha \Psi(t) &= \omega \Psi(t) + F(\Psi(t)) \\ \Psi(t_0) &= \Psi_0, \end{aligned} \tag{9}$$

where

$$\omega = \begin{bmatrix} -J_{11} & 0 & 0 & 0 & 0 & -J_{16} & 0 & 0 \\ J_{21} & -J_{22} & 0 & 0 & 0 & J_{26} & 0 & 0 \\ 0 & 0 & -J_{33} & 0 & 0 & -J_{36} & 0 & 0 \\ 0 & 0 & J_{43} & -J_{44} & 0 & J_{46} & 0 & 0 \\ 0 & -J_{52} & 0 & -J_{54} & -J_{55} & 0 & 0 & 0 \\ 0 & J_{62} & 0 & J_{64} & J_{65} & -J_{66} & 0 & 0 \\ 0 & 0 & 0 & 0 & 0 & J_{76} & -J_{77} & 0 \\ 0 & 0 & 0 & 0 & 0 & J_{86} & J_{87} & -J_{88} \end{bmatrix},$$

where $J_{i,j}$'s i,j = 1, 2, 3,..., 8 are explained in Section 6.1.4.

$$F(\Psi(t)) = \begin{bmatrix} -\frac{\alpha_i \rho_{m_h} \Psi_1 \Psi_6}{T_h} \\ \frac{\alpha_i \rho_{m_h} \Psi_1 \Psi_6}{T_h} \\ -\frac{\alpha_u \rho_{m_h} \Psi_3 \Psi_6}{T_h} \\ \frac{\alpha_u \rho_{m_h} \Psi_3 \Psi_6}{T_h} \\ -\frac{\alpha_i \rho_{m_i} \Psi_2 \Psi_5}{T_h} - \frac{\alpha_u \rho_{m_u} \Psi_4 \Psi_5}{T_h} \\ \frac{\alpha_i \rho_{m_i} \Psi_2 \Psi_5}{T_h} + \frac{\alpha_u \rho_{m_u} \Psi_4 \Psi_5}{T_h} \\ 0 \\ 0 \end{bmatrix}.$$

Theorem 3. *The system* (9) *is assumed to be satisfy that the function* $F(\Psi(t))$ *is Lipschitz-bounded. That is, for any* $\mu_1, \mu_2 \in \mathbb{R}^n$ *there exists* θ *such that*

$$||F(\mu_1) - F(\mu_2)|| \leq ||\theta(\mu_1 - \mu_2)||. \tag{10}$$

Then, there exists a positive definite matrix Θ *and a scalar* $\sigma > 0$ *that satisfies the below-mentioned inequality:*

$$\tilde{\Pi} = \begin{bmatrix} 2\Theta\omega & \Theta & \sigma\theta \\ \star & -\sigma & 0 \\ \star & \star & -\sigma \end{bmatrix} \tag{11}$$

such that our system (9) *is globally stable.*

Proof. By the following transformation function, $\Phi(t) = \Psi(t) - \psi^*$, we modified system (9) as

$$\begin{aligned} {}_a^c D_t^\alpha \Phi(t) &= \omega \Phi(t) + F(\Phi(t)) \\ \Phi(t_0) &= \Phi_0 \in \mathbb{Z}^*, \end{aligned} \tag{12}$$

where $\Phi(t) = [\Psi_1(t), \Psi_2(t), \Psi_3(t), \Psi_4(t), \Psi_5(t), \Psi_6(t), \Psi_7(t), \Psi_8(t)]^\top$,
$F(\Phi(t)) = [F(\Psi_1(t)), F(\Psi_2(t)), F(\Psi_3(t)), F(\Psi_4(t)), F(\Psi_5(t)), F(\Psi_6(t)), F(\Psi_7(t)), F(\Psi_8(t))]^\top$ and $\Phi_0 = \Psi_0 - \Psi^*$. Let us consider a Lyapunov candidate as:

$$\mathcal{V}(t) = \Phi^\top(t) \Theta \Phi(t) \tag{13}$$

Let us derive the time derivative of the system, along with the trajectory, as

$$\begin{aligned} {}_{a}^{c}D_{t}^{\alpha}\mathcal{V}(t) &\leq {}_{a}^{c}D_{t}^{\alpha}\Phi^{\top}(t)\Theta{}_{a}^{c}D_{t}^{\alpha}\Phi(t) \\ &= \Phi^{\top}(t)2\Theta[\omega\Phi(t) + F(\Phi(t))] \\ &= \Phi^{\top}(t)(2\Theta\omega)\Phi(t) + \Phi^{\top}(t)(2\Theta)F(\Phi(t)) \end{aligned} \tag{14}$$

By implementing Lemma 3,

$$\Phi^{\top}(t)(2\Theta)F(\Phi(t)) \leq \frac{1}{\sigma}\Phi^{\top}(t)(\Theta\Theta^{\top})\Phi(t) + \sigma F^{\top}(\Phi(t))F(\Phi(t)) \tag{15}$$

Using the assumption of boundedness,

$$\begin{aligned} F^{\top}(\Phi(t))F(\Phi(t)) &= \langle F(\Psi(t)) - F(\Psi^{*}), F(\Psi(t)) - F(\Psi^{*})\rangle \\ &= \langle F(\Phi(t) + \Psi^{*}) - F(\Psi^{*}), F(\Phi(t) + \Psi^{*}) - F(\Psi^{*})\rangle \\ &\leq \Phi^{\top}(t)\theta^{\top}\theta\Phi(t) \end{aligned} \tag{16}$$

By substituting (15) and (16) into (14), we obtain

$$\begin{aligned} {}_{a}^{c}D_{t}^{\alpha}\mathcal{V}(t) &\leq \Phi^{\top}(t)(2\Theta\omega)\Phi(t) + \Phi^{\top}(t)(\sigma^{-1}\Theta\Theta^{-1})\Phi(t) + \Phi^{\top}(t)(\sigma\theta^{\top}\theta)\Phi(t) \\ &= \Phi^{\top}(t)(2\Theta\omega + \sigma^{-1}\Theta\Theta^{\top} + \sigma\theta^{\top}\theta)\Phi(t) \end{aligned} \tag{17}$$

Let us consider

$$\Pi = 2\Theta\omega + \sigma^{-1}\Theta\Theta^{\top} + \sigma\theta^{\top}\theta$$

and we can rewrite it as

$$\Pi = \begin{bmatrix} 2\Theta\omega & \Theta & \theta \\ \star & -\sigma & 0 \\ \star & \star & \sigma^{-1} \end{bmatrix}$$

By pre- and post-multiplying $diag\{I, I, \sigma\}$ with $\tilde{\Pi}$, we derive

$$\tilde{\Pi} = \begin{bmatrix} 2\Theta\omega & \Theta & \sigma\theta \\ \star & -\sigma & 0 \\ \star & \star & -\sigma \end{bmatrix}$$

Finally, $\tilde{\Pi} < 0$ (Schur compliment Lemma 2). This implies that

$$\begin{aligned} {}_{a}^{c}D_{t}^{\alpha}\mathcal{V}(t) &\leq \Phi^{\top}(t)\tilde{\Pi}\Phi(t) \\ &= -[\Phi^{\top}(t)\Theta^{\frac{1}{2}}(-\Theta^{-\frac{1}{2}}\tilde{\Pi}\Theta^{-\frac{1}{2}})\Theta^{\frac{1}{2}}\Phi(t)]. \end{aligned}$$

Denote $\xi = \lambda_{min}(-\Theta^{-\frac{1}{2}}\tilde{\Pi}\Theta^{-\frac{1}{2}})$. Then, we obtain

$${}_{a}^{c}D_{t}^{\alpha}\mathcal{V}(t) \leq -\xi\mathcal{V}(t). \tag{18}$$

Since, $\mathcal{V}(t) = \Phi^{\top}(t)\Theta\Phi(t)$. Here, $\mathcal{V}(t) \geq 0$ and ${}_{a}^{c}D_{t}^{\alpha}\mathcal{V}(t) \leq 0$. By the Lyapunov direct method, our system is globally stable, hence the proof. □

7. Sensitivity Analysis

This section is devoted to analyzing the sensitivity of the model to its parameters. By the partial-rank correlation coefficient method, we have analyzed system (2) to find sensitive parameters. For that, we considered $k_1 = 0.000012 + 0.0904 + 0.0154$, $S_h = 0.8$, $T_h = 1$, $\alpha_i = 0.5985$, $\alpha_u = 0.76$, $\rho_{m_h} = 0.24$, $\lambda_{m_i} = 0.07854$, $\rho_{m_i} = 0.90.27$, $M_{i,s} = 0.4$,

$\lambda_{m_u} = 0.0714$, $\rho_{m_u} = 0.01$ and $M_{u,s} = 0.4$; and we found the partial derivative of R_0 with respect to the involved parameters.

That is, the basic reproduction number is

$$R_0 = \frac{1}{T_h}\sqrt{\frac{S_h^* \rho_{m_h}\left(\alpha_i^2 \rho_{m_i} M_{i_s}^* \lambda_{m_u} + \alpha_u^2 \lambda_{m_i} \rho_{m_u} M_{u_s}^*\right)}{k_1 \lambda_{m_i} \lambda_{m_u}}} \tag{19}$$

$$\partial R_0|_{\rho_{m_i}} = \frac{S_h \alpha_i^2 \rho_{m_h} M_{i_s}}{2k_1 T_h \lambda_{m_i} \sqrt{\frac{S_h \rho_{m_h}\left(\alpha_i^2 \rho_{m_i} M_{i_s} \lambda_{mu} + \alpha_u^2 \lambda_{m_i} \rho_{mu} M_{us}\right)}{k_1 \lambda_{m_i} \lambda_{mu}}}} = 1.78156,$$

$$\partial R_0|_{\rho_{m_u}} = \frac{S_h \alpha_u^2 \rho_{m_h} M_{u_s}}{2k_1 T_h \lambda_{m_u} \sqrt{\frac{S_h \rho_{m_h}\left(\alpha_i^2 \rho_{m_i} M_{i_s} \lambda_{mu} + \alpha_u^2 \lambda_{m_i} \rho_{mu} M_{us}\right)}{k_1 \lambda_{m_i} \lambda_{mu}}}} = 3.16003,$$

$$\partial R_0|_{\rho_{m_h}} = \frac{S_h\left(\alpha_i^2 \rho_{m_i} M_{i_s} \lambda_{m_u} + \alpha_u^2 \lambda_{m_i} \rho_{m_u} M_{u_s}\right)}{2k_1 T_h \lambda_{m_i} \lambda_{m_u} \sqrt{\frac{S_h \rho_{m_h}\left(\alpha_i^2 \rho_{m_i} M_{i_s} \lambda_{mu} + \alpha_u^2 \lambda_{m_i} \rho_{mu} M_{us}\right)}{k_1 \lambda_{m_i} \lambda_{mu}}}} = 1.9355,$$

$$\partial R_0|_{\lambda_{m_u}} = \frac{\frac{S_h \alpha_i^2 \rho_{m_h} \rho_{m_i} M_{i_s}}{k_1 \lambda_{m_i} \lambda_{mu}} - \frac{S_h \rho_{m_h}\left(\alpha_i^2 \rho_{m_i} M_{i_s} \lambda_{mu} + \alpha_u^2 \lambda_{m_i} \rho_{mu} M_{us}\right)}{k_1 \lambda_{m_i} \lambda_{mu}^2}}{2T_h \sqrt{\frac{S_h \rho_{m_h}\left(\alpha_i^2 \rho_{m_i} M_{i_s} \lambda_{mu} + \alpha_u^2 \lambda_{m_i} \rho_{mu} M_{us}\right)}{k_1 \lambda_{m_i} \lambda_{mu}}}} = -0.442582,$$

$$\partial R_0|_{\lambda_{m_i}} = \frac{\frac{S_h \alpha_u^2 \rho_{m_h} \rho_{mu} M_{us}}{k_1 \lambda_{m_i} \lambda_{mu}} - \frac{S_h \rho_{m_h}\left(\alpha_i^2 \rho_{m_i} M_{i_s} \lambda_{mu} + \alpha_u^2 \lambda_{m_i} \rho_{mu} M_{us}\right)}{k_1 \lambda_{m_i}^2 \lambda_{mu}}}{2T_h \sqrt{\frac{S_h \rho_{m_h}\left(\alpha_i^2 \rho_{m_i} M_{i_s} \lambda_{mu} + \alpha_u^2 \lambda_{m_i} \rho_{mu} M_{us}\right)}{k_1 \lambda_{m_i} \lambda_{mu}}}} = -5.51208,$$

$$\partial R_0|_{\alpha_u} = \frac{S_h \alpha_u \rho_{m_h} \rho_{m_u} M_{u_s}}{k_1 T_h \lambda_{m_u} \sqrt{\frac{S_h \rho_{m_h}\left(\alpha_i^2 \rho_{m_i} M_{i_s} \lambda_{mu} + \alpha_u^2 \lambda_{m_i} \rho_{mu} M_{us}\right)}{k_1 \lambda_{m_i} \lambda_{mu}}}} = 0.0831588,$$

$$\partial R_0|_{\alpha_i} = \frac{S_h \alpha_i \rho_{m_h} \rho_{m_i} M_{i_s}}{k_1 T_h \lambda_{m_i} \sqrt{\frac{S_h \rho_{m_h}\left(\alpha_i^2 \rho_{m_i} M_{i_s} \lambda_{mu} + \alpha_u^2 \lambda_{m_i} \rho_{mu} M_{us}\right)}{k_1 \lambda_{m_i} \lambda_{mu}}}} = 1.44668,$$

$$\partial R_0|_{T_h} = -\frac{\sqrt{\frac{S_h \rho_{m_h}\left(\alpha_i^2 \rho_{m_i} M_{i_s} \lambda_{mu} + \alpha_u^2 \lambda_{m_i} \rho_{mu} M_{us}\right)}{k_1 \lambda_{m_i} \lambda_{mu}}}}{T_h^2} = -0.929038,$$

According to the PRCC analysis (Ref. Figure 5), the most influential parameters are α_i, α_u, ρ_{m_h}, ρ_{m_u} and ρ_i.

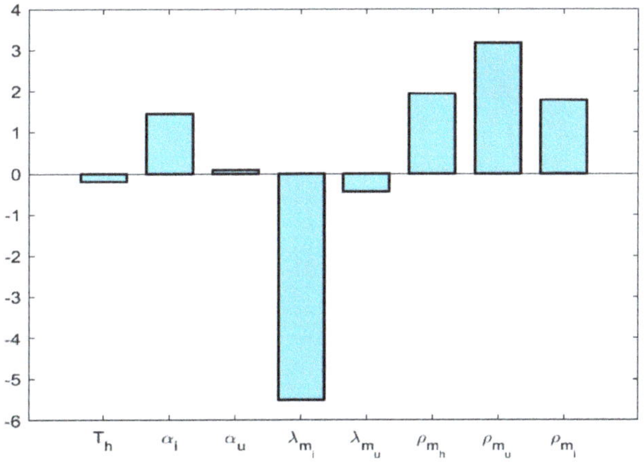

Figure 5. Sensitivity of system parameters.

8. Numerical Simulation

By considering the numerical values quoted in Table 2, the following time series plots were evaluated using MATLAB and Mathematica software. The initial population sizes were $M_i = 0.5, 0.4$, $M_u = 0.5, 0.6$, $M_{i,s} = 0.4,$, $M_{i,i} = 0.1$, $M_{u,s} = 0.4$, $M_{u,i} = 0.1$, $S_h = 0.8$, $I_h = 0.1$, $H_h = 0.1$ and $R_h = 0$. The model was analyzed in five different initial conditions and compared with the single initial conditions.

In Figure 6, the phase plot portrays the time evaluation of aquatic stage *Wolbachia*-infected mosquitoes at various fractional states (left) and under various initial conditions (right). This phase portrays shows that the M_i population is globally stable.

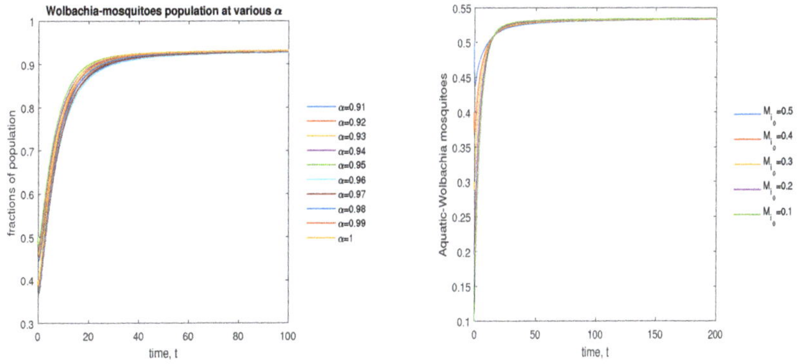

Single initial condition for various α | Several initial condition at $\alpha = 0.95$

Figure 6. Phase plot of aquatic-stage *Wolbachia*-infected mosquitoes with various values of order, α.

In Figure 7, the phase plot portrays the time evaluation of aquatic stage non-*Wolbachia* mosquitoes at various fractional states (left) and under various initial conditions (right). This phase portrays shows that the M_u population is globally stable.

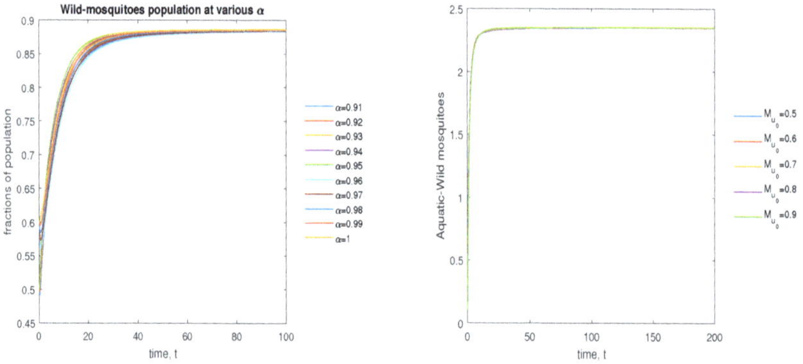

Single initial condition for various α Several initial condition at $\alpha = 0.95$

Figure 7. Phase plot of aquatic-stage wild mosquitoes with various values of order α.

In Figure 8, the phase plot portrays the time evaluation of susceptible *Wolbachia*-infected mosquitoes at various fractional states (left) and under various initial conditions (right). This phase portrait shows that the $M_{i,s}$ population is globally stable.

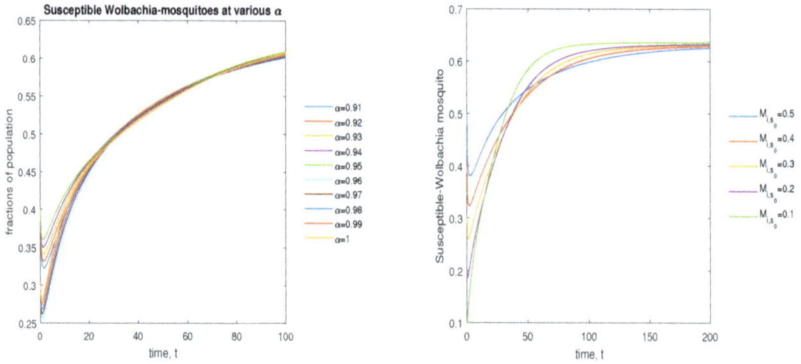

Single initial condition for various α Several initial condition at $\alpha = 0.95$

Figure 8. Phase plot of susceptible *Wolbachia* mosquitoes with various values of order α.

In Figure 9, the phase plot portrays the time evaluation of infectious *Wolbachia*-infected mosquitoes at various fractional states (left) and under various initial conditions (right). This phase portrait shows that the $M_{i,i}$ population is globally stable.

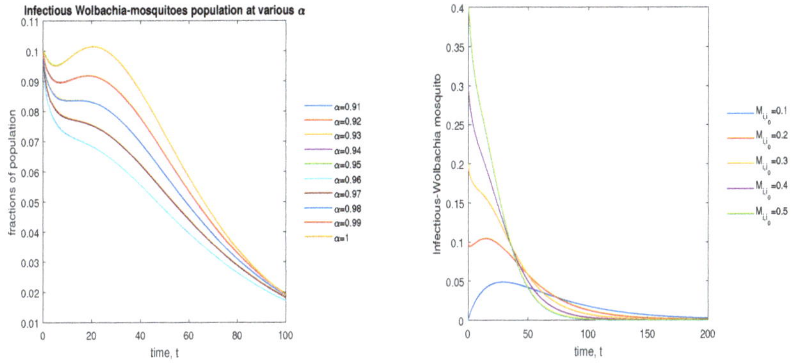

Single initial condition for various α Several initial condition at $\alpha = 0.95$

Figure 9. Phase plot of infectious *Wolbachia* mosquitoes with various values of order α.

In Figure 10, the phase plot portrays the time evaluation of susceptible non-*Wolbachia* mosquitoes at various fractional states (left) and under various initial conditions (right). This phase portrait shows that the $M_{u,s}$ population is globally stable.

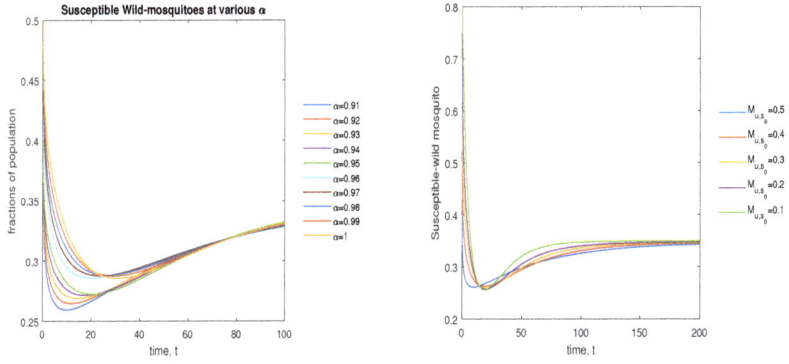

Single initial condition for various α Several initial condition at $\alpha = 0.95$

Figure 10. Phase plot of susceptible wild mosquitoes with various values of order α.

In Figure 11, the phase plot portrays the time evaluation of infectious non-*Wolbachia* mosquitoes at various fractional states (left) and under various initial conditions (right). This phase portrait shows that the $M_{u,1}$ population is globally stable.

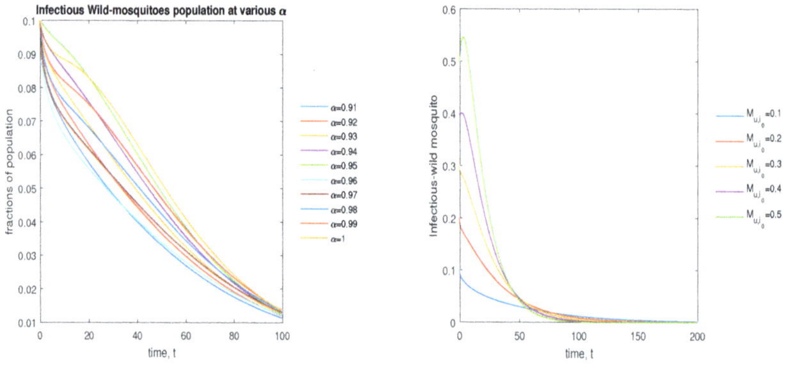

Single initial condition for various α Several initial condition at $\alpha = 0.95$

Figure 11. Phase plot of infectious wild mosquitoes with various values of order α.

In Figure 12, the phase plot portrays the time evaluation of the susceptible human population at various fractional states (left) and under various initial conditions (right). This phase portrait shows that the S_h population is globally stable.

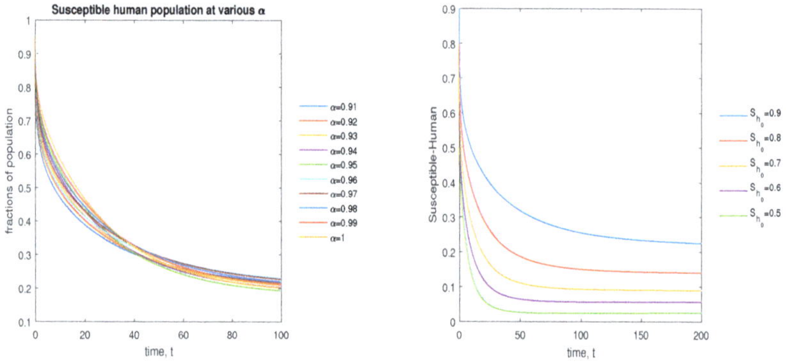

Single initial condition for various α Several initial condition at $\alpha = 0.95$

Figure 12. Phase plot of the susceptible human population with various values of order α.

In Figure 13, the phase plot portrays the time evaluation of the infectious human population at various fractional states (left) and under various initial conditions (right). This phase portrait shows that the I_h population is globally stable.

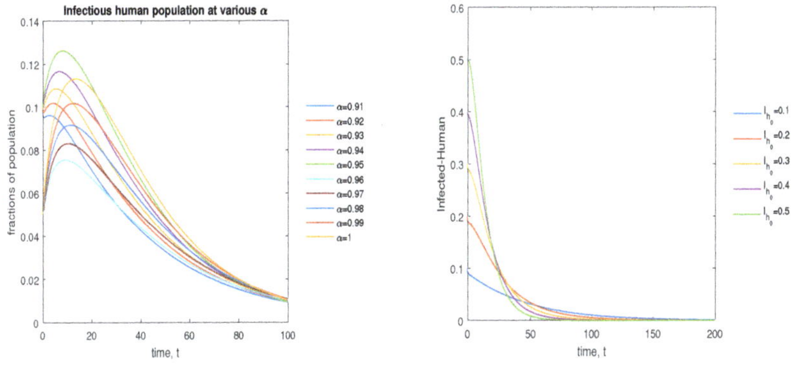

Single initial condition for various α Several initial condition at $\alpha = 0.95$

Figure 13. Phase plot of the infectious human population with various values of order α.

In Figure 14, the phase plot portrays the time evaluation of hospitalized human population at various fractional states (left) and under various initial conditions (right). This phase portrait shows that the H_h population is globally stable.

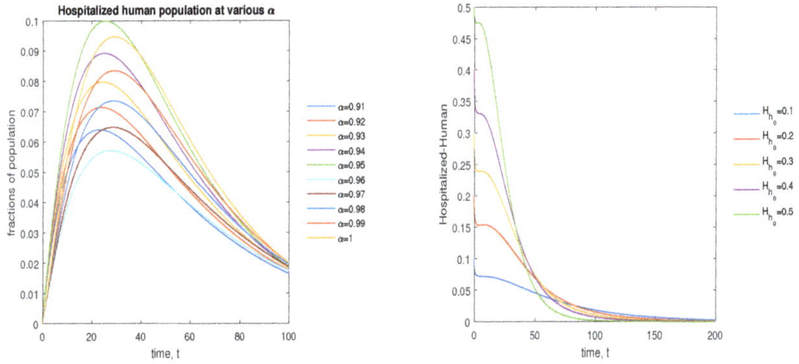

Single initial condition for various α Several initial condition at $\alpha = 0.95$

Figure 14. Phase plot of hospitalized human population with various values of order α.

In Figure 15, the phase plot portrays the time evaluation of the recovered human population at various fractional states (left) and under various initial conditions (right). This phase portrait shows that the R_h population is globally stable.

To find a suitable strain, we included a parameter c_y in both M_i and M_u to measure the cytoplasmic incompatibility created by an injected *Wolbachia* strain. For instance, we considered five different strains of *Wolbachia*, as mentioned in [64]. The values were

These CI values from Table 3 were implemented in a system (2), and the corresponding time series plots are depicted in Figure 16. From Figure 16, we can understand that the *Wolbachia* strain $wAlbB$ is the best strain economically because of its complete CI. In the above figure (left), the aquatic-stage mosquitoes with increased *Wolbachia* for the CI value of $wAlbB$, and in the next figure (Right), the aquatic non-*Wolbachia* mosquitoes are decreased and maintained at a particular level to sustain hereditary. Due to these reasons, the strain $wAlbB$ is one of the best strains economically in a real-world situation.

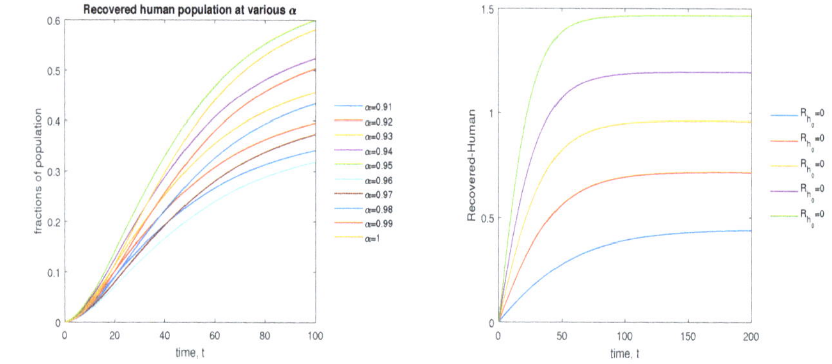

Single initial condition for various α Several initial condition at $\alpha = 0.95$

Figure 15. Phase plot of recovered human population with various values of order α.

Table 3. The values of CI created by various strains.

S. No	Strain	CI
1.	wMelCS	0.20–0.83
2.	wAlbB	0.20–0.88
3.	wMel	0.826–2.516
4.	wPip	0.367–0.681

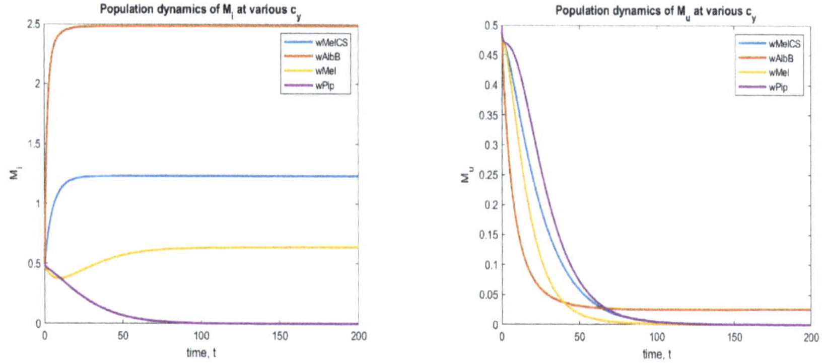

Wolbachia-infected mosquitoes Non-*Wolbachia* mosquitoes

Figure 16. Phase plots of both *Wolbachia* and non-*Wolbachia* mosquitoes for various strains.

9. Conclusions

A novel density-dependent, fractional-order mathematical model incorporating the complete cytoplasmic incompatibility was developed. To analytically solve the proposed model, the Caputo fractional derivative was utilized. Various mathematical analyses, such as positiveness and boundedness, were performed to support the fact that our developed model is as similar to a real-world phenomenon as possible. In the light of next-generation matrix theory, the basic reproduction number (BRN) was derived. The BRNs of disease-free and endemic equilibriums were analyzed by eight possible cases. From this analysis, our model shows that whenever *Wolbachia* mosquitoes exist, there is a notable decrease in disease spread, as the BRN is derived at *Wolbachia* alone and the coexistence state (both *Wolbachia* and non-*Wolbachia*) equilibrium points to the values of $R_0 < 1$. This means that zero disease transmission exists. In another case, suppose there exist non-*Wolbachia* mosquitoes with values of $R_0 > 1$. There is a hike in the disease-spread rate. The local stability of the proposed equilibrium points was derived via the Routh–Hurwitz criterion, and the global stability results were proved via the LMI approach. Moreover, to understand the disease-spread's dynamics, we can vary the fractional-order α, and can see how gradually the population size increases and decreases. Through numerical analysis, we proved that the particular strain $wAlbB$ is the best strain among all existing strains by having high CI and a high ability to block the virus inside the mosquitoes. Through our results, we proved that *Wolbachia* is an effective method to control Mosquito-borne diseases and $wAlbB$ is an economically suitable strain.

Author Contributions: Conceptualization, D.J. and R.R.; methodology, D.J. and S.A.J.; software, D.J.; validation, R.R., J.A. and H.K.; formal analysis, D.J.; investigation, R.R.; resources, D.J.; data curation, D.J.; writing—original draft preparation, D.J.; writing—review and editing, J.A.; visualization, D.J. and S.A.J.; supervision,J.A.; project administration, J.A.; funding acquisition, J.A. All authors have read and agreed to the published version of the manuscript.

Funding: This article has been written with the joint partial financial support of Center for Nonlinear Systems, the Chennai Institute of Technology, India, vide funding number CIT/CNS/2022/RP-017, RUSA-Phase 2.0 grant sanctioned vide letter No. F 24-51/2014-U, Policy (TN Multi-Gen), Dept. of Edn. Govt. of India. J.A. and H.K. would like to thank Prince Sultan University and OSTIM Technical University for their endless support.

Data Availability Statement: Not applicable.

Conflicts of Interest: The authors declare no conflict of interest.

References

1. Bhatt, S.; Gething, P.W.; Brady, O.J.; Messina, J.P.; Farlow, A.W.; Moyes, C.L.; Drake, J.M.; Brownstein, J.S.; Hoen, A.G.; Sankoh, O. The global distribution and burden of dengue. *Nature* **2013**, *496*, 504–507. [CrossRef] [PubMed]
2. Cattarino, L.; Rodriguez-Barraquer, I.; Imai, N.; Cummings, D.A.T.; Ferguson, N.M. Mapping global variation in dengue transmission intensity. *Sci. Transl. Med.* **2020**, *12*, 105788. [CrossRef]
3. Evelyn, M.; Murray, A.; Quam, M.B.; Wilder-Smith, A. Epidemiology of dengue: Past, present and future prospects. *Clin. Epidemiol.* **2013**, *5*, 299.
4. Shepard, D.S.; Undurraga, E.A.; Halasa, Y.A.; Stanaway, J.D. The global economic burden of dengue: A systematic analysis. *Lancet Infect. Dis.* **2016**, *16*, 935–941. [CrossRef]
5. Souza-Neto, J.A.; Powell, J.R.; Bonizzoni, M. *Aedes Aegypti* Vector Competence Stud. A Rev. Infection. *Genet. Sel. Evol.* **2019**, *67*, 191–209. [CrossRef] [PubMed]
6. World Health Organization, Vector-Borne Diseases Fact Sheet. Available online: https://www.who.int/news-room/fact-sheets/detail/vector-borne-diseases (accessed on 12 December 2022).
7. Jose, S.A.; Raja, R.; Omede, B.I.; Agarwal, R.P.; Alzabut, J.; Cao, J. Balas, V.E. Mathematical Modeling on Co-infection: Transmission Dynamics of Zika virus and Dengue fever. *Nonlinear Dyn.* **2022**. [CrossRef]
8. Baldacchino, F.; Caputo, B.; Chandre, F.; Drago, A.; Torre, A.D.; Montarsi, F.; Rizzoli, A. Control methods against invasive *Aedes* mosquitoes in Europe: A review. *Pest Manag. Sci.* **2015**, *71*, 1471–1485. [CrossRef] [PubMed]
9. Somwang, P.; Yanola, J.; Suwan, W.; Walton, C.; Lumjuan, N.; Prapanthadara, L.A.; Somboon, P. Enzymes-based resistant mechanism in pyrethroid resistant and susceptible *Aedes aegypti* strains from northern Thailand. *Parasitol. Res.* **2011**, *109*, 531–537. [CrossRef]
10. Silva, J.V.J., Jr.; Lopes, T.R.R.; de Oliveira-Filho, E.F.; Oliveira, R.A.S.; Duraes-Carvalho, R.; Gil, L.H.V.G. Current status, challenges and perspectives in the development of vaccines against yellow fever, dengue, Zika, and chikungunya viruses. *Acta Trop.* **2018**, *182*, 257–263. [CrossRef]
11. Joubert, D.A.; Walker, T.; Carrington, L.B.; De Bruyne, J.T.; Kien, D.H.T.; Hoang, N.L.T.; Chau, N.V.V.; Iturbe-Ormaetxe, I.; Simmons, C.P.; O'Neill, S.L. Establishment of a *Wolbachia* superinfection in *Aedes Aegypti* Mosquitoes A Potential Approach Future Resist. Management. *PLoS Pathog.* **2016**, *12*, e1005434. [CrossRef] [PubMed]
12. World Mosquito Program, How *Wolbachia* Method Works. Available online: https://www.worldmosquitoprogram.org/en/work/wolbachia-method (accessed on 12 December 2022).
13. Xi, Z.; Khoo, C.C.; Dobson, S.L. *Wolbachia* establishment and invasion in an *Aedes Aegypti* Lab. Population. *Science* **2005**, *310*, 326–328. [CrossRef] [PubMed]

14. Jimenez, N.E.; Gerdtzen, Z.P.; Olivera-Nappa, A.; Salgado, J.C.; Concaa, C. Novel symbiotic genome-scale model reveals *Wolbachia's* arboviral pathogen blocking mechanism in *Aedes Aegypti*. *MBio* **2021**, *12*, e01563-21. [CrossRef]
15. Hoffmann, A.A.; Montgomery, B.L.; Popovici, J.; Iturbeormaetxe, I.; Johnson, P.H.; Muzzi, F.; Greenfield, M.; Durkan, M.; Leong, Y.S.; Dong, Y. Successful establishment of *Wolbachia* in *Aedes* populations to suppress dengue transmission. *Nature* **2011**, *476*, 454–457. [CrossRef] [PubMed]
16. Crawford, J.E.; Clarke, D.W.; Criswell, V.; Desnoyer, M.; Cornel, D.; Deegan, B.; Gong, K.; Hopkins, K.C.; Howell, P.; Hyde, J.S.J.S. Efficient production of male *Wolbachia*-infected *Aedes Aegypti* Mosquitoes Enables Large-Scale Suppr. Wild Populations. *Nat. Biotechnol.* **2020**, *38*, 482–492. [CrossRef] [PubMed]
17. Dianavinnarasi, J.; Raja, R.; Alzabut, J.; Niezabitowski, M.; Selvam, G.; Bagdasar, O. An LMI Approach-Based Mathematical Model to Control *Aedes Aegypti* Mosquitoes Popul. Via Biol. Control. *Math. Probl. Eng.* **2021**, *2021*, 5565949. [CrossRef]
18. Dianavinnarasi, J.; Raja, R.; Alzabut, J.; Niezabitowski, M.; Bagdasar, O. Controlling *Wolbachia* transmission and invasion dynamics among *Aedes aegypti* population via impulsive control strategy. *Symmetry* **2021**, *13*, 434. [CrossRef]
19. Pagendam, D.E.; Trewin, B.J.; Snoad, N.; Ritchie, S.A.; Hoffmann, A.A.; Staunton, K.M.; Paton, C.; Beebe, N. Modelling the *Wolbachia* incompatible insect technique: Strategies for effective mosquito population elimination. *BMC Biol.* **2020**, *18*, 161. [CrossRef]
20. Jose, S.A.; Raja, R.; Dianavinnarasi, J.; Baleanu, D.; Jirawattanapanit, A. Mathematical Modeling of Chickenpox in Phuket: Efficacy of Precautionary Measures and Bifurcation Analysis. *Biomed. Signal. Proces.* **2023**, *84*, 104714. [CrossRef]
21. Sadek, L.; Sadek, O.; Alaoui, H.T.; Abdo, M.S.; Shah, K.; Abdeljawad, T. Fractional Order Modeling of Predicting COVID-19 with Isolation and Vaccination Strategies in Morocco. *CMES-Comput. Model. Eng. Sci.* **2023**, *136*, 1931–1950. [CrossRef]
22. Abdeljawad, T.; Abdo, M.S.; Shah, K. Theoretical and numerical analysis for transmission dynamics of COVID-19 mathematical model involving Caputo-Fabrizio derivative. *Adv. Differ. Equ.* **2021**, *2021*, 1–17.
23. Thirthar, A.A.; Abboubakar, H.; Khan, A.; Abdeljawad, T. Mathematical modeling of the COVID-19 epidemic with fear impact. *AIMS Math.* **2023**, *8*, 6447–6465. [CrossRef]
24. Magin, R.L. Fractional calculus models of complex dynamics in biological tissues. *Comput. Math. Appl.* **2010**, *59*, 1586–1593. [CrossRef]
25. Heydari, M.H.; Razzaghi, M.; Avazzadeh, Z. Numerical investigation of variable-order fractional Benjamin–Bona–Mahony–Burgers equation using a pseudo-spectral method. *Math Meth. Appl. Sci.* **2021**, 1–15. [CrossRef]
26. Ghafoor, A.; Khan, N.; Hussain, M.; Ullah, R. A hybrid collocation method for the computational study of multi-term time fractional partial differential equations. *Comput. Math. Appl.* **2022**, *128*, 130–144. [CrossRef]
27. Haq, S.; Ghafoor, A.; Hussain, M. Numerical solutions of variable order time fractional (1+1)- and (1+2)-dimensional advection dispersion and diffusion models. *Appl. Math. Comput.* **2019**, *360*, 107–121. [CrossRef]
28. Barclay, H.J. The sterile insect release method on species with two-stage life cycles. *Popul. Ecol.* **1980**, *21*, 165–180. [CrossRef]
29. Barclay, H.J.; Mackauer, M. The sterile insect release method for pest control: A density-dependent model. *Environ. Entomol.* **1980**, *9*, 810–817. [CrossRef]
30. Barclay, H.J. Pest population stability under sterile releases. *Popul. Ecol.* **1982**, *24*, 405–416. [CrossRef]
31. Barclay, H.J. Modeling incomplete sterility in a sterile release program: Interactions with other factors. *Popul. Ecol.* **2001**, *43*, 197–206. [CrossRef]
32. Barclay, H.J. Mathematical models for the use of sterile insects, in Sterile Insect Technique. In *Principles and Practice in Area-Wide Integrated Pest Management*; Dyck, V.A., Hendrichs, J., Robinson, A.S., Eds.; Springer: Berlin/Heidelberg, Germany, 2005; pp. 147–174.
33. Dame, D.A.; Curtis, C.F.; Benedict, M.Q.; Robinson, A.S.; Knols, B.G. Historical applications of induced sterilization in field populations of mosquitoes. *Malar. J.* **2009**, *8*, S2. [CrossRef]
34. Ranathunge, T.; Harishchandra, J.; Maiga, H.; Bouyer, J.; Gunawardena, Y.I.N.S.; Hapugoda, M. Development of the Sterile Insect Technique to control the dengue vector *Aedes Aegypti* (Linnaeus) Sri Lanka. *PLoS ONE* **2022**, *17*, e0265244. [CrossRef] [PubMed]
35. Zhu, Z.; Yan, R.; Feng, X. Existence and stability of two periodic solutions for an interactive wild and sterile mosquitoes model. *J. Biol. Dyn.* **2022**, *16*, 277–293. [CrossRef] [PubMed]
36. Cai, L.; Ai, S.; Li, J. Dynamics of mosquitoes populations with different strategies for releasing sterile mosquitoes. *SIAP* **2014**, *74*, 1786–1809. [CrossRef]
37. Li, J. New revised simple models for interactive wild and sterile mosquito populations and their dynamics. *J. Biol. Dyn.* **2017**, *11*, 316–333. [CrossRef]
38. Ndii, M.Z.; Hickson, R.I.; Mercer, G.N. Modelling the introduction of *Wolbachia* into *Aedes aegypti* mosquitoes to reduce dengue transmission. *ANZIAM J.* **2012**, *53*, 213–227.
39. Ndii, M.Z.; Hickson, R.I.; Allingham, D.; Mercer, G.N. Modelling the transmission dynamics of dengue in the presence of *Wolbachia*. *Math. Biosci.* **2015**, *262*, 157–166. [CrossRef] [PubMed]
40. Ndii, M.Z.; Allingham, D.; Hickson, R.I.; Glass, K. The effect of *Wolbachia* on dengue outbreaks when dengue is repeatedly introduced. *Theor. Popul. Biol.* **2016**, *111*, 9–15. [CrossRef]
41. Ndii, M.Z.; Allingham, D.; Hickson, R.I.; Glass, K. The effect of *Wolbachia* on dengue dynamics in the presence of two serotypes of dengue: Symmetric and asymmetric epidemiological characteristics. *Epidemiol. Infect.* **2016**, *144*, 2874–2882. [CrossRef]

42. Ndii, M.Z.; Wiraningsih, E.D.; Anggriani, N.; Supriatna, A.K. *Dengue Fever-a Resilient Threat in the Face of Innovation: Mathematical Model as a Tool for the Control of Vector-Borne Diseases: Wolbachia Example*; Intechopen: London, UK, 2018.
43. Ndii, M.Z. Modelling the Use of Vaccine and Wolbachia on Dengue Transmission Dynamics. *Infect. Dis. Trop. Med.* **2020**, *5*, 78. [CrossRef]
44. Ndii, M.Z.; Messakh, J.J.; Djahi, B.S. Effects of vaccination on dengue transmission dynamics. *JPCS* **2020**, *1490*, 012048. [CrossRef]
45. Ndii, M.Z.; Supriatna, A.K. Stochastic Dengue Mathematical Model in the Presence of *Wolbachia*: Exploring the Disease Extinction. *Nonlinear Dyn. Syst. Theory* **2020**, *20*, 214–227.
46. Su, Y.; Zheng, B.; Zou, X. Wolbachia Dynamics in Mosquitoes with Incomplete CI and Imperfect Maternal Transmission by a DDE System. *Bull. Math. Biol.* **2022**, 84–95. [CrossRef] [PubMed]
47. Yu, J.; Zheng, B. Modeling Wolbachia infection in mosquito population via discrete dynamical models. *J. Differ. Equ.* **2019**, *25*, 1549–1567. [CrossRef]
48. Ai, S.; Li, J.; Yu, J.; Zheng, B. Stage-structured models for interactive wild and periodically and impulsively released sterile mosquitoes. *Discret. Contin. Dyn. Syst. Ser. B* **2022**, *27*, 3039–3052. [CrossRef]
49. Hoffmann, A.A.; Ross, P.A.; Rasic, G. *Wolbachia* strains for disease control: Ecological and evolutionary considerations. *Evol. Appl.* **2015**, *8*, 751–768. [CrossRef]
50. Van-Driessche, D.; Watmough, J. Reproduction numbers and subthreshold endemic equilibria for compartmental models of disease transmission. *Math. Biosci.* **2002**, *180*, 29–48. [CrossRef] [PubMed]
51. Podlubny, I. *An Introduction to Fractiorlal Derivatives, Fractiorlal Differential Eqnations, to Methods of Their Solutiori and Some of Their Applications*; Academic Press: London, UK, 1999.
52. Caputo, M. Linear model of dissipation whose *Q* is almost frequency independent-II. *Geophys. J. R. Astron. Soc.* **1967**, *13*, 529–539. [CrossRef]
53. Boyd, S.; Ghaoui, L.; Feron, E.; Balakrishnan, V. *Linear Matrix Inequalities in System and Control Theory*; SIAM: Philadelphia, PA, USA, 1994.
54. Wu, H.; Zhang, X.; Xue, S.; Wang, L.; Wang, Y. LMI conditions to global Mittag–Leffler stability of fractional-order neural networks with impulses. *Neurocomputing* **2016**, *193*, 148–154. [CrossRef]
55. Ross, P.A.; Gu, X.; Robinson, K.L.; Yang, Q.; Cottingham, E.; Zhang, Y.; Yeap, H.L.; Xu, X.; Endersby-Harshman, N.M.; Hoffmann, A.A. A *w*AlbB *Wolbachia* Transinfection Displays Stable Phenotypic Effects across Divergent *Aedes Aegypti* Mosq. Backgrounds. *Appl. Environ. Microbiol.* **2021**, *87*, e0126421. [CrossRef]
56. Walker, T.; Johnson, P.H.; Moreira, L.A.; Iturbe-Ormaetxe, I.; Frentiu, F.D.; McMeniman, C.J.; Leong, Y.S.; Dong, Y.; Axford, J.; Kriesner, P.; et al. The wMel Wolbachia strain blocks dengue and invades caged Aedes aegypti populations. *Nature* **2011**, *476*, 450–453. [CrossRef]
57. Yang, H.M.; Macoris, M.L.G.; Galvani, K.C.; Andrighetti, M.T.M.; Wanderley, D.M.V. Assessing the effects of temperature on the population of Aedes aegypti, the vector of dengue. *Epidemiol. Infect.* **2009**, *137*, 1188–1202. [CrossRef] [PubMed]
58. Scott, T.W.; Amerasinghe, P.H.; Morrison, A.C.; Lorenz, L.H.; Clark, G.G.; Strickman, D.; Kittayapong, P.; Edman, J.D. Longitudinal studies of *Aedes Aegypti* (*Diptera: Culicidae*) Thail. Puerto Rico: Blood Feed. Frequency. *J. Med. Entomol.* **2000**, *37*, 89–101. [CrossRef]
59. Turley, A.P.; Moreira, L.A.; O'Neill, S.L.; McGraw, E.A. *Wolbachia* infection reduces blood-feeding success in the dengue fever mosquito, Aedes aegypti. *PLoS Negl. Trop. Dis.* **2009**, *3*, e516. [CrossRef] [PubMed]
60. Bian, G.; Xu, Y.; Lu, P.; Xie, Y.; Xi, Z. The endosymbiotic bacterium *Wolbachia* induces resistance to dengue virus in *Aedes Aegypti*. *PLoS Pathog.* **2010**, *6*, e1000833. [CrossRef]
61. Yeap, H.L.; Mee, P.; Walker, T.; Weeks, A.R.; O'Neill, S.L.; Johnson, P.; Ritchie, S.A.; Richardson, K.M.; Doig, C.; Endersby, N.M. Dynamics of the 'popcorn' Wolbachia infection in outbred Aedes aegypti informs prospects for mosquito vector control. *Genetics* **2011**, *187*, 583–595. [CrossRef] [PubMed]
62. United Nations, Human Birth and Death Rates. Available online: https://population.un.org/wpp/Download/Standard/Population/ (accessed on 12 December 2022).
63. Khan, M.A.; Fatmawati, C. Dengue infection modeling and its optimal control analysis in East Java, Indonesia. *Heliyon* **2021**, *7*, e06023. [CrossRef]
64. Liang, X.; Liu, J.; Bian, G.; Xi, Z. *Wolbachia* Inter-strain competition and inhibition of expression of cytoplasmic incompatibility in the mosquito. *Front Microbiol.* **2020**, *11*, 1638. [CrossRef] [PubMed]

found by Birajdar that the highly non-linear temporal fractional diffusion equation is stable [27]. Discrete Adomain decomposition was also used by Dhaigue and Birajdar [28–30] to solve several kinds of fractional partial differential equations. Recently, an analytical solution to fractional differential equations was discovered by Dhaigue and Birajdar [31]. Mehmood et al. [32] worked on a partial differential equation. Boulares et al. [33], Abuasbeh et al. [34–36], and Alnahdi et al. [37] investigated the existence–uniqueness of the fractional evolution equations.

In spite of the fact that the formalism of constant-order fraction calculus can be used to solve certain extremely pertinent physical problems, it cannot account for a significant class of physical events where the order itself is determined by either dependent or independent variables. For example, it has been discovered that the reaction kinetics of proteins exhibit relaxation mechanisms that can be accurately represented by temperature-dependent fractional orders [38]. As a result, temperature affects the underlying physics of reaction kinetics. Hence, it makes sense that a differential equation with operators that update their order as a function of temperature will provide a more accurate representation of protein dynamics. Despite their simplicity, variable-order operators may be more appropriate for expressing certain categories of physical problems.

There are a limited number of papers on numerical solutions for variable-order fractional diffusion equations. The existing research articles include that of Lin et al. [39], who created an explicit finite difference method for variable-order non-linear fractional diffusion equations and evaluated its stability and convergence. Zhuang et al. [40] developed numerical techniques for the variable-order fractional advection–diffusion equation with a non-linear source term. Sun et al. [41] proposed a model for variable-order fractional diffusion equations with a variable order in both time and space. Chen et al. [42] developed a numerical scheme for the variable-order anomalous sub-diffusion equation with high spatial accuracy. Chen et al. [42] also developed numerical techniques for a two-dimensional variable-order anomalous sub-diffusion equation. Additionally, Chen et al. [43] proposed a numerical scheme for the variable-order non-linear reaction sub-diffusion equation. Shen et al. [41] solved the variable-order time-fractional diffusion equation, while Sun et al. [44] examined explicit, implicit, and Crank–Nicolson schemes for the variable-order time-fractional linear diffusion equation, including a discussion of their stability and convergence. However, some authors, such as Diaz and Coimnra [45], and Soon et al. [46,47], have not addressed the stability of numerical solutions. This issue is addressed in the current paper.

Approximate solutions of linear time-fractional differential equations are given in [45]. It explores the application of a numerical method for resolving linear time-fractional differential equations based on the Caputo sense. A theorem is presented in the paper that illustrates the relationship between the Kamal transform and nth-order Caputo derivatives. New group iterative schemes for the numerical solution of a two-dimensional anomalous fractional sub-diffusion equation with specific initial and boundary conditions are developed in [48]. These schemes are a combination of standard and rotated (skewed) five-point modified implicit finite difference approximations. An alternating direction implicit (ADI) method for solving multi-dimensional fractional integro-differential problems is proposed in [49]. The solution is discretized in two stages: the fractional integral term and time-fractional derivative are discretized using the convolution quadrature and Grunwald formula, while the spatial discretization is obtained through finite difference. The ADI algorithms aim to reduce computational burden, and the convergence of the method is analyzed through the energy method. A new extended cubic B-spline approximation for the numerical solution of the time-fractional Fisher equation is given [50]. A non-linear PDE is converted to a linear one using Taylor series expansion and the time-fractional derivative is approximated using Caputo sense [50]. The space dimension is calculated using the new B-spline. This approximation is unconditionally stable and convergent, and its accuracy is measured through errors.

The research in question seeks to address two major challenges in the field of fractional differential equations. Firstly, while there are numerous methods available for solving fractional differential equations, many of them lack stability analysis. In this research work, the authors not only develop a model for solving time-fractional initial boundary value problems, but also discuss the stability of the implicit finite difference scheme. Secondly, the authors design a model that can be applied to both linear and semi-linear equations. While similar models have been applied to semi-linear equations by other authors, the authors here apply this model to linear equations and present numerical results. Linear time-fractional equations have several advantages over semi-linear time-fractional equations. They are easier to solve, as standard numerical methods can be used, whereas semi-linear equations require more advanced methods. Furthermore, linear time-fractional equations have a simpler mathematical structure and can be used to model a broad range of physical and biological processes. In contrast, semi-linear time-fractional equations are typically limited to more specific applications. Additionally, linear time-fractional equations are well-posed, meaning that solutions exist, are unique, and depend continuously on the initial conditions, while the well-posedness of semi-linear time-fractional equations can be more challenging to establish. The aim of this paper is to present a novel implicit finite difference method for solving linear/semi-linear variable-order time-fractional initial boundary value problems. The paper is organized in a clear and comprehensive manner, as follows: Section 2 develops the implicit finite difference scheme, which utilizes central finite difference approximations for space derivatives and Caputo's concept for time-fractional derivatives. The stability of the scheme is thoroughly evaluated to ensure its accuracy and reliability. In Section 3, several numerical problems are addressed using the method developed in Section 2. The numerical solutions are obtained using MATLAB and graphically visualized to provide a clear understanding of the results. The final section summarizes the key findings and provides a discussion of the implications of the results, serving as a conclusion to the research and highlighting the importance of the work presented in the paper.

2. Methodology

The first part of this section is devoted to the derivation of the scheme, and the second part contains the method to check the stability of the proposed scheme.

2.1. Implicit Finite Difference Scheme

We augment the implicit numerical scheme in this section. Let us take a variable-order time-fractional diffusion equation as an example:

$$\frac{\partial^{\beta(x,t)}\phi(x,t)}{\partial t^{\beta(x,t)}} = c(x,t)\phi_{xx} + f(\phi), \tag{1}$$

where

$$0 < x < L_x, \quad 0 < t \leq T, \quad 0 < \beta(x,t) \leq 1,$$

$$\phi(x,0) = s(x),$$

$$\phi(0,t) = 0 = \phi(L_x,t),$$

or

$$\phi(0,t) = 0 = \frac{\partial\phi(L_x,t)}{\partial x}.$$

The function $f(\phi)$ is non-linear. In absence of the function $f(\phi)$, the Equation (1) is linear.

2.2. Discretization

Let $[0,1]$ be the domain of interest. We discretize the domain first. We define $x_i = ih$, where $0 \le i \le M$, $Mh = Lx$, $t_j = jk$, $0 \le j \le N$, $Nk = T$,k represent the time step size and h represents the space step length. Let us assume that ϕ_i^j is the numerical approximation of $\phi(x_i, t_j)$ and $f_i^j(\phi_i^j) = f(x_i, t_j, \phi_i^j)$. Further suppose that the non-linear function $f_i^j(\phi_i^j)$ satisfies the Lipschitz condition. $\mid f_i^j(\phi_i^j) - f_i^j(\bar{\phi}_i^j) \mid \le L_p \mid \phi_i^j - \bar{\phi}_i^j \mid$, L_p is a non-negative Lipschitz constant.

2.3. Development of the Scheme

Consider the fractional-order diffusion Equation (1), where β is fractional order. The variable-order fractional derivative of order $\beta(x,t)$ is defined by Coimbra in views of Caputo and is written as

$$\frac{\partial^{\beta}\phi(x,t)}{\partial t^{\beta}} = \begin{cases} \dfrac{1}{\Gamma(1-\beta(x,t))} \int_0^t \dfrac{\phi_{\xi} d\xi}{(t-\xi)^{\beta(x,t)}} & \text{if} \quad 0 < \beta(x,t) < 1, \\ \phi_t, & \text{if} \quad \beta(x,t) = 1. \end{cases} \tag{2}$$

The Caputo derivative is a popular fractional derivative operator and has several advantages over other advanced operators. One advantage is that it has a well-defined initial condition, which is important in the numerical solution of fractional differential equations. The Caputo derivative is defined using a standard integer-order derivative and is therefore easier to understand and compute compared with other advanced operators that are defined using more complex mathematical concepts. Additionally, the Caputo derivative has a more intuitive physical interpretation than other fractional derivative operators, as it models the memory and hereditary properties of a system, which are important in many real-world applications. Furthermore, the Caputo derivative has been widely studied in the literature and has well-established mathematical properties, making it a reliable and widely accepted choice for modeling fractional dynamic systems.

Initially, as the boundary value problem needs to be discretized to be able to solve (1), it is first necessary to discretize the variable-order time-fractional derivative (2) as follows:

$$\begin{aligned} \frac{\partial^{\beta(x_i,t_{j+1})}\phi(x_i,t_{j+1})}{\partial t^{\beta(x_i,t_{j+1})}} &= \frac{1}{\Gamma(1-\beta(x_i,t_{j+1}))} \int_0^{t_j} \frac{\phi_{\xi} d\xi}{(t_{j+1}-\xi)^{\beta(x_i,t_{j+1})}}, \\ &= \frac{1}{\Gamma(1-\beta(x_i,t_{j+1}))} \sum_{n=0}^{j-1} \int_{n(k)}^{(n+1)k} \frac{\partial\phi(x_i,\xi)}{\partial\xi} \frac{d\xi}{(t_{j+1}-\xi)^{\beta(x_i,t_{j+1})}}. \end{aligned}$$

Here, we can use the forward difference approximation

$$\begin{aligned} \frac{\partial^{\beta(x_i,t_{j+1})}\phi(x_i,t_{j+1})}{\partial t^{\beta(x_i,t_{j+1})}} &= \frac{1}{\Gamma(1-\beta(x_i,t_{j+1}))} \sum_{n=0}^{j-1} \left(\frac{\phi(x_i,t_{n+1}) - \phi(x_i,t_n)}{k} \right) \\ &\quad \times \int_{n(k)}^{(n+1)k} \frac{d\xi}{(t_{j+1}-\xi)^{\beta(x_i,t_{j+1})}}, \\ &= \frac{1}{\Gamma(1-\beta(x_i,t_j))} \sum_{n=0}^{j-1} \frac{\phi_i^{n+1} - \phi_i^n}{k} \int_{(j-n-1)k}^{(j-n)k} \frac{d\eta}{\eta^{\beta(x_i,t_j)}}. \end{aligned}$$

Equivalently, the above expression can also be written as

$$\frac{\partial^{\beta(x_i,t_{j+1})}\phi(x_i,t_{j+1})}{\partial t^{\beta(x_i,t_{j+1})}} = \frac{1}{\Gamma(1-\beta(x_i,t_j))} \sum_{n=0}^{j-1} \frac{\phi_i^{j-n} - \phi_i^{j-n-1}}{k} \int_{(n)k}^{(n+1)k} \eta^{-\beta(x_i,t_j)} d\eta.$$

Integration yields

$$\frac{\partial^{\beta(x_i,t_{j+1})}u(x_i,t_{j+1})}{\partial t^{\beta(x_i,t_{j+1})}} = \frac{1}{\Gamma(1-\beta(x_i,t_j))}\sum_{n=0}^{j-1}\frac{\phi_i^{j-n}-\phi_i^{j-n-1}}{k} \times \frac{((n+1)k)^{1-\beta(x_i,t_j)}-((n)k)^{1-\beta(x_i,t_j)}}{1-\beta(x_i,t_j)}.$$

Using $\Gamma(1+\beta)=\beta\Gamma(\beta)$ and expanding the summation for $n=0$, we reach

$$\begin{aligned}\frac{\partial^{\beta(x_i,t_{j+1})}\phi(x_i,t_{j+1})}{\partial t^{\beta(x_i,t_{j+1})}} &= \frac{1}{\Gamma(2-\beta(x_i,t_j))}\frac{\phi_i^j-\phi_i^{j-n-1}}{k}k^{1-\beta(x_i,t_j)} \\ &+\frac{1}{\Gamma(2-\beta(x_i,t_j))}\sum_{n=1}^{j-1}\frac{\phi_i^{j-n}-\phi_i^{j-n-1}}{k}\quad((n+1)k)^{1-\beta(x_i,t_j)}-((n)k)^{1-\beta(x_i,t_j)}, \\ &= \frac{k^{-\beta(x_i,t_j)}}{\Gamma(2-\beta(x_i,t_j))}[(\phi_i^j-\phi_i^{j-1}) \\ &+\sum_{n=1}^{j-1}(\phi_n^{j-l}-\phi_n^{j-n-1})\Big(((n+1)k)^{1-\beta(x_i,t_j)}-((n)k)^{1-\beta(x_i,t_j)}\Big)].\end{aligned}$$

Replacing j by j + 1

$$\begin{aligned}\frac{\partial^{\beta(x_i,t_{j+1})}\phi(x_i,t_{j+1})}{\partial t^{\beta(x_i,t_{j+1})}} &= \frac{k^{-\beta(x_i,t_{j+1})}}{\Gamma(2-\beta(x_i,t_{j+1}))}[(\phi_i^{j+1}-\phi_i^j) \\ &+\sum_{n=1}^{j}(\phi_n^{j+1-n}-\phi_n^{j-n})(((n+1)k)^{1-\beta(x_i,t_{j+1})}-((n)k)^{1-\beta(x_i,t_{j+1})})].\end{aligned}$$

or

$$\frac{\partial^{\beta(x_i,t_{j+1})}\phi(x_i,t_{j+1})}{\partial t^{\beta(x_i,t_{j+1})}} = \frac{k^{-\beta(x_i,t_{j+1})}}{\Gamma(2-\beta(x_i,t_{j+1}))}\left[(\phi_i^{j+1}-u_i^j)+\sum_{n=1}^{j}(\phi_n^{j+1-n}-\phi_n^{j-n})(b_l^{i,j+1})\right]. \quad (3)$$

where

$$b_l^{i,j+1} = ((n+1)k)^{1-\beta(x_i,t_{j+1})}-((n)k)^{1-\beta(x_i,t_{j+1})},\quad i=0,1,\ldots,M; j=0,1,\ldots N.$$

Discretization of non-linear function $f(\phi)$is given as

$$f(x_i,t_j,\phi(x_i,t_j)) = f_i^j(\phi_i^j)+O(k).$$

The second-order finite difference approximation of space derivative is as follows:

$$\phi_{xx} = \frac{\phi_{i-1}^{j+1}-2\phi_i^{j+1}+\phi_{i+1}^{j+1}}{h^2}+O(h^2). \quad (4)$$

Using approximations (3) and (4), the semi-linear diffusion Equation (1) takes the form

$$\frac{k^{-\beta_i^{j+1}}}{\Gamma(2-\beta_i^{j+1})}\left[(\phi_i^{j+1}-\phi_i^j)+\sum_{n=1}^{j}(\phi_n^{j+1-n}-\phi_n^{j-n})b_n^{i,j+1}\right] = c_i^j\left(\frac{\phi_{i-1}^j-2\phi_i^j+\phi_{i+1}^j}{h^2}\right)+f_i^j(\phi_i^j).$$

or

$$(\phi_i^{j+1}-\phi_i^j)+\sum_{n=1}^{j}(\phi_n^{j+1-n}-\phi_n^{j-n})(b_n^{i,j+1}) = r_i^{j+1}\left[\phi_{i-1}^j-2\phi_i^j+\phi_{i+1}^j\right]+f_i^j(\phi_i^j)k^{\beta_i^{j+1}}\Gamma(2-\beta_i^{j+1}).$$

where

$$r_i^{j+1} = \frac{c_i^j k^{\beta_i^{j+1}} \Gamma(2-\beta_i^{j+1})}{h^2}.$$

Through the rearranging of the terms,

$$-r_i^{j+1}\phi_{i-1}^{j+1} + (1+2r_i^{j+1})\phi_i^{j+1} - r_i^{j+1}\phi_{i+1}^{j+1} = \phi_i^j + f_i^j(\phi_i^j)k^{\beta_i^{j+1}}\Gamma(2-\beta_i^{j+1}) \\ - \sum_{n=1}^{j}(\phi_n^{j+1-n} - \phi_n^{j-n})(b_n^{i,j+1}). \quad (5)$$

Assuming initial conditions,

$$\phi_i^0 = s(x_i) \qquad i = 0, 1, \ldots, M. \quad (6)$$

Conditions at the boundary are

$$\phi_0^j = 0 = \phi_M^j \qquad j = 0, 1, \ldots, N. \quad (7)$$

The method of solution is summarized in the below Algorithm 1.

Algorithm 1 Fractional Model of Solving Time-Fractional Initial Boundary Value Problems.

(1) Input: Time-fractional IBVP, step sizes h and k, fractional-order β, coefficient matrix A, and right-hand side matrix b;
Output: Plot of the numerical solution;
Initialize the variables: h, x, T, k, t, β.

(2) Discretize the domain $[0, 1]$ by defining the space and time step size.

(3) Discretize the variable-order time-fractional Caputo derivative and non-linear function;
Set and discretize the initial and boundary condition.

(4) Write the numerical approximation of the given equation and non-linear function.

(5) Use the forward difference approximation for variable-order time-fractional Caputo derivative.

(6) Use central difference approximation for second-order space derivative.

(7) Rearrange terms to obtain the solution of the semi-linear time-fractional diffusion equation.

Initialize the coefficient matrix A and right-hand side matrix b with zeros;
Calculate $r = (k^\beta * \Gamma(2-\beta))/h^2$;
Initialize Solution;
Implicit Scheme;
Set $A(i,i); A(i,i-1); A(i,i+1); b(i,1); A(Lx,Lx); A(Lx,Lx-1)$;
Calculate the solution for time step $j+1 : \phi(j+1,:) = (inv(A) * b)'$;
Store the solution for different values of fractional-order β;
Plot the surface solution plot.

The comparison of the proposed method with previous techniques is given in Table 1 below.

Table 1. Proposed method comparison with previous methods.

Techniques	Formulation	Benefits and Drawbacks
Cubic B-spline approximation for the numerical solution of the time-fractional Fisher equation.	The time-fractional derivative is approximated in Caputo's sense while the space dimension is calculated using a new extended cubic B-spline.	Unconditionally stable and convergent. Applied to non-linear time-fractional partial differential equation.
Efficient ADI numerical methods for multi-dimensional fractional integro-differential problems.	The Riemann–Liouville fractional integral and distributed-order fractional derivative are discretized using the second-order convolution quadrature and weighted Grünwald formula. Spatial discretization is achieved through a centered finite difference technique.	The method is computationally efficient and convergent. Stability of this method is not verified.
New group iterative methods developed for solving the two-dimensional sub-diffusion equation with fractional derivatives and specific boundary conditions.	New iterative schemes using a combination of standard and rotated five-point approximations are developed for numerical solution of two-dimensional fractional sub-diffusion equations.	Computationally efficient. Stability analysis of the method is not provided.
Approximate solutions of linear time-fractional differential equations. The method is suitable for specific boundary conditions.	The numerical approach for solving linear time-fractional differential equations (of Caputo type) was studied and a theorem was established to demonstrate the Kamal transform of the nth-order Caputo derivatives.	High-accuracy solutions for linear time-fractional differential equations are obtained through the proposed numerical scheme. Stability analysis of the scheme is not provided. The method is only applicable to linear time-fractional differential equations.
Proposed	The central finite difference method is used for approximating the second-order spatial derivative and the forward difference for approximating the Caputo derivative of variable order in time.	Applicable to both linear and semi-linear equations. The stability of the scheme is verified. The method is not restricted to specific boundary conditions.

In the next section, we investigate stability of the scheme governed by the discrete Equations (5)–(7).

3. Stability Analysis

For stability, let us assume that $\rho_i^j = \phi_i^j - U_i^j$, where U_i^j is the exact solution at (x_i, t_j). By using the Fourier method, we examine the stability of the scheme. The function $\rho^j(x_i^*)$ is defined as

$$\rho^j(x_i^*) = \begin{cases} \rho_i^j & \text{if} \quad x_i - \frac{h}{2} < x_i^* \leq x_i + \frac{h}{2}, \\ 0, & \text{if} \quad 0 \leq x \leq \frac{h}{2} \quad or \quad L_x - \frac{h}{2} < x_i^* \leq L_x. \end{cases} \tag{8}$$

In the Fourier series, the discrete function (8) may be enlarged:

$$\rho^j(x_i^*) = \sum_{m=-\infty}^{\infty} \xi_j(m) exp\left(\frac{2\pi\iota m}{L_x}\right),$$

where

$$\xi_j(m) = \frac{1}{L_x}\int_0^{L_x} \rho^j(x_i^*) exp\left(\frac{2\pi\iota m}{L_x}\right)dx, \qquad \|\rho^j(m)\|_2^2 = \sum_{-\infty}^{\infty} |\xi_j(m)|^2. \tag{9}$$

Properties of the coefficients r_i^j and $d_n^{i,j}$:
(1) $r_i^j > 0, \quad 0 < b_n^{i,j} < d_{n-1}^{i,j} < 1;$
where

$$d_n^{i,j+1} = b_n^{i,j+1} - b_n^{i,j+1}, \quad \forall i = 1,2,\ldots,M, n = 1,2,\ldots,N.$$

(2) $0 < d_n^{i,j} < 1, \quad \sum_{j=0}^{k-1} d_{n+1}^{i,j+1} = 1 - b_n^{i,j+1}.$
Property (2) can be proved easily.

Stability of the Scheme

We examine the stability of the proposed scheme in this subsection. We obtain the following round-off error equation from (5).

$$\begin{aligned} -r_i^{j+1}\rho_{i-1}^{j+1} + (1+2r_i^{j+1})\rho_i^{j+1} - r_i^{j+1}\rho_{i+1}^{j+1} &= \rho_i^j + \left[f(x_i,t_j,\phi(x_i,t_j)) - f_i^j(\phi_i^j)\right]k^{\beta_i^{j+1}}\Gamma(2-\beta_i^{j+1}) \\ &- \sum_{n=1}^{j}(\rho_n^{j+1-n} - \rho_n^{j-n})b_n^{i,j+1}. \end{aligned}$$

Evaluating sum for $n = 0$, we obtain

$$\begin{aligned} -r_i^{j+1}\rho_{i-1}^{j+1} + (1+2r_i^{j+1})\rho_i^{j+1} - r_i^{j+1}\rho_{i+1}^{j+1} &= \rho_i^j + \left[f(x_i,t_j,\phi(x_i,t_j)) - f_i^j(\phi_i^j)\right]k^{\beta_i^{j+1}}\Gamma(2-\beta_i^{j+1}) \\ &- (\rho_n^1 - \rho_n^0)b_j^{i,j+1} - \sum_{n=1}^{j-1}(\rho_n^{j+1-n} - \rho_n^{j-n})b_n^{i,j+1}. \end{aligned}$$

Simplification yields

$$\begin{aligned} -r_i^{j+1}\rho_{i-1}^{j+1} + (1+2r_i^{j+1})\rho_i^{j+1} - r_i^{j+1}\rho_{i+1}^{j+1} &= \rho_i^j + \left[f(x_i,t_j,\phi(x_i,t_j)) - f_i^j(\phi_i^j)\right]k^{\beta_i^{j+1}} \\ &\times \Gamma(2-\beta_i^{j+1}) - \rho_n^1 b_j^{i,j+1} + \rho_n^0 b_j^{i,j+1} \\ &- \sum_{n=1}^{j-1}\rho_n^{j+1-n}b_n^{i,j+1} + \sum_{n=1}^{j-1}\rho_n^{j-n}b_n^{i,j+1}. \end{aligned} \tag{10}$$

Since

$$\begin{aligned} -\sum_{n=1}^{j-1}\rho_i^{j+1-n}b_n^{i,j+1} - \rho_i^1 b_j^{i,j+1} &= -\sum_{n=1}^{j}\rho_i^{j+1-n}b_n^{i,j+1}, \\ &= -\sum_{n=0}^{j-1}\rho_i^{j-n}b_{n+1}^{i,j+1}, \\ &= -b_1^{i,j+1}\rho_i^j - \sum_{n=1}^{j-1}\rho_i^{j-n}b_{n+1}^{i,j+1}. \end{aligned} \tag{11}$$

Using (11) in Equation (10), we obtain

$$\begin{aligned} -r_i^{j+1}\rho_{i-1}^{j+1} + (1+2r_i^{j+1})\rho_i^{j+1} - r_{i+1}^{j+1}\rho_i^{j+1} &= \rho_i^j + \left[f(x_i,t_j,\phi(x_i,t_j)) - f_i^j(\phi_i^j)\right]k^{\beta_i^{j+1}}\Gamma(2-\beta_i^{j+1}) \\ &+\rho_n^0 b_j^{i,j+1} + \sum_{n=1}^{j-1}\rho_n^{j-n}b_n^{i,j+1} - b_1^{i,j+1}\rho_i^j - \sum_{n=1}^{j-1}\rho_i^{j-n}b_{n+1}^{i,j+1}. \end{aligned}$$

This can be further simplified to reach

$$-r_i^{j+1}\rho_{i-1}^{j+1} + (1+2r_i^{j+1})\rho_i^{j+1} - r_i^{j+1}\rho_{i+1}^{j+1} = \rho_i^j(1-b_1^{i,j+1}) + \left[f(x_i,t_j,\phi(x_i,t_j) - f_i^j(\phi_i^j)\right] \times k^{\beta_i^{j+1}}\Gamma(2-\beta_i^{j+1}) + \rho_n^0(b_j^{i,j+1}) + \sum_{n=1}^{j-1}\rho_i^{j-n}d_{n+1}^{i,j+1}. \quad (12)$$

where

$$d_{n+1}^{i,j+1} = b_n^{i,j+1} - b_{n+1}^{i,j+1}.$$

Let the solutions at grid points be of the form

$$\rho_i^j = \xi^j e^{\iota\lambda ih}. \quad (13)$$

Replacing (13) in Equation (12), we have

$$-r_i^{j+1}\xi^{j+1}e^{\iota\lambda(i-1)h} + (1+2r_i^{j+1})\xi^{j+1}e^{\iota\lambda ih} - r_i^{j+1}\xi^{j+1}e^{\iota\lambda(i+1)h}$$
$$= \xi^j e^{\iota\lambda ih}(1-b_1^{i,j+1}) + \left[f(x_i,t_j,u(x_i,t_j) - f_i^j(u_i^j\right] \times k^{\beta_i^{j+1}}\Gamma(2-\beta_i^{j+1}) + \xi^0 e^{\iota\lambda nh}b_j^{i,j+1} + \sum_{n=1}^{j-1}\xi^{j-n}e^{\iota\lambda ih}d_{n+1}^{i,j+1}.$$

By simplifying and reorganizing the terms, we arrive at

$$\xi^{j+1}\left[-r_i^{j+1}(e^{-\iota\lambda h}+e^{\iota\lambda h}) + (1+2r_i^{j+1})\right] = \xi^j\left(1-b_1^{i,j+1}\right) + \left[f(x_i,t_j,\phi(x_i,t_j)) - f_i^j(\phi_i^j)\right] \times k^{\beta_i^{j+1}}\Gamma(2-\beta_i^{j+1})e^{-\iota\lambda ih} + \xi^0 b_j^{i,j+1} + \sum_{n=1}^{j-1}\xi^{j-n}d_{n+1}^{i,j+1}.$$

Using identity, $e^{ix} = cosx + isinx$ and again arranging the terms, we obtain

$$\xi^{j+1}\left[1+4r_i^{j+1}\sin^2(\frac{\lambda h}{2})\right] = \xi^j\left(1-b_1^{i,j+1}\right) + \left[f(x_i,t_j,\phi(x_i,t_j)) - f_i^j(\phi_i^j)\right] \times k^{\beta_i^{j+1}}\Gamma(2-\beta_i^{j+1})e^{-\iota\lambda ih} + \xi^0 b_j^{i,j+1} + \sum_{n=1}^{j-1}\xi^{j-n}d_{n+1}^{i,j+1}.$$

or

$$\xi^{j+1}\left[1+4r_i^{j+1}\sin^2(\frac{\lambda h}{2})\right] = \xi^j\left(1-b_1^{i,j+1}\right) + \left[f(x_i,t_j,\phi(x_i,t_j)) - f_i^j(\phi_i^j)\right] \times k^{\beta_i^{j+1}}\Gamma(2-\beta_i^{j+1})e^{-\iota\lambda ih} + \xi^0 b_j^{i,j+1} + \sum_{n=1}^{j-1}\xi^{j-1}d_{n+1}^{i,j+1}. \quad (14)$$

where the result has been used $\sum_{n=0}^{j-1} d_{n+1}^{i,j+1} = 1 - b_j^{i,j+1}$.

In order to verify the stability of the implicit finite difference scheme presented in this paper, we prove the following lemma. This lemma provides a framework for evaluating the stability of the scheme and serves as a crucial step in the overall stability analysis.

Lemma 1. *Assume that $\xi^j, (j = 1,2,\ldots,N-1)$ is the solution to the Equation (14); then, $|\xi^j| \le C^*|\xi^0|$, and the following holds true $j = 1,2,\ldots,N-1$.*

Proof. Using mathematical induction, we have proven this lemma.
For $j = 0$, the Equation (14) reduces to

$$\xi^1\left[1+4r_i^1\sin^2\left(\frac{\lambda h}{2}\right)\right] = \left[f(x_i,t_0,\phi(x_i,t_0)) - f_i^0(\phi_i^0)\right]k^{\beta_i^1}\Gamma(2-\beta_i^1)e^{-\iota\lambda ih} + \xi^0.$$

Solving for ξ^1, we obtain

$$\xi^1 = \frac{\left[f(x_i,t_j,\phi(x_i,t_j) - f_i^j(\phi_i^j)\right]k^{\beta_i^{j+1}}\Gamma(2-\beta_i^{j+1})e^{-\iota\lambda ih}}{1+4r_i^{j+1}\sin^2\left(\dfrac{\lambda h}{2}\right)} + \frac{\xi^0}{1+4r_i^{j+1}\sin^2\left(\dfrac{\lambda h}{2}\right)}.$$

By taking the modulus on both sides

$$\begin{aligned}|\xi^1| &= \left|\frac{\left[f(x_i,t_j,\phi(x_i,t_j) - f_i^j(\phi_i^j)\right]k^{\beta_i^{j+1}}\Gamma(2-\beta_i^{j+1})e^{-\iota\lambda ih}}{1+4r_i^{j+1}\sin^2\left(\dfrac{\lambda h}{2}\right)} + \frac{\xi^0}{1+4r_i^{j+1}\sin^2\left(\dfrac{\lambda h}{2}\right)}\right|,\\
&\leq \frac{\left|\left[f(x_i,t_j,\phi(x_i,t_j) - f_i^j(\phi_i^j)\right] \mid\mid k^{\beta_i^{j+1}}\Gamma(2-\beta_i^{j+1})e^{-\iota\lambda ih}\right| + \mid \xi^0 \mid}{\left|1+4r_i^{j+1}\sin^2\left(\dfrac{\lambda(h)}{2}\right)\right|},\\
&\leq \frac{\left[1+L_p k^{\beta_i^1}\Gamma(2-\beta_i^1)\right] \mid \xi^0 \mid}{1+4r_i^{j+1}\sin^2\left(\dfrac{\lambda(h)}{2}\right)},\\
&\leq C^0 \mid \xi^0 \mid,\end{aligned}$$

where

$$C^0 = \frac{\left[1+L_p k^{\beta_i^1}\Gamma(2-\beta_i^1)\right]}{1+4r_i^{j+1}\sin^2\left(\dfrac{\lambda h}{2}\right)}.$$

For $j > 0$, Equation (14) can be written as

$$\begin{aligned}&\xi^{j+1}\left[1+4r_i^{j+1}\sin^2\left(\frac{\lambda h}{2}\right)\right] = \\
&\left[\xi^j(d_1^{i,j+1}) + \left[f(x_i,t_j,\phi(x_i,t_j) - f_i^j(\phi_i^j)\right]k^{\beta_i^1}\Gamma(2-\beta_i^{j+1})e^{-\iota\lambda ih} + \xi^0 b_j^{i,j+1}\right] + \sum_{n=1}^{j-1}\xi^{j-n}d_n^{i,j+1}.\end{aligned}$$

Solving for ξ^{j+1}, we obtain

$$\begin{aligned}\xi^{j+1} = &\frac{\xi^j(d_1^{i,j+1})}{1+4r_i^{j+1}\sin^2\left(\dfrac{\lambda h}{2}\right)} + \frac{\left[f(x_i,t_j,\phi(x_i,t_j) - f_i^j(\beta_i^j)\right]k^{\beta_i^{j+1}}\Gamma(2-\beta_i^{j+1})e^{-\iota\lambda ih}}{1+4r_i^{j+1}\sin^2\left(\dfrac{\lambda h}{2}\right)}\\
&+\frac{\xi^0 b_j^{i,j+1}}{1+4r_i^{j+1}\sin^2\left(\dfrac{\lambda h}{2}\right)} + \frac{\sum_{n=1}^{j-1}\xi^{j-n}d_n^{i,j+1}}{1+4r_i^{j+1}\sin^2\left(\dfrac{\lambda h}{2}\right)}.\end{aligned} \tag{15}$$

Let us now assume that the given result holds for j and prove it for $j+1$, i.e., it holds $\mid \xi^j \mid\leq C^0 \mid \xi^0 \mid$ and we are going to show that $\mid \xi^{j+1} \mid\leq C^* \mid \xi^0 \mid$. We take the modulus on both sides of (15), i.e.,

$$|\xi^{j+1}| = \left| \frac{\left[f(x_i,t_j,\phi(x_i,t_j)) - f_i^j(\phi_i^j)\right] k^{\beta_i^{j+1}} \Gamma(2-\beta_i^{j+1}) e^{-\iota\lambda i h}}{1+4r_i^{j+1}\sin^2\left(\frac{\lambda h}{2}\right)} + \frac{\xi^0 b_j^{i,j+1}}{1+4r_i^{j+1}\sin^2\left(\frac{\lambda h}{2}\right)} + \frac{\sum_{n=1}^{j-1}\xi^{j-n} d_{i+1}^{i,j+1}}{1+4r_i^{j+1}\sin^2\left(\frac{\lambda h}{2}\right)} \right|,$$

$$\leq \left| \frac{\left[f(x_i,t_j,\phi(x_i,t_j) - f_i^j(\phi_i^j)\right] k^{\beta_i^{j+1}} \Gamma(2-\beta_i^{j+1}) e^{-\iota\lambda i h}}{1+4r_i^{j+1}\sin^2\left(\frac{\lambda h}{2}\right)} \right| + \left| \frac{\xi^0 b_j^{i,j+1}}{1+4r_i^{j+1}\sin^2\left(\frac{\lambda h}{2}\right)} \right| + \left| \frac{\sum_{n=1}^{j-1}\xi^{j-n} d_{n+1}^{i,j+1}}{1+4r_i^{j+1}\sin^2\left(\frac{\lambda h}{2}\right)} \right|,$$

$$\leq \frac{\left|\left[f(x_i,t_j,\phi(x_i,t_j) - f_i^j(\phi_i^j)\right]\right| \left| k^{\beta_i^{j+1}} \Gamma(2-\beta_i^{j+1}) e^{-\iota\lambda i h}\right|}{\left[1+4r_i^{j+1}\sin^2\left(\frac{\lambda h}{2}\right)\right]} + \frac{|\xi^0| b_j^{i,j+1}}{1+4r_i^{j+1}\sin^2\left(\frac{\lambda h}{2}\right)} + \frac{\sum_{n=1}^{j-1}|\xi^{j-n}| d_{n+1}^{i,j+1}}{1+4r_i^{j+1}\sin^2\left(\frac{\lambda h}{2}\right)}.$$

We know that $|\xi^j| \leq C^* |\xi^0|$ for all $j > 1$; so,

$$|\xi^{j+1}| \leq \frac{\sum_{n=0}^{j-1} d_{n+1}^{i,j+1} \bar{C}^* |\xi^0| + b_n^{i,j+1} |\xi^0| + k^{\beta_i^{j+1}} \Gamma(2-\beta_i^{j+1}) L_p |\xi^0|}{1+4r_i^{j+1}\sin^2\left(\frac{\lambda h}{2}\right)}.$$

or

$$|\xi^{j+1}| \leq \left[\frac{\sum_{n=0}^{j-1} d_{n+1}^{i,j+1} \bar{C}^* + b_n^{i,j+1} + k^{\beta_i^{j+1}} \Gamma(2-\beta_i^{j+1}) L_p}{1+4r_i^{j+1}\sin^2\left(\frac{\lambda h}{2}\right)} \right] |\xi^0|. \tag{16}$$

Since $\sum_{j=0}^{k-1} d_{n+1}^{i,j+1} = 1 - b_n^{i,j+1} < 1$, and Equation (16) can be written as

$$|\xi^{j+1}| \leq \left[\frac{\bar{C}^*\left(1 - b_n^{i,j+1}\right) + b_n^{i,j+1} + k^{\beta_i^{j+1}} \Gamma(2-\beta_i^{j+1}) L_p}{1+4r_i^{j+1}\sin^2\left(\frac{\lambda h}{2}\right)} \right] |\xi^0|$$
$$\leq C^* |\xi^0|.$$

where

$$C^* = \frac{\bar{C}^*\left(1 - b_n^{i,j+1}\right) + b_n^{i,j+1} + k^{\beta_i^{j+1}} \Gamma(2-\beta_i^{j+1}) L_p}{1+4r_i^{j+1}\sin^2\left(\frac{\lambda h}{2}\right)}.$$

□

By this method, the Lemma can be proved by induction.

Theorem 1. *The implicit finite difference scheme is unconditionally stable—(12) to (14).*

Proof. Based on the above Lemma:

$$\|\rho^j\| \leq C^* \|\rho^0\|, \quad k = 1, 2, \ldots, N.$$

The system is always stable, as shown by this observation. As a result of the proof, it can be concluded that the implicit finite difference scheme is unconditionally stable, and can be used to obtain accurate solutions for semi-linear variable-order initial boundary value problems. This provides a solid foundation for the application of the method in future research and practical applications. □

4. Numerical Experiments

The numerical solution of fractional model of heat equation using an implicit scheme with different initial and boundary conditions is given in this section. The equations are solved for different values of the fractional-order β from 0 to 1. The spatial domain is discretized into $N = 10$ intervals with step size h and the solution is obtained for final time T. The solution is stored for each value fractional-order β in the matrix. The solution is then plotted against the spatial variable x with different lines representing the solutions for different values of fractional order.

Several time-fractional boundary value problems are considered in this section and approximated using a newly developed implicit finite difference algorithm. The solution curves are also plotted for distinct values of fractional-order β.

All the tests are performed on Windows 10 Pro and Matlab version (R2016b) running on an Intel(R) Core(TM) i5-7200U CPU @ 2.5 GHz with 8 GB RAM.

Example 1. *The given equation is the linear fractional diffusion equation. It describes the time evolution of a scalar field $\phi(x,t)$ in one spatial dimension and fractional time derivatives. The fractional-order β determines the strength of the diffusion process and can be any value between 0 and 1. The equation also contains a first-order spatial derivative term in addition to the second-order spatial derivative. The initial condition is a piece-wise linear function defined at time $t = 0$. The boundary conditions specify that the field is zero at the two boundaries of the spatial domain. The purpose of this equation is to model physical phenomena that exhibit non-local diffusion, such as heat transfer and fluid flow in porous media. Let us examine the linear diffusion equation:*

$$\frac{\partial^{\beta}\phi}{\partial t^{\beta}} = \frac{\partial^2\phi}{\partial x^2} + \frac{\partial\phi}{\partial x}, \tag{17}$$

Based on the initial condition,

$$\phi(x,0) = \begin{cases} x, & 0 \le x \le 1/2, \\ 1-x, & 1/2 \le x \le 1. \end{cases}$$

Conditions at the boundary are

$$\phi(0,t) = 0 = \phi(1,t), \qquad t \ge 0.$$

Proof. Using time-fractional approximation (3) of time derivative and the central difference approximations of space derivatives, the discrete form of Equation (17) can be written as

$$\frac{k^{-\beta_i^{j+1}}}{\Gamma(2-\beta_i^{j+1})}\left[\left(\phi_i^{j+1}-\phi_i^j\right)+\sum_{n=1}^{j}\left(\phi_n^{j+1-n}-\phi_n^{j-n}\right)b_n^{i,j+1}\right] = \frac{\phi_{i-1}^{j+1}-2\phi_i^{j+1}+\phi_{i+1}^{j+1}}{h^2}+\frac{\phi_{i+1}^{j+1}-\phi_{i-1}^{j+1}}{2h}.$$

As a result of rearranging the terms

$$\left(-r_i^{j+1}+\frac{h}{2}r_i^{j+1}\right)\phi_{i-1}^{j+1}+\left(1+2r_i^{j+1}\right)\phi_i^{j+1}+\left(-r_{i+1}^{j+1}-\frac{h}{2}r_i^{j+1}\right)\phi_{i+1}^{j+1} = \phi_i^j-\sum_{n=1}^{j}\left(\phi_n^{j+1-n}-\phi_n^{j-n}\right)b_n^{i,j+1}$$

with

$$\phi_i^0 = \begin{cases} x_i, & 0 \le x_i \le 1/2, \\ 1-x_i, & 1/2 \le x_i \le 1. \end{cases} \quad i = 0,1,\ldots,M,$$

$\phi_0^j = 0 = \phi_M^j$, where

$$r_i^{j+1} = \frac{k^{\beta_i^{j+1}}\Gamma(2-\beta_i^{j+1})}{h^2}.$$

Matrix form of the discrete problem is defined as

$$\begin{bmatrix} d_1^{j+1} & b_1^{j+1} & 0 & 0 & . & . & 0 \\ a_2^{j+1} & d_2^{j+1} & b_2^{j+1} & 0 & . & . & 0 \\ . & . & . & . & . & . & . \\ . & . & . & . & . & . & . \\ . & . & . & . & . & . & . \\ 0 & 0 & 0 & 0 & . & a_{M-1}^{j+1} & d_{M-1}^{j+1} \end{bmatrix} \begin{bmatrix} \phi_1^{j+1} \\ \phi_2^{j+1} \\ . \\ . \\ . \\ \phi_{M-1}^{j+1} \end{bmatrix}$$

$$= \begin{bmatrix} \phi_1^j - \sum_{n=1}^{j}(\phi_n^{j+1-n} - \phi_n^{j-n})b_n^{1,j+1} \\ \phi_2^j - \sum_{n=1}^{j}(\phi_n^{j+1-n} - \phi_n^{j-n})b_n^{2,j+1} \\ . \\ . \\ . \\ \phi_{M-1}^j - \sum_{n=1}^{j}(\phi_n^{j+1-n} - \phi_n^{j-n})b_n^{M-1,j+1} \end{bmatrix}$$

and, after incorporating the conditions, the matrix system is given as

$$\begin{bmatrix} 1 & 0 & 0 & 0 & . & . & . & 0 & 0 \\ a_1^{j+1} & d_1^{j+1} & b_1^{j+1} & 0 & 0 & . & . & 0 & 0 \\ 0 & a_2^{j+1} & d_2^{j+1} & b_2^{j+1} & 0 & . & . & 0 & 0 \\ . & . & . & . & . & . & . & . & \\ . & . & . & . & . & . & . & . & \\ 0 & 0 & 0 & 0 & 0 & . & a_{M-1}^{j+1} & d_{M-1}^{j+1} & b_{M-1}^{j+1} \\ 0 & 0 & 0 & 0 & . & . & . & 0 & 1 \end{bmatrix}$$

$$\begin{bmatrix} \phi_0^{j+1} \\ \phi_1^{j+1} \\ . \\ . \\ . \\ \phi_{M-1}^{j+1} \\ \phi_M^{j+1} \end{bmatrix} = \begin{bmatrix} 0 \\ \phi_1^j - \sum_{n=1}^{j}(\phi_n^{j+1-n} - \phi_n^{j-n})b_n^{1,j+1} \\ i_3^j - \sum_{n=1}^{j}(\phi_n^{j+1-n} - \phi_n^{j-n})b_n^{2,j+1} \\ . \\ . \\ . \\ \phi_{M-1}^j - \sum_{n=1}^{j}(\phi_n^{j+1-n} - \phi_n^{j-n})b_n^{M-1,j+1} \\ 0 \end{bmatrix}$$

where $a_i^{j+1} = -r_i^{j+1} + \frac{h}{2}r_i^{j+1}$, $d_i^{j+1} = 1 + 2r_i^{j+1}$, $b_i^{j+1} = -r_i^{j+1} - \frac{h}{2}r_i^{j+1}$.

The matrix system can also be written as

$$\phi^{j+1}A^{j+1} = B^j.$$

We use MATLAB code to solve for ϕ_i^{j+1} using the equation $A^{j+1}\phi_i^{j+1} = 0$, where A^{j+1} is an invertible matrix. The numerical solution is plotted in Figure 1 for distinct values of the fractional-order β at final time $T = 0.2$ with $h = 0.01$ and $k = 0.01$. □

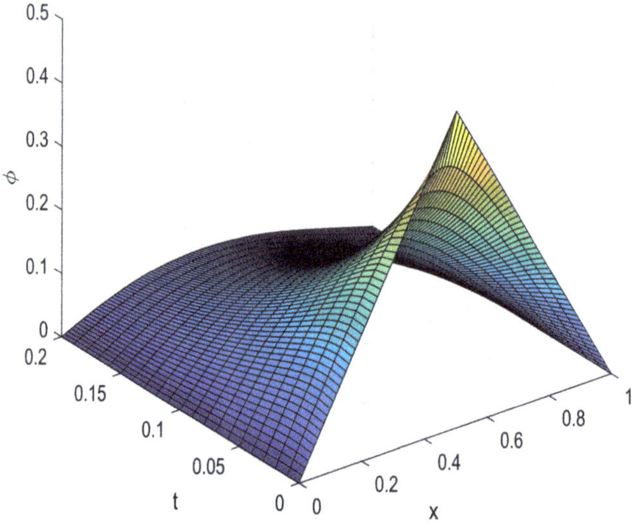

Figure 1. The numerical solution for various values of the fractional-order β at the final time T = 0.2 with h = 0.01, k= 0.01.

Example 2. *The given equation represents the time evolution of a field $\phi(x,t)$ in a one-dimensional space, described by a fractional partial derivative with respect to time, β. The right-hand side of the equation describes the spatial spread of the field due to a combination of diffusion (represented by $\partial^2\phi/\partial x^2$) and decay ($-\phi$). The initial condition specifies the shape of the field at time $t = 0$, and the boundary conditions specify the behavior of the field at the edges of the spatial domain (i.e., $x = 0$ and $x = 1$). The significance of this equation lies in its ability to describe a wide range of physical phenomena, such as heat transfer, fluid flow, and electromagnetic wave propagation, which can be modeled using the combination of diffusion and decay.*

$$\frac{\partial^\beta \phi}{\partial t^\beta} = \frac{\partial^2 \phi}{\partial x^2} - \phi, \tag{18}$$

with respect to the initial conditions

$$\phi(x,0) = x^2, \qquad 0 \le x \le 1,$$

where the conditions of the boundary are

$$\phi(0,t) = 0, \qquad \phi_x(1,t) = 1 - \phi, \qquad t \ge 0.$$

Proof. Using time-fractional approximation (4) for the time derivative and the central difference approximations (5) for space derivative, Equation (18) can be written in discrete form as

$$\frac{k^{-\beta_i^{j+1}}}{\Gamma(2-\beta_i^{j+1})}\left[(\phi_i^{j+1} - \phi_i^j) + \sum_{n=1}^{j}(\phi_n^{j+1-n} - \phi_n^{j-n})(b_n^{i,j+1})\right] = \left[\frac{\phi_{i-1}^{j+1} - 2\phi_i^{j+1} + \phi_{i+1}^{j+1}}{h^2}\right]\phi_i^{j+1}.$$

After rearranging the terms, we obtain

$$-r_i^{j+1}\phi_{i-1}^{j+1} + \left(1 + 2r_i^{j+1} + h^2 r_i^{j+1}\right)\phi_i^{j+1} - r_i^{j+1}\phi_{i+1}^{j+1} = \phi_i^j - \sum_{n=1}^{j}\left(\phi_n^{j+1-n} - \phi_n^{j-n}\right)b_n^{i,j+1}.$$

with

$$\phi_i^0 = x_i^2, \qquad i = 0, 1, \ldots, M,$$

$$\phi_0^j = 0, \qquad (\phi_M^i)_x = 1 - \phi_M^j, \qquad j = 0, 1, \ldots, N.$$

where

$$r_i^{j+1} = \frac{k^{\beta_i^{j+1}}\Gamma(2 - \beta_i^{j+1})}{h^2}.$$

The matrix form of the discrete problem, after adding the boundary conditions, is defined as follows:

$$\begin{bmatrix} 1 & 0 & 0 & 0 & . & . & . & 0 & 0 \\ a_1^{j+1} & d_1^{j+1} & a_1^{j+1} & 0 & 0 & . & . & 0 & 0 \\ 0 & a_2^{j+1} & d_2^{j+1} & a_2^{j+1} & 0 & . & . & 0 & 0 \\ . & . & . & . & . & . & . & & \\ . & . & . & . & . & . & . & & \\ . & . & . & . & . & . & . & & \\ 0 & 0 & 0 & 0 & 0 & . & a_{M-1}^{j+1} & d_{M-1}^{j+1} & a_{M-1}^{j+1} \\ 0 & 0 & 0 & 0 & . & . & . & -2r_M^{j+1} & d_M^{j+1} + 2h_M^{j+1} \end{bmatrix}$$

$$\begin{bmatrix} \phi_0^{j+1} \\ \phi_1^{j+1} \\ . \\ . \\ . \\ \phi_{M-1}^{j+1} \\ \phi_M^{j+1} \end{bmatrix} = \begin{bmatrix} 0 \\ \phi_1^j - \sum_{n=1}^{j}(\phi_n^{j+1-n} - \phi_n^{j-n})b_n^{1,j+1} \\ . \\ . \\ . \\ \phi_{M-1}^j - \sum_{n=1}^{j}(\phi_n^{j+1-n} - \phi_n^{j-n})b_n^{M-1,j+1} \\ \phi_M^j - \sum_{n=1}^{j}(\phi_n^{j+1-n} - \phi_n^{j-n})b_n^{M,j+1} + 2hr_M^j \end{bmatrix}$$

where $a_i^{j+1} = -r_i^{j+1}$ and $d_i^{j+1} = 1 + 2r_i^{j+1} + h^2 r_i^{j+1}$,

Matrix systems can also be expressed as

$$\phi^{j+1}A^{j+1} = B^j,$$

We use MATLAB to solve for ϕ_i^{j+1} by solving the equation $A^{j+1}\phi_i^{j+1} = 0$, where A^{j+1} is an invertible matrix. The resulting numerical solution is plotted in Figure 2 for various values of the fractional-order β at the final time $T = 0.1$ with $h = 0.01, k = 0.01$. □

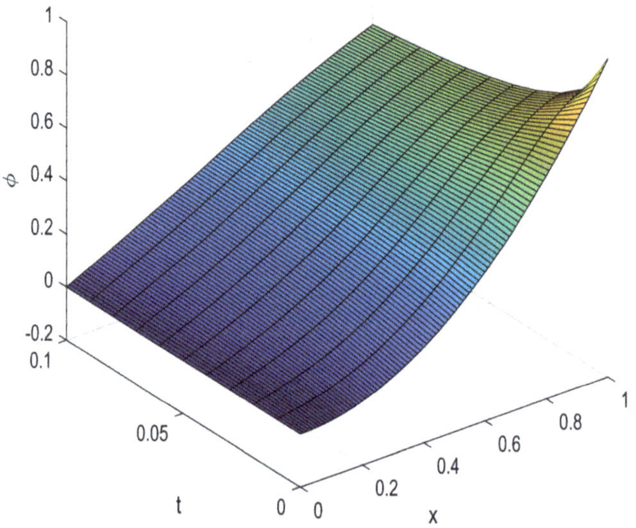

Figure 2. The numerical solution for various values of the fractional-order β at the final time T = 0.1 with h = 0.01, k= 0.01.

Example 3. *The purpose of this equation is to describe the diffusion of a quantity ϕ over space and time, where the diffusion process is characterized by the fractional derivative with respect to time. The initial condition $\phi(x,0) = 1 - x^2$ defines the initial distribution of ϕ over the space interval $0 \leq x \leq 1$. The conditions at the boundary, $\phi_x(0,t) = 0$ and $\phi(1,t) = 0$, define the behavior of ϕ at the boundary points over time.*

$$\frac{\partial^\beta \phi}{\partial t^\beta} = \frac{\partial^2 \phi}{\partial x^2} - \frac{1}{x}\frac{\partial \phi}{\partial x}. \tag{19}$$

The initial condition is

$$\phi(x,0) = 1 - x^2, \qquad 0 \leq x \leq 1,$$

with conditions at the boundary of

$$\phi_x(0,t) = 0, \qquad \phi(1,t) = 0.$$

Proof. Using (3) and (19), we obtain

$$\frac{k^{-\beta_i^{j+1}}}{\Gamma(2-\beta_i^{j+1})}\left[\left(\phi_i^{j+1} - \phi_i^j\right) + sum_{n=1}^{j}\left(\phi_n^{j+1-n} - \phi_n^{j-n}\right)b_n^{i,j+1}\right] = \left[\frac{\phi_{i-1}^{j+1} - 2\phi_i^{j+1} + \phi_{i+1}^{j+1}}{h^2}\right] - \frac{1}{x_i}\frac{\phi_{i+1}^{j+1} - \phi_{i-1}^{j+1}}{2h}.$$

The following implicit form is obtained after rearranging the terms

$$\left(-r_i^{j+1} - \frac{h}{2x_i} r_i^{j+1}\right)\phi_{i-1}^{j+1} + \left(1 + 2r_i^{j+1}\right)\phi_i^{j+1} + \left(-r_i^{j+1} + \frac{h}{2x_i} r_i^{j+1}\right)\phi_{i+1}^{j+1}$$
$$= \phi_i^j - \sum_{n=1}^{j}\left(\phi_n^{j+1-n} - \phi_n^{j-n}\right) b_n^{i,j+1}.$$

with

$$\phi_i^0 = 1 - x_i^2, \qquad i = 0, 1, \ldots, M.$$

$$\left(\phi_i^0\right)_x = 0, \qquad \phi_M^j = 0, \qquad j = 0, 1, \ldots, N.$$

where

$$r_i^{j+1} = \frac{k^{\beta_i^{j+1}} \Gamma\left(2 - \beta_i^{j+1}\right)}{h^2}.$$

Adding boundary conditions to the discrete problem results in a matrix form:

$$\begin{bmatrix} d_0^{j+1} & -2r_0^{j+1} & 0 & 0 & . & . & . & 0 & 0 \\ a_1^{j+1} & d_1^{j+1} & b_1^{j+1} & 0 & 0 & . & . & 0 & 0 \\ 0 & a_2^{j+1} & d_2^{j+1} & b_2^{j+1} & . & . & 0 & 0 & \\ . & . & . & . & . & . & . & & \\ . & . & . & . & . & . & . & & \\ . & . & . & . & . & . & . & & \\ 0 & 0 & 0 & 0 & 0 & . & a_{M-1}^{j+1} & d_{M-1}^{j+1} & b_{M-1}^{j+1} \\ 0 & 0 & 0 & 0 & . & . & . & 0 & 1 \end{bmatrix}$$

$$\begin{bmatrix} \phi_0^{j+1} \\ \phi_1^{j+1} \\ \phi_2^{j+1} \\ . \\ . \\ . \\ \phi_{M-1}^{j+1} \\ \phi_M^{j+1} \end{bmatrix} = \begin{bmatrix} \phi_0^j - \sum_{n=1}^{j}\left(\phi_n^{j+1-n} - \phi_n^{j-n}\right) b_n^{0,j+1} \\ \phi_1^j - \sum_{n=1}^{j}\left(\phi_n^{j+1-n} - \phi_n^{j-n}\right) b_n^{1,j+1} \\ \phi_2^j - \sum_{n=1}^{j}\left(\phi_n^{j+1-n} - \phi_n^{j-n}\right) b_n^{2,j+1} \\ . \\ . \\ . \\ \phi_{M-1}^j - \sum_{n=1}^{j}\left(\phi_n^{j+1-n} - \phi_n^{j-n}\right) b_n^{M-1,j+1} \\ 0 \end{bmatrix}.$$

where $a_i^{j+1} = -r_i^{j+1}\left(1 + \frac{h}{2x_i}\right)$, $d_i^{j+1} = 1 + 2r_i^{j+1}$, and $b_i^{j+1} = -r_i^{j+1}\left(1 - \frac{h}{2x_i}\right)$.

Matrix systems can also be expressed as

$$\phi^{j+1} A^{j+1} = B^j, \tag{20}$$

We use MATLAB to solve for ϕ_i^{j+1} by solving the matrix Equation (20), which is represented as $A^{j+1}\phi_i^{j+1} = 0$, where A^{j+1} is an invertible matrix. The numerical solution obtained is plotted in Figure 3 for various values of the fractional-order β at the final time $T = 0.3$ with $h = 0.05, k = 0.05$. □

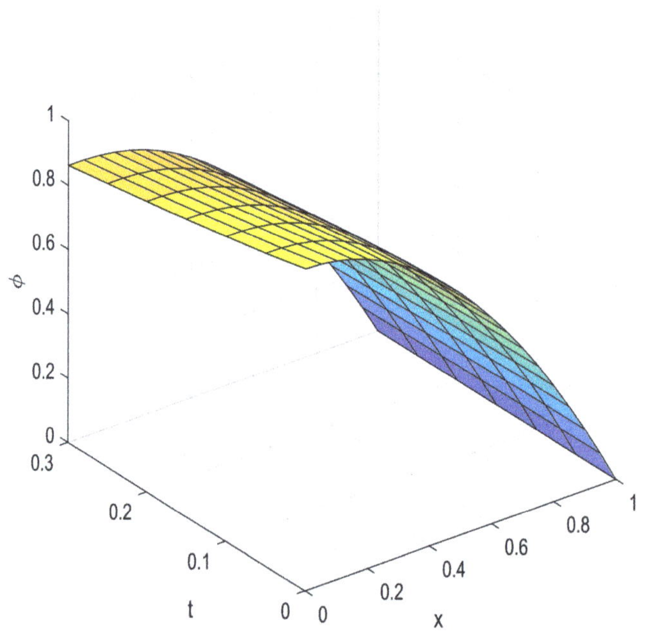

Figure 3. The numerical solution for various values of the fractional-order β at the final time T = 0.3 with h = 0.05, k= 0.05.

5. Conclusions

The purpose of this paper is to present a new implicit finite difference scheme for resolving variable-order time-fractional linear and semi-linear partial differential equations. The scheme is shown to be unconditionally stable by means of the Fourier method. To demonstrate the effectiveness of the proposed method, the authors present a series of numerical examples and display the results graphically using MATLAB. To further highlight the behavior of the solution under different conditions, the authors plot solution curves for varying values of the fractional-order parameter β. The implicit finite difference method and the Fourier method used in this study provide a versatile tool for solving variable-order time-fractional partial differential equations, which have applications in a wide range of physics and engineering problems.

6. Future Directions

The method presented in this paper can be extended to solve non-linear fractional differential equations, which are commonly encountered in real-world problems. This could provide new insights into the behavior of non-linear systems with memory and non-locality. Further research can be conducted to improve the stability analysis of the implicit finite difference method and to explore other methods for evaluating stability. The implicit finite difference method can be parallelized—this will make calculations fast and efficient. This could lead to the development of large-scale simulations and the solution of complex problems in a shorter amount of time. The implicit finite difference method can be applied to a wide range of real-world problems, such as heat transfer, diffusion, and wave propagation. This could lead to new insights and applications in various fields, including physics, engineering, and material science.

Author Contributions: R.S.; Methodology, R.S.; Software, A.K.; Formal analysis, B.T. and M.A.; Investigation, R.S. and A.K.; Resources, R.S.; Writing—original draft, A.K.; Writing—review & editing, R.S.; Visualization, M.A.; Supervision, M.A.A.; Project administration, K.A.; Funding acquisition, K.A. All authors have read and agreed to the published version of the manuscript.

Funding: This work was supported by the Deanship of Scientific Research, Vice Presidency for Graduate Studies and Scientific Research, King Faisal University, Saudi Arabia (Grant No. 2764).

Data Availability Statement: No new data were created for this study.

Conflicts of Interest: The authors declare that they have no known competing financial interests or personal relationships that could have appeared to influence the work reported in this paper.

References

1. Lazarević, M.P.; Rapaić, M.R.; Šekara, T.B.; Mladenov, V.; Mastorakis, N. Introduction to fractional calculus with brief historical background. In *Advanced Topics on Applications of Fractional Calculus on Control Problems, System Stability and Modeling*; WSEAS Press: Attica, Greece, 2014.
2. Calcagni, G. Geometry of fractional spaces. *Adv. Theor. Math. Phys.* **2012**, *16*, 549–644. [CrossRef]
3. Sar, E.Y.; Giresunlu, I.B. Fractional differential equations. *Pramana J. Phys.* **2016**, *87*.
4. Klafter, J.; Lim, S.C.; Metzler, R. (Eds.) *Fractional Dynamics: Recent Advances*; World Scientific: Singapre, 2012.
5. Tarasov, V.E. On history of mathematical economics: Application of fractional calculus. *Mathematics* **2019**, *7*, 509. [CrossRef]
6. Dalir, M.; Bashour, M. Applications of fractional calculus. *Appl. Math. Sci.* **2010**, *4*, 1021–1032.
7. Wharmby, A.W.; Bagley, R.L. Generalization of a theoretical basis for the application of fractional calculus to viscoelasticity. *J. Rheol.* **2013**, *57*, 1429.. [CrossRef]
8. Sun, H.; Zhang, Y.; Baleanu, D.; Chen, W.; Chen, Y. A new collection of real world applications of fractional calculus in science and engineering. *Commun. Nonlinear Sci. Numer. Simul.* **2018**, *64*, 213–231. [CrossRef]
9. Yilmaz B. A new type electromagnetic curves in optical fiber and rotation of the polarization plane using fractional calculus. *Optik* **2021**, *247*, 168026. [CrossRef]
10. Gonzalez-Lee, M.; Vazquez-Leal, H.; Morales-Mendoza, LJ.; Nakano-Miyatake, M.; Perez-Meana, H.; Laguna-Camacho, J.R. Statistical assessment of discrimination capabilities of a fractional calculus based image watermarking system for Gaussian watermarks. *Entropy* **2021**, *23*, 255. [CrossRef]
11. Valério, D.; Machado, J.T.; Kiryakova, V. Some pioneers of the applications of fractional calculus. *Fract. Calc. Appl. Anal.* **2014**, *17*, 552–578. [CrossRef]
12. Tarasov, V.E. (Ed.) *Handbook of Fractional Calculus with Applications*; De Gruyter: Berlin, Germany, 2019.
13. Chávez-Vázquez, S.; Gómez-Aguilar, J.F.; Lavín-Delgado, J.E.; Escobar-Jiménez, R.F.; Olivares-Peregrino, V.H. Applications of fractional operators in robotics: A review. *J. Intell. Robot. Syst.* **2022**, *104*, 63. [CrossRef]
14. Mishra, S.U.; Mishra, L.N.; Mishra, R.K.; Patnaik, S.R. Some applications of fractional calculus in technological development. *J. Fract. Calc. Appl.* **2019**, *10*, 228–235.
15. Ionescu, C.; Lopes, A.; Copot, D.; Machado, J.T.; Bates, J.H. The role of fractional calculus in modeling biological phenomena: A review. *Commun. Nonlinear Sci. Numer. Simul.* **2017**, *51*, 141–159. [CrossRef]
16. Katugampola, U.N. New approach to a generalized fractional integral. *Appl. Math. Comput.* **2011**, *218*, 860–865. [CrossRef]
17. Ross, B. The development of fractional calculus 1695–1900. *Hist. Math.* **1977**, *4*, 75–89. [CrossRef]
18. Baleanu, D.; Diethelm, K.; Scalas, E.; Trujillo, J.J. *Fractional Calculus: Models and Numerical Methods*; World Scientific: London, UK, 2012.
19. Chen, C.; Liu, F.; Burrage, K. Finite difference methods and a Fourier analysis for the fractional reaction–subdiffusion equation. *Appl. Math. Comput.* **2008**, *198*, 754–769. [CrossRef]
20. Birajdar, G.A.; Dhaigude, D.B. An implicit numerical method for semi-linear fractional diffusion equation. In Proceedings of the International Conference on Mathematical Sciences, Chennai, India, 17–19 July 2014.
21. Zhang, H.M.; Liu, F. Numerical simulation of the Riesz fractional diffusion equation with a nonlinear source term. *J. Appl. Math. Comput.* **2008**, *26*, 1–14.
22. Liu, F.; Shen, S.; Anh, V.; Turner, I. Analysis of a discrete non-Markovian random walk approximation for the time-fractional diffusion equation. *Anziam J.* **2004**, *46*, C488–C504. [CrossRef]
23. Lin, Y.; Xu, C. Finite difference/spectral approximations for the time-fractional diffusion equation. *J. Comput. Phys.* **2007**, *225*, 1533–1552. [CrossRef]
24. Zhuang, P.; Liu, F. Implicit difference approximation for the two-dimensional space-time-fractional diffusion equation. *J. Appl. Math. Comput.* **2007**, *25*, 269–282. [CrossRef]
25. Zhuang, P.; Liu, F.; Anh, V.; Turner, I. New solution and analytical techniques of the implicit numerical method for the anomalous subdiffusion equation. *Siam J. Numer. Anal.* **2008**, *46*, 1079-1095. [CrossRef]
26. Murio, D.A. Implicit finite difference approximation for time-fractional diffusion equations. *Comput. Math. Appl.* **2008**, *56*, 1138–1145. [CrossRef]

27. Sweilam, N.H.; Khader, M.M.; Mahdy, A.M. Crank-Nicolson finite difference method for solving time-fractional diffusion equation. *J. Fract. Calc. Appl.* **2012**, *2*, 1–9.
28. Birajdar, G.A. Stability of nonlinear fractional diffusion equation. *Lib. Math.* **2016**, *36*, 1–12.
29. Dhaigude, D.B.; Birajdar, G.A.; Nikam, V.R. Adomain decomposition method for fractional Benjamin-Bona-Mahony-Burger's equations. *Int. J. Appl. Math. Mech.* **2012**, *8*, 42–51.
30. Dhaigude, D.B.; Birajdar, G.A. Numerical solution of system of fractional partial differential equations by discrete Adomian decomposition method. *J. Frac. Cal. Appl.* **2012**, *3*, 1–11.
31. Dhaigude, D.B.; Birajdar, G.A. Numerical solution of fractional partial differential equations by discrete Adomian decomposition method. *Adv. Appl. Math. Mech.* **2014**, *6*, 107–119. [CrossRef]
32. Mehmood, Y.; Shafqat, R.; Sarris, I.E.; Bilal, M.; Sajid, T.; Akhtar, T. Numerical Investigation of MWCNT and SWCNT Fluid Flow along with the Activation Energy Effects over Quartic Auto Catalytic Endothermic and Exothermic Chemical Reactions. *Mathematics* **2022**, *10*, 4636. [CrossRef]
33. Boulares, H.; Benchaabane, A.; Pakkaranang, N.; Shafqat, R.; Panyanak, B. Qualitative properties of positive solutions of a kind for fractional pantograph problems using technique fixed point theory. *Fractal Fract.* **2022**, *6*, 593. [CrossRef]
34. Abuasbeh, K.; Shafqat, R. Fractional Brownian motion for a system of fuzzy fractional stochastic differential equation. *J. Math.* **2022**, *2022*, 3559035. [CrossRef]
35. Abuasbeh, K.; Shafqat, R.; Alsinai, A.; Awadalla, M. Analysis of Controllability of Fractional Functional Random Integroevolution Equations with Delay. *Symmetry* **2023**, *15*, 290. [CrossRef]
36. Abuasbeh, K.; Shafqat, R.; Alsinai, A.; Awadalla, M. Analysis of the Mathematical Modelling of COVID-19 by Using Mild Solution with Delay Caputo Operator. *Symmetry* **2023**, *15*, 286. [CrossRef]
37. Alnahdi, A.S.; Shafqat, R.; Niazi, A.U.K.; Jeelani, M.B. Pattern Formation Induced by Fuzzy Fractional-Order Model of COVID-19. *Axioms* **2022**, *11*, 313. [CrossRef]
38. Kumar, S.; Kumar, A.; Baleanu, D. Two analytical methods for time-fractional nonlinear coupled Boussinesq–Burger's equations arise in propagation of shallow water waves. *Nonlinear Dyn.* **2016**, *85*, 699–715. [CrossRef]
39. Lin, R.; Liu, F.; Anh, V.; Turner, I. Stability and convergence of a new explicit finite-difference approximation for the variable-order nonlinear fractional diffusion equation. *Appl. Math. Comput.* **2009**, *212*, 435–445. [CrossRef]
40. Zhuang, P.; Liu, F.; Anh, V.; Turner, I. Numerical methods for the variable-order fractional advection-diffusion equation with a nonlinear source term. *Siam J. Numer. Anal.* **2009**, *47*, 1760–1781. [CrossRef]
41. Sun, H.; Chen, W.; Chen, Y. Variable-order fractional differential operators in anomalous diffusion modeling. *Phys. Stat. Mech. Its Appl.* **2009**, *388*, 4586–4592. [CrossRef]
42. Chen, C.M.; Liu, F.; Turner, I.; Anh, V.; Chen, Y. Numerical approximation for a variable-order nonlinear reaction–subdiffusion equation. *Numer. Algorithms* **2013**, *63*, 265–290. [CrossRef]
43. Chen, C.M.; Liu, F.; Anh, V.; Turner, I. Numerical methods for solving a two-dimensional variable-order anomalous subdiffusion equation. *Math. Comput.* **2012**, *81*, 345–366. [CrossRef]
44. Sun, H.; Chen, W.; Li, C.; Chen, Y. Finite difference schemes for variable-order time-fractional diffusion equation. *Int. J. Bifurc. Chaos* **2012**, *22*, 1250085. [CrossRef]
45. Diaz, G.; Coimbra, C.F. Nonlinear dynamics and control of a variable-order oscillator with application to the van der Pol equation. *Nonlinear Dyn.* **2009**, *56*, 145–157. [CrossRef]
46. Soon, C.M.; Coimbra, C.F.; Kobayashi, M.H. The variable viscoelasticity oscillator. *Ann. Phys.* **2005**, *14*, 378–389. [CrossRef]
47. Oderinu, R.A.; Owolabi, J.A.; Taiwo, M. Approximate solutions of linear time-fractional differential equations. *J. Math. Comput. Sci.* **2023**, *29*, 60–72. [CrossRef]
48. Alia, A.; Abbasb, M.; Akramc, T. New group iterative schemes for solving the two-dimensional anomalous fractional sub-diffusion equation. *J. Math. Comp. Sci.* **2021**, *22*, 119–127. [CrossRef]
49. Guo, T.; Nikan, O.; Avazzadeh, Z.; Qiu, W. Efficient alternating direction implicit numerical approaches for multi-dimensional distributed-order fractional integro differential problems. *Comput. Appl. Math.* **2022**, *41*, 236. [CrossRef]
50. Akram, T.; Abbas, M.; Ali, A. A numerical study on time-fractional Fisher equation using an extended cubic B-spline approximation. *J. Math. Comput. Sci.* **2021**, *22*, 85–96. [CrossRef]

symmetry MDPI

Article

Unknown Input Observer Scheme for a Class of Nonlinear Generalized Proportional Fractional Order Systems

Ali Omar M. Alsharif [1,2], Assaad Jmal [1], Omar Naifar [1,*], Abdellatif Ben Makhlouf [3], Mohamed Rhaima [4] and Lassaad Mchiri [5]

1 Control and Energy Management Laboratory (CEM Lab), Engineering National School, Electrical Engineering Department, Sfax University, Sfax 3038, Tunisia; assaad.jmal@enis.tn (A.J.)
2 Department of Electrical & Computer Engineering, Faculty of Engineering, Elmergib University, Alkhums 7206, Libya
3 Department of Mathematics, Faculty of Sciences, Sfax University, Sfax 1171, Tunisia; benmakhloufabdellatif@gmail.com
4 Department of Statistics and Operations Research, College of Sciences, King Saud University, Riyadh 11451, Saudi Arabia; mrhaima.c@ksu.edu.sa
5 ENSIIE, University of Evry-Val-d'Essonne, 1 Square de la Résistance, CEDEX, 91025 Évry-Courcouronnes, France; lassaad.mchiri@ensiie.fr
* Correspondence: omar.naifar@enis.tn

Abstract: In this study, an unknown input observer is proposed for a class of nonlinear GPFOSs. For this class of systems, both full-order and reduced-order observers have been established. The investigated system satisfies the one-sided Lipschitz nonlinear condition, which is an improvement of the classic Lipschitz condition. Sufficient conditions have been proposed to ensure the error dynamics' Mittag–Leffler stability. The value of this work lies in the fact that, to the best of the authors' knowledge, this is the first research work that investigates the issue of Observer Design (OD) for GPFOSs. To exemplify the usefulness of the suggested observers, an illustrative numerical example is suggested.

Keywords: GPFOSs; unknown input observer; one-sided Lipschitz nonlinear system; Mittag–Leffler stability

Citation: Alsharif, A.O.M.; Jmal, A.; Naifar, O.; Ben Makhlouf, A.; Rhaima, M.; Mchiri, L. Unknown Input Observer Scheme for a Class of Nonlinear Generalized Proportional Fractional Order Systems. *Symmetry* **2023**, *15*, 1233. https://doi.org/10.3390/sym15061233

Academic Editor: Dongfang Li

Received: 5 May 2023
Revised: 2 June 2023
Accepted: 6 June 2023
Published: 9 June 2023

1. Introduction

Generalized Proportional Fractional Differential Equations (GPFDEs) are a class of differential equations that extend the concept of fractional calculus to encompass proportional fractional derivatives. These equations involve fractional derivatives with variable-order parameters, allowing for a more flexible and adaptable modeling of complex systems and processes. In their paper [1] Jarad, Abdeljawad, and Alzabut released the "Generalized Proportional Fractional Derivative (GPFD)". This revolutionary derivative retains the semigroup feature while embracing its non-locality. In [2], it has been observed that the function easily transitions to its derivative in limiting cases. This transition is made possible by a fractional derivative known as Generalized Proportional Fractional Derivative (GPFD), which incorporates a non-singular kernel function and a non-local operator. In comparison to traditional derivatives like the integer-order derivative and the Caputo fractional derivative, the GPFD offers a more versatile and generic approach to describing intricate processes. Its usefulness lies in its ability to handle systems with memory and non-locality, such as diffusion processes, viscoelasticity, and anomalous transport. Moreover, the GPFD allows for the consideration of derivatives with varying orders, enabling the capturing of different degrees of smoothness or roughness in the underlying signal. The GPFD finds application in modeling and analyzing complex systems in physics, engineering, and finance [3–5].

Numerous academics have recently examined the stability of Generalized Proportional Caputo Fractional Differential Equations (GPCFDEs). For instance, Donchev and Hristova obtained adequate requirements for the practical stability of GPCFDEs in [6] using Lyapunov functions. In [7], Bohner and Hristova investigated the stability of GPCFDEs using integro-differential equations with fractional delays. Agarwal, Hristova, and O'Regan examined GPCFDE stability using Lyapunov functions in [8]. Agarwal, Hristova, and O'Regan used the Razumikhin approach in [9] to investigate the stability of GPCFDEs with delay. These investigations have demonstrated the versatility of GPCFDE stability. The system's stability may be impacted by the Lyapunov function selection, which is why it is crucial. The system's stability may also be impacted by the delay term, therefore it's crucial to pick a delay that's not too long. Given that these equations are utilized to simulate a wide range of events in research and engineering, the stability of GPCFDEs is a significant issue. The research mentioned above have significantly advanced our knowledge of the stability of GPCFDEs and offer insightful information for the development of stable systems.

On the other hand, two subjects in control theory, that are strongly connected to each other, are observer design and stability analysis [10–14]. A novel observer design strategy, for instance, has been put out in [15] for a class of uncertain Nonlinear Systems (NSs) with sampled-delayed output. In this work [15], low-pass filter and a high-gain observer were used to create the suggested observer. The results of using the observer with a quadrotor UAV are encouraging. The suggested observer can be utilized to enhance the performance and stability of quadrotor UAVs. Additionally, the topic of OD for a class of nonlinear delayed systems was examined in [16]. In that work, a Lyapunov-Krasovskii functional was used to create the suggested observer. The error between the estimated states and the genuine states converges to a small region of the origin since the observer has been demonstrated to be virtually stable.

In the same context, the Unknown Input Observer (UIO) is a well-known type of observers that has drawn a lot of interest recently, see for instance [17–21]. Ref. [22] is a very interesting UIO research work, where the authors have used an UIO to control quadrotors. In another noteworthy work [23], the authors have designed an UIO for discrete-time interval type-2 takagi–sugeno fuzzy systems. Finally, the authors can't go on without mentioning [24], where it has been question of using an UIO for distributed tube-based model predictive control of heterogeneous vehicle platoons. It is important to note, in the end of this paragraph, that, to the best of the authors' knowledge, there are not yet published researches in the literature, dealing with the observer design issue for GPFOSs (GPFOSs). For more information, UIO design has been a topic of interest in control systems research. One approach is the interval observer-based UIO design proposed by Zhu, Fu, and Dinh in [25]. The study presents an asymptotic convergence UIO design that can handle input disturbances and measurement noise. Another approach is the full-order impulsive observer design for impulsive systems with unknown inputs, as proposed by Tong et al., in [26]. Their proposed observer design can estimate both the state and unknown input of the system. Ren et al., in [27] proposed a disturbance observer-based intelligent control for nonstrict-feedback nonlinear systems. The proposed method combines a disturbance observer and an intelligent control law to achieve robustness against uncertainties and disturbances. Huang et al., in [28] proposed a combination of functional and disturbance observers for positive systems with disturbances. Their proposed observer design can estimate the state, unknown input, and disturbances of the system. Finally, Wang et al., in [29] proposed a finite-time observer-based H_∞ fault-tolerant output formation tracking control for heterogeneous nonlinear multi-agent systems. Their proposed observer-based control method can ensure finite-time convergence and robustness against faults and disturbances.

There has been a surge of interest in One-Sided Lipschitz (OSL) NSs in recent years. OSL NSs are a type of nonlinear systems distinguished by the fact that their nonlinear function satisfies the one-sided Lipschitz nonlinear condition. One major advantage of the class of OSL systems is that it has been proved in the literature that the OSL condition is more general than the Lipschitz one. Furthermore, many real-world systems may be represented as one-sided Lipschitz nonlinear systems. OSL NSs, for example, have been used to describe the dynamics of robotic manipulators, power systems, and chemical processes, as shown in [30–34]. In other words, OSL is a mathematical concept used in the analysis of differential equations and control systems. According to [35], a OSL condition is a weaker form of the standard Lipschitz condition, which requires that the difference between the values of a function at two points be no greater than the product of the distance between the points and a constant. [36] explains that OSL conditions are particularly useful in the analysis of impulsive systems, which are systems that experience sudden changes in their state variables at certain times. [37] shows how one-sided Lipschitz conditions can be used to prove stability of a class of nonlinear systems. Finally, [38] presents an application of OSL conditions to the analysis and control of mechanical systems.

Various aspects have motivated the authors to produce the present study. First, to the best of the authors' knowledge, the observer design problem has not yet been investigated in the literature. Second, the authors have thought about developing a research method that is applicable to a wide range of systems. Indeed, this work investigates OSL systems, which correspond to an extension of the classical Lipschitz systems. Furthermore, the used UIO allows us to not only investigate disturbance-free systems but also systems with unknown inputs.

Based on the points made above, the contributions and advantages of the proposed work are summarized as follows:

- To the best of the authors' knowledge, this is the first time that an observer has been synthesized for Generalized Proportional Fractional-Order Systems.
- A full-order observer is developed, as well as a reduced-order one.
- The considered class of systems is one-sided Lipschitz nonlinear systems—an extension of the traditional Lipschitz systems.
- The developed observer (the UIO) is efficient, even for systems with unknown inputs, and this is thanks to the inner property of the UIOs. Indeed, the UIO has the ability to decouple the estimation error from these unknown inputs.

2. Preliminaries and Problem Formulation

This section presents the basic explanation and concept, along with a discussion on the derivative related to the GPFOSs called the Generalized Proportional Fractional Derivative (GPFD). The operators of GPFD for a function $\in AC([a,b],\mathrm{R})$ $a < b$, are defined in the following manner (refer to [39]):

$$D_{0,t}^{\mathrm{n},h}d(t) = I_{t_0,t}^{1-\mathrm{n},h}D_t^{1,h}d(t) = \frac{1}{h^{1-\mathrm{n}}\Gamma(1-\mathrm{n})}\int_0^t e^{\frac{h-1}{h}(t-s)}(t-s)^{-\mathrm{n}}D_t^{1,h}d(s)ds.$$

$$for\ t \in (a,b],\ 0 < \mathrm{n} < 1,\ 0 < h \leq 1$$

where $D_t^{1,h}d(s) = (1-h)d(s) + hd'(s)$.

This formula outlines the GPFD as a broadened version of the Caputo fractional derivative with ($h = 1$).

Lemma 1 [39]. *Let $0 < \mathrm{n} < 1, 0 < h \leq 1$ and S be a constant and symmetric, definite positive matrix. Then,*

$$^C D_{0,t}^{\mathrm{n},h} d^T S d(t) \leq 2d^T(t) S\ ^C D_{0,t}^{\mathrm{n},h} d(t)$$

Definition 1. *The Mittag–Leffler function can be defined in two ways, either with one parameter or with two parameters. These two versions are given below with $\mathrm{n} > 0$ and $\beta > 0$*

$$E_{\mathrm{n}}(z) = \sum_{k=0}^{\infty}\frac{z^k}{\Gamma(1+k\mathrm{n})}\ and\ E_{\mathrm{n},\beta}(z) = \sum_{k=0}^{\infty}\frac{z^k}{\Gamma(\beta+k\mathrm{n})} \tag{1}$$

In the rest of this paper, attention is given to a nonlinear system that is valid for $t \geq t_0$

$$ {}^{C}D^{\mathrm{n},h}_{0,t} w(t) = Aw(t) + Bu(t) + D_g g(Gw,u) + Dd(t) y(t) = Cw(t) \tag{2} $$

where $w(t) \in \mathrm{R}^{\mathrm{n}}$ denotes the state, $u(t) \in \mathrm{R}^{\mathrm{m}}$ denotes the input, $y(t) \in \mathrm{R}^{\mathrm{q}}$ denotes the output, $d(\mathrm{t}) \in \mathrm{R}^{\mathrm{S}}$ denotes the disturbance. $A \in \mathrm{R}^{\mathrm{n}\times\mathrm{n}}$, $B \in \mathrm{R}^{\mathrm{n}\times\mathrm{m}}$, $\mathrm{C} \in \mathrm{R}^{\mathrm{q}\times\mathrm{n}}$, $\mathrm{D} \in \mathrm{R}^{\mathrm{n}\times\mathrm{S}}$, D_g, and G are known matrices, and the nonlinear portion of the system is denoted by $g(Gw,u)$. It is assumed that the input matrix D, which is unknown, has a complete column rank.

Definition 2. *The function $g(Gw,u)$ is OSL in R^n, with a OSL constant ρ, i.e.,*

$$ \langle g(G\hat{w},u) - g(Gw,u), G(\hat{w} - w) \rangle \leq \rho \| G(\hat{w} - w) \|^2 \tag{3} $$

Definition 3. *The function $g(Gw,u)$ is said to be quadratically inner bounded in R^n if, for any w in R^n and u in the domain of g, there exists the positive constants γ and β so that the following inequality holds:*

$$ \| g(G\hat{w},u) - g(Gw,u) \|^2 \leq \beta \| G(\hat{w} - w) \|^2 + \gamma \langle g(G\hat{w},u) - g(Gw,u), G(\hat{w} - w) \rangle \tag{4} $$

where β and γ are known scalars.

3. Unknown Input Observer (UIO) Design

3.1. Full-Order UIO

Consider the UIO for the GPFOS (2), which is formulated as follows:

$$ {}^{C}D^{\mathrm{n},h}_{0,t} \xi(t) = R\xi(t) + Hy(t) + QD_g g(G\hat{w},u) + QBu(t)\hat{w}(t) = \xi(t) - Ey(t) \tag{5} $$

Here, $\xi(\mathrm{t}) \in \mathrm{R}^{\mathrm{n}}$ denotes the observer's state vector, and $\hat{w}(t) \in \mathrm{R}^{\mathrm{n}}$ represents the estimated value of $w(t)$. R, H, and Q are matrices, which satisfy the following constraints:

$$ R = QA - KC \tag{6} $$

$$ H = K(I + CE) - QAE \tag{7} $$

$$ Q = I + EC \tag{8} $$

Matrices K and E will be constructed later on. Let us define the state estimation error as:

$$ e(t) = \hat{w}(t) - w(t) = \xi(t) - Qw(t) $$

By defining $\Delta g = g(Gw,u) - g(Gw,u)$, we can express the error dynamics as follows:

$$ {}^{C}D^{\mathrm{n},h}_{0,t} e(t) = {}^{C}D^{\mathrm{n},h}_{0,t} \xi(t) - Q\,{}^{C}D^{\mathrm{n},h}_{0,t} w(t) = Re + (RQ + HC - QA)x + QD_g\Delta g - QDd $$

From Equations (6)–(8), it follows that $RQ + HC - QA = 0$, which implies that:

$$ {}^{C}D^{\mathrm{n},h}_{0,t} e(t) = Re + QD_g\Delta g - QDd \tag{9} $$

The following theorem gives a necessary condition for the error dynamic Mittag–Leffler stability (9):

Theorem 1. *Onesupposes the GPFOS (2), which verifies (3) and (4), with the unknown input observer (5). If* $\exists P = P^T > 0$ *and matrices E and K with appropriate dimensions and* $\tau_1, \tau_2, \varepsilon > 0$*, the following is assumed:*

$$\begin{bmatrix} R^T P + PR + 2\eta G^T G + \varepsilon I & \sigma G^T + PQD_g \\ * & -2\tau_2 I \end{bmatrix} < 0 \tag{10}$$

$$ECD = -D \tag{11}$$

where $\eta = \tau_1\rho + \tau_2\beta$ *and* $\sigma = \tau_2\gamma - \tau_1$*, then*

$$\|e(t)\| \le m(\|(e(0)\|)e^{c\frac{h-1}{h}t}(E_{\mathrm{n}}(-\mu t^{\mathrm{n}}))^{\delta}, t \ge 0$$

where $m(s) \ge 0, m(0) = 0$*, m is a locally Lipschitz function,* $\mu > 0, \delta > 0, c > 0$*.*

Proof. It can be inferred from Equations (8) and (11) that $QD = 0$. Consequently, by utilizing Equation (9), we can obtain:

$${}^{C}D_{0,t}^{\mathrm{n},h} e(t) = Re + QD_g\Delta g \tag{12}$$

Let the Lyapunov function be $V = e^T Pe$. Based on Lemma 1, $\forall t \ge 0$ and $\forall \mathrm{n} \in (0,1)$, the Fractional order derivative of $V(t)$ is given by:

$${}^{C}D_{0,t}^{\mathrm{n},h} V(t) \le 2e^T P\left(Re + QD_g\Delta g\right) \le e^T\left(R^T P + PR\right)e + \Delta g^{\mathrm{T}}\left(QD_g\right)^{\mathrm{T}} Pe + e^T PQD_g\Delta g \tag{13}$$

Now, by condition (3), we have, for a positive scalar, τ_1:

$$2\tau_1\left(\rho e^T G^T Ge - e^T G^T \Delta g\right) \ge 0 \tag{14}$$

Similarly, condition (4) yields $\tau_2 > 0$:

$$2\tau_2\left(\beta e^T G^T Ge + \gamma e^T G^T \Delta g - \Delta g^T \Delta g\right) \ge 0 \tag{15}$$

The sum of the left-hand sides of (14) and (15) can be added to the right-hand side of (13) to give:

$$\begin{aligned} {}^{C}D_{0,t}^{\mathrm{n},h} V(t) &\le e^T(R^T P + PR + 2\eta G^T G)e - 2\tau_2\Delta g^T\Delta g + 2e^T(\sigma G^T + PQD_g)\Delta g \\ &\le \begin{bmatrix} e \\ \Delta g \end{bmatrix}^T \begin{bmatrix} R^T P + PR + 2\eta G^T G & \sigma G^T + PQD_g \\ * & -2\tau_2 I \end{bmatrix} \times \begin{bmatrix} e \\ \Delta g \end{bmatrix} \end{aligned}$$

Based on the previous equations, for any positive scalar ε, one can obtain the following inequality:

$${}^{C}D_{0,t}^{\mathrm{n},h} V(t) \le \begin{bmatrix} e \\ \Delta g \end{bmatrix}^T \Lambda \begin{bmatrix} e \\ \Delta g \end{bmatrix} - \varepsilon\|e\|^2$$

where:

$$\Lambda = \begin{bmatrix} R^T P + PR + 2\eta G^T G + \varepsilon I & \sigma G^T + PQD_g \\ * & -2\tau_2 I \end{bmatrix}$$

The condition (10) guarantees that ${}^{C}D_{0,t}^{\mathrm{n},h} V(t) \le -\varepsilon\|e\|^2$. Therefore, using Corollary 2 in [8], we can obtain the required estimation. □

Remark 1. *Condition (10) in the previous theorem is a Nonlinear Matrix Inequality. To solve (10) by means of an available software, such as the MATLAB toolbox, it needs to be converted into a*

Linear Matrix Inequality (LMI). The following theorem provides a method to transform the NMI into an LMI.

Theorem 2. *One supposes that conditions (3) and (4) are verified and that CD has a full column rank. If* $\exists P = P^T > 0$*, matrices* W_1 *and* W_2*, and* $\tau_1, \tau_2, \varepsilon > 0$ *that satisfy the following inequality holds:*

$$\begin{bmatrix} \Theta & \sigma G^T + P\Delta_T + W_1\Delta_2 \\ * & -2\tau_2 I \end{bmatrix} < 0 \tag{16}$$

where:

$$\Theta = \Delta_N{}^T P + P\Delta_N + W_1\Delta_1 + \Delta_1{}^T W_1{}^T - W_2C - C^T W_2{}^T + 2\eta G^T G + \varepsilon I$$

$$\Delta_N = A - D(CD)^{-1}CA \tag{17}$$

$$\Delta_T = \left[I - D(CD)^{-1}C\right]D_g \tag{18}$$

$$\Delta_1 = \left[I - (CD)(CD)^{-1}\right]CA \tag{19}$$

$$\Delta_2 = \left[I - (CD)(CD)^{-1}\right]CD_g \tag{20}$$

with $(CD)^{-1}$ *as the generalized inverse of CD satisfying* $CD(CD)^{-1}CD = CD$*.*

Then:

$$\|e(t)\| \le m(\|(e(0)\|)e^{c\frac{h-1}{h}t}\left(\mathrm{E_n}\left(-\mu t^{\mathrm{n}}\right)\right)^{\delta}, t \ge 0$$

where $m(s) \ge 0$*,* $m(0) = 0$*,m is a locally Lipschitz function,* $\mu > 0, \delta > 0, c > 0$*.*

Proof. If D is a matrix of full column rank, then to have $ECD = -D$, matrix CD should be also a matrix of full column rank. Then, the solution of Equation (11) can be expressed as:

$$E = -D(CD)^{-1} + Y\left[I - (CD)(CD)^{-1}\right], \tag{21}$$

where a real matrix, Y, has the appropriate dimensions. By using Equations (6), (8), and (21), we can deduce that:

$$R = \left[I - D(CD)^{-1}C + Y\left(I - (CD)(CD)^{-1}\right)C\right]A - KC = \Delta_N + Y\Delta_1 - KC. \tag{22}$$

Using Equations (8) and (21), it follows that:

$$QD_g = \left[I - D(CD)^{-1}C + Y\left(I - (CD)(CD)^{-1}\right)C\right]D_g = \Delta_T + Y\Delta_2 \tag{23}$$

One substitutes Equations (22) and (23) into (10) and one defines $W_1 = PY$ and $W_2 = PK$, one can obtain the LMI (16). □.

Remark 2. *If the feasibility of condition (16) can be obtained, then it is possible to compute* $Y = P^{-1}W_1$ *and* $K = P^{-1}W_2$*. This will allow us to calculate E, R, Q, and H easily, and use the unknown input observer (5).*

3.2. Reduced-Order UIO

Since matrix C has a complete row rank, it is ensured that a suitable transformation can be found for the coordinates of the system's states, meaning that C can be expressed as $C = \begin{bmatrix} I_p & 0 \end{bmatrix}$. In this situation, the state vector can be represented as $w = \begin{bmatrix} y \\ l \end{bmatrix}$, where the sub-vector $l \in R^{n-p}$ consists of the states that are unmeasurable. Consequently, Equation (2) can be restated as follows:

$$ {}^{C}D_{0,t}^{n,h}\begin{bmatrix} y \\ l \end{bmatrix} = \begin{bmatrix} A_{11} & A_{12} \\ A_{21} & A_{22} \end{bmatrix}\begin{bmatrix} y \\ l \end{bmatrix} + \begin{bmatrix} B_1 \\ B_2 \end{bmatrix}u + \begin{bmatrix} D_{g1} \\ D_{g2} \end{bmatrix}f(G_1y + G_2l, u) + \begin{bmatrix} D_1 \\ D_2 \end{bmatrix}d \quad (24) $$

where the matrices A_{11}, B_1, and D_1 have dimensions of $p \times p, p \times m$, and $p \times q$, respectively, while D_{g1}, D_{g2}, G_1, and G_2 are known matrices. The objective of this part is to reconstruct the non-measurable sub-states, denoted by $l(t)$, by considering the unknown input vector $d(t)$. For this purpose, a reduced-order estimator is proposed as follows:

$$ \begin{cases} {}^{C}D_{0,t}^{n,h}\hat{z}_2 = (A_{22} + LA_{12})\hat{z}_2 + Uy + (LB_1 + B_2)u + D_Lg\left(\hat{l}, u\right) \\ \hat{l} = G_1y + G_2(\hat{z}_2 - Ly) \\ \hat{w} = \binom{y}{\hat{z}_2 - Ly} \end{cases} \quad (25) $$

The gain of matrix L can be determined later as follows:

$$ U = L(A_{11} - A_{12}L) + A_{21} - A_{22}L \quad (26) $$

$$ D_L = LD_{g1} + D_{g2} \quad (27) $$

Theorem 3. *Consider the GPFOS (2) under the nonlinear conditions (3) and (4) and with the UIO (25), provided that* $C = \begin{bmatrix} I_p & 0 \end{bmatrix}$. *If* $\exists \tau_1, \tau_2, \varepsilon > 0$ *and* $P = P^T > 0$ *and a matrix L, so that conditions (28) and (29) are satisfied:*

$$ \begin{bmatrix} (A_{22} + LA_{12})^T P + P(A_{22} + LA_{12}) + 2\eta {G_2}^T G_2 + \varepsilon I & \sigma {G_2}^T + PD_L \\ * & -2\tau_2 I \end{bmatrix} < 0, \quad (28) $$

$$ LD_1 + D_2 = 0 \quad (29) $$

where $\eta = \tau_1\rho + \tau_2\beta$ *and* $\sigma = \tau_2\gamma + \tau_1$.
Then:

$$ \left\|\tilde{z}_2(t)\right\| \le m\left(\left\|\left(\tilde{z}_2(0)\right\|\right)e^{c\frac{h-1}{h}t}\left(E_n\left(-\mu t^n\right)\right)^{\delta}, t \ge 0 $$

where $\tilde{z}_2 = \hat{z}_2 - z_2 =$ *with* $z_2 = Ly + l$. $m(s) \ge 0, m(0) = 0$, *m is a locally Lipschitz function,* $\mu > 0, \delta > 0, c > 0$.

Proof. The subsequent coordinate transformation is being considered: $\begin{bmatrix} z_1 \\ z_2 \end{bmatrix} = \begin{bmatrix} I_p & 0 \\ L & I_{n-p} \end{bmatrix}\begin{bmatrix} y \\ l \end{bmatrix}$. It can be observed that $z_2 = Ly + l$. Utilizing Equation (24), it is possible to derive the following expression for the derivative of z_2:

$$ {}^{C}D_{0,t}^{n,h}z_2 = (A_{22} + LA_{12})z_2 + Uy + (LB_1 + B_2)u + D_Lg(l, u) + (LD_1 + D_2)d, \quad (30) $$

In which, we have: $l = G_1y + G_2(z_2 - Ly)$. Given the first equation in (25), along with Equations (29) and (30), it can be concluded that the dynamics of the error $\tilde{z}_2 = \hat{z}_2 - z_2 = \hat{l} - l$ are defined by:

$$ {}^{C}D_{0,t}^{n,h}\tilde{z}_2(t) = (A_{22} + LA_{12})\tilde{z}_2 + D_L\Delta g \quad (31) $$

Let $\Delta g = g\left(\hat{l}, u\right) - g(l, u)$. Consider the Lyapunov function candidate $V = \tilde{z}_2^{\,T} P\tilde{z}_2$. By lemma 1, for every time $t \ge t_0$ and scalar $n \in (0, 1)$, the dynamics of this function are defined by:

$$ {}^{C}D_{0,t}^{n,h}V(t) \le 2\tilde{z}_2^{\,T}P\left[(A_{22} + LA_{12})\tilde{z}_2 + D_L\Delta g\right] \le \tilde{z}_2^{\,T}\left[P(A_{22} + LA_{12}) + (A_{22} + LA_{12})^T P\right]\tilde{z}_2 + \Delta g^T {D_L}^T P\tilde{z}_2 + \tilde{z}_2^{\,T} PD_L\Delta g \quad (32) $$

By utilizing the One-sided Lipschitz property (3), it is possible to determine:

$$\left\langle \Delta f, G\begin{pmatrix} 0 \\ \tilde{z}_2 \end{pmatrix} \right\rangle \le \rho \left\| G\begin{pmatrix} 0 \\ \tilde{z}_2 \end{pmatrix} \right\|^2,$$

Therefore, for any positive scalar τ_1, it can be inferred that:

$$2\tau_1\left(\rho \tilde{z}_2^{\,T} G_2{}^T G_2 \tilde{z}_2 - \tilde{z}_2^{\,T} G_2{}^T \Delta g\right) \ge 0 \tag{33}$$

Similarly, by making use of the quadratic inner boundedness inequality (4), it is possible to determine:

$$\Delta g^T \Delta g \le \beta \left\| G\begin{pmatrix} 0 \\ \tilde{z}_2 \end{pmatrix} \right\|^2 + \gamma \left\langle \Delta g, G\begin{pmatrix} 0 \\ \tilde{z}_2 \end{pmatrix} \right\rangle,$$

Hence, for any positive scalar $\tau_2 > 0$, it can be inferred that:

$$2\tau_2\left(\beta \tilde{z}_2^{\,T} G_2{}^T G_2 \tilde{z}_2 + \gamma \tilde{z}_2^{\,T} G_2{}^T \Delta g - \Delta g^T \Delta g\right) \ge 0 \tag{34}$$

Subsequently, by employing Equations (32)–(34), it is possible to obtain:

$${}^{C}D_{0,t}^{\mathfrak{n},h} V(t) \le \tilde{z}_2^{\,T}\left[(A_{22} + LA_{12})^T P + P(A_{22} + LA_{12}) + 2\eta G_2{}^T G_2\right]\tilde{z}_2 - 2\tau_2 \Delta g^T \Delta g + 2\tilde{z}_2^{\,T}\left(\sigma G_2{}^T + PD_L\right)\Delta g$$

Let $J = (A_{22} + LA_{12})^T P + P(A_{22} + LA_{12})$, then:

$${}^{C}D_{0,t}^{\mathfrak{n},h} V(t) \le \begin{bmatrix} \tilde{z}_2 \\ \Delta g \end{bmatrix}^T \begin{bmatrix} J + 2\eta G_2{}^T G_2 & \sigma G_2{}^T + PD_L \\ * & -2\tau_2 I \end{bmatrix} \begin{bmatrix} \tilde{z}_2 \\ \Delta g \end{bmatrix}$$

Therefore, for any positive value of ε, one can derive:

$${}^{C}D_{0,t}^{\mathfrak{n},h} V(t) \le \begin{bmatrix} \tilde{z}_2 \\ \Delta g \end{bmatrix}^T \Lambda \begin{bmatrix} \tilde{z}_2 \\ \Delta g \end{bmatrix} - \varepsilon \left\| \tilde{z}_2 \right\|^2$$

where $\Lambda = \begin{bmatrix} J + 2\eta G_2{}^T G_2 + \varepsilon I & \sigma G_2{}^T + PD_L \\ * & -2\tau_2 I \end{bmatrix}$. Therefore, if condition (28) is satisfied, then it guarantees that the inequality ${}^{C}D_{0,t}^{\mathfrak{n},h} V(t) \le -\varepsilon \left\| \tilde{z}_2 \right\|^2$ holds, which implies that the origin $\tilde{z}_2 = 0$ is globally Mittag–Leffler stable. □

Remark 3. *Condition (28), involved in Theorem 3, is a Nonlinear Matrix Inequality. However, to solve this condition by using available software packages such as MATLAB, it needs to be transformed into a Linear Matrix Inequality (LMI). By means of an appropriate transformation technique, Theorem 4 will provide a LMI stability condition.*

Theorem 4. *Consider GPFOS (2), and conditions (3) and (4) and that* $\text{rank}(D_1) = q$ *and that* $C = \begin{bmatrix} I_p & 0 \end{bmatrix}$*. If* $\exists \tau_1, \tau_2, \varepsilon > 0$ *and* $P = P^T > 0$*, and a matrix S, so that the linear matrix inequality (35) is feasible.*

$$\begin{bmatrix} \theta & \sigma G_2{}^T + P\Delta_D + S\Delta_G \\ * & -2\tau_2 I \end{bmatrix} < 0 \tag{35}$$

where:

$$\theta = \Delta_U{}^T P + P\Delta_U + SV_D A_{12} + A_{12}{}^T V_D{}^T S^T + 2\eta G_2{}^T G_2 + \varepsilon I$$

$$\Delta_U = A_{22} - D_2\overline{D}_1 A_{12} \tag{36}$$

$$V_D = I_p - D_1\overline{D}_1 \tag{37}$$

$$\Delta_D = D_{g2} - D_2\overline{D}_1 D_{g1} \tag{38}$$

$$\Delta_G = \left[I_p - D_1\overline{D}_1\right] D_{g1} \tag{39}$$

The symbol $\overline{D}_1$ denotes the generalized inverse of D_1, which satisfies the property $D_1\overline{D}_1 D_1 = D_1$. Then:

$$\left\|\tilde{z}_2(t)\right\| \le m\left(\left\|\left(\tilde{z}_2(0)\right\|\right)e^{c\frac{h-1}{h}t}\left(E_n\left(-\mu t^n\right)\right)\right)^{\delta}, t \ge 0$$

where $\tilde{z}_2 = \hat{z}_2 - z_2 =$ with $z_2 = Ly + l$. $m(s) \ge 0, m(0) = 0$, m is a locally Lipschitz function, $\mu > 0, \delta > 0, c > 0$.

Proof. If the rank of $rank(D_1) = rank(D) = q$, it is possible to find a matrix L such that $LD_1 + D_2 = 0$. Then, the solution of Equation (29) is:

$$L = -D_2\overline{D}_1 + Z(I_p - D_1\overline{D}_1), = -D_2\overline{D}_1 + ZV_D \tag{40}$$

In which, Z is a real matrix. If one exploits Equation (27), one can find:

$$D_L = -D_2\overline{D}_1 D_{g1} + D_{g2} + ZV_D D_{g1} = \Delta_D + Z\Delta_G \tag{41}$$

By substituting Equations (40) and (41) into the matrix inequality (28) and defining $S = PZ$, one can obtain the LMI (35). □

Remark 4. *Whenever the linear matrix inequality (LMI) given by Equation (35) is satisfied, it is possible to determine the matrix $Z = P^{-1}S$. This then enables the calculation of matrix L using Equation (40), which, in turn, allows for the computation of matrices U and D_L using Equations (26) and (27). Once these matrices are obtained, the unknown input observer (UIO) specified by Equation (25) can be utilized to estimate the state of the system.*

The next section includes a simulation study, which serves as additional evidence to support the effectiveness of the adopted approach.

4. Numerical Example and Simulations

Here, the authors provide a numerical example to verify the effectiveness of the fractional UIO. The system being studied is described by the GPFOS (2) and is as follows:

$$A = \begin{bmatrix} -3 & 1 \\ 0 & -6 \end{bmatrix}, B = \begin{bmatrix} 0.7 \\ 1 \end{bmatrix}, D_g = G = I_2,$$

$$C = \begin{bmatrix} 1 \\ 0 \end{bmatrix}^T, D = \begin{bmatrix} 1 \\ 0 \end{bmatrix},$$

$$g(Gw, u) = \begin{bmatrix} sinw_1 - 2w_1 \\ -2w_2 + cosw_2 \end{bmatrix},$$

The values $\rho = -1, \beta = 9$, and $\gamma = 0$ fulfill conditions (10) and (11). Moreover, CD, D, and $D_1 = 1$ all have a rank equal to one, enabling the utilization of Theorems 2 and 4.

4.1. Full-Order Observer Design Case

The UIFO concept for Nonlinear GPFOS is based on the estimate of a system's states and unknown inputs using the measurements data. Based on existing output measurements and known system dynamics, the UIFO attempts to rebuild the unmeasured states and unknown inputs of the system. Thus, we should design a full-order observer (also known as a state estimator) for the system. The observer should be capable of estimating all the system states based on the available output measurements. This can be achieved by constructing an observer with the same structure as the original system model. This fact is described in Equation (5). Then, derive the error dynamics of the observer, which describes the evolution of the estimation error between the estimated states and the actual states of the system. This task can be completed by analyzing the difference between the observer equations and the system equations, as shown in Equation (9). After that, analyze the stability of the UIFO by examining the stability properties of the error dynamics. Stability ensures that the estimation error converges to zero, indicating accurate estimation of the states, as investigated by the result of Theorem 1. The previous theorem's condition (10) is a Nonlinear Matrix Inequality; therefore, it must be turned into a Linear Matrix Inequality (LMI) before it can be solved using existing software, such as the MATLAB toolbox. Theorem 2 describes how to convert an NMI to an LMI. Thus, we can obtain the LMI (16).

To proceed, the initial action is to solve LMI (16) using MATLAB, which yields the following result:

$$E = \begin{bmatrix} -1 \\ 0 \end{bmatrix}, Q = \begin{bmatrix} 0 & 0 \\ 0 & 1 \end{bmatrix}, K = \begin{bmatrix} 0.79 \\ 0 \end{bmatrix},$$

$$R = \begin{bmatrix} -0.7892 & 0 \\ 0 & -6 \end{bmatrix}, H = \begin{bmatrix} 0 \\ 0 \end{bmatrix},$$

Subsequently, one can formulate the estimator (5).

The simulation is initialized with the conditions $w_1(0) = 2$ and $w_2(0) = -1$. The values of n and h are chosen so that $\mathrm{n} = 0.5$ and $h = 0.2$. We have generated simulations of the trajectories of w_1 and w_2 for the interval $[0\,1]$, with a time step of 10^{-8}. These simulations are visually represented in Figure 1. The curves of the errors are shown in Figure 2.

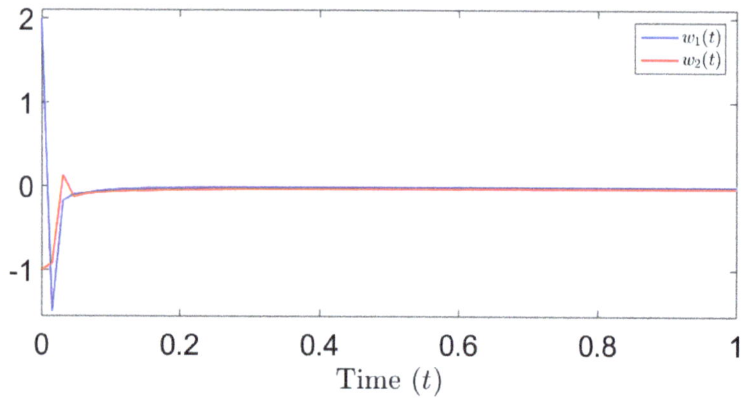

Figure 1. The evolution of the states $w_1(t)$ and $w_2(t)$.

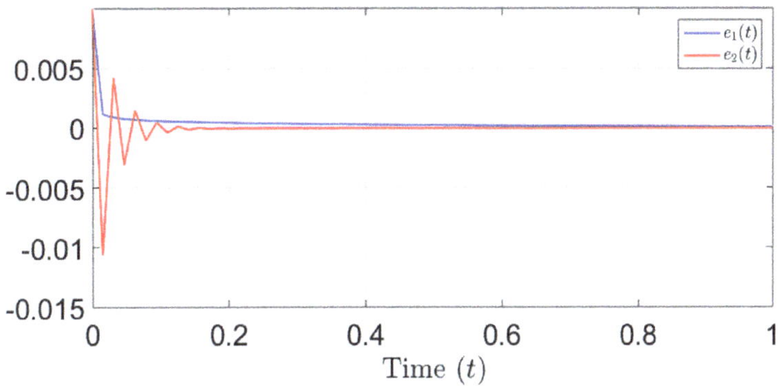

Figure 2. The evolution of the errors $e_1(t)$ and $e_2(t)$.

Based on Figures 1 and 2, we can easily see the result of Theorem 2. Indeed, Figure 2 clearly illustrates the exponential stability of the error dynamics, as the curves converge exponentially towards zero. This result is in line with Theorem 2.

4.2. Reduced-Order Observer Design Case

The principle of the UIRO for Nonlinear GPFOS is similar to the UIFO, but with the distinction that the UIRO estimates the system states using a reduced-order observer structure. This means that the observer only estimates a subset of the system states instead of all the states. The UIRO aims to reconstruct the unmeasured states and unknown inputs of a GPFOS based on the available output measurements and the known system dynamics. Thus, it is essential to design a reduced-order observer (also known as a state estimator) for the GPFOS system, as shown in Equation (25). The observer structure should be chosen in a way that facilitates the estimation of a subset of the system states rather than all the states. The choice of which states to estimate depends on observability considerations and the specific requirements of the application. After that, derive the error dynamics of the observer, describing the evolution of the estimation error between the estimated states and the actual states of the system. This task can be completed by analyzing the difference between the observer equations and the system equations. Then, analyze the stability of the UIRO by examining the stability properties of the error dynamics (31). Stability ensures that the estimation error converges to zero exponentially, indicating accurate estimation of the states. Condition (28), which is a Nonlinear Matrix Inequality, is implicated in Theorem 3. However, in order to solve this condition using accessible software tools such as MATLAB, it must first be turned into a Linear Matrix Inequality (LMI). Theorem 4 will provide an LMI stability condition using an appropriate transformation approach. When the LMI provided by Equation (35) is met, the matrix $Z = P^{-1}S$ may be determined. This allows for the calculation of matrix L using Equation (40), which, in turn, allows for the construction of matrices U and D_L using Equations (26) and (27), respectively. After obtaining these matrices, the UIO indicated by Equation (25) may be used to estimate the system's state.

The initial step in constructing the observer (25) is to solve (35) using MATLAB. The feasibility of LMI (35) is confirmed with:

$$P = 71.82,\ \tau_1 = 80.69,\ \tau_2 = 47.59 \text{ and } \varepsilon = 83.35$$

meaning that Mittag–Leffler stability can be achieved. In this instance, $L = 0$ since $V_D = 0$. Consequently, from (26) and (27), we obtain $U = 0$ and $D_L = \begin{bmatrix} 0 & 1 \end{bmatrix}$. Subsequently, the observer (25) can be designed for implementation.

The simulation is initialized with the condition $w_2(0) = -1$. The values of $\mathfrak{n}$ and h are chosen so that $\mathfrak{n} = 0.5$ and $h = 0.2$. We have generated simulations of the trajectory of w_2

for the interval [0 1], with a time step of 10^{-8}. These simulations are visually represented in Figure 3. The curves of the error $\tilde{z}_2$ are shown in Figure 4.

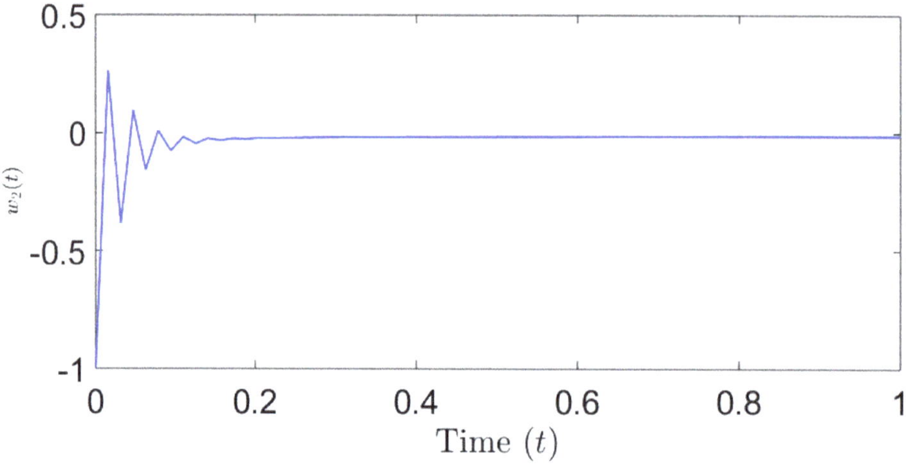

Figure 3. The evolution of the state $w_2(t)$.

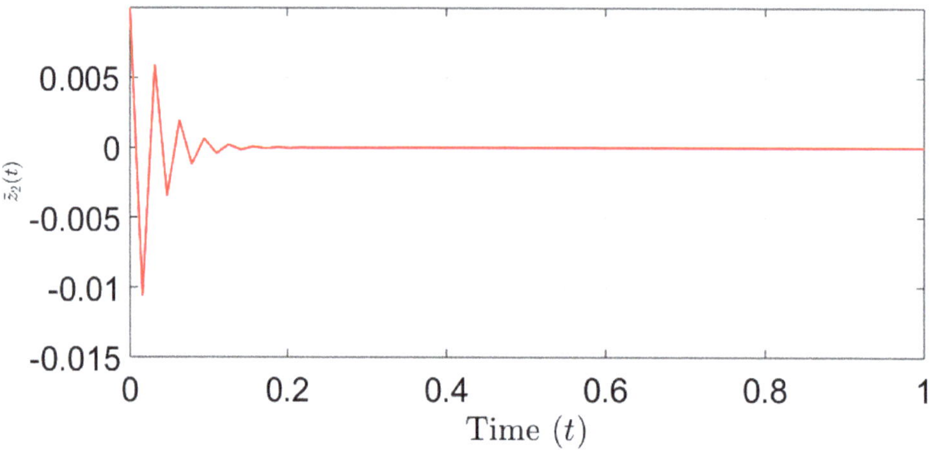

Figure 4. The evolution of the error $\tilde{z}_2(t)$.

Based on Figures 3 and 4, we can easily see the result of Theorem 4. In fact, the graphical representation provided in Figure 4 serves as visual evidence for the exponential stability of the error dynamics. The curve depicted in this figure exhibits a clear and consistent pattern of exponential convergence towards zero, which supports the conclusion drawn from Theorem 4. This observation provides strong empirical evidence to support the theoretical framework outlined in Theorem 4 and reinforces the notion that the error dynamics of the system are indeed exponentially stable.

5. Conclusions

In the present study, an UIO for Generalized Proportional Fractional-Order Systems has been developed. Regarding nonlinearity, the proposed system satisfies the One-Sided Lipschitz condition, which is an extension of the Lipschitz one. Both a full-order observer and a reduced-order observer have been established. The main contribution of this work is that it presents the first scheme to design observers for Generalized Proportional Fractional-Order Systems. A numerical example with simulations has been provided at the end of the paper to further clarify the efficiency of the developed scheme.

Author Contributions: Conceptualization, O.N. and A.J.; methodology, A.B.M.; software, M.R.; validation, L.M.; formal analysis, A.O.M.A.; investigation, A.B.M.; resources, L.M.; writing—original draft preparation, O.N. and A.O.M.A.; writing—review and editing, A.J. All authors have read and agreed to the published version of the manuscript.

Funding: This research is funded by "Researchers Supporting Project number (RSPD2023R683), King Saud University, Riyadh, Saudi Arabia".

Data Availability Statement: Not applicable.

Acknowledgments: The authors extend their appreciation to King Saud University in Riyadh, Saudi Arabia for funding this research work through Researchers Supporting Project number (RSPD2023R683).

Conflicts of Interest: The authors declare no conflict of interest.

Abbreviations

OD	Observer Design
GPFDEs	Generalized Proportional Fractional Differential Equations
GPCFDEs	Generalized Proportional Caputo Fractional Differential Equations
GPFD	Generalized Proportional Fractional Derivative
NSs	Nonlinear Systems
UIO	Unknown Input Observer
OSL	One-Sided Lipschitz
LMI	Linear Matrix Inequality
NMI	Nonlinear Matrix Inequality
UIFO	Unknown Input Full Order Observer
GPFOS	Generalized Proportional Fractional Order Systems
UIRO	Unknown Input Reduced Order Observer

References

1. Jarad, F.; Abdeljawad, T.; Alzabut, J. Generalized fractional derivatives generated by a class of local proportional derivatives. *Eur. Phys. J. Spéc. Top.* **2017**, *226*, 3457–3471. [CrossRef]
2. Alzabut, J.; Abdeljawad, T.; Jarad, F.; Sudsutad, W. A Gronwall inequality via the generalized proportional fractional derivative with applications. *J. Inequalities Appl.* **2019**, *2019*, 101. [CrossRef]
3. Tarasov, V.E. Exact Solutions of Bernoulli and Logistic Fractional Differential Equations with Power Law Coefficients. *Mathematics* **2020**, *8*, 2231. [CrossRef]
4. Atangana, A.; Baleanu, D. New fractional derivatives with nonlocal and non-singular kernel: Theory and application to heat transfer model. *Therm. Sci.* **2016**, *20*, 763–769. [CrossRef]
5. Rashid, S.; Jarad, F.; Hammouch, Z. Some new bounds analogous to generalized proportional fractional integral operator with respect to another function. *Discret. Contin. Dyn. Syst. Ser. S* **2021**, *14*, 3703. [CrossRef]
6. Donchev, T.; Hristova, S. Practical Stability of Generalized Proportional Caputo Fractional Differential Equations by Lyapunov Functions. In *New Trends in the Applications of Differential Equations in Sciences: NTADES 2022, Sozopol, Bulgaria, June 14–17*; Springer International Publishing: Cham, Switzerland, 2023; pp. 425–432. [CrossRef]
7. Bohner, M.; Hristova, S. Stability for generalized Caputo proportional fractional delay integro-differential equations. *Bound. Value Probl.* **2022**, *2022*, 14. [CrossRef]
8. Agarwal, R.; Hristova, S.; O'regan, D. Stability of Generalized Proportional Caputo Fractional Differential Equations by Lyapunov Functions. *Fractal Fract.* **2022**, *6*, 34. [CrossRef]
9. Agarwal, R.; Hristova, S.; O'regan, D. Generalized Proportional Caputo Fractional Differential Equations with Delay and Practical Stability by the Razumikhin Method. *Mathematics* **2022**, *10*, 1849. [CrossRef]
10. Kahouli, O.; Naifar, O.; Ben Makhlouf, A.; Bouteraa, Y.; Aloui, A.; Rebhi, A. A Robust and Non-Fragile Observer Design for Nonlinear Fractional-Order Systems. *Symmetry* **2022**, *14*, 1795. [CrossRef]

11. Sergiyenko, O.; Zhirabok, A.; Ibraheem, I.K.; Zuev, A.; Filaretov, V.; Azar, A.T.; Hameed, I.A. Interval Observers for Discrete-Time Linear Systems with Uncertainties. *Symmetry* **2022**, *14*, 2131. [CrossRef]
12. Xu, L.; Xiong, W.; Zhou, M.; Chen, L. A Continuous Terminal Sliding-Mode Observer-Based Anomaly Detection Approach for Industrial Communication Networks. *Symmetry* **2022**, *14*, 124. [CrossRef]
13. Akremi, R.; Lamouchi, R.; Amairi, M.; Dinh, T.N.; Raïssi, T. Functional interval observer design for multivariable linear parameter-varying systems. *Eur. J. Control* **2023**, *71*, 100794. [CrossRef]
14. Zhang, Y.; Nie, Y.; Chen, L. Adaptive Fuzzy Fault-Tolerant Control against Time-Varying Faults via a New Sliding Mode Observer Method. *Symmetry* **2021**, *13*, 1615. [CrossRef]
15. Dam, Q.T.; Thabet, R.E.H.; Ali, S.A.; Guerin, F. Observer design for a class of uncertain nonlinear systems with sampled-delayed output using High-Gain Observer and low-pass filter: Application for a quadrotor UAV. *IEEE Trans. Ind. Electron.* **2023**, 1–10. [CrossRef]
16. Echi, N. Observer design and practical stability of nonlinear systems under unknown time-delay. *Asian J. Control* **2021**, *23*, 685–696. [CrossRef]
17. Xia, J.; Jiang, B.; Zhang, K. UIO-Based Practical Fixed-Time Fault Estimation Observer Design of Nonlinear Systems. *Symmetry* **2022**, *14*, 1618. [CrossRef]
18. Zhao, S.; Yu, J.; Wang, Z.; Gao, D. Unknown input observer based distributed fault detection for nonlinear multi-agent systems with probabilistic time delay. *J. Frankl. Inst.* **2023**, *360*, 1058–1076. [CrossRef]
19. Houda, K.; Saifia, D.; Chadli, M.; Labiod, S. Unknown input observer based robust control for fuzzy descriptor systems subject to actuator saturation. *Math. Comput. Simul.* **2023**, *203*, 150–173. [CrossRef]
20. Ríos, H.; Dávila, J.; Fridman, L. Finite–and fixed–time observers for uncertain multiple–outputs linear systems with unknown inputs. *Int. J. Robust Nonlinear Control* **2023**, 1–26. [CrossRef]
21. Essabre, M.; Hmaiddouch, I.; El Assoudi, A.; El Yaagoubi, E.H. Design of unknown input observer for discrete-time Takagi Sugeno implicit systems with unmeasurable premise variables. *Bull. Electr. Eng. Inform.* **2022**, *12*, 59–68. [CrossRef]
22. Zhang, W.; Shao, X.; Zhang, W.; Qi, J.; Li, H. Unknown input observer-based appointed-time funnel control for quadrotors. *Aerosp. Sci. Technol.* **2022**, *126*, 107351. [CrossRef]
23. Li, Y.; Yuan, M.; Chadli, M.C.; Wang, Z.-P.; Zhao, D. Unknown Input Functional Observer Design for Discrete-Time Interval Type-2 Takagi–Sugeno Fuzzy Systems. *IEEE Trans. Fuzzy Syst.* **2022**, *30*, 4690–4701. [CrossRef]
24. Luo, Q.; Nguyen, A.-T.; Fleming, J.; Zhang, H. Unknown Input Observer Based Approach for Distributed Tube-Based Model Predictive Control of Heterogeneous Vehicle Platoons. *IEEE Trans. Veh. Technol.* **2021**, *70*, 2930–2944. [CrossRef]
25. Zhu, F.; Fu, Y.; Dinh, T.N. Asymptotic convergence unknown input observer design via interval observer. *Automatica* **2023**, *147*, 110744. [CrossRef]
26. Tong, L.; Liu, B.; Yan, C.; Liu, D. Full-order impulsive observers for impulsive systems with unknown inputs. *Asian J. Control* **2023**, 1–12. [CrossRef]
27. Ren, H.; Ma, H.; Li, H.; Lu, R. A disturbance observer based intelligent control for nonstrict-feedback nonlinear systems. *Sci. China Technol. Sci.* **2023**, *66*, 456–467. [CrossRef]
28. Huang, L.; Zhao, X.; Lin, F.; Zhang, J. Combination of Functional and Disturbance Observer for Positive Systems with Disturbances. *Mathematics* **2022**, *11*, 200. [CrossRef]
29. Wang, Q.; Dong, X.; Wang, B.; Hua, Y.; Ren, Z. Finite-time Observer-based H_∞ Fault-tolerant Output Formation Tracking Control for Heterogeneous Nonlinear Multi-agent Systems. *IEEE Trans. Netw. Sci. Eng.* **2023**, 1–13. [CrossRef]
30. Zhang, W.; Su, H.; Zhu, F.; Azar, G.M. Unknown input observer design for one-sided Lipschitz nonlinear systems. *Nonlinear Dyn.* **2015**, *79*, 1469–1479. [CrossRef]
31. Yang, Y.; Lin, C.; Chen, B.; Zhao, X. H_∞ observer design for uncertain one-sided Lipschitz nonlinear systems with time-varying delay. *Appl. Math. Comput.* **2020**, *375*, 125066. [CrossRef]
32. Li, J.; Han, T.; Xiao, B.; Yang, Q.; Yan, H. Observer-based time-varying group formation tracking for one-sided Lipschitz nonlinear second-order multi-agent systems. *Trans. Inst. Meas. Control* **2023**, 01423312231162896. [CrossRef]
33. Iqbal, W.; Ghous, I.; Ansari, E.A.; Duan, Z.; Imran, M.; Khan, A.A.; Humayun, M.T. Robust nonlinear observer-based controller design for one-sided Lipschitz switched systems with time-varying delays. *J. Frankl. Inst.* **2023**, *360*, 2046–2067. [CrossRef]
34. Razaq, M.A.; Rehan, M.; Hussain, M.; Ahmed, S.; Hong, K.S. Observer-based leader-following consensus of one-sided Lipschitz multi-agent systems over input saturation and directed graphs. *Asian J. Control* **2023**, 1–17. [CrossRef]
35. Wang, M.; Yang, X.; Mao, S.; Yiu, K.F.C.; Park, J.H. Consensus of multi-Agent systems with one-Sided lipschitz nonlinearity via nonidentical double event-Triggered control subject to deception attacks. *J. Frankl. Inst.* **2023**, *360*, 6275–6295. [CrossRef]
36. Li, H.; Cao, J. Event-triggered group consensus for one-sided Lipschitz multi-agent systems with input saturation. *Commun. Nonlinear Sci. Numer. Simul.* **2023**, *121*, 107234. [CrossRef]
37. Yang, W.; Dong, J.; Meng, F. Dynamic edge event-triggered consensus for one-sided Lipschitz multiagent systems with disturbances. *Int. J. Robust Nonlinear Control.* **2023**, *33*, 5305–5321. [CrossRef]

38. Phuong, N.T.; Sau, N.H.; Thuan, M.V. Finite-time dissipative control design for one-sided Lipschitz nonlinear singular Caputo fractional order systems. *Int. J. Syst. Sci.* **2023**, *54*, 1694–1712. [CrossRef]
39. Almeida, R.; Agarwal, R.P.; Hristova, S.; O'regan, D. Quadratic Lyapunov Functions for Stability of the Generalized Proportional Fractional Differential Equations with Applications to Neural Networks. *Axioms* **2021**, *10*, 322. [CrossRef]

symmetry MDPI

Article

Numerical Approach for Solving a Fractional-Order Norovirus Epidemic Model with Vaccination and Asymptomatic Carriers

Aeshah A. Raezah [1], Rahat Zarin [2,*] and Zehba Raizah [1]

[1] Department of Mathematics, Faculty of Science, King Khalid University, Abha 62529, Saudi Arabia
[2] Department of Mathematics, Faculty of Science, King Mongkut's University of Technology Thonburi (KMUTT), 126 Pracha-Uthit Road, Bang Mod, Thrung Khru, Bangkok 10140, Thailand
* Correspondence: rahat.zarin@uetpeshawar.edu.pk

Abstract: This paper explored the impact of population symmetry on the spread and control of a norovirus epidemic. The study proposed a mathematical model for the norovirus epidemic that takes into account asymptomatic infected individuals and vaccination effects using a non-singular fractional operator of Atanganaa–Baleanu Caputo (ABC). Fixed point theory, specifically Schauder and Banach's fixed point theory, was used to investigate the existence and uniqueness of solutions for the proposed model. The study employed MATLAB software to generate simulation results and demonstrate the effectiveness of the fractional order q. A general numerical algorithm based on Adams–Bashforth and Newton's Polynomial method was developed to approximate the solution. Furthermore, the stability of the proposed model was analyzed using Ulam–Hyers stability techniques. The basic reproductive number was calculated with the help of next-generation matrix techniques. The sensitivity analysis of the model parameters was performed to test which parameter is the most sensitive for the epidemic. The values of the parameters were estimated with the help of least square curve fitting tools. The results of the study provide valuable insights into the behavior of the proposed model and demonstrate the potential applications of fractional calculus in solving complex problems related to disease transmission.

Keywords: Mittag–Leffler kernel; fractional norovirus epidemic model; ABC-fractional derivative; iterative solution; numerical scheme

Citation: Raezah, A.A.; Zarin, R.; Raizah, Z. Numerical Approach for Solving a Fractional-Order Norovirus Epidemic Model with Vaccination and Asymptomatic Carriers. *Symmetry* **2023**, *15*, 1208. https://doi.org/10.3390/sym15061208

Academic Editors: Hassen Fourati, Abdellatif Ben Makhlouf and Omar Naifar

Received: 9 May 2023
Revised: 30 May 2023
Accepted: 31 May 2023
Published: 5 June 2023

1. Introduction

The most dangerous infectious diseases were listed by medical sciences researchers through testing by various laboratories. Among them, one of the diseases of the stomach is caused by noroviruses (NoV), which enter through fecal–oral paths and interact with human feeding. These types of viruses may also be found in the shedding of vomitus. Besides these sources, the contamination of used food or water and contact with fomites or direct contact with any infected individuals may also cause this type of epidemic [1]. The local significance for each of these paths has been discussed but it is widely known that the NoV group of viruses alone is responsible for a huge epidemic due to food consumption and creates a burden on health in various countries [2,3]. The acute viral gastroenteritis viruses are related to three types of foods, which can cause an epidemic:

A_1 : The shells of molluscs are contaminated with different impurities during production.
A_2 : Fresh food items can be contaminated at the time of packing, collection, and harvesting.
A_3 : Taking more time to prepare and cook food can lead to contamination.

Poor practical and personal hygiene when handling foods is the main cause of contaminated food, which can lead to the transmission of an NoV epidemic. This type of food contamination will depend on many factors such as personal hygiene habits, the output of the virus, time of virus transfer, duration of the existence of the virus, time of inactivation for the virus, the shedding effect of the virus and many other factors. The contamination of hands may contaminate different surfaces depending upon the degree of touching and contamination of hands. The hands in this situation may contribute to the epidemic as well as receiving the disease [4]. The spreading of norovirus (NoV) and its results may depend on many factors. It may also depend on weather conditions and nearly half of the cases may occur in the winter season [5].

Mathematical models of epidemiological problems have been applied to the prediction and control of infectious diseases [6–10]. Different global problems of epidemic diseases have very interesting outcomes as represented by mathematical formulations given in the past literature. Some aspects of this concept include stochastic representation which have impacts, such as global humidity, perceptions, heat occurrence, etc., which affect the strength of the immune system against infective diseases. This idea will enable us to write the deterministic idea in the form of random situations which have more realistic outcomes. This will include all the other external impacts in the form of mathematical formulation. This will cause vibration in the parameters from the environment or some variation in the infectious models or due to the given system [11,12]. This approach of modeling provides more choices for selection and gives more realistic results as compared to the idealistic approach of deterministic models. Therefore, the stochastic concepts that are perturbed by white noise or Brownian motion are well represented in the literature, for detail one can see [13].

The relationship between symmetry and epidemic models relates to how the distribution of susceptible, infected, and recovered individuals in a population are affected by factors such as demographic and environmental symmetry. Symmetry considerations can play a role in the modeling of disease transmission dynamics, as they can affect the spatial and temporal spread of an epidemic. For example, if a population is asymmetric with respect to some underlying factor, such as age or location, this could lead to differences in the transmission of a disease and impact the effectiveness of control strategies. In the context of mathematical modeling, accounting for symmetry in the population being modeled can help to improve the accuracy of epidemic models and provide valuable insights into the spread and control of infectious diseases [14–16]. Fractional calculus, as used in the paper abstract mentioned earlier, is one approach to modeling the impact of symmetry in disease transmission dynamics. By developing models that account for the effects of asymmetry, researchers can gain a better understanding of the underlying mechanisms driving epidemics and develop more effective strategies to prevent and control their spread.

As we describe any system having different choices for the selection of the order of the derivative, the extra degrees will be obtained in the complex dynamics. This extra variety of choices can be studied in modern calculus in the form of non-natural order derivative expressions whose outcomes must be obtained as the whole density of the quantities [17–19]. Due to this, modern calculus will be superior to classical calculus. The medical sciences and natural sciences dynamical systems require more and more information, therefore these can be well investigated using different fractional operators for the internal behavior of the system; for the last few decades, this has been the central focus of many researchers as compared to the integer order analysis. In this field, the investigation is related to unique and solution existence, positivity, boundedness, numerical solution, and the realistic approach of feasibility. To date, various problems of small micro species, logistic population problems, HBV, TB, HCV, SIR, SEIR, SI, and many cancer problems have been investigated in the sense of fractional order derivatives [20–24]. These problems are tested for theoretical and approximate solutions in the non-integer order parameters sensed by the application of various techniques. Some examples are the Adams–Bashforth, corrector-predictor method, various transformations, and series solution techniques [25,26]. The analysis of COVID-19 problems has been investigated recently through fractional operators as can be seen in [27–29]. The literature is full of articles related to infectious disease problems and their analysis for different dynamics [30,31].

A fractional derivative is a generalization of the standard derivative to non-integer orders. It is defined using the Riemann–Liouville fractional integral, which is a generalization of the standard integral to non-integer orders [17,18]. The fractional derivative has applications in many areas of science and engineering, including mathematical biology. In mathematical biology, fractional derivatives are used to model various phenomena such as diffusion in porous media, blood flow in vessels, and the spread of diseases. For example, in the study of tumor growth, a fractional derivative model can be used to describe the diffusion of nutrients and oxygen through the tumor tissue, which is a non-local process. Additionally, in the study of the spread of infectious diseases, a fractional derivative model can be used to describe the spread of the disease through a population, which is also a non-local process. There have been a variety of fractional operators proposed in the literature with both nonsingular and singular kernels [20–24,32]. The work of [25,26,33–35] and references cited therein present a comprehensive study and the application of these fractional order operators as well as a detailed analysis of their implementation.

The Atangana–Baleanu fractional derivative is a particular type of fractional derivative that is defined using a Caputo–Fabrizio type of kernel function. It is named after its inventors, Atangana and Baleanu, who introduced it in their 2016 paper [25]. This fractional derivative is a generalization of the Caputo fractional derivative, which is one of the most widely used fractional derivatives in mathematical biology. It can be used to model various phenomena such as diffusion in porous media, blood flow in vessels, and the spread of diseases. In mathematical biology, the Atangana-Baleanu fractional derivative has been used to model various phenomena such as the spread of infectious diseases, tumor growth, and the spread of pollutants in a porous medium. For example, in the study of the spread of infectious diseases, a fractional derivative model can be used to describe the spread of the disease through a population, which is a non-local process. Additionally, in the study of tumor growth, the Atangana–Baleanu fractional derivative can be used to describe the diffusion of nutrients and oxygen through the tumor tissue, which is also a non-local process. In the study of the spread of pollutants in a porous medium, the Atangana–Baleanu fractional derivative can be used to describe the diffusion of pollutants through the porous medium, which is also a non-local process. It has been found that in many cases that the Atangana–Baleanu fractional derivative provides a better fit than other types of fractional derivatives, such as the Caputo fractional derivative, for the above-mentioned phenomena.

As for the motivation of our work, we kept in mind the above significance of fractional calculus and took a novel problem related to the norovirus (NoV) using the Atangana–Baleanu arbitrary order differentiation by applying the conditions of asymptomatic and vaccinated classes. For the discussion, different aspects of NoV mathematical formulation have been used. Here, we discuss the said epidemic with the inclusion of two classes of asymptomatic carriers and vaccinated classes for more effective analysis. There is a duration of 30–180 days in which the signs of NoV virus and the risk of infection by an infectious person with a chance of death can manifest [36,37]. On reviewing the literature, we have formulated a new problem for the NoV viruses with two new compartments [9,12,30,31]. Firstly, the problem was constructed for the integer order and, after that, it was modified and extended to the fractional version of the Atangana–Baleanu derivative. The main objective of this article was to evaluate the mathematical formulation, testing the problem on public health with vaccination and dilation of time for controlling an NoV epidemic.

The novelty of this paper is in the extension of the deterministic stochastic model [38] to the Atanga–Beleanu fractional model, which offers a more realistic approach to epidemic modeling. The ABC fractional operator model provides several advantages over stochastic models in the context of epidemic modeling. First of all, it provides a deterministic framework that makes it possible to precisely and deterministically analyze the dynamics of epidemics, especially when examining how population symmetry affects spread and control. Contrarily, stochastic models introduce randomness and variability, creating uncertainties and making it difficult to comprehend the effects of population symmetry. Second, for better comprehension and management of epidemics, the ABC fractional operator model incorporates critical elements such as asymptomatic infected individuals and vaccination effects. This thorough representation takes into account the sizeable portion of infected people who might not show any symptoms. Stochastic models have limitations in accurately determining the effectiveness of control strategies and interventions because they do not explicitly take into account asymptomatic individuals or vaccination effects. Furthermore, the ABC model benefits from the application of fixed point theory, such as Schauder and Banach's fixed point theory, to analyze the existence and uniqueness of solutions. This mathematical approach provides rigorous foundations, ensuring reliable and valid outcomes. In contrast, stochastic models heavily rely on probabilistic methods and simulations, which can be computationally intensive and susceptible to statistical fluctuations. Moreover, the utilization of MATLAB software in the ABC model enables efficient computation and visualization of epidemic dynamics. This capability facilitates insights into model behavior under various scenarios and interventions, supporting informed decision-making in epidemic control. Collectively, the advantages of the ABC fractional operator model make it a valuable tool for epidemic modeling, offering greater realism and enhanced analytical capabilities compared to stochastic models.

The organization of this paper is as follows: Ii Section 2, we will formulate a novel mathematical model. Section 3 presents some basic definitions of fractional operators. In Section 4, the mathematical analysis determines whether there is a solution that exists and how certain terms can be optimized (3). The qualitative theory is studied in Section 5. The basic reproductive number and sensitivity analysis of the model are presented in Section 6. Section 7 studied the approximate solution of the model (3). Section 8 presented the parameter estimation of the model. In Section 9, we verify our theoretical results using numerical simulations. At the end of this paper, we summarize the main findings of our research in a section titled Conclusions.

2. Model Formulation

We extended Cui et al.'s model [38] which has five equations that are applicable to the considered infection mathematical model describing norovirus (NoV). All the density of individuals is distributed in five different compartmental agents, namely: Susceptible class ($\mathcal{H}$), Vaccinated individuals ($\mathcal{V}$), Asymptomatic or Exposed individuals ($\mathcal{U}$), Symptomatic or Infectious individuals ($\mathcal{A}$), and the Recovered class ($\mathcal{C}$), i.e., $H(t) + V(t) + U(t) + A(t) + C(t)) = N(t)$. The equations describing the model are

$$\begin{aligned}
\acute{\mathcal{H}} &= \Lambda - \frac{\eta\mathcal{H}(t)\mathcal{A}(t)}{N} - \mathcal{H}(t)(\rho + d), \\
\acute{\mathcal{V}} &= \rho\mathcal{H}(t) - \frac{(1-\tau)\eta\mathcal{A}(t)}{N} - d\mathcal{V}(t), \\
\acute{\mathcal{U}} &= \frac{\eta\mathcal{H}(t)\mathcal{A}(t)}{N} + \frac{(1-\tau)\eta\mathcal{V}(t)\mathcal{A}(t)}{N} - (\alpha + d)\mathcal{U}(t), \\
\acute{\mathcal{A}} &= \alpha\mathcal{U}(t) - (q+d)\mathcal{A}(t), \\
\acute{\mathcal{C}} &= \delta\mathcal{A}(t) - d\mathcal{C}(t),
\end{aligned} \tag{1}$$

with the starting approximation,

$$H(0) \geq 0, \;\; V(0) \geq 0, \;\; A(0) \geq 0, \;\; U(0) \geq 0, \;\; R(0) \geq 0, \tag{2}$$

where Λ is the recruitment rate representing the rate at which individuals enter the susceptible population. η is the transmission rate representing the probability of transmission per contact between susceptible individuals and infected individuals. $\mathcal{H}(t)$ represents the density of individuals in the susceptible (healthy) class at time t. The rate of change of $\mathcal{H}(t)$ is determined by the balance between recruitment (Λ), transmission $\frac{\eta\mathcal{H}(t)\mathcal{A}(t)}{N}$, and the natural removal $\mathcal{H}(t)(\rho + d)$ of individuals. $\mathcal{V}(t)$ represents the density of vaccinated individuals at time t. The balance between transmission from susceptible individuals $\rho\mathcal{H}(t)$, transmission from immunized individuals $\frac{[(1-\tau)\eta\mathcal{A}(t)]}{N}$, and natural removal of individuals $d\mathcal{V}(t)$ determines the rate of change of $\mathcal{V}(t)$. The density of people who are asymptomatic or exposed at time t is represented by $\mathcal{U}(t)$. The balance between transmission from susceptible individuals and $\mathcal{U}(t)$ determines the rate of change of this variable. $\frac{\eta\mathcal{H}(t)\mathcal{A}(t)}{N}$, transmission from immunized people $\frac{[(1-\tau)\eta\mathcal{V}(t)\mathcal{A}(t)}{N}$, recovery of people $(\alpha+d)\mathcal{U}(t)$, and natural removal. $\mathcal{A}(t)$ indicates the proportion of people who are symptomatic or contagious at time t. The balance between natural removal, $\frac{[(q+d)\mathcal{A}(t)]}{N}$, and transmission to susceptible individuals $\alpha\mathcal{U}(t)$ determines the rate of change of $\mathcal{A}(t)$. $\mathcal{C}(t)$ represents the density of people who have been found at time t. The recovery of individuals $\delta\mathcal{A}(t)$ and natural removal $d\mathcal{C}(t)$ determine the rate of change of $\mathcal{C}(t)$. The system of equations captures the interactions between those who are susceptible, those who have received vaccinations, those who are asymptomatic, those who are symptomatic, and those who have recovered to describe the dynamics of the norovirus epidemic. The spread and management of the epidemic over time are influenced by the rates of transmission, recovery, and removal as well as the population size N. The behavior's transition points are shown in Figure 1.

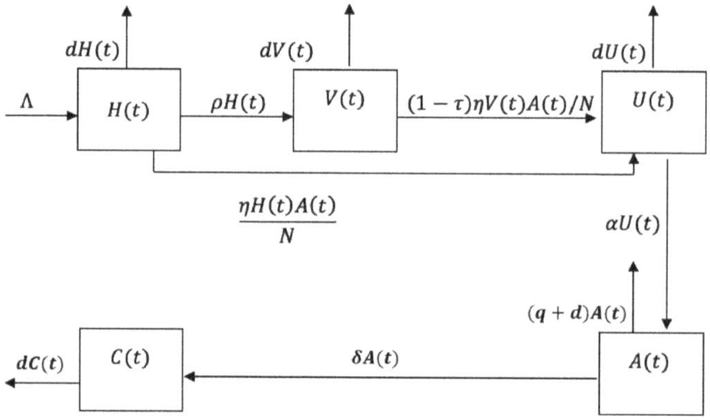

Figure 1. Schematic diagram of the model.

The key objective was to construct a new numerical system (1) using the ABC fractional derivative for an extra degree of choices of dynamical behavior. The qualitative analysis will be derived by the application of fixed point theory. The considered numerical problem will be analyzed, having a general derivative order of η as follows:

$$\begin{cases} {}^{ABC}D^{q}\mathcal{H}(t) = \Lambda - \dfrac{\eta\mathcal{H}(t)\mathcal{A}(t)}{N} - (\rho+d)\mathcal{H}(t), \\ {}^{ABC}D^{q}\mathcal{V}(t) = \rho\mathcal{H}(t) - \dfrac{(1-\tau)\eta\mathcal{A}(t)}{N} - d\mathcal{V}(t), \\ {}^{ABC}D^{q}\mathcal{U}(t) = \dfrac{\eta\mathcal{H}(t)\mathcal{A}(t)}{N} + \dfrac{(1-\tau)\eta\mathcal{V}(t)\mathcal{A}(t)}{N} - (\alpha+d)\mathcal{U}(t), \\ {}^{ABC}D^{q}\mathcal{A}(t) = \alpha\mathcal{U}(t) - (q+d)\mathcal{A}(t), \\ {}^{ABC}D^{q}\mathcal{C}(t) = \delta\mathcal{A}(t) - d\mathcal{C}(t). \end{cases} \tag{3}$$

3. Preliminaries

This section introduces the $\mathcal{ABC}$ operator and its properties, along with the numerical approximation method for solving fractional order differential equations.

Definition 1. *If $\Pi(t) \in \mathfrak{G}^1(0,\mathcal{T})$ and $q \in (0,1]$, then $\mathcal{ABC}$ is formulated as*

$$^{ABC}D^{q}_{+0}\Pi(t) = \frac{M(q)}{1-q}\int_0^t \frac{d}{dx}\Pi(y)M_q\left[\frac{-q}{1-q}(t-y)\right]dy, \tag{4}$$

replacing $M_q\left[\frac{-q}{1-q}(t-y)\right]dy$ by $M_1 = exp\left[\frac{-q}{1-q}(t-y)\right]$, we obtain the Caputo–Fabrizo fractional derivative. It should be noticed that

$$^{ABC}D^{q}_{+0}[Constant] = 0;$$

here, $M(q)$ is named the normal mapping given as $M(0) = M(1) = 1$. M_q represents Mittag–Leffler mapping, the generalized exponent mapping [39–41].

In Definition 1, the $\mathcal{ABC}$ operator is defined as a fractional derivative operator, denoted by $^{ABC}D^{q}_{+0}$, where $\Pi(t)$ is a function belonging to the space $\mathfrak{G}^1(0,\mathcal{T})$ and q is a parameter in the range $(0,1]$. The operator is expressed as an integral involving the derivative of Π and a Mittag–Leffler mapping M_q, with M_1 representing the exponential function. The lemma also states the behavior of the operator for constant values.

Lemma 1. *[42] Solution of the given equation for $1 > q > 0$,*

$$\begin{aligned} ^{ABC}D^{q}_{+0}\mathfrak{Z}(t) &= x(t), \ t \in [0,T], \\ \mathfrak{Z}(0) &= \mathfrak{Z}_0, \end{aligned} \tag{5}$$

is given by

$$\mathfrak{Z}(t) = \mathfrak{Z}_0 + \frac{(1-q)}{M(q)}x(t) + \frac{q}{\Gamma(q)M(q)}\int_0^t (t-y)^{q-1}x(y)dy.$$

Lemma 1 provides the solution to a fractional differential equation in terms of the $\mathcal{ABC}$ operator. The equation $^{ABC}D^{q}_{+0}\mathfrak{Z}(t) = x(t)$ represents a fractional order differential equation, where $\mathfrak{Z}(t)$ is the unknown function and $x(t)$ is a given function. The lemma presents the explicit solution $\mathfrak{Z}(t)$ in terms of the initial condition $\mathfrak{Z}_0$, the function $x(t)$, and the parameters q, $M(q)$, and $\Gamma(q)$.

Definition 2. *We can convert the fractional order DEs with order q in the form of the ABC derivative as*

$$\begin{aligned} ^{ABC}D^{q}\mathcal{Y}(t) &= f(t,\mathcal{Y}(t)) \\ \mathcal{Y}(0) &= \mathcal{Y}_0. \end{aligned} \tag{6}$$

Then, the approximate solution of (6) is given as follows:

$$\begin{aligned} \mathcal{Y}(t_{m+1}) &= \mathcal{Y}_0 + \frac{1-q}{M(q)}f(t_m,\mathcal{Y}(t_m)) \\ &+ \frac{q}{\Gamma(q)M(q)}\sum_{k=0}^{m}\left(\frac{h^q f(t_k,\mathcal{Y}_k)}{\Gamma(q+2)}\Big((1+m-k)^q(-k+m+2+q)\right. \\ &- (-k+m)^q(-k+m+2+2q)\Big) \\ &\left.- \frac{h^q f(t_{k-1},\mathcal{Y}_{k-1})}{\Gamma(q+2)}\Big((1+m-k)^{q+1} - (-k+m)^q(-k+m+1+q)\Big)\right). \end{aligned} \tag{7}$$

Definition 2 introduces the conversion of fractional order differential equations to the ABC derivative form. The equation $^{ABC}D^{q}\mathcal{Y}(t) = f(t,\mathcal{Y}(t))$ represents a fractional order differential equation with the unknown function $\mathcal{Y}(t)$ and the function $f(t,\mathcal{Y}(t))$ on the right-hand side. The definition provides an approximation method for solving such equations using the $\mathcal{ABC}$ operator. The approximate solution $\mathcal{Y}(t_{m+1})$ is expressed recursively in terms of the initial condition $\mathcal{Y}_0$, the function $f(t, \mathcal{Y}(t))$, and parameters q, $M(q)$, $\Gamma(q)$, and h.

4. The Theory of Existence of Solution

The existence of the solutions for the given fractional order model is presented in this part of the paper; for this purpose, we try to define a function as follows:

$$\begin{cases} \Pi_1(t,\mathcal{H},\mathcal{V},\mathcal{U},\mathcal{A},\mathcal{C}) = \Lambda - \dfrac{\eta\mathcal{H}(t)\mathcal{A}(t)}{N} - \mathcal{H}(t)(\rho + d), \\ \Pi_2(t,\mathcal{H},\mathcal{V},\mathcal{U},\mathcal{A},\mathcal{C}) = \rho\mathcal{H}(t) - \dfrac{(1-\tau)\eta\mathcal{A}(t)}{N} - d\mathcal{V}(t), \\ \Pi_3(t,\mathcal{H},\mathcal{V},\mathcal{U},\mathcal{A},\mathcal{C}) = \dfrac{\eta\mathcal{H}(t)\mathcal{A}(t)}{N} + \dfrac{(1-\tau)\eta\mathcal{V}(t)\mathcal{A}(t)}{N} - \mathcal{U}(t)(\alpha + d), \\ \Pi_4(t,\mathcal{H},\mathcal{V},\mathcal{U},\mathcal{A},\mathcal{C}) = \alpha\mathcal{U}(t) - (q + d)\mathcal{A}(t), \\ \Pi_5(t,\mathcal{H},\mathcal{V},\mathcal{U},\mathcal{A},\mathcal{C}) = \delta\mathcal{A}(t) - d\mathcal{C}(t). \end{cases} \tag{8}$$

Using (8), the model is expressed as follows:

$$\begin{aligned} {}^{ABC}D^q_{+0}\mathfrak{Z}(t) &= \Pi(t, \mathfrak{Z}(t)),\ t \in [0, T],\ 0 < q \le 1, \\ \mathfrak{Z}(0) &= \mathfrak{Z}_0. \end{aligned} \tag{9}$$

Using Lemma (1), Equation (9) becomes

$$\mathfrak{Z}(t) = \mathfrak{Z}_0(t) + \Big[\Pi((t, \mathfrak{Z}(t)) - \Pi_0(t)\Big]\frac{1-q}{M(q)} + \frac{q}{M(q)\Gamma(q)}\int_0^t (t-y)^{q-1}\Pi(y, \mathfrak{Z}(y))dy,\ \ for\ 0 \le y \le t \le 1, \tag{10}$$

where

$$\mathfrak{Z}(t) = \begin{cases} \mathcal{H}(t) \\ \mathcal{V}(t) \\ \mathcal{U}(t) \\ \mathcal{A}(t) \\ \mathcal{CR}(t) \end{cases}, \mathfrak{Z}_0(t) = \begin{cases} \mathcal{H}_0 \\ \mathcal{V}_0 \\ \mathcal{U}_0 \\ \mathcal{A}_0 \\ \mathcal{C}_0 \end{cases}, \Pi(t, \mathfrak{Z}(t)) = \begin{cases} \Pi_1(t,\mathcal{H},\mathcal{V},\mathcal{U},\mathcal{A},\mathcal{C}) \\ \Pi_2(t,\mathcal{H},\mathcal{V},\mathcal{U},\mathcal{A},\mathcal{C}) \\ \Pi_3(t,\mathcal{H},\mathcal{V},\mathcal{U},\mathcal{A},\mathcal{C}) \\ \Pi_4(t,\mathcal{H},\mathcal{V},\mathcal{U},\mathcal{A},\mathcal{C}) \\ \Pi_5(t,\mathcal{H},\mathcal{V},\mathcal{U},\mathcal{A},\mathcal{C}) \end{cases}, \Pi_0(t) \begin{cases} \Pi_1(0,\mathcal{H}_0,\mathcal{V}_0,\mathcal{U}_0,\mathcal{A}_0,\mathcal{C}_0) \\ \Pi_2(0,\mathcal{H}_0,\mathcal{V}_0,\mathcal{U}_0,\mathcal{A}_0,\mathcal{C}_0) \\ \Pi_3(0,\mathcal{H}_0,\mathcal{V}_0,\mathcal{U}_0,\mathcal{A}_0,\mathcal{C}_0) \\ \Pi_4(0,\mathcal{H}_0,\mathcal{V}_0,\mathcal{U}_0,\mathcal{A}_0,\mathcal{C}_0) \\ \Pi_5(0,\mathcal{H}_0,\mathcal{V}_0,\mathcal{U}_0,\mathcal{A}_0,\mathcal{C}_0) \end{cases} \tag{11}$$

Using (10) and (11), define two operators $\mathcal{F}$ and $\mathscr{G}$, using (10)

$$\begin{aligned} \mathcal{F}\mathfrak{Z} &= \mathfrak{Z}_0(t) + \Big[\Pi(t, \mathfrak{Z}(t)) - \Pi_0(t)\Big]\frac{1-q}{M(q)}, \\ \mathscr{G}\mathfrak{Z} &= \frac{q}{M(q)\Gamma(q)}\int_0^t (t-y)^{q-1}\Pi(y, \mathfrak{Z}(y))dy. \end{aligned} \tag{12}$$

Furthermore, we reassume that the conditions $\mathbf{D}_1$ and $\mathbf{D}_2$ holds

($\mathbf{D}_1$) If fixed σ_1 and σ_2, as

$$|\Pi(t, \mathfrak{Z}(t))| \le \sigma_1|\mathfrak{Z}(t)| + \sigma_2.$$

($\mathbf{D}_2$) If fixed $\kappa > 0$, for all $\mathfrak{Z}, \mathfrak{Z}_1 \in \mathbb{X}$, as

$$|\Pi(t, \mathfrak{Z}(t)) - \Pi(t, \mathfrak{Z}_1(t))| \le \kappa||\mathfrak{Z} - \mathfrak{Z}_1||.$$

Theorem 1. *If* ($\mathbf{D}_1$) *and* ($\mathbf{D}_2$) *are fulfilled, then system* (10) *will have at least a unique root, implying that our problem* (3) *has at least one root if*

$$\frac{(1-q)\kappa}{M(q)} < 1.$$

Proof. For the derivation of $\mathcal{F}$ to be a contraction operator, let $\mathfrak{z}_1 \in \mathbb{B}$, while $\mathbb{B} = \{\mathfrak{z} \in \mathbb{Y} : ||\mathfrak{z}|| \leq r, r > 0\}$ is a closed convex set. Applying the result of $\mathcal{F}$ from (12), as

$$\begin{aligned} ||\mathcal{F}\mathfrak{z} - \mathcal{F}\mathfrak{z}_1|| &= \frac{(1-q)}{M(q)} \max_{t\in[0,T]} \left|\Pi(t,\mathfrak{z}(t)) - \Pi(t,\mathfrak{z}_1(t))\right|, \\ &\leq \frac{(1-q)_P}{M(q)}||\mathfrak{z} - \mathfrak{z}_1||. \end{aligned} \tag{13}$$

Therefore, $\mathcal{F}$ is a contraction operator. Next, to derive the relative compactness of $\mathscr{G}$, we must prove that $\mathscr{G}$ has its bounds, and define on their domain. For achieving the result, consider as given under:

As $\mathscr{G}$ is continuous as Π is defined on their domain, for $u \in \mathbb{B}$,

$$\begin{aligned} |\mathscr{G}(\mathfrak{z})| &= \max_{t\in[0,T]} \frac{q}{M(q)\Gamma(q)} \left|\left| \int_0^t (t-y)^{q-1}\Pi(y,\mathfrak{z}(y))dy \right|\right| \\ &\leq \frac{q}{M(q)\Gamma(q)} \int_0^T (T-y)^{q-1}|\Pi(y,\mathfrak{z}(y))|dy \\ &\leq \frac{qT^q}{M(q)\Gamma(q)}[\sigma_1 r + \sigma_2]. \end{aligned} \tag{14}$$

Hence, (14) shows that $\mathscr{G}$ has bound; for equi-continuity, let $t_1 > t_2 \in [0,T]$, as

$$\begin{aligned} |\mathscr{G}\mathfrak{z}(t_1) - \mathscr{G}\mathfrak{z}(t_2)| &= \frac{q}{M(q)\Gamma(q)} \left| \int_0^{t_1} (t_1-y)^{q-1}\Pi(y),\mathfrak{z}(y)dy - \int_0^{t_2} (t_2-y)^{q-1}\Pi(y,\mathfrak{z}(y))dy \right| \\ &\leq \frac{[\sigma_1 r + \sigma_2]}{M(q)\Gamma(q)}[t_1^q - t_2^q]. \end{aligned} \tag{15}$$

As $t_1 \to t_2$, the (15) approaches zero, also $\mathscr{G}$ is defined on their domain, and so

$$|\mathscr{G}\mathfrak{z}(t_1) - \mathscr{G}\mathfrak{z}(t_2)| \to 0, \ \ as \ \ t_1 \to t_2.$$

So, $\mathscr{G}$ has bounds and is defined on its domain, hence $\mathscr{G}$ is uniformly continuous and has bounds. The Arzelà–Ascoli theorem $\mathscr{G}$ is relatively compact and therefore completely continuous. Applying Theorem 1, the integration Equation (10) has at least one zero and so the model has at least one zero. □

For a unique solution, we proceed as follows:

Theorem 2. *By condition* (D_2)*, the integration Equation* (10) *has one root which provides that the proposed model* (3) *has one solution if*

$$\left[\frac{(1-q)\kappa}{M(q)} + \frac{qT^q\kappa}{M(q)\Gamma(q)}\right] < 1.$$

Proof. Take $\mathbb{T} : \mathbb{Y} \to \mathbb{Y}$ by

$$\mathbb{T}\mathfrak{z}(t) = \mathfrak{z}_0(t) + \Big[\Pi(t,\mathfrak{z}(t)) - \Pi_0(t)\Big]\frac{1-q}{M(q)} + \frac{q}{M(q)\Gamma(q)}\int_0^t (t-y)^{q-1}\Pi(y,\mathfrak{z}(y))dy, \ t \in [0,T]. \tag{16}$$

Let $\mathfrak{z}, \mathfrak{z}_1 \in \mathbb{Y}$, then

$$\begin{aligned}||\mathbb{T}\mathfrak{Z}-\mathbb{T}\mathfrak{Z}_1|| &\le \frac{(1-q)}{M(\Gamma(q))}\max_{t\in[0,T]}\left|\Pi(t,\mathfrak{Z}(t))-\Pi(t,\mathfrak{Z}_1(t))\right| \\ &+\frac{q}{M(q)\Gamma(q)}\max_{t\in[0,T]}\left|\int_0^t (t-y)^{q-1}\Pi(y,\mathfrak{Z}(y))dy-\int_0^t (t-y)^{q-1}\Pi(y,\mathfrak{Z}_1(y))dy\right| \\ &\le \left[\frac{(1-q)\kappa}{M(q)}+\frac{qT^q\kappa}{M(q)\Gamma(q)}\right]||\mathfrak{Z}-\mathfrak{Z}_1|| \\ &\le \varphi||\mathfrak{Z}-\mathfrak{Z}_1||,\end{aligned} \tag{17}$$

where

$$\varphi=\left[\frac{(1-q)\kappa}{M(q)}+\frac{qT^q\kappa}{M(q)\Gamma(q)}\right]. \tag{18}$$

So by (17), $\mathbb{T}$ is a contraction operator. Therefore, the integration Equation (10) has one root. Hence, problem (3) has one root. □

5. Stability Analysis

Hyers–Ulam stability, also known as Hyers–Ulam–Rassias stability, is a concept in the field of functional analysis that deals with the stability of functional equations. It is named after David Hyers, Stanislaw Ulam, and Themistocles Rassias, who independently proved that the Cauchy equation for functional equations is stable in certain cases. In other words, it states that if a function is close to a solution of a functional equation, then it is also a solution of that equation. This concept has been extended to include various types of functional equations, including those involving nonlinear operations. Overall, Hyers–Ulam stability plays an important role in the study of functional equations and has been applied in various areas of mathematics and science.

The proposed model stability is assured by the consideration of a small perturbation $\alpha \in C[0,T]$, related to the root of $\alpha(0)=0$. Consider

(i) $|\alpha(t)| \le \mu, for\ \ \mu > 0,$

(ii) ${}^{ABC}D^q_{+0}(\mathfrak{Z}(t)) = \Pi(t,\mathfrak{Z}(t))+\alpha(t), \forall\ t\in[0,T].$

Lemma 2. *The root of the perturbed model,*

$$\begin{cases} {}^{ABC}_{0}D^q_{+0}\mathfrak{Z}(t)=\Pi(t,\mathfrak{Z}(t))+\alpha(t), \\ \mathfrak{Z}(0)=\mathfrak{Z}_0, \end{cases} \tag{19}$$

satisfies the following expression,

$$\left|\mathfrak{Z}(t)-\left(\mathfrak{Z}_0(t)+\left[\Pi(t,\mathfrak{Z}(t))-\Pi_0(t)\right]\frac{1-q}{M(q)}+\frac{q}{M(q)\Gamma(q)}\int_0^t (t-y)^{q-1}\Pi(y,\mathfrak{Z}(y))dy\right)\right| \le \mu_{T,q}, \tag{20}$$

where

$$\mu_{T,q}=\frac{\Gamma(q)(1-q)+T^q}{M(q)\Gamma(q)}.$$

Proof. The derivation is straight forward, so we skip it. □

Theorem 3. *Using* (D_2) *and* (20) *in lemma* (2), *the root of concerned integration Equation* (10) *is U-H stable and, so, the solution of the concerned problem is U-H stable if* $\varphi < 1$.

Proof. Consider $\mathfrak{Z}_1 \in \mathbb{Y}$ to be one root and u $\in \mathbb{Y}$ to be zero of (10), then

$$
\begin{aligned}
|\mathfrak{z}(t)-\mathfrak{z}_1(t)| &= \left|\mathfrak{z}(t)-\left(\mathfrak{z}_0(t)+\left[\Pi(t,\mathfrak{z}_1(t))-\Pi_0(t)\right]\frac{1-q}{M(q)}+\frac{q}{M(q)\Gamma(q)}\int_0^t (t-y)^{q-1}\Pi(y,\mathfrak{z}_1(y))dy\right)\right| \\
&\le \left|\mathfrak{z}(t)-\left(\mathfrak{z}_0(t)+\left[\Pi(t,\mathfrak{z}(t))-\Pi_0(t)\right]\frac{1-q}{M(q)}+\frac{q}{M(q)\Gamma(q)}\int_0^t (t-y)^{q-1}\Pi(y,\mathfrak{z}(y))dy\right)\right| \\
&+\left|\left(\mathfrak{z}_0(t)+\left[\Pi(t,\mathfrak{z}(t))-\Pi_0(t)\right]\frac{1-q}{M(q)}+\frac{q}{M(q)\Gamma(q)}\int_0^t (t-y)^{q-1}\Pi(y,\mathfrak{z}(y))dy\right)\right. \\
&-\left.\left(\mathfrak{z}_0(t)+\left[\Pi(t,\mathfrak{z}_1(t))-\Pi_0(t)\right]\frac{1-q}{M(q)}+\frac{q}{M(q)\Gamma(q)}\int_0^t (t-y)^{q-1}\Pi(y,\mathfrak{z}_1(y))dy\right)\right| \\
&\le \mu_{T,q}+\frac{(1-q)\kappa}{M(q)}||\mathfrak{z}-\mathfrak{z}_1||+\frac{qT^q\kappa}{M(q)\Gamma(q)}||\mathfrak{z}-\mathfrak{z}_1|| \\
&\le \mu_{T,q}+\varphi||\mathfrak{z}-\mathfrak{z}_1||.
\end{aligned} \tag{21}
$$

From (21), we can write

$$||\mathfrak{z}-\mathfrak{z}_1|| \le \frac{\mu_{T,q}}{1-\varphi}. \tag{22}$$

By (22), we say that the zero of (10) is U-H stable and hence generalized U-H stable by applying $\Pi_U(\mu)=\mu_{T,q}, \Pi_U(0)=0$, implying that the zero of the considered system is U-H stable and so generalized U-H stable. □

Considering

(i) $|\alpha(t)| \le \Omega(t)\mu, for\ \mu>0,$
(ii) ${}^{ABC}D^q_{+0}(\mathfrak{z}(t))=\Pi(t,\mathfrak{z}(t))+\alpha(t), \forall\ t\in[0,T].$

Lemma 3. *The below equation holds for* (19)

$$
\begin{aligned}
&\left|\mathfrak{z}(t)-\left(\mathfrak{z}_0(t)+\left[\Pi(t,\mathfrak{z}(t))-\Pi_0(t)\right]\frac{1-q}{M(q)}+\frac{q}{M(q)\Gamma(q)}\int_0^t (t-y)^{q-1}\Pi(y,\mathfrak{z}(y))dy\right)\right| \\
&\le \Omega(t)\mu_{T,q}.
\end{aligned} \tag{23}
$$

Proof. This is also straight forward. □

Theorem 4. *By Lemma* (3)*, the root of the given model is U-H-Rassias stable and therefore, generalized U-H-Rassias stable.*

Proof. Consider $\mathfrak{z}_1 \in \mathbb{Y}$ to be one root and u $\in \mathbb{Y}$ to be the root of (10), then

$$
\begin{aligned}
|\mathfrak{z}(t)-\mathfrak{z}_1(t)| &= \left|\mathfrak{z}(t)-\left(\mathfrak{z}_0(t)+\left[\Pi(t,\mathfrak{z}_1(t))-\Pi_0(t)\right]\frac{1-q}{M(q)}+\frac{q}{M(q)\Gamma(q)}\int_0^t (t-y)^{q-1}\Pi(y,\mathfrak{z}_1(y))dy\right)\right| \\
&\le \left|\mathfrak{z}(t)-\left(\mathfrak{z}_0(t)+\left[\Pi(t,\mathfrak{z}(t))-\Pi_0(t)\right]\frac{1-q}{M(q)}+\frac{q}{M(q)\Gamma(q)}\int_0^t (t-y)^{q-1}\Pi(y,\mathfrak{z}(y))dy\right)\right| \\
&+\left|\left(\mathfrak{z}_0(t)+\left[\Pi(t,\mathfrak{z}(t))-\Pi_0(t)\right]\frac{1-q}{M(q)}+\frac{q}{M(q)\Gamma(q)}\int_0^t (t-y)^{q-1}\Pi(y,\mathfrak{z}(y))dy\right)\right. \\
&-\left.\left(\mathfrak{z}_0(t)+\left[\Pi(t,\mathfrak{z}_1(t))-\Pi_0(t)\right]\frac{1-q}{M(q)}+\frac{q}{M(q)\Gamma(q)}\int_0^t (t-y)^{q-1}\Pi(y,\mathfrak{z}_1(y))dy\right)\right| \\
&\le \Omega(t)\mu_{T,q}+\frac{(1-q)\kappa}{M(q)}||\mathfrak{z}-\mathfrak{z}_1||+\frac{qT^q\kappa}{M(q)\Gamma(q)}||\mathfrak{z}-\mathfrak{z}_1|| \\
&\le \Omega(t)\mu_{T,q}+\varphi||\mathfrak{z}-\mathfrak{z}_1||,
\end{aligned} \tag{24}
$$

we can write, from (24),

$$||\mathfrak{Z} - \mathfrak{Z}_1|| \leq \frac{\Omega(t)\mu_{T,\mathfrak{q}}}{1-\varphi}. \tag{25}$$

Hence, the solution of (10) is U-H-Rassias stable and so generalized U-H-Rassias stable. □

6. Basic Reproductive Number

The disease-free equilibrium, denoted as E_0, can be determined by setting the right-hand side of the equations in system (3) equal to zero, yielding the following equations:

$$E_0 = (\mathcal{S}_0, \mathcal{V}_0, \mathcal{U}_0, \mathcal{A}_0, \mathcal{C}_0) = \left(\frac{\Lambda}{\rho+d}, \frac{\rho\Lambda}{d(\rho+d)}, 0, 0, 0\right).$$

We determined the basic reproductive ratio, abbreviated R_0, using the next-generation matrix approach. This estimate is solely based on the two equations that correspond to the compartments $\mathcal{U}$ and $\mathcal{A}$ classes that were derived from system (3).

$$\mathbf{F} = \begin{bmatrix} 0 & \frac{\eta\Lambda[d+(1-\tau)\rho]}{d(\rho+d)} \\ 0 & 0 \end{bmatrix},$$

$$\mathbf{V} = \begin{bmatrix} d+\alpha & 0 \\ -\alpha & d+\delta \end{bmatrix},$$

$$\mathbf{V}^{-1} = \begin{bmatrix} \frac{1}{d+\alpha} & 0 \\ \frac{\alpha}{(d+\alpha)(d+\delta)} & \frac{1}{d+\delta} \end{bmatrix}.$$

The spectral radius of the matrix $\mathbf{FV}^{-1}$, which corresponds to the basic reproductive ratio, is calculated as follows:

$$R_0 = \rho\left(\mathbf{FV}^{-1}\right) = \frac{\alpha\eta\Lambda[d+(1-\tau)\rho]}{d(\rho+d)(d+\alpha)(d+\delta)}. \tag{26}$$

Sensitivity Analysis

We must ascertain the sensitivity of R_0 with respect to each relevant parameter in order to perform sensitivity analysis for the given expression of R_0. The sensitivity quantifies the impact of a parameter's changes on the value of R_0. We can use the idea of partial derivatives to determine the sensitivity of R_0 with respect to each parameter. If all other parameters are held constant, the partial derivative of R_0 with respect to a parameter represents the rate of change of R_0 with respect to that parameter. Let us determine how each parameter affects the sensitivity of R_0:

- Sensitivity with respect to α: $\frac{\partial R_0}{\partial \alpha} = \frac{\eta\Lambda[d+(1-\tau)\rho]}{d(\rho+d)(d+\alpha)(d+\delta)} = 0.002$.
- Sensitivity with respect to η: $\frac{\partial R_0}{\partial \eta} = \frac{\alpha\Lambda[d+(1-\tau)\rho]}{d(\rho+d)(d+\alpha)(d+\delta)} = 0.004$.
- Sensitivity with respect to Λ: $\frac{\partial R_0}{\partial \Lambda} = \frac{\alpha\eta[d+(1-\tau)\rho]}{d(\rho+d)(d+\alpha)(d+\delta)} = 0.0016$.
- Sensitivity with respect to d: $\frac{\partial R_0}{\partial d} = \frac{\alpha\eta\Lambda[(1-\tau)\rho-d(\rho+d)]}{d^2(\rho+d)^2(d+\alpha)(d+\delta)} = -0.292$.
- Sensitivity with respect to ρ: $\frac{\partial R_0}{\partial \rho} = \frac{\alpha\eta\Lambda(1-\tau)}{d(\rho+d)(d+\alpha)(d+\delta)} = 0.022$.
- Sensitivity with respect to τ: $\frac{\partial R_0}{\partial \tau} = -\frac{\alpha\eta\Lambda\rho}{d(\rho+d)(d+\alpha)(d+\delta)} = -0.0044$.
- Sensitivity with respect to δ: $\frac{\partial R_0}{\partial \delta} = -\frac{\alpha\eta\Lambda(1-\tau)}{d(\rho+d)(d+\alpha)(d+\delta)^2} = -0.0244$.

The sensitivities of R_0 with respect to each parameter are represented by these partial derivatives. They show how each parameter's changes affect the value of R_0. Positive sensitivities predict an increase in R_0 as the parameter increases, whereas negative sensitivities predict the opposite. Please be aware that when calculating the sensitivity with respect to a specific parameter, these calculations make the assumption that the other parameters remain constant. Sensitivity analysis aids in understanding how changes in these parameters can affect the spread and control of the virus by illuminating the relative importance of each parameter in determining the value of R_0. Figure 2 shows the graphic results of parameter versus R_0.

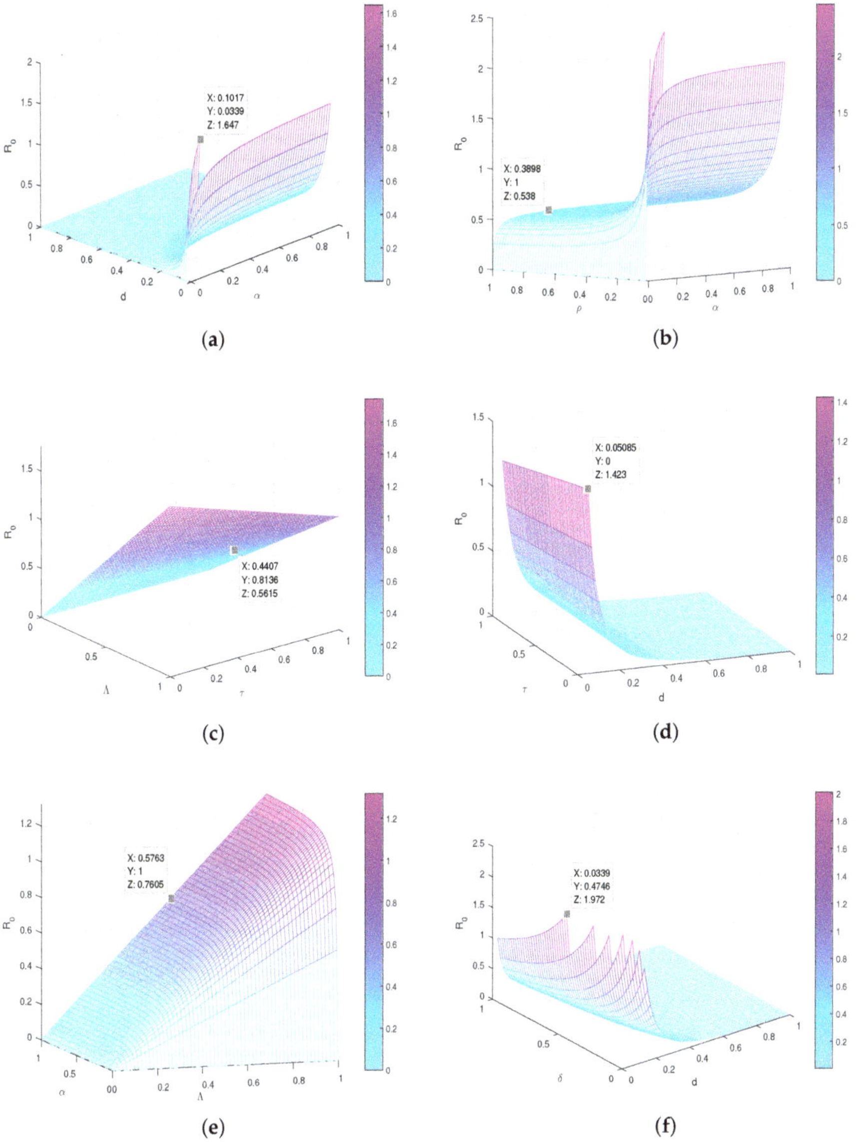

Figure 2. The plots examine how changes in various parameters relate to R_0 through sensitivity analysis. (**a**) R_0 versus sensitive parameters d and α. (**b**) R_0 versus sensitive parameters ρ and α. (**c**) R_0 versus sensitive parameters Λ and τ. (**d**) R_0 versus sensitive parameters τ and d. (**e**) R_0 versus sensitive parameters α and Λ. (**f**) R_0 versus sensitive parameters δ and d.

7. Approximate Solution by ABM Method

The numerical scheme used in this article is a fractional Adams–Bashforth–Moulton (ABM) method. The ABM method has a long history in numerical analysis, dating back to the work of Adams in the late 19th century. The method was further developed by Bashforth and Moulton in the early 20th century, and it has since been widely used in a variety of applications, including fluid dynamics, chemical kinetics, and population dynamics. Advantages of the ABM method include its simplicity and efficiency, as well as its ability to handle stiff equations. The method is based on the extrapolation of previous time steps, and it can be easily implemented using standard software packages. The fractional version of the ABM method used in this article is a relatively new development, arising from recent advances in fractional calculus. This version of the method is well-suited to problems involving fractional derivatives, which arise in many areas of science and engineering.

In this section of the article, we present the approximate solution; for this we can write model (3)

$$\begin{aligned}
{}^{ABC}D^q\mathcal{H}(t) &= \Lambda - \frac{\eta\mathcal{H}(t)\mathcal{A}(t)}{N} - (\rho + d)\mathcal{H}(t),\\
{}^{ABC}D^q\mathcal{V}(t) &= \rho\mathcal{H}(t) - \frac{(1-\tau)\eta\mathcal{A}(t)}{N} - d\mathcal{V}(t),\\
{}^{ABC}D^q\mathcal{U}(t) &= \frac{\eta\mathcal{H}(t)\mathcal{A}(t)}{N} + \frac{(1-\tau)\eta\mathcal{V}(t)\mathcal{A}(t)}{N} - (\alpha + d)\mathcal{U}(t),\\
{}^{ABC}D^q\mathcal{A}(t) &= \alpha\mathcal{U}(t) - (q + d)\mathcal{A}(t),\\
{}^{ABC}D^q\mathcal{C}(t) &= \delta\mathcal{A}(t) - d\mathcal{C}(t).
\end{aligned} \tag{27}$$

Using the basic theorem of the generalized calculus known as fractional calculus, we can now obtain

$$\begin{aligned}
\mathcal{H}(t) &= \mathcal{H}_0 + \frac{1-q}{M(q)}\mathfrak{E}_1(t,\mathcal{H}(t)) + \frac{q}{\Gamma(q)M(q)}\int_0^t \mathfrak{E}_1(\phi,\mathcal{H}(\phi))(t-\phi)^{q-1}d\phi,\\
\mathcal{V}(t) &= \mathcal{V}_0 + \frac{1-q}{M(q)}\mathfrak{E}_2(t,\mathcal{V}(t)) + \frac{q}{\Gamma(q)M(q)}\int_0^t \mathfrak{E}_2(\phi,\mathcal{V}(\phi))(t-\phi)^{q-1}d\phi,\\
\mathcal{U}(t) &= \mathcal{U}_0 + \frac{1-q}{M(q)}\mathfrak{E}_3(t,\mathcal{U}(t)) + \frac{q}{\Gamma(q)M(q)}\int_0^t \mathfrak{E}_3(\phi,\mathcal{U}(\phi))(t-\phi)^{q-1}d\phi,\\
\mathcal{A}(t) &= \mathcal{A}_0 + \frac{1-q}{M(q)}\mathfrak{E}_4(t,\mathcal{A}(t)) + \frac{q}{\Gamma(q)M(q)}\int_0^t \mathfrak{E}_4(\phi,\mathcal{A}(\phi))(t-\phi)^{q-1}d\phi,\\
\mathcal{C}(t) &= \mathcal{C}_0 + \frac{1-q}{M(q)}\mathfrak{E}_5(t,\mathcal{C}(t)) + \frac{q}{\Gamma(q)M(q)}\int_0^t \mathfrak{E}_5(\phi,\mathcal{A}(\phi))(t-\phi)^{q-1}d\phi.
\end{aligned}$$

At the moment $t = tm + 1$, we obtain our result as follows:

$$\begin{aligned}
\mathcal{H}(t_{m+1}) &= \mathcal{H}_0 + \frac{1-q}{M(q)}\mathfrak{E}_1(t_m,\mathcal{H}(t_m)) + \frac{q}{\Gamma(q)M(q)}\sum_{k=0}^{m}\int_{t_k}^{t_{k+1}} \mathfrak{E}_1(\phi,\mathcal{H}(\phi))(t_{m+1}-\phi)^{q-1}d\phi,\\
\mathcal{V}(t_{m+1}) &= \mathcal{V}_0 + \frac{1-q}{M(q)}\mathfrak{E}_2(t_m,\mathcal{V}(t_m)) + \frac{q}{\Gamma(q)M(q)}\sum_{k=0}^{m}\int_{t_k}^{t_{k+1}} \mathfrak{E}_2(\phi,\mathcal{V}(\phi))(t_{m+1}-\phi)^{q-1}d\phi,\\
\mathcal{U}(t_{m+1}) &= \mathcal{U}_0 + \frac{1-q}{M(q)}\mathfrak{E}_3(t_m,\mathcal{U}(t_m)) + \frac{q}{\Gamma(q)M(q)}\sum_{k=0}^{m}\int_{t_k}^{t_{k+1}} \mathfrak{E}_3(\phi,\mathcal{U}(\phi))(t_{m+1}-\phi)^{q-1}d\phi,\\
\mathcal{A}(t_{m+1}) &= \mathcal{A}_0 + \frac{1-q}{M(q)}\mathfrak{E}_4(t_m,\mathcal{A}(t_m)) + \frac{q}{\Gamma(q)M(q)}\sum_{k=0}^{m}\int_{t_k}^{t_{k+1}} \mathfrak{E}_4(\phi,\mathcal{A}(\phi))(t_{m+1}-\phi)^{q-1}d\phi,\\
\mathcal{C}(t_{m+1}) &= \mathcal{C}_0 + \frac{1-q}{M(q)}\mathfrak{E}_5(t_m,\mathcal{C}(t_m)) + \frac{q}{\Gamma(q)M(q)}\sum_{k=0}^{m}\int_{t_k}^{t_{k+1}} \mathfrak{E}_5(\phi,\mathcal{A}(\phi))(t_{m+1}-\phi)^{q-1}d\phi.
\end{aligned} \tag{28}$$

By approximating $\mathfrak{E}_1 - \mathfrak{E}_5$ in two stages of the interpolation of Lagrange polynomials in $[t_k, t_{k+1}]$, and after reentering it into (28), we have the following:

$$
\begin{aligned}
\mathcal{H}(t_{m+1}) &= \mathcal{H}_0 + \frac{1-q}{M(q)}\mathfrak{E}_1(t_m, \mathcal{H}(t_m)) + \frac{q}{\Gamma(q)M(q)}\sum_{k=0}^{m}\left(\frac{\mathfrak{E}_1(t_k, \mathcal{H}_k)}{h}\int_{t_k}^{t_{k+1}}(\phi - t_{k-1})(t_{m+1}-\phi)^{q-1}d\phi\right. \\
&\quad \left. - \frac{\mathfrak{E}_1(t_{k-1}, \mathcal{H}_{k-1})}{h}\int_{t_k}^{t_{k+1}}(\phi - t_k)(t_{m+1}-\phi)^{q-1}d\phi\right), \\
\mathcal{V}(t_{m+1}) &= \mathcal{V}_0 + \frac{1-q}{M(q)}\mathfrak{E}_2(t_m, \mathcal{V}(t_m)) + \frac{q}{\Gamma(q)M(q)}\sum_{k=0}^{m}\left(\frac{\mathfrak{E}_2(t_k, \mathcal{V}_k)}{h}\int_{t_k}^{t_{k+1}}(\phi - t_{k-1})(t_{m+1}-\phi)^{q-1}d\phi\right. \\
&\quad \left. - \frac{\mathfrak{E}_2(t_{k-1}, \mathcal{V}_{k-1})}{h}\int_{t_k}^{t_{k+1}}(\phi - t_k)(t_{m+1}-\phi)^{q-1}d\phi\right), \\
\mathcal{U}(t_{m+1}) &= \mathcal{U}_0 + \frac{1-q}{M(q)}\mathfrak{E}_3(t_m, \mathcal{U}(t_m)) + \frac{q}{\Gamma(q)M(q)}\sum_{k=0}^{m}\left(\frac{\mathfrak{E}_3(t_k, \mathcal{A}_k)}{h}\int_{t_k}^{t_{k+1}}(\phi - t_{k-1})(t_{m+1}-\phi)^{q-1}d\phi\right. \\
&\quad \left. - \frac{\mathfrak{E}_3(t_{k-1}, \mathcal{A}_{k-1})}{h}\int_{t_k}^{t_{k+1}}(\phi - t_k)(t_{m+1}-\phi)^{q-1}d\phi\right), \\
\mathcal{A}(t_{m+1}) &= \mathcal{A}_0 + \frac{1-q}{M(q)}\mathfrak{E}_4(t_m, \mathcal{A}(t_m)) + \frac{q}{\Gamma(q)M(q)}\sum_{k=0}^{m}\left(\frac{\mathfrak{E}_4(t_k, \mathcal{A}_k)}{h}\int_{t_k}^{t_{k+1}}(\phi - t_{k-1})(t_{m+1}-\phi)^{q-1}d\phi\right. \\
&\quad \left. - \frac{\mathfrak{E}_4(t_{k-1}, \mathcal{A}_{k-1})}{h}\int_{t_k}^{t_{k+1}}(\phi - t_k)(t_{m+1}-\phi)^{q-1}d\phi\right), \\
\mathcal{C}(t_{m+1}) &= \mathcal{C}_0 + \frac{1-q}{M(q)}\mathfrak{E}_5(t_m, \mathcal{C}(t_m)) + \frac{q}{\Gamma(q)M(q)}\sum_{k=0}^{m}\left(\frac{\mathfrak{E}_5(t_k, \mathcal{C}_k)}{h}\int_{t_k}^{t_{k+1}}(\phi - t_{k-1})(t_{m+1}-\phi)^{q-1}d\phi\right. \\
&\quad \left. - \frac{\mathfrak{E}_5(t_{k-1}, \mathcal{C}_{k-1})}{h}\int_{t_k}^{t_{k+1}}(\phi - t_k)(t_{m+1}-\phi)^{q-1}d\phi\right).
\end{aligned}
\tag{29}
$$

The following outcome is obtained by integrating the terms contained in (29) and plugging them back into it.

$$
\begin{aligned}
\mathcal{H}(t_{m+1}) &= \mathcal{H}_0 + \frac{1-q}{M(q)}\mathfrak{E}_1(t_m, \mathcal{H}(t_m)) + \frac{q}{\Gamma(q)M(q)}\sum_{k=0}^{m}\left(\frac{h^q\mathfrak{E}_1(t_k, \mathcal{H}_k)}{\Gamma(q+2)}((m+1-k)^q(m-k+2+q)-\right. \\
&\quad \left.(m-k)^q(m-k+2+2q)) - \frac{h^q\mathfrak{E}_1(t_{k-1}, \mathcal{H}_{k-1})}{\Gamma(q+2)}((m+1-k)^{q+1}-(m-k)^q(m-k+1+q))\right), \\
\mathcal{V}(t_{m+1}) &= \mathcal{V}_0 + \frac{1-q}{M(q)}\mathfrak{E}_2(t_m, \mathcal{V}(t_m)) + \frac{q}{\Gamma(q)M(q)}\sum_{k=0}^{m}\left(\frac{h^q\mathfrak{E}_1(t_k, \mathcal{V}_k)}{\Gamma(q+2)}((m+1-k)^q(m-k+2+q)-\right. \\
&\quad \left.(m-k)^q(m-k+2+2q)) - \frac{h^q\mathfrak{E}_2(t_{k-1}, \mathcal{V}_{k-1})}{\Gamma(q+2)}((m+1-k)^{q+1}-(m-k)^q(m-k+1+q))\right), \\
\mathcal{U}(t_{m+1}) &= \mathcal{U}_0 + \frac{1-q}{M(q)}\mathfrak{E}_3(t_m, \mathcal{U}(t_m)) + \frac{q}{\Gamma(q)M(q)}\sum_{k=0}^{m}\left(\frac{h^q\mathfrak{E}_3(t_k, \mathcal{U}_k)}{\Gamma(q+2)}((m+1-k)^q(m-k+2+q)-\right. \\
&\quad \left.(m-k)^q(m-k+2+2q)) - \frac{h^q\mathfrak{E}_3(t_{k-1}, \mathcal{U}_{k-1})}{\Gamma(q+2)}((m+1-k)^{q+1}-(m-k)^q(m-k+1+q))\right), \\
\mathcal{A}(t_{m+1}) &= \mathcal{A}_0 + \frac{1-q}{M(q)}\mathfrak{E}_4(t_m, \mathcal{A}(t_m)) + \frac{q}{\Gamma(q)M(q)}\sum_{k=0}^{m}\left(\frac{h^q\mathfrak{E}_4(t_k, \mathcal{A}_k)}{\Gamma(q+2)}((m+1-k)^q(m-k+2+q)-\right. \\
&\quad \left.(m-k)^q(m-k+2+2q)) - \frac{h^q\mathfrak{E}_4(t_{k-1}, \mathcal{A}_{k-1})}{\Gamma(q+2)}((m+1-k)^{q+1}-(m-k)^q(m-k+1+q))\right), \\
\mathcal{C}(t_{m+1}) &= \mathcal{C}_0 + \frac{1-q}{M(q)}\mathfrak{E}_5(t_m, \mathcal{C}(t_m)) + \frac{q}{\Gamma(q)M(q)}\sum_{k=0}^{m}\left(\frac{h^q\mathfrak{E}_5(t_k, \mathcal{C}_k)}{\Gamma(q+2)}((m+1-k)^q(m-k+2+q)-\right. \\
&\quad \left.(m-k)^q(m-k+2+2q)) - \frac{h^q\mathfrak{E}_5(t_{k-1}, \mathcal{C}_{k-1})}{\Gamma(q+2)}((m+1-k)^{q+1}-(m-k)^q(m-k+1+q))\right),
\end{aligned}
\tag{30}
$$

where

$$\begin{aligned}
\mathfrak{E}_1 &= \Lambda - \frac{\eta\mathcal{H}(t)\mathcal{A}(t)}{N} - (\rho+d)\mathcal{H}(t), \\
\mathfrak{E}_2 &= \rho\mathcal{H}(t) - \frac{(1-\tau)\eta\mathcal{A}(t)}{N} - d\mathcal{V}(t), \\
\mathfrak{E}_3 &= \frac{\eta\mathcal{H}(t)\mathcal{A}(t)}{N} + \frac{(1-\tau)\eta\mathcal{V}(t)\mathcal{A}(t)}{N} - (\alpha+d)\mathcal{U}(t), \\
\mathfrak{E}_4 &= \alpha\mathcal{U}(t) - (q+d)\mathcal{A}(t), \\
\mathfrak{E}_5 &= \delta\mathcal{A}(t) - d\mathcal{C}(t).
\end{aligned}$$

Approximate Solution by Newton's Polynomial Method

Newton's polynomial method is a numerical technique used to interpolate a set of data points using a polynomial function. The method involves constructing an nth degree polynomial that passes through $n+1$ data points. This polynomial can be evaluated at any point within the range of the data points to estimate the corresponding function value. The advantage of this method is its simplicity and efficiency, as it only requires basic algebraic operations to construct the polynomial. Additionally, it can accurately approximate complex functions with a high degree of precision. The method was first introduced by Sir Isaac Newton in the 17th century and has since been widely used in various fields, including engineering, physics, and computer science. There are several advantages of using Newton's polynomial numerical methods. Firstly, it allows for accurate approximation of the values of functions, making it a useful tool in various fields such as engineering, physics, and economics. Secondly, the method is relatively simple to use and understand, making it accessible to a wider audience of mathematicians and scientists. Thirdly, the method can be applied to a wide range of functions and is not limited to specific types or classes. Fourthly, the method allows for easy and efficient calculation of the derivatives of the function, which can be useful in many applications. Finally, the method can be extended to higher dimensions, making it suitable for problems in multiple variables.

We derive the numerical scheme for the case of Mittag–Leffler as follows:

$$\begin{aligned}
\mathcal{H}^{v+1} &= \frac{1-q}{AB(q)} + \mathcal{H}^*(t_v, \mathcal{H}^v, \mathcal{V}^v, \mathcal{U}^v, \mathcal{A}^v, \mathcal{C}^v) \\
&+ \frac{q(\Delta t)^q}{AB(q)\Gamma(q+1)} \sum_{u=2}^{v} \mathcal{H}^*(t_{u-2}, \mathcal{H}^{u-2}, \mathcal{V}^{u-2}, \mathcal{U}^{u-2}, \mathcal{A}^{u-2}, \mathcal{C}^{u-2})\Pi \\
&+ \frac{q(\Delta t)^q}{AB(q)\Gamma(q+2)} \sum_{u=2}^{v} \begin{bmatrix} \mathcal{H}^*(t_{u-1}, \mathcal{H}^{u-1}, \mathcal{V}^{u-1}, \mathcal{U}^{u-1}, \mathcal{A}^{u-1}, \mathcal{C}^{u-1}) \\ -\mathcal{H}^*(t_{u-2}, \mathcal{H}^{u-2}, \mathcal{V}^{u-2}, \mathcal{U}^{u-2}, \mathcal{A}^{u-2}, \mathcal{C}^{u-2}) \end{bmatrix} \Sigma \\
&+ \frac{q(\Delta t)^q}{2AB(q)\Gamma(q+3)} \sum_{u=2}^{v} \left\{ \begin{matrix} \mathcal{H}^*(t_u, \mathcal{H}^u, \mathcal{V}^u, \mathcal{U}^u, \mathcal{A}^u, \mathcal{C}^u) \\ -2\mathcal{H}^*(t_{u-1}, \mathcal{H}^{u-1}, \mathcal{V}^{u-1}, \mathcal{U}^{u-1}, \mathcal{A}^{u-1}, \mathcal{C}^{u-1}) \\ +\mathcal{H}^*(t_{u-2}, \mathcal{H}^{u-2}, \mathcal{V}^{u-2}, \mathcal{U}^{u-2}, \mathcal{A}^{u-2}, \mathcal{C}^{u-2}) \end{matrix} \right\} \Delta \\
\mathcal{V}^{v+1} &= \frac{1-q}{AB(q)} + \mathcal{V}^*(t_v, \mathcal{H}^v, \mathcal{V}^v, \mathcal{U}^v, \mathcal{A}^v, \mathcal{C}^v) \\
&+ \frac{q(\Delta t)^q}{AB(q)\Gamma(q+1)} \sum_{u=2}^{v} \mathcal{V}^*(t_{u-2}, \mathcal{H}^{u-2}, \mathcal{V}^{u-2}, \mathcal{U}^{u-2}, \mathcal{A}^{u-2}, \mathcal{C}^{u-2})\Pi \\
&+ \frac{q(\Delta t)^q}{AB(q)\Gamma(q+2)} \sum_{u=2}^{v} \begin{bmatrix} \mathcal{V}^*(t_{u-1}, \mathcal{H}^{u-1}, \mathcal{V}^{u-1}, \mathcal{U}^{u-1}, \mathcal{A}^{u-1}, \mathcal{C}^{u-1}) \\ -\mathcal{V}^*(t_{u-2}, \mathcal{H}^{u-2}, \mathcal{V}^{u-2}, \mathcal{U}^{u-2}, \mathcal{A}^{u-2}, \mathcal{C}^{u-2}) \end{bmatrix} \Sigma \\
&+ \frac{q(\Delta t)^q}{2AB(q)\Gamma(q+3)} \sum_{u=2}^{v} \left\{ \begin{matrix} \mathcal{V}^*(t_u, \mathcal{H}^u, \mathcal{V}^u, \mathcal{U}^u, \mathcal{A}^u, \mathcal{C}^u) \\ -2\mathcal{V}^*(t_{u-1}, \mathcal{H}^{u-1}, \mathcal{V}^{u-1}, \mathcal{U}^{u-1}, \mathcal{A}^{u-1}, \mathcal{C}^{u-1}) \\ +\mathcal{V}^*(t_{u-2}, \mathcal{H}^{u-2}, \mathcal{V}^{u-2}, \mathcal{U}^{u-2}, \mathcal{A}^{u-2}, \mathcal{C}^{u-2}) \end{matrix} \right\} \Delta
\end{aligned}$$

$$
\begin{aligned}
\mathcal{U}^{v+1} &= \frac{1-q}{AB(q)} + \mathcal{U}^*(t_v, \mathcal{H}^v, \mathcal{V}^v, \mathcal{U}^v, \mathcal{A}^v, \mathcal{C}^v) \\
&+ \frac{q(\Delta t)^q}{AB(q)\Gamma(q+1)} \sum_{u=2}^{v} \mathcal{U}^*(t_{u-2}, \mathcal{H}^{u-2}, \mathcal{V}^{u-2}, \mathcal{U}^{u-2}, \mathcal{A}^{u-2}, \mathcal{C}^{u-2})\Pi \\
&+ \frac{q(\Delta t)^q}{AB(q)\Gamma(q+2)} \sum_{u=2}^{v} \begin{bmatrix} \mathcal{U}^*(t_{u-1}, \mathcal{H}^{u-1}, \mathcal{V}^{u-1}, \mathcal{U}^{u-1}, \mathcal{A}^{u-1}, \mathcal{C}^{u-1}) \\ -\mathcal{U}^*(t_{u-2}, \mathcal{H}^{u-2}, \mathcal{V}^{u-2}, \mathcal{U}^{u-2}, \mathcal{A}^{u-2}, \mathcal{C}^{u-2}) \end{bmatrix} \Sigma \\
&+ \frac{q(\Delta t)^q}{2AB(q)\Gamma(q+3)} \sum_{u=2}^{v} \begin{Bmatrix} \mathcal{U}^*(t_u, \mathcal{H}^u, \mathcal{V}^u, \mathcal{U}^u, \mathcal{A}^u, \mathcal{C}^u) \\ -2\mathcal{U}^*(t_{u-1}, \mathcal{H}^{u-1}, \mathcal{V}^{u-1}, \mathcal{U}^{u-1}, \mathcal{A}^{u-1}, \mathcal{C}^{u-1}) \\ +\mathcal{U}^*(t_{u-2}, \mathcal{H}^{u-2}, \mathcal{V}^{u-2}, \mathcal{U}^{u-2}, \mathcal{A}^{u-2}, \mathcal{C}^{u-2}) \end{Bmatrix} \Delta \\
\mathcal{A}^{v+1} &= \frac{1-q}{AB(q)} + \mathcal{A}^*(t_v, \mathcal{H}^v, \mathcal{V}^v, \mathcal{U}^v, \mathcal{A}^v, \mathcal{C}^v) \\
&+ \frac{q(\Delta t)^q}{AB(q)\Gamma(q+1)} \sum_{u=2}^{v} \mathcal{A}^*(t_{u-2}, \mathcal{H}^{u-2}, \mathcal{V}^{u-2}, \mathcal{U}^{u-2}, \mathcal{A}^{u-2}, \mathcal{C}^{u-2})\Pi \\
&+ \frac{q(\Delta t)^q}{AB(q)\Gamma(q+2)} \sum_{u=2}^{v} \begin{bmatrix} \mathcal{A}^*(t_{u-1}, \mathcal{H}^{u-1}, \mathcal{V}^{u-1}, \mathcal{U}^{u-1}, \mathcal{A}^{u-1}, \mathcal{C}^{u-1}) \\ -\mathcal{A}^*(t_{u-2}, \mathcal{H}^{u-2}, \mathcal{V}^{u-2}, \mathcal{U}^{u-2}, \mathcal{A}^{u-2}, \mathcal{C}^{u-2}) \end{bmatrix} \Sigma \\
&+ \frac{q(\Delta t)^q}{2AB(q)\Gamma(q+3)} \sum_{u=2}^{v} \begin{Bmatrix} \mathcal{A}^*(t_u, \mathcal{H}^u, \mathcal{V}^u, \mathcal{U}^u, \mathcal{A}^u, \mathcal{C}^u) \\ -2\mathcal{A}^*(t_{u-1}, \mathcal{H}^{u-1}, \mathcal{V}^{u-1}, \mathcal{U}^{u-1}, \mathcal{A}^{u-1}, \mathcal{C}^{u-1}) \\ +\mathcal{A}^*(t_{u-2}, \mathcal{H}^{u-2}, \mathcal{V}^{u-2}, \mathcal{U}^{u-2}, \mathcal{A}^{u-2}, \mathcal{C}^{u-2}) \end{Bmatrix} \Delta \\
\mathcal{C}^{v+1} &= \frac{1-q}{AB(q)} + \mathcal{C}^*(t_v, \mathcal{H}^v, \mathcal{V}^v, \mathcal{U}^v, \mathcal{A}^v, \mathcal{C}^v) \\
&+ \frac{q(\Delta t)^q}{AB(q)\Gamma(q+1)} \sum_{u=2}^{v} \mathcal{C}^*(t_{u-2}, \mathcal{H}^{u-2}, \mathcal{V}^{u-2}, \mathcal{U}^{u-2}, \mathcal{A}^{u-2}, \mathcal{C}^{u-2})\Pi \\
&+ \frac{q(\Delta t)^q}{AB(q)\Gamma(q+2)} \sum_{u=2}^{v} \begin{bmatrix} \mathcal{C}^*(t_{u-1}, \mathcal{H}^{u-1}, \mathcal{V}^{u-1}, \mathcal{U}^{u-1}, \mathcal{A}^{u-1}, \mathcal{C}^{u-1}) \\ -\mathcal{C}^*(t_{u-2}, \mathcal{H}^{u-2}, \mathcal{V}^{u-2}, \mathcal{U}^{u-2}, \mathcal{A}^{u-2}, \mathcal{C}^{u-2}) \end{bmatrix} \Sigma \\
&+ \frac{q(\Delta t)^q}{2AB(q)\Gamma(q+3)} \sum_{u=2}^{v} \begin{Bmatrix} \mathcal{C}^*(t_u, \mathcal{H}^u, \mathcal{V}^u, \mathcal{U}^u, \mathcal{A}^u, \mathcal{C}^u) \\ -2\mathcal{C}^*(t_{u-1}, \mathcal{H}^{u-1}, \mathcal{V}^{u-1}, \mathcal{U}^{u-1}, \mathcal{A}^{u-1}, \mathcal{C}^{u-1}) \\ +\mathcal{C}^*(t_{u-2}, \mathcal{H}^{u-2}, \mathcal{V}^{u-2}, \mathcal{U}^{u-2}, \mathcal{A}^{u-2}, \mathcal{C}^{u-2}) \end{Bmatrix} \Delta,
\end{aligned}
$$

where

$$
\Delta = \begin{bmatrix} (v-u+1)^q \begin{bmatrix} 2(v-u)^2 + (3q+10)(v-u) \\ +2\delta^2 + 9q + 12 \end{bmatrix} \\ -(v-u)^q \begin{bmatrix} 2(v-u)^2 + (5q+10)(v-u) \\ +6\delta^2 + 18q + 12 \end{bmatrix} \end{bmatrix},
$$

$$
\Sigma = \begin{bmatrix} (v-u+1)^q (v-u+3+2\delta) \\ -(v-u)^q (v-u+3+3\delta) \end{bmatrix}, \Pi = [(v-u+1)^q - (v-u)^q].
$$

8. Parameter Estimation

Parameter estimation is a process of determining the values of unknown parameters in a model, based on available data. This process is essential in many fields of science and engineering, including epidemiology, physics, economics, and engineering. Parameter estimation allows researchers to quantify the underlying characteristics of a system or process and make predictions about its behavior under different conditions. There are many different methods for parameter estimation, including maximum likelihood estimation, Bayesian inference, and least squares estimation. The choice of method depends on the type of data available, the assumptions of the model, and the desired level of precision. Overall, parameter estimation plays a crucial role in improving our understanding of complex systems and in making informed decisions in a wide range of applications. We have taken the real data from the Norovirus laboratory reports in England by week during 2021/2022 [43]. The optimized curve that best fits the data is shown in Figure 3. We employed the least squares curve fitting technique to analyze the reported cases of norovirus in this section. The estimated parameters of system (1) were obtained from the available data of reported cases. The ordinary least squares

(OLS) method was applied to minimize the daily report errors, and the goodness of fit was evaluated by analyzing the relative error.

$$\min\left(\frac{\sum_{i=1}^{n}\left(\mathcal{A}_i-\hat{\mathcal{A}}_i\right)^2}{\sum_{i=1}^{n}\mathcal{A}_i^2}\right). \tag{31}$$

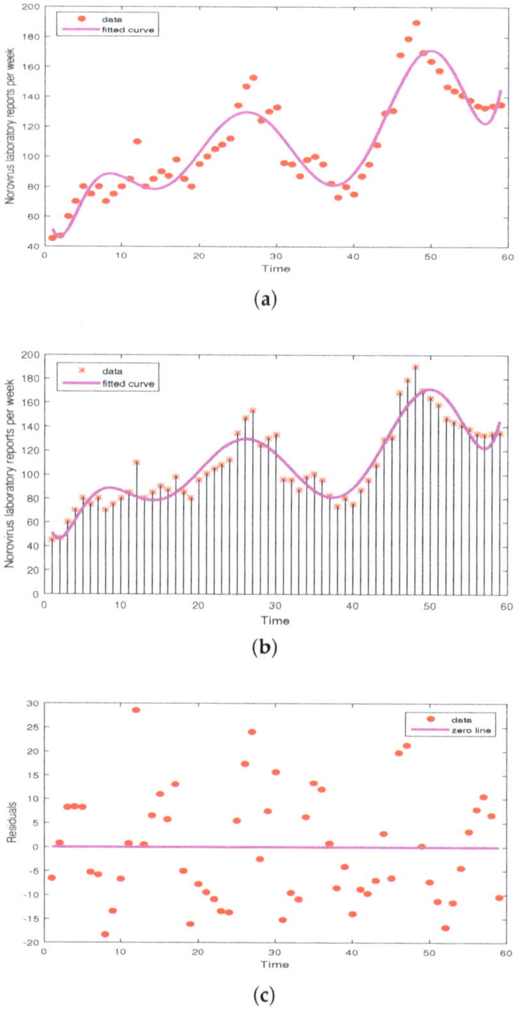

Figure 3. The graph presents the optimized curve that best fits the data, along with the residuals depicting the discrepancies between the simulated results and the recorded daily cumulative cases within the corresponding timescale. (**a**,**b**) Represents the model fit with the Norovirus laboratory-reported cases per week, and (**c**) represents the Residuals.

9. Numerical Simulation

In this section of the article, our aim was to find the approximate solution for the non-integer-order NoV (Norovirus) system using the ABC derivative of model (3). The simulation was performed over a time interval ranging from 0 to 60 steps, utilizing MATLAB 2019. The system parameters are provided in Table 1, and these values are used for graphical representation. The numerical simulation was conducted for various orders of q, and the results indicate that the non-integer-order fractional derivative yields favorable outcomes for controlling the infected class. The dynamics of each class in the system (3), for different values of q such as $0.90, 0.85, 0.80, 0.75, 0.70, 0.65, 0.60, 0.55, 0.50$, are depicted in Figure 4a–e. Figure 4a illustrates an increasing trend in the number of healthy individuals with a decay occurring in the fractional order q. Figure 4c demonstrates the growth of the exposed class for arbitrary values of q; however, after a certain time interval (around 20), the exposed class starts to decrease. The population of the infected class decreases over time as the values of q decrease in Figure 4d. Additionally, Figure 4b illustrates how newborns can immunize themselves by being carried by their mothers. This implies that proper care for carrier mothers could result in the vaccination-induced recovery of newborns in as little as a day. Similar to this, Figure 4e represents the recovery class and illustrates how people recover from infections. The approximative results show clear system deviations for various non-integer order parameter q values. The long-term simulation results obtained using ABM methods are also shown in Figure 5. Additionally, Figure 6 compares the simulation outcomes attained using the Newton polynomial and ABM approaches. Figures 7 and 8 show the simulation results specifically for the Newton polynomial method. Additionally, Figures 9 and 10 show, for each state variable, the effects of the transmission parameter *eta* and the natural removal rate d, respectively, on the results of the simulation.

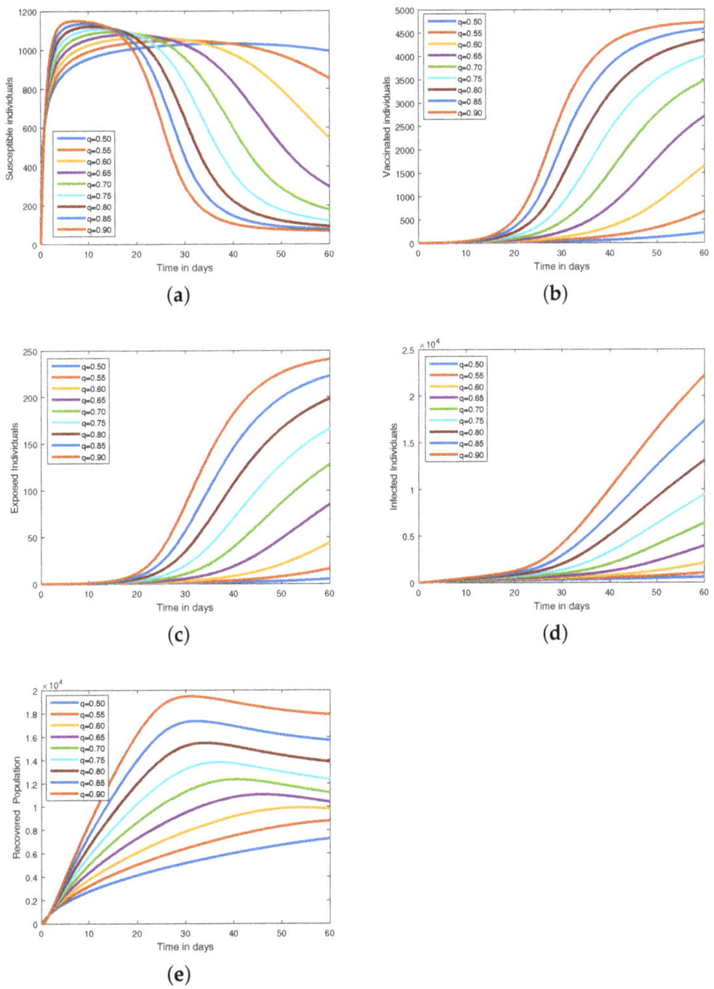

Figure 4. Paths for the solution of system (3) for $t = 60$, when $q = 0.90, 0.85, 0.80, 0.75, 0.70, 0.65, 0.60, 0.55, 0.50$. (**a**) Susceptible individuals. (**b**) Vaccinated individuals. (**c**) Exposed individuals. (**d**) Infected individuals. (**e**) Recovered individuals.

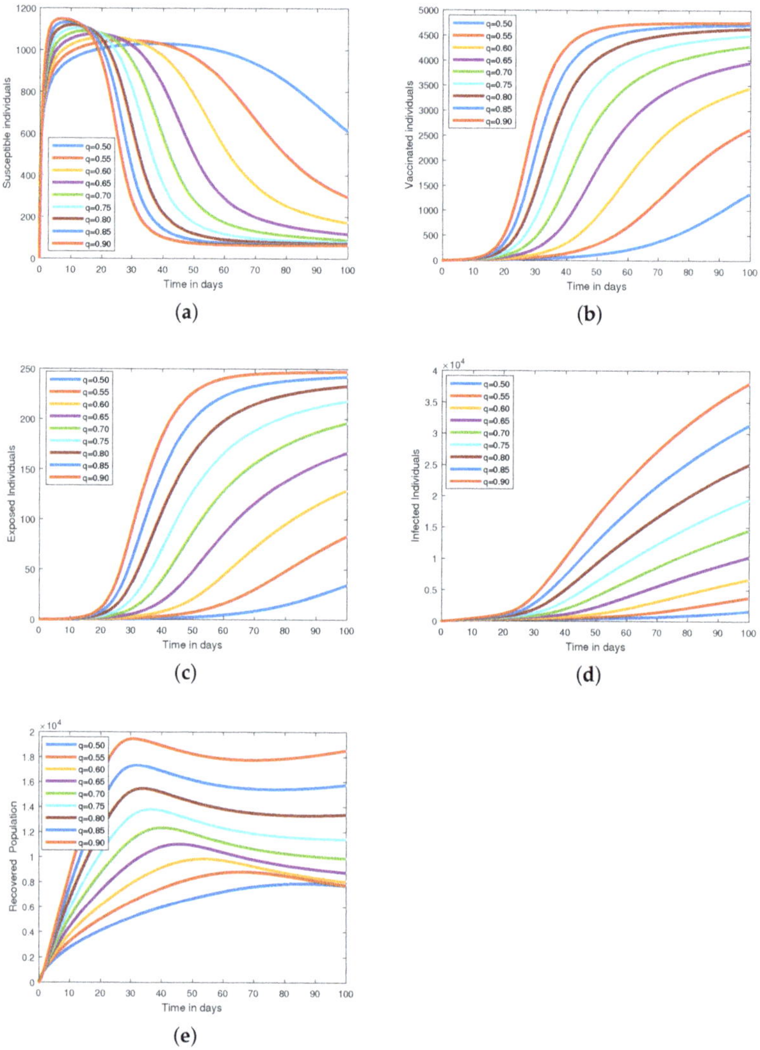

Figure 5. Paths for the solution of system (3) for a long time $t = 100$, when $q = 0.90, 0.85, 0.80, 0.75, 0.70, 0.65, 0.60, 0.55, 0.50$. (**a**) Susceptible individuals. (**b**) Vaccinated individuals. (**c**) Exposed individuals. (**d**) Infected individuals. (**e**) Recovered individuals.

Table 1. The table represents the parameters values and initial conditions of the state variable given in model (1).

Parameters	Description	Value	Source
Λ	The recruitment rate	125.66/day	Fitted
η	The rate of effectively contacts	0.02/day	Estimated
ρ	The vaccinated converging rate	0.01/day	Estimated
d	The natural mortality rate	0.02/day	Estimated
δ	The recovery rate	0.5/day	Estimated

Table 1. *Cont.*

Parameters	Description	Value	Source
α	Developing clinical symptoms	0.2/day	[38]
τ	The vaccine efficiency	0.90/day	Estimated
$\mathcal{H}(0)$	IC	75	[38]
$\mathcal{V}(0)$	IC	20	[38]
$\mathcal{U}(0)$	IC	55	[38]
$\mathcal{A}(0)$	IC	30	[38]
$\mathcal{C}(0)$	IC	20	[38]

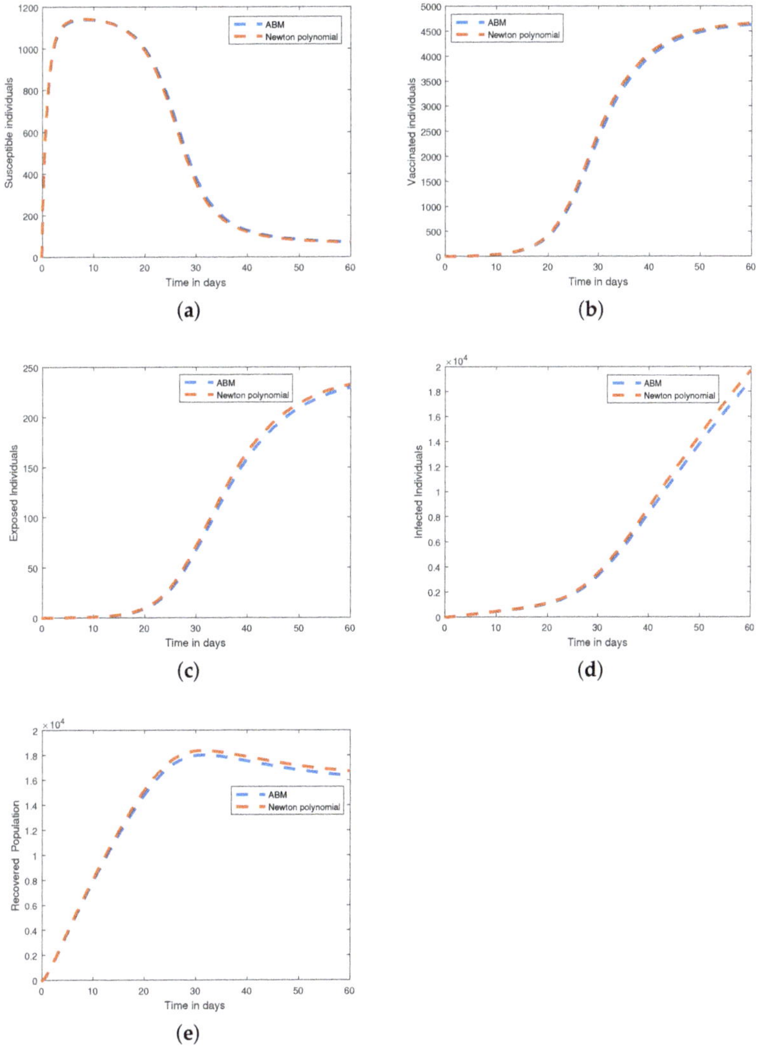

Figure 6. The plots represents the caparison of ABM and Newton's polynomial numerical methods on each state variable at fractional order $q = 0.95$. (**a**) Susceptible individuals. (**b**) Vaccinated individuals. (**c**) Exposed individuals. (**d**) Infected individuals. (**e**) Recovered individuals.

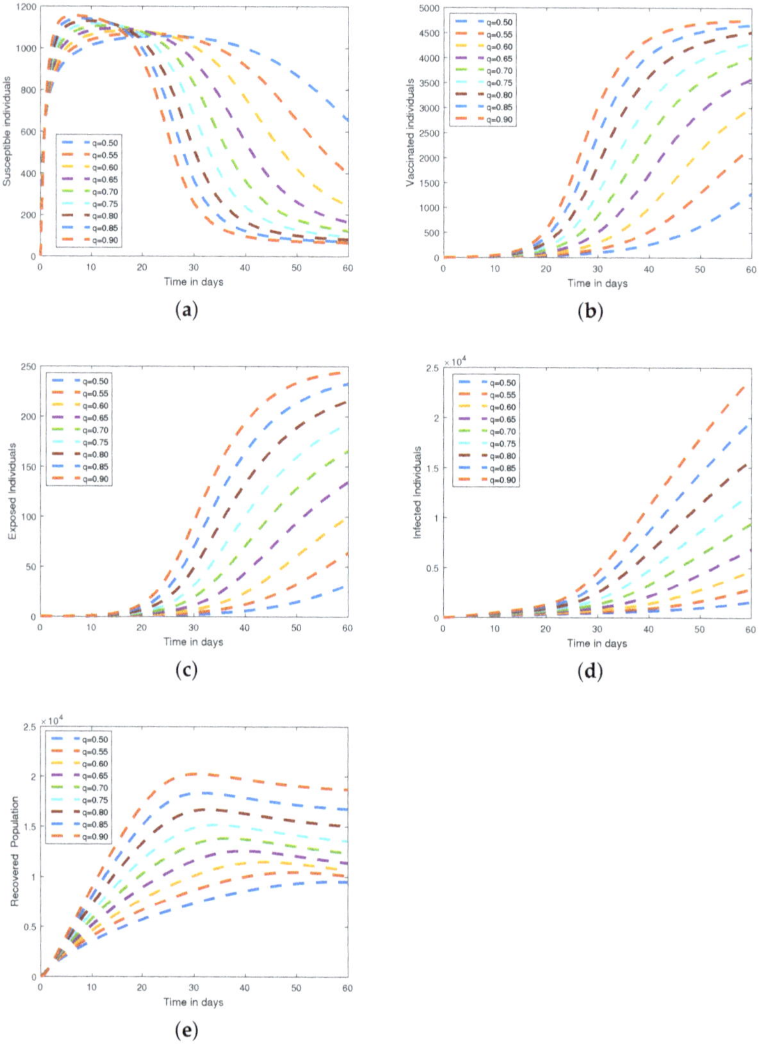

Figure 7. Paths for the solution of system (3) via Newton's Polynomial numerical method for a long time t = 60, when q = 0.90, 0.85, 0.80, 0.75, 0.70, 0.65, 0.60, 0.55, 0.50. (**a**) Susceptible individuals. (**b**) Vaccinated individuals. (**c**) Exposed individuals. (**d**) Infected individuals. (**e**) Recovered individuals.

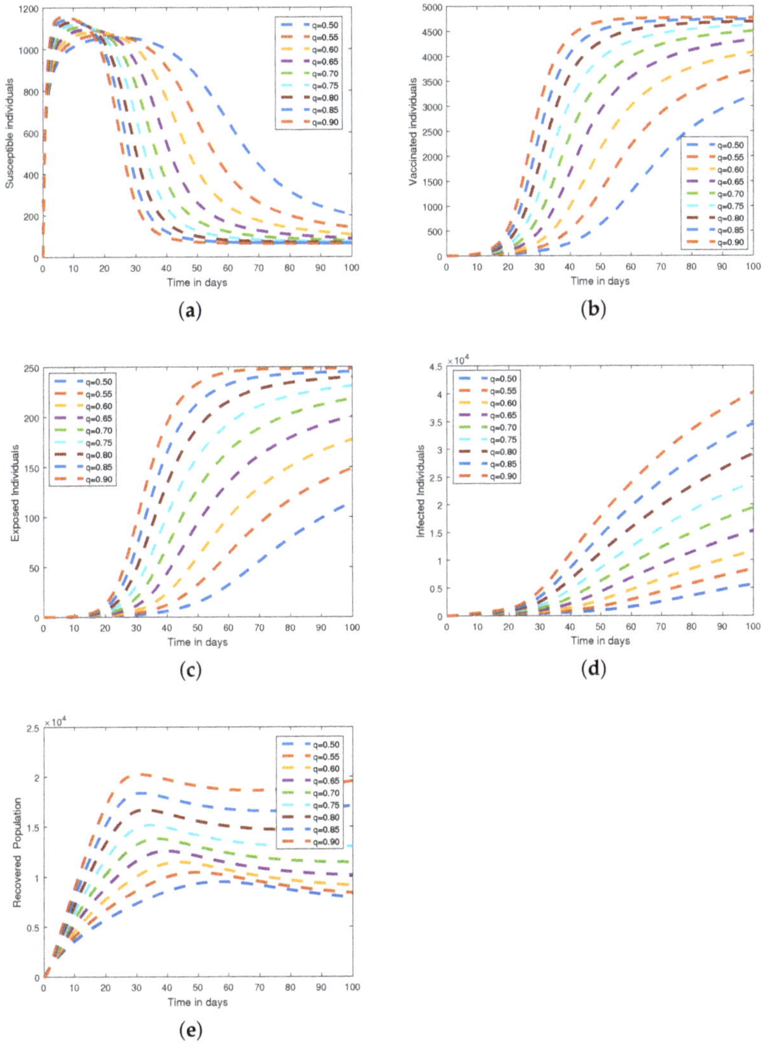

Figure 8. Paths for the solution of system (3) via Newton's Polynomial numerical method for a long time t = 100, when q = 0.90,0.85,0.80,0.75, 0.70, 0.65, 0.60, 0.55, 0.50. (**a**) Susceptible individuals. (**b**) Vaccinated individuals. (**c**) Exposed individuals. (**d**) Infected individuals. (**e**) Recovered individuals.

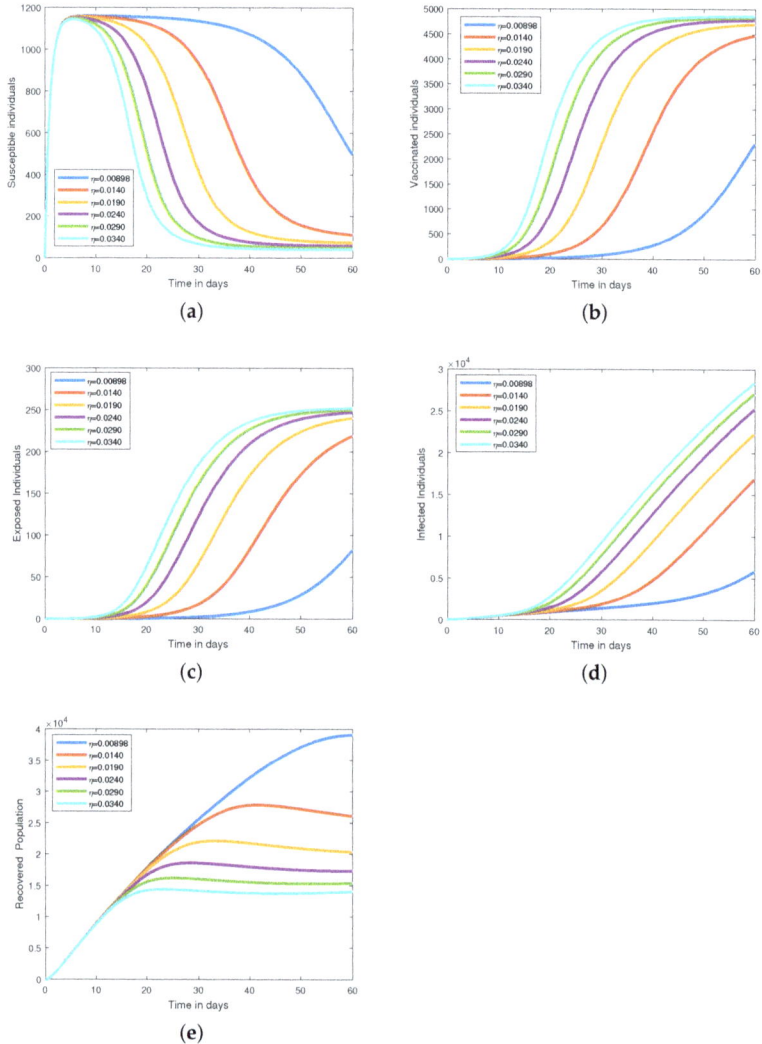

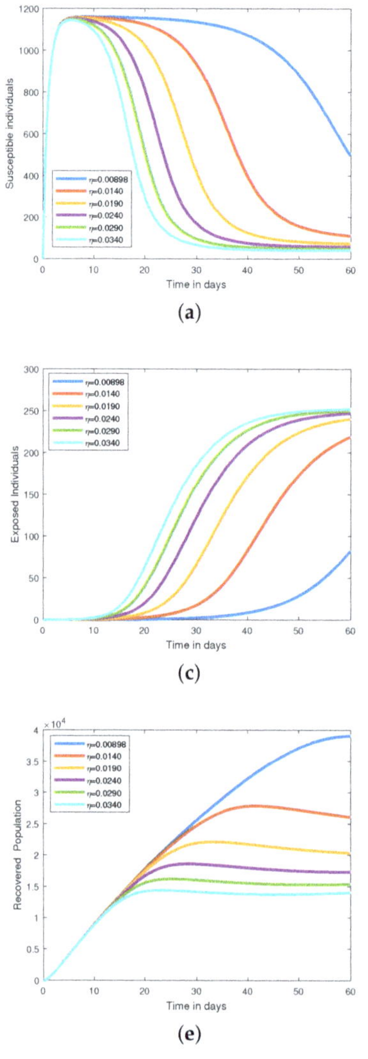

Figure 9. Impact of the parameter η which represent the rate of effectively contacts on each state variable at fractional order $q = 1$. (**a**) Susceptible individuals. (**b**) Vaccinated individuals. (**c**) Exposed individuals. (**d**) Infected individuals. (**e**) Recovered individuals.

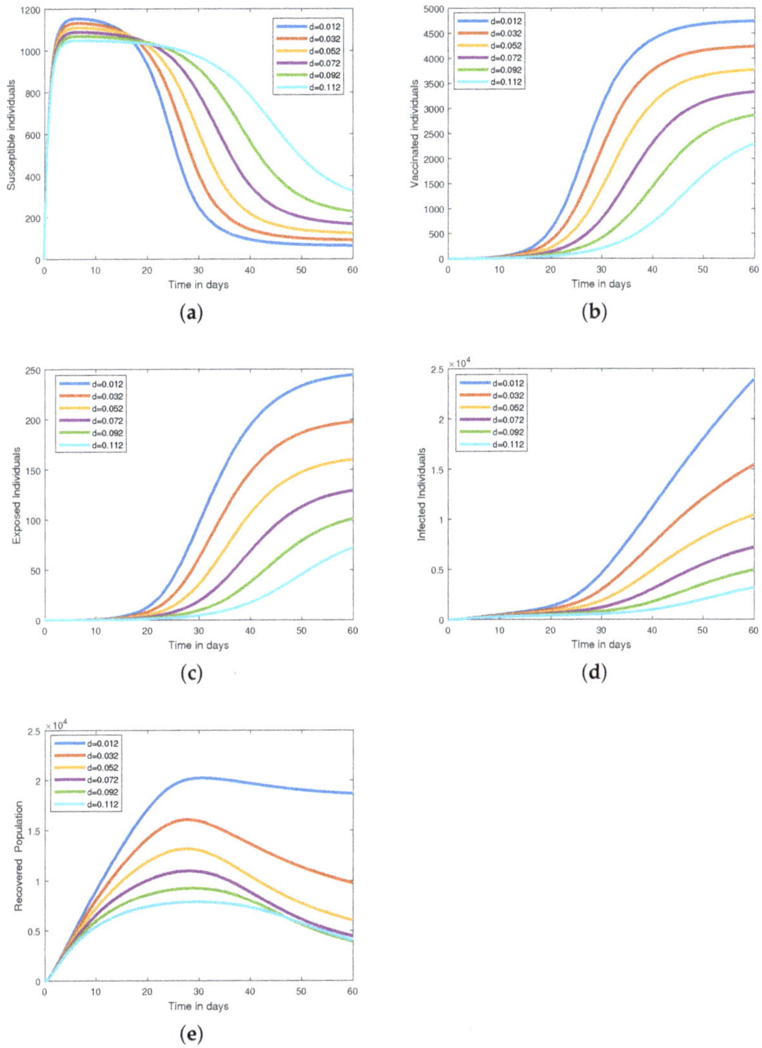

Figure 10. Impact of the parameter d which represents the natural death on each state variable at fractional order $q = 1$. (**a**) Susceptible individuals. (**b**) Vaccinated individuals. (**c**) Exposed individuals. (**d**) Infected individuals. (**e**) Recovered individuals.

10. Conclusions

In this paper, we have conducted a thorough investigation into the dynamics of Norovirus (NoV), taking into account the presence of asymptomatic carriers and the effects of vaccination. Our study utilized the Atangana–Baleanu–Caputo (ABC) fractional order derivative and applied fixed point theory to derive qualitative analysis for the positive solution of the system. To obtain an approximate solution, we have employed an iterative numerical method. Furthermore, we have presented graphical results for each system quantity at different fractional orders, revealing a convergence of curves to the integer order curves as the order increases. Our findings demonstrate a significant reduction in the number of infected cases through vaccination, emphasizing its positive impact. Consequently, this article provides valuable guidance for public health authorities in promoting and ensuring widespread vaccination within communities. Educating both rural and urban areas about the importance of vaccination and proper treatment is crucial for effectively controlling and preventing NoV outbreaks. The use of Atangana–Baleanu fractional derivatives demonstrates their usefulness as a tool for researching the dynamics of norovirus disease transmission, and our work highlights several crucial features of the fractional model. These include the model's creation, the fixed-point theorem's proof of the existence and uniqueness of solutions, stability and sensitivity analyses, and the basic reproduction number. Notably, the basic reproduction number is most sensitive to the disease transmission rate (η), whereas the basic reproduction number is least sensitive to the natural mortality rate (d) and the recovery rate of isolated individuals (δ). Additionally, because an increase in the fractional parameter results in an overall increase in the indices of all parameters, the fractional parameter has a significant impact on the sensitivity indices.

Author Contributions: Conceptualization, R.Z.; Formal analysis, A.A.R.; Methodology, A.A.R.; Project administration, Z.R.; Software, R.Z.; Supervision, Z.R.; Writing — original draft, R.Z.; Writing — review and editing, R.Z. All authors have read and agreed to the published version of the manuscript.

Funding: This research was funded by the Ministry of Education in KSA, project number (KKU-IFP2-H-9).

Data Availability Statement: Not applicable.

Acknowledgments: The authors extend their appreciation to the Ministry of Education in KSA for funding this research work through the project number (KKU-IFP2-H-9).

Conflicts of Interest: The authors declare no conflict of interest.

References

1. Ahmed S.M.; Lopman B.A.; Levy, K. A systematic review and meta-analysis of the global seasonality of norovirus. *PLoS ONE* **2013**, *8*, 75922. [CrossRef] [PubMed]
2. Marshall, J.A.; Bruggink, L.D. The dynamics of norovirus outbreak epidemics: Recent insights. *Int. J. Environ. Res. Public Health* **2011**, *8*, 1141–1149. [CrossRef] [PubMed]
3. Rohayem, J. Norovirus seasonality and the potential impact of climate change. *Clin. Microbiol. Infect.* **2009**, *18*, 524–527. [CrossRef] [PubMed]
4. Carmona-Vicente, N.; Fernåndez-Jiménez, M.; Ribes, J.M. Norovirus infections and seroprevalence of genotype GII.4–Specific antibodies in a Spanish population. *J. Med. Virol.* **2015**, *8*, 675–682. [CrossRef]
5. Anwarud, D.; Li, Y. Stochastic optimal control for norovirus transmission dynamics by contaminated food and water. *Chin. Phys. B* **2021**, *31*, 020202.
6. Hossein, J.; Daftardar-Gejji, V. Solving linear and nonlinear fractional diffusion and wave equations by Adomian decomposition. *Appl. Math. Comput.* **2006**, *180*, 488–497.
7. Li, X.-P.; Wang, Y.; Khan, M.A.; Alshahrani, M.Y.; Muhammad, T. A dynamical study of SARS-CoV-2: A study of third wave. *Results Phys.* **2021**, *29*, 104705. [CrossRef]
8. Razia, B.; Tunç, O.; Khan, H.; Gulzar, H.; Khan, A. A fractional order Zika virus model with Mittag–Leffler kernel. *Chaos Solitons Fractals* **2021**, *146*, 110898.
9. Osman, T.; Tunç, C. Ulam stabilities of nonlinear iterative integro-differential equations. *Rev. Real Acad. Cienc. Exactas Físicas Nat. Ser. Matemáticas* **2023**, *117*, 118.
10. Muhammad Shoaib, A.; Raza, A.; Rafiq, M.; Bibi, M. A reliable numerical analysis for stochastic hepatitis B virus epidemic model with the migration effect. *Iran. J. Sci. Technol. Trans. A Sci.* **2019**, *43*, 2477–2492.
11. Lu, Q. Stability of SIRS system with random perturbations. *Phys. A Stat. Mech. Its Appl.* **2009**, *388*, 3677–3686. [CrossRef]
12. Liu, P.; Din, A.; Zarin, R. Numerical dynamics and fractional modeling of hepatitis B virus model with non-singular and non-local kernels. *Results Phys.* **2022**, *39*, 105757. [CrossRef]
13. Zhang, X.-B.; Wang, X.-D.; Huo, H.-F. Extinction and stationary distribution of a stochastic SIRS epidemic model with standard incidence rate and partial immunity. *Phys. A Stat. Mech. Its Appl.* **2019**, *531*, 121548. [CrossRef]
14. Raizah, Z.; Zarin, R. Advancing COVID-19 Understanding: Simulating Omicron Variant Spread Using Fractional-Order Models and Haar Wavelet Collocation. *Mathematics* **2023**, *11*, 1925. [CrossRef]
15. Simone, G.; Fusè, M.; Mazzeo, G.; Abbate, S.; Longhi, G. MCD and Induced CD of a Tetraphenoxyperylene-Based Dye in Chiral Solvents: An Experimental and Computational Study. *Symmetry* **2023**, *14*, 1108. [CrossRef]
16. Zarin, R.; Khaliq, H.; Khan, A.; Ahmed, I. and Humphries, U.W. A numerical study based on haar wavelet collocation methods of fractional-order antidotal computer virus model. *Symmetry* **2023**, *15*, 621. [CrossRef]
17. Hossein, J.; Daftardar-Gejji, V. Solving a system of nonlinear fractional differential equations using Adomian decomposition *J. Comput. Appl. Math.* **2006**, *196*, 644–651.
18. Hossein, J.; Yousefi, S.A.; Firoozjaee, M.A.; Momani, S.; Masood Khalique, C. Application of Legendre wavelets for solving fractional differential equations. *Comput. Math. Appl.* **2011**, *62*, 1038–1045.

19. Khan, A.; Zarin, R.; Humphries, U.W.; Akgül, A.; Saeed, A.; Gul, T. Fractional optimal control of COVID-19 pandemic model with generalized Mittag-Leffler function. *Adv. Differ. Equ.* **2021**, *2021*, 387 . [CrossRef]
20. Khan, A.; Zarin, R.; Hussain, G.; Ahmad, N.A.; Mohd, M.H.; Yusuf, A. Stability analysis and optimal control of COVID-19 with convex incidence rate in Khyber Pakhtunkhawa (Pakistan). *Results Phys.* **2021**, *20*, 103703. [CrossRef]
21. Hossein, J.; Masood Khalique, C.; Nazari, M. Application of the Laplace decomposition method for solving linear and nonlinear fractional diffusion–Wave equations. *Appl. Math. Lett.* **2011**, *24*, 1799–1805.
22. Hossein, Y.; Daftardar-Gejji, V. Revised Adomian decomposition method for solving systems of ordinary and fractional differential equations. *Appl. Math. Comput.* **2006**, *181*, 598–608.
23. Shen, H.; Chu, Y.-M.; Khan, M.A.; Muhammad, S.; Al- Hartomy, O.A.; Higazy, M. Mathematical modeling and optimal control of the COVID-19 dynamics. *Results Phy.* **2021**, *31*, 105026. [CrossRef]
24. Zarin, R.; Khan, A.; Inc, M.; Humphries, U.W.; Karite, T. Dynamics of five grade leishmania epidemic model using fractional operator with Mittag–Leffler kernel. *Chaos Solitons Fractals* **2021**, *147*, 110985. [CrossRef]
25. Abdon, A.; Baleanu, D. New fractional derivatives with nonlocal and non-singular kernel: Theory and application to heat transfer model. *arXiv* **2016**, arXiv:1602.03408.
26. Abdon, A.; Koca, I. Chaos in a simple nonlinear system with Atangana–Baleanu derivatives with fractional order. *Chaos Solitons Fractals* **2016**, *89*, 447–454.
27. Gu, Y.; Khan, M.; Zarin, R.; Khan, A.; Yusuf, A.; Humphries, U.W. Mathematical analysis of a new nonlinear dengue epidemic model via deterministic and fractional approach. *Alex. Eng. J.***2023**, *67*, 1–21. [CrossRef]
28. Hossein, J.; Nazari, M.; Baleanu, D.; Masood Khalique, C. A new approach for solving a system of fractional partial differential equations. *Comput. Math. Appl.* **2013**, *66*, 838–843.
29. Afshin, B.; Jafari, H.; Ahmadi, M. A fractional order HIV/AIDS model based on the effect of screening of unaware infectives. *Math. Methods Appl. Sci.* **2019**, *42*, 2334–2343.
30. Anwarud, D.; Li, Y.; Muhammad Khan, F.; Ullah Khan, Z.; Liu, P. On Analysis of fractional order mathematical model of Hepatitis B using Atangana–Baleanu Caputo (ABC) derivative. *Fractals* **2022**, *30*, 2240017.
31. Anwarud, D.; Li, Y.; Yusuf, A.; Isa Ali, A. Caputo type fractional operator applied to Hepatitis B system. *Fractals* **2022**, *30*, 2240023.
32. Can, N.H.; Nikan, O.; Rasoulizadeh, M.N.; Jafari, H.; Gasimov, Y.S. Numerical computation of the time non-linear fractional generalized equal width model arising in shallow water channel. *Therm. Sci.* **2020**, *24* (Suppl. S1), 49–58. [CrossRef]
33. Salama, F.M.; Ali, N.H.M.; Abd Hamid, N.N. Fast O (N) hybrid Laplace transform-finite difference method in solving 2D time fractional diffusion equation. *J. Math. Comput. Sci.* **2021**, *23*, 110–123. [CrossRef]
34. Jassim, H.K.; Shareef, M.A. On approximate solutions for fractional system of differential equations with Caputo-Fabrizio fractional operator. *J. Math. Comput. Sci.* **2021**, *23*, 58–66. [CrossRef]
35. Akram, T.; Abbas, M.; Ali, A. A numerical study on time fractional Fisher equation using an extended cubic B-spline approximation. *J. Math. Comput. Sci.* **2021**, *22*, 85–96. [CrossRef]
36. Colin, S.; Edgar, W.; Simard, P.; Finelli, L.; Fiore, A.E.; Bell, B.P. Hepatitis B virus infection: Epidemiology and vaccination. *Epidemiol. Rev.* **2006**, *28*, 112–125.
37. Shapiro, C.N. Epidemiology of hepatitis B. *Pediatr. Infect. Dis. J.* **1993**, *12*, 433–437. [CrossRef]
38. Ting, C.; Liu, P.; Din, A. Fractal–fractional and stochastic analysis of norovirus transmission epidemic model with vaccination effects. *Sci. Rep.* **2021**, *11*, 1–25.
39. Biazar, J. Solution of the epidemic model by Adomian decomposition method. *Appl. Math. and Comp.* **2006**, *173*, 1101–1106. [CrossRef]
40. Rafei, M.; Ganji, D.D.; Daniali, H. Solution of the epidemic model by homotopy perturbation method. *Appl. Math. and Comp.* **2007**, *187*, 1056–1062. [CrossRef]
41. Ahmed, A. Adomian Decomposition Method: Convergence Analysis and Numerical Approximation. Master's Thesis, McMaster University, Hamilton, ON, USA , 2008.
42. Ali, Z.; Zada, A.; Shah, K. Ulam stability to a toppled systems of nonlinear implicit fractional order boundary value problem. *Bound. Value Probl.* **2018**, *175*, 1–16. [CrossRef]
43. National Norovirus and Rotavirus Report, Week 4 Report: Data up to Week 2 (15 January 2023). Available online: https://www.gov.uk/government/statistics/national-norovirus-and-rotavirus-surveillance-reports-2022-to-2023-season/national-norovirus-and-rotavirus-report-week-4-report-data-up-to-week-2-15-january-2023 (accessed on 23 August 2022).

symmetry MDPI

Article

Symmetrical Solutions for Non-Local Fractional Integro-Differential Equations via Caputo–Katugampola Derivatives

Khalil S. Al-Ghafri [1], Awad T. Alabdala [2], Saleh S. Redhwan [3,4], Omar Bazighifan [5,6], Ali Hasan Ali [7,8] and Loredana Florentina Iambor [9,*]

1 University of Technology and Applied Sciences, P.O. Box 14, Ibri 516, Oman
2 Management Department, Université Française d'Égypte, El Shorouk 11837, Egypt
3 Department of Mathematics, Al-Mahweet University, Al-Mahweet, Yemen
4 Department of Mathematics, Dr. Babasaheb Ambedkar Marathwada University, Aurangabad 431001, India
5 Department of Mathematics, Faculty of Education, Seiyun University, Hadhramout 50512, Yemen
6 Department of Mathematics, International Telematic University Uninettuno, CorsoVittorio Emanuele II, 39, 00186 Roma, Italy
7 Department of Mathematics, College of Education for Pure Sciences, University of Basrah, Basrah 61001, Iraq
8 Institute of Mathematics, University of Debrecen, Pf. 400, H-4002 Debrecen, Hungary
9 Department of Mathematics and Computer Science, University of Oradea, 1 University Street, 410087 Oradea, Romania
* Correspondence: iambor.loredana@gmail.com

Abstract: Fractional calculus, which deals with the concept of fractional derivatives and integrals, has become an important area of research, due to its ability to capture memory effects and non-local behavior in the modeling of real-world phenomena. In this work, we study a new class of fractional Volterra–Fredholm integro-differential equations, involving the Caputo–Katugampola fractional derivative. By applying the Krasnoselskii and Banach fixed-point theorems, we prove the existence and uniqueness of solutions to this problem. The modified Adomian decomposition method is used, to solve the resulting fractional differential equations. This technique rapidly provides convergent successive approximations of the exact solution to the given problem; therefore, we investigate the convergence of approximate solutions, using the modified Adomian decomposition method. Finally, we provide an example, to demonstrate our results. Our findings contribute to the current understanding of fractional integro-differential equations and their solutions, and have the potential to inform future research in this area.

Keywords: Katugampola operator; uniqueness of solutions; Banach space; integro-differential equations; existence theorem; Adomian decomposition; fractional operator; fixed point

MSC: 34A12; 34B18; 34A12; 47H10

Citation: Al-Ghafri, K.S.; Alabdala, A.T.; Redhwan, S.S.; Bazighifan, O.; Ali, A.H.; Iambor, L.F. Symmetrical Solutions for Non-Local Fractional Integro-Differential Equations via Caputo–Katugampola Derivatives. *Symmetry* **2023**, *15*, 662. https://doi.org/10.3390/sym15030662

Academic Editors: Hassen Fourati, Abdellatif Ben Makhlouf and Omar Naifar

Received: 12 February 2023
Revised: 23 February 2023
Accepted: 4 March 2023
Published: 6 March 2023

1. Introduction

Fractional calculus is a branch of mathematics that has gained significant attention in recent times, due to its wide range of applications in various fields. It deals with the concept of fractional derivatives and integrals, which are generalized versions of the standard notions of derivatives and integrals. These tools are useful for describing phenomena that exhibit memory or non-local behavior, such as those described by differential equations with power law kernels or fractional order operators. In [1,2], a generalized Riemann–Liouville fractional integral and corresponding fractional derivatives were introduced, which generalized the Riemann–Liouville and Hadamard integrals. The properties of the Katugampola fractional derivative (KFD), and its potential applications to quantum mechanics, were studied by Anderson et al. in [3]. Janaki et al. established the existence and uniqueness of solutions to impulsive differential equations with inclusions in [4], and also established conditions for the existence and uniqueness of solutions to a class of fractional implicit differential equations with KFD, in [5]. Vivek et al. recently investigated the existence and stability of solutions to impulsive type integro-differential equations in [6], and in [7], the existence and Ulam stability of solutions for impulsive type pantograph equations were studied. Fractional differential equations have been widely applied in various fields, due to their ability to capture memory effects often observed in real-world systems. Examples of phenomena that have been modeled using these equations include anomalous diffusion, viscoelastic behavior, and the spread of epidemics. The following articles [8–10] and their references discuss a number of interesting and new findings on the existence of various types of FDEs.

Recently, Basim [11] investigated the following Caputo fractional Volterra–Fredholm integro-differential equation

$$\begin{cases} {}^{C}\mathcal{D}^{\nu}_{0^+}\omega(\varkappa) = g(\varkappa) + \Pi_1\omega(\varkappa) + \Pi_2\omega(\varkappa), \ \varkappa \in \hbar = [0,1], \\ \omega(0) = \omega_0 + y(\omega), \end{cases}$$

where $0 < \nu < 1$, ${}^{C}\mathcal{D}^{\nu}_{0^+}$ is the Caputo fractional derivative of order ν, $g : \hbar \to \mathbb{R}$, $y : \mathbb{C}(\hbar, \mathbb{R}) \to \mathbb{R}$, $\chi_1, \chi_2 : \hbar \times \hbar \to \mathbb{R}$ are continuous functions, and $\mathcal{N}_1, \mathcal{N}_2 : \mathbb{R} \to \mathbb{R}$, $j = 1,2$ are Lipschitz continuous functions. In short, they put

$$\Pi_1\omega(\varkappa) := \int_0^{\varkappa} \chi_1(\varkappa, \xi)\mathcal{N}_1(\omega(\xi))d\xi,$$

and

$$\Pi_2\omega(\varkappa) := \int_0^{1} \chi_2(\varkappa, \xi)\mathcal{N}_2(\omega(\xi))d\xi.$$

Here, we confirm that the objective of the present study is to investigate the uniqueness and existence of the solution, by applying Banach's and Krasnoselskii's fixed-point theorems (FPTs), after which, we use the method of modified Adomian decomposition (MADM) for the Caputo–Katugampola fractional Volterra–Fredholm integro-differential equation (CK fractional VFIDE), which is given by

$$\begin{cases} {}^{C}\mathcal{D}^{\nu;\varsigma}_{0^+}\omega(\varkappa) = g(\varkappa) + \Pi_1\omega(\varkappa) + \Pi_2\omega(\varkappa), \ \varkappa \in \hbar = [0,1], \\ \omega(0) = \omega_0 + y(\omega), \end{cases} \tag{1}$$

where $0 < \nu < 1$, ${}^{C}\mathcal{D}^{\nu;\varsigma}_{0^+}$ is the CK fractional derivative of order ν, with a parameter ς, $g : \hbar \to \mathbb{R}$, $y : \mathbb{C}(\hbar, \mathbb{R}) \to \mathbb{R}$, $\chi_1, \chi_2 : \hbar \times \hbar \to \mathbb{R}$ are continuous functions, and $\mathcal{N}_1, \mathcal{N}_2 : \mathbb{R} \to \mathbb{R}$, $j = 1,2$ are Lipschitz continuous functions. In brief, we put

$$\Pi_1\omega(\varkappa) := \int_0^{\varkappa} \chi_1(\varkappa, \xi)\mathcal{N}_1(\omega(\xi))d\xi,$$

and

$$\Pi_2\omega(\varkappa) := \int_0^{1} \chi_2(\varkappa, \xi)\mathcal{N}_2(\omega(\xi))d\xi.$$

Amongst the other fractional derivatives, this new fractional differential operator (Caputo–Katugampola fractional derivative ${}^{C}\mathcal{D}^{\nu;\varsigma}_{0^+}$) is advantageous, because it combines and unites the Caputo and Caputo–Hadamard fractional differential operators, and preserves some basic and fundamental properties of the Caputo and Caputo–Hadamard fractional derivatives; therefore, the Caputo–Katugampola fractional derivative is a generalization of the following fractional derivatives: standard Caputo ($\varsigma \to 1$) [1]; Caputo–Hadamard ($\varsigma \to 0^+$) [12]; Caputo–Liouville ($\varsigma \to 1, a \to 0$) [1]; Caputo–Wey ($\varsigma \to 1, a \to -\infty$) [13].

Additionally, numerous studies have been conducted, using George Adomian's approach of Adomian decomposition (AD), to estimate the solution to this type of equation [14], and other numerical methods (see, for instance, [15–24]). The style and simplicity of the AD approach make it attractive. The answer is given as a series, where each equation may be calculated with ease, using Adomian polynomials that are appropriate for nonlinear components (see [14,25–29]). In [30], Wazwaz introduced the MADM, which entails splitting the first term of the series into two second terms, one of which is kept, to define the second term of the series. This approach's primary goals are to perform fewer operations, and to accelerate convergence on the precise solution to the stated problem. For instance, we quote [31] when discussing the application of the MADM. Many authors have used fixed-point methods to study findings on the presence of solutions to CK fractional differential equations: recent papers can be found at [32–34]. In this paper, we establish the existence and uniqueness solution of problem (1), using a contemporary methodology. We arrive at a few prerequisites that are necessary for fractional integro-differential equations with non-local conditions to obtain solutions. To acquire a rough solution, the MADM is utilized. The FPTs of Krasnoselskii and Banach are also used, to assess our findings.

1.1. Significance of This Paper

It appears that the issues indicated by the fractional operator are more difficult than those indicated by the ordinary operator. Some authors have recently considered the applications of fractional derivatives in a variety of scientific fields, such as the fractional Volterra–Fredholm integro-differential equation, the fractional quadratic integral equation, and mechanical applications. Among these are numerous works on numerical techniques for a specific class of fractional differential equations and other types of equations, such as [11,35,36].

1.2. Structurization of the Paper

The remainder of the paper is structured as follows. In Section 2, we review some fractional calculus notations, definitions, and lemmas that are relevant to our research. In Section 3, we provide an important lemma that enables us to convert the fractional Volterra–Fredholm integro-differential equation defined in Equation (1) into an equivalent integral equation. This section also contains the primary existence and uniqueness results for the problem (1), attained by applying the Krasnoselskii and Banach fixed-point theorems. In Section 4, we discuss the modified Adomian decomposition method, and prove that the series generated by this method converges to the exact solution of the problem. A numerical example is presented, to demonstrate the result, in Section 5. Concluding remarks are presented in Section 6.

2. Preliminaries

Denoting $\mathbb{C}(\hbar,\mathbb{R})$ as the Banach space of all continuous functions on $\hbar$. For $z \in \mathbb{C}(\hbar,\mathbb{R})$, we have

$$\|z\|_{\mathbb{C}} = \sup_{\varkappa\in\hbar}|z(\varkappa)| : \varkappa \in \hbar\}.$$

For $a < b, c \in \mathbb{R}^+$ and $1 \leq p < \infty$, define the function space

$$X_c^p(a,b) = \left\{ z : \hbar \to \mathbb{R} : \|z\|_{X_c^p} = \left(\int_a^b |\varkappa^c z(\varkappa)|^p \frac{d\varkappa}{\varkappa} \right)^{\frac{1}{p}} < \infty \right\},$$

for $p = \infty$,

$$\|z\|_{X_c^p} = ess \sup_{a\leq\varkappa\leq T} [|\varkappa^c z(\varkappa)|].$$

Definition 1 ([37]). *Let $\nu > 0$, $\varsigma > 0$, $c \in \mathbb{R}^+$ and $z \in X_c^p(a,b)$. Then, the definition of the Katugampola fractional integral of order ν with parameter ς is given by*

$$\mathcal{I}_{a^+}^{\nu;\varsigma} z(\varkappa) = \int_a^\varkappa \frac{\eta^{\varsigma-1}}{\Gamma(\nu)} \left(\frac{\varkappa^\varsigma - \eta^\varsigma}{\varsigma} \right)^{\nu-1} z(\eta) d\eta.$$

Now, when $\varsigma = 0$, we arrive at the standard Riemann–Liouville fractional integral, which is used to define both the Riemann–Liouville and Caputo fractional derivatives [1,2]. Using L'hospital rule, when $\varsigma \to 0^+$, we have

$$\begin{aligned} & \lim_{\varsigma \to -0^+} \int_a^{\varkappa} \frac{\eta^{\varsigma-1}}{\Gamma(\nu)} \left(\frac{\varkappa^\varsigma - \eta^\varsigma}{\varsigma} \right)^{\nu-1} z(\eta) d\eta \\ = & \frac{1}{\Gamma(\nu)} \int_a^{\varkappa} \lim_{\varsigma \to -0^+} \eta^{\varsigma-1} \left(\frac{\varkappa^\varsigma - \eta^\varsigma}{\varsigma} \right)^{\nu-1} z(\eta) d\eta \\ = & \frac{1}{\Gamma(\nu)} \int_a^{\varkappa} \left(\log \frac{\varkappa}{\eta} \right)^{\nu-1} \frac{z(\eta)}{\eta} d\eta. \end{aligned}$$

This is the well-known Hadamard fractional integral.

Definition 2 ([38])**.** *Let $n-1 < \nu < n$, $(n = [\nu]+1)$, $\varsigma > 0$, $c \in \mathbb{R}^+$ and $z \in X_c^p(a,b)$. Then, the definitions of Katugampola and the CK fractional derivative of order ν, with a parameter ς, are given by*

$$\mathcal{D}_{a^+}^{\nu;\varsigma} z(\varkappa) = \left(\varkappa^{1-\varsigma} \frac{d}{d\varkappa} \right)^n \mathcal{I}_{a^+}^{n-\nu;\varsigma} z(\varkappa),$$

and

$$\mathcal{D}_{a^+}^{\nu;\varsigma} z(\varkappa) = \mathcal{I}_{a^+}^{n-\nu;\varsigma} z_\varsigma^{(n)}(\varkappa),$$

respectively, where $z_\varsigma^{(n)}(\varkappa) = \left(\varkappa^{1-\varsigma} \frac{d}{d\varkappa} \right)^n z(\varkappa)$. For example, if we take $z(\varkappa) = \varkappa^\tau$ where $\tau \in \mathbb{R}$, then the generalized derivative of the function $z(\varkappa)$ can be found as follows:

$$\mathcal{D}_{a^+}^{\nu;\varsigma} \varkappa^\tau = \frac{(\varsigma+1)^\nu}{\Gamma(1-\nu)} \frac{d}{d\varkappa} \int_a^{\varkappa} \frac{\eta^\varsigma}{(\varkappa^{\varsigma+1} - \eta^{\varsigma+1})^\nu} \eta^\tau d\eta.$$

To evaluate the inner integral, we use the substitution $u = \frac{\eta^{\varsigma+1}}{\varkappa^{\varsigma+1}}$, to obtain

$$\begin{aligned} \int_a^{\varkappa} \frac{\eta^\varsigma}{(\varkappa^{\varsigma+1} - \eta^{\varsigma+1})^\nu} \eta^\tau d\eta &= \frac{\varkappa^{(\varsigma+1)(1-\nu)+\tau}}{\varsigma+1} \int_0^1 \frac{u^{\frac{\tau}{\varsigma+1}}}{(1-u)^\nu} du \\ &= \frac{\varkappa^{(\varsigma+1)(1-\nu)+\tau}}{\varsigma+1} \int_0^1 u^{\frac{\tau+\varsigma+1}{\varsigma+1}-1} (1-u)^{(1-\nu)-1} du \\ &= \frac{\varkappa^{(\varsigma+1)(1-\nu)+\tau}}{\varsigma+1} B\left(1-\nu, \frac{\tau+\varsigma+1}{\varsigma+1}\right), \end{aligned}$$

where $B(\cdot,\cdot)$ is the Beta function.

Lemma 1 ([39])**.** *Let $z \in \mathbb{C}^n[a,b]$, $\varsigma > 0$, Then*

$$\left(\mathcal{I}_{a^+}^{\nu;\varsigma} \, {}^C\mathcal{D}_{a^+}^{\nu;\varsigma} \right) z(\varkappa) = z(\varkappa) - \sum_{k=0}^{n-1} \frac{\varsigma^{-k}}{k!} (\varkappa^\varsigma - a^\varsigma)^k z_\varsigma^{(n)}(a).$$

Lemma 2 ([37])**.** *Let $\nu, \delta, \beta > 0$ and $z \in X_c^p(a,b)$. Then:*

1. $\mathcal{I}_{a^+}^{\nu;\varsigma}$ *is bounded on the function space $X_c^p(a,b)$;*
2. $\mathcal{I}_{a^+}^{\nu;\varsigma} \mathcal{I}_{a^+}^{\beta;\varsigma} z(\varkappa) = \mathcal{I}_{a^+}^{\nu+\beta;\varsigma} z(\varkappa)$;
3. $\mathcal{I}_{a^+}^{\nu;\varsigma} \left(\frac{\varkappa^\varsigma - a^\varsigma}{\varsigma} \right)^{\delta-1} = \frac{\Gamma(\delta)}{\Gamma(\delta+\nu)} \left(\frac{\varkappa^\varsigma - a^\varsigma}{\varsigma} \right)^{\nu+\delta-1}$.

3. Existence Result

We start by assuming the following:

(H$_1$) Let $\mathcal{N}_1(\omega(\varkappa)), \mathcal{N}_2(\omega(\varkappa))$ be continuous nonlinearity terms, and there exist constants $\ell_{\mathcal{N}_1} > 0$ and $\ell_{\mathcal{N}_2} > 0$, such that

$$|\mathcal{N}_j(\omega_1(\varkappa)) - \mathcal{N}_j(\omega_2(\varkappa))| \leq \ell_{\mathcal{N}_j}|\omega_1 - \omega_2|,\ j = 1,2,\ \forall \omega_1, \omega_2 \in \mathbb{R};$$

(H$_2$) The kernels $\chi_1(\varkappa, \xi)$ and $\chi_1(\varkappa, \xi)$ are continuous on $\hbar \times \hbar$, and there exist two positive constants, χ_1^* and χ_2^*, in $\hbar \times \hbar$, such that

$$\chi_j^* = \sup_{\varkappa \in \hbar} \int_0^{\varkappa} |\chi_j(\varkappa, \xi)| d\xi < \infty,\ j = 1,2;$$

(H$_3$) $g : \hbar \to \mathbb{R}$ is continuous on $\hbar$;

(H$_4$) $y : \mathbb{C}(\hbar, \mathbb{R}) \to \mathbb{R}$ is continuous on $\mathbb{C}(\hbar)$, and there exists a constant $0 < \ell_y < 1$, such that

$$|y(\omega_1(\varkappa)) - y(\omega_2(\varkappa))| \leq \ell_y|\omega_1 - \omega_2|,\ \forall \omega_1, \omega_2 \in \mathbb{C}(\hbar, \mathbb{R}),\ \varkappa \in \hbar.$$

Problem (1) and the integral equation are equivalent, according to the next lemma. The proof for this lemma is disregarded, as it resembles some traditional arguments that are known from the literature.

Lemma 3. *The function $\omega \in \mathbb{C}(\hbar, \mathbb{R})$ is the CK fractional VFIDE's (1) solution if and only if ω is the integral equation's solution, which is given by*

$$\begin{aligned}\omega(\varkappa) &= \omega_0 + y(\omega) + \frac{1}{\Gamma(\nu)} \int_0^{\varkappa} \eta^{\varsigma-1} \left(\frac{\varkappa^{\varsigma} - \eta^{\varsigma}}{\varsigma} \right)^{\nu-1} g(\eta) d\eta \\ &+ \frac{1}{\Gamma(\nu)} \int_0^{\varkappa} \eta^{\varsigma-1} \left(\frac{\varkappa^{\varsigma} - \eta^{\varsigma}}{\varsigma} \right)^{\nu-1} \left\{ \int_0^{\eta} \chi_1(\eta, \zeta) \mathcal{N}_1(\omega(\zeta)) d\zeta \right. \\ &\left. + \int_0^1 \chi_2(\eta, \zeta) \mathcal{N}_2(\omega(\zeta)) d\zeta \right\} d\eta.\end{aligned}$$

Our first result relates to existence based on the Krasnoselkii's FPT [40].

Theorem 1. *If conditions (H$_1$)–(H$_4$) are met, then there is at least one solution on $\hbar$ to the problem defined in Equation (1) if*

$$\Lambda_1 := \left(\ell_y + \frac{\sum_{j=1}^{2} \ell_{\mathcal{N}_j} \chi_j^*}{\varsigma^{\nu} \Gamma(\nu + 1)} \right) < 1. \tag{2}$$

Proof. Think about the ball:

$$\mathcal{S}_{\gamma} = \{\omega \in \mathbb{C}(\hbar, \mathbb{R}) : \|\omega\|_{\infty} \leq \gamma\} \subset \mathbb{C}(\hbar, \mathbb{R}). \tag{3}$$

Apparently, $\mathcal{S}_{\gamma}$ is a subset that is closed, convex, non-empty, and of $\mathbb{C}(\hbar, \mathbb{R})$. Select γ in a way where $\gamma \geq \frac{\Lambda_2}{1-\Lambda_1}$, where $\Lambda_1 < 1$,

$$\Lambda_2 := \mu_0 + \frac{\mu_g + \sum_{j=1}^{2} \mu_{\mathcal{N}_j} \chi_j^*}{\varsigma^{\nu} \Gamma(\nu + 1)}, \tag{4}$$

$\mu_g := \sup_{\varkappa \in [0,1]} |g(\varkappa)|$, $\mu_0 := |\omega_0| + \mu_y$, $\mu_y = |y(0)|$, $\mu_{\mathcal{N}_1} := |\mathcal{N}_1(0)|$, and $\mu_{\mathcal{N}_2} := |\mathcal{N}_2(0)|$.

Using Lemma 3, we can express the equivalent fractional integral equation for the problem defined in Equation (1) as an operator equation in the following form:

$$\omega = \mathbb{T}_1 \omega + \mathbb{T}_2 \omega,\ \ \omega \in \mathcal{S}_{\gamma} \subset \mathbb{C}(\hbar, \mathbb{R}), \tag{5}$$

where $\mathbb{T}_1$ and $\mathbb{T}_2$ are two operators on $\mathcal{S}_\gamma$ defined by

$$\begin{aligned}(\mathbb{T}_1\omega)(\varkappa) &= \frac{1}{\Gamma(\nu)}\int_0^{\varkappa}\eta^{\varsigma-1}\left(\frac{\varkappa^{\varsigma}-\eta^{\varsigma}}{\varsigma}\right)^{\nu-1}\left\{\int_0^{\eta}\chi_1(\eta,\zeta)\mathcal{N}_1(\omega(\zeta))d\zeta\right.\\ &\quad\left.+\int_0^1\chi_2(\eta,\zeta)\mathcal{N}_2(\omega(\zeta))d\zeta\right\}d\eta,\end{aligned}$$

and

$$(\mathbb{T}_2\omega)(\varkappa) = \omega_0 + y(\omega) + \frac{1}{\Gamma(\nu)}\int_0^{\varkappa}\eta^{\varsigma-1}\left(\frac{\varkappa^{\varsigma}-\eta^{\varsigma}}{\varsigma}\right)^{\nu-1}g(\eta)d\eta.$$

Applying the conditions of Theorem 2, we can find the fixed point of the operator Equation (5), in the following way:

Step 1: We claim that $\mathbb{T}_1\omega + \mathbb{T}_2\varpi \in \mathcal{S}_\gamma$ for each $\omega, \varpi \in \mathcal{S}_\gamma$. By (H_1), and for any $\omega, \varpi \in \mathcal{S}_\gamma$, we have

$$\begin{aligned}|\mathcal{N}_j(\omega(\varkappa))| &\le |\mathcal{N}_j(\omega(\varkappa)) - \mathcal{N}_j(0)| + |\mathcal{N}_j(0)|\\ &\le \ell_{\mathcal{N}_j}\|\omega\|_\infty + |\mathcal{N}_j(0)|\\ &\le \ell_{\mathcal{N}_j}\gamma + \mu_{\mathcal{N}_j},\ \text{for all } (j = 1,2),\end{aligned}$$

and

$$\begin{aligned}|y(\varpi(\varkappa))| &\le |y(\varpi(\varkappa)) - y(0)| + |y(0)|\\ &\le \ell_y\|\varpi\|_\infty + |y(0)|\\ &\le \ell_y\gamma + \mu_y.\end{aligned}$$

Let $\omega, \varpi \in \mathcal{S}_\gamma$. Then,

$$\begin{aligned}&|(\mathbb{T}_1\omega)(\varkappa) + (\mathbb{T}_2\varpi)(\varkappa)|\\ &\le \frac{1}{\Gamma(\nu)}\int_0^{\varkappa}\eta^{\varsigma-1}\left(\frac{\varkappa^{\varsigma}-\eta^{\varsigma}}{\varsigma}\right)^{\nu-1}\left\{\int_0^{\eta}\chi_1(\eta,\zeta)\mathcal{N}_1(\omega(\zeta))d\zeta\right.\\ &\quad\left.+\int_0^1\chi_2(\eta,\zeta)\mathcal{N}_2(\omega(\zeta))d\zeta\right\}d\eta.\\ &\quad+|\omega_0| + |y(\varpi)| + \frac{1}{\Gamma(\nu)}\int_0^{\varkappa}\eta^{\varsigma-1}\left(\frac{\varkappa^{\varsigma}-\eta^{\varsigma}}{\varsigma}\right)^{\nu-1}g(\eta)d\eta\\ &\le \mu_0 + \ell_y\gamma + \frac{\mu_g + \sum_{j=1}^{2}\left(\ell_{\mathcal{N}_j}\gamma + \mu_{\mathcal{N}_j}\right)\chi_j^*}{\varsigma^{\nu}\Gamma(\nu+1)}\varkappa^{\nu\varsigma},\end{aligned}$$

which implies

$$\begin{aligned}&\|\mathbb{T}_1\omega + \mathbb{T}_2\varpi\|_\infty\\ &\le \mu_0 + \frac{\mu_g + \sum_{j=1}^{2}\mu_{\mathcal{N}_j}\chi_j^*}{\varsigma^{\nu}\Gamma(\nu+1)} + \left(\ell_y + \frac{\sum_{j=1}^{2}\ell_{\mathcal{N}_j}\chi_j^*}{\varsigma^{\nu}\Gamma(\nu+1)}\right)\gamma\\ &\le \Lambda_2 + \Lambda_1\gamma \le \gamma.\end{aligned}$$

Consequently,

$$\mathbb{T}_1\omega + \mathbb{T}_2\varpi \in \mathcal{S}_\gamma.$$

Step 2: We demonstrate that $\mathbb{T}_2$ is a contraction on $\mathcal{S}_\gamma$.

Let $\omega, \omega^* \in \mathcal{S}_\gamma$. It follows from ($H_4$) that

$$\begin{aligned}\|\mathbb{T}_2\omega - \mathbb{T}_2\omega^*\|_\infty &= \sup_{\varkappa\in\hbar}|\mathbb{T}_2\omega(\varkappa) - \mathbb{T}_2\omega(\varkappa)| = \sup_{\varkappa\in\hbar}|y(\omega(\varkappa)) - y(\omega^*(\varkappa))| \\ &\le \ell_y\|\omega - \omega^*\|_\infty.\end{aligned}$$

This implies that $\mathbb{T}_2$ is a contraction mapping, as $\ell_y < 1$.

Step 3: We claim that $\mathbb{T}_1$ is completely continuous on $\mathcal{S}_\gamma$, which we will prove in three stages.

Stage 1—we prove that $\mathbb{T}_1$ is continuous. Let (ω_n) be a sequence, such that $\omega_n \to \omega$ in $\mathbb{C}(\hbar, \mathbb{R})$. Then, for any $\varkappa \in \hbar$, and for every $\omega_n, \omega \in \mathbb{C}(\hbar, \mathbb{R})$, we deduce

$$\begin{aligned}&|(\mathbb{T}_1\omega_n)(\varkappa) - (\mathbb{T}_1\omega)(\varkappa)| \\ \le\ & \frac{1}{\Gamma(\nu)}\int_0^\varkappa \eta^{\varsigma-1}\left(\frac{\varkappa^\varsigma - \eta^\varsigma}{\varsigma}\right)^{\nu-1}\left(\int_0^\eta |\chi_1(\eta,\zeta)||\mathcal{N}_1(\omega_n(\zeta)) - \mathcal{N}_1(\omega(\zeta))|d\zeta\right. \\ &\left.+\int_0^1 |\chi_2(\eta,\zeta)||\mathcal{N}_2(\omega_n(\zeta)) - \mathcal{N}_2(\omega(\zeta))|d\zeta\right)d\eta \\ \le\ & \frac{\sum_{j=1}^2 \ell_{\mathcal{N}_j}\chi_j^*}{\varsigma^\nu\Gamma(\nu+1)}\|\omega_n - \omega\|_\infty.\end{aligned}$$

As $\omega_n \to \omega$ as $n \to \infty$, $\|\mathbb{T}_1\omega_n - \mathbb{T}_1\omega\|_\infty \to 0$, as $n \to \infty$, this shows that $\mathbb{T}_1$ is continuous on $\mathbb{C}(\hbar, \mathbb{R})$.

Stage 2—from Step 1, we observe that

$$\begin{aligned}&|(\mathbb{T}_1\omega)(\varkappa)| \\ \le\ & \frac{1}{\Gamma(\nu)}\int_0^\varkappa \eta^{\varsigma-1}\left(\frac{\varkappa^\varsigma - \eta^\varsigma}{\varsigma}\right)^{\nu-1}\left(\int_0^\eta |\chi_1(\eta,\zeta)||\mathcal{N}_1(\omega(\zeta))|d\zeta\right. \\ &\left.+\int_0^1 |\chi_2(\eta,\zeta)||\mathcal{N}_2(\omega(\zeta))|d\zeta\right)d\eta \\ \le\ & \frac{\sum_{j=1}^2\left(\ell_{\mathcal{N}_j}\gamma + \mu_{\mathcal{N}_j}\right)\chi_j^*}{\varsigma^\nu\Gamma(\nu+1)}\varkappa^{\varsigma\nu}.\end{aligned}$$

Thus,

$$\|\mathbb{T}_1\omega\|_\infty \le \frac{\sum_{j=1}^2\left(\ell_{\mathcal{N}_j}\gamma + \mu_{\mathcal{N}_j}\right)\chi_j^*}{\varsigma^\nu\Gamma(\nu+1)}.$$

This proves that $(\mathbb{T}_1\mathcal{S}_\gamma)$ is uniformly bounded.

Stage 3—we show that $(\mathbb{T}_1\mathcal{S}_\gamma)$ is equicontinuous. Let $\omega \in \mathcal{S}_\gamma$. Then, for $\varkappa_1, \varkappa_2 \in \hbar$ with $\varkappa_1 \le \varkappa_2$, we have

$$\begin{aligned}&|(\mathbb{T}_1\omega)(\varkappa_2) - (\mathbb{T}_1\omega)(\varkappa_1)| \\ =\ & \left|\frac{1}{\Gamma(\nu)}\int_0^{\varkappa_2} \eta^{\varsigma-1}\left(\frac{\varkappa_2^\varsigma - \eta^\varsigma}{\varsigma}\right)^{\nu-1}\left(\int_0^\eta |\chi_1(\eta,\zeta)||\mathcal{N}_1(\omega(\zeta))|d\zeta\right.\right. \\ &\left.+\int_0^1 |\chi_2(\eta,\zeta)||\mathcal{N}_2(\omega(\zeta))|d\zeta\right)d\eta \\ &-\frac{1}{\Gamma(\nu)}\int_0^{\varkappa_1} \eta^{\varsigma-1}\left(\frac{\varkappa_1^\varsigma - \eta^\varsigma}{\varsigma}\right)^{\nu-1}\left(\int_0^\eta |\chi_1(\eta,\zeta)||\mathcal{N}_1(\omega(\zeta))|d\zeta\right. \\ &\left.\left.+\int_0^1 |\chi_2(\eta,\zeta)||\mathcal{N}_2(\omega(\zeta))|d\zeta\right)d\eta\right|\end{aligned}$$

$$\begin{aligned}
&|(\mathbb{T}_1\omega)(\varkappa_2) - (\mathbb{T}_1\omega)(\varkappa_1)| \\
\leq\ & \frac{1}{\Gamma(\nu)}\left(\int_{\varkappa_1}^{\varkappa_2} \eta^{\varsigma-1}\left(\frac{\varkappa_2^{\varsigma}-\eta^{\varsigma}}{\varsigma}\right)^{\nu-1} \int_0^{\eta} |\chi_1(\eta,\zeta)||\mathcal{N}_1(\omega(\zeta))|d\zeta d\eta \right.\\
&\left. + \int_0^{\varkappa_1} \eta^{\varsigma-1}\left|\left(\frac{\varkappa_2^{\varsigma}-\eta^{\varsigma}}{\varsigma}\right)^{\nu-1} - \left(\frac{\varkappa_1^{\varsigma}-\eta^{\varsigma}}{\varsigma}\right)^{\nu-1}\right| \int_0^{\eta} |\chi_1(\eta,\zeta)||\mathcal{N}_1(\omega(\zeta))|d\zeta d\eta\right) \\
& + \frac{1}{\Gamma(\nu)}\left(\int_{\varkappa_1}^{\varkappa_2} \eta^{\varsigma-1}\left(\frac{\varkappa_2^{\varsigma}-\eta^{\varsigma}}{\varsigma}\right)^{\nu-1} \int_0^{\eta} |\chi_2(\eta,\zeta)||\mathcal{N}_2(\omega(\zeta))|d\zeta d\eta \right.\\
&\left. + \int_0^{\varkappa_1} \eta^{\varsigma-1}\left|\left(\frac{\varkappa_2^{\varsigma}-\eta^{\varsigma}}{\varsigma}\right)^{\nu-1} - \left(\frac{\varkappa_1^{\varsigma}-\eta^{\varsigma}}{\varsigma}\right)^{\nu-1}\right| \int_0^{\eta} |\chi_2(\eta,\zeta)||\mathcal{N}_2(\omega(\zeta))|d\zeta d\eta\right)
\end{aligned}$$

which implies

$$\begin{aligned}
|(\mathbb{T}_1\omega)(\varkappa_2) - (\mathbb{T}_1\omega)(\varkappa_1)| \leq\ & \frac{(\ell_{\mathcal{N}_1}\gamma + \mu_{\mathcal{N}_1})\chi_1^*}{\Gamma(\nu)}\left(\int_{\varkappa_1}^{\varkappa_2} \eta^{\varsigma-1}\left(\frac{\varkappa_2^{\varsigma}-\eta^{\varsigma}}{\varsigma}\right)^{\nu-1} d\eta\right.\\
&\left. + \int_0^{\varkappa_1} \eta^{\varsigma-1}\left|\left(\frac{\varkappa_2^{\varsigma}-\eta^{\varsigma}}{\varsigma}\right)^{\nu-1} - \left(\frac{\varkappa_1^{\varsigma}-\eta^{\varsigma}}{\varsigma}\right)^{\nu-1}\right| d\eta\right) \\
& + \frac{(\ell_{\mathcal{N}_2}\gamma + \mu_{\mathcal{N}_2})\chi_2^*}{\Gamma(\nu)}\left(\int_{\varkappa_1}^{\varkappa_2} \eta^{\varsigma-1}\left(\frac{\varkappa_2^{\varsigma}-\eta^{\varsigma}}{\varsigma}\right)^{\nu-1} d\eta\right.\\
&\left. + \int_0^{\varkappa_1} \eta^{\varsigma-1}\left|\left(\frac{\varkappa_2^{\varsigma}-\eta^{\varsigma}}{\varsigma}\right)^{\nu-1} - \left(\frac{\varkappa_1^{\varsigma}-\eta^{\varsigma}}{\varsigma}\right)^{\nu-1}\right| d\eta\right) \\
\leq\ & \left(\frac{(\ell_{\mathcal{N}_1}\gamma + \mu_{\mathcal{N}_1})\chi_1^*}{\varsigma^{\nu}\Gamma(\nu+1)} + \frac{(\ell_{\mathcal{N}_2}\gamma + \mu_{\mathcal{N}_2})\chi_2^*}{\varsigma^{\nu}\Gamma(\nu+1)}\right) \\
& \times\left(\frac{(\varkappa_2^{\varsigma}-\varkappa_1^{\varsigma})^{\nu}}{\nu} + \frac{\varkappa_1^{\varsigma}}{\nu} - \frac{\varkappa_2^{\varsigma}}{\nu} + \frac{(\varkappa_2^{\varsigma}-\varkappa_1^{\varsigma})^{\nu}}{\nu}\right) \\
\leq\ & \frac{2\sum_{j=1}^{2}\left(\ell_{\mathcal{N}_j}\gamma + \mu_{\mathcal{N}_j}\right)\chi_j^*}{\varsigma^{\nu}\Gamma(\nu+1)}(\varkappa_2^{\varsigma}-\varkappa_1^{\varsigma})^{\nu},
\end{aligned}$$

which tends to zero, as $\varkappa_2 - \varkappa_1 \to 0$. Thus, $\mathbb{T}_1\mathcal{S}_\gamma$ is equicontinuous. Consequently, by the Arzela–Ascoli alternative, the operator $\mathbb{T}_1$ is continuous and completely continuous. Thus, by Krasnoselskii's FPT, $\mathbb{T}_1$ has a fixed point ω in $\mathcal{S}_\gamma$ which is a solution of the problem (1). End the proof. □

In the following result, we provide the uniqueness of the solution of our problem (1), and its proof is based on Banach's FPT [40].

Theorem 2. *Suppose that* (H_1)–(H_4) *hold. If*

$$\Lambda_1 < 1, \tag{6}$$

then there is a unique solution to the problem defined in Equation (1) on $\hbar$.

Proof. Using Lemma 3, we can express the equivalent fractional integral equation for the problem defined in Equation (1) as an operator equation in the following form:

$$\omega = \Upsilon\omega, \ \ \omega \in \mathbb{C}(\hbar, \mathbb{R}),$$

such that the operator $\Upsilon : \mathbb{C}(\hbar, \mathbb{R}) \to \mathbb{C}(\hbar, \mathbb{R})$, is defined by

$$\begin{aligned}(\Upsilon\omega)(\varkappa) &= \omega_0 + y(\omega) + \frac{1}{\Gamma(\nu)} \int_0^{\varkappa} \eta^{\varsigma-1} \left(\frac{\varkappa^{\varsigma} - \eta^{\varsigma}}{\varsigma} \right)^{\nu-1} g(\eta) d\eta \\ &+ \frac{1}{\Gamma(\nu)} \int_0^{\varkappa} \eta^{\varsigma-1} \left(\frac{\varkappa^{\varsigma} - \eta^{\varsigma}}{\varsigma} \right)^{\nu-1} \left(\int_0^{\eta} \chi_1(\eta, \zeta) \mathcal{N}_1(\omega(\zeta)) d\zeta \right. \\ &+ \left. \int_0^1 \chi_2(\eta, \zeta) \mathcal{N}_2(\omega(\zeta)) d\zeta \right) d\eta,\end{aligned}$$

for all $\varkappa \in \hbar$. Let $\omega, \omega^* \in \mathbb{C}(\hbar, \mathbb{R})$. Then, for each $\varkappa \in \hbar$, we have

$$\begin{aligned}&|\Upsilon\omega(\varkappa) - \Upsilon\omega^*(\varkappa)| \\ \leq\ & |y(\omega(\varkappa)) - y(\omega^*(\varkappa))| \\ &+ \frac{1}{\Gamma(\nu)} \int_0^{\varkappa} \eta^{\varsigma-1} \left(\frac{\varkappa^{\varsigma} - \eta^{\varsigma}}{\varsigma} \right)^{\nu-1} \left(\int_0^{\eta} \chi_1(\eta, \zeta) |\mathcal{N}_1(\omega(\zeta)) - \mathcal{N}_1(\omega^*(\zeta))| d\zeta \right) d\eta \\ &+ \frac{1}{\Gamma(\nu)} \int_0^{\varkappa} \eta^{\varsigma-1} \left(\frac{\varkappa^{\varsigma} - \eta^{\varsigma}}{\varsigma} \right)^{\nu-1} \left(\int_0^{1} \chi_2(\eta, \zeta) |\mathcal{N}_2(\omega(\zeta)) - \mathcal{N}_2(\omega^*(\zeta))| d\zeta \right) d\eta \\ \leq\ & \ell_y \|\omega - \omega^*\|_\infty + \frac{1}{\Gamma(\nu)} \int_0^{\varkappa} \eta^{\varsigma-1} \left(\frac{\varkappa^{\varsigma} - \eta^{\varsigma}}{\varsigma} \right)^{\nu-1} \chi_1^* \ell_{\mathcal{N}_1} \|\omega - \omega^*\|_\infty d\eta \\ &+ \frac{1}{\Gamma(\nu)} \int_0^{\varkappa} \eta^{\varsigma-1} \left(\frac{\varkappa^{\varsigma} - \eta^{\varsigma}}{\varsigma} \right)^{\nu-1} \chi_2^* \ell_{\mathcal{N}_2} \|\omega - \omega^*\|_\infty d\eta \\ \leq\ & \left(\ell_y + \frac{\chi_1^* \ell_{\mathcal{N}_1} + \chi_2^* \ell_{\mathcal{N}_2}}{\varsigma^{\nu} \Gamma(\nu+1)} \varkappa^{\varsigma\nu} \right) \|\omega - \omega^*\|_\infty,\end{aligned}$$

which implies

$$\|\Upsilon\omega - \Upsilon\omega^*\|_\infty \leq \left(\ell_y + \frac{\sum_{j=1}^{2} \ell_{\mathcal{N}_j} \chi_j^*}{\varsigma^{\nu} \Gamma(\nu+1)} \right) \|\omega - \omega^*\|_\infty.$$

The inequality (6) shows that Υ is a contraction mapping on $\mathbb{C}(\hbar, \mathbb{R})$. As a result of Banach's FPT, Υ will have a unique fixed point that is the solution of the problem (1). □

4. Approximate Solution

In this section, we use the fractional AD technique to derive an approximate solution to the CK fractional VFIDE that is defined in (1). We start by recalling the classical AD technique, which represents the solution to the problem as a series:

$$\omega = \sum_{n=0}^{\infty} \omega_n, \tag{7}$$

and the nonlinear terms $\mathcal{N}_1, \mathcal{N}_2$, and y are decomposed as

$$\mathcal{N}_1 = \sum_{n=0}^{\infty} A_n,\ \mathcal{N}_2 = \sum_{n=0}^{\infty} B_n,\ y = \sum_{n=0}^{\infty} D_n, \tag{8}$$

such that each of A_n, B_n, and D_n are called as Adomian polynomials for every non-negative and non-zero integer n, where this implies that

$$\omega = \omega(\lambda) = \sum_{n=0}^{\infty} \lambda^n \omega_n = \omega_0 + \lambda\omega_1 + \lambda^2\omega_2 + \cdots + \lambda^k \omega_k + \cdots \tag{9}$$

$$\mathcal{N}_1 = \mathcal{N}_1(\lambda) = \sum_{n=0}^{\infty} \lambda^n A_n = A_0 + \lambda A_1 + \lambda^2 A_2 + \cdots + \lambda^k A_k + \cdots \tag{10}$$

$$\mathcal{N}_2 = \mathcal{N}_2(\lambda) = \sum_{n=0}^{\infty} \lambda^n B_n = B_0 + \lambda B_1 + \lambda^2 B_2 + \cdots + \lambda^k B_k + \cdots \tag{11}$$

$$y = y(\lambda) = \sum_{n=0}^{\infty} \lambda^n D_n = D_0 + \lambda D_1 + \lambda^2 D_2 + \cdots + \lambda^k D_k + \cdots \tag{12}$$

Using the previous formulas (9), (10), (11), and (12), we can conclude that

$$A_n = \frac{1}{n!}\left[\frac{d^n}{d\lambda^n}\left(\mathcal{N}_1 \sum_{j=0}^{\infty} \lambda^j \omega_j\right)\right]_{\lambda=0},$$

$$B_n = \frac{1}{n!}\left[\frac{d^n}{d\lambda^n}\left(\mathcal{N}_2 \sum_{j=0}^{\infty} \lambda^j \omega_j\right)\right]_{\lambda=0},$$

and

$$D_n = \frac{1}{n!}\left[\frac{d^n}{d\lambda^n}\left(y \sum_{j=0}^{\infty} \lambda^j \omega_j\right)\right]_{\lambda=0},$$

where $\omega_0, \omega_1, \omega_2, \ldots$ are repeatedly specified by

$$\begin{cases} \omega_0(\varkappa) = \omega_0 + \mathcal{I}_{0^+}^{\nu;\varsigma}(g(\varkappa)) \\ \omega_{k+1}(\varkappa) = D_k + \mathcal{I}_{0^+}^{\nu;\varsigma}\left(\int_0^{\varkappa} \chi_1(\varkappa,\xi) A_k d\xi\right) \\ \quad +\mathcal{I}_{0^+}^{\nu;\varsigma}\left(\int_0^1 \chi_2(\varkappa,\xi) B_k d\xi\right), \ k \geq 1. \end{cases} \tag{13}$$

Now, we use the modified AD method, and the scheme (13) yields

$$\begin{cases} \omega_0(\varkappa) = \omega_0 + R_1(\varkappa), \\ \omega_1(\varkappa) = R_2(\varkappa) + D_0 + \mathcal{I}_{0^+}^{\nu;\varsigma}\left(\int_0^{\varkappa} \chi_1(\varkappa,\xi) A_0 d\xi\right) \\ \quad +\mathcal{I}_{0^+}^{\nu;\varsigma}\left(\int_0^1 \chi_2(\varkappa,\xi) B_0 d\xi\right), \\ \omega_{k+1}(\varkappa) = D_k + \mathcal{I}_{0^+}^{\nu;\varsigma}\left(\int_0^{\varkappa} \chi_1(\varkappa,\xi) A_k d\xi\right) \\ \quad +\mathcal{I}_{0^+}^{\nu;\varsigma}\left(\int_0^1 \chi_2(\varkappa,\xi) B_k d\xi\right), \ k \geq 1. \end{cases} \tag{14}$$

We will now turn our attention to the convergence of the solution, using the modified Adomian decomposition method.

Theorem 3. *Suppose that* $(H_1) - (H_4)$ *and (2) are all satisfied, if the solution* $\omega(\varkappa) = \sum_{j=0}^{\infty} \omega_j(\varkappa)$ *and* $\|\omega\|_\infty < \infty$ *of the Caputo–Katugampola fractional Volterra–Fredholm integro-differential equation converges, it will converge to the true solution of the equation (1).*

Proof. We omit the proof because it is similar to the proof provided in other works, such as [15]. □

5. An Example

Example 1. *Take into consideration the following integro-differential equation with the CK fractional derivative,*

$$\begin{cases} {}^{C}\mathcal{D}_{0^+}^{\frac{1}{2};\frac{1}{3}}\omega(\varkappa) = \frac{3}{\sqrt{\pi}}\left(\frac{5\varkappa^{\frac{3}{2}}}{\Gamma(7)} + \varkappa^{\frac{1}{2}}\right) + \frac{\varkappa^3}{\Gamma(8)} + \frac{\varkappa}{\Gamma(9)} \\ +\frac{1}{5}\int_0^{\varkappa}(1+\varkappa-\eta)\omega(\eta)d\eta + \frac{7}{20}\int_0^1 e^{\eta-\varkappa}\omega^2(\eta)d\eta, \end{cases} \tag{15}$$

with the non-local condition,

$$\omega(0) = \frac{1}{5}\omega(\frac{1}{4}), \tag{16}$$

where

$$\begin{aligned}
\nu &= \frac{1}{2}, \varsigma = \frac{1}{3}, \; \omega_0 = 0, \; y(\omega(\varkappa)) = \frac{1}{5}\omega(\frac{1}{4}), \\
g(\varkappa) &= \frac{3}{\sqrt{\pi}}\left(\frac{5\varkappa^{\frac{3}{2}}}{\Gamma(7)} + \varkappa^{\frac{1}{2}}\right) + \frac{\varkappa^3}{\Gamma(8)} + \frac{\varkappa}{\Gamma(9)}, \\
\chi_1(\varkappa,\xi) &= \frac{1}{5}(1+\varkappa-\xi), \; \chi_2(\varkappa,\xi) = \frac{7}{20}e^{\xi-\varkappa}.
\end{aligned}$$

Clearly, $\ell_{\mathcal{N}_1} = \ell_{\mathcal{N}_2} = 1$, $\ell_y = \frac{1}{5}$.

$$\begin{aligned}
\mu_g \; &: = \sup_{\varkappa\in[0,1]} |g(\varkappa)| = \|g\|_\infty \\
&= \frac{3}{\sqrt{\pi}}\left(\frac{5}{\Gamma(7)} + 1\right) + \frac{1}{\Gamma(8)} + \frac{1}{\Gamma(9)} \\
&= \frac{3\sqrt{\pi} + 40\,600}{13\,440\sqrt{\pi}}
\end{aligned}$$

and

$$\begin{aligned}
\chi_1^* &= \frac{1}{5}\sup_{\varkappa\in\hbar}\int_0^{\varkappa} |1+\varkappa-\xi| d\xi = \frac{1}{10}. \\
\chi_2^* &= \frac{7}{20}\sup_{\varkappa\in\hbar}\int_0^{\varkappa}\left|e^{\xi-\varkappa}\right| d\xi = \frac{7}{20}\sup_{\varkappa\in\hbar} e^{-\varkappa}\int_0^{\varkappa}\left|e^{\xi}\right| d\xi \\
&= \frac{7}{20}(1-\frac{1}{e}).
\end{aligned}$$

Hence,

$$\Lambda_1 := \left(\ell_y + \frac{\sum_{j=1}^2 \ell_{\mathcal{N}_j}\chi_j^*}{\varsigma^\nu\Gamma(\nu+1)}\right) \approx 0.656\,70 < 1.$$

As a consequence of Theorem 2, the problem (15)–(16) has a unique solution in $[0,1]$. *Applying the operator* $\mathcal{I}_{0^+}^{\frac{1}{2};\frac{1}{3}}$ *to both sides of Equation (15), we get*

$$\begin{aligned}
\omega(\varkappa) &= \frac{1}{5}\omega(\frac{1}{4}) + \mathcal{I}_{0^+}^{\frac{1}{2};\frac{1}{3}}\left(\frac{3}{\sqrt{\pi}}\left(\frac{5\varkappa^{\frac{3}{2}}}{\Gamma(7)} + \varkappa^{\frac{1}{2}}\right) + \frac{\varkappa^3}{\Gamma(8)} + \frac{\varkappa}{\Gamma(9)}\right) \\
&\quad + \mathcal{I}_{0^+}^{\frac{1}{2};\frac{1}{3}}\left(\frac{1}{5}\int_0^{\varkappa}(1+\varkappa-\eta)\omega(\eta)d\eta\right) + \mathcal{I}_{0^+}^{\frac{1}{2};\frac{1}{3}}\left(\frac{7}{20}\int_0^1 e^{\eta-\varkappa}\omega^2(\eta)d\eta\right).
\end{aligned}$$

Suppose

$$\begin{aligned}
R(\varkappa) &= \mathcal{I}_{0^+}^{\frac{1}{2};\frac{1}{3}}\left(\frac{3}{\sqrt{\pi}}\left(\frac{5\varkappa^{\frac{3}{2}}}{\Gamma(7)}+\varkappa^{\frac{1}{2}}\right)+\frac{\varkappa^3}{\Gamma(8)}+\frac{\varkappa}{\Gamma(9)}\right)\\
&= \frac{3}{\sqrt{\pi}}\frac{5}{\Gamma(7)}\left(\mathcal{I}_{0^+}^{\frac{1}{2};\frac{1}{3}}\eta^{\frac{3}{2}}\right)(\varkappa)+\frac{3}{\sqrt{\pi}}\left(\mathcal{I}_{0^+}^{\frac{1}{2};\frac{1}{3}}\eta^{\frac{1}{2}}\right)(\varkappa)\\
&\quad+\frac{1}{\Gamma(8)}\left(\mathcal{I}_{0^+}^{\frac{1}{2};\frac{1}{3}}\eta^{3}\right)(\varkappa)+\frac{1}{\Gamma(9)}\left(\mathcal{I}_{0^+}^{\frac{1}{2};\frac{1}{3}}\eta\right)(\varkappa)\\
&= \frac{3}{\sqrt{\pi}}\frac{5}{\Gamma(7)}\left(\frac{\Gamma(\frac{11}{2})}{\left(\frac{1}{3}\right)^{\frac{1}{2}}\Gamma(6)}\varkappa^{\frac{5}{3}}\right)+\frac{3}{\sqrt{\pi}}\left(\frac{\Gamma(\frac{5}{2})}{\left(\frac{1}{3}\right)^{\frac{1}{2}}\Gamma(3)}\varkappa^{\frac{2}{3}}\right)\\
&\quad+\frac{1}{\Gamma(8)}\left(\frac{\Gamma(10)}{\left(\frac{1}{3}\right)^{\frac{1}{2}}\Gamma(\frac{21}{2})}\varkappa^{\frac{19}{6}}\right)+\frac{1}{\Gamma(9)}\left(\frac{\Gamma(4)}{\left(\frac{1}{3}\right)^{\frac{1}{2}}\Gamma(\frac{9}{2})}\varkappa^{\frac{7}{6}}\right).
\end{aligned}$$

Now, we apply the modified AD method,

$$R(\varkappa) = R_1(\varkappa) + R_2(\varkappa),$$

where

$$R_1(\varkappa) = \frac{15}{\sqrt{\pi}}\frac{\Gamma(\frac{11}{2})}{\left(\frac{1}{3}\right)^{\frac{1}{2}}\Gamma(7)\Gamma(6)}\varkappa^{\frac{5}{3}},$$

and

$$R_2(\varkappa) = \frac{3}{\sqrt{\pi}}\frac{\Gamma(\frac{5}{2})}{\left(\frac{1}{3}\right)^{\frac{1}{2}}\Gamma(3)}\varkappa^{\frac{2}{3}}+\frac{\Gamma(10)}{\left(\frac{1}{3}\right)^{\frac{1}{2}}\Gamma(8)\Gamma(\frac{21}{2})}\varkappa^{\frac{19}{6}}+\frac{\Gamma(4)}{\left(\frac{1}{3}\right)^{\frac{1}{2}}\Gamma(9)\Gamma(\frac{9}{2})}\varkappa^{\frac{7}{6}}.$$

The modified recursive relation

$$\omega_0(\varkappa) = R_1(\varkappa) = \frac{15}{\sqrt{\pi}}\frac{\Gamma(\frac{11}{2})}{\left(\frac{1}{3}\right)^{\frac{1}{2}}\Gamma(7)\Gamma(6)}\varkappa^{\frac{5}{3}},$$

$$\begin{aligned}
\omega_1(\varkappa) &= R_2(\varkappa)+\mathcal{I}_{0^+}^{\frac{1}{2};\frac{1}{3}}\left(\frac{1}{5}\int_0^{\varkappa}(1+\varkappa-\eta)A_0(\eta)d\eta\right)\\
&\quad+\mathcal{I}_{0^+}^{\frac{1}{2};\frac{1}{3}}\left(\frac{7}{20}\int_0^{1}e^{\eta-\varkappa}B_0(\eta)d\eta\right)+D_0(\varkappa)\\
&= \frac{3}{\sqrt{\pi}}\frac{\Gamma(\frac{5}{2})}{\left(\frac{1}{3}\right)^{\frac{1}{2}}\Gamma(3)}\varkappa^{\frac{2}{3}}+\frac{\Gamma(10)}{\left(\frac{1}{3}\right)^{\frac{1}{2}}\Gamma(8)\Gamma(\frac{21}{2})}\varkappa^{\frac{19}{6}}+\frac{\Gamma(4)}{\left(\frac{1}{3}\right)^{\frac{1}{2}}\Gamma(9)\Gamma(\frac{9}{2})}\varkappa^{\frac{7}{6}}\\
&\quad+\mathcal{I}_{0^+}^{\frac{1}{2};\frac{1}{3}}\left(\frac{1}{5}\int_0^{\varkappa}(1+\varkappa-\eta)\omega_0(\eta)d\eta\right)\\
&\quad+\mathcal{I}_{0^+}^{\frac{1}{2};\frac{1}{3}}\left(\frac{7}{20}\int_0^{1}e^{\eta-\varkappa}\omega_0(\eta)d\eta\right)+\frac{1}{5}\omega_0(\frac{1}{4})
\end{aligned}$$

which gives

$$
\begin{aligned}
\omega_1(\varkappa) &= \frac{3}{\sqrt{\pi}}\frac{\Gamma(\frac{5}{2})}{\left(\frac{1}{3}\right)^{\frac{1}{2}}\Gamma(3)}\varkappa^{\frac{2}{3}} + \frac{\Gamma(10)}{\left(\frac{1}{3}\right)^{\frac{1}{2}}\Gamma(8)\Gamma(\frac{21}{2})}\varkappa^{\frac{19}{6}} + \frac{\Gamma(4)}{\left(\frac{1}{3}\right)^{\frac{1}{2}}\Gamma(9)\Gamma(\frac{9}{2})}\varkappa^{\frac{7}{6}} \\
&+ \mathcal{I}_{0^+}^{\frac{1}{2};\frac{1}{3}}\left(\frac{1}{5}\int_0^{\varkappa}(1+\varkappa-\eta)\left(\frac{15}{\sqrt{\pi}}\frac{\Gamma(\frac{11}{2})}{\left(\frac{1}{3}\right)^{\frac{1}{2}}\Gamma(7)\Gamma(6)}\eta^{\frac{5}{3}}\right)d\eta\right) \\
&+ \mathcal{I}_{0^+}^{\frac{1}{2};\frac{1}{3}}\left(\frac{5}{18}\int_0^{1}e^{\eta-\varkappa}\left(\frac{15}{\sqrt{\pi}}\frac{\Gamma(\frac{11}{2})}{\left(\frac{1}{3}\right)^{\frac{1}{2}}\Gamma(7)\Gamma(6)}\eta^{\frac{5}{3}}\right)d\eta\right) \\
&+ \frac{1}{5}\left(\frac{15}{\sqrt{\pi}}\frac{\Gamma(\frac{11}{2})}{\left(\frac{1}{3}\right)^{\frac{1}{2}}\Gamma(7)\Gamma(6)}\right)\left(\frac{1}{4}\right)^{\frac{5}{3}} \\
&= 0,
\end{aligned}
$$

$$\omega_2(\varkappa) = 0,$$

$$\vdots$$

$$\omega_n(\varkappa) = 0.$$

Therefore, the obtained solution is

$$\omega(\varkappa) = \sum_{j=0}^{\infty}\omega_j(\varkappa) = \frac{15}{\sqrt{\pi}}\frac{\Gamma(\frac{11}{2})}{\left(\frac{1}{3}\right)^{\frac{1}{2}}\Gamma(7)\Gamma(6)}\varkappa^{\frac{5}{3}}.$$

6. Conclusions

In this work, we examine a fractional Volterra–Fredholm integro-differential equation, involving the Caputo–Katugampola fractional derivative, as shown in Equation (1). We derive a representation of the solution to this equation, and establish the convergence of approximated solutions and the existence of solutions using classic fixed-point theorems, such as Banach and Krasnoselskii, in addition to the fractional AD technique. We also provide an example, to demonstrate the relevance of these results.

Overall, the study of fractional differential equations has become an important area of research, due to their ability to capture memory effects and non-local behavior in the modeling of real-world phenomena. These equations have a wide range of applications in fields such as physics, engineering, and biology, and further research is necessary, to fully understand and utilize their potential in understanding complex systems. In conclusion, our work adds to the current understanding of fractional integro-differential equations and their solutions.

Author Contributions: Conceptualization, K.S.A.-G. and A.T.A.; Data curation, A.H.A.; Formal analysis, S.S.R. and O.B.; Funding acquisition, L.F.I.; Investigation, S.S.R. and O.B.; Methodology, K.S.A.-G. and A.T.A.; Project administration, L.F.I.; Resources, O.B. and A.H.A.; Supervision, L.F.I.; Validation, S.S.R.; Writing—review & editing, A.H.A. All authors have read and agreed to the published version of the manuscript.

Funding: This research was funded by the University of Oradea.

Institutional Review Board Statement: Not applicable.

Informed Consent Statement: Not applicable.

Data Availability Statement: Not applicable.

Conflicts of Interest: The authors declare no conflict of interest.

References

1. Kilbas, A.A.; Srivastava, H.M.; Trujillo, J.J. *Theory and Applications of Fractional Differential Equations*; Elsevier: Amsterdam, The Netherlands, 2006; Volume 204.
2. Samko, S.G.; Kilbas, A.A.; Marichev, O.I. *Fractional Integrals and Derivatives: Theory and Applications*; Gordon and Breach Science Publishers: Basel, Switzerland; Philadelphia, PA, USA, 1993; ISBN 9782881248641.
3. Anderson, D.R.; Ulness, D.J. Properties of Katugampola fractional derivative with potential application in quantum mechanics. *J. Math. Phys.* **2015**, *56*, 063502. [CrossRef]
4. Janaki, M.; Kanagarajan, K.; Elsayed, E.M. Existence criteria for Katugampola fractional type impulsive differential equations with inclusions. *Math. Sci. Model.* **2019** 2, 51–63.
5. Janaki, M.; Kanagarajan, K.; Vivek, D. Analytic study on fractional implicit differential equations with impulses via Katugampola fractional Derivative. *Int. J. Math. Appl.* **2018**, *6*, 53–62.
6. Vivek, D.; Elsayed, E.M.; Kanagarajan, K. Dynamics and stability results for impulsive type integro-differential equations with generalized fractional derivative. *Math. Nat. Sci.* **2019**, *4*, 1–12. [CrossRef]
7. Vivek, D.; Kanagarajan, K.; Harikrishnan, S. Theory and analysis of impulsive type pantograph equations with Katugampola fractioanl derivative. *J. Vabration Test. Syst. Dyn.* **2018**, *2*, 9–20. [CrossRef]
8. Wang, L.; Liu, G.; Xue, J.; Wong, K.-K. Channel Prediction Using Ordinary Differential Equations for MIMO Systems. *IEEE Trans. Veh. Technol.* **2023**, *72*, 2111–2119. [CrossRef]
9. Li, X.; Dong, Z.Q.; Wang, L.P.; Niu, X.D.; Yamaguchi, H.; Li, D.C.; Yu, P. A magnetic field coupling fractional step lattice Boltzmann model for the complex interfacial behavior in magnetic multiphase flows. *Appl. Math. Model.* **2023**, *117*, 219–250. [CrossRef]
10. Xie, X.; Wang, T.; Zhang, W. Existence of solutions for the (p, q)-Laplacian equation with nonlocal Choquard reaction. *Appl. Math. Lett.* **2023**, *135*, 108418. [CrossRef]
11. Abood, B.N. Approximate solutions and existence of solution for a Caputo nonlocal fractional volterra fredholm integro-differential equation. *Int. J. Appl. Math.* **2020** *33*, 1049. [CrossRef]
12. Gambo, Y.Y.; Jarad, F.; Baleanu, D.; Abdeljawad, T. On Caputo modification of the Hadamard fractional derivatives. *Adv. Differ. Equ.* **2014**, *2014*, 10. [CrossRef]
13. Hilfer, R. Threefold introduction to fractional derivatives. *Anomalous Transp. Found. Appl.* **2008**, 17–73. [CrossRef]
14. Adomian, G. A review of the decomposition method in applied mathematics. *J. Math. Anal. Appl.* **1988**, *135*, 501–544. [CrossRef]
15. Suvinthra, M.; Balachandran K.; Lizzy, R.M. Large deviations for stochastic fractional integrodifferential equations. *AIMS Math.* **2018**, *2*, 348–364. [CrossRef]
16. Almarri, B.; Ali, A.H.; Al-Ghafri, K.S.; Almutairi, A.; Bazighifan, O.; Awrejcewicz, J. Symmetric and Non-Oscillatory Characteristics of the Neutral Differential Equations Solutions Related to p-Laplacian Operators. *Symmetry* **2022**, *14*, 566. [CrossRef]
17. Almarri, B.; Ali, A.H.; Lopes, A.M.; Bazighifan, O. Nonlinear Differential Equations with Distributed Delay: Some New Oscillatory Solutions. *Mathematics* **2022**, *10*, 995. [CrossRef]
18. Almarri, B.; Janaki, S.; Ganesan, V.; Ali, A.H.; Nonlaopon, K.; Bazighifan, O. Novel Oscillation Theorems and Symmetric Properties of Nonlinear Delay Differential Equations of Fourth-Order with a Middle Term. *Symmetry* **2022**, *14*, 585. [CrossRef]
19. Bazighifan, O.; Ali, A.H.; Mofarreh, F.; Raffoul, Y.N. Extended Approach to the Asymptotic Behavior and Symmetric Solutions of Advanced Differential Equations. *Symmetry* **2022**, *14*, 686. [CrossRef]
20. Khan, F.S.; Khalid, M.; Al-Moneef, A.A.; Ali, A.H.; Bazighifan, O. Freelance Model with Atangana–Baleanu Caputo Fractional Derivative. *Symmetry* **2022**, *14*, 2424. [CrossRef]
21. Arshad, U.; Sultana, M.; Ali, A.H.; Bazighifan, O.; Al-moneef, A.A.; Nonlaopon, K. Numerical Solutions of Fractional-Order Electrical RLC Circuit Equations via Three Numerical Techniques. *Mathematics* **2022**, *10*, 3071. [CrossRef]
22. Sultana, M.; Arshad, U.; Ali, A.H.; Bazighifan, O.; Al-Moneef, A.A.; Nonlaopon, K. New Efficient Computations with Symmetrical and Dynamic Analysis for Solving Higher-Order Fractional Partial Differential Equations. *Symmetry* **2022**, *14*, 1653. [CrossRef]
23. Bazighifan, O.; Kumam, P. Oscillation Theorems for Advanced Differential Equations with p-Laplacian Like Operators. *Mathematics* **2020**, *8*, 821. [CrossRef]
24. Bazighifan, O.; Alotaibi, H.; Mousa, A.A.A. Neutral Delay Differential Equations: Oscillation Conditions for the Solutions. *Symmetry* **2021**, *13*, 101. [CrossRef]
25. Adomian, G.; Rach, R. Inversion of nonlinear stochastic operators. *J. Math. Anal. Appl.* **1983**, *91*, 39–46. [CrossRef]
26. Adomian, G.; Sarafyan, D. Numerical solution of differential equations in the deterministie limit of stochastic theory. *Appl. Math. Comput.* **1981**, *8*, 111–119.
27. Duan, J.S.; Rach, R.; Baleanu, D.; Wazwaz, A.M. A review of the Adomian decomposition method and its applications to fractional differential equations. *Commun. Frac. Calc.* **2012**, *3*, 73–99.
28. Mittal, R.; Nigam, R. Solution of fractional integro-differential equations by Adomian decomposition method. *Int. J. Appl. Math. Mech.* **2008**, *4*, 87–94.

29. Rach, R. On the Adomian decomposition method and comparisons with Picard's method. *J. Math. Anal. Appl.* **1987**, *128*, 480–483. [CrossRef]
30. Wazwaz, A.M. A reliable modification of Adomian decomposition method. *Appl. Math. Comput.* **1999**, *102*, 77–86. [CrossRef]
31. Ismail, H.N.A.; Youssef, I.K.; Rageh, T.M. Modification on Adomian decomposition method for solving fractional Riccati differential equation. *Int. Adv. Res. J. Sci. Technol.* **2017**, *4*, 1–10.
32. Redhwan, S.S.; Shaikh, S.; Mohammed, A.B.D.O. Caputo-Katugampola-type implicit fractional differential equation with anti-periodic boundary conditions. *Results Nonlinear Anal.* **2022**, *5*, 12–28. [CrossRef]
33. Redhwan, S.S.; Shaikh, S.L.; Abdo, M.S. Implicit fractional differential equation with anti-periodic boundary condition involving Caputo-Katugampola type. *Aims Math* **2020**, *5*, 3714–3730. [CrossRef]
34. Redhwan, S.S.; Shaikh, S.L.; Abdo, M.S. Theory of Nonlinear Caputo-Katugampola Fractional Differential Equations. *arXiv* **2020**, arXiv:1911.08884.
35. Abood, B.N.; Redhwan, S.S.; Abdo, M.S. Analytical and approximate solutions for generalized fractional quadratic integral equation. *Nonlinear Funct. Anal. Appl.* **2021**, *26*, 497–512.
36. Abdul-Hassan, N.Y.; Ali, A.H.; Park C. A New Fifth-Order Iterative Method Free from Second Derivative for Solving Nonlinear Equations. *J. Appl. Math. Comput.* **2022**, *68*, 2877–2886 [CrossRef]
37. Katugampola, U.N. New approach to a generalized fractional integral. *Appl. Math. Comput.* **2011**, *3*, 860–865. [CrossRef]
38. Katugampola, U.N. A new approach to generalized fractional derivatives. *Bull. Math. Anal. Appl.* **2014**, *6*, 1–15.
39. Almeida R. A Gronwall inequality for a general Caputo fractional operator. *arXiv* **2017**, arXiv:1705.10079.
40. Smart, D.R. *Fixed Point Theorems*; Cambridge University Press: Cambridge, UK, 1980; Volume 66.

symmetry

MDPI

Article

State Feedback Controller Design for a Class of Generalized Proportional Fractional Order Nonlinear Systems

Ali Omar M. Alsharif [1,2], Assaad Jmal [1], Omar Naifar [1], Abdellatif Ben Makhlouf [3,*], Mohamed Rhaima [4] and Lassaad Mchiri [5]

1 Control and Energy Management Laboratory (CEM Lab), Electrical Engineering Department, Engineering National School, Sfax University, Sfax 3038, Tunisia; omar.naifar@enis.tn (O.N.)
2 Department of Electrical & Computer Engineering, Faculty of Engineering, Elmergib University, Alkhums 7206, Libya
3 Department of Mathematics, Faculty of Sciences, Sfax University, Sfax 1171, Tunisia
4 Department of Statistics and Operations Research, College of Sciences, King Saud University, Riyadh 11451, Saudi Arabia; mrhaima.c@ksu.edu.sa
5 ENSIIE, University of Evry-Val-d'Essonne, 1 Square de la Résistance, CEDEX, 91025 Évry-Courcouronnes, France; lassaad.mchiri@ensiie.fr
* Correspondence: abdellatif.benmakhlouf@fss.usf.tn

Abstract: The state feedback controller design for a class of Generalized Proportional Fractional Order (GPFO) Nonlinear Systems is presented in this paper. The design is based on the combination of the One-Sided Lipschitz (OSL) system class with GPFO modeling. The main contribution of this study is that, to the best of the authors' knowledge, this work presents the first state feedback control design for GPFO systems. The suggested state feedback controller is intended to ensure the system's generalized Mittag Leffler (GML) stability and to deliver optimal performance. The findings of this paper show that the proposed strategy is effective in stabilizing Generalized Proportional Fractional Order Nonlinear Systems. A numerical example is presented to demonstrate the usefulness of the stated theoretical conclusions.

Keywords: Generalized Proportional Fractional Differential Equations; Generalized Proportional Fractional Derivative; state feedback controller; Lipschitz; One-Sided Lipschitz

Citation: Alsharif, A.O.M.; Jmal, A.; Naifar, O.; Ben Makhlouf, A.; Rhaima, M.; Mchiri, L. State Feedback Controller Design for a Class of Generalized Proportional Fractional Order Nonlinear Systems. *Symmetry* **2023**, *15*, 1168. https://doi.org/10.3390/sym15061168

Academic Editors: Dongfang Li and Junesang Choi

Received: 6 May 2023
Revised: 20 May 2023
Accepted: 26 May 2023
Published: 29 May 2023

1. Introduction

GPFDEs (Generalized Proportional Fractional Differential Equations) are a form of mathematical equation that describes the temporal evolution of a system using fractional derivatives of non-integer order. These equations are used to simulate a wide range of physical and biological phenomena, such as anomalous diffusion, fractional oscillators, and aging processes. GPFDEs are broader than classical differential equations and can describe systems with memory and non-local interactions more accurately. In [1], the authors have introduced a revolutionary fractional derivative. This new derivative, dubbed the "Generalized Proportional Fractional Derivative (GPFD)", retains the semigroup feature while embracing its nonlocality. As a result, under limiting cases, it easily transitions from the original function to its derivative, as seen in [2]. A fractional derivative with a non-singular kernel function and a non-local operator is known as a GPFD. When compared to traditional derivatives such as the integer-order derivative and the Caputo Fractional Derivative (CFD), it is a more generic and versatile tool for describing complicated processes. GPFD is very beneficial for dealing with memory and non-locality systems, such as diffusion processes, viscoelasticity, and anomalous transport. Furthermore, the GPFD allows for the consideration of varying order derivatives, allowing for the capture of various degrees of smoothness or roughness in the underlying signal. Overall, the GPFD is an effective tool for modeling and evaluating complex systems in physics, engineering, and finance [3–5].

State Feedback Controller Design for Nonlinear Systems, on the other hand, is a hard and active topic of study in control systems engineering. Because of nonlinearities, uncertainties, and disturbances, nonlinear systems display complicated behaviors and are frequently difficult to manage. Numerous research has been conducted in recent years with the goal of establishing state feedback control techniques for nonlinear systems. Refs. [6–9] are some recent references on this subject. These references highlight current attempts to create nonlinear state feedback control techniques. Ref. [6] offers a state-feedback control technique for nonlinear systems based on adaptive dynamic programming and feedback linearization. Ref. [7] provides an adaptive state-feedback control approach for nonlinear systems with time-varying delay, whereas [8] develops a state-feedback control technique for nonlinear neural network systems. These recent breakthroughs in state feedback control design for nonlinear systems emphasize ongoing research efforts in this subject and the creation of new and improved control techniques for solving nonlinear system difficulties. In [9], the authors have suggested an LMI-based study about state feedback stability for Lipschitz uncertain systems, with time delay. On the other hand, some other works have focused on output feedback control, rather than state feedback control. This is the case in [10], where the authors have investigated the output-tracking problem of high-order time-delayed nonlinear systems. Another interesting work [11] has tackled the output feedback control problem for uncertain linear systems, using the separation principle.

Stabilization has gained a lot of attention in recent years when it comes to Fractional Order Nonlinear Systems (FONSs). Fractional calculus has shown to be a useful tool for modeling complicated systems, with numerous applications in physics, engineering, and biology. In a noteworthy study [3], the authors have investigated the stability of a class of Fractional-Order delayed artificial neural networks. Control and design of FONSs rely heavily on stability analysis. Several strategies for stabilizing FONSs have been presented in recent years. One of the most recent references is Zhang et al. [12], where the authors proposed a sliding mode control technique for the stabilization of fractional order chaotic systems. The authors conducted a theoretical study of fractional order chaotic system stability and demonstrated that the suggested sliding mode control rule may successfully stabilize the system. Another recent reference is the work of Liu et al. [13], which presented a backstepping control approach for the stabilization of FONSs with uncertainties. The authors formulated necessary requirements for the stability of FONSs and demonstrated that the suggested backstepping control rule may successfully stabilize the system even when uncertainties exist. In a noteworthy study, Wang et al. [14] suggested a fuzzy control approach for the stabilization of FONSs with uncertainties in their study. The authors performed a stability analysis of FONSs and demon strated that the suggested fuzzy control rule may successfully stabilize the system even when uncertainties exist. The recent paper [15] investigated the synchronous control of a class of fractional chaotic systems. In the end of this paragraph, it is important to highlight that more study is needed to solve the issues of FONS stabilization and to create more efficient control approaches. Finally, in [16], the authors have tackled the synchronization of a class of Fractional-Order delayed artificial neural networks.

Some criteria may be taken into account while stabilizing nonlinear systems. Regarding the linearity aspect, writers typically utilize the nonlinear Lipschitz condition or the One-sided Lipschitz (OSL) condition. The OSL system class is a large category of nonlinear systems. The OSL constant can be smaller than the Lipschitz constant, and this difference can have a major influence even in basic nonlinear systems [17–19]. The importance of the OSL condition arises from its capacity to ensure the stability of nonlinear systems. This condition establishes constraints on the system's behavior, allowing predictions and preventing instability. The OSL condition is frequently used in the field of control and optimization because it provides a helpful tool for constructing stable nonlinear control systems. Furthermore, the combination of fractional order modeling with the OSL condition can improve the stability of nonlinear systems, making it a viable alternative for dealing with complicated control and optimization issues. The OSL condition is a feature of particular functions that can provide varied benefits in specific applications. The advantages of the OSL class of systems include, first and foremost, a broader range of systems than the standard Lipschitz category. Second, =algorithm convergence should be considered: because many optimization techniques rely on the Lipschitz continuity of the gradient or Jacobian function to ensure convergence, the OSL condition can help ensure the convergence of these algorithms.

The combination of the OSL class of systems with the Generalized Proportional (GP) Fractional Order modeling to solve the stabilization challenge for a wide variety of FONSs is this work's main contribution. No previous study, to the best of our knowledge, has addressed the state feedback control problem for Generalized Proportional FONSs.

2. Preliminaries and System Description

In this part, the basic Definitions and Lemmas are presented, as well as some Remarks related to the GPFD and the Generalized Fractional Proportional Integral (GFPI).

Thus, we remember that the GP fractional operators of the function $\in AC([a,b],\mathbb{R})$, $a<b$, are defined as follows (see [20]):

- The GFPI:

$$I_{t_0,t}^{\alpha,\lambda}v(t)=\frac{1}{\lambda^{\alpha}\Gamma(\alpha)}\int_{t_0}^{t}e^{\frac{\lambda-1}{\lambda}(t-s)}(t-s)^{\alpha-1}v(s)ds,\ for\ t\in(a,b],\ \alpha>0,\ 0<\lambda\le 1.$$

- The GPFD:

$$^{C}D_{t_0,t}^{\alpha,\lambda}v(t)=I_{t_0,t}^{1-\alpha,\lambda}D_t^{1,\lambda}v(t)=\frac{1}{\lambda^{1-\alpha}\Gamma(1-\alpha)}\int_{t_0}^{t}e^{\frac{\lambda-1}{\lambda}(t-s)}(t-s)^{-\alpha}D_t^{1,\lambda}v(s)ds,\ for\ t\in(a,b],\ 0<\alpha<1,\ 0<\lambda\le 1,$$

where $D_t^{1,\lambda}v(s)=(1-\lambda)v(s)+\lambda v'(s)$.

The previous equation defines the GPFD as an extension of the CFD ($\lambda=1$).

Lemma 1 [21]. *Let $0<\alpha<1,\ 0<\lambda\le 1$ and S be a constant and symmetric, definite positive matrix. Then,*

$$^{C}D_{0,t}^{\alpha,\lambda}v^{T}Sv(t)\le 2v^{T}(t)S\,{}^{C}D_{0,t}^{\alpha,\lambda}v(t).$$

Definition 1 [2]. *The Mittag-Leffler (ML) functions can be defined with one or two parameters, respectively, as follows:*

$$E_{\alpha}(z)=\sum_{k=0}^{\infty}\frac{z^k}{\Gamma(1+k\alpha)}\ \text{and}\ E_{\alpha,\beta}(z)=\sum_{k=0}^{\infty}\frac{z^k}{\Gamma(\beta+k\alpha)}.$$

Consider the system:

$$^{C}D_{0,t}^{\alpha,\lambda}w(t)=\phi(w,t)\ \text{for}\ t\ge 0,\ \lambda\in(0,1),\alpha\in(0,1] \qquad (*)$$

Definition 2 [22]. *Let $\alpha\in(0,1)$ and $\lambda\in(0,1]$. The equilibrium point $w=0$ of (*) is called GML stable if $\exists\ h,\mu,\gamma>0$ such that for $\forall\ w(\cdot)$ of (*), the inequality.*

$$\|w(t)\|\le m(\|(w(0)\|)e^{h\,\frac{\lambda-1}{\lambda}\,t}(E_{\alpha}(-\mu t^{\alpha}))^{\gamma},t\ge 0,$$

is satisfied, where $E_{\alpha}(z)$ is the ML function with one parameter, $m(s)\ge 0, m(0)=0$, is a given locally Lipschitz function.

Lemma 2 [9,10]. *(Schur Complement Lemma): Given constant matrices M, N, and Q, of appropriate dimensions, where M and Q are symmetric, then:*

$$\begin{cases} Q > 0 \\ M + N^T Q^{-1} N < 0 \end{cases} \text{if and only if} \begin{bmatrix} M & N^T \\ N & -Q \end{bmatrix} < 0$$

Lemma 3 [20]. *For any matrices* $x \in \mathbb{R}^n$ *and* $y \in \mathbb{R}^n$ *and any* $P \in \mathbb{R}_+^{n\times n}$ *the following is true:*

$$2x^T y \leq x^T P x + y^T P^{-1} y$$

Talking about nonlinearity, most of published research works use the classical Lipschitz nonlinearity (given in Definition 3). In this work, we rather assume that the system nonlinearity verifies the OSL condition and the "Quadratically Inner Bounded" condition, as detailed in the next lines.

Definition 3. *A nonlinear function* $f(x)$ *is a Lipschitz in* $\mathbb{R}^n$ *with a Lipschitz constant* $\widetilde{\alpha}$, *i.e.,*

$$\|f(x_1) - f(x_2)\| \leq \widetilde{\alpha}\|x_1 - x_2\| \tag{1}$$

Assumption 1. *The nonlinear function* $f(x,u)$ *is OSL in* $\mathbb{R}^n$ *with a OSL constant* ρ, *i.e.,*

$$\langle f(x_1,u) - f(x_2,u), x_1 - x_2\rangle \leq \rho\|x_1 - x_2\|^2 \tag{2}$$

Assumption 2. *The nonlinear function* $f(x,u)$ *is Quadratically Inner Bounded (QIB) in* $\mathbb{R}^n$, *i.e.,*

$$\|f(x_1,u) - f(x_2,u)\|^2 \leq \beta\|x_1 - x_2\|^2 + \gamma\langle f(x_1,u) - f(x_2,u), x_1 - x_2\rangle \tag{3}$$

This study focuses on the examination of the nonlinear fractional order system presented below:

$$\begin{cases} {}^C D_{0,t}^{\alpha,\lambda} x(t) = Ax(t) + Bu(t) + f(x(t)), \\ y(t) = Cx(t), \end{cases} \tag{4}$$

where $x(t) \in \mathbb{R}^n$, $u(t) \in \mathbb{R}^m$, and $y(t) \in \mathbb{R}^p$. $A \in \mathbb{R}^{n\times n}, B \in \mathbb{R}^{n\times m}$, and $C \in \mathbb{R}^{p\times n}$ are assumed to be known constant matrices. Additionally, it is supposed that (A, B) is stabilizable and $f(\cdot) : \mathbb{R}^n \rightarrow \mathbb{R}^n$.

3. State Feedback Controller Design for Lipschitz Fractional Order Nonlinear System

In this section, the nonlinear part is assumed to be Lipschitz satisfying the condition (2). A state feedback controller is proposed. Regarding this objective, the state feedback control input is considered to be:

$$u(t) = -Kx(t), \tag{5}$$

where $K \in \mathbb{R}^{m\times n}$ is the constant matrix gain as determined by Theorem 1.

Theorem 1. *Consider the system described in Equation (4) with the control input described in Equation (5). Under condition (1), if a constant positive scalar* ζ, *a matrix* $G \in \mathbb{R}^{m\times n}$, *and a symmetric positive definite matrix* $Q \in \mathbb{R}^{m\times n}$ *exist, then the origin of the system of Equation (1) is GML stable if*:

$$\begin{pmatrix} AQ + QA^T - G^T B^T - BG + \frac{1}{\zeta} I_n & Q \\ Q & -\frac{1}{\widetilde{\alpha}^2 \zeta} \end{pmatrix} < 0, \tag{6}$$

where the gain K is obtained from $K = GQ^{-1}$.

Proof. The closed-loop dynamical system is obtained from substitution of Equation (5) in Equation (4) as:

$$^C D_{0,t}^{\alpha,\lambda} x(t) = (A - BK)x(t) + f(x(t)) \tag{7}$$

One selects the Lyapunov candidate function $V(t,x) = x^T P x$ where $P \in \mathbb{R}^{n\times n}$ such as $P = P^T > 0$. Using Lemma 1, and substituting $f(x(t))$ by f, the derivative of V along (6) is obtained:

$$\begin{aligned} {}^C D_{0,t}^{\alpha,\lambda} V(t,x) &\leq x^T \left[(A - BK)^T P + P(A - BK) \right] x + 2fPx \\ &\leq x^T \left[(A - BK)^T P + P(A - BK) + \widetilde{\alpha}^2 \zeta I_n + \tfrac{1}{\zeta} P^2 \right] x \\ &= x^T \Lambda x, \end{aligned} \tag{8}$$

where $\zeta > 0$ and $\Lambda = (A - BK)^T P + P(A - BK) + \widetilde{\alpha}^2 \zeta I_n + \frac{1}{\zeta} P^2$.

Note that, according to Lemma 3, the following fact was utilized:

$$\begin{aligned} 2fPx &\leq 2\|f\|\|Px\| \\ &\leq 2\widetilde{\alpha}\|x\|\|Px\| \\ &\leq x^T \left[\widetilde{\alpha}^2 \zeta I_n + \tfrac{1}{\zeta} P^2 \right] x, \end{aligned} \tag{9}$$

To ensure the stability of the controlled system, we must have $\Lambda < 0$. This matrix inequality may be rewritten as:

$$AQ + QA^T - G^T B^T - BG + \widetilde{\alpha}^2 \zeta Q^2 + \frac{1}{\zeta} I_n < 0, \tag{10}$$

where $Q = P^{-1}$ and $G = KQ$.

In this case, $\exists r > 0$ such that ${}^C D_{0,t}^{\alpha,\lambda} V(t,x) < -rV(t,x)$. Using Lemma 2, inequality (10) is equivalent to (6). Therefore, it follows from Corollary 2 in [22] that the origin of the system is GML stable. □

Remark 1. *Theorem 1 presents a fundamental extension of the classical feedback control law for Lipschitz nonlinear systems [23], providing a comprehensive generalization. Specifically, in the context of Generalized Proportional Fractional order nonlinear systems, this unique generalization has not been addressed in existing literature.*

4. State Feedback Controller Design for OSL Fractional Order Nonlinear System

In this section, the nonlinear part is assumed to be OSL and QIB satisfying conditions (2) and (3). The same state feedback controller is proposed (5).

The following Theorem shows our main result for this section:

Theorem 2. *One considers the system (4). Under conditions (2) and (3), the control law (5) stabilizes system (4) if there exist matrices $Q = Q^T > 0$, W and positive scalars τ_1, τ_2 and ε, such that the following LMI holds:*

$$\begin{pmatrix} QA^T + AQ - WB^T - BW^T & P + 2(\tau_2\gamma - \tau_1)I & Q \\ * & -2\tau_2 I & 0 \\ * & * & -\dfrac{1}{\mu + \varepsilon} I \end{pmatrix} < 0, \tag{11}$$

where $Q = P^{-1}$ and $W = P^{-1}K^T$, and $\mu = 2\tau_1\rho + 2\tau_2\beta$.

Proof. Let: $V(t,x) = x^T P x$. Using (4), (5), and Lemma 1, and substituting $f(x(t))$ by f, we obtain:

$$\begin{aligned} {}^C D_{0,t}^{\alpha,\lambda} V(t,x) &\leq {}^C D_{0,t}^{\alpha,\lambda} x^T P x + x^T p \, {}^C D_{0,t}^{\alpha,\lambda} x \\ &\leq ((A - BK)x + f)^T P x + x^T P((A - BK)x + f) \\ &\leq x^T ((A - BK)^T P + P(A - BK))x + 2f^T P x \end{aligned} \tag{12}$$

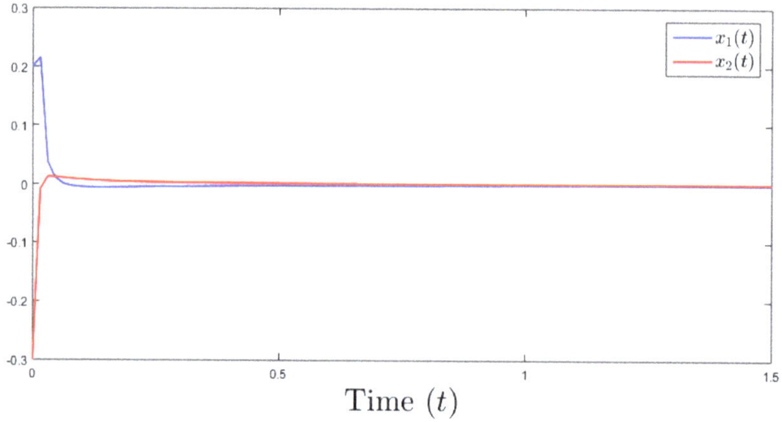

Figure 2. The trajectory simulation of x_1 and x_2 for $\alpha = 0.4$ and $\lambda = 1$.

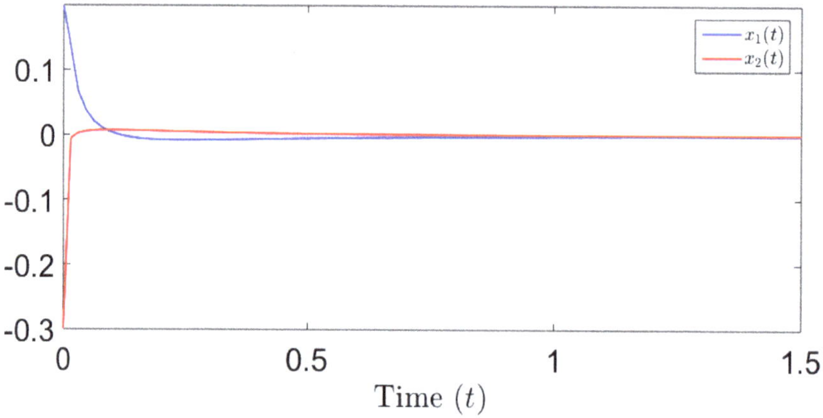

Figure 3. The trajectory simulation of x_1 and x_2 for $\alpha = 0.7$ and $\lambda = 0.7$.

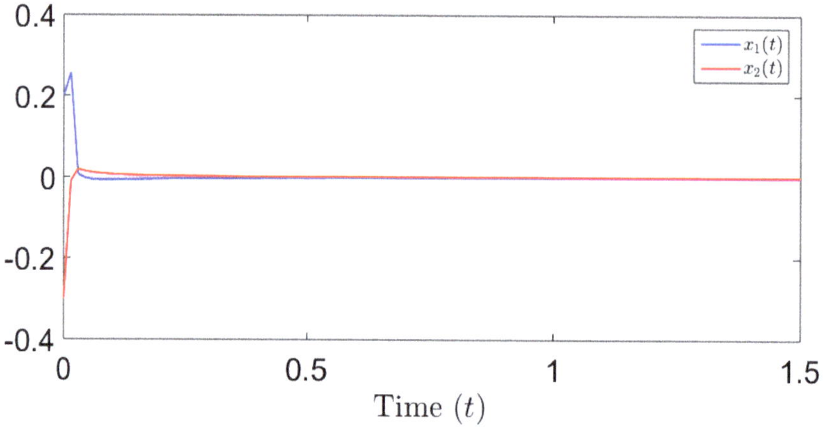

Figure 4. The trajectory simulation of x_1 and x_2 for $\alpha = 0.3$ and $\lambda = 0.8$.

The figures presented, namely Figures 1–4, showcase the convergence of the system states towards zero with various values of α and λ. Specifically, the Mittag-Leffler convergence of the system states is observed through these figures. The results presented in the figures provide strong evidence for the efficacy of the proposed control approach.

6. Conclusions

In this work, a state feedback controller has been designed for a category of GPFO Nonlinear Systems. The design has been based on the integration of the OSL class of systems and GPFO modeling. This study aims to stabilize a broad range of fractional order nonlinear systems, which has not been tackled in prior research. The stabilization method has been designed to guarantee the GML stability of the system and achieve desirable performance. The outcomes of this work showcase the feasibility and efficiency of the suggested approach in stabilizing GPFO nonlinear systems. To guarantee the practicality of the proposed theoretical results, an illustrative numerical example has been presented. As a future outlook, this work can be expanded to include other control techniques such as fuzzy control, sliding mode control, backstepping control, etc. Furthermore, the inclusion of a practical example would offer an opportunity to showcase the real-world applicability of our theoretical framework, enabling practitioners to witness firsthand its effectiveness in solving practical problems. Moreover, incorporating a practical example in future research endeavors would not only serve as a means of validating our theoretical findings but also facilitate the identification of potential challenges, limitations, and avenues for further improvement, ultimately enhancing the practical value and impact of our work.

Author Contributions: Conceptualization, O.N. and A.J.; methodology, A.B.M.; software, M.R.; validation, L.M.; formal analysis, A.O.M.A.; investigation, A.B.M.; resources, L.M.; writing—original draft preparation, O.N. and A.O.M.A.; writing—review and editing, A.J. All authors have read and agreed to the published version of the manuscript.

Funding: This research is funded by "Researchers Supporting Project number (RSPD2023R683), King Saud University, Riyadh, Saudi Arabia".

Data Availability Statement: Not applicable.

Acknowledgments: The authors extend their appreciation to King Saud University in Riyadh, Saudi Arabia for funding this research work through Researchers Supporting Project number (RSPD2023R683).

Conflicts of Interest: The authors declare no conflict of interest.

References

1. Jarad, F.; Abdeljawad, T.; Alzabut, J. Generalized fractional derivatives generated by a class of local proportional derivatives. *Eur. Phys. J. Spec. Top.* **2017**, *226*, 3457–3471. [CrossRef]
2. Alzabut, J.; Abdeljawad, T.; Jarad, F.; Sudsutad, W. A Gronwall inequality via the generalized proportional fractional derivative with applications. *Inequalities* **2019**, *2019*, 101. [CrossRef]
3. Xu, Y.; Yu, J.; Li, W.; Feng, J. Global asymptotic stability of fractional-order competitive neural networks with multiple time-varying-delay links. *Appl. Math. Comput.* **2021**, *389*, 125498. [CrossRef]
4. Atangana, A.; Baleanu, B. New fractional derivatives with non-local and non-singular kernel: Theory and application to heat transfer model. *Therm. Sci.* **2016**, *20*, 763–769. [CrossRef]
5. Rashid, S.; Jarad, F.; Hammouch, Z. Some new bounds analogous to generalized proportional fractional integral operator with respect to another function. *Discret. Contin. Dyn. Syst. Ser. S* **2021**, *14*, 3703–3718. [CrossRef]
6. Zhang, L.; Chen, Y.; Zhang, X. State-feedback stabilization control of nonlinear systems via adaptive dynamic programming and feedback linearization. *Int. J. Control.* **2019**, *95*, 751–761.
7. Elias, L.J.; Faria, F.A.; Magossi, R.F.; Oliveira, V.A. Switched control design for nonlinear systems using state feedback. *J. Control. Autom. Electr. Syst.* **2022**, *33*, 733–742. [CrossRef]
8. Gao, S.; Zhao, D.; Yan, X.; Spurgeon, S.K. Model-Free Adaptive State Feedback Control for a Class of Nonlinear Systems. In *IEEE Transactions on Automation Science and Engineering*; IEEE: Piscataway, NJ, USA, 2023.
9. Golestani, M.; Mobayen, S.; HosseinNia, S.H.; Shamaghdari, S. An LMI approach to nonlinear state-feedback stability of uncertain time-delay systems in the presence of Lipschitzian nonlinearities. *Symmetry* **2020**, *12*, 1883. [CrossRef]
10. Alimhan, K.; Mamyrbayev, O.J.; Abdenova, G.A.; Akmetkalyeva, A. Output tracking control for high-order nonlinear systems with time delay via output feedback design. *Symmetry* **2021**, *13*, 675. [CrossRef]

11. Krokavec, D.; Filasova, A. On the Separation Principle in Dynamic Output Controller Design for Uncertain Linear Systems. *Symmetry* **2022**, *14*, 2239. [CrossRef]
12. Yin, C.; Zhong, S.; Chen, W. Design of sliding mode controller for a class of fractional-order chaotic systems. *Commun. Nonlinear Sci. Numer. Simul.* **2012**, *17*, 356–366. [CrossRef]
13. Zirkohi, M.M. Robust adaptive backstepping control of uncertain fractional-order nonlinear systems with input time delay. *Math. Comput. Simul.* **2022**, *196*, 251–272. [CrossRef]
14. Li, L.; Sun, Y. Adaptive Fuzzy Control for Nonlinear Fractional-Order Uncertain Systems with Unknown Uncertainties and External Disturbance. *Entropy* **2015**, *17*, 5580–5592. [CrossRef]
15. Lei, T.; Mao, B.; Zhou, X.; Fu, H. Dynamics Analysis and Synchronous Control of Fractional-Order Entanglement Symmetrical Chaotic Systems. *Symmetry* **2021**, *13*, 1996. [CrossRef]
16. Guo, Y.; Li, Y. Bipartite leader-following synchronization of fractional-order delayed multilayer signed networks by adaptive and impulsive controllers. *Appl. Math. Comput.* **2022**, *430*, 127243. [CrossRef]
17. Hairer, E.; Norsett, S.P.; Wanner, G. *Solving Ordinary Differntial Equations II: Stiff and DAE Problems*; Springer: Berlin/Heidelberg, Germany, 1993.
18. Dekker, K.; Verwer, J.G. *Stability of Runge-Kutta Methods for Stiff Nonlinear Differetial Equations*; North-Holland: Amsterdam, The Netherlands, 1984.
19. Dong, Y.; Liu, W.; Liang, S. Nonlinear observer design for one-sided Lipschitz systems with time-varying delay and uncertainties. *Int. J. Robust Nonlinear Control* **2017**, *27*, 1974–1998. [CrossRef]
20. Khosrowjerdi, M.J.; Barzegary, S. Fault tolerant control using virtual actuator for continuous-time Lipschitz nonlinear systems. *Int. J. Robust Nonlinear Control* **2014**, *24*, 2597–2607. [CrossRef]
21. Almeida, R.; Agarwal, R.P.; Hristova, S.; O'Regan, D. Quadratic Lyapunov Functions for Stability of the Generalized Proportional Fractional Differential Equations with Applications to Neural Networks. *Axioms* **2021**, *10*, 322. [CrossRef]
22. Agarwal, R.; Hristova, S.; O'Regan, D. Stability of Generalized Proportional Caputo Fractional Differential Equations by Lyapunov Functions. *Fractal Fract.* **2022**, *6*, 34. [CrossRef]
23. Yadegar, M.; Afshar, A.; Davoodi, M. Observer-based tracking controller design for a class of Lipschitz nonlinear systems. *J. Vib. Control.* **2018**, *24*, 2112–2119. [CrossRef]

symmetry

Article

Analysis of the Mathematical Modelling of COVID-19 by Using Mild Solution with Delay Caputo Operator

Kinda Abuasbeh [1,*], Ramsha Shafqat [2,*], Ammar Alsinai [3,*] and Muath Awadalla [1]

1 Department of Mathematics and Statistics, College of Science, King Faisal University, Hafuf 31982, Al Ahsa, Saudi Arabia
2 Department of Mathematics and Statistics, The University of Lahore, Sargodha 40100, Pakistan
3 Department of Studies in Mathematics, University of Mysore, Manasagangotri, Mysore 570006, India
* Correspondence: kabuasbeh@kfu.edu.sa (K.A.); ramshawarriach@gmail.com (R.S.); aliiammar1985@gmail.com (A.A.)

Abstract: This work investigates a mathematical fractional-order model that depicts the Caputo growth of a new coronavirus (COVID-19). We studied the existence and uniqueness of the linked solution using the fixed point theory method. Using the Laplace Adomian decomposition method (LADM), we explored the precise solution of our model and obtained results that are stated in terms of infinite series. Numerical data were then used to demonstrate the use of the new derivative and the symmetric structure that we created. When compared to the traditional order derivatives, our results under the new hypothesis show that the innovative coronavirus model performs better.

Keywords: COVID-19; fractional epidemic model; Caputo operator; existence and uniqueness; numerical simulations

MSC: 34K37; 34B15

Citation: Abuasbeh, K.; Shafqat, R.; Alsinai, A.; Awadalla, M. Analysis of the Mathematical Modelling of COVID-19 by Using Mild Solution with Delay Caputo Operator. *Symmetry* **2023**, *15*, 286. https://doi.org/10.3390/sym15020286

Academic Editor: Dumitru Baleanu

Received: 28 December 2022
Revised: 12 January 2023
Accepted: 15 January 2023
Published: 19 January 2023

1. Introduction

In the last month of 2019, a severe respiratory disease outbreak started in Wuhan City, Hubei Province, China [1]. At the beginning of January 2020, the clinical diagnosis was identified and isolated from a single patient, and the disease was termed COVID-19 or the novel coronavirus. Animals were the first source of this virus's spread. However, the ratio of reported cases increased as a result of human interaction [2]. According to recent research, the virus has nearly reached every corner of the globe. Up to 7 December 2020, approximately 66,243,918 people have been reported as infected with the disease, which has resulted in 1,528,984 deaths. Because of its widespread distribution, the infection is contagious and has been revealed as a global epidemic by the WHO. Generally, virus symptoms may include fever, fatigue, coughing, and respiratory problems, among others. Studies have focused on infectious diseases because of their danger to civilization and novel aspects. See, for example, [3,4] for a review article on infection prevention epidemiology. Fractional calculus, fractional differential and integro-differential equations, and the qualitative theory of these equations have all been included in the discipline of mathematical analysis over the past three decades, both on a theoretical level and in terms of its practical applications. Fundamentally, the theory of fractional calculus, the qualitative theory of fractional differential and fractional integro-differential equations and their numerical simulations, and symmetry analyses are all mathematical analysis tools that are used to study arbitrary order integrals and derivatives. Moreover, they unify and generalize the traditional notions of differentiation and integration. Nonlinear operators with fractional order are more practical than classical formulations. Numerous scientific disciplines, including fluid mechanics, viscoelasticity, physics, biology, chemistry, dynamical systems, signal processing, entropy theory, and others, can involve qualitative theory of fractional differential equations, fractional integro-differential equations, and fractional order operators. Because of this, the applications of the theory of fractional calculus and the qualitative theory of the aforementioned equations have drawn the attention of academics throughout the world, and many scholars have included them in their latest study. Numerous studies have used different analytical techniques to analyze the existing coronavirus pandemic [5,6]. There are several mathematical models in the research for the existing global epidemic that predict the disease's future. Several researchers [7,8] have provided different control techniques. Previously, Khan et al. [9] described the spectral transfer of information of a novel coronavirus using a mathematical model and introduced control techniques to exterminate the infection. Their model is describe as follows:

$$\begin{aligned} \frac{dS_h(v)}{dv} &= \Pi^* - \beta_1^* I_h(v) + d^* + \beta_2^* W(v) S_h(v), \\ \frac{dI_h(v)}{dv} &= \beta_1^* I_h(v) + \beta_2^* W(v) S_h(v) - (\sigma^* + d_1^* + d^*) I_h(v), \\ \frac{dR_h(v)}{dv} &= \sigma^* I_h(v) - d^* R_h(v), \\ \frac{dW(v)}{dv} &= \alpha^* I_h(v) - \eta^* W(v). \end{aligned} \tag{1}$$

In model (1), the letters $S_h(v)$, $I_h(v)$, and $R_h(v)$ represent the susceptible, infected, and recovered populations, respectively, whereas $W(v)$ represents the reservoir compartment. The parameter Π^* denotes the rate of newborns considered to be susceptible. The variables $\beta1^*$ and $\beta2^*$ represent the rates of the transmission of infection from reservoirs and infected individuals to susceptible populations, respectively. The natural mortality rate is represented by the symbol d^*, whereas disease-related death is represented by the symbol d_1^*. Similarly, the recovery rate is σ^*, the virus removal rate is η^*, and the amount that the virus contributed to the seafood market is α^*.

First, we demonstrate that model (1)'s strategies are bounded. Consider that $N(v)$ is the entire population at time v. By taking the sequential derivative of $N(v)$ and utilizing values from the fitted model, we have

$$\frac{dN(v)}{dv} - dN \leq \Pi^*.$$

The solution of this equation under the boundary conditions $S_h(0) \geq 0, I_h(0) \geq 0, R_h(0) \geq 0, W(0) \geq 0$ and $N(0) = N_0$ has the form

$$N(v) \leq \frac{\Pi^*}{d^*} + \left(N_0 - \frac{\Pi^*}{d^*}\right) e^{-d^* v}.$$

When v expands without limitation, this solution will be bounded. For the above model (1), the feasible uniform states (i.e., disease-free (DFE) and inherent) and the threshold amount (basic breeding amount) have been discussed, along with a detailed qualitative analysis. When the v parameter rises without a bound, the solution $(S_{h0}, 0, 0, 0, 0)$, where $\frac{\Pi^*}{d^*}$ becomes constrained:

$$\begin{aligned} R_0 &= \frac{\beta_1 \Pi^*}{d^*(\sigma^* + d^* + d_1^*)} + \frac{\alpha^* \beta_2^* \Pi^*}{\eta^* d^* (\sigma^* + d^* + d_1^*)}, \\ S_h^* &= \frac{\eta^*(\sigma^* + d^* + d_1^*)}{\eta^* \beta_1^* + \alpha^* \beta_2^*}, \\ I_h^* &= \frac{\eta^* d^* (\sigma^* + d^* + d_1^*)(R_0 - 1)}{\sigma \beta_1^* \eta^* + \sigma^* \beta_1^* \alpha^* + d^* \beta_1^* \alpha^* + d_1^* \beta_1^* \eta^* + d_1^* \beta_2^* \alpha^*}, \\ R_h^* &= \frac{\sigma^*}{d^*} I_h^*, \\ W^* &= \frac{\alpha^* \eta^* (\sigma^* + d^* + d_1^*)(R_0 - 1)}{\sigma^* \beta_1^* \eta^* + \sigma^* \beta_1^* \alpha^* + d^* \beta_1^* \alpha^* + d_1^* \beta_1^* \eta^* + d_1^* \beta_2^* \alpha^*}, \\ R_h^* &= \frac{\sigma^*}{d^*} I_h^*. \end{aligned} \tag{2}$$

Lebniz tried to draw researchers interest toward fractional-order derivatives. Owing to the unavailability of solutions for fractional-order differential equations, scientists did not commonly work in the area. When fractional-order derivatives and integrals were established, the field was mainly concentrated because the classic models did not clarify them correctly and came with many mistakes. Fractional order epidemic models contribute better to a deeper understanding of models while accounting for all lacking factors. As a result, a few scientists have been drawn to the field and contribute to microbiology. Discovering a real scenario that can be clarified by a fractional-order model, on the other hand, is a complex job. These models are more autonomous than traditional models. These models have the capacity to use the mathematical strategy to address non-integer order nonlinear systems. This scenario has prompted numerous investigators to use the fractional-order system when modifying the integral order models. In particular, integer-order derivatives do not explore evolution more precisely than fractional derivatives. A number of theoretical physicists have used factors determined by fractional derivatives in describing numerous numerical solutions. Caputo, Hadamard, Riemann, and Liouville (RL), among others [10,11], have introduced numerous beneficial concepts. A variety of methods, such as iterative and numerical methods, were used to examine fractional mathematical models in the traditional Caputo derivative notion, as shown in [12]. The aforementioned derivative has a singular kernel, which complicates fractional-order derivatives. Caputo and Fabrizio presented a novel concept for the fractional-order derivative known as the non-kernel [13,14]. Based on the Caputo–Fabrizio (CF) fractional integral, some significant results have been mentioned. These investigations demonstrate that the aforementioned operator is, in essence, the function's fractional estimate with a fractional integral in the RL context. The aforementioned derivative has been revealed to have potential advantages in heat transfer and fabric sciences [15]. LADM is a beneficial tool for solving analytically estimated nonlinear problems. This model has been widely applied to solve problems involving fractional and classical differential equations [16,17]. Avinash [18] and Chellamani [19] worked on the COVID-19 model. Nonetheless, the aforementioned method is rarely applied to fractional-order differential equations with nonsingular kernels [20]. Fractional calculus is a growing field that has been extensively used to extend traditional remedy concepts. The method of [21,22] is noteworthy in this respect. We examined a fractional variant of the novel coronavirus model 1 in this manuscript and employed the concept of a fractional CF derivative [23], which is now being used by many scientists to examine a wide variety of issues in biological and physical sciences; for example, [24–26]. The concept of a CF derivative has already been used numerous times to explain the motion of different highly infectious infections [27,28]. CF derivatives have been used to examine the stability, existence, and uniqueness of various mathematical models [29]. Bedi et al. [30] and Devi et al. [31] studied the fractional-order vector-borne diseases model and transmission of worms in a wireless sensor network, respectively. Mehmood et al. [32] worked on a partial differential equation. Niazi et al.[33], Iqbal et al. [34], Shafqat et al. [35], Alnahdi [36], Khan [37], and Abuasbeh et al. [38–40] investigated the existence and uniqueness of the fractional evolution equations. In many cases, fractional-order models are more useful for better describing the evolution of numerous actual issues. The justification for this is that fractional-order derivatives have a higher level of freedom than classical integer order derivatives. Rather than ordinary derivatives, the new type of non-singular derivatives of a fractional order has been considered satisfactory for studying thermal concerns. Rehman et al. [41] collaborated on the mathematical modeling of COVID-19 with a CF fractional extension of the model (1), which has the below form:

$$
\begin{aligned}
{}^{CF}D_v^q S_h(v) &= \Pi^{*q} - \beta_1^{*q} I_h(v) + \beta + \beta_2^{*q} W(v) + d^{*q} S(v), \\
{}^{CF}D_v^q R_h(v) &= (\beta_1^{*q} I_h(v) + \beta_2^{*q} W(v) + d^{*q}) S(v) - (\sigma^{*q} + d^{*q} + d_1^{*q}) I_h(v), \\
{}^{CF}D_v^q R_h(v) &= \sigma^{*q} I_h(t) - d^{*q} R_h(v), \\
{}^{CF}D_v^q W(v) &= \alpha^{*q} I_h(t) - \eta^{*q} W(v),
\end{aligned}
\tag{3}
$$

by using the following initial conditions

$$S_0 = S(0), I_0 = I(0), R_0 = R(0), W_0 = W(0).$$

Our current article is organized as follows. In Section 2, we review the basic definitions and concepts used in the article. In Section 3, the modeling formulation is presented. Section 4 investigates the existence and uniqueness of the involved solution using a fixed point theory approach. In Section 5, we investigate the analytical solution of the results of the model using the Adomian decomposition technique and the Laplace integral transform. In Section 6, we use current information to run numerical computations to support and validate our analytical findings. At the end, in Section 7, the conclusion is presented.

2. Preliminaries

The results that we remember are listed below.

Definition 1 ([42]). *The fractional RL derivative is defined as*

$$ {}_aD^p_\omega\chi(\omega) = \frac{1}{\Gamma(n-p+1)}\left(\frac{d}{d\omega}\right)^{n+1}\int_a^\omega (\omega-\tau)^{n-p}\chi(\tau)d\tau,\ n\leqslant p\leqslant n+1. $$

Definition 2 ([42]). *The Caputo fractional derivatives ${}^C_aD^\alpha_\omega\chi(\omega)$ of order $\alpha\in\mathbb{R}^+$ are defined by*

$$ {}^C_aD^\alpha_\omega\chi(\omega) = {}_aD^\alpha_\omega\left(\chi(\omega) - \sum_{j=0}^{k-1}\frac{\chi^{(j)}(a)}{j!}(\omega-a)^j\right), $$

in which $k=[\alpha]+1$.

Definition 3 ([43]). *The Wright function, ψ_α is defined by*

$$ \begin{aligned} \psi_\alpha(\kappa) &= \sum_{j=0}^{\infty}\frac{(-\kappa)^j}{j!\Gamma(-\alpha j+1-\alpha)} \\ &= \frac{1}{\pi}\sum_{j=1}^{\infty}\frac{(-\kappa)^j}{(j-1)!}\Gamma(j\alpha)\sin(j\pi\alpha),\ \alpha\in(0,1),\kappa\in\mathbb{C}. \end{aligned} $$

Lemma 1 ((Gronwall lemma) [44]). *Assume $\mu, y\in\mathcal{H}([0,1],\mathbb{R}_+)$ and let μ be increasing. If $u\in\mathcal{H}([0,1],\mathbb{R}_+)$ satisfies*

$$ u(\omega)\leqslant\mu(\omega)+\int_0^\omega y(s)u(s)ds,\ \omega\in[0,1], $$

then

$$ u(\omega)\leqslant\mu(\omega)\exp\int_0^\omega y(s)u(s)ds,\ \omega\in[0,1]. $$

Lemma 2 ([45]). *Consider $\{\mathcal{H}(\omega)\}_{\omega\in\mathbb{R}}$ as a strongly continuous cosine category in X fulfilling $\|\mathcal{H}(\omega)\|_{L_b(X)}\leq Me^{\Omega|\omega|}, \omega\in\mathbb{R}$, and $\mathcal{A}$ as an infinitesimal generator of $\{\mathcal{H}(\omega)\}_{\omega\in\mathbb{R}}$. Then, for $\mathrm{Re}(\lambda)>\omega$ and $\lambda^2\in\rho(A)$,*

$$ \lambda R(\lambda^2;\mathcal{A})x = \int_0^\infty e^{-\lambda\omega}\mathcal{H}(\omega)xd\omega,\ R(\lambda^2;\mathcal{A})x = \int_0^\infty e^{-\lambda\omega}S(\omega)xd\omega. $$

Theorem 1. *If $X(v)$ fulfills Equation (4), then $Y(v)$ is given by*

$$ Y(v) = Y_0+(Y_1+m\varpi(Y))v+\frac{1}{\Gamma(\beta)}\int_0^v (v-s)^{q-1}P_q(v-s)\Omega(x,Y(x))dx,\ v\in[0,\infty), $$

If this holds, then

$$ Y(v) = C_q(v)Y_0+K_q(v)(Y_1+m\varpi(Y))+\int_0^v (v-s)^{q-1}P_q(v-s)\Omega(x,Y(x))dx, $$

$\forall\, t \in [0, b]$, *such that*

$$C_q(v) = \int_0^{\infty} M_q(\theta) C(v^q \theta) d\theta,\; K_q(v) = \int_0^{v} C_q(s) ds,\; P_q(v) = \int_0^{\infty} q\theta M_q(\theta) C(v^q \theta) d\theta,$$

where $C_q(v)$ *and* $K_q(v)$ *are continuous with* $K(0) = I$ *and* $C(0) = I$, $|C_q(v)| \leqslant c, c > 1$ *and* $|K_q(v)| \leqslant c, c > 1$, $\forall\, v \in [0, \Im]$.

3. Modeling Formulation

In light of the article [41], we evaluated the following model:

$$\begin{aligned}
{}^{c}D_v^q S(v) &= \wedge - (\xi + \mu) S(v - \tau) - \beta S(v - \tau) E(v - \tau),\\
{}^{c}D_v^q E(v) &= \beta S(v - \tau) E(v - \tau) - (\gamma + \mu + \eta + \sigma) E(v - \tau),\\
{}^{c}D_v^q Q(v) &= \xi S(v - \tau) + \gamma E(v - \tau) - (\mu + v + \theta) Q(v),\\
{}^{c}D_v^q I_A(v) &= \sigma E(v - \tau) + \theta Q(v) - (\mu + r_1) I_A(v),\\
{}^{c}D_v^q I_S(v) &= \eta E(v - \tau) + v Q(v) - (\delta + \mu + r_2) I_S(v),\\
{}^{c}D_v^q R(v) &= r_1 I_A(v) + r_2 I_S(v) - \mu R(v).
\end{aligned} \tag{4}$$

For $q \in (1, 2)$ and $v \in [-\tau, 0]$, we studied the model underneath the basic initial conditions

$$\begin{aligned}
&S(0) = S_0 + m\varpi_1(S),\; E(0) = E_0 + m\varpi_2(E),\; Q(0) = Q_0 + m\varpi_3(Q),\; I_A(0) = I_{A_0} + m\varpi_4(I_A),\\
&I_S(0) = I_{S_0} + m\varpi_5(I_S),\; R(0) = R_0 + \varpi_6(R),\\
&S'(0) = S_1,\; E'(0) = E_1,\; Q'(0) = Q_1,\; I'_A(0) = I_{A_1},\; I'_S(0) = I_{S_1},\; R'(0) = R_1.
\end{aligned}$$

Let $N(v)$ stands for the total number of people. This population is made up of seven classes: susceptible individuals $S(v)$, individuals who have been exposed to COVID-19 $E(v)$, individuals who have asymptotically contracted the disease $I_A(v)$, individuals who have demonstrated symptoms $I_S(v)$, and individuals who have recovered or been saved from COVID-19 $R(v)$. In light of this, the population as a whole is

$$N(v) = S(v) + E(v) + Q(v) + I_A(v) + I_S(v) + R(v).$$

The terms $\wedge$ and μ stand for the natural natality and mortality rates of humans, respectively. People who are susceptible (S) either contract the disease after enough contact with exposed people (E) at a rate of β or they simply move to a class that is quarantined at a rate of τ. The exposed individuals (E) have the option of moving to the quarantined (Q) class first or contracting the infection at rates of γ, σ, and η, respectively, either asymptomatically (I_A) or symptomatically (I_S). Additionally, individuals who have been placed under quarantine (Q) could test positive for infection at rates of v and θ with symptoms (I_S) or (I_A), respectively(see Table 1 and Figure 1).

Table 1. Notations used and their meanings (4).

Parameter	Parameters Description
ξ	Transfer ratio from susceptible people to quarantine
β	Contact ratio between susceptible people and exposed individuals
δ	Mortality ratio due to coronavirus in symptomatic infected people class
γ	Ratio of transfer of exposed people to quarantine
η	Ratio of transfer of exposed people from exposed class to symptomatic infected people class
θ	Ratio of quarantined people to asymptomatic infected people class
μ	Natural mortality

Table 1. *Cont.*

Parameter	Parameters Description
υ	Ratio of transfer of quarantined people to symptomatic infected people class
σ	Ratio of transfer of exposed people to asymptomatic infected people class
$\wedge$	Recruitment (natality) ratio
r_1	Recovery ratio of asymptomatic infected people
r_2	Recovery ratio of symptomatic infected people

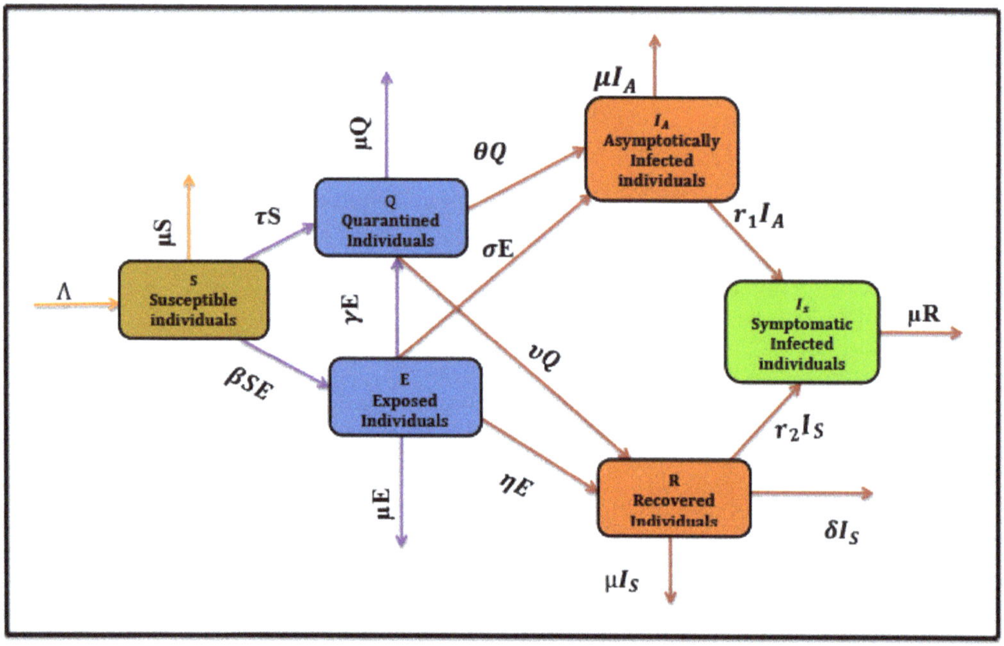

Figure 1. Transmission pattern of COVID-19.

4. Existence and Uniqueness Results for the Model

It is critical to understand whether or not a mathematical model has a solution. The fixed point theory approach can be used to solve this problem. We studied the uniqueness and existence of the involved solution. The Banach fixed point theorem was used to meet the target. We investigated the existence and uniqueness of the results using Picard's operator method on the proposed model (4). Allow us to define

$$\begin{aligned}
{}^cD_\upsilon^q S(\upsilon) &= g_1(\upsilon, S(\upsilon)) = \wedge - (\xi + \mu)S(\upsilon - \tau) - \beta S(\upsilon)E(\upsilon - \tau), \\
{}^cD_\upsilon^q E(\upsilon) &= g_2(\upsilon, E(\upsilon)) = \beta S(\upsilon)E(\upsilon - \tau) - (\gamma + \mu + \eta + \sigma)E(\upsilon - \tau), \\
{}^cD_\upsilon^q Q(\upsilon) &= g_3(\upsilon, Q(\upsilon)) = \xi S(\upsilon - \tau) + \gamma E(\upsilon - \tau) - (\mu + v + \theta)Q(\upsilon), \\
{}^cD_\upsilon^q I_A(\upsilon) &= g_4(\upsilon, I_A(\upsilon)) = \sigma E(\upsilon - \tau) + \theta Q(\upsilon) - (\mu + r_1)I_A(\upsilon), \\
{}^cD_\upsilon^q I_S(\upsilon) &= g_5(\upsilon, I_S(\upsilon)) = \eta E(\upsilon - \tau) + v Q(\upsilon) - (\delta + \mu + r_2)I_S(\upsilon), \\
{}^cD_\upsilon^q R(\upsilon) &= g_6(\upsilon, R(\upsilon)) = r_1 I_A(\upsilon) + r_2 I_S(\upsilon) - \mu R(\upsilon).
\end{aligned} \tag{5}$$

We further set

$$Q_j = \sup_{C \in [d, b_j]} \| g_1(\upsilon, S(\upsilon), E(\upsilon), Q(\upsilon), I_A(\upsilon), I_S(\upsilon), R(\upsilon) \|, \; for\; j = 1,2,3,4,5,6,$$

where

$$C[d, b_j] = [v - d, v + d] \times [u - c_j, u + c_j] = D \times D_j, \; for \; j = 1,2,3,4,5,6. \tag{6}$$

After that, we describe the norm on $C \in [d, b_j]$ for $j = 1,2,3,4,5,6$ using the Banach fixed point theorem to demonstrate the existence and uniqueness of the solution:

$$\|H\|_\infty = \sup_{v \in [v-d, v+b]} |\phi(v)|. \tag{7}$$

In view of (5), by applying I^q to all of the equations in model (4), we obtained

$$\begin{aligned}
S(v) &= S(0) + S'(0)v + I^q\Big[g_1(v, S(v), E(v), Q(v), I_A(v), I_S(v), R(v))\Big],\\
E(v) &= E(0) + E'(0)v + I^q\Big[g_2(v, S(v), E(v), Q(v), I_A(v), I_S(v), R(v))\Big],\\
Q(v) &= Q(0) + Q'(0)v + I^q\Big[g_3(v, S(v), E(v), Q(v), I_A(v), I_S(v), R(v))\Big],\\
I_A(v) &= I_A(0) + I'_A(0)v + I^q\Big[g_4(v, S(v), E(v), Q(v), I_A(v), I_S(v), R(v))\Big],\\
I_S(v) &= I_S(0) + I'_S(0)v + I^q\Big[g_5(v, S(v), E(v), Q(v), I_A(v), I_S(v), R(v))\Big],\\
R(v) &= R(0) + R'(0)v + I^q\Big[g_6(v, S(v), E(v), Q(v), I_A(v), I_S(v), R(v))\Big].
\end{aligned} \tag{8}$$

We obtained this by analyzing the right-hand side of (8) and writing it in the format provided below:

$$Y(v) = C_q(v)Y_0 + K_q(v)(Y_1 + m\varpi(Y)) + \frac{1}{\sqrt{\gamma}} \int_0^v (v-s)^{q-1} P_q(v-s)\Omega(x, Y(x))dx, \tag{9}$$

where

$$\begin{aligned}
&Y(v) = (S(v), E(v), Q(v), I_A(v), I_S(v), R(v))^T,\\
&Y_0(v) = ((S(v), E(v), Q(v), I_A(v), I_S(v), R(v)) + m(S))^T,\\
&Y_1(v) = (S'(v), E'(v), Q'(v), I'_A(v), I'_S(v), R'(v))^T,\\
&\Omega(v, Y(v)) = g_j(v, S(v), E(v), Q(v), I_A(v), I_S(v), R(v)), \; j = 1,2,3,4,5,6.
\end{aligned} \tag{10}$$

Let us define the Picard's operator as

$$A : C(V, V_1, V_2, V_3, V_4, V_5, V_6) \to C(V, V_1, V_2, V_3, V_4, V_5, V_6). \tag{11}$$

The operator in (11) is defined by using (9) and (10):

$$Y(v) = C_q(v)Y_0 + K_q(v(Y_1 + m\varpi(Y)) + \frac{1}{\sqrt{\gamma}} \int_0^v (v-s)^{q-1} P_q(v-s)\Omega(x, Y(x))dx. \tag{12}$$

Suppose that the model that is being studied is effectively

$$\|Y\| \leq \max\{d_1, d_2, d_3, d_4, d_5, d_6\}, \tag{13}$$

Now,

$$\begin{aligned}
\|Y_0(v)-Z_0(v)\| &= \sup_{v\in D}\Big|C_q(v)Y_0+K_q(v)(Y_1+m\varpi(Y))+\frac{1}{\sqrt{\gamma}}\int_0^v (v-s)^{q-1}P_q(v-s)\Omega(x,Y(x))dx - \\
&\quad C_q(v)Z_0-K_q(v)(Z_1+m\varpi(Z))-\frac{1}{\sqrt{\gamma}}\int_0^v (v-s)^{q-1}P_q(v-s)\Omega(x,Z(x))dx\Big|,\\
&\le M_1|Y_0-Z_0|+M_1|Y_0-Z_0|v+\frac{M_1}{\Gamma(2q)}|Y_0-Z_0|v^q,\\
&< M_1|Y_0-Z_0|(1+v+\frac{1}{\Gamma(2q)}v^q)\\
&< M_1|Y_0-Z_0|c,\ M_1=\max\{M_j\}\ for\ j=1,2,\ldots,7,\\
&\le \max\{d_1,d_2,d_3,d_4,d_5,d_6,d_7\}\\
&= \bar{c},\ v_0=\sup\{|v|:v\in D\}.
\end{aligned} \tag{14}$$

In Equation (14), we have defined $c=(1+v+\frac{1}{\Gamma(2q)}v^q)$. It follows that

$$c<\frac{\bar{c}}{M_1}.$$

Furthermore, in order to evaluate the equality given by

$$\|AY_1-AZ_1\|=\sup_{v\in D}|Y_1-Z_1|, \tag{15}$$

we make use of (9) and can write

$$\begin{aligned}
\|AY_1-AZ_1\| &= \sup_{v\in D}\Big|C_q(v)Y_1+K_q[(v)(Y_1+m\varpi(Y))+\\
&\quad +\frac{1}{\sqrt{\gamma}}\int_0^v (v-s)^{q-1}P_q(v-s)\Omega(x,Y_1(v)(x))dx, C_q(v)Z_1+\\
&\quad K_q(v)(Z_1+m\varpi(Z))+\frac{1}{\sqrt{\gamma}}\int_0^v (v-s)^{q-1}P_q(v-s)\Omega(x,Z_1(v)(x))dx\Big|,\\
&\le M_1k|Y_1-Z_1|+M_1k|Y_1-Z_1|v+\frac{M_1}{\Gamma(2q)}k|Y_1-Z_1|v^q,\ M=\max\{M_j\}\ for\ j=1,2,\ldots,7,\\
&< M_1k|Y_1-Z_1|(1+v+\frac{1}{\Gamma(2q)}v^q)\\
&< ck\|Y_1-Z_1\|.
\end{aligned}$$

One can infer that operator A is also a closure because Ω is a closure, which leads to $ck<1$. This implies that the system's (8) solution is unique.

5. Analytical Solution of Model (4)

Here, we computed the numerical solutions to our model. Model (4) can be written with the normalization value $M(q)=1$, and the Laplace transform on both sides is

$$\begin{aligned}
L[D_t^qS(v)] &= \tfrac{S(0)}{s}+\tfrac{S'(0)+m\varpi S}{s^2}+\tfrac{s+q(1-s)}{s}L[\wedge-(\xi+\mu)S(v-\tau)-\beta S(v-\tau)E(v-\tau)],\\
L[D_v^qE(v)] &= \tfrac{E(0)}{s}+\tfrac{E'(0)+m\varpi(E)}{s^2}+\tfrac{s+q(1-s)}{s}L[\beta S(v)E(v-\tau)-(\gamma+\mu+\eta+\sigma)E(v-\tau)],\\
L[D_v^qQ(v)] &= \tfrac{Q(0)}{s}+\tfrac{Q'(0)+m\varpi(Q)}{s^2}+\tfrac{s+q(1-s)}{s^2}L[\xi S(v-\tau)+\gamma E(v-\tau)-(\mu+v+\theta)Q(v)],\\
L[D_v^qI_A(v)] &= \tfrac{I_A(0)}{s}+\tfrac{I_A'(0)+m\varpi(I_A)}{s^2}+\tfrac{s+q(1-s)}{s}L[\sigma E(v-\tau)+\theta Q(v)-(\mu+r_1)I_A(v)],\\
L[D_v^qI_S(v)] &= \tfrac{I_S(0)}{s}+\tfrac{I_S'(0)+m\varpi(I_S)}{s^2}+\tfrac{s+q(1-s)}{s}L[\eta E(v-\tau)+\nu Q(v)-(\delta+\mu+r_2)I_S(v)],\\
L[D_v^qR(v)] &= \tfrac{R(0)}{s}+\tfrac{R'(0)+m\varpi(R)}{s^2}+\tfrac{s+q(1-s)}{s}L[r_1I_A(v)+r_2I_S(v)-\mu R(v)].
\end{aligned} \tag{16}$$

In the following section, we solve, in series form, for every class of the system under consideration:

$$
\begin{aligned}
&S(v)=\sum_{q=0}^{\infty} S_q(v)+m\varpi_1(S),\;\; E(v)=\sum_{q=0}^{\infty} E_q(v)+m\varpi_2(E),\;\; Q(v)=\sum_{q=0}^{\infty} Q_q(v)+m\varpi_3(Q),\\
&I_A(v)=\sum_{q=0}^{\infty} I_{Aq}(v)+m\varpi_4(I_A),\;\; W(v)=\sum_{q=0}^{\infty} I_{S_q}(v)+m\varpi_5(I_s),\;\; R(v)=\sum_{q=0}^{\infty} R_q(v)+m\varpi_6(R),\\
&S'(v)=\sum_{q=0}^{\infty} S'_q(v),\;\; E'(v)=\sum_{q=0}^{\infty} E'_q(v),\;\; Q'(v)=\sum_{q=0}^{\infty} Q'_q(v), I'_A(v)=\sum_{q=0}^{\infty} I'_{A_q}(v),\\
&W'(v)=\sum_{q=0}^{\infty} I'_{S_q}(v),\;\; R'(v))=\sum_{q=0}^{\infty} R'_q(v).
\end{aligned}
\tag{17}
$$

Using the Adomian polynomials method, the nonlinear terms $E(v)S(v), Q(v)S(v)$, and $R(v)S(v)$ can be decomposed as follows:

$$
E(v)S(v)=\sum_{q=0}^{\infty} X_q(E,S),\;\; Q(v)S(v)=\sum_{q=0}^{\infty} Y_q(Q,S),\;\; R(v)S(v)=\sum_{q=0}^{\infty} Z_q(R,S), \tag{18}
$$

where the Adomian polynomial $X_q(E,S), Q_q(W,S), R_q(W,S)$ may be written as

$$
\begin{aligned}
X_q(E,S)&=\frac{1}{q!}\frac{d^q}{d\lambda^q}\left[\sum_{k=0}^{q}\lambda^k E_k(v)\sum_{k=0}^{q}\lambda^k S_k(v)\right]_{\lambda=0},\\
Y_q(Q,S)&=\frac{1}{q!}\frac{d^q}{d\lambda^q}\left[\sum_{k=0}^{q}\lambda^k Q_k(v)\sum_{k=0}^{q}\lambda^k S_k(v)\right]_{\lambda=0},\\
Z_q(R,S)&=\frac{1}{q!}\frac{d^q}{d\lambda^q}\left[\sum_{k=0}^{q}\lambda^k R_k(v)\sum_{k=0}^{q}\lambda^k S_k(v)\right]_{\lambda=0}.
\end{aligned}
$$

Equations (17) and (18) are used to create the following system (16):

$$
\begin{aligned}
L\left[\textstyle\sum_{q=0}^{\infty} S_q(v)\right]&=\tfrac{S(0)}{s}+\tfrac{S'(0)+m\varpi_1(S)}{s^2}+\tfrac{s+q(1-s)}{s}L\left[\wedge-(\xi+\mu)\textstyle\sum_{q=0}^{\infty} S_q(v-\tau)-\beta\sum_{q=0}^{\infty} S_q(v-\tau)\sum_{q=0}^{\infty} X_q(v)\right],\\
L\left[\textstyle\sum_{q=0}^{\infty} E_q(v)\right]&=\tfrac{E(0)}{s}+\tfrac{E'(0)+m\varpi_2(E)}{s^2}+\tfrac{s+q(1-s)}{s}L\left[\beta\textstyle\sum_{q=0}^{\infty} S_q(v-\tau)\sum_{q=0}^{\infty} X_q(v)-(\gamma+\mu+\eta+\sigma)\sum_{q=0}^{\infty} X_q(v)\right],\\
L\left[\textstyle\sum_{q=0}^{\infty} Q_q(v)\right]&=\tfrac{Q(0)}{s}+\tfrac{Q'(0)+m\varpi_3(Q)}{s^2}+\tfrac{s+q(1-s)}{s}L\left[\xi\textstyle\sum_{q=0}^{\infty} S_q(v-\tau)+\gamma\sum_{q=0}^{\infty} X_q(v)-(\mu+v+\theta)\sum_{q=0}^{\infty} Y_q(v)\right],\\
L\left[\textstyle\sum_{q=0}^{\infty} I_{A_q}(v)\right]&=\tfrac{I_A(0)}{s}+\tfrac{I'_A(0)+m\varpi_4(I_A)}{s^2}+\tfrac{s+q(1-s)}{s}L\left[\sigma\textstyle\sum_{q=0}^{\infty} X_q(v)+\theta\sum_{q=0}^{\infty} Y_q(v)-(\mu+r_1)\sum_{q=0}^{\infty} I_{A_q}(v)\right],\\
L\left[\textstyle\sum_{q=0}^{\infty} I_{S_q}(v)\right]&=\tfrac{I_S(0)}{s}+\tfrac{I'_S(0)+m\varpi_5(I_S)}{s^2}+\tfrac{s+q(1-s)}{s}L\left[\eta\textstyle\sum_{q=0}^{\infty} X_q(v)+\nu\sum_{q=0}^{\infty} Y_q(v)-(\delta+\mu+r_2)\sum_{q=0}^{\infty} I_{S_q}(v)\right],\\
L\left[\textstyle\sum_{q=0}^{\infty} R_q(v)\right]&=\tfrac{R(0)}{s}+\tfrac{R'(0)+m\varpi_6(R)}{s^2}+\tfrac{s+q(1-s)}{s}L\left[r_1\textstyle\sum_{q=0}^{\infty} I_{A_q}(v)+r_2\sum_{q=0}^{\infty} I_{S_q}(v)-\mu\sum_{q=0}^{\infty} Z_q(\tau)\right].
\end{aligned}
\tag{19}
$$

On both sides of (19), if we equalize like terms, we can write

$$
\begin{aligned}
&L[S_0(v)]=\frac{S_0}{s},\;\; L[E_0(v)]=\frac{E_0}{s},\;\; L[Q_0(v)]=\frac{Q_0}{s},\;\; L[I_{A_0}(v)]=\frac{I_{A_0}}{s},\;\; L[I_{S_0}(v)]=\frac{I_{S_0}}{s},\\
&L[R_0(v)]=\frac{R_0}{s},\;\; L[S'_0(v)]=\frac{S_1+m\varpi_1(S)}{s^2},\;\; L[E'_0(v)]=\frac{E_1+m\varpi_2(E)}{s^2},\\
&L[Q'_0(v)]=\frac{Q_1+m\varpi_3(Q)}{s^2},\;\; L[I'_{A_0}(v)]=\frac{I_{A_1}+m\varpi_4(I_A)}{s^2},\;\; L[I'_{S_0}(v)]=\frac{I_{S_1}+m\varpi_5(I_S)}{s^2},\\
&L[R'_0(v)]=\frac{R_1+m\varpi_6(R)}{s^2},
\end{aligned}
$$

$$
\begin{aligned}
L[S_1(v)] &= \frac{s+q(1-s)}{s} L\Big[\wedge - (\xi+\mu)[(S_0(v)-m(S))+S_0(v)] - \beta[(S_0(v)-m(S))+S_0(v)] \\
&\quad [(E_0(v)-m(E))+E_0(v)]\Big], \\
L[E_1(v)] &= \frac{s+q(1-s)}{s} L\Big[\beta[(S_0(v)-m(S))+S_0(v)][(X_0(v)-m(X))+X_0(v)] - (\gamma+\mu+\eta+\sigma) \\
&\quad [(X_0(t)-m(X))+X_0(v)]\Big], \\
L[Q_1(v)] &= \frac{s+q(1-s)}{s} L\Big[\xi[(S_0(v)-m(S))+S_0(v)] + \gamma[(X_0(v)-m(X))+X_0(v)] - (\mu+v+\theta) \\
&\quad [(Y_0(v)-m(Y))+Y_0(v)]\Big], \\
L[I_{A_1}(v)] &= \frac{s+q(1-s)}{s} L\Big[\sigma[(X_0(v)-m(X))+X_0(v)] + \theta[(Y_0(v)-m(Y))+Y_0(v)] - (\mu+r_1) \\
&\quad [(I_{A_0}(v)-m(I_A))+I_{A_0}(v)]\Big], \\
L[I_{S_1}(v)] &= \frac{s+q(1-s)}{s} L\Big[\eta[(X_0(v)-m(X))+S_0(v)] + \nu[(Y_0(v)-m(Y))+Y_0(v)] - (\delta+\mu+r_2) \\
&\quad [(I_{S_0}(v)-m(I_s))+I_{S_0}(v)]\Big], \\
L[R_1(v)] &= \frac{s+q(1-s)}{s} L\Big[r_1[(I_{A_0}(v)-m(I_A))+I_{A_0}(v)] + r_2[(I_{S_0}(v)-m(I_S))+I_{S_0}(v)] \\
&\quad -\mu[(Z_0(v)-m(Z))+Z_0(v)]\Big], \\
&\vdots \\
L[S_{q+1}(v)] &= \frac{s+q(1-s)}{s} L\Big[\wedge - (\xi+\mu)[(S_q(v)-m(S))+S_q(v)] - \beta[(S_q(v)-m(S))+S_q(v)] \\
&\quad [(X_q(v)-m(X))+X_q(v)]\Big], \\
L[E_{q+1}(v)] &= \frac{s+q(1-s)}{s} L\Big[\beta[(S_q(v)-m(S))+S_q(v)][(X_q(v)-m(X))+X_q(v)] - (\gamma+\mu+\eta+\sigma) \\
&\quad [(X_q(v)-m(X))+X_q(v)]\Big], \\
L[Q_{q+1}(v)] &= \frac{s+q(1-s)}{s} L\Big[\tau[(S_q(v)-m(S))+S_q(v)] + \gamma[(Y_q(v)-m(Y))+Y_q(v)] - (\mu+v+\theta) \\
&\quad [(Y_q(v)-m(Y))+Y_q(v)]\Big], \\
L[I_{A_{q+1}}(v)] &= \frac{s+q(1-s)}{s} L\Big[\sigma[(X_q(t)-m(X))+X_q(v)] + \theta[(Y_q(v)-m(Y))+Y_q(v)] - (\mu+r_1) \\
&\quad [(I_A(t)-m(I_A))+I_{A_q}(v)]\Big],
\end{aligned} \tag{20}
$$

$$
\begin{aligned}
L[I_{S_{q+1}}(v)] &= \frac{s+q(1-s)}{s}L\Big[\eta[(X_q(t)-m(X))+X_q(v)]+v[(Y_q(v)-m(Y))+Y_q(v)]-(\delta+\mu+r_2)\\
&\quad [(I_S(v)-m(I_S))+I_{S_q}(v)]\Big],\\
L[R_{q+1}(v)] &= \frac{s+q(1-s)}{s}L\Big[r_1[(I_{A_q}(v)-mI_A)+I_{A_q}(v)]+r_2[(I_{S_q}(v)-mI_S)+I_{S_q}(v)]\\
&\quad -\mu[(Z_q(v)-m(Z))+Z_q(v)]\Big].
\end{aligned}
$$

Now, we calculate (20)'s Laplace transform and find

$$
\begin{aligned}
&S_0=N_1,\ E_0=N_2,\ Q_0=N_3,\ I_{A_0}=N_{A_4}, I_{S_5}=N_{S_5},\ R_0=N_6,\\
&S_0'=N_1+m\varpi_1(N_1),\ E_0'=N_2+m\varpi_2(N_2),\ Q_0'=N_3+m\varpi_3(N_3),\ I_{A_0}'=N_{A_4}+m\varpi_4(N_{A_4}),\\
&I_{S_5}'=N_{S_5}+m\varpi_5(N_{S_5}),\ R_0(t)'=N_6+m\varpi_6(N_6),\\
&S_1=\Big[\wedge-(\xi+\mu)[N_1+(N_1+m\varpi_1(N_1))]-\beta[N_1(N_1+m\varpi_1(N_1))][N_2+(N_2+m\varpi_2(N_2))]\Big](1+q(1-s)),\\
&E_1=\Big[\beta[N_1+(N_1+m\varpi_1(N_1))][N_2+(N_2+m\varpi_2(N_2))]-(\gamma+\mu+\eta+\sigma)[N_2+(N_2+m\varpi_2(N_2))]\Big]\\
&(1+q(1-s)),\\
&Q_1=\Big[\xi[N_1+(N_1+m\varpi_1(N_1))]+\gamma[N_2+(N_2+m\varpi_2(N_2))]-(\mu+v+\theta)[N_3+(N_3+m\varpi_3(N_3))]\Big]\\
&(1+q(1-s)),\\
&I_{A_1}=\Big[\sigma[N_2+(N_2+m\varpi_2(N_2))]+\theta[N_3+(N_3+m\varpi_3(N_3))]-(\mu+r_1)[N_{A_4})+N_{A_4}(N_{A_4}+m\varpi_4(N_{A_4}))]\Big]\\
&(1+q(1-s)),\\
&I_{S_1}=\Big[\eta[N_1+(N_1+m\varpi_1(N_1))]+v[N_3+(N_3+m\varpi_3(N_3))]-(\delta+\mu+r_2)[N_5+(N_5+m\varpi_5(N_5))]\Big]\\
&(1+q(1-s)),\\
&R_1=\Big[r_1[N_{A_4}+(N_{A_4}+m\varpi_1(N_{A_4}))]+r_2[N_{S_5}+(N_{S_5}+m\varpi_1(N_{S_5}))]-\mu[N_6+(N_6+m\varpi_1(N_6))]\Big]\\
&(1+q(1-s)),\\
&S_2=\wedge(1+q(1-s))-\Big((\tau+\mu)[s_{11})+(s_{11}+m\varpi s_{11})]-\beta\Big([N_2+(N_2+m\varpi_2(N_2))][s_{11}+(s_{11}+m\varpi s_{11})]\\
&+[N_1+(N_1+m\varpi_1(N_1))][e_{11}+(e_{11}+m\varpi e_{11})]\Big)\Big)\times\Big(\tfrac{1}{2}q^2v^2-2q^2v+2qv+(q-1)^2\Big),\\
&E_2=\Big(\beta\Big([N_2+(N_2+m\varpi_2(N_2))][s_{11})+(s_{11}+m\varpi s_{11})]+[N_1+(N_1+m\varpi_1(N_1))][e_{11}+(e_{11}+m\varpi e_{11})]\Big)\\
&-(\gamma+\mu+\eta+\sigma)[e_{11}+(e_{11}+m\varpi e_{11})]\Big)\times\Big(\tfrac{1}{2}q^2v^2-2q^2v+2qv+(q-1)^2\Big),\\
&Q_2=\Big(\xi[s_{11}+(s_{11}+m\varpi s_{11})]+\gamma[e_{11})+(e_{11}+m\varpi e_{11})]-(\mu+v+\theta)[q_{11}+(q_{11}+m\varpi q_{11})]\Big)\times\\
&\Big(\tfrac{1}{2}q^2v^2-2q^2v+2qv+(q-1)^2\Big),\\
&I_{A_2}=\Big(\sigma[s_{11}+(s_{11}+m\varpi s_{11})]+\theta[q_{11}+(q_{11}+m\varpi q_{11})]-(\mu+r_1)[i_{A_{11}}+(i_{A_{11}}+m\varpi i_{A_{11}})]\Big)\times\\
&\Big(\tfrac{1}{2}q^2v^2-2q^2v+2qv+(q-1)^2\Big),\\
&I_{S_2}=\Big(\eta[s_{11}+(s_{11}+m\varpi s_{11})]+v[q_{11}+(q_{11}+m\varpi q_{11})]-(\delta+\mu+r_2)[i_{s_{11}}+(i_{s_{11}}+m\varpi i_{s_{11}})]\Big)\times\\
&\Big(\tfrac{1}{2}q^2v^2-2q^2v+2qv+(q-1)^2\Big),
\end{aligned}
\tag{21}
$$

$$R_2 = \left(r_1[i_{A_{11}} + (i_{A_{11}} + m\varpi i_{A_{11}})] + r_2[i_{S_{11}} + (i_{S_{11}} + m\varpi i_{S_{11}})] - \mu[r_{11} + (r_{11} + m\varpi r_{11})] \right) \times \left(\frac{1}{2} q^2 v^2 - 2q^2 v + 2qv + (q-1)^2 \right),$$

The same procedures can be used to determine additional series solution terms. The unknown values in Equation (21) above are determined as follows:

$$\begin{aligned}
s_{11}(v) &= \wedge - (\xi + \mu)[N_1 + (N_1 + m\varpi N_1)] - \beta[N_1 + (N_1 + m\varpi N_1)][N_2 + (N_2 + m\varpi N_2)], \\
e_{11}(v) &= \beta[N_1 + (N_1 + m\varpi N_1)][N_2 + (N_2 + m\varpi N_2)] - (\gamma + \mu + \eta + \sigma)[N_2 + (N_2 + m\varpi N_2)], \\
w_{11}(v) &= \xi[N_1 + (N_1 + m\varpi N_1)] + \gamma[N_2 + (N_2 + m\varpi N_2)] - (\mu + v + \theta)[N_3 + (N_3 + m\varpi N_3)], \\
i_{A_{11}}(v) &= \sigma[N_2 + (N_2 + m\varpi N_2)] + \theta[N_3 + (N_3 + m\varpi N_3)] - (\mu + r_1)[N_4 + (N_4 + m\varpi N_4)], \\
i_{S_{11}}(v) &= \eta[N_1 + (N_1 + m\varpi N_1)] + \nu[N_3 + (N_3 + m\varpi N_3)] - (\delta + \mu + r_2)[N_5 + (N_5 + m\varpi N_5)], \\
r_{11}(v) &= r_1[N_4 + (N_4 + m\varpi N_4)] + r_2[N_5 + (N_5 + m\varpi N_5)] - \mu[N_6 + (N_6 + m\varpi N_6)].
\end{aligned} \tag{22}$$

6. Numerical Simulations and Discussion

This section of our manuscript is designed to run computational modeling to validate the analytical findings in the preceding sections. Initially, we introduced the semi-analytical solution to the first equations of each compartment in (4), as well as the data in Table 2 with various order derivatives, using the Laplace Adomian decomposition method. The outcomes are depicted in Figures 2–7. Continuing along the same lines, we take values from Table 3 and plot our results in Figures 8–13. Red line shows susceptible individuals $S(v)$ and blue line individuals who have been exposed to COVID-19 $E(v)$.

Table 2. Statistical parameters for our model (4).

Parameters Description	Numerical Value
$\wedge$	4.21×10^{-6}
τ	0.000761
μ	0.2516
β	0.00073
γ	3.50×10^{-3}
η	0.01
σ	0.00039
v	0.00404720925
θ	0.009567816
δ	0.09871
r_1	5.7341
r_2	1.6728

Table 3. Statistical parameters for our model (4).

Parameters Description	Numerical Value
$\wedge$	4.21×10^{-6}
τ	0.000761
μ	0.2516
β	0.700
γ	3.0050×10^{-6}
η	0.01
σ	0.00039
v	0.00404720925
θ	0.009567816
δ	0.09871
r_1	5.7341
r_2	1.6728

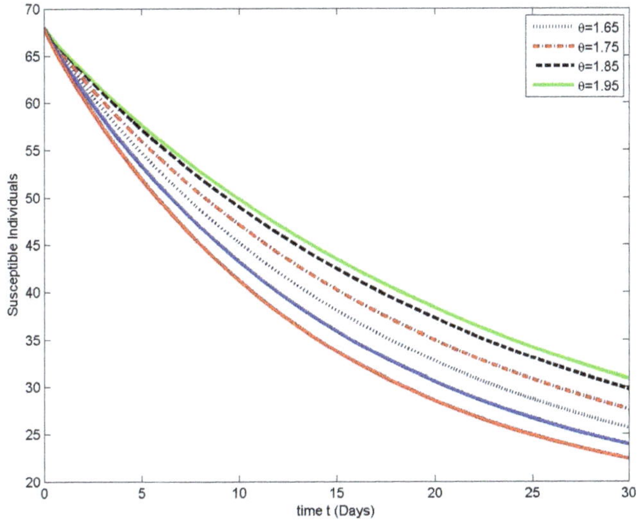

Figure 2. Illustration of susceptible individual solutions for six terms at given uncertainty levels $\vartheta \in [1,2]$ versus fractional order.

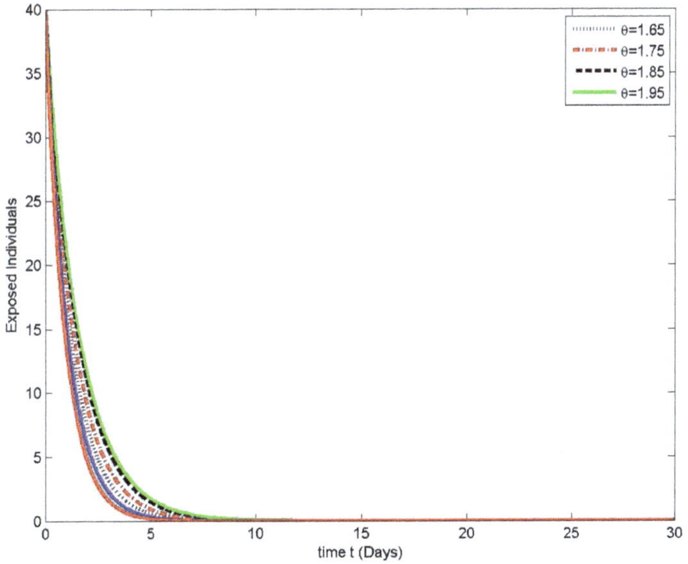

Figure 3. Illustration of exposed individual solutions for six terms at given uncertainty levels $\vartheta \in [1,2]$ versus fractional order.

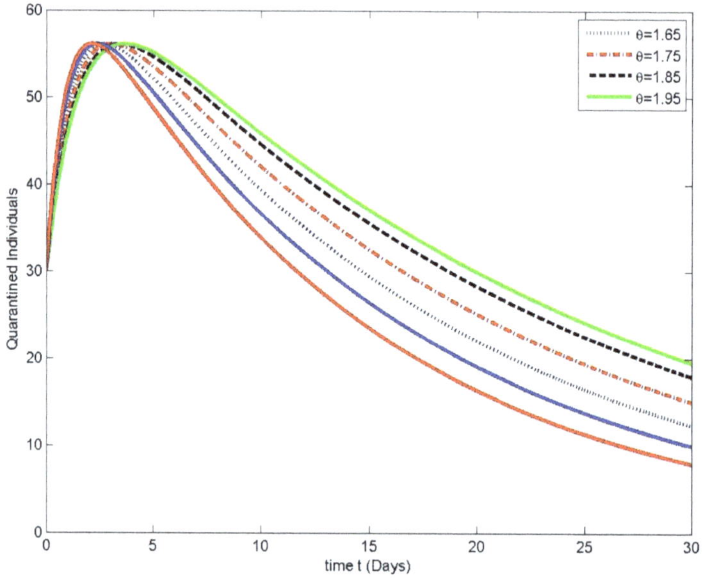

Figure 4. Illustration of quarantined individual solutions for six terms at given uncertainty levels $\vartheta \in [1,2]$ versus fractional order.

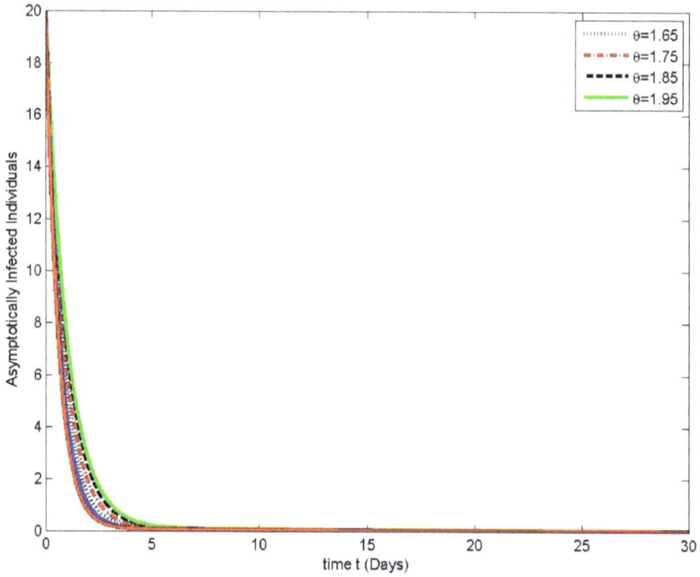

Figure 5. Illustration of asymptotically infected individual solutions for six terms at given uncertainty levels $\vartheta \in [1,2]$ versus fractional order.

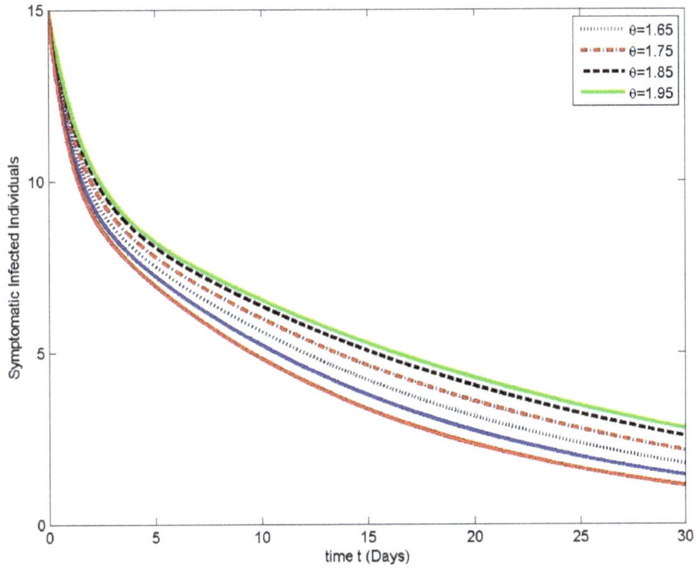

Figure 6. Illustration of symptomatic infected individual solutions for six terms at given uncertainty levels $\vartheta \in [1,2]$ versus fractional order.

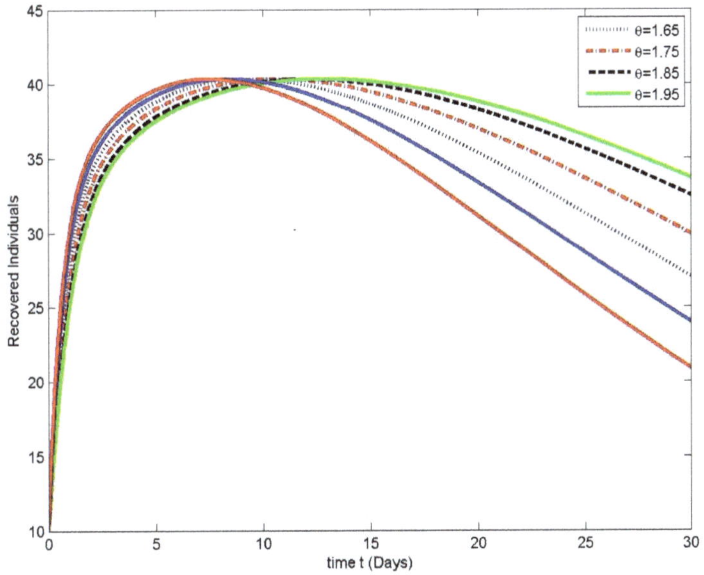

Figure 7. Illustration of recovered individual solutions for six terms at given uncertainty levels $\vartheta \in [1,2]$ versus fractional order.

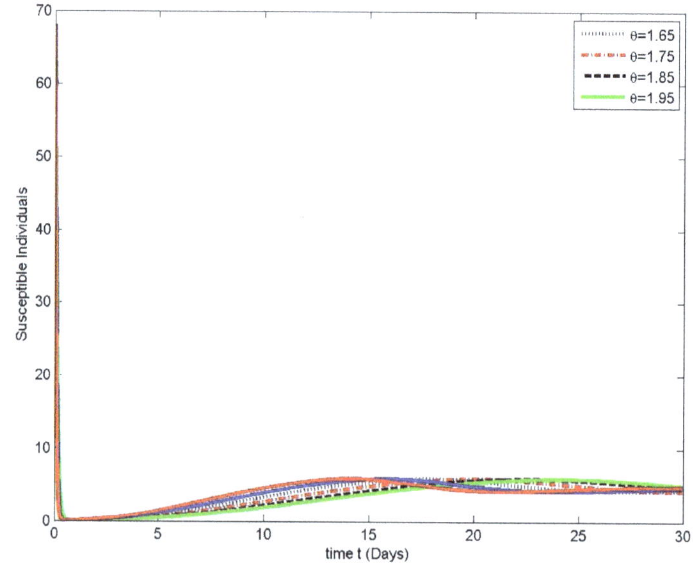

Figure 8. Illustration of susceptible individual solutions for six terms at given uncertainty levels $\vartheta \in [1,2]$ versus fractional order.

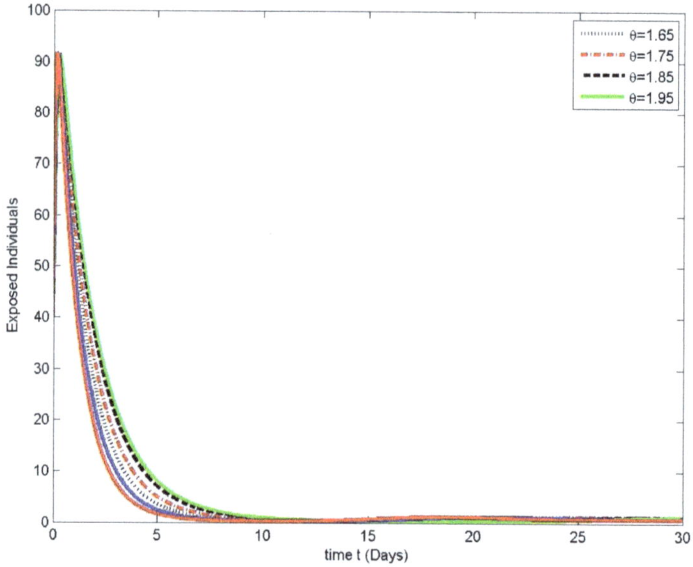

Figure 9. Illustration of exposed individual solutions for six terms at given uncertainty levels $\vartheta \in [1,2]$ versus fractional order.

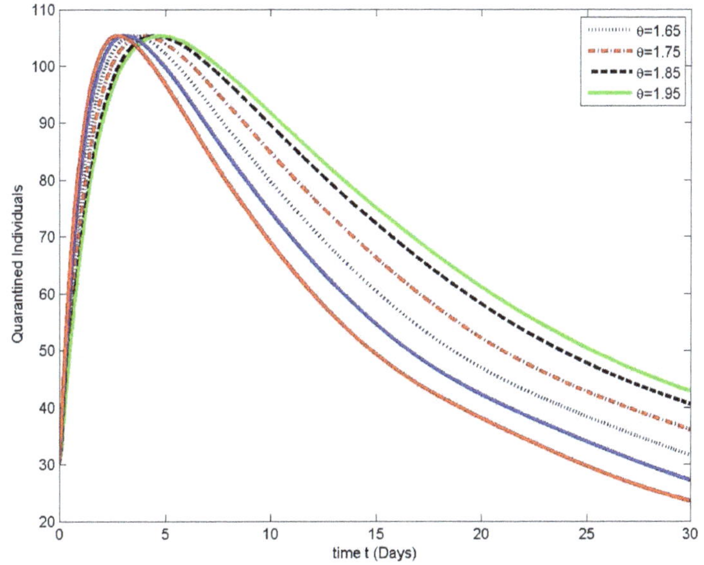

Figure 10. Illustration of quarantined individual solutions for six terms at given uncertainty levels $\vartheta \in [1,2]$ versus fractional order.

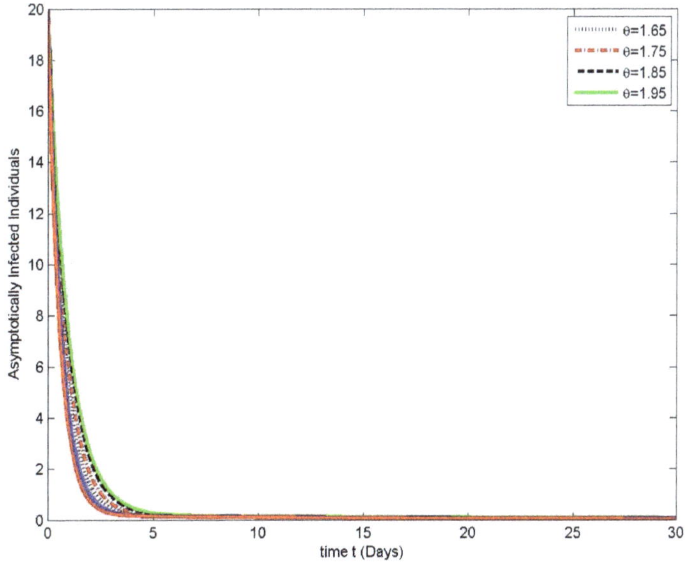

Figure 11. Illustration of asymptotically infected individual solutions for six terms at given uncertainty levels $\vartheta \in [1,2]$ versus fractional order.

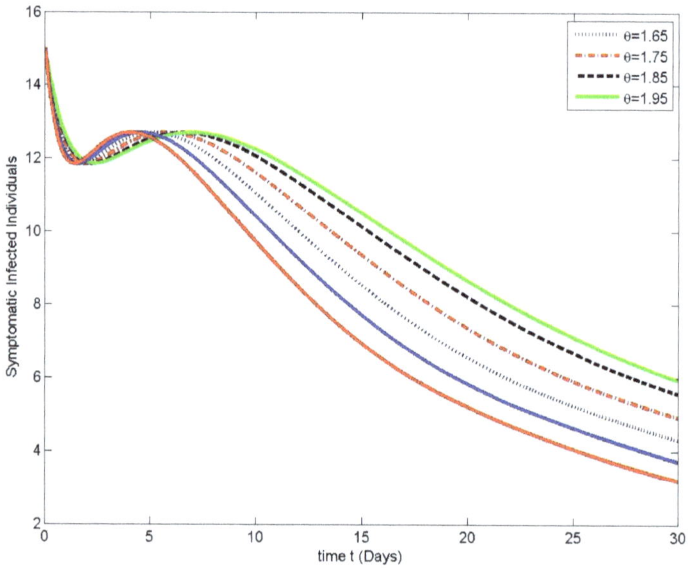

Figure 12. Illustration of symptomatic infected individual solutions for six terms at given uncertainty levels $\vartheta \in [1, 2]$ versus fractional order.

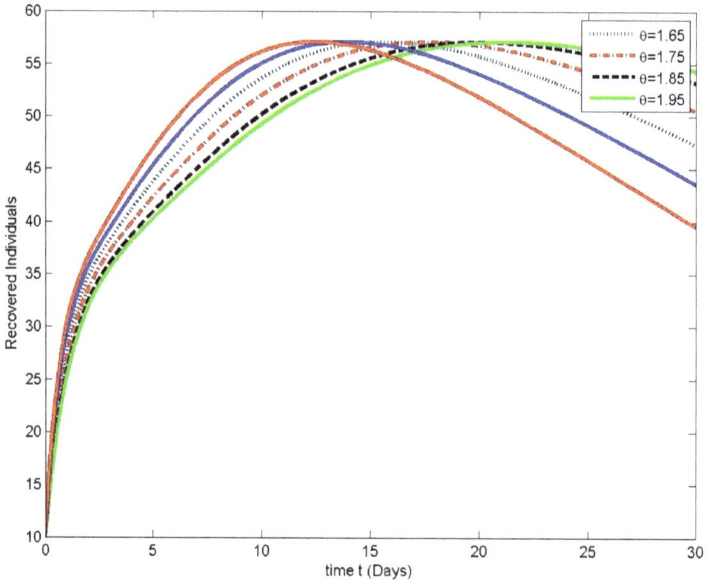

Figure 13. Illustration of recovered individual solutions for six terms at given uncertainty levels $\vartheta \in [1, 2]$ versus fractional order.

The susceptible population is shown in Figure 2, followed by the exposed population in Figure 3, the quarantined population in Figure 4, the asymptotically infected population in Figure 5, the symptomatically infected population in Figure 6, and the recovered population in Figure 7 as a function of days at 1.65, 1.75, 1.85, and 1.95. The class gradually decreases over a brief period of time, and the solution stabilizes. Using information from Table 3 and a plot for time t in the range of 0 to 30, the four classes shown in Figures 8–13 were all determined. Figure 8 shows the susceptible population versus days. Figures 9 show the exposed population versus days, Figures 10 show the quarantined population versus days, Figure 11 shows the quarantined population versus days, Figure 12 shows the symptomatic infected population versus days, and Figure 13 shows the recovered population versus days at 1.65, 1.75, 1.85, and 1.95.

7. Conclusions

In this paper, we investigated a mathematical model for COVID-19 under the Caputo fractional-order derivative. The qualitative approach, basic reproductive quantity, and equations of the proposed model were all addressed. The fixed point theory approach was used to determine the existence and uniqueness of the involved solution. The Laplace Adomian decomposition method was used to evaluate an approximation of a solution to the model's results. We ran computational modeling for our model and explained the findings temporarily for numerous fractional-order derivative values. Our graphical representations show that, compared to the conventional integer-order COVID-19 model, the fractional-order derivative of the Caputo type enables a more precise assessment. To predict the future spread of infectious diseases, the health department can apply the best control methods. The concept of optimum control is applicable to the model that we are considering. This problem is being worked on, and it will be covered in a subsequent manuscript.

Author Contributions: Conceptualization, R.S.; Methodology, R.S.; Software, A.A.; Formal analysis, A.A. and M.A.; Investigation, R.S. and A.A.; Resources, R.S.; Writing—original draft, R.S.; Writing—review & editing, R.S.; Visualization, M.A.; Supervision, A.A.; Project administration, K.A.; Funding acquisition, K.A. All authors have read and agreed to the published version of the manuscript.

Funding: This work was supported by the Deanship of Scientific Research, Vice Presidency for Graduate Studies and Scientific Research, King Faisal University, Saudi Arabia [Grant No. 2385].

Data Availability Statement: No new data were created this study.

Conflicts of Interest: The authors declare that they have no known competing financial interests or personal relationships that could have appeared to influence the work reported in this paper.

References

1. Backer, J.A.; Klinkenberg, D.; Wallinga, J. Incubation period of 2019 novel coronavirus (2019-nCoV) infections among travellers from Wuhan, China, 20–28 January 2020. *Eurosurveillance* **2020**, *25*, 2000062. [CrossRef] [PubMed]
2. Ali Mohamed Abdel-Rahman, M. Academic attitudes toward the role of social media in shaping electronic public opinion about crises an applied study on (corona virus crisis). *Inf. Sci. Lett.* **2020**, *9*, 11.
3. Din, A.; Li, Y.; Khan, T.; Zaman, G. Mathematical analysis of spread and control of the novel corona virus (COVID-19) in China. *Chaos Solitons Fractals* **2020**, *141*, 110286. [CrossRef]
4. Silva, P.C.L.; Batista, P.V.C.; Lima, H.S.; Alves, M.A.; Guimarães, F.G.; Silva, R.C.P. COVID-ABS: An agent-based model of COVID-19 epidemic to simulate health and economic effects of social distancing interventions. *Chaos Solitons Fractals* **2020**, *139*, 110088. [CrossRef]
5. Abdulwasaa, M.A.; Abdo, M.S.; Shah, K.; Nofal, T.A.; Panchal, S.K.; Kawale, S.V.; Abdel-Aty, A. Fractal-fractional mathematical modeling and forecasting of new cases and deaths of COVID-19 epidemic outbreaks in India. *Results Phys.* **2021**, *20*, 103702. [CrossRef]
6. Shahzad, M.; Abdel-Aty, A.-H.; Attia, R.A.M.; Khoshnaw, S.H.A.; Aldila, D.; Ali, M.; Sultan, F. Dynamics models for identifying the key transmission parameters of the COVID-19 disease. *Alex. Eng. J.* **2021**, *60*, 757–765. [CrossRef]
7. Ameen, I.G.; Ali, H.M.; Alharthi, M.R.; Abdel-Aty, A.-H.; Elshehabey, H.M. Investigation of the dynamics of COVID-19 with a fractional mathematical model: A comparative study with actual data. *Results Phys.* **2021**, *23*, 103976. [CrossRef] [PubMed]
8. Ahmad, S.; Owyed, S.; Abdel-Aty, A.; Mahmoud, E.E.; Shah, K.; Alrabaiah, H. Mathematical analysis of COVID-19 via new mathematical model. *Chaos Solitons Fractals* **2021**, *143*, 110585.
9. Peter, O.J.; Shaikh, A.S.; Ibrahim, M.O.; Nisar, K.S.; Baleanu, D.; Khan, I.; Abioye, A.I. Analysis and dynamics of fractional order mathematical model of COVID-19 in Nigeria using atangana-baleanu operator. *Comput. Mater. Contin.* **2021**, *66*, 1823–1848. [CrossRef]

10. Podlubny, I. *Fractional Differential Equations, Mathematics in Science and Engineering*; Academic Press: San Diego, CA, USA, 1999; p. 340.
11. Kilbas, A.A.; Srivastava, H.M.; Trujillo, J.J. *Theory and Applications of Fractional Differential Equations*; Elsevier: Amsterdam, The Netherlands, 2006; Volume 204.
12. Caputo, M.; Fabrizio, M. On the singular kernels for fractional derivatives. Some applications to partial differential equations. *Prog. Fract. Differ. Appl.* **2021**, *7*, 79–82. [CrossRef]
13. Caputo, M.; Fabrizio, M. A new definition of fractional derivative without singular kernel. *Prog. Fract. Differ. Appl.* **2015**, *1*, 73–85.
14. Caputo, M.; Fabrizio, M. Applications of new time and spatial fractional derivatives with exponential kernels. *Prog. Fract. Differ. Appl.* **2016**, *2*, 1–11. [CrossRef]
15. Toledo-Hernandez, R.; Rico-Ramirez, V.; Iglesias-Silva, G.A.; Diwekar, U.M. A fractional calculus approach to the dynamic optimization of biological reactive systems. Part I: Fractional models for biological reactions. *Chem. Eng. Sci.* **2014**, *117*, 217–228. [CrossRef]
16. Korpinar, Z. On numerical solutions for the Caputo-Fabrizio fractional heat-like equation. *Therm. Sci.* **2018**, *22* (Suppl. 1), 87–95. [CrossRef]
17. Kiymaz, O. An algorithm for solving initial value problems using Laplace Adomian decomposition method. *Appl. Math. Sci.* **2009**, *3*, 1453–1459.
18. Avinash, N.; Xavier, G.B.A.; Alsinai, A.; Ahmed, H.; Sherine, V.R.; Chellamani, P. Dynamics of COVID-19 Using SEIQR Epidemic Model. *J. Math.* **2022**, *2022*, 2138165. [CrossRef]
19. Chellamani, P.; Julietraja, K.; Alsinai, A.; Ahmed, H. A Fuzzy Fractional Order Approach to SIDARTHE Epidemic Model for COVID-19. *Complexity* **2022**, *2022*, 5468696. [CrossRef]
20. Shaikh, A.; Tassaddiq, A.; Nisar, K.S.; Baleanu, D. Analysis of differential equations involving Caputo–Fabrizio fractional operator and its applications to reaction–diffusion equations. *Adv. Differ. Equ.* **2019**, *2019*, 178. [CrossRef]
21. Baleanu, D.; Mohammadi, H.; Rezapour, S. Analysis of the model of HIV-1 infection of CD4+ $CD4^+$ T-cell with a new approach of fractional derivative. *Adv. Differ. Equ.* **2020**, *2020*, 71. [CrossRef]
22. Baleanu, D.; Jajarmi, A.; Mohammadi, H.; Rezapour, S. A new study on the mathematical modelling of human liver with Caputo–Fabrizio fractional derivative. *Chaos Solitons Fractals* **2020**, *134*, 109705. [CrossRef]
23. Alshabanat, A.; Jleli, M.; Kumar, S.; Samet, B. Generalization of Caputo-Fabrizio fractional derivative and applications to electrical circuits. *Front. Phys.* **2020**, *8*, 64. [CrossRef]
24. Baleanu, D.; Rezapour, S.; Saberpour, Z. On fractional integro-differential inclusions via the extended fractional Caputo–Fabrizio derivation. *Bound. Value Probl.* **2019**, *2019*, 79. [CrossRef]
25. Qiao, H.; Liu, Z.; Cheng, A. Two unconditionally stable difference schemes for time distributed-order differential equation based on Caputo–Fabrizio fractional derivative. *Adv. Differ. Equ.* **2020**, *2020*, 36. [CrossRef]
26. Al Sawoor, A. Stability analysis of fractional-order linear neutral delay differential–algebraic system described by the Caputo–Fabrizio derivative. *Adv. Differ. Equ.* **2020**, *2020*, 531. [CrossRef]
27. Ucar, E.; Özdemir, N.; Altun, E. Fractional order model of immune cells influenced by cancer cells. *Math. Model. Nat. Phenom.* **2019**, *14*, 308. [CrossRef]
28. Moore, E.J.; Sirisubtawee, S.; Koonprasert, S. A Caputo–Fabrizio fractional differential equation model for HIV/AIDS with treatment compartment. *Adv. Differ. Equ.* **2019**, *2019*, 200. [CrossRef]
29. Shah, K.; Alqudah, M.A.; Jarad, F.; Abdeljawad, T. Semi-analytical study of Pine Wilt Disease model with convex rate under Caputo–Febrizio fractional order derivative. *Chaos Solitons Fractals* **2020**, *135*, 109754. [CrossRef]
30. Bedi, P.; Khan, A.; Kumar, A.; Abdeljawad, T. Computational Study Of Fractional-Order Vector Borne Diseases Model. *Fractals* **2022**, *30*, 2240149. [CrossRef]
31. Amita Devi, A.; Kumar, A.; Abdeljawad, T. Numerical approximation of fractional order transmission of worms in wireless sensor network in sense of Caputo operator. *Prog. Fract. Differ. Appl.* **2022**, *1*, 1–15. [CrossRef]
32. Mehmood, Y.; Shafqat, R.; Sarris, I.E.; Bilal, M.; Sajid, T.; Akhtar, T. Numerical Investigation of MWCNT and SWCNT Fluid Flow along with the Activation Energy Effects over Quartic Auto Catalytic Endothermic and Exothermic Chemical Reactions. *Mathematics* **2022**, *10*, 4636.
33. Niazi, A.U.K.; He, J.; Shafqat, R.; Ahmed, B. Existence, Uniqueness, and E q–Ulam-Type Stability of Fuzzy Fractional Differential Equation. *Fractal Fract.* **2021**, *5*, 66. [CrossRef]
34. Iqbal, N.; Niazi, A.U.K.; Shafqat, R.; Zaland, S. Existence and uniqueness of mild solution for fractional-order controlled fuzzy evolution equation. *J. Funct. Spaces* **2021**, *2021*. [CrossRef]
35. Shafqat, R.; Niazi, A.U.K.; Jeelani, M.B.; Alharthi, N.H. Existence and Uniqueness of Mild Solution Where $\alpha \in (1,2)$ for Fuzzy Fractional Evolution Equations with Uncertainty. *Fractal Fract.* **2022**, *6*, 65. [CrossRef]
36. Alnahdi, A.S.; Shafqat, R.; Niazi, A.U.K.; Jeelani, M.B. Pattern formation induced by fuzzy fractional-order model of COVID-19. *Axioms* **2022**, *11*, 313. [CrossRef]
37. Khan, A.; Shafqat, R.; Niazi, A.U.K. Existence Results of Fuzzy Delay Impulsive Fractional Differential Equation by Fixed Point Theory Approach. *J. Funct. Spaces* **2022**, *2022*, 4123949. [CrossRef]
38. Abuasbeh, K.; Shafqat, R.; Niazi, A.U.K.; Awadalla, M. Nonlocal fuzzy fractional stochastic evolution equations with fractional Brownian motion of order (1, 2). *Aims Math.* **2022**, *7*, 19344–19358. [CrossRef]

39. Abuasbeh, K.; Shafqat, R.; Niazi, A.U.K.; Awadalla, M. Local and global existence and uniqueness of solution for class of fuzzy fractional functional evolution equation. *J. Funct. Spaces* **2022**, *2022*, 7512754. [CrossRef]
40. Abuasbeh, K.; Shafqat, R.; Niazi, A.U.K.; Awadalla, M. Local and global existence and uniqueness of solution for time-fractional fuzzy Navier–Stokes equations. *Fractal Fract.* **2022**, *6*, 330. [CrossRef]
41. ur Rahman, M.; Ahmad, S.; Matoog, R.T.; Alshehri, N.A.; Khan, T. Study on the mathematical modelling of COVID-19 with Caputo-Fabrizio operator. *Chaos Solitons Fractals* **2021**, *150*, 111121. [CrossRef]
42. Podlubny, I. Fractional differential equations. *Math. Sci. Eng.* **1999**, *198*, 41–119. [CrossRef]
43. Mainardi, F.; Paradisi, P.; Gorenflo, R. Probability distributions generated by fractional diffusion equations. *arXiv* **2007**, arXiv:0704.0320.
44. Otrocol, D.; Ilea, V. Ulam stability for a delay differential equation. *Open Math.* **2013**, *11*, 1296–1303.
45. Travis, C.C.; Webb, G.F. Cosine families and abstract nonlinear second order differential equations. *Acta Math. Hung.* **1978**, *32*, 75–96. [CrossRef]

symmetry

MDPI

Article

Existence and Ulam–Hyers Stability Results for a System of Coupled Generalized Liouville–Caputo Fractional Langevin Equations with Multipoint Boundary Conditions

Muath Awadalla [1], Muthaiah Subramanian [2,*] and Kinda Abuasbeh [1]

1 Department of Mathematics and Statistics, College of Science, King Faisal University, Hafuf 31982, Al Ahsa, Saudi Arabia
2 Department of Mathematics, KPR Institute of Engineering and Technology, Coimbatore 641407, Tamilnadu, India
* Correspondence: mawadalla@kfu.edu.sa (M.A.); subramanian.m@kpriet.ac.in (M.S.)

Abstract: We study the existence and uniqueness of solutions for coupled Langevin differential equations of fractional order with multipoint boundary conditions involving generalized Liouville–Caputo fractional derivatives. Furthermore, we discuss Ulam–Hyers stability in the context of the problem at hand. The results are shown with examples. Results are asymmetric when a generalized Liouville–Caputo fractional derivative (ρ) parameter is changed.

Keywords: coupled system; Langevin equations; generalized fractional integrals; generalized fractional derivatives; stability; existence; fixed point

MSC: 26A33; 34A08; 34B10

Citation: Awadalla, M.; Subramanian, M.; Abuasbeh, K. Existence and Ulam–Hyers Stability Results for a System of Coupled Generalized Liouville–Caputo Fractional Langevin Equations with Multipoint Boundary Conditions. *Symmetry* **2023**, *15*, 198. https://doi.org/10.3390/sym15010198

Academic Editors: Hassen Fourati, Abdellatif Ben Makhlouf and Omar Naifar

Received: 15 December 2022
Revised: 5 January 2023
Accepted: 6 January 2023
Published: 9 January 2023

1. Introduction

The study of operators of fractional order, including integral and derivative, over either real or complex domains is the focus of fractional calculus. Due to its active development and applications in the fields of physics, mechanics, chemistry, engineering, etc., fractional differential equations (FDEs) have become a popular topic of study among scholars. The books [1–7] are recommended for readers interested in the systematic development of the topic. In mathematical physics, the Langevin equation (LE) is a potent tool for modelling anomalous diffusion and other phenomena in a systematic way. Harmonic oscillators, price index variations [8], and other related processes are examples of this type of process. The theory of critical dynamics also extensively makes use of a general Langevin equation for noise sources with correlations [9]. To comprehend the nature of the quantum noise, a generalized Langevin equation (GLE) [10] can be employed. The LE has a highly elegant and rich role in fractional systems, such as fractional reaction–diffusion systems [11,12]. It is suggested that the fractional analogue of the standard LE, also known as the stochastic differential equation, be used in cases where the separation between microscopic and macroscopic time scales is not obvious; see, for instance, [13]. For a GLE of fractional order of the Liouville–Caputo fractional derivative, the author of [14] investigated moments, variances, location, and velocity correlation. Comparisons were made between the outcomes and those obtained for the same GLE. The aforementioned papers [15–21] and their relevant references contain recent studies on the LE with varied boundary conditions. The study of fractional calculus has become a significant area of study because of the multiple applications it has in the technical sciences, social sciences, and engineering professions. Differential and integral operators based on a fractional order are thought to be more realistic and useful than their integer-order counterparts because they can show the history of ongoing phenomena and processes. Recently, the literature on the subject has included Hadamard, Caputo(Liouville–Caputo), Riemann–Liouville type derivatives, among others, as well as FDEs. See citations [22–30], as well as the references, for a few recent publications on the topic. The authors in [31] discussed the existence of solutions for Langevin FDEs using Liouville–Caputo derivatives:

$$\begin{cases} {}^{\rho}_{c}\mathcal{D}^{\alpha}_{a^+}({}^{\rho}_{c}\mathcal{D}^{\beta}_{a^+}+\lambda)x(t)=f(t,x(t)), t\in\mathcal{J}:=[a,T], \\ \lambda\in\mathbb{R},\ 1<\alpha\leq 2,\ 0<\beta<1,\ \rho>0 \end{cases} \tag{1}$$

$$\left\{ x(a)=0,\ x(\eta)=0,\ x(T)=\mu^{\rho}\mathcal{I}^{\gamma}_{a^+}x(\xi),\ \gamma>0, \rho>0, \right. \tag{2}$$

where ${}^{\rho}_{c}\mathcal{D}^{\alpha}_{a^+}, {}^{\rho}_{c}\mathcal{D}^{\beta}_{a^+}$ denote the generalized Liouville–Caputo fractional derivatives (GLCFD), ${}^{\rho}\mathcal{I}^{\gamma}_{a^+}$ is the generalized fractional integral (GFI). The main results were proven using a fixed-point index theory. Applications to differential equations in science inevitably lead to multipoint boundary value problems. A dynamical system with m degrees of freedom, for instance, might have exactly m examples that are seen at m different times. An m-point boundary value problem is a mathematical representation of such problems. Multipoint problems for differential equations are a subset of interface problems and are therefore amenable to a variety of solutions. The study of fractional differential equations with multipoint boundary conditions has attracted the interest of numerous researchers (see [32–35] and the references given therein). We demonstrate the existence, uniqueness of solutions and Ulam–Hyers stability for the following generalized Langevin fractional differential system with multipoint boundary conditions, which was inspired by previous research, by utilizing the fixed-point theorems:

$$\begin{cases} {}^{\rho}_{C}\mathcal{D}^{\xi_1}_{0^+}({}^{\rho}_{C}\mathcal{D}^{\zeta_1}_{0^+}+\phi_1)x(\iota)=f(\iota,x(\iota),y(\iota)), \iota\in\mathcal{E}:=[0,\mathcal{S}], \\ {}^{\rho}_{C}\mathcal{D}^{\xi_2}_{0^+}({}^{\rho}_{C}\mathcal{D}^{\zeta_2}_{0^+}+\phi_2)y(\iota)=g(\iota,x(\iota),y(\iota)), \iota\in\mathcal{E}:=[0,\mathcal{S}], \end{cases} \tag{3}$$

$$\begin{cases} x(0)=0, \quad y(0)=0,\ x(\mathcal{S})=\epsilon\sum_{j=1}^{k}\varsigma_j y(\varpi_j),\ y(\mathcal{S})=\pi\sum_{j=1}^{k}\varrho_j x(\sigma_j), \\ 0<\sigma_1<\varpi_1<\cdots<\sigma_k<\varpi_k<\mathcal{S}, \end{cases} \tag{4}$$

where ${}^{\rho}_{C}\mathcal{D}^{\xi_1}_{0^+}, {}^{\rho}_{C}\mathcal{D}^{\xi_2}_{0^+}, {}^{\rho}_{C}\mathcal{D}^{\zeta_1}_{0^+}, {}^{\rho}_{C}\mathcal{D}^{\zeta_2}_{0^+}$ are the GLCFD of order $1<\xi_1,\xi_2\leq 2$, $0<\zeta_1,\zeta_2<1$, and $f,g:\mathcal{E}\times\mathbb{R}\times\mathbb{R}\to\mathbb{R}$ are continuous functions, $\epsilon,\pi\in\mathbb{R}$. The requirement states that the unknown function's value at the right endpoint of the specified interval, $\iota=\mathcal{S}$, must be proportional to its values on different multipoint values of unknown functions with σ_j,ϖ_j, $j=1,2,\cdots k$, where ς_j,ϱ_j, $j=1,2,\cdots k$ are arbitrary constants. The GLCFD is converted into the differentially effective Caputo sense when $\rho=1$. It should be noticed that the multipoint strip boundary condition in (4) is new in the context of generalized Liouville–Caputo fractional differential equations and can be understood as the value of a known function at $\mathcal{S}$ being proportional to the discrete values of the unknown function at ϖ_i,σ_i, $i=1,2,\ldots,k$. By employing the fixed-point technique, we investigate the existence and uniqueness solutions of nonlocal generalized Liouville–Caputo fractional boundary value problem with discrete boundary conditions (3) and (4). Differently from the above mentioned works, we obtain the Ulam–Hyers stability solutions of the nonlocal boundary value problem of the generalized Liouville–Caputo type fractional differential Equations (3) and (4) by using conventional functional analysis. To the best of our knowledge, boundary value problems' (BVPs) stability analysis is still in its early development. The fundamental contribution of this research is to investigate the existence of Ulam–Hyers stability solutions. In addition, we show the problems (3) and (4) used by the fixed-point theorems of Leray–Schauder and Banach to demonstrate the existence and uniqueness of the solutions. The remainder of the paper is structured as follows: In Section 2, we review some fundamental ideas of fractional calculus and find the integral solutions to the given problems' linear versions. The existence results for problems (3) and (4) derived by using Leray–Schauder's nonlinear alternative and Banach's contraction mapping principle are presented in Section 3. Section 4 looks at the Ulam–Hyers stability of the provided systems (3) and (4) under particular circumstances. Examples are provided in Section 6 to further clarify the study's findings.

2. Preliminaries

This section begins with the fundamental definitions of fractional calculus. Later, we demonstrate an auxiliary lemma that is crucial in formulating a fixed-point problem related to the topic at hand. We define space $\mathcal{P} = \{x(\iota) : x(\iota) \in \mathcal{C}(\mathcal{E}, \mathbb{R})\}$ equipped with the norm $||x|| = \sup\{|x(\iota)|, \iota \in \mathcal{E}\}$ as a Banach space. Moreover, $\mathcal{Q} = \{y(\iota) : y(\iota) \in \mathcal{C}(\mathcal{E}, \mathbb{R})\}$ equipped with the norm $||y|| = \sup\{|y(\iota)|, \iota \in \mathcal{E}\}$ is a Banach space. Then, the product space $(\mathcal{P} \times \mathcal{Q}, ||(x, y)||)$ is also a Banach space with norm $||(x, y)|| = ||x|| + ||y||$.

Definition 1 ([36]). *The left- and right-sided GFIs of $f \in \mathcal{Z}_b^y(c, d)$ of order $\xi > 0$ and $\rho > 0$, for $-\infty < c < \iota < d < \infty$, are defined as follows:*

$$({}^{\rho}\mathcal{I}_{c^+}^{\xi} f)(\iota) = \frac{\rho^{1-\xi}}{\Gamma(\xi)} \int_c^{\iota} \frac{\theta^{\rho-1}}{(\iota^{\rho} - \theta^{\rho})^{1-\xi}} f(\theta) d\theta, \tag{5}$$

$$({}^{\rho}\mathcal{I}_{d^-}^{\zeta} f)(\iota) = \frac{\rho^{1-\xi}}{\Gamma(\xi)} \int_{\iota}^{d} \frac{\theta^{\rho-1}}{(\theta^{\rho} - \iota^{\rho})^{1-\xi}} f(\theta) d\theta. \tag{6}$$

Definition 2 ([37]). *The generalized fractional derivatives (GFDs) which are associated with GFIs (5) and (6), for $0 \leq c < \iota < d < \infty$, are defined as follows:*

$$\begin{aligned} ({}^{\rho}\mathcal{D}_{c^+}^{\zeta} f)(\iota) &= \left(\iota^{1-\rho} \frac{d}{d\iota}\right)^n ({}^{\rho}\mathcal{I}_{c^+}^{n-\zeta} f)(\iota) \\ &= \frac{\rho^{\zeta-n+1}}{\Gamma(n-\zeta)} \left(\iota^{1-\rho} \frac{d}{d\iota}\right)^n \int_c^{\iota} \frac{\theta^{\rho-1}}{(\iota^{\rho} - \theta^{\rho})^{\zeta-n+1}} f(\theta) d\theta, \end{aligned} \tag{7}$$

$$\begin{aligned} ({}^{\rho}\mathcal{D}_{d^-}^{\zeta} f)(\iota) &= \left(-\iota^{1-\rho} \frac{d}{d\iota}\right)^n ({}^{\rho}\mathcal{I}_{d^-}^{n-\zeta} f)(\iota) \\ &= \frac{\rho^{\zeta-n+1}}{\Gamma(n-\zeta)} \left(-\iota^{1-\rho} \frac{d}{d\iota}\right)^n \int_{\iota}^{d} \frac{\theta^{\rho-1}}{(\iota^{\rho} - \theta^{\rho})^{\zeta-n+1}} f(\theta) d\theta, \end{aligned} \tag{8}$$

if the integrals exist.

Definition 3 ([38]). *The above GFDs define the left- and right-sided generalized Liouville–Caputo type fractional derivatives of $f \in \mathcal{AC}_{\gamma}^n[c, d]$ of order $\zeta \geq 0$*

$${}_{C}^{\rho}\mathcal{D}_{c^+}^{\zeta} f(z) = {}^{\rho}\mathcal{D}_{c^+}^{\zeta} \left[f(\iota) - \sum_{k=0}^{n-1} \frac{\gamma^k f(c)}{k!} \left(\frac{\iota^{\rho} - c^{\rho}}{\rho} \right)^k \right](z), \gamma = z^{1-\rho} \frac{d}{dz}, \tag{9}$$

$${}_{C}^{\rho}\mathcal{D}_{d^-}^{\zeta} f(z) = {}^{\rho}\mathcal{D}_{d^-}^{\zeta} \left[f(\iota) - \sum_{k=0}^{n-1} \frac{(-1)^k \gamma^k f(d)}{k!} \left(\frac{d^{\rho} - \iota^{\rho}}{\rho} \right)^k \right](z), \gamma = z^{1-\rho} \frac{d}{dz}, \tag{10}$$

when $n = [\zeta] + 1$.

Lemma 1 ([38]). *1.* *If $\zeta \notin \mathbb{N}$,*

$$ {}^{\rho}_{C}\mathcal{D}^{\zeta}_{c+}f(\iota) = \frac{1}{\Gamma(n-\zeta)} \int_{c}^{\iota} \left(\frac{\iota^{\rho} - \theta^{\rho}}{\rho} \right)^{n-\zeta-1} \frac{(\gamma^{n} f)(\theta) d\theta}{\theta^{1-\rho}} = {}^{\rho}\mathcal{I}^{n-\zeta}_{c+}(\gamma^{n} f)(\iota), \tag{11} $$

$$ {}^{\rho}_{C}\mathcal{D}^{\zeta}_{d-}f(\iota) = \frac{1}{\Gamma(n-\zeta)} \int_{\iota}^{d} \left(\frac{\theta^{\rho} - \iota^{\rho}}{\rho} \right)^{n-\zeta-1} \frac{(-1)^{n}(\gamma^{n} f)(\theta) d\theta}{\theta^{1-\rho}} = {}^{\rho}\mathcal{I}^{n-\zeta}_{d-}(\gamma^{n} f)(\iota). \tag{12} $$

2. *If $\zeta \in \mathbb{N}$,*

$$ {}^{\rho}_{C}\mathcal{D}^{\zeta}_{c+}f = \gamma^{n} f, \qquad {}^{\rho}_{C}\mathcal{D}^{\zeta}_{d-}f = (-1)^{n}\gamma^{n} f. \tag{13} $$

Lemma 2 ([38]). *Let $f \in \mathcal{AC}^{n}_{\gamma}[c,d]$ or $\mathcal{C}^{n}_{\gamma}[c,d]$ and $\zeta \in \mathbb{R}$. Then,*

$$ {}^{\rho}\mathcal{I}^{\zeta}_{c+}\,{}^{\rho}_{C}\mathcal{D}^{\zeta}_{c+}f(\iota) = f(\iota) - \sum_{k=0}^{n-1} \frac{\gamma^{k} f(c)}{k!} \left(\frac{\iota^{\rho} - c^{\rho}}{\rho} \right)^{k}, $$

$$ {}^{\rho}\mathcal{I}^{\zeta}_{d-}\,{}^{\rho}_{C}\mathcal{D}^{\zeta}_{d-}f(\iota) = f(\iota) - \sum_{k=0}^{n-1} \frac{(-1)^{k}\gamma^{k} f(d)}{k!} \left(\frac{d^{\rho} - \iota^{\rho}}{\rho} \right)^{k}. $$

In particular, for $0 < \zeta \leq 1$, we have

$$ {}^{\rho}\mathcal{I}^{\zeta}_{c+}\,{}^{\rho}_{C}\mathcal{D}^{\zeta}_{c+}f(\iota) = f(\iota) - f(c), \qquad {}^{\rho}\mathcal{I}^{\zeta}_{d-}\,{}^{\rho}_{C}\mathcal{D}^{\zeta}_{d-}f(\iota) = f(\iota) - f(d). $$

In order to facilitate the computation, we present the following notations:

$$ \widehat{\mathcal{E}}_{1} = \frac{\mathcal{S}^{\rho\zeta_{1}}}{\rho^{\zeta_{1}}\Gamma(\zeta_{1}+1)}, \; \widehat{\mathcal{E}}_{2} = \frac{\pi \sum_{j=1}^{k} \varrho_{j} \sigma_{j}^{\rho(\zeta_{1})}}{\rho^{\zeta_{1}}\Gamma(\zeta_{1}+1)}, \tag{14} $$

$$ \mathcal{E}_{1} = \frac{\mathcal{S}^{\rho\zeta_{2}}}{\rho^{\zeta_{2}}\Gamma(\zeta_{2}+1)}, \; \mathcal{E}_{2} = \frac{\epsilon \sum_{j=1}^{k} \varsigma_{j} \varpi_{j}^{\rho(\zeta_{2})}}{\rho^{\zeta_{2}}\Gamma(\zeta_{2}+1)}, \tag{15} $$

$$ \mathcal{G} = \widehat{\mathcal{E}}_{1}\mathcal{E}_{2} - \mathcal{E}_{1}\widehat{\mathcal{E}}_{2} \neq 0, \tag{16} $$

$$ \delta_{1}(\iota) = \left(\frac{\iota^{\rho\zeta_{1}}}{\rho^{\zeta_{1}}\Gamma(\zeta_{1}+1)\mathcal{G}} \right), \; \delta_{2}(\iota) = \left(\frac{\iota^{\rho\zeta_{2}}}{\rho^{\zeta_{2}}\Gamma(\zeta_{2}+1)\mathcal{G}} \right). \tag{17} $$

Lemma 3. *Let $\hat{f}, \hat{g} \in C(0,\mathcal{S}) \cup \mathcal{L}(0,\mathcal{S}), x, y \in \mathcal{AC}^{2}_{\gamma}(\mathcal{E})$, and $\Lambda \neq 0$. The solution of the system of coupled Langevin fractional BVP:*

$$ \begin{cases} {}^{\rho}_{C}\mathcal{D}^{\xi_{1}}_{0+}({}^{\rho}_{C}\mathcal{D}^{\zeta_{1}}_{0+} + \phi_{1})x(\iota) = \hat{f}(\iota), \iota \in \mathcal{E} := [0,\mathcal{S}], \\ {}^{\rho}_{C}\mathcal{D}^{\xi_{2}}_{0+}({}^{\rho}_{C}\mathcal{D}^{\zeta_{2}}_{0+} + \phi_{2})y(\iota) = \hat{g}(\iota), \iota \in \mathcal{E} := [0,\mathcal{S}], \\ x(0) = 0, \quad y(0) = 0, \; x(\mathcal{S}) = \epsilon \sum_{j=1}^{k} \varsigma_{j} y(\varpi_{j}), \; y(\mathcal{S}) = \pi \sum_{j=1}^{k} \varrho_{j} x(\sigma_{j}), \\ 0 < \sigma_{1} < \varpi_{1} < \cdots < \sigma_{k} < \varpi_{k} < \mathcal{S}, \end{cases} \tag{18} $$

is given by

$$\begin{aligned}x(\iota) =& {}^{\rho}\mathcal{I}_{0^+}^{\xi_1+\zeta_1}\hat{f}(\iota) - \phi_1^{\rho}\mathcal{I}_{0^+}^{\zeta_1}x(\iota)\\&+\delta_1(\iota)\Bigg[\mathcal{E}_2\Bigg(\epsilon\sum_{j=1}^{k}\varsigma_j{}^{\rho}\mathcal{I}_{0^+}^{\xi_2+\zeta_2}\hat{g}(\varpi_j) - \epsilon\phi_2\sum_{j=1}^{k}\varsigma_j^{\rho}\mathcal{I}_{0^+}^{\zeta_2}y(\varpi_j) - {}^{\rho}\mathcal{I}_{0^+}^{\xi_1+\zeta_1}\hat{f}(\mathcal{S}) + \phi_1^{\rho}\mathcal{I}_{0^+}^{\zeta_1}x(\mathcal{S})\Bigg)\\&+\mathcal{E}_1\Bigg(\pi\sum_{j=1}^{k}\varrho_j{}^{\rho}\mathcal{I}_{0^+}^{\xi_1+\zeta_1}\hat{f}(\sigma_j) - \pi\phi_1\sum_{j=1}^{k}\varrho_j^{\rho}\mathcal{I}_{0^+}^{\zeta_1}x(\sigma_j) - {}^{\rho}\mathcal{I}_{0^+}^{\xi_2+\zeta_2}\hat{g}(\mathcal{S}) + \phi_2^{\rho}\mathcal{I}_{0^+}^{\zeta_2}y(\mathcal{S})\Bigg)\Bigg]\end{aligned} \tag{19}$$

and

$$\begin{aligned}y(\iota) =& {}^{\rho}\mathcal{I}_{0^+}^{\xi_2+\zeta_2}\hat{g}(\iota) - \phi_2^{\rho}\mathcal{I}_{0^+}^{\zeta_2}y(\iota)\\&+\delta_2(\iota)\Bigg[\widehat{\mathcal{E}}_2\Bigg(\epsilon\sum_{j=1}^{k}\varsigma_j{}^{\rho}\mathcal{I}_{0^+}^{\xi_2+\zeta_2}\hat{g}(\varpi_j) - \epsilon\phi_2\sum_{j=1}^{k}\varsigma_j^{\rho}\mathcal{I}_{0^+}^{\zeta_2}y(\varpi_j) - {}^{\rho}\mathcal{I}_{0^+}^{\xi_1+\zeta_1}\hat{f}(\mathcal{S}) + \phi_1^{\rho}\mathcal{I}_{0^+}^{\zeta_1}x(\mathcal{S})\Bigg)\\&+\widehat{\mathcal{E}}_1\Bigg(\pi\sum_{j=1}^{k}\varrho_j{}^{\rho}\mathcal{I}_{0^+}^{\xi_1+\zeta_1}\hat{f}(\sigma_j) - \pi\phi_1\sum_{j=1}^{k}\varrho_j^{\rho}\mathcal{I}_{0^+}^{\zeta_1}x(\sigma_j) - {}^{\rho}\mathcal{I}_{0^+}^{\xi_2+\zeta_2}\hat{g}(\mathcal{S}) + \phi_2^{\rho}\mathcal{I}_{0^+}^{\zeta_2}y(\mathcal{S})\Bigg)\Bigg].\end{aligned} \tag{20}$$

Proof. Applying operators ${}^{\rho}\mathcal{I}_{0^+}^{\xi_1}, {}^{\rho}\mathcal{I}_{0^+}^{\xi_2}$ to (18) and using Lemma 2, we get

$$({}^{\rho}_{C}\mathcal{D}_{0^+}^{\zeta_1} + \phi_1)x(\iota) = {}^{\rho}\mathcal{I}_{0^+}^{\xi_1}\hat{f}(\iota) + a_1, \tag{21}$$

$$({}^{\rho}_{C}\mathcal{D}_{0^+}^{\zeta_2} + \phi_2)y(\iota) = {}^{\rho}\mathcal{I}_{0^+}^{\xi_2}\hat{g}(\iota) + b_1, \tag{22}$$

respectively, for some $a_1, b_1 \in \mathcal{R}$. When ${}^{\rho}\mathcal{I}_{0^+}^{\zeta_1}, {}^{\rho}\mathcal{I}_{0^+}^{\zeta_2}$ are applied to the FDEs in (21) and (22), the solution of the Langevin FDEs in (18) for $\iota \in \mathcal{E}$ is

$$x(\iota) = {}^{\rho}\mathcal{I}_{0^+}^{\xi_1+\zeta_1}\hat{f}(\iota) - \phi_1^{\rho}\mathcal{I}_{0^+}^{\zeta_1}x(\iota) + a_1\frac{\iota^{\rho\zeta_1}}{\rho^{\zeta_1}\Gamma(\zeta_1+1)} + a_2, \tag{23}$$

$$y(\iota) = {}^{\rho}\mathcal{I}_{0^+}^{\xi_2+\zeta_2}\hat{g}(\iota) - \phi_2^{\rho}\mathcal{I}_{0^+}^{\zeta_2}y(\iota) + b_1\frac{\iota^{\rho\zeta_2}}{\rho^{\zeta_2}\Gamma(\zeta_2+1)} + b_2, \tag{24}$$

respectively, for some $a_2, b_2 \in \mathcal{R}$. By utilizing the conditions $x(0) = y(0) = 0$ in (23) and (24), respectively, we get $a_2 = b_2 = 0$. Then, using the multipoint boundary conditions, we get:

$$\sum_{j=1}^{k}\varrho_j x(\sigma_j) = \sum_{j=1}^{k}\varrho_j{}^{\rho}\mathcal{I}_{0^+}^{\xi_1+\zeta_1}\hat{f}(\sigma_j) - \phi_1\sum_{j=1}^{k}\varrho_j^{\rho}\mathcal{I}_{0^+}^{\zeta_1}x(\sigma_j) + a_1\sum_{j=1}^{k}\frac{\varrho_j\sigma_j^{\rho(\zeta_1)}}{\rho^{\zeta_1}\Gamma(\zeta_1+1)}, \tag{25}$$

$$\sum_{j=1}^{k}\varsigma_j y(\varpi_j) = \sum_{j=1}^{k}\varsigma_j{}^{\rho}\mathcal{I}_{0^+}^{\xi_2+\zeta_2}\hat{g}(\varpi_j) - \phi_2\sum_{j=1}^{k}\varsigma_j^{\rho}\mathcal{I}_{0^+}^{\zeta_2}y(\varpi_j) + b_1\sum_{j=1}^{k}\frac{\varsigma_j\varpi_j^{\rho(\zeta_2)}}{\rho^{\zeta_2}\Gamma(\zeta_2+1)}, \tag{26}$$

which, when combined with the boundary conditions $x(\mathcal{S}) = \epsilon\sum_{j=1}^{k} y(\varpi_j)$, $y(\mathcal{S}) = \pi\sum_{j=1}^{k} x(\sigma_j)$, gives the following results:

$$^{\rho}\mathcal{I}_{0^+}^{\xi_1+\zeta_1}\hat{f}(\mathcal{S}) - \phi_1^{\rho}\mathcal{I}_{0^+}^{\zeta_1}x(\mathcal{S}) + a_1\frac{\mathcal{S}^{\rho\zeta_1}}{\rho^{\zeta_1}\Gamma(\zeta_1+1)} = \epsilon\sum_{j=1}^{k}\varsigma_j{}^{\rho}\mathcal{I}_{0^+}^{\xi_2+\zeta_2}\hat{g}(\varpi_j) - \epsilon\phi_2\sum_{j=1}^{k}\varsigma_j^{\rho}\mathcal{I}_{0^+}^{\zeta_2}y(\varpi_j) + b_1\epsilon\sum_{j=1}^{k}\frac{\varsigma_j\varpi_j^{\rho(\zeta_2)}}{\rho^{\zeta_2}\Gamma(\zeta_2+1)}, \tag{27}$$

$$^{\rho}\mathcal{I}_{0^+}^{\xi_2+\zeta_2}\hat{g}(\mathcal{S}) - \phi_2^{\rho}\mathcal{I}_{0^+}^{\zeta_2}y(\mathcal{S}) + b_1\frac{\mathcal{S}^{\rho\zeta_2}}{\rho^{\zeta_2}\Gamma(\zeta_2+1)} = \pi\sum_{j=1}^{k}\varrho_j{}^{\rho}\mathcal{I}_{0^+}^{\xi_1+\zeta_1}\hat{f}(\sigma_j) - \pi\phi_1\sum_{j=1}^{k}\varrho_j^{\rho}\mathcal{I}_{0^+}^{\zeta_1}x(\sigma_j) + a_1\pi\sum_{j=1}^{k}\frac{\varrho_j\sigma_j^{\rho(\zeta_1)}}{\rho^{\zeta_1}\Gamma(\zeta_1+1)}. \tag{28}$$

Next, we obtain

$$a_1\widehat{\mathcal{E}_1} - b_1\mathcal{E}_1 = \epsilon\sum_{j=1}^{k}\varsigma_j{}^{\rho}\mathcal{I}_{0^+}^{\xi_2+\zeta_2}\hat{g}(\varpi_j) - \epsilon\phi_2\sum_{j=1}^{k}\varsigma_j^{\rho}\mathcal{I}_{0^+}^{\zeta_2}y(\varpi_j) -^{\rho}\mathcal{I}_{0^+}^{\xi_1+\zeta_1}\hat{f}(\mathcal{S}) + \phi_1^{\rho}\mathcal{I}_{0^+}^{\zeta_1}x(\mathcal{S}), \tag{29}$$

$$b_1\mathcal{E}_2 - a_2\widehat{\mathcal{E}_2} = \pi\sum_{j=1}^{k}\varrho_j{}^{\rho}\mathcal{I}_{0^+}^{\xi_1+\zeta_1}\hat{f}(\sigma_j) - \pi\phi_1\sum_{j=1}^{k}\varrho_j^{\rho}\mathcal{I}_{0^+}^{\zeta_1}x(\sigma_j) -^{\rho}\mathcal{I}_{0^+}^{\xi_2+\zeta_2}\hat{g}(\mathcal{S}) + \phi_2^{\rho}\mathcal{I}_{0^+}^{\zeta_2}y(\mathcal{S}), \tag{30}$$

using the notations (15) in (27) and (28), respectively. When the system of equations is solved, we find that (29) and (30) for a_1 and b_1 are

$$\begin{aligned} a_1 =& \frac{1}{\mathcal{G}}\Bigg[\mathcal{E}_2\Bigg(\epsilon\sum_{j=1}^{k}\varsigma_j{}^{\rho}\mathcal{I}_{0^+}^{\xi_2+\zeta_2}\hat{g}(\varpi_j) - \epsilon\phi_2\sum_{j=1}^{k}\varsigma_j^{\rho}\mathcal{I}_{0^+}^{\zeta_2}y(\varpi_j) -^{\rho}\mathcal{I}_{0^+}^{\xi_1+\zeta_1}\hat{f}(\mathcal{S}) + \phi_1^{\rho}\mathcal{I}_{0^+}^{\zeta_1}x(\mathcal{S})\Bigg) \\ &+ \mathcal{E}_1\Bigg(\pi\sum_{j=1}^{k}\varrho_j{}^{\rho}\mathcal{I}_{0^+}^{\xi_1+\zeta_1}\hat{f}(\sigma_j) - \pi\phi_1\sum_{j=1}^{k}\varrho_j^{\rho}\mathcal{I}_{0^+}^{\zeta_1}x(\sigma_j) -^{\rho}\mathcal{I}_{0^+}^{\xi_2+\zeta_2}\hat{g}(\mathcal{S}) + \phi_2^{\rho}\mathcal{I}_{0^+}^{\zeta_2}y(\mathcal{S})\Bigg)\Bigg], \end{aligned} \tag{31}$$

$$\begin{aligned} b_1 =& \frac{1}{\mathcal{G}}\Bigg[\widehat{\mathcal{E}_2}\Bigg(\epsilon\sum_{j=1}^{k}\varsigma_j{}^{\rho}\mathcal{I}_{0^+}^{\xi_2+\zeta_2}\hat{g}(\varpi_j) - \epsilon\phi_2\sum_{j=1}^{k}\varsigma_j^{\rho}\mathcal{I}_{0^+}^{\zeta_2}y(\varpi_j) -^{\rho}\mathcal{I}_{0^+}^{\xi_1+\zeta_1}\hat{f}(\mathcal{S}) + \phi_1^{\rho}\mathcal{I}_{0^+}^{\zeta_1}x(\mathcal{S})\Bigg) \\ &+ \widehat{\mathcal{E}_1}\Bigg(\pi\sum_{j=1}^{k}\varrho_j{}^{\rho}\mathcal{I}_{0^+}^{\xi_1+\zeta_1}\hat{f}(\sigma_j) - \pi\phi_1\sum_{j=1}^{k}\varrho_j^{\rho}\mathcal{I}_{0^+}^{\zeta_1}x(\sigma_j) -^{\rho}\mathcal{I}_{0^+}^{\xi_2+\zeta_2}\hat{g}(\mathcal{S}) + \phi_2^{\rho}\mathcal{I}_{0^+}^{\zeta_2}y(\mathcal{S})\Bigg)\Bigg]. \end{aligned} \tag{32}$$

Substituting the values of a_1, b_1 in (23) and (24), respectively, we obtain the BVP solution (18). □

3. Main Results

We propose a fixed-point problem relevant to the problem in Lemma 3 as follows: $\Psi : \mathcal{P} \times \mathcal{Q} \to \mathcal{P} \times \mathcal{Q}$ by

$$\Psi(x,y)(\iota) = (\Psi_1(x,y)(\iota), \Psi_2(x,y)(\iota)), \tag{33}$$

where

$$\Psi_1(x,y)(\iota) = {}^{\rho}\mathcal{I}_{0^+}^{\xi_1+\zeta_1} f(\iota, x(\iota), y(\iota)) - \phi_1^{\rho}\mathcal{I}_{0^+}^{\zeta_1} x(\iota) + \delta_1(\iota)\Bigg[\mathcal{E}_2\Bigg(\epsilon \sum_{j=1}^{k} \varsigma_j {}^{\rho}\mathcal{I}_{0^+}^{\xi_2+\zeta_2} g(\varpi_j, x(\varpi_j), y(\varpi_j))$$
$$- \epsilon\phi_2 \sum_{j=1}^{k} \varsigma_j^{\rho}\mathcal{I}_{0^+}^{\zeta_2} y(\varpi_j) - {}^{\rho}\mathcal{I}_{0^+}^{\xi_1+\zeta_1} f(\mathcal{S}, x(\mathcal{S}), y(\mathcal{S})) + \phi_1^{\rho}\mathcal{I}_{0^+}^{\zeta_1} x(\mathcal{S})\Bigg)$$
$$+ \mathcal{E}_1\Bigg(\pi \sum_{j=1}^{k} \varrho_j {}^{\rho}\mathcal{I}_{0^+}^{\xi_1+\zeta_1} f(\sigma_j, x(\sigma_j), y(\sigma_j)) - \pi\phi_1 \sum_{j=1}^{k} \varrho_j^{\rho}\mathcal{I}_{0^+}^{\zeta_1} x(\sigma_j) \tag{34}$$
$$- {}^{\rho}\mathcal{I}_{0^+}^{\xi_2+\zeta_2} g(\mathcal{S}, x(\mathcal{S}), y(\mathcal{S})) + \phi_2^{\rho}\mathcal{I}_{0^+}^{\zeta_2} y(\mathcal{S})\Bigg)\Bigg],$$

$$\Psi_2(x,y)(\iota) = {}^{\rho}\mathcal{I}_{0^+}^{\xi_2+\zeta_2} g(\iota, x(\iota), y(\iota)) - \phi_2^{\rho}\mathcal{I}_{0^+}^{\zeta_2} y(\iota) + \delta_2(\iota)\Bigg[\widehat{\mathcal{E}_2}\Bigg(\epsilon \sum_{j=1}^{k} \varsigma_j {}^{\rho}\mathcal{I}_{0^+}^{\xi_2+\zeta_2} g(\varpi_j, x(\varpi_j), y(\varpi_j))$$
$$- \epsilon\phi_2 \sum_{j=1}^{k} \varsigma_j^{\rho}\mathcal{I}_{0^+}^{\zeta_2} y(\varpi_j) - {}^{\rho}\mathcal{I}_{0^+}^{\xi_1+\zeta_1} f(\mathcal{S}, x(\mathcal{S}), y(\mathcal{S})) + \phi_1^{\rho}\mathcal{I}_{0^+}^{\zeta_1} x(\mathcal{S})\Bigg)$$
$$+ \widehat{\mathcal{E}_1}\Bigg(\pi \sum_{j=1}^{k} \varrho_j {}^{\rho}\mathcal{I}_{0^+}^{\xi_1+\zeta_1} f(\sigma_j, x(\sigma_j), y(\sigma_j)) - \pi\phi_1 \sum_{j=1}^{k} \varrho_j^{\rho}\mathcal{I}_{0^+}^{\zeta_1} x(\sigma_j) \tag{35}$$
$$- {}^{\rho}\mathcal{I}_{0^+}^{\xi_2+\zeta_2} g(\mathcal{S}, x(\mathcal{S}), y(\mathcal{S})) + \phi_2^{\rho}\mathcal{I}_{0^+}^{\zeta_2} y(\mathcal{S})\Bigg)\Bigg].$$

For brevity, we use these notations:

$$\mathcal{U}_1 = \frac{\left(\mathcal{S}^{\rho(\xi_1+\zeta_1)}(1 + |\delta_1||\mathcal{E}_2|)\right)}{\rho^{\xi_1+\zeta_1}\Gamma(\xi_1+\zeta_1+1)} + \frac{|\delta_1||\pi||\mathcal{E}_1| \sum_{j=1}^{k} \varrho_j \sigma_j^{\rho(\xi_1+\zeta_1)}}{\rho^{\xi_1+\zeta_1}\Gamma(\xi_1+\zeta_1+1)}, \tag{36}$$

$$\mathcal{V}_1 = |\delta_1|\left(\frac{|\mathcal{E}_1|\mathcal{S}^{\rho(\xi_2+\zeta_2)}}{\rho^{\xi_2+\zeta_2}\Gamma(\xi_2+\zeta_2+1)} + \frac{|\mathcal{E}_2||\epsilon| \sum_{j=1}^{k} \varsigma_j \varpi_j^{\rho(\xi_2+\zeta_2)}}{\rho^{\xi_2+\zeta_2}\Gamma(\xi_2+\zeta_2+1)}\right), \tag{37}$$

$$\widehat{\mathcal{U}_1} = |\phi_1|\left(\frac{(\mathcal{S}^{\rho\zeta_1}(1 + |\delta_1||\mathcal{E}_2|))}{\rho^{\zeta_1}\Gamma(\zeta_1+1)} + \frac{|\delta_1||\pi||\mathcal{E}_1| \sum_{j=1}^{k} \varrho_j \sigma_j^{\rho(\zeta_1)}}{\rho^{\zeta_1}\Gamma(\zeta_1+1)}\right), \tag{38}$$

$$\widehat{\mathcal{V}_1} = |\delta_1||\phi_2|\left(\frac{|\mathcal{E}_1|\mathcal{S}^{\rho\zeta_2}}{\rho^{\zeta_2}\Gamma(\zeta_2+1)} + \frac{|\mathcal{E}_2||\epsilon| \sum_{j=1}^{k} \varsigma_j \varpi_j^{\rho(\zeta_2)}}{\rho^{\zeta_2}\Gamma(\zeta_2+1)}\right), \tag{39}$$

$$\mathcal{U}_2 = |\delta_2|\left(\frac{\mathcal{S}^{\rho(\xi_1+\zeta_1)}|\widehat{\mathcal{E}_2}|}{\rho^{\xi_1+\zeta_1}\Gamma(\xi_1+\zeta_1+1)} + \frac{|\pi||\widehat{\mathcal{E}_1}| \sum_{j=1}^{k} \varrho_j \sigma_j^{\rho(\xi_1+\zeta_1)}}{\rho^{\xi_1+\zeta_1}\Gamma(\xi_1+\zeta_1+1)}\right), \tag{40}$$

$$\mathcal{V}_2 = \frac{(1 + |\delta_2||\widehat{\mathcal{E}_1}|)\mathcal{S}^{\rho(\xi_2+\zeta_2)}}{\rho^{\xi_2+\zeta_2}\Gamma(\xi_2+\zeta_2+1)} + \frac{|\delta_2||\widehat{\mathcal{E}_2}||\epsilon| \sum_{j=1}^{k} \varsigma_j \varpi_j^{\rho(\xi_2+\zeta_2)}}{\rho^{\xi_2+\zeta_2}\Gamma(\xi_2+\zeta_2+1)}, \tag{41}$$

$$\widehat{\mathcal{U}_2} = |\delta_2||\phi_1|\left(\frac{\mathcal{S}^{\rho\zeta_1}|\widehat{\mathcal{E}_2}|}{\rho^{\zeta_1}\Gamma(\zeta_1+1)} + \frac{|\pi||\widehat{\mathcal{E}_1}|\sum_{j=1}^{k}\varrho_j\sigma_j^{\rho(\zeta_1)}}{\rho^{\zeta_1}\Gamma(\zeta_1+1)}\right), \tag{42}$$

$$\widehat{\mathcal{V}_2} = |\phi_2|\left(\frac{(1+|\delta_2||\widehat{\mathcal{E}_1}|)\mathcal{S}^{\rho\zeta_2}}{\rho^{\zeta_2}\Gamma(\zeta_2+1)} + \frac{|\delta_2||\widehat{\mathcal{E}_2}||\epsilon|\sum_{j=1}^{k}\varsigma_j\varpi_j^{\rho(\zeta_2)}}{\rho^{\zeta_2}\Gamma(\zeta_2+1)}\right), \tag{43}$$

$$\begin{aligned}\Phi = \min\{&1-[\psi_1(\mathcal{U}_1+\mathcal{U}_2)+\hat{\psi}_1(\mathcal{V}_1+\mathcal{V}_2)+\widehat{\mathcal{U}_1}+\widehat{\mathcal{U}_2}],\\ &1-[\psi_2(\mathcal{U}_1+\mathcal{U}_2)+\hat{\psi}_2(\mathcal{V}_1+\mathcal{V}_2)+\widehat{\mathcal{V}_1}+\widehat{\mathcal{V}_2}]\}.\end{aligned} \tag{44}$$

Let $f, g : \mathcal{E}\times\mathbb{R}\times\mathbb{R}\to\mathbb{R}$ be continuous functions.

- $(\mathcal{A}_1)$ there exist constants $\psi_m, \hat{\psi}_m \geq 0 (m = 1,2)$ and $\psi_0, \hat{\psi}_0 > 0$ such that

$$\begin{aligned}&|f(\iota, o_1, o_2)| \leq \psi_0 + \psi_1|o_1| + \psi_2|o_2|,\\ &|g(\iota, o_1, o_2)| \leq \hat{\psi}_0 + \hat{\psi}_1|o_1| + \hat{\psi}_2|o_2|, \forall o_m \in \mathbb{R}, m = 1,2.\end{aligned}$$

- $(\mathcal{A}_2)$ there exist constants $\psi_m, \hat{\psi}_m \geq 0 (m = 1,2)$ such that

$$\begin{aligned}|f(\iota, o_1, o_2) - f(\iota, \hat{o}_1, \hat{o}_2)| \leq& \psi_1|o_1 - \hat{o}_1| + \psi_2|o_2 - \hat{o}_2|,\\ |g(\iota, o_1, o_2) - g(\iota, \hat{o}_1, \hat{o}_2)| \leq& \hat{\psi}_1|o_1 - \hat{o}_1| + \hat{\psi}_2|o_2 - \hat{o}_2|, \forall o_m, \hat{o}_m \in \mathbb{R}, m = 1,2.\end{aligned}$$

Theorem 1. *If the assumption* $(\mathcal{A}_1)$ *is satisfied, then the problem in (3) and (4) has at least one solution on* $\mathcal{E}$ *if* $\psi_1(\mathcal{U}_1+\mathcal{U}_2)+\hat{\psi}_1(\mathcal{V}_1+\mathcal{V}_2)+\widehat{\mathcal{U}_1}+\widehat{\mathcal{U}_2} < 1$, $\psi_2(\mathcal{U}_1+\mathcal{U}_2)+\hat{\psi}_2(\mathcal{V}_1+\mathcal{V}_2)+\widehat{\mathcal{V}_1}+\widehat{\mathcal{V}_2} < 1$, *where* $\mathcal{U}_1, \mathcal{V}_1, \widehat{\mathcal{U}_1}, \widehat{\mathcal{V}_1}, \mathcal{U}_2, \mathcal{V}_2, \widehat{\mathcal{U}_2}, \widehat{\mathcal{V}_2}$ *are given by (36)–(43), respectively.*

Proof. In the first phase, we define operator $\Psi : \mathcal{P}\times\mathcal{Q}\to\mathcal{P}\times\mathcal{Q}$ as being completely continuous. The operators Ψ_1 and Ψ_2 are continuous because the functions f and g are continuous. The operator Ψ is continuous as a result. For the purpose of illustrating how the uniformly bounded operator Ψ works, consider the bounded set $\Psi \subset \mathcal{P}\times\mathcal{Q}$. Then, $\hat{\mathcal{N}}_1$ and $\hat{\mathcal{N}}_2$ are positive constants such that $|f(\iota, x(\iota), y(\iota))| \leq \hat{\mathcal{N}}_1, |g(\iota, x(\iota), y(\iota))| \leq \hat{\mathcal{N}}_2$, $\forall(x,y)\in\Psi$. Then, we have

$$\begin{aligned}|\Psi_1(x,y)(\iota)| \leq& {}^{\rho}\mathcal{I}_{0^+}^{\xi_1+\zeta_1}|f(\iota, x(\iota), y(\iota))| + |\phi_1|^{\rho}\mathcal{I}_{0^+}^{\zeta_1}|x(\iota)|\\ &+|\delta_1(\iota)|\Bigg[|\mathcal{E}_2|\Bigg(|\epsilon|\sum_{j=1}^{k}\varsigma_j{}^{\rho}\mathcal{I}_{0^+}^{\xi_2+\zeta_2}|g(\varpi_j, x(\varpi_j), y(\varpi_j))|\\ &+|\epsilon||\phi_2|\sum_{j=1}^{k}\varsigma_j{}^{\rho}\mathcal{I}_{0^+}^{\zeta_2}|y(\varpi_j)| + {}^{\rho}\mathcal{I}_{0^+}^{\xi_1+\zeta_1}|f(\mathcal{S}, x(\mathcal{S}), y(\mathcal{S}))| + |\phi_1|^{\rho}\mathcal{I}_{0^+}^{\zeta_1}|x(\mathcal{S})|\Bigg)\\ &+|\mathcal{E}_1|\Bigg(|\pi|\sum_{j=1}^{k}\varrho_j^{\rho}\mathcal{I}_{0^+}^{\xi_1+\zeta_1}|f(\sigma_j, x(\sigma_j), y(\sigma_j))| + |\pi||\phi_1|\sum_{j=1}^{k}\varrho_j{}^{\rho}\mathcal{I}_{0^+}^{\zeta_1}|x(\sigma_j)|\\ &+{}^{\rho}\mathcal{I}_{0^+}^{\xi_2+\zeta_2}|g(\mathcal{S}, x(\mathcal{S}), y(\mathcal{S}))| + |\phi_2|^{\rho}\mathcal{I}_{0^+}^{\zeta_2}|y(\mathcal{S})|\Bigg)\Bigg]\\ \leq& \hat{\mathcal{N}}_1\left\{\frac{\left(\mathcal{S}^{\rho(\xi_1+\zeta_1)}(1+|\delta_1||\mathcal{E}_2|)\right)}{\rho^{\xi_1+\zeta_1}\Gamma(\xi_1+\zeta_1+1)} + \frac{|\delta_1||\pi||\mathcal{E}_1|\sum_{j=1}^{k}\varrho_j\sigma_j^{\rho(\xi_1+\zeta_1)}}{\rho^{\xi_1+\zeta_1}\Gamma(\xi_1+\zeta_1+1)}\right\}\end{aligned}$$

$$+\hat{\mathcal{N}_2}\left\{|\delta_1|\left(\frac{|\mathcal{E}_1|\mathcal{S}^{\rho(\xi_2+\zeta_2)}}{\rho^{\xi_2+\zeta_2}\Gamma(\xi_2+\zeta_2+1)}+\frac{|\mathcal{E}_2||\epsilon|\sum_{j=1}^{k}\varsigma_j\varpi_j^{\rho(\xi_2+\zeta_2)}}{\rho^{\xi_2+\zeta_2}\Gamma(\xi_2+\zeta_2+1)}\right)\right\}$$
$$+\left\{|\phi_1|\left(\frac{(\mathcal{S}^{\rho\zeta_1}(1+|\delta_1||\mathcal{E}_2|))}{\rho^{\zeta_1}\Gamma(\zeta_1+1)}+\frac{|\delta_1||\pi||\mathcal{E}_1|\sum_{j=1}^{k}\varrho_j\sigma_j^{\rho(\zeta_1)}}{\rho^{\zeta_1}\Gamma(\zeta_1+1)}\right)\right\}\|x\|$$
$$+\left\{|\delta_1||\phi_2|\left(\frac{|\mathcal{E}_1|\mathcal{S}^{\rho\zeta_2}}{\rho^{\zeta_2}\Gamma(\zeta_2+1)}+\frac{|\mathcal{E}_2||\epsilon|\sum_{j=1}^{k}\varsigma_j\varpi_j^{\rho(\zeta_2)}}{\rho^{\zeta_2}\Gamma(\zeta_2+1)}\right)\right\}\|y\|,$$

when taking the norm and using (36)–(39), which yields for $(x,y)\in\Psi$,

$$||\Psi_1(x,y)||\le\mathcal{U}_1\hat{\mathcal{N}_1}+\widehat{\mathcal{U}_1}\|x\|+\mathcal{V}_1\hat{\mathcal{N}_2}+\widehat{\mathcal{V}_1}\|y\|. \tag{45}$$

Likewise, we obtain

$$\begin{aligned}||\Psi_2(x,y)||\le&\hat{\mathcal{N}_2}\left\{\frac{(1+|\delta_2||\widehat{\mathcal{E}_1}|)\mathcal{S}^{\rho(\xi_2+\zeta_2)}}{\rho^{\xi_2+\zeta_2}\Gamma(\xi_2+\zeta_2+1)}+\frac{|\delta_2||\widehat{\mathcal{E}_2}||\epsilon|\sum_{j=1}^{k}\varsigma_j\varpi_j^{\rho(\xi_2+\zeta_2)}}{\rho^{\xi_2+\zeta_2}\Gamma(\xi_2+\zeta_2+1)}\right\}\\&+\hat{\mathcal{N}_1}\left\{|\delta_2|\left(\frac{\mathcal{S}^{\rho(\xi_1+\zeta_1)}|\widehat{\mathcal{E}_2}|}{\rho^{\xi_1+\zeta_1}\Gamma(\xi_1+\zeta_1+1)}+\frac{|\pi||\widehat{\mathcal{E}_1}|\sum_{j=1}^{k}\varrho_j\sigma_j^{\rho(\xi_1+\zeta_1)}}{\rho^{\xi_1+\zeta_1}\Gamma(\xi_1+\zeta_1+1)}\right)\right\}\\&+\left\{|\phi_2|\left(\frac{(1+|\delta_2||\widehat{\mathcal{E}_1}|)\mathcal{S}^{\rho\zeta_2}}{\rho^{\zeta_2}\Gamma(\zeta_2+1)}+\frac{|\delta_2||\widehat{\mathcal{E}_2}||\epsilon|\sum_{j=1}^{k}\varsigma_j\varpi_j^{\rho(\zeta_2)}}{\rho^{\zeta_2}\Gamma(\zeta_2+1)}\right)\right\}\|y\|\\&+\left\{|\delta_2||\phi_1|\left(\frac{\mathcal{S}^{\rho\zeta_1}|\widehat{\mathcal{E}_2}|}{\rho^{\zeta_1}\Gamma(\zeta_1+1)}+\frac{|\pi||\widehat{\mathcal{E}_1}|\sum_{j=1}^{k}\varrho_j\sigma_j^{\rho(\zeta_1)}}{\rho^{\zeta_1}\Gamma(\zeta_1+1)}\right)\right\}\|x\|\\\le&\mathcal{U}_2\hat{\mathcal{N}_1}+\widehat{\mathcal{U}_2}\|x\|+\mathcal{V}_2\hat{\mathcal{N}_2}+\widehat{\mathcal{V}_2}\|y\|,\end{aligned} \tag{46}$$

using (40)–(43). We may infer that Ψ_1 and Ψ_2 are uniformly bounded based on the inequalities (45) and (46), which means that the operator Ψ is also uniformly bounded. Following that, we demonstrate that Ψ is equicontinuous. Let $\iota_1,\iota_2\in\mathcal{E}$ with $\iota_1<\iota_2$. Then, we have

$$\begin{aligned}&|\Psi_1(x,y)(\iota_2)-\Psi_1(x,y)(\iota_1)|\\&\le|{}^{\rho}\mathcal{I}_{0+}^{\xi_1+\zeta_1}f(\iota_2,x(\iota_2),y(\iota_2))-{}^{\rho}\mathcal{I}_{0+}^{\xi_1+\zeta_1}f(\iota_1,x(\iota_1),y(\iota_1))|+|\phi_1||{}^{\rho}\mathcal{I}_{0+}^{\zeta_1}x(\iota_2)-{}^{\rho}\mathcal{I}_{0+}^{\zeta_1}x(\iota_1)|\\&+|\delta_1(\iota_2)-\delta_1(\iota_1)|\Bigg[|\mathcal{E}_2|\Bigg(|\epsilon|\sum_{j=1}^{k}\varsigma_j^{\rho}\mathcal{I}_{0+}^{\xi_2+\zeta_2}|g(\varpi_j,x(\varpi_j),y(\varpi_j))|\\&+|\epsilon||\phi_2|\sum_{j=1}^{k}\varsigma_j{}^{\rho}\mathcal{I}_{0+}^{\zeta_2}|y(\varpi_j)|+{}^{\rho}\mathcal{I}_{0+}^{\xi_1+\zeta_1}|f(\mathcal{S},x(\mathcal{S}),y(\mathcal{S}))|+|\phi_1|{}^{\rho}\mathcal{I}_{0+}^{\zeta_1}|x(\mathcal{S})|\Bigg)\\&+|\mathcal{E}_1|\Bigg(|\pi|\sum_{j=1}^{k}\varrho_j^{\rho}\mathcal{I}_{0+}^{\xi_1+\zeta_1}|f(\sigma_j,x(\sigma_j),y(\sigma_j))|+|\pi||\phi_1|\sum_{j=1}^{k}\varrho_j{}^{\rho}\mathcal{I}_{0+}^{\zeta_1}|x(\sigma_j)|\\&+{}^{\rho}\mathcal{I}_{0+}^{\xi_2+\zeta_2}|g(\mathcal{S},x(\mathcal{S}),y(\mathcal{S}))|+|\phi_2|{}^{\rho}\mathcal{I}_{0+}^{\zeta_2}|y(\mathcal{S})|\Bigg)\Bigg]\\&\le\frac{\rho^{1-(\xi_1+\zeta_1)}\hat{\mathcal{N}_1}}{\Gamma(\xi_1+\zeta_1)}\left|\int_0^{\iota_1}\left[\frac{\theta^{\rho-1}}{(\iota_2^{\rho}-\theta^{\rho})^{1-(\xi_1+\zeta_1)}}-\frac{\theta^{\rho-1}}{(\iota_1^{\rho}-\theta^{\rho})^{1-(\xi_1+\zeta_1)}}\right]d\theta\right.\\&\left.+\int_{\iota_1}^{\iota_2}\frac{\theta^{\rho-1}}{(\iota_2^{\rho}-\theta^{\rho})^{1-(\zeta_1)}}d\theta\right|\end{aligned}$$

$$
\begin{aligned}
&\frac{\rho^{1-(\zeta_1)}\|x\|}{\Gamma(\zeta_1)}\left|\int_0^{\iota_1}\left[\frac{\theta^{\rho-1}}{(\iota_2^{\rho}-\theta^{\rho})^{1-(\zeta_1)}}-\frac{\theta^{\rho-1}}{(\iota_1^{\rho}-\theta^{\rho})^{1-(\zeta_1)}}\right]d\theta\right.\\
&\left.+\int_{\iota_1}^{\iota_2}\frac{\theta^{\rho-1}}{(\iota_2^{\rho}-\theta^{\rho})^{1-(\zeta_1)}}d\theta\right| \qquad (47)\\
&+|\delta_1(\iota_2)-\delta_1(\iota_1)|\left[\hat{\mathcal{N}_1}\left\{\frac{\left(\mathcal{S}^{\rho(\xi_1+\zeta_1)}(|\delta_1||\mathcal{E}_2|)\right)}{\rho^{\xi_1+\zeta_1}\Gamma(\xi_1+\zeta_1+1)}+\frac{|\delta_1||\pi||\mathcal{E}_1|\sum_{j=1}^{k}\varrho_j\sigma_j^{\rho(\xi_1+\zeta_1)}}{\rho^{\xi_1+\zeta_1}\Gamma(\xi_1+\zeta_1+1)}\right\}\right.\\
&+\hat{\mathcal{N}_2}\left\{|\delta_1|\left(\frac{|\mathcal{E}_1|\mathcal{S}^{\rho(\xi_2+\zeta_2)}}{\rho^{\xi_2+\zeta_2}\Gamma(\xi_2+\zeta_2+1)}+\frac{|\mathcal{E}_2||\epsilon|\sum_{j=1}^{k}\varsigma_j\varpi_j^{\rho(\xi_2+\zeta_2)}}{\rho^{\xi_2+\zeta_2}\Gamma(\xi_2+\zeta_2+1)}\right)\right\}\\
&+\left\{|\phi_1|\left(\frac{(\mathcal{S}^{\rho\zeta_1}(1+|\delta_1||\mathcal{E}_2|))}{\rho^{\zeta_1}\Gamma(\zeta_1+1)}+\frac{|\delta_1||\pi||\mathcal{E}_1|\sum_{j=1}^{k}\varrho_j\sigma_j^{\rho(\zeta_1)}}{\rho^{\zeta_1}\Gamma(\zeta_1+1)}\right)\right\}\|x\|\\
&\left.+\left\{|\delta_1||\phi_2|\left(\frac{|\mathcal{E}_1|\mathcal{S}^{\rho\zeta_2}}{\rho^{\zeta_2}\Gamma(\zeta_2+1)}+\frac{|\mathcal{E}_2||\epsilon|\sum_{j=1}^{k}\varsigma_j\varpi_j^{\rho(\zeta_2)}}{\rho^{\zeta_2}\Gamma(\zeta_2+1)}\right)\right\}\|y\|\right]\\
&\to 0 \text{ as } \iota_2\to\iota_1.
\end{aligned}
$$

independent of (x,y) with respect to $|f(\iota,x(\iota_1),y(\iota_1))|\le\hat{\mathcal{N}_1}$ and $|g(\iota,x(\iota_1),y(\iota_1))|\le\hat{\mathcal{N}_2}$. Similarly, we can express $|\Psi_2(x,y)(\iota_2)-\Psi_2(x,y)(\iota_1)|\to 0$ as $\iota_2\to\iota_1$ independent of (x,y) in terms of the boundedness of f and g. The operator Ψ is equicontinuous due to the equicontinuity of Ψ_1 and Ψ_2. The operator is compact as a result of the Arzela–Ascoli theorem. Finally, we show that the set $\Pi(\Psi)=\{(x,y)\in\mathcal{P}\times\mathcal{Q}:\lambda\Psi(x,y);0<\lambda<1\}$ is bounded. Let $(x,y)\in\Pi(\Psi)$. Then, $(x,y)=\lambda\Psi(x,y)$. For any $\iota\in\mathcal{E}$, we have $x(\iota)=\lambda\Psi_1(x,y)(\iota), y(\iota)=\lambda\Psi_2(x,y)(\iota)$. By utilizing $(\mathcal{A}_1)$ in (34), we obtain

$$
\begin{aligned}
|x(\iota)|\le&{}^{\rho}\mathcal{I}_{0^+}^{\xi_1+\zeta_1}(\psi_0,\psi_1|x(\iota)|,\psi_2|y(\iota)|)+|\phi_1|^{\rho}\mathcal{I}_{0^+}^{\zeta_1}|x(\iota)|\\
&+|\delta_1(\iota)|\left[|\mathcal{E}_2|\left(|\epsilon|\sum_{j=1}^{k}\varsigma_j^{\rho}\mathcal{I}_{0^+}^{\xi_2+\zeta_2}(\hat{\psi}_0+\hat{\psi}_1|x(\varpi_j)|+\hat{\psi}_2|y(\varpi_j)|)\right.\right.\\
&\left.+|\epsilon||\phi_2|\sum_{j=1}^{k}\varsigma_j{}^{\rho}\mathcal{I}_{0^+}^{\zeta_2}|y(\varpi_j)|+{}^{\rho}\mathcal{I}_{0^+}^{\xi_1+\zeta_1}(\psi_0,\psi_1|x(\mathcal{S})|,\psi_2|y(\mathcal{S})|)+|\phi_1|^{\rho}\mathcal{I}_{0^+}^{\zeta_1}|x(\mathcal{S})|\right)\\
&+|\mathcal{E}_1|\left(|\pi|\sum_{j=1}^{k}\varrho_j^{\rho}\mathcal{I}_{0^+}^{\xi_1+\zeta_1}(\psi_0,\psi_1|x(\sigma_j)|,\psi_2|y(\sigma_j)|)+|\pi||\phi_1|\sum_{j=1}^{k}\varrho_j{}^{\rho}\mathcal{I}_{0^+}^{\zeta_1}|x(\sigma_j)|\right.\\
&\left.\left.+{}^{\rho}\mathcal{I}_{0^+}^{\xi_2+\zeta_2}(\hat{\psi}_0+\hat{\psi}_1|x(\mathcal{S})|+\hat{\psi}_2|y(\mathcal{S})|)+|\phi_2|^{\rho}\mathcal{I}_{0^+}^{\zeta_2}|y(\mathcal{S})|\right)\right],
\end{aligned}
$$

which is obtained when the norm for $\iota\in\mathcal{E}$ is taken,

$$
||x||\le(\psi_0+\psi_1||x||+\psi_2||y||)\mathcal{U}_1+(\hat{\psi}_0+\hat{\psi}_1||x||+\hat{\psi}_2||y||)\mathcal{V}_1+||x||\widehat{\mathcal{U}_1}+||y||\widehat{\mathcal{V}_1}. \qquad (48)
$$

Likewise, we have the ability to get

$$
||y||\le(\hat{\psi}_0+\hat{\psi}_1||x||+\hat{\psi}_2||y||)\mathcal{V}_2+(\psi_0+\psi_1||x||+\psi_2||y||)\mathcal{U}_2+||x||\widehat{\mathcal{U}_2}+||y||\widehat{\mathcal{V}_2}. \qquad (49)
$$

From (48) and (49), we get

$$
\begin{aligned}
||x||+||y||=&\psi_0(\mathcal{U}_1+\mathcal{U}_2)+\hat{\psi}_0(\mathcal{V}_1+\mathcal{V}_2)+||x||\left[\psi_1(\mathcal{U}_1+\mathcal{U}_2)+\hat{\psi}_1(\mathcal{V}_1+\mathcal{V}_2)+\widehat{\mathcal{U}_1}+\widehat{\mathcal{U}_2}\right]\\
&+||y||\left[\psi_1(\mathcal{U}_1+\mathcal{U}_2)+\hat{\psi}_1(\mathcal{V}_1+\mathcal{V}_2)+\widehat{\mathcal{V}_1}+\widehat{\mathcal{V}_2}\right],
\end{aligned}
$$

which results, with $||(x,y)|| = ||x|| + ||y||$, in

$$||(x,y)|| \leq \frac{\psi_0(\mathcal{U}_1 + \mathcal{U}_2) + \hat{\psi}_0(\mathcal{V}_1 + \mathcal{V}_2)}{\Phi}.$$

Thus, $\Pi(\Psi)$ is bounded. Hence the operator Ψ has a fixed point by Leray–Schauder's nonlinear alternative [39], which corresponds to at least one solution of the problem in (3) and (4) on $\mathcal{E}$. □

Theorem 2. *If the assumption* $(\mathcal{A}_2)$ *is satisfied, then the problem in (3) and (4) has a unique solution on* $\mathcal{E}$*, and there exist* $\mathcal{S}_1, \mathcal{S}_2 > 0$ *such that* $|f(\iota,0,0)| \leq \mathcal{S}_1, |g(\iota,0,0)| \leq \mathcal{S}_2$*, Then, given that*

$$(\mathcal{U}_1 + \mathcal{U}_2)(\psi_1 + \psi_2) + (\mathcal{V}_1 + \mathcal{V}_2)(\hat{\psi}_1 + \hat{\psi}_2) + (\widehat{\mathcal{U}_1} + \widehat{\mathcal{U}_2}) + (\widehat{\mathcal{V}_1} + \widehat{\mathcal{V}_2}) < 1, \tag{50}$$

where $\mathcal{U}_1, \mathcal{V}_1, \widehat{\mathcal{U}_1}, \widehat{\mathcal{V}_1}, \mathcal{U}_2, \mathcal{V}_2, \widehat{\mathcal{U}_2}, \widehat{\mathcal{V}_2}$ *are given by (36)–(43), respectively.*

Proof. Let us fix $\varphi \leq \frac{(\mathcal{U}_1+\mathcal{U}_2)\mathcal{S}_1+(\mathcal{V}_1+\mathcal{V}_2)\mathcal{S}_2}{1-((\mathcal{U}_1+\mathcal{U}_2)(\psi_1+\psi_2)+(\mathcal{V}_1+\mathcal{V}_2)(\hat{\psi}_1+\hat{\psi}_2)+\widehat{\mathcal{U}_2})+(\widehat{\mathcal{V}_1}+\widehat{\mathcal{V}_2}))}$ and demonstrate that $\Psi\mathcal{B}_\varphi \subset \mathcal{B}_\varphi$ when operator Ψ is given by (33) and $\mathcal{B}_\varphi = \{(x,y) \in \mathcal{P} \times \mathcal{Q} : ||(x,y)|| \leq \varphi\}$. For $(x,y) \in \mathcal{B}_\varphi, \iota \in \mathcal{E}$

$$\begin{aligned} |f(\iota, x(\iota), y(\iota))| &\leq \psi_1|x(\iota)| + \psi_2|y(\iota)| + \mathcal{S}_1 \\ &\leq \psi_1||x|| + \psi_2||y|| + \mathcal{S}_1, \end{aligned}$$

and

$$\begin{aligned} |g(\iota, x(\iota), y(\iota))| &\leq \hat{\psi}_1|x(\iota)| + \hat{\psi}_2|y(\iota)| + \mathcal{S}_2 \\ &\leq \hat{\psi}_1||x|| + \hat{\psi}_2||y|| + \mathcal{S}_2. \end{aligned} \tag{51}$$

This leads to

$$\begin{aligned}
&|\Psi_1(x,y)(\iota)| \\
\leq& {}^\rho\mathcal{I}_{0^+}^{\xi_1+\zeta_1}|f(\iota,x(\iota),y(\iota)) - f(\iota,0,0)| + |f(\iota,0,0)| + |\phi_1|{}^\rho\mathcal{I}_{0^+}^{\zeta_1}|x(\iota)| \\
&+ |\delta_1(\iota)|\Bigg[|\mathcal{E}_2|\Bigg(|\epsilon|\sum_{j=1}^{k}\varsigma_j^\rho\mathcal{I}_{0^+}^{\xi_2+\zeta_2}|g((\varpi_j,x(\varpi_j),y(\varpi_j)) - g(\varpi_j,0,0)| + |g(\varpi_j,0,0)|) \\
&+ |\epsilon||\phi_2|\sum_{j=1}^{k}\varsigma_j{}^\rho\mathcal{I}_{0^+}^{\zeta_2}|y(\varpi_j)| + {}^\rho\mathcal{I}_{0^+}^{\xi_1+\zeta_1}|f(\mathcal{S},x(\mathcal{S}),y(\mathcal{S})) - f(\mathcal{S},0,0)| + |f(\mathcal{S},0,0)| \\
&+ |\phi_1|{}^\rho\mathcal{I}_{0^+}^{\zeta_1}|x(\mathcal{S})|\Bigg) \\
&+ |\mathcal{E}_1|\Bigg(|\pi|\sum_{j=1}^{k}\varrho_j^\rho\mathcal{I}_{0^+}^{\xi_1+\zeta_1}|f(\sigma_j,x(\sigma_j),y(\sigma_j)) - f(\sigma_j,0,0)| + |f(\sigma_j,0,0)| \\
&+ |\pi||\phi_1|\sum_{j=1}^{k}\varrho_j{}^\rho\mathcal{I}_{0^+}^{\zeta_1}|x(\sigma_j)| \\
&+ {}^\rho\mathcal{I}_{0^+}^{\xi_2+\zeta_2}|g((\mathcal{S},x(\mathcal{S}),y(\mathcal{S})) - g(\mathcal{S},0,0)| + |g(\mathcal{S},0,0)|) + |\phi_2|{}^\rho\mathcal{I}_{0^+}^{\zeta_2}|y(\mathcal{S})|\Bigg)\Bigg] \\
\leq& (\psi_1||x|| + \psi_2||y|| + \mathcal{S}_1)\left\{\frac{\left(\mathcal{S}^{\rho(\xi_1+\zeta_1)}(1 + |\delta_1||\mathcal{E}_2|)\right)}{\rho^{\xi_1+\zeta_1}\Gamma(\xi_1+\zeta_1+1)} + \frac{|\delta_1||\pi||\mathcal{E}_1|\sum_{j=1}^{k}\varrho_j\sigma_j^{\rho(\xi_1+\zeta_1)}}{\rho^{\xi_1+\zeta_1}\Gamma(\xi_1+\zeta_1+1)}\right\}
\end{aligned}$$

$$+ (\hat{\psi}_1||x|| + \hat{\psi}_2||y|| + \mathcal{S}_2)\left\{ |\delta_1| \left(\frac{|\mathcal{E}_1|\mathcal{S}^{\rho(\xi_2+\zeta_2)}}{\rho^{\xi_2+\zeta_2}\Gamma(\xi_2+\zeta_2+1)} + \frac{|\mathcal{E}_2||\epsilon|\sum_{j=1}^{k}\varsigma_j\omega_j^{\rho(\xi_2+\zeta_2)}}{\rho^{\xi_2+\zeta_2}\Gamma(\xi_2+\zeta_2+1)} \right) \right\}$$
$$+ \left\{ |\phi_1| \left(\frac{(\mathcal{S}^{\rho\zeta_1}(1+|\delta_1||\mathcal{E}_2|))}{\rho^{\zeta_1}\Gamma(\zeta_1+1)} + \frac{|\delta_1||\pi||\mathcal{E}_1|\sum_{j=1}^{k}\varrho_j\sigma_j^{\rho(\zeta_1)}}{\rho^{\zeta_1}\Gamma(\zeta_1+1)} \right) \right\} ||x||$$
$$+ \left\{ |\delta_1||\phi_2| \left(\frac{|\mathcal{E}_1|\mathcal{S}^{\rho\zeta_2}}{\rho^{\zeta_2}\Gamma(\zeta_2+1)} + \frac{|\mathcal{E}_2||\epsilon|\sum_{j=1}^{k}\varsigma_j\omega_j^{\rho(\zeta_2)}}{\rho^{\zeta_2}\Gamma(\zeta_2+1)} \right) \right\} ||y||$$

$$||\Psi_1(x,y)|| \leq (\psi_1||x|| + \psi_2||y|| + \mathcal{S}_1)\mathcal{U}_1 + (\hat{\psi}_1||x|| + \hat{\psi}_2||y|| + \mathcal{S}_2)\mathcal{V}_1 + ||x||\widehat{\mathcal{U}_1} + ||y||\widehat{\mathcal{V}_1}. \tag{52}$$

Similarly, we obtain

$$|\Psi_2(x,y)(\iota)| \leq (\hat{\psi}_1||x|| + \hat{\psi}_2||y|| + \mathcal{S}_2)\left\{ \frac{(1+|\delta_2||\widehat{\mathcal{E}_1}|)\mathcal{S}^{\rho(\xi_2+\zeta_2)}}{\rho^{\xi_2+\zeta_2}\Gamma(\xi_2+\zeta_2+1)} + \frac{|\delta_2||\widehat{\mathcal{E}_2}||\epsilon|\sum_{j=1}^{k}\varsigma_j\omega_j^{\rho(\xi_2+\zeta_2)}}{\rho^{\xi_2+\zeta_2}\Gamma(\xi_2+\zeta_2+1)} \right\}$$
$$+ (\psi_1||x|| + \psi_2||y|| + \mathcal{S}_1)\left\{ |\delta_2| \left(\frac{\mathcal{S}^{\rho(\xi_1+\zeta_1)}|\widehat{\mathcal{E}_2}|}{\rho^{\xi_1+\zeta_1}\Gamma(\xi_1+\zeta_1+1)} + \frac{|\pi||\widehat{\mathcal{E}_1}|\sum_{j=1}^{k}\varrho_j\sigma_j^{\rho(\xi_1+\zeta_1)}}{\rho^{\xi_1+\zeta_1}\Gamma(\xi_1+\zeta_1+1)} \right) \right\}$$
$$+ \left\{ |\phi_2| \left(\frac{(1+|\delta_2||\widehat{\mathcal{E}_1}|)\mathcal{S}^{\rho\zeta_2}}{\rho^{\zeta_2}\Gamma(\zeta_2+1)} + \frac{|\delta_2||\widehat{\mathcal{E}_2}||\epsilon|\sum_{j=1}^{k}\varsigma_j\omega_j^{\rho(\zeta_2)}}{\rho^{\zeta_2}\Gamma(\zeta_2+1)} \right) \right\} ||y|| \tag{53}$$
$$+ \left\{ |\delta_2||\phi_1| \left(\frac{\mathcal{S}^{\rho\zeta_1}|\widehat{\mathcal{E}_2}|}{\rho^{\zeta_1}\Gamma(\zeta_1+1)} + \frac{|\pi||\widehat{\mathcal{E}_1}|\sum_{j=1}^{k}\varrho_j\sigma_j^{\rho(\zeta_1)}}{\rho^{\zeta_1}\Gamma(\zeta_1+1)} \right) \right\} ||x||$$
$$||\Psi_2(x,y)|| \leq (\hat{\psi}_1||x|| + \hat{\psi}_2||y|| + \mathcal{S}_2)\mathcal{K}_2 + (\psi_1||x|| + \psi_2||y|| + \mathcal{S}_1)\mathcal{J}_2 + ||x||\widehat{\mathcal{U}_2} + ||y||\widehat{\mathcal{V}_2}.$$

As a result, (52) and (53) follow $||\Psi(x,y)|| \leq \varphi$, and thus $\Psi\mathcal{B}_\varphi \subset \mathcal{B}_\varphi$. Now, for $(x_1,y_1),(x_2,y_2) \in \mathcal{P} \times \mathcal{Q}$ and any $\iota \in \mathcal{E}$, we get

$$|\Psi_1(x_1,y_1)(\iota) - \Psi_1(x_2,y_2)(\iota)|$$
$$\leq {}^{\rho}\mathcal{I}_{0^+}^{\xi_1+\zeta_1}|f(\iota,x_1(\iota),y_1(\iota)) - f(\iota,x_2(\iota),y_2(\iota))| + |\phi_1|{}^{\rho}\mathcal{I}_{0^+}^{\zeta_1}|x_1(\iota) - x_2(\iota)|$$
$$+ |\delta_1(\iota)|\Bigg[|\mathcal{E}_2|\Big(|\epsilon|\sum_{j=1}^{k}\varsigma_j^{\rho}\mathcal{I}_{0^+}^{\xi_2+\zeta_2}|g(\omega_j,x_1(\omega_j),y_1(\omega_j)) - g(\omega_j,x_2(\omega_j),y_2(\omega_j))|$$
$$+ |\epsilon||\phi_2|\sum_{j=1}^{k}\varrho_j{}^{\rho}\mathcal{I}_{0^+}^{\zeta_2}|y_1(\omega_j) - y_2(\omega_j)|$$
$$+ {}^{\rho}\mathcal{I}_{0^+}^{\xi_1+\zeta_1}|f(\mathcal{S},x_1(\mathcal{S}),y_1(\mathcal{S})) - f(\mathcal{S},x_2(\mathcal{S}),y_2(\mathcal{S}))| + |\phi_1|{}^{\rho}\mathcal{I}_{0^+}^{\zeta_1}|x_1(\mathcal{S}) - x_2(\mathcal{S})|\Big)$$
$$+ |\mathcal{E}_1|\Big(|\pi|\sum_{j=1}^{k}\varrho_j^{\rho}\mathcal{I}_{0^+}^{\xi_1+\zeta_1}|f(\sigma_j,x_1(\sigma_j),y_1(\sigma_j)) - f(\sigma_j,x_2(\sigma_j),y_2(\sigma_j))|$$
$$+ |\pi||\phi_1|\sum_{j=1}^{k}\varrho_j{}^{\rho}\mathcal{I}_{0^+}^{\zeta_1}|x_1(\sigma_j) - x_2(\sigma_j)|$$
$$+ {}^{\rho}\mathcal{I}_{0^+}^{\xi_2+\zeta_2}|g(\mathcal{S},x_1(\mathcal{S}),y_1(\mathcal{S})) - g(\mathcal{S},x_2(\mathcal{S}),y_2(\mathcal{S}))| + |\phi_2|{}^{\rho}\mathcal{I}_{0^+}^{\zeta_2}|y_1(\mathcal{S}) - y_2(\mathcal{S})|\Big)\Bigg]$$

$$
\begin{aligned}
&\leq (\psi_1 ||x_1 - x_2|| + \psi_2 ||y_1 - y_2||) \left\{ \frac{\left(\mathcal{S}^{\rho(\xi_1+\zeta_1)}(1 + |\delta_1||\mathcal{E}_2|)\right)}{\rho^{\xi_1+\zeta_1}\Gamma(\xi_1+\zeta_1+1)} + \frac{|\delta_1||\pi||\mathcal{E}_1| \sum_{j=1}^{k} \varrho_j \sigma_j^{\rho(\xi_1+\zeta_1)}}{\rho^{\xi_1+\zeta_1}\Gamma(\xi_1+\zeta_1+1)} \right\} \\
&+ (\hat{\psi}_1 ||x_1 - x_2|| + \hat{\psi}_2 ||y_1 - y_2||) \left\{ |\delta_1| \left(\frac{|\mathcal{E}_1| \mathcal{S}^{\rho(\xi_2+\zeta_2)}}{\rho^{\xi_2+\zeta_2}\Gamma(\xi_2+\zeta_2+1)} + \frac{|\mathcal{E}_2||\epsilon| \sum_{j=1}^{k} \varsigma_j \varpi_j^{\rho(\xi_2+\zeta_2)}}{\rho^{\xi_2+\zeta_2}\Gamma(\xi_2+\zeta_2+1)} \right) \right\} \\
&+ \left\{ |\phi_1| \left(\frac{(\mathcal{S}^{\rho\zeta_1}(1 + |\delta_1||\mathcal{E}_2|))}{\rho^{\zeta_1}\Gamma(\zeta_1+1)} + \frac{|\delta_1||\pi||\mathcal{E}_1| \sum_{j=1}^{k} \varrho_j \sigma_j^{\rho(\zeta_1)}}{\rho^{\zeta_1}\Gamma(\zeta_1+1)} \right) \right\} ||x_1 - x_2|| \\
&+ \left\{ |\delta_1||\phi_2| \left(\frac{|\mathcal{E}_1| \mathcal{S}^{\rho\zeta_2}}{\rho^{\zeta_2}\Gamma(\zeta_2+1)} + \frac{|\mathcal{E}_2||\epsilon| \sum_{j=1}^{k} \varsigma_j \varpi_j^{\rho(\zeta_2)}}{\rho^{\zeta_2}\Gamma(\zeta_2+1)} \right) \right\} ||y_1 - y_2||
\end{aligned}
$$

$$
\leq (\mathcal{U}_1(\psi_1 + \psi_2) + \mathcal{V}_1(\hat{\psi}_1 + \hat{\psi}_2) + \widehat{\mathcal{U}_1} + \widehat{\mathcal{V}_1})(||x_1 - x_2|| + ||y_1 - y_2||).
$$

Similarly, we obtain

$$
\begin{aligned}
&|\Psi_2(x_1, y_1)(\iota) - \Psi_2(x_2, y_2)(\iota)| \\
&\leq (\hat{\psi}_1 ||x_1 - x_2|| + \hat{\psi}_2 ||y_1 - y_2||) \left\{ \frac{(1 + |\delta_2||\widehat{\mathcal{E}_1}|)\mathcal{S}^{\rho(\xi_2+\zeta_2)}}{\rho^{\xi_2+\zeta_2}\Gamma(\xi_2+\zeta_2+1)} + \frac{|\delta_2||\widehat{\mathcal{E}_2}||\epsilon| \sum_{j=1}^{k} \varsigma_j \varpi_j^{\rho(\xi_2+\zeta_2)}}{\rho^{\xi_2+\zeta_2}\Gamma(\xi_2+\zeta_2+1)} \right\} \\
&+ (\psi_1 ||x_1 - x_2|| + \psi_2 ||y_1 - y_2||) \left\{ |\delta_2| \left(\frac{\mathcal{S}^{\rho(\xi_1+\zeta_1)} |\widehat{\mathcal{E}_2}|}{\rho^{\xi_1+\zeta_1}\Gamma(\xi_1+\zeta_1+1)} + \frac{|\pi||\widehat{\mathcal{E}_1}| \sum_{j=1}^{k} \varrho_j \sigma_j^{\rho(\xi_1+\zeta_1)}}{\rho^{\xi_1+\zeta_1}\Gamma(\xi_1+\zeta_1+1)} \right) \right\} \\
&+ \left\{ |\phi_2| \left(\frac{(1 + |\delta_2||\widehat{\mathcal{E}_1}|)\mathcal{S}^{\rho\zeta_2}}{\rho^{\zeta_2}\Gamma(\zeta_2+1)} + \frac{|\delta_2||\widehat{\mathcal{E}_2}||\epsilon| \sum_{j=1}^{k} \varsigma_j \varpi_j^{\rho(\zeta_2)}}{\rho^{\zeta_2}\Gamma(\zeta_2+1)} \right) \right\} ||y_1 - y_2|| \\
&+ \left\{ |\delta_2||\phi_1| \left(\frac{\mathcal{S}^{\rho\zeta_1} |\widehat{\mathcal{E}_2}|}{\rho^{\zeta_1}\Gamma(\zeta_1+1)} + \frac{|\pi||\widehat{\mathcal{E}_1}| \sum_{j=1}^{k} \varrho_j \sigma_j^{\rho(\zeta_1)}}{\rho^{\zeta_1}\Gamma(\zeta_1+1)} \right) \right\} ||x_1 - x_2|| \\
&\leq (\mathcal{U}_2(\psi_1 + \psi_2) + \mathcal{V}_2(\hat{\psi}_1 + \hat{\psi}_2) + \widehat{\mathcal{U}_2} + \widehat{\mathcal{V}_2})(||x_1 - x_2|| + ||y_1 - y_2||).
\end{aligned}
$$

Thus, we obtain

$$
\begin{aligned}
||\Psi_1(x_1, y_1)(\iota) - \Psi_1(x_2, y_2)(\iota)|| \leq & (\mathcal{U}_1(\psi_1 + \psi_2) + \mathcal{V}_1(\hat{\psi}_1 + \hat{\psi}_2) + \widehat{\mathcal{U}_1} + \widehat{\mathcal{V}_1}) \\
& (||x_1 - x_2|| + ||y_1 - y_2||). \qquad (54)
\end{aligned}
$$

In a similar manner,

$$
\begin{aligned}
||\Psi_2(x_1, y_1)(\iota) - \Psi_2(x_2, y_2)(\iota)|| \leq & (\mathcal{U}_2(\psi_1 + \psi_2) + \mathcal{V}_2(\hat{\psi}_1 + \hat{\psi}_2) + \widehat{\mathcal{U}_2} + \widehat{\mathcal{V}_2}) \\
& (||x_1 - x_2|| + ||y_1 - y_2||). \qquad (55)
\end{aligned}
$$

Hence, using (54) and (55) we can get

$$
\begin{aligned}
||\Psi(x_1, y_1)(\iota) - \Psi(x_2, y_2)(\iota)|| \leq & ((\mathcal{U}_1 + \mathcal{U}_2)(\psi_1 + \psi_2) + (\mathcal{V}_1 + \mathcal{V}_2)(\hat{\psi}_1 + \hat{\psi}_2) \\
& + (\widehat{\mathcal{U}_1} + \widehat{\mathcal{U}_2}) + (\widehat{\mathcal{V}_1} + \widehat{\mathcal{V}_2}))(||x_1 - x_2|| + ||y_1 - y_2||).
\end{aligned}
$$

As a consequence of condition $((\mathcal{U}_1 + \mathcal{U}_2)(\psi_1 + \psi_2) + (\mathcal{V}_1 + \mathcal{V}_2)(\hat{\psi}_1 + \hat{\psi}_2) + (\widehat{\mathcal{U}_1} + \widehat{\mathcal{U}_2}) + (\widehat{\mathcal{V}_1} + \widehat{\mathcal{V}_2})) < 1$, Ψ is a contraction operator. Hence, the operator has a unique fixed point by Banach's contraction principle [39], which corresponds to a unique solution of the problem in (3) and (4). □

4. Example

Consider the following system of coupled generalized Liouville–Caputo type Langevin FDEs:

$$\begin{cases} {}^{\frac{39}{50}}_{C}\mathcal{D}^{\frac{63}{50}}_{0+}\left({}^{\frac{39}{50}}_{C}\mathcal{D}^{\frac{3}{5}}_{0+} + \frac{1}{100}\right)x(\iota) = f(\iota, x(\iota), y(\iota)), \iota \in \mathcal{E} := [0,1], \\ {}^{\frac{39}{50}}_{C}\mathcal{D}^{\frac{44}{25}}_{0+}\left({}^{\frac{39}{50}}_{C}\mathcal{D}^{\frac{17}{20}}_{0+} + \frac{1}{150}\right)y(\iota) = g(\iota, x(\iota), y(\iota)), \iota \in \mathcal{E} := [0,1], \end{cases} \tag{56}$$

augmented with boundary conditions

$$\left\{ x(0) = 0,\ y(0) = 0,\ x(1) = \tfrac{9}{50}\textstyle\sum_{j=1}^{k} \varsigma_j y(\varpi_j),\ y(1) = \tfrac{4}{25}\sum_{j=1}^{k} \varrho_j x(\sigma_j), \right. \tag{57}$$

where $\xi_1 = \frac{63}{50}, \xi_2 = \frac{44}{25}, \zeta_1 = \frac{3}{5}, \zeta_2 = \frac{17}{20}, \rho = \frac{39}{50}, \mathcal{S} = 1, \epsilon = \frac{9}{50}, \pi = \frac{4}{25}, \varpi_1 = \frac{8}{25}, \varpi_2 = \frac{21}{50}, \varpi_3 = \frac{13}{25}, \varpi_4 = \frac{31}{50}, \sigma_1 = \frac{7}{20}, \sigma_2 = \frac{9}{20}, \sigma_3 = \frac{11}{20}, \sigma_4 = \frac{13}{20}, \varsigma_1 = \frac{6}{25}, \varsigma_2 = \frac{17}{50}, \varsigma_3 = \frac{11}{25}, \varsigma_4 = \frac{12}{25}, \varrho_1 = \frac{7}{50}, \varrho_2 = \frac{4}{25}, \varrho_3 = \frac{1}{5}, \varrho_4 = \frac{11}{50}$, and

$$f(\iota, x(\iota), y(\iota)) = \frac{(\iota+1)}{200}\left(\frac{|y(\iota)|}{1+|y(\iota)|} + \frac{1}{4}\cos(x(\iota)) + 5\iota\right), \tag{58}$$

$$g(\iota, x(\iota), y(\iota)) = \frac{e^{-\iota}}{100}\left(\frac{1+\sqrt{\iota}}{4} + \frac{1}{7}\cos(y(\iota)) + \frac{|x(\iota)|}{3(1+|x(\iota)|)}\right). \tag{59}$$

with $\psi_0 = \frac{1}{40}, \psi_1 = \frac{1}{800}, \psi_2 = \frac{1}{200}, \hat{\psi}_0 = \frac{1}{400}, \hat{\psi}_1 = \frac{1}{300}$, and $\hat{\psi}_2 = \frac{1}{700}$, using condition $(\mathcal{A}_1)$. Next, we find that $\mathcal{U}_1 = 7.17720698699361, \mathcal{V}_1 = 15.76278111144004, \mathcal{U}_2 = 3.062775121234468, \mathcal{V}_2 = 17.146905979118152, \widehat{\mathcal{U}_1} = 0.06427770462505382, \widehat{\mathcal{V}_1} = 0.12551798367318132, \widehat{\mathcal{U}_2} = 0.030350664250901854, \widehat{\mathcal{V}_2} = 0.1356913209638917$, $\mathcal{U}_i, \mathcal{V}_i, \widehat{\mathcal{U}_i}, \widehat{\mathcal{V}_i} (i = 1,2)$ are, respectively, given by (36)–(43). Thus, $\psi_1(\mathcal{U}_1 + \mathcal{U}_2) + \hat{\psi}_1(\mathcal{V}_1 + \mathcal{V}_2) + \widehat{\mathcal{U}_1} + \widehat{\mathcal{U}_2} \approxeq 0.21712730347976808 < 1, \psi_2(\mathcal{U}_1 + \mathcal{U}_2) + \hat{\psi}_2(\mathcal{V}_1 + \mathcal{V}_2) + \widehat{\mathcal{V}_1} + \widehat{\mathcal{V}_2} \approxeq 0.35942305387901086 < 1$, and there is at least one solution for the problem in (56) and (57) on $[0,1]$ with f and g, which are, respectively, given by (58) and (59). Additionally, all of the requirements of Theorem 1 have been satisfied.

Moreover, we employ

$$f(\iota, x(\iota), y(\iota)) = \frac{\iota}{20} + \frac{1}{500}\frac{|y(\iota)|}{1+|y(\iota)|} + \frac{3}{800}\cos(x(\iota)), \tag{60}$$

$$g(\iota, x(\iota), y(\iota)) = \frac{(e^{-\iota}+1)}{50} + \frac{1}{400}\cos(y(\iota)) + \frac{1}{700}\frac{|x(\iota)|}{1+|x(\iota)|}, \tag{61}$$

to illustrate Theorem 2. Using assumption $(\mathcal{A}_2)$ with $\psi_1 = \frac{3}{800}, \psi_2 = \frac{1}{500}, \hat{\psi}_1 = \frac{1}{700}$, and $\hat{\psi}_2 = \frac{1}{400}$. The assumptions of Theorem 2 are also satisfied with $(\mathcal{U}_1 + \mathcal{U}_2)(\psi_1 + \psi_2) + (\mathcal{V}_1 + \mathcal{V}_2)(\hat{\psi}_1 + \hat{\psi}_2) + (\widehat{\mathcal{U}_1} + \widehat{\mathcal{U}_2}) + (\widehat{\mathcal{V}_1} + \widehat{\mathcal{V}_2}) \approxeq 0.5440056270625331 < 1$. Consequently, there exists a unique solution on $[0,1]$ to the problem in (56) and (57) with f and g supplied by (60) and (61), respectively, according to Theorem 2.

For brevity, we use these notations:

$$\begin{aligned} \mathcal{U}_1 = {} & \frac{\left(\mathcal{S}^{\rho(\xi_1+\zeta_1)}(1+|\delta_1||\mathcal{E}_2|)\right)}{\rho^{\xi_1+\zeta_1}\Gamma(\xi_1+\zeta_1+1)} + \frac{|\delta_1||\pi||\mathcal{E}_1|\sum_{j=1}^{k}\varrho_j\sigma_j^{\rho(\xi_1+\zeta_1)}}{\rho^{\xi_1+\zeta_1}\Gamma(\xi_1+\zeta_1+1)} \\ & + |\phi_1|\left(\frac{(\mathcal{S}^{\rho\zeta_1}(1+|\delta_1||\mathcal{E}_2|))}{\rho^{\zeta_1}\Gamma(\zeta_1+1)} + \frac{|\delta_1||\pi||\mathcal{E}_1|\sum_{j=1}^{k}\varrho_j\sigma_j^{\rho(\zeta_1)}}{\rho^{\zeta_1}\Gamma(\zeta_1+1)}\right), \end{aligned} \tag{62}$$

$$\mathcal{V}_1 = |\delta_1|\left(\frac{|\mathcal{E}_1|\mathcal{S}^{\rho(\xi_2+\zeta_2)}}{\rho^{\xi_2+\zeta_2}\Gamma(\xi_2+\zeta_2+1)} + \frac{|\mathcal{E}_2||\epsilon|\sum_{j=1}^{k}\varsigma_j\varpi_j^{\rho(\xi_2+\zeta_2)}}{\rho^{\xi_2+\zeta_2}\Gamma(\xi_2+\zeta_2+1)}\right)$$
$$+|\delta_1||\phi_2|\left(\frac{|\mathcal{E}_1|\mathcal{S}^{\rho\zeta_2}}{\rho^{\zeta_2}\Gamma(\zeta_2+1)} + \frac{|\mathcal{E}_2||\epsilon|\sum_{j=1}^{k}\varsigma_j\varpi_j^{\rho(\zeta_2)}}{\rho^{\zeta_2}\Gamma(\zeta_2+1)}\right), \tag{63}$$

$$\mathcal{U}_2 = |\delta_2|\left(\frac{\mathcal{S}^{\rho(\xi_1+\zeta_1)}|\widehat{\mathcal{E}}_2|}{\rho^{\xi_1+\zeta_1}\Gamma(\xi_1+\zeta_1+1)} + \frac{|\pi||\widehat{\mathcal{E}}_1|\sum_{j=1}^{k}\varrho_j\sigma_j^{\rho(\xi_1+\zeta_1)}}{\rho^{\xi_1+\zeta_1}\Gamma(\xi_1+\zeta_1+1)}\right)$$
$$+|\delta_2||\phi_1|\left(\frac{\mathcal{S}^{\rho\zeta_1}|\widehat{\mathcal{E}}_2|}{\rho^{\zeta_1}\Gamma(\zeta_1+1)} + \frac{|\pi||\widehat{\mathcal{E}}_1|\sum_{j=1}^{k}\varrho_j\sigma_j^{\rho(\zeta_1)}}{\rho^{\zeta_1}\Gamma(\zeta_1+1)}\right), \tag{64}$$

$$\mathcal{V}_2 = \frac{(1+|\delta_2||\widehat{\mathcal{E}}_1|)\mathcal{S}^{\rho(\xi_2+\zeta_2)}}{\rho^{\xi_2+\zeta_2}\Gamma(\xi_2+\zeta_2+1)} + \frac{|\delta_2||\widehat{\mathcal{E}}_2||\epsilon|\sum_{j=1}^{k}\varsigma_j\varpi_j^{\rho(\xi_2+\zeta_2)}}{\rho^{\xi_2+\zeta_2}\Gamma(\xi_2+\zeta_2+1)}$$
$$+|\phi_2|\left(\frac{(1+|\delta_2||\widehat{\mathcal{E}}_1|)\mathcal{S}^{\rho\zeta_2}}{\rho^{\zeta_2}\Gamma(\zeta_2+1)} + \frac{|\delta_2||\widehat{\mathcal{E}}_2||\epsilon|\sum_{j=1}^{k}\varsigma_j\varpi_j^{\rho(\zeta_2)}}{\rho^{\zeta_2}\Gamma(\zeta_2+1)}\right), \tag{65}$$

5. Ulam–Hyers Stability Results

With the help of an integral formulation of the solution provided by

$$x(\iota) = \Psi_1(x,y)(\iota),\ y(\iota) = \Psi_2(x,y)(\iota), \tag{66}$$

where Ψ_1 and Ψ_2 are given by (34) and (35), we analyse the Ulam–Hyers stability for problem (3) in this section. Consider the following definitions of nonlinear operators

$$\mathcal{H}_1, \mathcal{H}_2 \in \mathcal{C}(\mathcal{E},\mathbb{R}) \times \mathcal{C}(\mathcal{E},\mathbb{R}) \to \mathcal{C}(\mathcal{E},\mathbb{R}),$$

$$\begin{cases} {}_{C}^{\rho}\mathcal{D}_{0^+}^{\xi_1}({}_{C}^{\rho}\mathcal{D}_{0^+}^{\zeta_1} + \phi_1)x(\iota) - f(\iota,x(\iota),y(\iota)) = \mathcal{H}_1(x,y)(\iota), \iota \in \mathcal{E}, \\ {}_{C}^{\rho}\mathcal{D}_{0^+}^{\xi_2}({}_{C}^{\rho}\mathcal{D}_{0^+}^{\zeta_2} + \phi_2)y(\iota) - g(\iota,x(\iota),y(\iota)) = \mathcal{H}_1(x,y)(\iota), \iota \in \mathcal{E}. \end{cases}$$

For some $\hat{\lambda}_1, \hat{\lambda}_2 > 0$, taking into consideration the following inequality

$$||\mathcal{H}_1(x,y)|| \le \hat{\lambda}_1, ||\mathcal{H}_2(x,y)|| \le \hat{\lambda}_2, \tag{67}$$

Definition 4. *the system in (3) and (4) is UHS if $\mathcal{V}_1, \mathcal{V}_2 > 0$ and $\exists$ a unique solution $(x,y) \in \mathcal{C}(\mathcal{E},\mathbb{R})$ of the problem in (3) and (4) with*

$$||(x,y) - (x^*,y^*)|| \le \mathcal{V}_1\hat{\lambda}_1 + \mathcal{V}_2\hat{\lambda}_2,$$

$\forall (x,y) \in \mathcal{C}(\mathcal{E},\mathbb{R})$ of inequality (67).

Theorem 3. *If assumption $(\mathcal{A}_2)$ is satisfied, then the BVP (3) and (4) is UHS.*

Proof. Let $(x,y) \in \mathcal{C}(\mathcal{E},\mathbb{R}) \times \mathcal{C}(\mathcal{E},\mathbb{R})$ be the solution of the BVP (3) and (4) satisfying (34) and (35). Let (x,y) be any solution satisfying (67):

$$\begin{cases} {}_{C}^{\rho}\mathcal{D}_{0^+}^{\xi_1}({}_{C}^{\rho}\mathcal{D}_{0^+}^{\zeta_1} + \phi_1)x(\iota) = f(\iota,x(\iota),y(\iota)) + \mathcal{H}_1(x,y)(\iota), \iota \in \mathcal{E}, \\ {}_{C}^{\rho}\mathcal{D}_{0^+}^{\xi_2}({}_{C}^{\rho}\mathcal{D}_{0^+}^{\zeta_2} + \phi_2)y(\iota) = g(\iota,x(\iota),y(\iota)) + \mathcal{H}_1(x,y)(\iota), \iota \in \mathcal{E}, \end{cases}$$

thus,

$$
\begin{aligned}
x^*(\iota) = {} & \Psi_1(x^*,y^*)(\iota) +^\rho \mathcal{I}_{0^+}^{\xi_1+\zeta_1}\mathcal{H}_1(x,y)(\iota) - \phi_1^\rho \mathcal{I}_{0^+}^{\zeta_1} x(\iota) \\
& + \delta_1(\iota)\Bigg[\mathcal{E}_2\Big(\epsilon \sum_{j=1}^{k} \varsigma_j^\rho \mathcal{I}_{0^+}^{\xi_2+\zeta_2}\mathcal{H}_2(x,y)(\varpi_j) \\
& - \epsilon\phi_2 \sum_{j=1}^{k} \varsigma_j{}^\rho \mathcal{I}_{0^+}^{\zeta_2} y(\varpi_j) - {}^\rho\mathcal{I}_{0^+}^{\xi_1+\zeta_1}\mathcal{H}_1(x,y)(\mathcal{S}) + \phi_1^\rho \mathcal{I}_{0^+}^{\zeta_1} x(\mathcal{S})\Big) \\
& + \mathcal{E}_1\Big(\pi \sum_{j=1}^{k} \varrho_j^\rho \mathcal{I}_{0^+}^{\xi_1+\zeta_1}\mathcal{H}_1(x,y)(\sigma_j) - \pi\phi_1 \sum_{j=1}^{k} \varrho_j{}^\rho \mathcal{I}_{0^+}^{\zeta_1} x(\sigma_j) \\
& - {}^\rho\mathcal{I}_{0^+}^{\xi_2+\zeta_2}\mathcal{H}_2(x,y)(\mathcal{S}) + \phi_2^\rho \mathcal{I}_{0^+}^{\zeta_2} y(\mathcal{S})\Big)\Bigg].
\end{aligned}
$$

It follows that

$$
\begin{aligned}
& |\Psi_1(x^*,y^*)(\iota) - x^*(\iota)| \\
\leq & {}^\rho\mathcal{I}_{0^+}^{\xi_1+\zeta_1}|\mathcal{H}_1(x,y)(\iota)| + |\phi_1|^\rho \mathcal{I}_{0^+}^{\zeta_1}|x(\iota)| \\
& + |\delta_1(\iota)|\Bigg[|\mathcal{E}_2|\Big(|\epsilon| \sum_{j=1}^{k} \varsigma_j^\rho \mathcal{I}_{0^+}^{\xi_2+\zeta_2}|\mathcal{H}_2(x,y)(\varpi_j)| \\
& + |\epsilon||\phi_2| \sum_{j=1}^{k} \varsigma_j{}^\rho \mathcal{I}_{0^+}^{\zeta_2}|y(\varpi_j)| + {}^\rho\mathcal{I}_{0^+}^{\xi_1+\zeta_1}|\mathcal{H}_1(x,y)(\mathcal{S})| + |\phi_1|^\rho \mathcal{I}_{0^+}^{\zeta_1}|x(\mathcal{S})|\Big) \\
& + |\mathcal{E}_1|\Big(|\pi| \sum_{j=1}^{k} \varrho_j^\rho \mathcal{I}_{0^+}^{\xi_1+\zeta_1}\mathcal{H}_1(x,y)(\sigma_j) + |\pi||\phi_1| \sum_{j=1}^{k} \varrho_j{}^\rho \mathcal{I}_{0^+}^{\zeta_1}|x(\sigma_j)| \\
& + {}^\rho\mathcal{I}_{0^+}^{\xi_2+\zeta_2}|\mathcal{H}_2(x,y)(\mathcal{S})| + |\phi_2|^\rho \mathcal{I}_{0^+}^{\zeta_2}|y(\mathcal{S})|\Big)\Bigg] \\
\leq & \ \hat{\lambda}_1\Bigg\{\frac{\Big(\mathcal{S}^{\rho(\xi_1+\zeta_1)}(1+|\delta_1||\mathcal{E}_2|)\Big)}{\rho^{\xi_1+\zeta_1}\Gamma(\xi_1+\zeta_1+1)} + \frac{|\delta_1||\pi||\mathcal{E}_1|\sum_{j=1}^{k}\varrho_j\sigma_j^{\rho(\xi_1+\zeta_1)}}{\rho^{\xi_1+\zeta_1}\Gamma(\xi_1+\zeta_1+1)} \\
& + |\phi_1|\Bigg(\frac{(\mathcal{S}^{\rho\zeta_1}(1+|\delta_1||\mathcal{E}_2|))}{\rho^{\zeta_1}\Gamma(\zeta_1+1)} + \frac{|\delta_1||\pi||\mathcal{E}_1|\sum_{j=1}^{k}\varrho_j\sigma_j^{\rho(\zeta_1)}}{\rho^{\zeta_1}\Gamma(\zeta_1+1)}\Bigg)\Bigg\} \\
& + \hat{\lambda}_2\Bigg\{|\delta_1|\Bigg(\frac{|\mathcal{E}_1|\mathcal{S}^{\rho(\xi_2+\zeta_2)}}{\rho^{\xi_2+\zeta_2}\Gamma(\xi_2+\zeta_2+1)} + \frac{|\mathcal{E}_2||\epsilon|\sum_{j=1}^{k}\varsigma_j\varpi_j^{\rho(\xi_2+\zeta_2)}}{\rho^{\xi_2+\zeta_2}\Gamma(\xi_2+\zeta_2+1)}\Bigg) \\
& + |\delta_1||\phi_2|\Bigg(\frac{|\mathcal{E}_1|\mathcal{S}^{\rho\zeta_2}}{\rho^{\zeta_2}\Gamma(\zeta_2+1)} + \frac{|\mathcal{E}_2||\epsilon|\sum_{j=1}^{k}\varsigma_j\varpi_j^{\rho(\zeta_2)}}{\rho^{\zeta_2}\Gamma(\zeta_2+1)}\Bigg)\Bigg\} \\
\leq & \,\mathcal{U}_1\hat{\lambda}_1 + \mathcal{V}_1\hat{\lambda}_2.
\end{aligned}
$$

Similarly , we obtain

$$
\begin{aligned}
&|\Psi_2(x^*,y^*)(\iota)-y^*(\iota)|\\
\leq&\hat{\lambda}_2\left\{\frac{(1+|\delta_2||\widehat{\mathcal{E}}_1|)\mathcal{S}^{\rho(\xi_2+\zeta_2)}}{\rho^{\xi_2+\zeta_2}\Gamma(\xi_2+\zeta_2+1)}+\frac{|\delta_2||\widehat{\mathcal{E}}_2||\epsilon|\sum_{j=1}^{k}\varsigma_j\varpi_j^{\rho(\xi_2+\zeta_2)}}{\rho^{\xi_2+\zeta_2}\Gamma(\xi_2+\zeta_2+1)}\right.\\
&\left.+|\phi_2|\left(\frac{(1+|\delta_2||\widehat{\mathcal{E}}_1|)\mathcal{S}^{\rho\zeta_2}}{\rho^{\zeta_2}\Gamma(\zeta_2+1)}+\frac{|\delta_2||\widehat{\mathcal{E}}_2||\epsilon|\sum_{j=1}^{k}\varsigma_j\varpi_j^{\rho(\zeta_2)}}{\rho^{\zeta_2}\Gamma(\zeta_2+1)}\right)\right\}\\
&+\hat{\lambda}_1\left\{|\delta_2|\left(\frac{\mathcal{S}^{\rho(\xi_1+\zeta_1)}|\widehat{\mathcal{E}}_2|}{\rho^{\xi_1+\zeta_1}\Gamma(\xi_1+\zeta_1+1)}+\frac{|\pi||\widehat{\mathcal{E}}_1|\sum_{j=1}^{k}\varrho_j\sigma_j^{\rho(\xi_1+\zeta_1)}}{\rho^{\xi_1+\zeta_1}\Gamma(\xi_1+\zeta_1+1)}\right)\right.\\
&\left.+|\delta_2||\phi_1|\left(\frac{\mathcal{S}^{\rho\zeta_1}|\widehat{\mathcal{E}}_2|}{\rho^{\zeta_1}\Gamma(\zeta_1+1)}+\frac{|\pi||\widehat{\mathcal{E}}_1|\sum_{j=1}^{k}\varrho_j\sigma_j^{\rho(\zeta_1)}}{\rho^{\zeta_1}\Gamma(\zeta_1+1)}\right)\right\}\\
\leq&\mathcal{U}_2\hat{\lambda}_1+\mathcal{V}_2\hat{\lambda}_2,
\end{aligned}
$$

where $\mathcal{U}_1,\mathcal{V}_1,\mathcal{U}_2$, and $\mathcal{V}_2$ are defined in (62)–(65), respectively. Consequently, based on the fixed-point property of the operator Ψ, provided in (34) and (35), we derive

$$
\begin{aligned}
|x(\iota)-x^*(\iota)|=&|x(\iota)-\Psi_1(x^*,y^*)(\iota)+\Psi_1(x^*,y^*)(\iota)-x^*(\iota)|\\
\leq&|\Psi_1(x,y)(\iota)-\Psi_1(x^*,y^*)(\iota)|+|\Psi_1(x^*,y^*)(\iota)-x^*(\iota)|\\
\leq&((\mathcal{U}_1\psi_1+\mathcal{V}_1\hat{\psi}_1)+(\mathcal{U}_1\psi_2+\mathcal{V}_1\hat{\psi}_2))||(x,y)-(x^*,y^*)||\\
&+\mathcal{U}_1\hat{\lambda}_1+\mathcal{V}_1\hat{\lambda}_2.
\end{aligned}
\tag{68}
$$

$$
\begin{aligned}
|y(\iota)-y^*(\iota)|=&|y(\iota)-\Psi_2(x^*,y^*)(\iota)+\Psi_2(x^*,y^*)(\iota)-y^*(\iota)|\\
\leq&|\Psi_2(x,y)(\iota)-\Psi_2(x^*,y^*)(\iota)|+|\Psi_2(x^*,y^*)(\iota)-y^*(\iota)|\\
\leq&((\mathcal{U}_2\psi_1+\mathcal{V}_2\hat{\psi}_1)+(\mathcal{U}_2\psi_2+\mathcal{V}_2\hat{\psi}_2))||(x,y)-(x^*,y^*)||\\
&+\mathcal{U}_2\hat{\lambda}_1+\mathcal{V}_2\hat{\lambda}_2.
\end{aligned}
\tag{69}
$$

From the above equations (68) and (69) it follows that

$$
\begin{aligned}
||(x,y)-(x^*,y^*)||\leq&(\mathcal{U}_1+\mathcal{U}_2)\hat{\lambda}_1+(\mathcal{V}_1+\mathcal{V}_2)\hat{\lambda}_2\\
&+((\mathcal{U}_1+\mathcal{U}_2)(\psi_1+\psi_2)+(\mathcal{V}_1+\mathcal{V}_2)(\hat{\psi}_1+\hat{\psi}_2))||(x,y)-(x^*,y^*)||.
\end{aligned}
$$

$$
\begin{aligned}
||(x,y)-(x^*,y^*)||\leq&\frac{(\mathcal{U}_1+\mathcal{U}_2)\hat{\lambda}_1+(\mathcal{V}_1+\mathcal{V}_2)\hat{\lambda}_2}{1-((\mathcal{U}_1+\mathcal{U}_2)(\psi_1+\psi_2)+(\mathcal{V}_1+\mathcal{V}_2)(\hat{\psi}_1+\hat{\psi}_2))}\\
\leq&\mathcal{V}_1\hat{\lambda}_1+\mathcal{V}_2\hat{\lambda}_2,
\end{aligned}
$$

with

$$
\mathcal{V}_1=\frac{\mathcal{U}_1+\mathcal{U}_2}{1-((\mathcal{U}_1+\mathcal{U}_2)(\psi_1+\psi_2)+(\mathcal{V}_1+\mathcal{V}_2)(\hat{\psi}_1+\hat{\psi}_2))},
$$

$$
\mathcal{V}_2=\frac{\mathcal{V}_1+\mathcal{V}_2}{1-((\mathcal{U}_1+\mathcal{U}_2)(\psi_1+\psi_2)+(\mathcal{V}_1+\mathcal{V}_2)(\hat{\psi}_1+\hat{\psi}_2))}.
$$

Thus, the BVP (3) and (4) is UHS. □

6. Example

Consider the following system of coupled generalized Liouville–Caputo type Langevin FDEs:

$$\begin{cases} {}^{\frac{39}{50}}_{C}\mathcal{D}^{\frac{63}{50}}_{0+}\left({}^{\frac{39}{50}}_{C}\mathcal{D}^{\frac{3}{5}}_{0+} + \frac{1}{100}\right)x(\iota) = \frac{\sqrt{\iota}}{30} + \frac{1}{40(16+\iota)}\frac{|y(\iota)|}{1+|y(\iota)|} + \frac{4}{900}\cos(x(\iota)), \iota \in [0,1], \\ {}^{\frac{39}{50}}_{C}\mathcal{D}^{\frac{44}{25}}_{0+}\left({}^{\frac{39}{50}}_{C}\mathcal{D}^{\frac{17}{20}}_{0+} + \frac{1}{150}\right)y(\iota) = \frac{\iota}{70} + \frac{1}{400}\cos(y(\iota)) + \frac{1}{800}\frac{|x(\iota)|}{1+|x(\iota)|}, \iota \in [0,1], \end{cases} \tag{70}$$

augmented with boundary conditions:

$$\left\{ x(0) = 0,\ y(0) = 0,\ x(1) = \frac{9}{50}\sum_{j=1}^{k} \varsigma_j y(\varpi_j),\ y(1) = \frac{4}{25}\sum_{j=1}^{k} \varrho_j x(\sigma_j), \right. \tag{71}$$

where $\xi_1 = \frac{63}{50}, \xi_2 = \frac{44}{25}, \zeta_1 = \frac{3}{5}, \zeta_2 = \frac{17}{20}, \rho = \frac{39}{50}, \mathcal{S} = 1, \epsilon = \frac{9}{50}, \pi = \frac{4}{25}, \varpi_1 = \frac{8}{25}, \varpi_2 = \frac{21}{50}, \varpi_3 = \frac{13}{25}, \varpi_4 = \frac{31}{50}, \sigma_1 = \frac{7}{20}, \sigma_2 = \frac{9}{20}, \sigma_3 = \frac{11}{20}, \sigma_4 = \frac{13}{20}, \varsigma_1 = \frac{6}{25}, \varsigma_2 = \frac{17}{50}, \varsigma_3 = \frac{11}{25}, \varsigma_4 = \frac{12}{25}, \varrho_1 = \frac{7}{50}, \varrho_2 = \frac{4}{25}, \varrho_3 = \frac{1}{5}, \varrho_4 = \frac{11}{50}$ and

$$|f(\iota, x_1(\iota), y_1(\iota)) - f(\iota, x_2(\iota), y_2(\iota))| = \frac{4}{900}|x_1(\iota) - x_2(\iota)| + \frac{1}{640}|y_1(\iota) - y_2(\iota)|, \tag{72}$$

$$|g(\iota, x_1(\iota), y_1(\iota)) - g(\iota, x_2(\iota), y_2(\iota))| = \frac{1}{800}|x_1(\iota) - x_2(\iota)| + \frac{1}{400}|y_1(\iota) - y_2(\iota)|. \tag{73}$$

with $\psi_1 = \frac{4}{900}, \psi_2 = \frac{1}{640}, \hat{\psi}_1 = \frac{1}{800}$, and $\hat{\psi}_2 = \frac{1}{400}$, and using condition $(\mathcal{A}_2)$. Next, we find that $\mathcal{U}_1 = 7.241484691618664, \mathcal{V}_1 = 15.88829909511322, \mathcal{U}_2 = 3.0931257854853698, \mathcal{V}_2 = 17.282597300082045, \mathcal{U}_i, \mathcal{V}_i$ are, respectively, given by (62)–(65). Thus, $((\mathcal{U}_1 + \mathcal{U}_2)(\psi_1 + \psi_2) + (\mathcal{V}_1 + \mathcal{V}_2)(\hat{\psi}_1 + \hat{\psi}_2)) \approxeq 0.18647029247291969 < 1$. Consequently, there exists a unique solution on $[0,1]$, to the problem in (70) and (71), which is stable for Ulam–Hyers, with f and g supplied by (72) and (73), respectively, according to Theorem 3.

7. Asymmetric Case

Remark 1. *If $\rho = 1$, the problem (3)'s generalized Langevin FDEs reduces to the Caputo Langevin FDEs.*

$$\begin{cases} {}_{C}\mathcal{D}^{\xi_1}_{0^+}({}_{C}\mathcal{D}^{\zeta_1}_{0^+} + \phi_1)x(\iota) = f(\iota, x(\iota), y(\iota)), \iota \in \mathcal{E} := [0, \mathcal{S}], \\ {}_{C}\mathcal{D}^{\xi_2}_{0^+}({}_{C}\mathcal{D}^{\zeta_2}_{0^+} + \phi_2)y(\iota) = g(\iota, x(\iota), y(\iota)), \iota \in \mathcal{E} := [0, \mathcal{S}]. \end{cases} \tag{74}$$

8. Conclusions

We discussed the existence and uniqueness of solutions for a Langevin coupled system of fractional order involving generalised Liouville–Caputo type and multipoint boundary conditions in our contribution. To get at our result, we used the Leray–Schauder and Banach fixed-point theorems, and we included examples to help explain our study results. By using a conventional functional analysis, we demonstrated Ulam–Hyers stability. Our findings in this context are original and contribute to the body of knowledge on generalised fractional integral operators that are used to resolve generalised fractional differential equations of coupled Langevin systems with nonlocal multipoint boundary conditions. We highlighted the topic's asymmetries in the remarks. The form of the solution in these kinds of statements can be used to conduct additional research on the positive solution and its asymmetry.

Author Contributions: Conceptualization, M.S.; formal analysis, M.A. and M.S.; methodology, M.A., M.S. and K.A. All authors have read and agreed to the published version of the manuscript.

Funding: This work was supported by the Deanship of Scientific Research, Vice Presidency for Graduate Studies and Scientific Research, King Faisal University, Saudi Arabia (Grant No. 2224).

Institutional Review Board Statement: Not applicable.

Informed Consent Statement: Not applicable.

Data Availability Statement: Not applicable.

Conflicts of Interest: The authors declare no conflict of interest.

References

1. Klafter, J.; Lim, S.; Metzler, R. *Fractional Dynamics: Recent Advances*; World Scientific: Singapore, 2012.
2. Podlubny, I. *Fractional Differential Equations: An Introduction to Fractional Derivatives, Fractional Differential Equations, to Methods of Their Solution and Some of Their Applications*; Elsevier: Amsterdam, The Netherlands, 1998.
3. Valerio, D.; Machado, J.T.; Kiryakova, V. Some pioneers of the applications of fractional calculus. *Fract. Calc. Appl. Anal.* **2014**, *17*, 552–578. [CrossRef]
4. Machado, J.T.; Kiryakova, V.; Mainardi, F. Recent history of fractional calculus. *Commun. Nonlinear Sci. Numer. Simul.* **2011**, *16*, 1140–1153. [CrossRef]
5. Kilbas, A.A.A.; Srivastava, H.M.; Trujillo, J.J. *Theory and Applications of Fractional Differential Equations*; Elsevier Science Limited: Amsterdam, The Netherlands, 2006; Volume 204.
6. Bitsadze, A.; Samarskii, A. On some simple generalizations of linear elliptic boundary problems. *Soviet Math. Dokl.* **1969**, *10*, 398–400.
7. Ciegis, R.; Bugajev, A. Numerical approximation of one model of bacterial self-organization. *Nonlinear Anal. Model. Control.* **2012**, *17*, 253–270. [CrossRef]
8. Vinales, A.D.; Esposito, M.A. Anomalous diffusion: Exact solution of the generalized Langevin equation for harmonically bounded particle. *Phys. Rev. E* **2006**, *73*, 016111. [CrossRef]
9. Hohenberg, P.C.; Halperin, B.I. Theory of dynamic critical phenomena. *Rev. Mod. Phys.* **1977**, *49*, 435–479. [CrossRef]
10. Metiu, H.; Schon, G. Description of Quantum noise by a Langevin equation. *Phys. Rev. Lett.* **1984**, *53*, 13. [CrossRef]
11. Datsko, B.; Gafiychuk, V. Complex nonlinear dynamics in subdiffusive activator–inhibitor systems. *Commun. Nonlinear Sci. Numer. Simul.* **2012**, *17*, 1673–1680. [CrossRef]
12. Datsko, B.; Gafiychuk, V. Complex spatio-temporal solutions in fractional reaction-diffusion systems near a bifurcation point. *Fract. Calc. Appl. Anal.* **2018**, *21*, 237–253. [CrossRef]
13. West, B.J.; Picozzi, S. Fractional Langevin model of memory in financial time series. *Phys. Rev. E* **2002**, *65*, 037106. [CrossRef]
14. Fa, K.S. Fractional Langevin equation and Riemann-Liouville fractional derivative. *Eur. Phys. J. E* **2007**, *24*, 139–143.
15. Theswan, S.; Ntouyas, S.K.; Ahmad, B.; Tariboon, J. Existence Results for Nonlinear Coupled Hilfer Fractional Differential Equations with Nonlocal Riemann–Liouville and Hadamard-Type Iterated Integral Boundary Conditions. *Symmetry* **2022**, *14*, 1948. [CrossRef]
16. Ahmad, B.; Nieto, J.J.; Alsaedi, A.; El-Shahed, M. A study of nonlinear Langevin equation involving two fractional orders in different intervals. *Nonlinear Anal. Real World Appl.* **2012**, *13*, 599–606. [CrossRef]
17. Wang, G.; Zhang, L.; Song, G. Boundary value problem of a nonlinear Langevin equation with two different fractional orders and impulses. *Fixed Point Theory Appl.* **2012**, *2012*, 200. [CrossRef]
18. Ahmad, B.; Ntouyas, S.K. New existence results for differential inclusions involving Langevin equation with two indices. *J. Nonlinear Convex Anal.* **2013**, *14*, 437–450.
19. Muensawat, T.; Ntouyas, S.K.; Tariboon, J. Systems of generalized Sturm-Liouville and Langevin fractional differential equations. *Adv. Differ. Equ.* **2017**, *2017*, 63. [CrossRef]
20. Fazli, H.; Nieto, J.J. Fractional Langevin equation with anti-periodic boundary conditions. *Chaos Solitons Fractals* **2018**, *114*, 332–337. [CrossRef]
21. Ahmad, B.; Alsaedi, A.; Salem, S. On a nonlocal integral boundary value problem of nonlinear Langevin equation with different fractional orders. *Adv. Differ. Equ.* **2019**, *2019*, 57. [CrossRef]
22. Arefin, M.A.; Sadiya, U.; Inc, M.; Uddin, M.H. Adequate soliton solutions to the space–time fractional telegraph equation and modified third-order KdV equation through a reliable technique. *Opt. Quantum Electron.* **2022**, *54*, 309. [CrossRef]
23. Khatun, M.A.; Arefin, M.A.; Uddin, M.H.; Inc, M.; Akbar, M.A. An analytical approach to the solution of fractional-coupled modified equal width and fractional-coupled Burgers equations. *J. Ocean. Eng. Sci.* **2022**, *in press*. [CrossRef]
24. Sadiya, U.; Inc, M.; Arefin, M.A.; Uddin, M.H. Consistent travelling waves solutions to the non-linear time fractional Klein–Gordon and Sine-Gordon equations through extended tanh-function approach. *J. Taibah Univ. Sci.* **2022**, *16*, 594–607. [CrossRef]
25. Duraisamy, P.; Gopal, T.N.; Subramanian, M. Analysis of fractional integro-differential equations with nonlocal Erdélyi-Kober type integral boundary conditions. *Fract. Calc. Appl. Anal.* **2020**, *23*, 1401–1415. [CrossRef]
26. Rahmani, A.; Du, W.S.; Khalladi, M.T.; Kostić, M.; Velinov, D. Proportional Caputo Fractional Differential Inclusions in Banach Spaces. *Symmetry* **2022**, *14*, 1941. [CrossRef]
27. Baleanu, D.; Hemalatha, S.; Duraisamy, P.; Pandian, P.; Muthaiah, S. Existence results for coupled differential equations of non-integer order with Riemann-Liouville, Erdélyi-Kober integral conditions. *AIMS Math.* **2021**, *6*, 13004–13023. [CrossRef]
28. Subramanian, M.; Kumar, A.V.; Gopal, T.N. A fundamental approach on non-integer order differential equation using nonlocal fractional sub-strips boundary conditions. *Discontinuity Nonlinearity Complex.* **2019**, *8*, 187–197. [CrossRef]

29. Awadalla, M.; Subramanian, M.; Abuasbeh, K.; Manigandan, M. On the Generalized Liouville–Caputo Type Fractional Differential Equations Supplemented with Katugampola Integral Boundary Conditions. *Symmetry* **2022**, *14*, 2273. [CrossRef]
30. Subramanian, M.; Aljoudi, S. Existence and Ulam–Hyers Stability Analysis for Coupled Differential Equations of Fractional-Order with Nonlocal Generalized Conditions via Generalized Liouville–Caputo Derivative. *Fractal Fract.* **2022**, *6*, 629. [CrossRef]
31. Ahmad, B.; Alghanmi, M.; Alsaedi, A.; Srivastava, H.M.; Ntouyas, S.K. The Langevin equation in terms of generalized Liouville–Caputo derivatives with nonlocal boundary conditions involving a generalized fractional integral. *Mathematics* **2019**, *7*, 533. [CrossRef]
32. Subramanian, M.; Kumar, A.V.; Gopal, T.N. Analysis of fractional boundary value problem with non local flux multi-point conditions on a caputo fractional differential equation. *Stud. Univ. Babes-Bolyai. Math.* **2019**, *64*, 511–527. [CrossRef]
33. Tudorache, A.; Luca, R. Positive Solutions for a Fractional Differential Equation with Sequential Derivatives and Nonlocal Boundary Conditions. *Symmetry* **2022**, *9*, 1779. [CrossRef]
34. Alsaedi, A.; Alghanmi, M.; Ahmad, B.; Ntouyas, S.K. Generalized liouville–caputo fractional differential equations and inclusions with nonlocal generalized fractional integral and multipoint boundary conditions. *Symmetry* **2018**, *10*, 667. [CrossRef]
35. Muthaiah, S.; Baleanu, D.; Thangaraj, N.G. Existence and Hyers-Ulam type stability results for nonlinear coupled system of Caputo-Hadamard type fractional differential equations. *AIMS Math.* **2020**, *6*, 168–194. [CrossRef]
36. Katugampola, U.N. New approach to a generalized fractional integral. *Appl. Math. Comput.* **2011**, *218*, 860–865. [CrossRef]
37. Katugampola, U.N. A new approach to generalized fractional derivatives. *arXiv* **2011**, arXiv:1106.0965.
38. Jarad, F.; Abdeljawad, T.; Baleanu, D. On the generalized fractional derivatives and their caputo modification. *J. Nonlinear Sci. Appl.* **2017**, *10*, 2607–2619. [CrossRef]
39. Granas, A.; Dugundji, J. *Fixed Point Theory*; Springer Science & Business Media: Berlin/Heidelberg, Germany, 2013.

symmetry MDPI

Article

On s-Convexity of Dual Simpson Type Integral Inequalities

Tarek Chiheb [1], Hamid Boulares [1], Moheddine Imsatfia [2], Badreddine Meftah [1] and Abdelkader Moumen [3,*]

1 Laboratory of Analysis and Control of Differential Equations "ACED", Faculty MISM, Department of Mathematics, University of 8 May 1945 Guelma, P.O. Box 401, Guelma 24000, Algeria; tchiheb@yahoo.fr (T.C.); boulareshamid@gmail.com (H.B.); badrimeftah@yahoo.fr (B.M.)
2 Mathematics Department, Faculty of Science, King Khalid University, P.O. Box 9004, Abha 61413, Saudi Arabia; mblgasim@kku.edu.sa
3 Department of Mathematics, Faculty of Science, University of Ha'il, Ha'il 55425, Saudi Arabia
* Correspondence: abdelkader.moumen@gmail.com

Abstract: Integral inequalities are a powerful tool for estimating errors of quadrature formulas. In this study, some symmetric dual Simpson type integral inequalities for the classes of s-convex, bounded and Lipschitzian functions are proposed. The obtained results are based on a new identity and the use of some standard techniques such as Hölder as well as power mean inequalities. We give at the end some applications to the estimation of quadrature rules and to particular means.

Keywords: dual Simpson inequality; Newton–Cotes quadrature; s-convex functions; Lipschitzian functions; bounded functions

Citation: Chiheb, T.; Boulares, H.; Imsatfia, M.; Meftah, B.; Moumen, A. On s-Convexity of Dual Simpson Type Integral Inequalities. *Symmetry* **2023**, *15*, 733. https://doi.org/10.3390/sym15030733

Academic Editors: Ioan Rașa, Hassen Fourati, Abdellatif Ben Makhlouf and Omar Naifar

Received: 10 February 2023
Revised: 25 February 2023
Accepted: 13 March 2023
Published: 15 March 2023

1. Introduction

The concept of convexity and its variants plays a fundamental and important role in the development of various fields of science and engineering in a direct or indirect way. This concept has a closed relationship in the development of the theory of inequalities, which is an important tool in the study of some qualitative properties of solutions for differential and integral equations as well as in numerical analysis for estimating the errors in quadrature formulas. Noting that the most used methods for evaluating the integrals by a numerical approach is that of Newton–Cotes, which comprises a group of formulas involving a certain numbers of equally spaced points.

Definition 1 ([1]). *A function $\Lambda : I \to \mathbb{R}$ is said to be convex, if*

$$\Lambda(ie + (1-i)k) \ \leq i\Lambda(e) + (1-i)\Lambda(k)$$

holds for all $e, k \in I$ and all $i \in [0,1]$.

Bakula et al. [2], studied the following general form of three point Newton–Cotes formula via weighted Montgomery identities:

$$\int_e^f w(j)\aleph(j)dj = C(\chi)(\aleph(\chi) + \aleph(e+f-\chi)) + (1-2C(\chi))\aleph\left(\tfrac{e+f}{2}\right) + \mathcal{R}(w,\aleph,\chi), \quad (1)$$

where $e < f$ and $\chi \in \left[e, \frac{e+f}{2}\right)$, $\mathcal{R}(w,\aleph,\chi)$ is the remainder term and $C(\chi)$ is an arbitrary real function defined on $\left[e, \frac{e+f}{2}\right)$ and gives the following results:

$$\left|\int_e^f w(j)\aleph(j)dj - C(\chi)(\aleph(\chi) + \aleph(e+f-\chi)) + (1-2C(\chi))\aleph\left(\tfrac{e+f}{2}\right) - g_n(\chi)\right|$$

$$\leq \frac{2B(\alpha+1,n-1)L}{(\alpha+n)(n-2)!}\left(|C(\chi)|\left((\chi-e)^{\alpha+n}+(f-\chi)^{\alpha+n}\right)+|1-2C(\chi)|\left(\frac{f-e}{2}\right)^{\alpha+n}\right),$$

where

$$\begin{aligned}
g_n(\chi) =& C(\chi)\left(\sum_{i=0}^{n-1}\frac{\aleph^{(i+1)}(f)}{i!}\left(\int_x^f(1-W(j))(j-f)^i dj+\int_{e+f-\chi}^{f}(1-W(j))(j-f)^i dj\right)\right.\\
&\left.-\sum_{i=0}^{n-1}\frac{\aleph^{(i+1)}(e)}{i!}\left(\int_e^{\chi}(1-W(j))(j-e)^i dj+\int_a^{e+f-\chi}(1-W(j))(j-e)^i dj\right)\right)\\
&+(1-2C(\chi))\left(\sum_{i=0}^{n-1}\frac{\aleph^{(i+1)}(f)}{i!}\int_{\frac{e+f}{2}}^{f}(1-W(j))(j-f)^i dj\right.\\
&\left.-\sum_{i=0}^{n-1}\frac{\aleph^{(i+1)}(f)}{i!}\int_e^{\frac{e+f}{2}}(1-W(j))(j-e)^i dj\right),
\end{aligned}$$

with $W(\chi)=\int_e^{\chi}w(j)dj$ for all $x\in[e,f]$ and $W(f)=1$. Additionally,

$$\begin{aligned}
&\left|\int_a^b w(j)\aleph(j)dj-C(\chi)(\aleph(\chi)+\aleph(e+f-\chi))+(1-2C(\chi))\aleph\left(\frac{e+f}{2}\right)-r_n(\chi)\right|\\
\leq& \frac{2B(\alpha+1,n-1)L}{(f-e)(\alpha+n+1)(n-2)!}\\
&\times\left(|C(\chi)|\left((\chi-e)^{\alpha+n+1}+(f-\chi)^{\alpha+n+1}\right)+|1-2C(\chi)|\left(\frac{f-e}{2}\right)^{\alpha+n+1}\right),
\end{aligned}$$

where

$$\begin{aligned}
r_n(\chi) =& C(\chi)\sum_{i=0}^{n-1}\frac{\left((-1)^i\aleph^{(i+1)}(f)-f^{(i+1)}(e)\right)\left((x-e)^{i+2}+(f-x)^{i+2}\right)}{i!(i+2)(f-e)}\\
&+(1-2C(\chi))\sum_{i=0}^{n-1}\frac{\left((-1)^i\aleph^{(i+1)}(f)-\aleph^{(i+1)}(e)\right)(f-e)^{i+2}}{i!(i+2)2^{i+2}}.
\end{aligned}$$

Obviously, if $C\left(\frac{3e+f}{4}\right)=\frac{2}{3}$, then identity (1) gives the weighted version of the dual Simpson inequality. Moreover, if we choose $w(j)=\frac{1}{f-e}$, we obtain the classical dual Simpson type inequality for functions whose n^{th} derivatives are α-L-Hölderians.

In [3], Pečarić and Vukelić used the Euler-type identities and gave some estimates of the general dual Simpson quadrature formula for functions as well as first derivatives are of bounded variation on $[0,1]$, L-Lipschitzian and R-integrable as follows.

In the case where $\aleph$ is L-Lipschitzian on $[0,1]$, we have

$$\left|\int_0^1\aleph(j)dj-\frac{1}{2u-v}\left(u\aleph\left(\frac{1}{4}\right)-v\aleph\left(\frac{1}{2}\right)+u\aleph\left(\frac{3}{4}\right)\right)\right|\leq\frac{2u+v}{8(2u-v)}L. \quad (2)$$

If $\aleph'$ is L-Lipschitzian on $[0,1]$, then

$$\begin{aligned}
&\left|\int_0^1\aleph(j)dj-\frac{1}{2u-v}\left(u\aleph\left(\frac{1}{4}\right)-v\aleph\left(\frac{1}{2}\right)+u\aleph\left(\frac{3}{4}\right)\right)\right|\\
\leq& \frac{2u^2\left(3v+\sqrt{2uv}\right)+uv\left(5v-\sqrt{2uv}\right)+2v^2\left(v+3\sqrt{2uv}\right)}{48(2u-v)\left(v+\sqrt{2uv}\right)\left(2u+v+2\sqrt{2uv}\right)}L. \quad (3)
\end{aligned}$$

If $\aleph$ is a continuous function of bounded variation on $[0,1]$, then

$$\left|\int_0^1 \aleph(j)dj - \frac{1}{2u-v}\left(u\aleph\left(\frac{1}{4}\right) - v\aleph\left(\frac{1}{2}\right) + u\aleph\left(\frac{3}{4}\right)\right)\right| \le \frac{2u+v}{4(2u-v)} \bigvee_0^1 (f). \tag{4}$$

If $\aleph'$ is a continuous function of bounded variation $[0,1]$, then

$$\left|\int_0^1 \aleph(j)dj - \frac{1}{2u-v}\left(u\aleph\left(\frac{1}{4}\right) - v\aleph\left(\frac{1}{2}\right) + u\aleph\left(\frac{3}{4}\right)\right)\right|$$
$$\le \frac{2u+3v+|2u-5v|}{64(2u-v)} \bigvee_0^1 (\aleph'). \tag{5}$$

By taking $u = 2$ and $v = 1$, inequalities (2)–(5) will be reduced to the classical dual Simpson inequality, of which the general form is as follows:

$$\left|\frac{1}{3}\left(2\aleph\left(\frac{3e+f}{4}\right) - \aleph\left(\frac{e+f}{2}\right) + 2\aleph\left(\frac{e+3f}{4}\right)\right) - \frac{1}{f-e}\int_e^f \aleph(j)dj\right| \le \frac{7(f-e)^4}{23040}\left\|\aleph^{(4)}\right\|_\infty, \tag{6}$$

where $\aleph$ is a four-times continuously differentiable function on (e,f), and $\left\|\aleph^{(4)}\right\|_\infty = \sup_{x\in(e,f)}\left|\aleph^{(4)}(x)\right|$, (see [4–6]).

In [7], Dragomir gave the following Simpson inequality for mapping of bounded variation:

$$\left|\frac{1}{6}\left(\aleph(e) + 4\aleph\left(\frac{e+f}{2}\right) + \aleph(f)\right) - \frac{1}{f-e}\int_e^f \aleph(j)dj\right| \le \frac{1}{3}(f-e)\bigvee_e^f (\aleph),$$

where $\bigvee_e^f\left(\aleph^{(n)}\right)$ is the total variation of function $\aleph$.

Pečarić and Varošanec [8] discussed the Simpson inequality for derivatives of bounded variation

$$\left|\frac{1}{6}\left(\aleph(e) + 4\aleph\left(\frac{e+f}{2}\right) + \aleph(f)\right) - \frac{1}{f-e}\int_e^f \aleph(j)dj\right| \le c_n(f-e)^n \bigvee_e^f \left(\aleph^{(n)}\right),$$

where $n \in \{0,1,2,3\}$ with $c_0 = \frac{1}{3}, c_1 = \frac{1}{24}, c_2 = \frac{1}{324}, c_3 = \frac{1}{1152}$ and $\bigvee_e^f\left(\aleph^{(n)}\right)$ is the total variation of function $\aleph^{(n)}$.

Regarding some papers dealing with three-point Newton–Cotes, we refer readers to [9–14] and references therein.

In this paper, by adopting a novel approach, we establish some dual Simpson-type inequalities for functions whose first derivatives are s-convex. The cases where the first derivatives are bounded as well as Lipschitzian functions are also discussed. Applications of the results are given.

2. Main Results

We recall that a non-negative function $\Lambda : I \subset [0,\infty) \to \mathbb{R}$ is said to be s-convex in the second sense for some fixed $s \in (0,1]$, if

$$\Lambda(ie + (1-i)k) \le i^s\Lambda(e) + (1-i)^s\Lambda(k),$$

holds for all $e, k \in I$ and $i \in [0,1]$ (see [15]).

Now, we prove the following identity, which is basic to establish our main results.

Lemma 1. *Let $\aleph : [\vartheta,\kappa] \to \mathbb{R}$ be a differentiable function on $[\vartheta,\kappa]$, with $\vartheta < \kappa$ and $\aleph' \in L^1[\vartheta,\kappa]$, then the following equality holds*

$$\frac{1}{3}\left(2\aleph\left(\frac{3\vartheta+\kappa}{4}\right)-\aleph\left(\frac{\vartheta+\kappa}{2}\right)+2\aleph\left(\frac{\vartheta+3\kappa}{4}\right)\right)-\frac{1}{\kappa-\vartheta}\int_{\vartheta}^{\kappa}\aleph(j)dj$$
$$=\frac{\kappa-\vartheta}{16}\left(\int_0^1 i\aleph'\left((1-i)\vartheta+i\frac{3\vartheta+\kappa}{4}\right)di+\int_0^1\left(i-\frac{5}{3}\right)\aleph'\left((1-i)\frac{3\vartheta+\kappa}{4}+i\frac{\vartheta+\kappa}{2}\right)di\right.$$
$$\left.+\int_0^1\left(i+\frac{2}{3}\right)\aleph'\left((1-i)\frac{\vartheta+\kappa}{2}+i\frac{\vartheta+3\kappa}{4}\right)di+\int_0^1(i-1)\aleph'\left((1-i)\frac{\vartheta+3\kappa}{4}+i\kappa\right)di\right).$$

Proof. Let

$$I_1=\int_0^1 i\aleph'\left((1-i)\vartheta+i\frac{3\vartheta+\kappa}{4}\right)di,$$
$$I_2=\int_0^1\left(i-\frac{5}{3}\right)\aleph'\left((1-i)\frac{3\vartheta+\kappa}{4}+i\frac{\vartheta+\kappa}{2}\right)di,$$
$$I_3=\int_0^1\left(i+\frac{2}{3}\right)\aleph'\left((1-i)\frac{\vartheta+\kappa}{2}+i\frac{\vartheta+3\kappa}{4}\right)di,$$
$$I_4=\int_0^1(i-1)\aleph'\left((1-i)\frac{\vartheta+3\kappa}{4}+i\kappa\right)di.$$

Integrating by parts I_1, we obtain

$$\begin{aligned}I_1&=\frac{4}{\kappa-\vartheta}i\aleph\left((1-i)\vartheta+i\frac{3\vartheta+\kappa}{4}\right)\Big|_{i=0}^{i=1}\\&-\frac{4}{\kappa-\vartheta}\int_0^1\aleph\left((1-i)\vartheta+i\frac{3\vartheta+\kappa}{4}\right)di\\&=\frac{4}{\kappa-\vartheta}\aleph\left(\frac{3\vartheta+\kappa}{4}\right)-\frac{4}{\kappa-\vartheta}\int_0^1\aleph\left((1-i)\vartheta+i\frac{3\vartheta+\kappa}{4}\right)di\\&=\frac{4}{\kappa-\vartheta}\aleph\left(\frac{3\vartheta+\kappa}{4}\right)-\frac{16}{(\kappa-\vartheta)^2}\int_{\vartheta}^{\frac{3\vartheta+\kappa}{4}}\aleph(j)dj.\end{aligned}\tag{7}$$

Similarly, we obtain

$$I_2=-\frac{8}{3(\kappa-\vartheta)}\aleph\left(\frac{\vartheta+\kappa}{2}\right)+\frac{20}{3(\kappa-\vartheta)}\aleph\left(\frac{3\vartheta+\kappa}{4}\right)-\frac{16}{(\kappa-\vartheta)^2}\int_{\frac{3\vartheta+\kappa}{4}}^{\frac{\vartheta+\kappa}{2}}\aleph(j)dj,\tag{8}$$

$$I_3=\frac{20}{3(\kappa-\vartheta)}\aleph\left(\frac{\vartheta+3\kappa}{4}\right)-\frac{8}{3(\kappa-\vartheta)}\aleph\left(\frac{\vartheta+\kappa}{2}\right)-\frac{16}{(\kappa-\vartheta)^2}\int_{\frac{\vartheta+\kappa}{2}}^{\frac{\vartheta+3\kappa}{4}}\aleph(j)dj,\tag{9}$$

and

$$I_4=\frac{4}{\kappa-\vartheta}\aleph\left(\frac{\vartheta+3\kappa}{4}\right)-\frac{16}{(\kappa-\vartheta)^2}\int_{\frac{\vartheta+3\kappa}{4}}^{\kappa}\aleph(j)dj.\tag{10}$$

Adding (7)–(10), multiplying the result by $\frac{\kappa-\vartheta}{16}$, we obtain the desired result. □

Theorem 1. *Let $\aleph$ be as in Lemma 1 with $0\leq\vartheta<\kappa$. If $|\aleph'|$ is s-convex in the second sense for some fixed $s\in(0,1]$, then we have*

$$\left|\frac{1}{3}\left(2\aleph\left(\frac{3\vartheta+\kappa}{4}\right)-\aleph\left(\frac{\vartheta+\kappa}{2}\right)+2\aleph\left(\frac{\vartheta+3\kappa}{4}\right)\right)-\frac{1}{\kappa-\vartheta}\int_{\vartheta}^{\kappa}\aleph(j)dj\right|$$
$$\leq\frac{\kappa-\vartheta}{16}\left(\frac{1}{(s+1)(s+2)}\left(|\aleph'(\vartheta)|+|\aleph'(\kappa)|\right)+\frac{4s+14}{3(s+1)(s+2)}\left|\aleph'\left(\frac{\vartheta+\kappa}{2}\right)\right|\right.$$

$$+\frac{8s+10}{3(s+1)(s+2)}\left(\left|\aleph'\left(\frac{3\vartheta+\kappa}{4}\right)\right|+\left|\aleph'\left(\frac{\vartheta+3\kappa}{4}\right)\right|\right)\right).$$

Proof. From Lemma 1, properties of modulus, and s-convexity in the second sense of $|\aleph'|$, we have

$$\left|\frac{1}{3}\left(2\aleph\left(\frac{3\vartheta+\kappa}{4}\right)-\aleph\left(\frac{\vartheta+\kappa}{2}\right)+2\aleph\left(\frac{\vartheta+3\kappa}{4}\right)\right)-\frac{1}{\kappa-\vartheta}\int_{\vartheta}^{\kappa}\aleph(j)dj\right|$$
$$\leq\frac{\kappa-\vartheta}{16}\left(\int_0^1 t\left|\aleph'\left((1-i)\vartheta+i\frac{3\vartheta+\kappa}{4}\right)\right|di+\int_0^1\left(\frac{5}{3}-i\right)\left|\aleph'\left((1-i)\frac{3\vartheta+\kappa}{4}+i\frac{\vartheta+\kappa}{2}\right)\right|di\right.$$
$$\left.+\int_0^1\left(i+\frac{2}{3}\right)\left|\aleph'\left((1-i)\frac{\vartheta+\kappa}{2}+i\frac{\vartheta+3\kappa}{4}\right)\right|di+\int_0^1(1-i)\left|\aleph'\left((1-i)\frac{\vartheta+3\kappa}{4}+i\kappa\right)\right|di\right)$$
$$\leq\frac{\kappa-\vartheta}{16}\left(\int_0^1 i\left((1-i)^s|\aleph'(\vartheta)|+i^s\left|\aleph'\left(\frac{3\vartheta+\kappa}{4}\right)\right|\right)di\right.$$
$$+\int_0^1\left(\frac{5}{3}-i\right)\left((1-i)^s\left|\aleph'\left(\frac{3\vartheta+\kappa}{4}\right)\right|+i^s\left|\aleph'\left(\frac{\vartheta+\kappa}{2}\right)\right|\right)di$$
$$+\int_0^1\left(i+\frac{2}{3}\right)\left((1-i)^s\left|\aleph'\left(\frac{\vartheta+\kappa}{2}\right)\right|+i^s\left|\aleph'\left(\frac{\vartheta+3\kappa}{4}\right)\right|\right)di$$
$$\left.+\int_0^1(1-i)\left((1-i)^s\left|\aleph'\left(\frac{\vartheta+3\kappa}{4}\right)\right|+i^s|\aleph'(\kappa)|\right)di\right)$$
$$=\frac{\kappa-\vartheta}{16}\left(\left(\int_0^1 i(1-i)^s di\right)|\aleph'(\vartheta)|+\left(\int_0^1 i^{s+1}di+\int_0^1\left(\frac{5}{3}-i\right)(1-i)^s di\right)\left|\aleph'\left(\frac{3\vartheta+\kappa}{4}\right)\right|\right.$$
$$+\left(\int_0^1\left(\frac{5}{3}-i\right)i^s di+\int_0^1\left(i+\frac{2}{3}\right)(1-i)^s di\right)\left|\aleph'\left(\frac{\vartheta+\kappa}{2}\right)\right|$$
$$\left.+\left(\int_0^1\left(i+\frac{2}{3}\right)i^s di+\int_0^1(1-i)^{s+1}di\right)\left|\aleph'\left(\frac{\vartheta+3\kappa}{4}\right)\right|+\left(\int_0^1(1-i)i^s di\right)|\aleph'(\kappa)|\right)$$
$$=\frac{\kappa-\vartheta}{16}\left(\frac{1}{(s+1)(s+2)}\left(|\aleph'(\vartheta)|+|\aleph'(\kappa)|\right)+\frac{4s+14}{3(s+1)(s+2)}\left|\aleph'\left(\frac{\vartheta+\kappa}{2}\right)\right|\right.$$
$$\left.+\frac{8s+10}{3(s+1)(s+2)}\left(\left|\aleph'\left(\frac{3\vartheta+\kappa}{4}\right)\right|+\left|\aleph'\left(\frac{\vartheta+3\kappa}{4}\right)\right|\right)\right),$$

where we have used the fact that

$$\int_0^1 i(1-i)^s di=\int_0^1 i^s(1-i)di=\frac{1}{(s+1)(s+2)},\tag{11}$$

$$\int_0^1 i^{s+1}di=\int_0^1(1-i)^{s+1}di=\frac{1}{s+2},\tag{12}$$

$$\int_0^1\left(\frac{5}{3}-i\right)(1-i)^s di=\int_0^1 i^s\left(i+\frac{2}{3}\right)di=\frac{5s+7}{3(s+1)(s+2)},\tag{13}$$

and

$$\int_0^1 i^s\left(\frac{5}{3}-i\right)di=\int_0^1\left(i+\frac{2}{3}\right)(1-i)^s di=\frac{2s+7}{3(s+1)(s+2)}.\tag{14}$$

The proof is completed. □

Corollary 1. *For $s=1$, Theorem 1 gives*

$$\left|\frac{1}{3}\left(2\aleph\left(\frac{3\vartheta+\kappa}{4}\right)-\aleph\left(\frac{\vartheta+\kappa}{2}\right)+2\aleph\left(\frac{\vartheta+3\kappa}{4}\right)\right)-\frac{1}{\kappa-\vartheta}\int_{\vartheta}^{\kappa}\aleph(j)dj\right|$$

$$\leq \frac{5(\kappa-\vartheta)}{24}\left(\frac{|\aleph'(\vartheta)|+6\left|\aleph'\left(\frac{3\vartheta+\kappa}{4}\right)\right|+6\left|\aleph'\left(\frac{\vartheta+\kappa}{2}\right)\right|+6\left|\aleph'\left(\frac{\vartheta+3\kappa}{4}\right)\right|+|\aleph'(\kappa)|}{20}\right).$$

Theorem 2. *Let $\aleph$ be as in Lemma 1 with $0 \leq \vartheta < \kappa$. If $|\aleph'|^q$ is s-convex in the second sense for some fixed $s \in (0,1]$ where $q > 1$ with $\frac{1}{p}+\frac{1}{q}=1$, then we have*

$$\begin{aligned}
&\left|\frac{1}{3}\left(2\aleph\left(\frac{3\vartheta+\kappa}{4}\right)-\aleph\left(\frac{\vartheta+\kappa}{2}\right)+2\aleph\left(\frac{\vartheta+3\kappa}{4}\right)\right)-\frac{1}{\kappa-\vartheta}\int_{\vartheta}^{\kappa}\aleph(j)dj\right| \\
&\leq \frac{\kappa-\vartheta}{16(p+1)^{\frac{1}{p}}}\left(\left(\frac{|\aleph'(\vartheta)|^q+\left|\aleph'\left(\frac{3\vartheta+\kappa}{4}\right)\right|^q}{1+s}\right)^{\frac{1}{q}}+\left(\frac{\left|\aleph'\left(\frac{\vartheta+3\kappa}{4}\right)\right|^q+|\aleph'(\kappa)|^q}{1+s}\right)^{\frac{1}{q}}\right. \\
&\left.+\left(\frac{5^{p+1}-2^{p+1}}{3^{p+1}}\right)^{\frac{1}{p}}\left(\left(\frac{\left|\aleph'\left(\frac{3\vartheta+\kappa}{4}\right)\right|^q+\left|\aleph'\left(\frac{\vartheta+\kappa}{2}\right)\right|^q}{1+s}\right)^{\frac{1}{q}}+\left(\frac{\left|\aleph'\left(\frac{\vartheta+\kappa}{2}\right)\right|^q+\left|\aleph'\left(\frac{\vartheta+3\kappa}{4}\right)\right|^q}{1+s}\right)^{\frac{1}{q}}\right)\right).
\end{aligned}$$

Proof. From Lemma 1, properties of modulus, Hölder's inequality, and s-convexity in the second sense of $|\aleph'|^q$, we have

$$\begin{aligned}
&\left|\frac{1}{3}\left(2\aleph\left(\frac{3\vartheta+\kappa}{4}\right)-\aleph\left(\frac{\vartheta+\kappa}{2}\right)+2\aleph\left(\frac{\vartheta+3\kappa}{4}\right)\right)-\frac{1}{\kappa-\vartheta}\int_{\vartheta}^{\kappa}\aleph(j)dj\right| \\
&\leq \frac{\kappa-\vartheta}{16}\left(\left(\int_0^1 i^p di\right)^{\frac{1}{p}}\left(\int_0^1\left|\aleph'\left((1-i)\vartheta+i\frac{3\vartheta+\kappa}{4}\right)\right|^q di\right)^{\frac{1}{q}}\right. \\
&+\left(\int_0^1\left(\tfrac{5}{3}-i\right)^p di\right)^{\frac{1}{p}}\left(\int_0^1\left|\aleph'\left((1-i)\frac{3\vartheta+\kappa}{4}+i\frac{\vartheta+\kappa}{2}\right)\right|^q di\right)^{\frac{1}{q}} \\
&+\left(\int_0^1\left(i+\tfrac{2}{3}\right)^p di\right)^{\frac{1}{p}}\left(\int_0^1\left|\aleph'\left((1-i)\frac{\vartheta+\kappa}{2}+i\frac{\vartheta+3\kappa}{4}\right)\right|^q di\right)^{\frac{1}{q}} \\
&\left.+\left(\int_0^1(1-i)^p di\right)^{\frac{1}{p}}\left(\int_0^1\left|\aleph'\left((1-i)\frac{\vartheta+3\kappa}{4}+i\kappa\right)\right|^q di\right)^{\frac{1}{q}}\right) \\
&\leq \frac{\kappa-\vartheta}{16(p+1)^{\frac{1}{p}}}\left(\left(\int_0^1\left((1-i)^s|\aleph'(\vartheta)|^q+i^s\left|\aleph'\left(\frac{3\vartheta+\kappa}{4}\right)\right|^q\right)di\right)^{\frac{1}{q}}\right. \\
&+\left(\frac{5^{p+1}-2^{p+1}}{3^{p+1}}\right)^{\frac{1}{p}}\left(\left(\int_0^1\left((1-i)^s\left|\aleph'\left(\frac{3\vartheta+\kappa}{4}\right)\right|^q+i^s\left|\aleph'\left(\frac{\vartheta+\kappa}{2}\right)\right|^q\right)di\right)^{\frac{1}{q}}\right. \\
&\left.+\left(\int_0^1\left((1-i)^s\left|\aleph'\left(\frac{\vartheta+\kappa}{2}\right)\right|^q+i^s\left|\aleph'\left(\frac{\vartheta+3\kappa}{4}\right)\right|^q\right)di\right)^{\frac{1}{q}}\right) \\
&\left.+\left(\int_0^1\left((1-i)^s\left|\aleph'\left(\frac{\vartheta+3\kappa}{4}\right)\right|^q+i^s|\aleph'(\kappa)|^q\right)di\right)^{\frac{1}{q}}\right) \\
&=\frac{\kappa-\vartheta}{16(p+1)^{\frac{1}{p}}}\left(\left(\frac{|\aleph'(\vartheta)|^q+\left|\aleph'\left(\frac{3\vartheta+\kappa}{4}\right)\right|^q}{1+s}\right)^{\frac{1}{q}}+\left(\frac{\left|\aleph'\left(\frac{\vartheta+3\kappa}{4}\right)\right|^q+|\aleph'(\kappa)|^q}{1+s}\right)^{\frac{1}{q}}\right. \\
&\left.+\left(\frac{5^{p+1}-2^{p+1}}{3^{p+1}}\right)^{\frac{1}{p}}\left(\left(\frac{\left|\aleph'\left(\frac{3\vartheta+\kappa}{4}\right)\right|^q+\left|\aleph'\left(\frac{\vartheta+\kappa}{2}\right)\right|^q}{1+s}\right)^{\frac{1}{q}}+\left(\frac{\left|\aleph'\left(\frac{\vartheta+\kappa}{2}\right)\right|^q+\left|\aleph'\left(\frac{\vartheta+3\kappa}{4}\right)\right|^q}{1+s}\right)^{\frac{1}{q}}\right)\right).
\end{aligned}$$

The proof is completed. □

Corollary 2. *For $s = 1$, Theorem 2 gives*

$$\left|\frac{1}{3}\left(2\aleph\left(\frac{3\vartheta+\kappa}{4}\right)-\aleph\left(\frac{\vartheta+\kappa}{2}\right)+2\aleph\left(\frac{\vartheta+3\kappa}{4}\right)\right)-\frac{1}{\kappa-\vartheta}\int_{\vartheta}^{\kappa}\aleph(j)dj\right|$$
$$\leq\frac{\kappa-\vartheta}{16(p+1)^{\frac{1}{p}}}\left(\left(\frac{|\aleph'(\vartheta)|^q+|\aleph'(\frac{3\vartheta+\kappa}{4})|^q}{2}\right)^{\frac{1}{q}}+\left(\frac{|\aleph'(\frac{\vartheta+3\kappa}{4})|^q+|\aleph'(\kappa)|^q}{2}\right)^{\frac{1}{q}}\right.$$
$$\left.+\left(\frac{5^{p+1}-2^{p+1}}{3^{p+1}}\right)^{\frac{1}{p}}\left(\left(\frac{|\aleph'(\frac{3\vartheta+\kappa}{4})|^q+|\aleph'(\frac{\vartheta+\kappa}{2})|^q}{2}\right)^{\frac{1}{q}}+\left(\frac{|\aleph'(\frac{\vartheta+\kappa}{2})|^q+|\aleph'(\frac{\vartheta+3\kappa}{4})|^q}{2}\right)^{\frac{1}{q}}\right)\right).$$

Theorem 3. *Let $\aleph$ be as in Lemma 1 with $0 \leq \vartheta < \kappa$. If $|\aleph'|^q$ is s-convex in the second sense for some fixed $s \in (0,1]$ where $q \geq 1$, then we have*

$$\left|\frac{1}{3}\left(2\aleph\left(\frac{3\vartheta+\kappa}{4}\right)-\aleph\left(\frac{\vartheta+\kappa}{2}\right)+2\aleph\left(\frac{\vartheta+3\kappa}{4}\right)\right)-\frac{1}{\kappa-\vartheta}\int_{\vartheta}^{\kappa}\aleph(j)dj\right|$$
$$\leq\frac{\kappa-\vartheta}{16}\left(\left(\frac{1}{2}\right)^{1-\frac{1}{q}}\left(\left(\frac{|\aleph'(\vartheta)|^q+(s+1)|\aleph'(\frac{3\vartheta+\kappa}{4})|^q}{(s+1)(s+2)}\right)^{\frac{1}{q}}+\left(\frac{(s+1)|\aleph'(\frac{\vartheta+3\kappa}{4})|^q+|\aleph'(\kappa)|^q}{(s+1)(s+2)}\right)^{\frac{1}{q}}\right)\right.$$
$$+\left(\frac{7}{6}\right)^{1-\frac{1}{q}}\left(\frac{(5s+7)|\aleph'(\frac{3\vartheta+\kappa}{4})|^q+(2s+7)|\aleph'(\frac{\vartheta+\kappa}{2})|^q}{3(s+1)(s+2)}\right)^{\frac{1}{q}}$$
$$\left.+\left(\frac{7}{6}\right)^{1-\frac{1}{q}}\left(\frac{(2s+7)|\aleph'(\frac{\vartheta+\kappa}{2})|^q+(5s+7)|\aleph'(\frac{\vartheta+3\kappa}{4})|^q}{3(s+1)(s+2)}\right)^{\frac{1}{q}}\right).$$

Proof. From Lemma 1, properties of modulus, power mean inequality, and s-convexity in the second sense of $|\aleph'|^q$, we have

$$\left|\frac{1}{3}\left(2\aleph\left(\frac{3\vartheta+\kappa}{4}\right)-\aleph\left(\frac{\vartheta+\kappa}{2}\right)+2\aleph\left(\frac{\vartheta+3\kappa}{4}\right)\right)-\frac{1}{\kappa-\vartheta}\int_{\vartheta}^{\kappa}\aleph(j)dj\right|$$
$$\leq\frac{\kappa-\vartheta}{16}\left(\left(\int_0^1 i\,di\right)^{1-\frac{1}{q}}\left(\int_0^1 i\left|\aleph'\left((1-i)\vartheta+i\frac{3\vartheta+\kappa}{4}\right)\right|^q di\right)^{\frac{1}{q}}\right.$$
$$+\left(\int_0^1\left(\frac{5}{3}-i\right)di\right)^{1-\frac{1}{q}}\left(\int_0^1\left(\frac{5}{3}-i\right)\left|\aleph'\left((1-i)\frac{3\vartheta+\kappa}{4}+i\frac{\vartheta+\kappa}{2}\right)\right|^q di\right)^{\frac{1}{q}}$$
$$+\left(\int_0^1\left(i+\frac{2}{3}\right)di\right)^{1-\frac{1}{q}}\left(\int_0^1\left(i+\frac{2}{3}\right)\left|\aleph'\left((1-i)\frac{\vartheta+\kappa}{2}+i\frac{\vartheta+3\kappa}{4}\right)\right|^q di\right)^{\frac{1}{q}}$$
$$\left.+\left(\int_0^1(1-i)di\right)^{1-\frac{1}{q}}\left(\int_0^1(1-i)\left|\aleph'\left((1-i)\frac{\vartheta+3\kappa}{4}+i\kappa\right)\right|^q di\right)^{\frac{1}{q}}\right)$$
$$\leq\frac{\kappa-\vartheta}{16}\left(\left(\frac{1}{2}\right)^{1-\frac{1}{q}}\left(\int_0^1 i\left((1-i)^s|\aleph'(\vartheta)|^q+i^s\left|\aleph'\left(\frac{3\vartheta+\kappa}{4}\right)\right|^q\right)di\right)^{\frac{1}{q}}\right.$$
$$+\left(\frac{7}{6}\right)^{1-\frac{1}{q}}\left(\int_0^1\left(\frac{5}{3}-i\right)\left((1-i)^s\left|\aleph'\left(\frac{3\vartheta+\kappa}{4}\right)\right|^q+i^s\left|\aleph'\left(\frac{\vartheta+\kappa}{2}\right)\right|^q\right)di\right)^{\frac{1}{q}}$$
$$+\left(\frac{7}{6}\right)^{1-\frac{1}{q}}\left(\int_0^1\left(i+\frac{2}{3}\right)\left((1-i)^s\left|\aleph'\left(\frac{\vartheta+\kappa}{2}\right)\right|^q+i^s\left|\aleph'\left(\frac{\vartheta+3\kappa}{4}\right)\right|^q\right)di\right)^{\frac{1}{q}}$$

$$+\left(\frac{1}{2}\right)^{1-\frac{1}{q}}\left(\int_0^1(1-i)\left((1-i)^s\left|\aleph'\left(\frac{\vartheta+3\kappa}{4}\right)\right|^q+i^s|\aleph'(\kappa)|^q\right)di\right)^{\frac{1}{q}}\Bigg)$$

$$=\frac{\kappa-\vartheta}{16}\left(\left(\frac{1}{2}\right)^{1-\frac{1}{q}}\left(|\aleph'(\vartheta)|^q\int_0^1 i(1-i)^s di+\left|\aleph'\left(\frac{3\vartheta+\kappa}{4}\right)\right|^q\int_0^1 i^{s+1}di\right)^{\frac{1}{q}}\right.$$

$$+\left(\frac{7}{6}\right)^{1-\frac{1}{q}}\left(\left|\aleph'\left(\frac{3\vartheta+\kappa}{4}\right)\right|^q\int_0^1\left(\frac{5}{3}-i\right)(1-i)^s di+\left|\aleph'\left(\frac{\vartheta+\kappa}{2}\right)\right|^q\int_0^1\left(\frac{5}{3}-i\right)i^s di\right)^{\frac{1}{q}}$$

$$+\left(\frac{7}{6}\right)^{1-\frac{1}{q}}\left(\left|\aleph'\left(\frac{\vartheta+\kappa}{2}\right)\right|^q\int_0^1\left(i+\frac{2}{3}\right)(1-i)^s di+\left|\aleph'\left(\frac{\vartheta+3\kappa}{4}\right)\right|^q\int_0^1\left(i+\frac{2}{3}\right)i^s di\right)^{\frac{1}{q}}$$

$$\left.+\left(\frac{1}{2}\right)^{1-\frac{1}{q}}\left(\left|\aleph'\left(\frac{\vartheta+3\kappa}{4}\right)\right|^q\int_0^1(1-i)^{s+1}di+|\aleph'(b)|^q\int_0^1(1-i)i^s di\right)^{\frac{1}{q}}\right)$$

$$=\frac{\kappa-\vartheta}{16}\left(\left(\frac{1}{2}\right)^{1-\frac{1}{q}}\left(\left(\frac{|\aleph'(\vartheta)|^q+(s+1)\left|\aleph'\left(\frac{3\vartheta+\kappa}{4}\right)\right|^q}{(s+1)(s+2)}\right)^{\frac{1}{q}}+\left(\frac{(s+1)\left|\aleph'\left(\frac{\vartheta+3\kappa}{4}\right)\right|^q+|\aleph'(\kappa)|^q}{(s+1)(s+2)}\right)^{\frac{1}{q}}\right)\right.$$

$$+\left(\frac{7}{6}\right)^{1-\frac{1}{q}}\left(\frac{(5s+7)\left|\aleph'\left(\frac{3\vartheta+\kappa}{4}\right)\right|^q+(2s+7)\left|\aleph'\left(\frac{\vartheta+\kappa}{2}\right)\right|^q}{3(s+1)(s+2)}\right)^{\frac{1}{q}}$$

$$\left.+\left(\frac{7}{6}\right)^{1-\frac{1}{q}}\left(\frac{(2s+7)\left|\aleph'\left(\frac{\vartheta+\kappa}{2}\right)\right|^q+(5s+7)\left|\aleph'\left(\frac{\vartheta+3\kappa}{4}\right)\right|^q}{3(s+1)(s+2)}\right)^{\frac{1}{q}}\right),$$

where we have used (11)–(14). The proof is achieved. □

Corollary 3. *For $s=1$, Theorem 3 gives*

$$\left|\frac{1}{3}\left(2\aleph\left(\frac{3\vartheta+\kappa}{4}\right)-\aleph\left(\frac{\vartheta+\kappa}{2}\right)+2\aleph\left(\frac{\vartheta+3\kappa}{4}\right)\right)-\frac{1}{\kappa-\vartheta}\int_\vartheta^\kappa\aleph(j)dj\right|$$

$$\leq\frac{\kappa-\vartheta}{32}\left(\left(\left(\frac{|\aleph'(\vartheta)|^q+2\left|\aleph'\left(\frac{3\vartheta+\kappa}{4}\right)\right|^q}{3}\right)^{\frac{1}{q}}+\left(\frac{2\left|\aleph'\left(\frac{\vartheta+3\kappa}{4}\right)\right|^q+|\aleph'(\kappa)|^q}{3}\right)^{\frac{1}{q}}\right)\right.$$

$$\left.+\frac{7}{3}\left(\left(\frac{4\left|\aleph'\left(\frac{3\vartheta+\kappa}{4}\right)\right|^q+3\left|\aleph'\left(\frac{\vartheta+\kappa}{2}\right)\right|^q}{7}\right)^{\frac{1}{q}}+\left(\frac{3\left|\aleph'\left(\frac{\vartheta+\kappa}{2}\right)\right|^q+4\left|\aleph'\left(\frac{\vartheta+3\kappa}{4}\right)\right|^q}{7}\right)^{\frac{1}{q}}\right)\right).$$

3. Further Results

In the following results, we will discuss the cases where $\aleph'(x)$ is bounded as well as $\aleph'(x)$ of L-Lipschitzian functions.

Theorem 4. *Let $\aleph$ be as in Lemma 1. If there exist constants $-\infty<m<M<+\infty$ such that $m\leq\aleph'(x)\leq M$ for all $x\in[\vartheta,\kappa]$, then we have*

$$\left|\frac{1}{3}\left(2\aleph\left(\frac{3\vartheta+\kappa}{4}\right)-\aleph\left(\frac{\vartheta+\kappa}{2}\right)+2\aleph\left(\frac{\vartheta+3\kappa}{4}\right)\right)-\frac{1}{\kappa-\vartheta}\int_\vartheta^\kappa\aleph(j)dj\right|\leq\frac{5(\kappa-\vartheta)(M-m)}{48}.$$

Proof. From Lemma 1, we have

$$\frac{1}{3}\left(2\aleph\left(\frac{3\vartheta+\kappa}{4}\right)-\aleph\left(\frac{\vartheta+\kappa}{2}\right)+2\aleph\left(\frac{\vartheta+3\kappa}{4}\right)\right)-\frac{1}{\kappa-\vartheta}\int_\vartheta^\kappa\aleph(j)dj$$

$$=\frac{\kappa-\vartheta}{16}\left(\int_0^1 i\aleph'\left((1-i)\vartheta+i\frac{3\vartheta+\kappa}{4}\right)di+\int_0^1\left(i-\frac{5}{3}\right)\aleph'\left((1-i)\frac{3\vartheta+\kappa}{4}+i\frac{\vartheta+\kappa}{2}\right)di\right.$$

$$
\begin{aligned}
&+\int_0^1 (i+\tfrac{2}{3})\aleph'\Big((1-i)\tfrac{\vartheta+\kappa}{2}+i\tfrac{\vartheta+3\kappa}{4}\Big)di+\int_0^1 (i-1)\aleph'\Big((1-i)\tfrac{\vartheta+3\kappa}{4}+i\kappa\Big)di\Bigg)\\
&=\tfrac{\kappa-\vartheta}{16}\Bigg(\int_0^1 i\Big(\aleph'\Big((1-i)\vartheta+i\tfrac{3\vartheta+\kappa}{4}\Big)-\tfrac{m+M}{2}+\tfrac{m+M}{2}\Big)di\\
&+\int_0^1 (i-\tfrac{5}{3})\Big(\aleph'\Big((1-i)\tfrac{3\vartheta+\kappa}{4}+i\tfrac{\vartheta+\kappa}{2}\Big)-\tfrac{m+M}{2}+\tfrac{m+M}{2}\Big)di\\
&+\int_0^1 (i+\tfrac{2}{3})\Big(\aleph'\Big((1-i)\tfrac{\vartheta+\kappa}{2}+i\tfrac{\vartheta+3\kappa}{4}\Big)-\tfrac{m+M}{2}+\tfrac{m+M}{2}\Big)di\\
&+\int_0^1 (i-1)\Big(\aleph'\Big((1-i)\tfrac{\vartheta+3\kappa}{4}+i\kappa\Big)-\tfrac{m+M}{2}+\tfrac{m+M}{2}\Big)di\Bigg)\\
&=\tfrac{\kappa-\vartheta}{16}\Bigg(\int_0^1 i\Big(\aleph'\Big((1-i)\vartheta+i\tfrac{3\vartheta+\kappa}{4}\Big)-\tfrac{m+M}{2}\Big)di\\
&+\int_0^1 (i-\tfrac{5}{3})\Big(\aleph'\Big((1-i)\tfrac{3\vartheta+\kappa}{4}+i\tfrac{\vartheta+\kappa}{2}\Big)-\tfrac{m+M}{2}\Big)di\\
&+\int_0^1 (i+\tfrac{2}{3})\Big(\aleph'\Big((1-i)\tfrac{\vartheta+\kappa}{2}+i\tfrac{\vartheta+3\kappa}{4}\Big)-\tfrac{m+M}{2}\Big)di\\
&+\int_0^1 (i-1)\Big(\aleph'\Big((1-i)\tfrac{\vartheta+3\kappa}{4}+i\kappa\Big)-\tfrac{m+M}{2}\Big)di,
\end{aligned}
\tag{15}
$$

where we have used the fact that

$$
\int_0^1 i\,di+\int_0^1 (i-\tfrac{5}{3})di+\int_0^1 (i+\tfrac{2}{3})di+\int_0^1 (i-1)di=\int_0^1 (4i-2)di=0.
$$

Applying the absolute value in both sides of (15), we obtain

$$
\begin{aligned}
&\left|\tfrac{1}{3}\Big(2\aleph\Big(\tfrac{3\vartheta+\kappa}{4}\Big)-\aleph\Big(\tfrac{\vartheta+\kappa}{2}\Big)+2\aleph\Big(\tfrac{\vartheta+3\kappa}{4}\Big)\Big)-\tfrac{1}{\kappa-\vartheta}\int_\vartheta^\kappa \aleph(j)dj\right|\\
&\leq\tfrac{\kappa-\vartheta}{16}\Bigg(\int_0^1 i\Big|\aleph'\Big((1-i)\vartheta+i\tfrac{3\vartheta+\kappa}{4}\Big)-\tfrac{m+M}{2}\Big|di\\
&+\int_0^1 (\tfrac{5}{3}-i)\Big|\aleph'\Big((1-i)\tfrac{3\vartheta+\kappa}{4}+i\tfrac{\vartheta+\kappa}{2}\Big)-\tfrac{m+M}{2}\Big|di\\
&+\int_0^1 (i+\tfrac{2}{3})\Big|\aleph'\Big((1-i)\tfrac{\vartheta+\kappa}{2}+i\tfrac{\vartheta+3\kappa}{4}\Big)-\tfrac{m+M}{2}\Big|di\\
&+\int_0^1 (1-i)\Big(\Big|\aleph'\Big((1-i)\tfrac{\vartheta+3\kappa}{4}+i\kappa\Big)-\tfrac{m+M}{2}\Big|\Big)di\Bigg).
\end{aligned}
\tag{16}
$$

Since $m \leq \aleph'(x) \leq M$ for all $x \in [\vartheta, \kappa]$, we have

$$
\Big|\aleph'\Big((1-i)\vartheta+i\tfrac{3\vartheta+\kappa}{4}\Big)-\tfrac{m+M}{2}\Big|\leq\tfrac{M-m}{2}, \tag{17}
$$

$$
\Big|\aleph'\Big((1-i)\tfrac{3\vartheta+\kappa}{4}+i\tfrac{\vartheta+\kappa}{2}\Big)-\tfrac{m+M}{2}\Big|\leq\tfrac{M-m}{2}, \tag{18}
$$

$$
\Big|\aleph'\Big((1-i)\tfrac{\vartheta+\kappa}{2}+i\tfrac{\vartheta+3\kappa}{4}\Big)-\tfrac{m+M}{2}\Big|\leq\tfrac{M-m}{2}, \tag{19}
$$

and

$$
\Big|\aleph'\Big((1-i)\tfrac{\vartheta+3\kappa}{4}+i\kappa\Big)-\tfrac{m+M}{2}\Big|\leq\tfrac{M-m}{2}. \tag{20}
$$

Using (17)–(20) in (16), we obtain

$$\begin{aligned}
&\left|\frac{1}{3}\left(2\aleph\left(\frac{3\vartheta+\kappa}{4}\right)-\aleph\left(\frac{\vartheta+\kappa}{2}\right)+2\aleph\left(\frac{\vartheta+3\kappa}{4}\right)\right)-\frac{1}{\kappa-\vartheta}\int_{\vartheta}^{\kappa}\aleph(j)dj\right| \\
&\leq\frac{(\kappa-\vartheta)(M-m)}{32}\left(\int_0^1 i di+\int_0^1\left(\frac{5}{3}-i\right)dt+\int_0^1\left(i+\frac{2}{3}\right)dt+\int_0^1(1-i)dt\right) \\
&=\frac{5(\kappa-\vartheta)(M-m)}{48}.
\end{aligned}$$

The proof is completed. □

Theorem 5. *Let $\aleph$ be as in Lemma 1. If $\aleph'$ is L-Lipschitzian function on $[\vartheta,\kappa]$, then we have*

$$\left|\frac{1}{3}\left(2\aleph\left(\frac{3\vartheta+\kappa}{4}\right)-\aleph\left(\frac{\vartheta+\kappa}{2}\right)+2\aleph\left(\frac{\vartheta+3\kappa}{4}\right)\right)-\frac{1}{\kappa-\vartheta}\int_{\vartheta}^{\kappa}\aleph(j)dj\right|\leq\frac{13(\kappa-\vartheta)^2}{192}L.$$

Proof. From Lemma 1, we have

$$\begin{aligned}
&\frac{1}{3}\left(2\aleph\left(\frac{3\vartheta+\kappa}{4}\right)-\aleph\left(\frac{\vartheta+\kappa}{2}\right)+2\aleph\left(\frac{\vartheta+3\kappa}{4}\right)\right)-\frac{1}{\kappa-\vartheta}\int_{\vartheta}^{\kappa}\aleph(j)dj \\
&=\frac{\kappa-\vartheta}{16}\left(\int_0^1 i\aleph'\left((1-i)\vartheta+i\frac{3\vartheta+\kappa}{4}\right)di+\int_0^1\left(i-\frac{5}{3}\right)\aleph'\left((1-i)\frac{3\vartheta+\kappa}{4}+i\frac{\vartheta+\kappa}{2}\right)di\right. \\
&\quad\left.+\int_0^1\left(i+\frac{2}{3}\right)\aleph'\left((1-i)\frac{\vartheta+\kappa}{2}+i\frac{\vartheta+3\kappa}{4}\right)di+\int_0^1(i-1)\aleph'\left((1-i)\frac{\vartheta+3\kappa}{4}+i\kappa\right)di\right) \\
&=\frac{\kappa-\vartheta}{16}\left(\int_0^1 i\left(\aleph'\left((1-i)\vartheta+i\frac{3\vartheta+\kappa}{4}\right)-\aleph'(\vartheta)+\aleph'(\vartheta)\right)di\right. \\
&\quad+\int_0^1\left(i-\frac{5}{3}\right)\left(\aleph'\left((1-i)\frac{3\vartheta+\kappa}{4}+i\frac{\vartheta+\kappa}{2}\right)-\aleph'\left(\frac{3\vartheta+\kappa}{4}\right)+\aleph'\left(\frac{\vartheta+3\kappa}{4}\right)\right)di \\
&\quad+\int_0^1\left(i+\frac{2}{3}\right)\left(\aleph'\left((1-i)\frac{\vartheta+\kappa}{2}+i\frac{\vartheta+3\kappa}{4}\right)-\aleph'\left(\frac{\vartheta+\kappa}{2}\right)+\aleph'\left(\frac{\vartheta+\kappa}{2}\right)\right)di \\
&\quad\left.+\int_0^1(i-1)\left(\aleph'\left((1-i)\frac{\vartheta+3\kappa}{4}+i\kappa\right)-\aleph'\left(\frac{\vartheta+3\kappa}{4}\right)+\aleph'\left(\frac{\vartheta+3\kappa}{4}\right)\right)di\right) \\
&=\frac{\kappa-\vartheta}{16}\left(\int_0^1 i\left(\aleph'\left((1-i)\vartheta+i\frac{3\vartheta+\kappa}{4}\right)-\aleph'(\vartheta)\right)di\right. \\
&\quad+\int_0^1\left(i-\frac{5}{3}\right)\left(\aleph'\left((1-i)\frac{3\vartheta+\kappa}{4}+i\frac{\vartheta+\kappa}{2}\right)-\aleph'\left(\frac{3\vartheta+\kappa}{4}\right)\right)di \\
&\quad+\int_0^1\left(i+\frac{2}{3}\right)\left(\aleph'\left((1-i)\frac{\vartheta+\kappa}{2}+i\frac{\vartheta+3\kappa}{4}\right)-\aleph'\left(\frac{\vartheta+\kappa}{2}\right)\right)di \\
&\quad+\int_0^1(i-1)\left(\aleph'\left((1-i)\frac{\vartheta+3\kappa}{4}+i\kappa\right)-\aleph'\left(\frac{\vartheta+3\kappa}{4}\right)\right)di \\
&\quad\left.+\frac{1}{2}\left(\aleph'(\vartheta)-\aleph'\left(\frac{\vartheta+3\kappa}{4}\right)\right)+\frac{7}{6}\left(\aleph'\left(\frac{\vartheta+\kappa}{2}\right)-\aleph'\left(\frac{3\vartheta+\kappa}{4}\right)\right)\right).
\end{aligned} \tag{21}$$

Applying the absolute value in both sides of (21), and by using the fact that $\aleph'$ is L-Lipschitzian on $[\vartheta,\kappa]$, we obtain

$$\left|\frac{1}{3}\left(2\aleph\left(\frac{3\vartheta+\kappa}{4}\right)-\aleph\left(\frac{\vartheta+\kappa}{2}\right)+2\aleph\left(\frac{\vartheta+3\kappa}{4}\right)\right)-\frac{1}{\kappa-\vartheta}\int_{\vartheta}^{\kappa}\aleph(j)dj\right|$$

$$\le \frac{\kappa-\vartheta}{16}\Bigg(\int_0^1 i\left|\aleph'\left((1-i)\vartheta+i\tfrac{3\vartheta+\kappa}{4}\right)-\aleph'(\vartheta)\right|di$$

$$+\int_0^1\left(\tfrac{5}{3}-i\right)\left|\aleph'\left((1-i)\tfrac{3\vartheta+\kappa}{4}+i\tfrac{\vartheta+\kappa}{2}\right)-\aleph'\left(\tfrac{3\vartheta+\kappa}{4}\right)\right|di$$

$$+\int_0^1\left(i+\tfrac{2}{3}\right)\left|\aleph'\left((1-i)\tfrac{\vartheta+\kappa}{2}+i\tfrac{\vartheta+3\kappa}{4}\right)-\aleph'\left(\tfrac{\vartheta+\kappa}{2}\right)\right|di$$

$$+\int_0^1(1-i)\left|\aleph'\left((1-i)\tfrac{\vartheta+3\kappa}{4}+i\kappa\right)-\aleph'\left(\tfrac{\vartheta+3\kappa}{4}\right)\right|di$$

$$+\tfrac{1}{2}\left|\aleph'(\vartheta)-\aleph'\left(\tfrac{\vartheta+3\kappa}{4}\right)\right|+\tfrac{7}{6}\left|\aleph'\left(\tfrac{\vartheta+\kappa}{2}\right)-\aleph'\left(\tfrac{3\vartheta+\kappa}{4}\right)\right|\Bigg)$$

$$\le \frac{\kappa-\vartheta}{16}\Bigg(\frac{(\kappa-\vartheta)L}{4}\int_0^1 i^2di+\frac{(\kappa-\vartheta)L}{4}\int_0^1\left(\tfrac{5}{3}-i\right)idi+\frac{(\kappa-\vartheta)L}{4}\int_0^1\left(i+\tfrac{2}{3}\right)idi$$

$$+\frac{(\kappa-\vartheta)L}{4}\int_0^1(1-i)idi+\frac{L}{2}\left|a-\frac{a+3b}{4}\right|+\frac{7L}{6}\left|\frac{a+b}{2}-\frac{3a+b}{4}\right|\Bigg)$$

$$=\frac{13(\kappa-\vartheta)^2}{192}L.$$

The proof is completed. □

4. Applications

Dual Simpson's quadrature formula

Let Λ be the partition of the points $\vartheta = e_0 < e_1 < \ldots < e_n = \kappa$ of the interval $[\vartheta,\kappa]$, and consider the quadrature formula

$$\int_\vartheta^\kappa \aleph(j)dj = \lambda(\aleph,\Lambda)+R(\aleph,\Lambda),$$

where

$$\lambda(\aleph,\Lambda)=\sum_{i=0}^{n-1}\frac{e_{i+1}-e_i}{3}\left(2\aleph\left(\frac{3e_i+e_{i+1}}{4}\right)-\aleph\left(\frac{e_i+e_{i+1}}{2}\right)+2\aleph\left(\frac{e_i+3e_{i+1}}{4}\right)\right),$$

and $R(\aleph,\Lambda)$ denotes the associated approximation error.

Proposition 1. *Let $n\in\mathbb{N}$ and $\aleph:[\vartheta,\kappa]\to\mathbb{R}$ be a differentiable function on (ϑ,κ) with $0\le\vartheta<\kappa$ and $\aleph'\in L^1[\vartheta,\kappa]$. If $|\aleph'|$ is s-convex function with $s\in(0,1]$, we have*

$$|R(\aleph,Y)|\le\sum_{i=0}^{n-1}\frac{(e_{i+1}-e_i)^2}{16}\left(\frac{1}{(s+1)(s+2)}\left(|\aleph'(e_i)|+|\aleph'(e_{i+1})|\right)+\frac{4s+14}{3(s+1)(s+2)}\left|\aleph'\left(\frac{e_i+e_{i+1}}{2}\right)\right|\right.$$

$$\left.+\frac{8s+10}{3(s+1)(s+2)}\left(\left|\aleph'\left(\frac{3e_i+e_{i+1}}{4}\right)\right|+\left|\aleph'\left(\frac{e_i+3e_{i+1}}{4}\right)\right|\right)\right).$$

Proof. Using Theorem 1 on $[e_i,e_{i+1}]$ $(i=0,1,\ldots,n-1)$, we obtain

$$\left|\frac{1}{3}\left(2\aleph\left(\frac{3e_i+e_{i+1}}{4}\right)-\aleph\left(\frac{e_i+e_{i+1}}{2}\right)+2\aleph\left(\frac{e_i+3e_{i+1}}{4}\right)\right)-\frac{1}{e_{i+1}-e_i}\int_{e_i}^{e_{i+1}}\aleph(j)dj\right|$$

$$\le\frac{e_{i+1}-e_i}{16}\left(\frac{1}{(s+1)(s+2)}\left(|\aleph'(e_i)|+|\aleph'(e_{i+1})|\right)+\frac{4s+14}{3(s+1)(s+2)}\left|\aleph'\left(\frac{e_i+e_{i+1}}{2}\right)\right|\right.$$

$$\left.+\frac{8s+10}{3(s+1)(s+2)}\left(\left|\aleph'\left(\frac{3e_i+e_{i+1}}{4}\right)\right|+\left|\aleph'\left(\frac{e_i+3e_{i+1}}{4}\right)\right|\right)\right).\tag{22}$$

Multiplying both sides of (22) by $(e_{i+1}-e_i)$, summing the obtained inequalities for all $i=0,1,\ldots,n-1$ and using the triangular inequality, we obtain the result. □

Application to special means

For arbitrary real numbers $e, e_1, e_2, ..., e_n, f$ we have:
The Arithmetic mean: $A(e_1, e_2, ..., e_n) = \frac{e_1+e_2+...+e_n}{n}$.
The p-Logarithmic mean: $L_p(e, f) = \left(\frac{f^{p+1}-e^{p+1}}{(p+1)(f-e)}\right)^{\frac{1}{p}}, e, f > 0, e \neq f$ and $p \in \mathbb{R}\setminus\{-1, 0\}$.

Proposition 2. *Let $e, f \in \mathbb{R}$ with $0 < e < f$, then we have*

$$\left|2A^{\frac{3}{2}}(e,e,e,f) - A^{\frac{3}{2}}(e,f) + 2A^{\frac{3}{2}}(e,f,f,f) - 3L^{\frac{3}{2}}_{\frac{3}{2}}(e,f)\right| \leq \frac{15(f-e)\left(\sqrt{f}-\sqrt{e}\right)}{32}.$$

Proof. Applying Theorem 4 to the function $\aleph(j) = j^{\frac{3}{2}}$ on $[e, f]$. □

5. Conclusions

Many practical studies and engineering problems often lead to calculations of integrals, most of which cannot be solved directly, requiring us to evaluate them by different quadrature rules, hence the need to estimate the error made to better circumvent and manage the problem. Thus, in this work, we have considered the dual Simpson quadrature rule. We have firstly established a novel identity. Based on this identity, we have derived some new dual Simpson type integral inequalities for functions whose first derivatives are -convex. We have also discussed the above-mentioned inequality when the first derivatives lie in the classes of bounded and Lipschitzian functions. We have provided at the end some applications to quadrature formulas and special means. We hope that the obtained results stimulate further research, as well as generalizations in various other types of calculus in this interesting field.

Author Contributions: Conceptualization, T.C., H.B., M.I., B.M. and A.M.; Methodology, T.C., H.B., B.M. and A.M.; Formal analysis, H.B. and B.M.; Writing—original draft, T.C., H.B., M.I., B.M. and A.M.; Writing—review and editing, T.C., H.B., M.I., B.M. and A.M.; supervision, A.M.; project administration, A.M. and M.I.; funding acquisition, A.M. and M.I. All authors have read and agreed to the published version of the manuscript.

Funding: This research received no external funding.

Data Availability Statement: Not applicable.

Acknowledgments: The authors extend their appreciation to the Deanship of Scientific Research at King Khalid University for funding this work through Small Groups.(RGP.1/350/43).

Conflicts of Interest: Authors declare that they have no conflict of interest.

References

1. Pećarixcx, J.E.; Proschan, F.; Tong, Y.L. *Convex Functions, Partial Orderings, and Statistical Applications; Mathematics in Science and Engineering*; Academic Press, Inc.: Boston, MA, USA, 1992; Volume 187.
2. Bakula, M.K.; Pećarixcx, J.; Penava, M.R. General three-point quadrature formulae with applications for α-L-Hölder type functions. *J. Math. Inequal.* **2008**, *2*, 343–361. [CrossRef]
3. Pećarixcx, J.; Vukelixcx, A. General dual Euler-Simpson formulae. *J. Math. Inequal.* **2008**, *2*, 511–526.
4. Dedić, L.; Matixcx, M.; Pexcxarixcx, J. On dual Euler-Simpson formulae. *Bull. Belg. Math. Soc. Simon Stevin* **2001**, *8*, 479–504. [CrossRef]
5. Li, Y. Schur convexity and the dual Simpson's formula. *J. Appl. Math. Phys.* **2016**, *4*, 623–629. [CrossRef]
6. Vukelić, A. Estimations of the error for general Simpson type formulae via pre-Grüss inequality. *J. Math. Inequal.* **2009**, *3*, 559–566. [CrossRef]
7. Dragomir, S.S. On Simpson's quadrature formula for mappings of bounded variation and applications. *Tamkang J. Math.* **1999**, *30*, 53–58. [CrossRef]
8. Pećarixcx, J.; Varošanec, S. A note on Simpson's inequality for functions of bounded variation. *Tamkang J. Math.* **2000**, *31*, 239–242.
9. Abdeljawad, T.; Rashid, S.; Hammouch, Z.; İşcan, İ.; Chu, Y.-M. Some new Simpson-type inequalities for generalized p-convex function on fractal sets with applications. *Adv. Differ. Equ.* **2020**, *2020*, 496. [CrossRef]
10. Alomari, M.; Darus, M.; Dragomir, S.S. New inequalities of Simpson's type for s-convex functions with applications. *Res. Rep.* **2009**, *12*, 4.

11. Boulares, H.; Meftah, B.; Moumen, A.; Shafqat, R.; Saber, H.; Alraqad, T.; Ali, E.E. Fractional Multiplicative Bullen-Type Inequalities for Multiplicative Differentiable Functions. *Symmetry* **2023**, *15*, 451. [CrossRef]
12. Hsu, K.-C.; Hwang, S.-R.; Tseng, K.-L. Some extended Simpson-type inequalities and applications. *Bull. Iran. Math. Soc.* **2017**, *43*, 409–425.
13. Luo, C.-Y.; Du, T.-S.; Kunt, M.; Zhang, Y. Certain new bounds considering the weighted Simpson-like type inequality and applications. *J. Inequal. Appl.* **2018**, *2018*, 332. [CrossRef] [PubMed]
14. Noor, M.A.; Noor, K.I.; Awan, M.U. Simpson-type inequalities for geometrically relative convex functions. *Ukr. Math. J.* **2018**, *70*, 1145–1154. [CrossRef]
15. Breckner, W.W. Stetigkeitsaussagen für eine Klasse verallgemeinerter konvexer Funktionen in topologischen linearen Räumen. *Publ. Inst. Math.* **1978**, *23*, 13–20. (In Germany)

symmetry

MDPI

Article

Multiplicatively Simpson Type Inequalities via Fractional Integral

Abdelkader Moumen [1,*], Hamid Boulares [2], Badreddine Meftah [2], Ramsha Shafqat [3], Tariq Alraqad [1], Ekram E. Ali [1] and Zennir Khaled [4]

[1] Department of Mathematics, Faculty of Sciences, University of Ha'il, Ha'il 55425, Saudi Arabia
[2] Laboratory of Analysis and Control of Differential Equations "ACED", Department of Mathematics, Faculty MISM, University of Guelma, Guelma 24000, Algeria
[3] Department of Mathematics and Statistics, University of Lahore, Sargodha 40100, Pakistan
[4] Department of Mathematics, College of Sciences and Arts, Qassim University, Ar Rass 58892, Saudi Arabia
* Correspondence: abdelkader.moumen@gmail.com

Abstract: Multiplicative calculus, also called non-Newtonian calculus, represents an alternative approach to the usual calculus of Newton (1643–1727) and Leibniz (1646–1716). This type of calculus was first introduced by Grossman and Katz and it provides a defined calculation, from the start, for positive real numbers only. In this investigation, we propose to study symmetrical fractional multiplicative inequalities of the Simpson type. For this, we first establish a new fractional identity for multiplicatively differentiable functions. Based on that identity, we derive new Simpson-type inequalities for multiplicatively convex functions via fractional integral operators. We finish the study by providing some applications to analytic inequalities.

Keywords: non-Newtonian calculus; Simpson inequality; multiplicatively convex functions

Citation: Moumen, A.; Boulares, H.; Meftah, B.; Shafqat, R.; Alraqad, T.; Ali, E.E.; Khaled, Z. Multiplicatively Simpson Type Inequalities via Fractional Integral. *Symmetry* **2023**, *15*, 460. https://doi.org/10.3390/sym15020460

Academic Editors: Hassen Fourati, Abdellatif Ben Makhlouf and Omar Naifar

Received: 6 January 2023
Revised: 31 January 2023
Accepted: 5 February 2023
Published: 9 February 2023

1. Introduction

Between 1967 and 1970, Grossman and Katz created the first non-Newtonian calculation system, called geometric calculation. Over the next few years they created an infinite family of non-Newtonian calculi, thus modifying the classical calculus introduced by Newton and Leibniz in the 17th century each of which differed markedly from the classical calculus of Newton and Leibniz known today as the non-Newtonian calculus or the multiplicative calculus, where the ordinary product and ratio are used, respectively, as sum and exponential difference over the domain of positive real numbers see [1]. This calculation is useful for dealing with exponentially varying functions. It is worth noting that the complete mathematical description of multiplicative calculus was given by Bashirov et al. [2]. We recall that the multiplicative derivatives ρ^* of positive function ρ is defined as follows:

$$\rho^*(t) = \lim_{h\to 0}\left(\frac{\rho(t+h)}{\rho(t)}\right)^{\frac{1}{h}}.$$

The relation between ρ^* and the ordinary derivative ρ' is as follows:

$$\rho^*(t) = e^{(\ln\rho(t))'} = e^{\frac{\rho'(t)}{\rho(t)}}.$$

Theorem 1. *Let $\rho : [l,k] \subset \mathbb{R} \to \mathbb{R}$ be four times continuously differentiable function on (l,k). Then we have*

$$\left|\frac{1}{6}\left(\rho(l) + 4\rho\left(\frac{l+k}{2}\right) + \rho(k)\right) - \frac{1}{k-l}\int_l^k \rho(u)du\right| \leq \frac{(k-l)^4}{2880}\left\|\rho^{(4)}\right\|_\infty, \tag{1}$$

where $\left\|\rho^{(4)}\right\|_\infty = \sup_{u\in[l,k]}\left|\rho^{(4)}(u)\right| < \infty.$

The above inequality is well known in the literature as Simpson's integral inequality. Regarding some results connected with inequality (1) and related inequalities, we refer readers to [3–17]. Shafqat et al. [18] investigated the existence and uniqueness of the Fuzzy fractional evolution equations. Boulares et al. [19,20] studied the existence and uniqueness of solutions for non-linear fractional differential equations.

The multiplicative derivative admits the following properties:

Theorem 2 ([2]). *Let ρ and ϑ be two multiplicatively differentiable functions, and c is an arbitrary constant. Then functions $c\rho, \rho\vartheta, \rho+\vartheta, \rho/\vartheta$ and ρ^{ϑ} are * differentiable and*

- $(c\rho)^*(t) = \rho^*(t)$,
- $(\rho\vartheta)^*(t) = \rho^*(t)\vartheta^*(t)$,
- $(\rho+\vartheta)^*(t) = \rho^*(t)^{\frac{\rho(t)}{\rho(t)+\vartheta(t)}}\vartheta^*(t)^{\frac{\vartheta(t)}{\rho(t)+\vartheta(t)}}$,
- $\left(\frac{\rho}{\vartheta}\right)^*(t) = \frac{\rho^*(t)}{\vartheta^*(t)}$,
- $\left(\rho^{\vartheta}\right)^*(t) = \rho^*(t)^{\vartheta(t)}\rho(t)^{\vartheta'(t)}$.

The multiplicative integral noted * integral $\int_l^k (\rho(t))^{dt}$ has the following relationship with the Riemann integral

$$\int_l^k (\rho(t))^{dt} = \exp\left\{\int_l^k \ln(\rho(t))dt\right\}.$$

The multiplicative integral enjoy the following properties:

Theorem 3 ([2]). *Let ρ be a positive and Riemann integrable on $[l,k]$, then ρ is multiplicative integrable on $[l,k]$ and*

- $\int_l^k ((\rho(t))^p)^{dt} = \left(\int_l^k (\rho(t))^{dt}\right)^p$,
- $\int_l^k (\rho(t)\vartheta(t))^{dt} = \int_l^k (\rho(t))^{dt}\int_l^k (\vartheta(t))^{dt}$,
- $\int_l^k \left(\frac{\rho(t)}{\vartheta(t)}\right)^{dt} = \frac{\int_l^k (\rho(t))^{dt}}{\int_l^k (\vartheta(t))^{dt}}$,
- $\int_l^k (\rho(t))^{dt} = \int_l^c (\rho(t))^{dt}\int_c^k (\rho(t))^{dt}, l < c < k$,
- $\int_l^l (\rho(t))^{dt} = 1$ and $\int_l^k (\rho(t))^{dt} = \left(\int_k^l (\rho(t))^{dt}\right)^{-1}$.

The multiplicative integration by parts is given by the following Theorem:

Theorem 4 ([2]). *Let $\rho : [l,k] \to \mathbb{R}$ be multiplicative differentiable, let $\vartheta : [l,k] \to \mathbb{R}$ be differentiable so the function ρ^{ϑ} is multiplicative integrable, and*

$$\int_l^k \left(\rho^*(t)^{\vartheta(t)}\right)^{dt} = \frac{\rho(k)^{\vartheta(k)}}{\rho(l)^{\vartheta(l)}} \times \frac{1}{\int_l^k \left(\rho(t)^{\vartheta'(t)}\right)^{dt}}.$$

Using the above result and the properties of multiplicative derivatives and integrals, Ali et al. [21], established an interesting identity given by the following lemma.

Lemma 1 ([21])**.** *Let $\rho : [l,k] \to \mathbb{R}$ be multiplicative differentiable, let $h : [l,k] \to \mathbb{R}$ and let $\vartheta : J \subset \mathbb{R} \to \mathbb{R}$ be two differentiable functions. Then we have*

$$\int_l^k \left(\rho^*(h(t))^{h'(t)\vartheta(t)}\right)^{dt} = \frac{\rho(h(k))^{\vartheta(k)}}{\rho(h(l))^{\vartheta(l)}} \times \frac{1}{\int_l^k \left(\rho(h(t))^{\vartheta'(t)}\right)^{dt}}.$$

In recent years, much interest has been given to the development of the theory and applications of multiplicative calculus. Aniszewska [22] presented the multiplicative version of the Runge–Kutta method and used it to solve multiplicative differential equations. Rıza et al. [23], gave the numerical solutions of multiplicative differential equations by introducing the multiplicative finite difference methods. Misirli and Gurefe [24] presented the multiplicative Adams Bashforth-Moulton methods. Bashirov and Norozpour [25] extended the multiplicative integral to complex valued functions. Bhat et al. defined multiplicative Fourier transform in [26] and multiplicative Sumudu transform [27]. Bashirov [28] studied double integrals in the sense of multiplicative calculus. In [29], Ali et al. introduced the multiplicative Hermite–Hadamard inequality for multiplicative integral as follows:

Theorem 5. *Let f be a positive and multiplicatively convex function on interval $[u_1, u_2]$, then following inequalities hold*

$$f\left(\frac{u_1+u_2}{2}\right) \le \left(\int_{u_1}^{u_2} (f(t))^{dt}\right)^{\frac{1}{u_2-u_1}} \le G(f(u_1), f(u_2)),$$

where $G(\cdot,\cdot)$ is a geometric mean.

In [30], Ali et al. generalized the obtained results in [29], via ϕ-convexity. In [31], Özcan generalized the results in [29] under the h-convexity. In [32], Özcan established the analogue preinvex of the Hermite–Hadamard inequality. In [33], Özcan generalized the results of [32] for h-preinvex functions.

In [34], Meftah studied the so-called Maclaurin type inequalities.

Theorem 6. *Let $f : [u_1, u_2] \to \mathbb{R}^+$ be a multiplicative differentiable mapping on $[u_1, u_2]$ with $u_1 < u_2$. If f^* is multiplicative convex on $[u_1, u_2]$, then we have*

$$\begin{aligned} &\left| \left(f\left(\frac{5u_1+u_2}{6}\right)^3 f\left(\frac{u_1+u_2}{2}\right)^2 f\left(\frac{u_1+5u_2}{6}\right)^3 \right)^{\frac{1}{8}} \left(\int_{u_1}^{u_2} f(t)^{dt}\right)^{\frac{1}{u_1-u_2}} \right| \\ \le\ & \left((f^*(u_1))^{64} \left(f^*\left(\frac{5u_1+u_2}{6}\right)\right)^{379} \left(f^*\left(\frac{u_1+u_2}{2}\right)\right)^{314} \left(f^*\left(\frac{u_1+5u_2}{6}\right)\right)^{379} \right. \\ & \left. \times (f^*(u_2))^{64} \right)^{\frac{u_2-u_1}{13824}}. \end{aligned}$$

In [21], Ali et al. gave some Ostrowski and Simpson type inequalities for multiplicative integrals as follow:

Theorem 7. *Let $f : I^\circ \subset \mathbb{R} \to \mathbb{R}^+$ be a multiplicative differentiable mapping on I°, $u_1, u_2 \in I^\circ$ with $u_1 < u_2$. If f is increasing on $[u_1, u_2]$ and $f^*$is multiplicatively convex on $[u_1, u_2]$, then the following Ostrowski type inequality for multiplicative integrals holds for all $x \in [u_1, u_2]$*

$$\left| f(x)\left(\int_{u_1}^{u_2}(f(t))^{dt}\right)^{\frac{1}{u_1-u_2}}\right| \leq (f^*(a))^{\frac{x-u_1}{2(u_2-u_1)}+\frac{(u_2-x)^3+(x-u_1)^3}{8(u_2-u_1)^2}}(f^*(b))^{\frac{u_2-x}{2(u_2-u_1)}+\frac{(u_2-x)^3+(x-u_1)^3}{8(u_2-u_1)^2}}.$$

Theorem 8. *Let $f : I^\circ \subset \mathbb{R} \to \mathbb{R}^+$ be a multiplicative differentiable mapping on I°, $u_1, u_2 \in I^\circ$ with $u_1 < u_2$. If f is increasing on $[u_1, u_2]$ and f^* is multiplicatively convex on $[u_1, u_2]$, then we the following Ostrowski type inequality for multiplicative integrals holds for all $x \in [u_1, u_2]$*

$$\left|\left(f(u_1)f^2\left(\frac{u_1+u_2}{2}\right)f(u_2)\right)\left(\int_{u_1}^{u_2}(f(t))^{dt}\right)^{\frac{1}{u_1-u_2}}\right| \leq ((f^*(a))(f^*(b)))^{\frac{5(u_2-u_1)}{72}}.$$

Recently, Abdeljawad and Grossman [35] introduced the multiplicative Riemann–Liouville fractional integrals as follows:

Definition 1. *The of order $\alpha \in \mathbb{C}$,$Re(\alpha) > 0$, respectively, are defined by*

$$({}_lI_*^\alpha\rho)(x) = e^{\left(J_{l+}^\alpha(\ln\circ\rho)\right)(x)}$$

and

$$({}_*I_k^\alpha\rho)(x) = e^{\left(J_{k-}^\alpha(\ln\circ\rho)\right)(x)},$$

where J_{l+}^α and J_{k-}^α denote the left and right Riemann–Liouville fractional integral, defined by

$$(J_{l+}^\alpha\rho)(x) = \frac{1}{\Gamma(\alpha)}\int_l^x (x-t)^{\alpha-1}\rho(t)dt, l < x$$

and

$$(J_{k-}^\alpha\rho)(x) = \frac{1}{\Gamma(\alpha)}\int_x^k (t-x)^{\alpha-1}\rho(t)dt, x < k.$$

Budak and Özçelik [36], used the above operator and presented some Hermite–Hadamard type inequalities for multiplicatively fractional integrals.

Hoping to stimulate future research in this direction and motivated by paper [21] and some of the existing results in the literature, in this study, we prove a new integral identity. Based on this, we establish some symmetrical fractional multiplicatively Simpson type inequalities for convex functions. Some applications to special means are proposed to demonstrate the effectiveness of our finding.

2. Main Results

We first recall that a positive function ρ is said to be multiplicatively convex, if the following inequality holds

$$\rho(tx + (1-t)y) \leq [\rho(x)]^t[\rho(y)]^{1-t}.$$

Lemma 2. *Let $\rho : [l, k] \to \mathbb{R}^+$ be a multiplicative differentiable mapping on $[l, k]$ with $l < k$. If ρ^* is multiplicative integrable on $[l, k]$, then we have the following identity for multiplicative integrals*

$$\left((\rho(l))\left(\rho\left(\frac{l+k}{2}\right)\right)^4(\rho(k))\right)^{\frac{1}{6}}\left(\left({}_lI_*^\alpha\rho\right)\left(\frac{l+k}{2}\right)\left({}_*I_{\frac{l+k}{2}}^\alpha\rho\right)(k)\right)^{-\frac{2^{\alpha-1}\Gamma(\alpha+1)}{(k-l)^\alpha}}$$

$$= \left(\int_0^1\left(\rho^*\left((1-t)l+t\frac{l+k}{2}\right)^{t^\alpha-\frac{1}{3}}\right)^{dt}\right)^{\frac{k-l}{4}}\left(\int_0^1\left(\rho^*\left((1-t)\frac{l+k}{2}+tk\right)^{\frac{1}{3}-(1-t)^\alpha}\right)^{dt}\right)^{\frac{k-l}{4}}.$$

Proof. Let

$$I_1 = \left(\int_0^1\left(\rho^*\left((1-t)l+t\frac{l+k}{2}\right)^{t^\alpha-\frac{1}{3}}\right)^{dt}\right)^{\frac{k-l}{4}}$$

and

$$I_2 = \left(\int_0^1\left(\rho^*\left((1-t)\frac{l+k}{2}+tk\right)^{\frac{1}{3}-(1-t)^\alpha}\right)^{dt}\right)^{\frac{k-l}{4}}.$$

Using the integration by parts for multiplicative integrals, I_1 gives

$$\begin{aligned}
I_1 &= \left(\int_0^1\left(\rho^*\left((1-t)l+t\frac{l+k}{2}\right)^{t^\alpha-\frac{1}{3}}\right)^{dt}\right)^{\frac{k-l}{4}} \\
&= \left(\int_0^1\left(\rho^*\left((1-t)l+t\frac{l+k}{2}\right)^{\frac{k-l}{2}\left(\frac{1}{2}t^\alpha-\frac{1}{6}\right)}\right)^{dt}\right) \\
&= \frac{\left(\rho\left(\frac{l+k}{2}\right)\right)^{\frac{1}{3}}}{(\rho(l))^{-\frac{1}{6}}}\cdot\frac{1}{\int_0^1\left(\rho\left(\left((1-t)l+t\frac{l+k}{2}\right)\right)^{\frac{\alpha}{2}t^{\alpha-1}}\right)^{dt}} \\
&= (\rho(l))^{\frac{1}{6}}\left(\rho\left(\frac{l+k}{2}\right)\right)^{\frac{1}{3}}\frac{1}{\exp\left\{\int_0^1\frac{\alpha}{2}(t)^{\alpha-1}\ln\left(\rho\left((1-t)l+t\frac{l+k}{2}\right)\right)dt\right\}} \\
&= (\rho(l))^{\frac{1}{6}}\left(\rho\left(\frac{l+k}{2}\right)\right)^{\frac{1}{3}}\frac{1}{\exp\left\{\frac{2^{\alpha-1}\alpha}{(k-l)^\alpha}\int_0^1(u-l)^{\alpha-1}\ln(\rho(u))du\right\}} \\
&= \frac{(\rho(l))^{\frac{1}{6}}\left(\rho\left(\frac{l+k}{2}\right)\right)^{\frac{1}{3}}}{\left(\exp\left\{\left(\frac{1}{\Gamma(\alpha)}\int_l^{\frac{l+k}{2}}(u-l)^{\alpha-1}\ln(\rho(u))du\right)\right\}\right)^{\frac{2^{\alpha-1}\Gamma(\alpha+1)}{(k-l)^\alpha}}} \\
&= (\rho(l))^{\frac{1}{6}}\left(\rho\left(\frac{l+k}{2}\right)\right)^{\frac{1}{3}}\left(\left({}_lI_*^\alpha\rho\right)\left(\frac{l+k}{2}\right)\right)^{-\frac{2^{\alpha-1}\Gamma(\alpha+1)}{(k-l)^\alpha}}.
\end{aligned}$$

Similarly, we obtain

$$I_2 = \left(\int_0^1\left(\rho^*\left((1-t)\frac{l+k}{2}+tk\right)^{\frac{1}{3}-(1-t)^\alpha}\right)^{dt}\right)^{\frac{k-l}{4}}$$

$$= \left(\int_0^1 \left(\rho^*\left((1-t)\frac{l+k}{2}+tk\right)^{\frac{k-l}{2}\left(\frac{1}{6}-\frac{1}{2}(1-t)^\alpha\right)}\right)^{dt}\right)$$

$$= \frac{(\rho(k))^{\frac{1}{6}}}{\left(\rho\left(\frac{l+k}{2}\right)\right)^{-\frac{1}{3}}}\cdot\frac{1}{\int_0^1\left(\rho\left((1-t)\frac{l+k}{2}+tk\right)^{\frac{\alpha}{2}(1-t)^{\alpha-1}}\right)^{dt}}$$

$$= \rho\left(\frac{l+k}{2}\right)^{\frac{1}{3}}\rho(k)^{\frac{1}{6}}\cdot\frac{1}{\exp\left\{\frac{\alpha}{2}\int_0^1(1-t)^{\alpha-1}\ln\rho\left((1-t)\frac{l+k}{2}+tk\right)dt\right\}}$$

$$= \rho\left(\frac{l+k}{2}\right)^{\frac{1}{3}}\rho(k)^{\frac{1}{6}}\cdot\frac{1}{\exp\left\{\frac{2^{\alpha-1}}{(k-l)^\alpha}\alpha\int_{\frac{l+k}{2}}^{k}(k-u)^{\alpha-1}\ln\rho(u)dt\right\}}$$

$$= \left(\rho\left(\frac{l+k}{2}\right)\right)^{\frac{n}{2(n+2)}}(\rho(k))^{\frac{1}{n+2}}\cdot\frac{1}{\exp\left\{\frac{2^{\alpha-1}\Gamma(\alpha+1)}{(k-l)^\alpha}\left(\frac{1}{\Gamma(\alpha)}\int_{\frac{l+k}{2}}^{k}(k-u)^{\alpha-1}\ln f(u)du\right)\right\}}$$

$$= \frac{\rho\left(\frac{l+k}{2}\right)^{\frac{1}{3}}\rho(k)^{\frac{1}{6}}}{\left(\exp\left\{\left(\frac{1}{\Gamma(\alpha)}\int_{\frac{l+k}{2}}^{k}(k-u)^{\alpha-1}\ln\rho(u)du\right)\right\}\right)^{\frac{2^{\alpha-1}\Gamma(\alpha+1)}{(k-l)^\alpha}}}.$$

$$= \rho\left(\frac{l+k}{2}\right)^{\frac{1}{3}}\rho(k)^{\frac{1}{6}}\cdot\left(\left({}_*I^\alpha_{\frac{l+k}{2}}\rho\right)(k)\right)^{-\frac{2^{\alpha-1}\Gamma(\alpha+1)}{(k-l)^\alpha}}.$$

Multiplying the above equalities, we obtain

$$I_1\times I_2 = (\rho(l))^{\frac{1}{6}}\left(\rho\left(\frac{l+k}{2}\right)\right)^{\frac{1}{3}}\left(({}_lI^\alpha_*\rho)\left(\frac{l+k}{2}\right)\right)^{-\frac{2^{\alpha-1}\Gamma(\alpha+1)}{(k-l)^\alpha}}$$
$$\times\left(\rho\left(\frac{l+k}{2}\right)\right)^{\frac{1}{3}}(\rho(k))^{\frac{1}{6}}\cdot\left(\left({}_*I^\alpha_{\frac{l+k}{2}}\rho\right)(k)\right)^{-\frac{2^{\alpha-1}\Gamma(\alpha+1)}{(k-l)^\alpha}}$$
$$= \left((\rho(l))\left(\rho\left(\frac{l+k}{2}\right)\right)^4(\rho(k))\right)^{\frac{1}{6}}\left(({}_lI^\alpha_*\rho)\left(\frac{l+k}{2}\right)\left({}_*I^\alpha_{\frac{l+k}{2}}\rho\right)(k)\right)^{-\frac{2^{\alpha-1}\Gamma(\alpha+1)}{(k-l)^\alpha}}.$$

which is the result. The proof is completed. □

Theorem 9. *Let $\rho:[l,k]\to\mathbb{R}^+$ be a multiplicatively differentiable mapping on $[l,k]$ with $l<k$. If $|\ln\rho^*|\le\ln\mathcal{M}$ on $[l,k]$, then we have*

$$\left|\left((\rho(l))\left(\rho\left(\frac{l+k}{2}\right)\right)^4(\rho(k))\right)^{\frac{1}{6}}\left(({}_lI^\alpha_*\rho)\left(\frac{l+k}{2}\right)\left({}_*I^\alpha_{\frac{l+k}{2}}\rho\right)(k)\right)^{-\frac{2^{\alpha-1}\Gamma(\alpha+1)}{(k-l)^\alpha}}\right|$$
$$\le \mathcal{M}^{\frac{k-l}{2}\left(\frac{\alpha+2}{3(\alpha+1)}+\frac{2\alpha}{\alpha+1}\left(\frac{1}{3}\right)^{\frac{1}{\alpha}+1}\right)}.$$

Proof. From Lemma 2, properties of multiplicative integral and using the fact that $|\ln f^*|\le\ln\mathcal{M}$, we have

$$
\begin{aligned}
&\left|\left((\rho(l))\left(\rho\left(\frac{l+k}{2}\right)\right)^{4}(\rho(k))\right)^{\frac{1}{6}}\left(\left({}_{l}I_{*}^{\alpha}\rho\right)\left(\frac{l+k}{2}\right)\left({}_{*}I_{\frac{l+k}{2}}^{\alpha}\rho\right)(k)\right)^{-\frac{2^{\alpha-1}\Gamma(\alpha+1)}{(k-l)^{\alpha}}}\right| \\
&= \left|\left(\int_{0}^{1}\left(\rho^{*}\left((1-t)l+t\frac{l+k}{2}\right)^{t^{\alpha}-\frac{1}{3}}\right)^{dt}\right)^{\frac{k-l}{4}}\right| \\
&\quad\times\left|\left(\int_{0}^{1}\left(\rho^{*}\left((1-t)\frac{l+k}{2}+tk\right)^{\frac{1}{3}-(1-t)^{\alpha}}\right)^{dt}\right)^{\frac{k-l}{4}}\right| \\
&= \left|\left(\int_{0}^{1}\left(\rho^{*}\left((1-t)l+t\frac{l+k}{2}\right)^{\frac{k-l}{4}\left(t^{\alpha}-\frac{1}{3}\right)}\right)^{dt}\right)\right| \\
&\quad\times\left|\left(\int_{0}^{1}\left(\rho^{*}\left((1-t)\frac{l+k}{2}+tk\right)^{\frac{k-l}{4}\left(\frac{1}{3}-(1-t)^{\alpha}\right)}\right)^{dt}\right)\right| \\
&\le \left(\exp\left\{\int_{0}^{1}\left|\frac{k-l}{4}\left(t^{\alpha}-\frac{1}{3}\right)\ln\left(\rho^{*}\left((1-t)l+t\frac{l+k}{2}\right)\right)\right|dt\right\}\right) \\
&\quad\times\left(\exp\left\{\int_{0}^{1}\left|\frac{k-l}{4}\left(\frac{1}{3}-(1-t)^{\alpha}\right)\ln\left(\rho^{*}\left((1-t)\frac{l+k}{2}+tk\right)\right)\right|dt\right\}\right) \\
&= \left(\exp\left\{\frac{k-l}{4}\int_{0}^{1}\left|t^{\alpha}-\frac{1}{3}\right|\left|\ln\left(\rho^{*}\left((1-t)l+t\frac{l+k}{2}\right)\right)\right|dt\right\}\right) \\
&\quad\times\left(\exp\left\{\frac{k-l}{4}\int_{0}^{1}\left|\frac{1}{3}-(1-t)^{\alpha}\right|\left|\ln\left(\rho^{*}\left((1-t)\frac{l+k}{2}+tk\right)\right)\right|dt\right\}\right) \\
&\le \left(\exp\left\{\frac{k-l}{4}\ln\mathcal{M}\int_{0}^{1}\left|t^{\alpha}-\frac{1}{3}\right|dt\right\}\right)\left(\exp\left\{\frac{k-l}{4}\ln\mathcal{M}\int_{0}^{1}\left|\frac{1}{3}-(1-t)^{\alpha}\right|dt\right\}\right) \\
&= \left(\exp\left\{\frac{k-l}{4}\ln\mathcal{M}\left(\int_{0}^{\left(\frac{1}{3}\right)^{\frac{1}{\alpha}}}\left(\frac{1}{3}-t^{\alpha}\right)dt+\int_{\left(\frac{1}{3}\right)^{\frac{1}{\alpha}}}^{1}\left(t^{\alpha}-\frac{1}{3}\right)dt\right)\right\}\right) \\
&\quad\times\left(\exp\left\{\frac{k-l}{4}\ln\mathcal{M}\left(\int_{0}^{1-\left(\frac{1}{3}\right)^{\frac{1}{\alpha}}}\left((1-t)^{\alpha}-\frac{1}{3}\right)dt+\int_{1-\left(\frac{1}{3}\right)^{\frac{1}{\alpha}}}^{1}\left(\frac{1}{3}-(1-t)^{\alpha}\right)dt\right)\right\}\right) \\
&= \left(\exp\left\{\frac{k-l}{4}\left(\frac{\alpha+2}{3(\alpha+1)}+\frac{2\alpha}{\alpha+1}\left(\frac{1}{3}\right)^{\frac{1}{\alpha}+1}\right)\ln\mathcal{M}\right\}\right) \\
&\quad\times\left(\exp\left\{\frac{k-l}{4}\left(\frac{\alpha+2}{3(\alpha+1)}+\frac{2\alpha}{\alpha+1}\left(\frac{1}{3}\right)^{1+\frac{1}{\alpha}}\right)\ln\mathcal{M}\right\}\right) \\
&= \mathcal{M}^{\frac{k-l}{2}\left(\frac{\alpha+2}{3(\alpha+1)}+\frac{2\alpha}{\alpha+1}\left(\frac{1}{3}\right)^{\frac{1}{\alpha}+1}\right)}.
\end{aligned}
$$

The proof is completed. □

Corollary 1. *In Theorem 9, if we take $\alpha = 1$, we obtain*

$$\left|\left((\rho(l))\left(\rho\left(\frac{l+k}{2}\right)\right)^4(\rho(k))\right)^{\frac{1}{6}}\left(\int_l^k \rho(u)^{du}\right)^{\frac{1}{l-k}}\right| \leq \mathcal{M}^{\frac{11}{36}(k-l)}.$$

Theorem 10. *Let $\rho : [l,k] \to \mathbb{R}^+$ be a multiplicative differentiable mapping on $[l,k]$ with $l < k$. If ρ^* is multiplicatively convex function on $[l,k]$, then we have*

$$\begin{aligned}
&\left|\left((\rho(l))\left(\rho\left(\frac{l+k}{2}\right)\right)^4(\rho(k))\right)^{\frac{1}{6}}\left(({}_lI_*^{\alpha}\rho)\left(\frac{l+k}{2}\right)\left({}_*I_{\frac{l+k}{2}}^{\alpha}\rho\right)(k)\right)^{-\frac{2^{\alpha-1}\Gamma(\alpha+1)}{(k-l)^{\alpha}}}\right| \\
\leq\ & [(\rho^*(l))(f^*(k))]^{\frac{k-l}{2}\left(\frac{4-\alpha^2-3\alpha}{12(\alpha+1)(\alpha+2)}+\frac{\alpha}{(\alpha+1)}\left(\frac{1}{3}\right)^{1+\frac{1}{\alpha}}-\frac{\alpha}{2(\alpha+2)}\left(\frac{1}{3}\right)^{1+\frac{2}{\alpha}}\right)} \\
&\times\left(f^*\left(\frac{l+k}{2}\right)\right)^{\frac{k-l}{2}\left(\frac{4-\alpha}{6(\alpha+2)}+\frac{\alpha}{\alpha+2}\left(\frac{1}{3}\right)^{1+\frac{2}{\alpha}}\right)}.
\end{aligned}$$

Proof. From Lemma 2, modulus and properties of multiplicative integral, we have

$$\begin{aligned}
&\left|\left((\rho(l))\left(\rho\left(\frac{l+k}{2}\right)\right)^4(\rho(k))\right)^{\frac{1}{6}}\left(({}_lI_*^{\alpha}\rho)\left(\frac{l+k}{2}\right)\left({}_*I_{\frac{l+k}{2}}^{\alpha}\rho\right)(k)\right)^{-\frac{2^{\alpha-1}\Gamma(\alpha+1)}{(k-l)^{\alpha}}}\right| \\
=\ & \left|\left(\int_0^1\left(\rho^*\left((1-t)l+t\frac{l+k}{2}\right)^{t^{\alpha}-\frac{1}{3}}\right)^{dt}\right)^{\frac{k-l}{4}}\right| \\
&\times\left|\left(\int_0^1\left(\rho^*\left((1-t)\frac{l+k}{2}+tk\right)^{\frac{1}{3}-(1-t)^{\alpha}}\right)^{dt}\right)^{\frac{k-l}{4}}\right| \\
=\ & \int_0^1\left|\rho^*\left((1-t)l+t\frac{l+k}{2}\right)^{\frac{k-l}{2}\left(\frac{1}{2}t^{\alpha}-\frac{1}{6}\right)}\right|^{dt} \\
&\times\int_0^1\left|\rho^*\left((1-t)\frac{l+k}{2}+tk\right)^{\frac{k-l}{2}\left(\frac{1}{6}-\frac{1}{2}(1-t)^{\alpha}\right)}\right|^{dt} \\
\leq\ & \left(\exp\left\{\frac{k-l}{2}\int_0^1\left|\left(\frac{1}{2}t^{\alpha}-\frac{1}{6}\right)\right|\left|\ln\rho^*\left((1-t)l+t\frac{l+k}{2}\right)\right|dt\right\}\right) \\
&\times\left(\exp\left\{\frac{k-l}{2}\int_0^1\left|\left(\frac{1}{6}-\frac{1}{2}(1-t)^{\alpha}\right)\right|\left|\ln\rho^*\left((1-t)\frac{l+k}{2}+tk\right)\right|dt\right\}\right).
\end{aligned} \tag{2}$$

From the multiplicative convexity of ρ^* and properties on ln, we have

$$\begin{aligned}
\left|\ln\rho^*\left((1-t)l+t\frac{l+k}{2}\right)\right| &\leq \left|\ln(\rho^*(l))^{(1-t)}\left(f^*\left(\frac{l+k}{2}\right)\right)^t\right| \\
&= \left((1-t)\ln(\rho^*(l))+t\ln\left(f^*\left(\frac{l+k}{2}\right)\right)\right)
\end{aligned} \tag{3}$$

and

$$\left|\ln\rho^*\left((1-t)\frac{l+k}{2}+tk\right)\right| \leq \left|\ln(\rho^*(l))^{(1-t)}\left(f^*\left(\frac{l+k}{2}\right)\right)^t\right| \tag{4}$$

$$= \left((1-t)\ln\left(\rho^*\left(\frac{l+k}{2}\right)\right) + t\ln(f^*(k))\right).$$

Combining (2)–(4), we obtain

$$\left|\left((\rho(l))\left(\rho\left(\frac{l+k}{2}\right)\right)^4(\rho(k))\right)^{\frac{1}{6}}\left(\left({}_lI^{\alpha}_{*}\rho\right)\left(\frac{l+k}{2}\right)\left({}_{*}I^{\alpha}_{\frac{l+k}{2}}\rho\right)(k)\right)^{-\frac{2^{\alpha-1}\Gamma(\alpha+1)}{(k-l)^{\alpha}}}\right|$$

$$\leq \exp\left\{\frac{k-l}{2}\left(\int_0^{\left(\frac{1}{3}\right)^{\frac{1}{\alpha}}}\left(\frac{1}{6}-\frac{1}{2}t^{\alpha}\right)\left((1-t)\ln(\rho^*(l)) + t\ln\left(f^*\left(\frac{l+k}{2}\right)\right)\right)dt\right.\right.$$

$$\left.\left.+\int_{\left(\frac{1}{3}\right)^{\frac{1}{\alpha}}}^{1}\left(\frac{1}{2}t^{\alpha}-\frac{1}{6}\right)\left((1-t)\ln(\rho^*(l)) + t\ln\left(f^*\left(\frac{l+k}{2}\right)\right)\right)dt\right)\right\}$$

$$\times\exp\left\{\frac{k-l}{2}\left(\int_0^{1-\left(\frac{1}{3}\right)^{\frac{1}{\alpha}}}\left(\frac{1}{2}(1-t)^{\alpha}-\frac{1}{6}\right)\left((1-t)\ln\left(\rho^*\left(\frac{l+k}{2}\right)\right) + t\ln(f^*(k))\right)dt\right.\right.$$

$$\left.\left.+\int_{1-\left(\frac{1}{3}\right)^{\frac{1}{\alpha}}}^{1}\left(\frac{1}{6}-\frac{1}{2}(1-t)^{\alpha}\right)\left((1-t)\ln\left(\rho^*\left(\frac{l+k}{2}\right)\right) + t\ln(f^*(k))\right)dt\right)\right\}$$

$$= \exp\left\{\frac{k-l}{2}\left(\left(\int_0^{\left(\frac{1}{3}\right)^{\frac{1}{\alpha}}}\left(\frac{1}{6}-\frac{1}{2}t^{\alpha}\right)(1-t)dt + \int_{\left(\frac{1}{3}\right)^{\frac{1}{\alpha}}}^{1}\left(\frac{1}{2}t^{\alpha}-\frac{1}{6}\right)(1-t)dt\right)\ln(\rho^*(l))\right.\right.$$

$$\left.\left.+\left(\int_0^{\left(\frac{1}{3}\right)^{\frac{1}{\alpha}}}\left(\frac{1}{6}-\frac{1}{2}t^{\alpha}\right)tdt + \int_{\left(\frac{1}{3}\right)^{\frac{1}{\alpha}}}^{1}\left(\frac{1}{2}t^{\alpha}-\frac{1}{6}\right)tdt\right)\ln\left(f^*\left(\frac{l+k}{2}\right)\right)\right)\right\}$$

$$\times\exp\left\{\ln\left(\rho^*\left(\frac{l+k}{2}\right)\right)\frac{k-l}{2}\left(\left(\int_0^{1-\left(\frac{1}{3}\right)^{\frac{1}{\alpha}}}\left(\frac{1}{2}(1-t)^{\alpha}-\frac{1}{6}\right)(1-t)dt\right.\right.\right.$$

$$\left.+\int_{1-\left(\frac{1}{3}\right)^{\frac{1}{\alpha}}}^{1}\left(\frac{1}{6}-\frac{1}{2}(1-t)^{\alpha}\right)(1-t)dt\right)$$

$$\left.\left.+\left(\int_0^{1-\left(\frac{1}{3}\right)^{\frac{1}{\alpha}}}\left(\frac{1}{2}(1-t)^{\alpha}-\frac{1}{n+2}\right)tdt + \int_{1-\left(\frac{1}{3}\right)^{\frac{1}{\alpha}}}^{1}\left(\frac{1}{6}-\frac{1}{2}(1-t)^{\alpha}\right)tdt\right)\ln(f^*(k))\right)\right\}$$

$$= \exp\left\{\frac{k-l}{2}\left(\ln(\rho^*(l))^{\left(\frac{4-\alpha^2-3\alpha}{12(\alpha+1)(\alpha+2)}+\frac{\alpha}{\alpha+1}\left(\frac{1}{3}\right)^{1+\frac{1}{\alpha}}-\frac{\alpha}{2(\alpha+2)}\left(\frac{1}{3}\right)^{1+\frac{2}{\alpha}}\right)}\right.\right.$$

$$
\begin{aligned}
&+\ln\left(f^*\left(\frac{l+k}{2}\right)\right)^{\frac{1}{2}\left(\frac{4-\alpha}{(n+2)(\alpha+2)}+\frac{\alpha}{\alpha+2}\left(\frac{1}{3}\right)^{1+\frac{2}{\alpha}}\right)}\Bigg)\Bigg\}\\
&\times\exp\Bigg\{\frac{k-l}{2}\Bigg(\ln\left(\rho^*\left(\frac{l+k}{2}\right)\right)^{\frac{1}{2}\left(\frac{4-\alpha}{(n+2)(\alpha+2)}+\frac{\alpha}{\alpha+2}\left(\frac{1}{3}\right)^{1+\frac{2}{\alpha}}\right)}\\
&+\ln(f^*(k))^{\left(\left(\frac{4-\alpha^2-3\alpha}{12(\alpha+1)(\alpha+2)}+\frac{\alpha}{\alpha+1}\left(\frac{1}{3}\right)^{1+\frac{1}{\alpha}}-\frac{\alpha}{2(\alpha+2)}\left(\frac{1}{3}\right)^{1+\frac{2}{\alpha}}\right)\right)}\Bigg)\Bigg\}\\
=\;&[(\rho^*(l))(f^*(k))]^{\frac{k-l}{2}\left(\frac{4-\alpha^2-3\alpha}{12(\alpha+1)(\alpha+2)}+\frac{\alpha}{\alpha+1}\left(\frac{1}{3}\right)^{1+\frac{1}{\alpha}}-\frac{\alpha}{2(\alpha+2)}\left(\frac{1}{3}\right)^{1+\frac{2}{\alpha}}\right)}\\
&\left(f^*\left(\frac{l+k}{2}\right)\right)^{\frac{k-l}{2}\left(\frac{4-\alpha}{6(\alpha+2)}+\frac{\alpha}{\alpha+2}\left(\frac{1}{3}\right)^{1+\frac{2}{\alpha}}\right)},
\end{aligned}
$$

where we have used

$$
\begin{aligned}
\int_0^{\left(\frac{1}{3}\right)^{\frac{1}{\alpha}}}\left(\frac{1}{6}-\frac{1}{2}t^\alpha\right)(1-t)dt &= \int_{1-\left(\frac{1}{3}\right)^{\frac{1}{\alpha}}}^{1}\left(\frac{1}{6}-\frac{1}{2}(1-t)^\alpha\right)tdt\\
&= \left(\frac{\alpha}{6(\alpha+1)}\left(\frac{1}{3}\right)^{\frac{1}{\alpha}}-\frac{\alpha}{12(\alpha+2)}\left(\frac{1}{3}\right)^{\frac{2}{\alpha}}\right),
\end{aligned}
$$

$$
\begin{aligned}
\int_0^{\left(\frac{1}{3}\right)^{\frac{1}{\alpha}}}\left(\frac{1}{n+2}-\frac{1}{2}t^\alpha\right)tdt &= \int_{1-\left(\frac{1}{3}\right)^{\frac{1}{\alpha}}}^{1}\left(\frac{1}{6}-\frac{1}{2}(1-t)^\alpha\right)(1-t)dt\\
&= \frac{\alpha}{12(\alpha+2)}\left(\frac{1}{3}\right)^{\frac{2}{\alpha}},
\end{aligned}
$$

$$
\begin{aligned}
&\int_{\left(\frac{1}{3}\right)^{\frac{1}{\alpha}}}^{1}\left(\frac{1}{2}t^\alpha-\frac{1}{6}\right)(1-t)dt = \int_0^{1-\left(\frac{1}{3}\right)^{\frac{1}{\alpha}}}\left(\frac{1}{2}(1-t)^\alpha-\frac{1}{6}\right)tdt\\
=\;&\frac{4-\alpha^2-3\alpha}{12(\alpha+1)(\alpha+2)}+\frac{\alpha}{6(\alpha+1)}\left(\frac{1}{3}\right)^{\frac{1}{\alpha}}-\frac{\alpha}{12(\alpha+2)}\left(\frac{1}{3}\right)^{\frac{2}{\alpha}}
\end{aligned}
$$

and

$$
\begin{aligned}
\int_{\left(\frac{1}{3}\right)^{\frac{1}{\alpha}}}^{1}\left(\frac{1}{2}t^\alpha-\frac{1}{6}\right)tdt &= \int_0^{1-\left(\frac{1}{3}\right)^{\frac{1}{\alpha}}}\left(\frac{1}{2}(1-t)^\alpha-\frac{1}{6}\right)(1-t)dt\\
&= \frac{4-\alpha}{12(\alpha+2)}+\frac{\alpha}{12(\alpha+2)}\left(\frac{1}{3}\right)^{\frac{2}{\alpha}}.
\end{aligned}
$$

The proof is completed. □

Corollary 2. *In Theorem 10, using the multiplicative convexity of* ρ^*, *i.e.*, $f^*\left(\frac{l+k}{2}\right) \leq \sqrt{\rho^*(l)\rho^*(k)}$, *we obtain*

$$\left| \left((\rho(l)) \left(\rho\left(\frac{l+k}{2}\right) \right)^4 (\rho(k)) \right)^{\frac{1}{6}} \left(({}_l I_*^\alpha \rho)\left(\frac{l+k}{2}\right) \left({}_* I_{\frac{l+k}{2}}^\alpha \rho \right)(k) \right)^{-\frac{2^{\alpha-1}\Gamma(\alpha+1)}{(k-l)^\alpha}} \right|$$

$$\leq \quad [(\rho^*(l))(f^*(k))]^{\frac{k-l}{2}\left(\frac{4-2\alpha}{12(\alpha+1)} + \frac{\alpha}{(\alpha+1)}\left(\frac{1}{3}\right)^{1+\frac{1}{\alpha}} \right)}.$$

Corollary 3. *In Theorem 10, if we take* $\alpha = 1$, *we obtain*

$$\left| \left((\rho(l)) \left(\rho\left(\frac{l+k}{2}\right) \right)^4 (\rho(k)) \right)^{\frac{1}{6}} \left(\int_l^k \rho(u)^{du} \right)^{\frac{1}{l-k}} \right|$$

$$\leq \quad [(\rho^*(l))(f^*(k))]^{\frac{2}{81}(k-l)} \left(f^*\left(\frac{l+k}{2}\right) \right)^{\frac{29}{324}(k-l)}.$$

Corollary 4. *In Corollary 3, using the multiplicative convexity of* f^*, *we obtain*

$$\left| \left((\rho(l)) \left(\rho\left(\frac{l+k}{2}\right) \right)^4 (\rho(k)) \right)^{\frac{1}{6}} \left(\int_l^k \rho(u)^{du} \right)^{\frac{1}{l-k}} \right| \leq [(\rho^*(l))(f^*(k))]^{\frac{5}{72}(k-l)}.$$

3. Applications to Special Means

We shall consider the means for arbitrary real numbers l, k.
The Arithmetic mean: $A(l,k) = \frac{l+k}{2}$.
The Harmonic mean: $H(l,k) = \frac{2lk}{l+k}$.
The logarithmic means: $L(l,k) = \frac{k-l}{\ln k - \ln l}$, $l, k > 0$, and $l \neq k$.
The p-Logarithmic mean: $L_p(l,k) = \left(\frac{k^{p+1} - l^{p+1}}{(p+1)(k-l)} \right)^{\frac{1}{p}}$, $l, k > 0, l \neq k$ and $p \in \mathbb{R} \setminus \{-1, 0\}$.

Proposition 1. *Let* $l, k \in \mathbb{R}$ *with* $0 < l < k$, *then we have*

$$\left| e^{\frac{1}{6}\left(2H^{-1}(l,k) - A^4(l,k)\right) - L^{-1}(l,k)} \right| \leq e^{-\frac{11}{36l^2}(k-l)}.$$

Proof. The assertion follows from Corollary 1 applied to the function $\rho(t) = e^{\frac{1}{t}}$ whose $\rho^*(t) = e^{-\frac{1}{t^2}}$, $\mathcal{M} = e^{-\frac{1}{l^2}}$ and $\left(\int_l^k \rho(u)^{du} \right)^{\frac{1}{l-k}} = \exp\{-L^{-1}(l,k)\}$. □

Proposition 2. *Let* $l, k \in \mathbb{R}$ *with* $0 < l < k$, *then we have*

$$\left| e^{\frac{1}{6}\left(2A(l^p,k^p) + A^{4p}(l,k)\right) - L_p^p(l,k)} \right| \leq e^{p\frac{5(k-l)\left(l^{p-1} + k^{p-1}\right)}{72}}.$$

Proof. The assertion follows from Corollary 4, applied to the function $\rho(t) = e^{t^p}$ with $p \geq 2$ whose $\rho^*(t) = e^{pt^{p-1}}$ and $\left(\int_l^k \rho(u)^{du} \right)^{\frac{1}{l-k}} = \exp\left\{ -L_p^p(l,k) \right\}$. □

4. Conclusions

Multiplicative calculus is an alternative to Newtonian calculus. Since its inception as one of the non-Newtonian calculus, a number of works have been devoted to different applications of multiplicative calculus. In this study, we discussed Simpson-type fractional integral inequalities for multiplicatively differentiable functions based on a new identity. Some special cases are derived and applications of our findings are provided. We hope that the new strategy formulated in this paper will inspire and stimulated further research in this promising field of multiplicative fractional inequalities.

Author Contributions: Conceptualization, A.M., H.B. and B.M.; methodology, A.M. and H.B.; writing—original draft preparation, R.S.; writing—review and editing, T.A., E.E.A. and Z.K. All authors have read and agreed to the published version of the manuscript.

Funding: This research has been funded by Scientific Research Deanship at University of Ha'il—Saudi Arabia through project number RG-21021.

Data Availability Statement: Not available.

Conflicts of Interest: The authors declare no conflict of interest.

References

1. Grossman, M.; Katz, R. *Non-Newtonian Calculus*; Lee Press: Pigeon Cove, MA, USA, 1972.
2. Bashirov, A.E.; Kurpınar, E.M.; Özyapıcı, A. Multiplicative calculus and its applications. *J. Math. Anal. Appl.* **2008**, *337*, 36–48.
3. Ali, M.A.; Kara, H.; Tariboon, J.; Asawasamrit, S.; Budak, H.; Hezenci, F. Some new Simpson's formula-type inequalities for twice-differentiable convex functions via generalized fractional operators. *Symmetry* **2021**, *13*, 2249. [CrossRef]
4. Bachar, M.; Guessab, A.; Mohammed, O.; Zaim, Y. New cubature formulas and Hermite-Hadamard type inequalities using integrals over some hyperplanes in the *d*-dimensional hyper-rectangle. *Appl. Math. Comput.* **2017**, *315*, 347–362. [CrossRef]
5. Chen, S.B.; Rashid, S.; Noor, M.A.; Ashraf, R.; Chu, Y.M. A new approach on fractional calculus and probability density function. *AIMS Math.* **2020**, *5*, 7041–7054. [CrossRef]
6. Guessab, A.; Schmeisser, G. Necessary and sufficient conditions for the validity of Jensen's inequality. *Arch. Math.* **2013**, *100*, 561–570.
7. Kashuri, A.; Meftah, B.; Mohammed, P.O. Some weighted Simpson type inequalities for differentiable *s*-convex functions and their applications. *J. Fract. Calc. Nonlinear Syst.* **2021**, *1*, 75–94.
8. Kashuri, A.; Meftah, B.; Mohammed, P.O.; Lupa, A.A.; Abdalla, B.; Hamed, Y.S.; Abdeljawad, T. Fractional weighted Ostrowski type inequalities and their applications. *Symmetry* **2021**, *13*, 968.
9. Kalsoom, H.; Wu, J.D.; Hussain, S.; Latif, M.A. Simpson's type inequalities for co-ordinated convex functions on quantum calculus. *Symmetry* **2019**, 11, 768. [CrossRef]
10. Meftah, B. Some new Ostrowski's inequalities for functions whose n^{th} derivatives are logarithmically convex. *Ann. Math. Sil.* **2017**, *32*, 275–284.
11. Meftah, B. Some new Ostrowski's inequalities for *n*-times differentiable mappings which are quasi-convex. *Facta Univ. Ser. Math. Inform.* **2017**, *32*, 319–327.
12. Meftah, B.; Azaizia, A. *Fractional Ostrowski Type Inequalities for Functions Whose First Derivatives Are MT-Preinvex*; Revista MATUA: Madrid, Spain, 2019; Volume 1, pp. 33–34. ISSN 2389-7422.
13. Nasir, J.; Qaisar, S.; Butt, S.I.; Khan, K.A.; Mabela, R.M. Some Simpson's Riemann-Liouville fractional integral inequalities with applications to special functions. *J. Funct. Spaces* **2022**, *2022*, 2113742. [CrossRef]
14. Rangel-Oliveros, Y.; Nwaeze, E.R. Simpson's type inequalities for exponentially convex functions with applications. *Open J. Math. Sci.* **2021**, *5*, 84–94. [CrossRef]
15. Şanlı, Z. Simpson type conformable fractional inequalities. *J. Funct. Spaces* **2022**, *2022*, 5707887. [CrossRef]
16. Soontharanon, J.; Ali, M.A.; Budak, H.; Nonlaopon, K.; Abdullah, Z. Simpson's and Newton's type tnequalities for (α, m) convex functions via quantum calculus. *Symmetry* **2022**, *14*, 736.
17. Vivas-Cortez, M.J.; Ali, M.A.; Qaisar, S.; Sial, I.B.; Jansem, S.; Mateen, A. On some new Simpson's formula type inequalities for convex functions in post-quantum calculus. *Symmetry* **2021**, *13*, 2419. [CrossRef]
18. Shafqat, R.; Niazi, A.U.K.; Yavuz, M.; Jeelani, M.B.; Saleem, K. Mild solution for the time-fractional Navier—Stokes equation incorporating MHD effects. *Fractal Fract.* **2022**, *6*, 580. [CrossRef]
19. Boulares, H.; Ardjouni, A.; Laskri, Y. Existence and uniqueness of solutions for nonlinear fractional nabla difference systems with initial conditions. *Fract. Differ. Calc.* **2017**, *7*, 247–263.
20. Boulares, H.; Ardjouni, A.; Laskri, Y. Existence and uniqueness of solutions to fractional order nonlinear neutral differential equations. *Appl. Math. E-Notes* **2018**, *18*, 25–33.
21. Ali, M.A.; Budak, H.; Sarikaya, M.Z.; Zhang, Z. Ostrowski and Simpson type inequalities for multiplicative integrals. *Proyecciones* **2021**, *40*, 743–763.
22. Aniszewska, D. Multiplicative runge—Kutta methods. *Nonlinear Dyn.* **2007**, *50*, 265–272.
23. Riza, M.; Özyapici, A.; Misirli, E. Multiplicative finite difference methods. *Quart. Appl. Math.* **2009**, 67, 745–754. [CrossRef]
24. Misirli, E.; Gurefe, Y. Multiplicative Adams Bashforth-Moulton methods. *Numer. Algorithms* **2011**, *57*, 425–439. [CrossRef]

25. Bashirov, A.E.; Norozpour, S. On complex multiplicative integration. *TWMS J. Appl. Eng. Math.* **2017**, *7*, 82–93.
26. Bhat, A.H.; Majid, J.; Shah, T.R.; Wani, I.A.; Jain, R. Multiplicative Fourier transform and its applications to multiplicative differential equations. *J. Comput. Math. Sci.* **2019**, *10*, 375–383.
27. Bhat, A.H.; Majid, J.; Wani, I.A. Multiplicative Sumudu transform and its Applications. *Emerg. Tech. Innov. Res.* **2019**, *6*, 579–589.
28. Bashirov, A.E. On line and double multiplicative integrals. *TWMS J. Appl. Eng. Math.* **2013**, *3*, 103–107.
29. Ali, M.A.; Abbas, M.; Zhang, Z.; Sial, I.B.; Arif, R. On integral inequalities for product and quotient of two multiplicatively convex functions. *Asian Res. J. Math.* **2019**, *12*, 1–11. [CrossRef]
30. Ali, M.A.; Abbas, M.; Zafer, A.A. On some Hermite-Hadamard integral inequalities in multiplicative calculus. *J. Ineq. Spec. Func.* **2019**, *10*, 111–122.
31. Özcan, S. Hermite-Hadamard type inequalities for multiplicatively *h*-convex functions. *Konuralp J. Math.* **2020**, *8*, 158–164.
32. Özcan, S. Some integral inequalities of Hermite-Hadamard type for multiplicatively preinvex functions. *AIMS Math.* **2020**, *5*, 1505–1518.
33. Özcan, S. Hermite-Hadamard type inequalities for multiplicatively *h*-preinvex functions. *Turk. J. Anal. Number Theory* **2021**, *9*, 65–70.
34. Meftah, B. Maclaurin type inequalities for multiplicatively convex functions. *Proc. Amer. Math. Soc., accepted paper*.
35. Abdeljawad, T.; Grossman, M. On geometric fractional calculus. *J. Semigroup Theory Appl.* **2016**, *2016*, 1–14.
36. Budak, H.; Özçelik, K. On Hermite-Hadamard type inequalities for multiplicative fractional integrals. *Miskolc Math. Notes* **2020**, *21*, 91–99. [CrossRef]

symmetry

MDPI

Article

Fractional Multiplicative Bullen-Type Inequalities for Multiplicative Differentiable Functions

Hamid Boulares [1,†], Badreddine Meftah [1,†], Abdelkader Moumen [2,*,†], Ramsha Shafqat [3], Hicham Saber [2], Tariq Alraqad [2] and Ekram E. Ali [2]

1 Laboratory of Analysis and Control of Differential Equations "ACED", Faculty MISM, Department of Mathematics, University of Guelma, Guelma 24000, Algeria
2 Department of Mathematics, Faculty of Science, University of Ha'il, Ha'il 55425, Saudi Arabia
3 Department of Mathematics and Statistics, University of Lahore, Sargodha 40100, Pakistan
* Correspondence: abdelkader.moumen@gmail.com
† These authors contributed equally to this work.

Abstract: Various scholars have lately employed a wide range of strategies to resolve specific types of symmetrical fractional differential equations. In this paper, we propose a new fractional identity for multiplicatively differentiable functions; based on this identity, we establish some new fractional multiplicative Bullen-type inequalities for multiplicative differentiable convex functions. Some applications of the obtained results are given.

Keywords: non-Newtonian calculus; Bullen inequality; multiplicatively convex functions

Citation: Boulares, H.; Meftah, B.; Moumen, A.; Shafqat, R.; Saber, H.; Alraqad, T.; Ahmad, E.E.A. Fractional Multiplicative Bullen-Type Inequalities for Multiplicative Differentiable Functions. *Symmetry* **2023**, *15*, 451. https://doi.org/10.3390/sym15020451

Academic Editor: Hassen Fourati, Abdellatif Ben Makhlouf, Omar Naifar, Ioan Raşa and Sergei D. Odintsov

Received: 28 December 2022
Revised: 18 January 2023
Accepted: 2 February 2023
Published: 8 February 2023

1. Introduction

Fractional calculus has been one of the main axes of mathematical analysis over the last three decades, both theoretically and in terms of practical applications. Basically, this theory, together with the qualitative theory of fractional differential and fractional integro-differential equations, their numerical simulations, and their symmetry represent a tool of mathematical analysis used to study integrals and derivatives of an arbitrary order, which unifies and generalizes the notions traditional ways of differentiation and integration. Fractional-order nonlinear operators are more convenient than classical formulations. Many scientific disciplines, including fluid mechanics, signal processing, and entropy theory, may involve the qualitative theory of fractional differential equations, fractional integro-differential equations, and fractional order operators. For this reason, the applications of the aforementioned fractional calculus theory and qualitative theory of equations have attracted the attention of scholars around the world.

Integrals play an essential and vital role in certain pure and applied fields combined with convexity, and their generalizations have been the subject of permanent research. As consequence, several papers dealing with convex inequalities in different types of computation have been published (in classical computation, see [1–6], for fractional computation [7–10] and for non-Newtonian calculus [11–16]).

Recently, Abdeljawad and Grossman [17] introduced the multiplicative Riemann–Liouville fractional integrals as follows:

Definition 1. *The multiplicative Riemann–Liouville fractional integrals of order $\alpha \in \mathbb{C}$, $\mathrm{Re}(\alpha) > 0$, respectively, are defined by*

$$\left({}_{f}I_{*}^{\alpha}\rho\right)(u) = e^{\left(J_{f^{+}}^{\alpha}(\ln\circ\rho)\right)(u)}$$

and

$$\left({}_{*}I_{k}^{\alpha}\rho\right)(u) = e^{\left(J_{k^{-}}^{\alpha}(\ln\circ\rho)\right)(u)},$$

where J^{α}_{l+} and J^{α}_{k-} represents the left and the right Riemann–Liouville fractional integral:

$$\left(J^{\alpha}_{f+}\rho\right)(u) = \frac{1}{\Gamma(\alpha)}\int_{f}^{u}(u-\varsigma)^{\alpha-1}\rho(\varsigma)d\varsigma, f < u$$

and

$$\left(J^{\alpha}_{k-}\rho\right)(u) = \frac{1}{\Gamma(\alpha)}\int_{u}^{k}(\varsigma-u)^{\alpha-1}\rho(\varsigma)d\varsigma, u < k.$$

Budak and Özçelik [18] used the above operator and established some Hermite–Hadamard-type inequalities for multiplicatively fractional integrals. Regarding some papers related to the applications concerning the non-Newtonian calculus, one can see [19–28].

The following inequality is known as the Bullen inequality:

$$\int_{l}^{k}\rho(x)dx \leq \frac{1}{2}\left[f\left(\frac{l+k}{2}\right) + \frac{f(l)+f(k)}{2}\right]. \tag{1}$$

In this paper, we propose the fractional multiplicative analogue of inequality (1). For this, we first prove a new fractional identity for multiplicative differentiable functions. Based on this equality, we provide some fractional Bullen-type inequalities for multiplicatively convex functions. We also give some examples of applications of the obtained results to analytical inequalities.

The non-Newtonian calculus was first presented by Grossman and Katz, where they created and studied the first non-Newtonian calculation system, called geometric calculation. Next, they created an infinite family of non-Newtonian calculi, thus modifying the classical calculus introduced by Newton and Leibniz in the 17th century, each of which differed markedly from the classical calculus of Newton and Leibniz known today as the non-Newtonian calculus or the multiplicative calculus, where the ordinary product and ratio are used, respectively, as the sum and exponential difference over the domain of positive real numbers see [29]. This calculation is useful for dealing with exponentially varying functions.

It is worth noting that the complete mathematical description of multiplicative calculus was given by Bashirov et al. [30]. The reader can also refer to the recent monographs [31,32].

Definition 2 ([30]). *Let $\rho : \mathbb{R} \to \mathbb{R}^{+}$ be a positive function. The multiplicative derivative ρ^{*} of the function ρ is defined as follows:*

$$\frac{d^{*}\rho}{dt} = \rho^{*}(\varsigma) = \lim_{h\to 0}\left(\frac{\rho(\varsigma+h)}{\rho(\varsigma)}\right)^{\frac{1}{h}}.$$

Remark 1. *The relation between the multiplicative derivative $\rho^{*}$and the ordinary derivative $\rho'$is as follows:*

$$\rho^{*}(\varsigma) = e^{(\ln\rho(\varsigma))'} = e^{\frac{\rho'(\varsigma)}{\rho(\varsigma)}}.$$

The multiplicative derivative admits the following properties:

Theorem 1 ([30]). *Let c be an arbitrary constant, and let ρ and ϑ be two multiplicatively differentiable functions. Then, functions $c\rho, \rho\vartheta, \rho+\vartheta, \rho/\vartheta$ and ρ^{ϑ} are * differentiable, and they satisfy*

- $(c\rho)^{*}(\varsigma) = \rho^{*}(\varsigma)$,
- $(\rho\vartheta)^{*}(\varsigma) = \rho^{*}(\varsigma)\vartheta^{*}(\varsigma)$,
- $(\rho+\vartheta)^{*}(\varsigma) = \rho^{*}(\varsigma)^{\frac{\rho(\varsigma)}{\rho(\varsigma)+\vartheta(\varsigma)}}\vartheta^{*}(\varsigma)^{\frac{\vartheta(\varsigma)}{\rho(\varsigma)+\vartheta(\varsigma)}}$,

- $\left(\frac{\rho}{\vartheta}\right)^{*}(\varsigma) = \frac{\rho^{*}(\varsigma)}{\vartheta^{*}(\varsigma)}$,
- $\left(\rho^{\vartheta}\right)^{*}(\varsigma) = \rho^{*}(\varsigma)^{\vartheta(\varsigma)}\rho(\varsigma)^{\vartheta'(\varsigma)}$.

In [30], Bashirov et al. introduced the concept of the * integral called the multiplicative integral, which is written as $\int_{l}^{k}(\rho(\varsigma))^{d\varsigma}$. It is clear that the sum in the classical Riemann integral of ρ over $[l,k]$, is replaced in the multiplicative integral of ρ over $[l,k]$ by the product. However, the product is represented by the raising to power.

The relationship between the Riemann integral and the multiplicative integral is as follows:

Proposition 1 ([30]). *If ρ is a Riemann integrable on $[l,k]$, then ρ is a multiplicative integrable on $[l,k]$ and*

$$\int_{l}^{k}(\rho(\varsigma))^{d\varsigma} = \exp\left\{\int_{l}^{k}\ln(\rho(\varsigma))d\varsigma\right\}.$$

Some properties of the multiplicative integral are given by the following theorem.

Theorem 2 ([30]). *Let ρ be a positive and a Riemann integrable on $[l,k]$; then, ρ is a multiplicative integrable on $[l,k]$ and*

- $\int_{l}^{k}((\rho(\varsigma))^{p})^{d\varsigma} = \left(\int_{l}^{k}(\rho(\varsigma))^{d\varsigma}\right)^{p}$,
- $\int_{l}^{k}(\rho(\varsigma)\vartheta(\varsigma))^{d\varsigma} = \int_{l}^{k}(\rho(\varsigma))^{d\varsigma}\int_{l}^{k}(\vartheta(\varsigma))^{d\varsigma}$,
- $\int_{l}^{k}\left(\frac{\rho(\varsigma)}{\vartheta(\varsigma)}\right)^{d\varsigma} = \frac{\int_{l}^{k}(\rho(\varsigma))^{d\varsigma}}{\int_{l}^{k}(\vartheta(\varsigma))^{d\varsigma}}$,
- $\int_{l}^{k}(\rho(\varsigma))^{d\varsigma} = \int_{l}^{c}(\rho(\varsigma))^{d\varsigma}\int_{c}^{k}(\rho(\varsigma))^{d\varsigma}, l < c < k$,
- $\int_{l}^{l}(\rho(\varsigma))^{d\varsigma} = 1$ and $\int_{l}^{k}(\rho(\varsigma))^{d\varsigma} = \left(\int_{k}^{l}(\rho(\varsigma))^{d\varsigma}\right)^{-1}$.

Theorem 3 ([30], multiplicative integration by parts). *Let $\rho : [l,k] \to \mathbb{R}$ be multiplicative differentiable, let $\vartheta : [l,k] \to \mathbb{R}$ be a differentiable so the function ρ^{ϑ} is a multiplicative integrable, and*

$$\int_{l}^{k}\left(\rho^{*}(\varsigma)^{\vartheta(\varsigma)}\right)^{d\varsigma} = \frac{\rho(k)^{\vartheta(k)}}{\rho(l)^{\vartheta(l)}} \times \frac{1}{\int_{l}^{k}\left(\rho(\varsigma)^{\vartheta'(\varsigma)}\right)^{d\varsigma}}.$$

Lemma 1 ([33]). *Let $\rho : [l,k] \to \mathbb{R}$ be multiplicative differentiable, let $h : [l,k] \to \mathbb{R}$, and let $\vartheta : J \subset \mathbb{R} \to \mathbb{R}$ be two differentiable functions. Then, we have*

$$\int_{l}^{k}\left(\rho^{*}(h(\varsigma))^{h'(\varsigma)\vartheta(\varsigma)}\right)^{d\varsigma} = \frac{\rho(h(k))^{\vartheta(k)}}{\rho(h(l))^{\vartheta(l)}} \times \frac{1}{\int_{l}^{k}\left(\rho(h(\varsigma))^{\vartheta'(\varsigma)}\right)^{d\varsigma}}.$$

Definition 3 ([33]). *A function $\rho : I \to [0,+\infty)$ is said to be multiplicatively convex or* log-*convex, if*

$$\rho(\varsigma x + (1-\varsigma)y) \leq [\rho(x)]^{\varsigma}[\rho(y)]^{1-\varsigma}$$

holds for all $x, y \in I$ and all $\varsigma \in [0,1]$.

2. Main Results

In order to prove our results, we need the following lemma.

Lemma 2. *Let $\rho : [l,k] \to \mathbb{R}^+$ be a multiplicative differentiable mapping on $[l,k]$ with $l < k$. If ρ^* is a multiplicative integrable on $[l,k]$, then we have the following identity for multiplicative integrals:*

$$\left((\rho(l))\left(\rho\left(\tfrac{l+k}{2}\right)\right)^2(\rho(k))\right)^{\frac{1}{4}}\left(\left({}_{l}I^{\alpha}_{*}\rho\right)\left(\tfrac{l+k}{2}\right)\left({}_{*}I^{\alpha}_{\frac{l+k}{2}}\rho\right)(k)\right)^{-\frac{2^{\alpha-1}\Gamma(\alpha+1)}{(k-l)^{\alpha}}}$$
$$=\left(\int_0^1\left(\rho^*\left((1-\varsigma)l+\varsigma\tfrac{l+k}{2}\right)^{\varsigma^{\alpha}-\frac{1}{2}}\right)^{d\varsigma}\right)^{\frac{k-l}{4}}$$
$$\times\left(\int_0^1\left(\rho^*\left((1-\varsigma)\tfrac{l+k}{2}+\varsigma k\right)^{\frac{1}{2}-(1-\varsigma)^{\alpha}}\right)^{d\varsigma}\right)^{\frac{k-l}{4}}.$$

Proof. Let

$$I_1=\left(\int_0^1\left(\rho^*\left((1-\varsigma)l+\varsigma\tfrac{l+k}{2}\right)^{\varsigma^{\alpha}-\frac{1}{2}}\right)^{d\varsigma}\right)^{\frac{k-l}{4}}$$

and

$$I_2=\left(\int_0^1\left(\rho^*\left((1-\varsigma)\tfrac{l+k}{2}+\varsigma k\right)^{\frac{1}{2}-(1-\varsigma)^{\alpha}}\right)^{d\varsigma}\right)^{\frac{k-l}{4}}.$$

Using the integration by parts for multiplicative integrals, from I_1 we have

$$I_1=\left(\int_0^1\left(\rho^*\left((1-\varsigma)l+\varsigma\tfrac{l+k}{2}\right)^{t^{\alpha}-\frac{1}{2}}\right)^{dt}\right)^{\frac{k-l}{4}}$$
$$=\left(\int_0^1\left(\rho^*\left((1-t)l+t\tfrac{l+k}{2}\right)^{\frac{k-l}{2}\left(\frac{1}{2}\varsigma^{\alpha}-\frac{1}{2}\right)}\right)^{d\varsigma}\right)$$
$$=\frac{\left(\rho\left(\frac{l+k}{2}\right)\right)^{\frac{1}{4}}}{(\rho(l))^{-\frac{1}{4}}}\cdot\frac{1}{\int_0^1\left(\rho\left(\left((1-\varsigma)l+\varsigma\frac{l+k}{2}\right)\right)^{\frac{\alpha}{2}\varsigma^{\alpha-1}}\right)^{d\varsigma}}$$
$$=(\rho(l))^{\frac{1}{4}}\left(\rho\left(\tfrac{l+k}{2}\right)\right)^{\frac{1}{4}}\frac{1}{\exp\left\{\int_0^1\frac{\alpha}{2}(\varsigma)^{\alpha-1}\ln\left(\rho\left((1-\varsigma)l+\varsigma\frac{l+k}{2}\right)\right)d\varsigma\right\}}$$
$$=(\rho(l))^{\frac{1}{4}}\left(\rho\left(\tfrac{l+k}{2}\right)\right)^{\frac{1}{4}}\frac{1}{\exp\left\{\frac{2^{\alpha-1}\alpha}{(k-l)^{\alpha}}\int_0^1(u-l)^{\alpha-1}\ln(\rho(u))du\right\}}$$
$$=\frac{(\rho(l))^{\frac{1}{4}}\left(\rho\left(\frac{l+k}{2}\right)\right)^{\frac{1}{4}}}{\left(\exp\left\{\left(\frac{1}{\Gamma(\alpha)}\int_l^{\frac{l+k}{2}}(u-l)^{\alpha-1}\ln(\rho(u))du\right)\right\}\right)^{\frac{2^{\alpha-1}\Gamma(\alpha+1)}{(k-l)^{\alpha}}}}$$
$$=(\rho(l))^{\frac{1}{4}}\left(\rho\left(\tfrac{l+k}{2}\right)\right)^{\frac{1}{4}}\left(\left({}_{l}I^{\alpha}_{*}\rho\right)\left(\tfrac{l+k}{2}\right)\right)^{-\frac{2^{\alpha-1}\Gamma(\alpha+1)}{(k-l)^{\alpha}}}.$$

Similarly, we obtain

$$
\begin{aligned}
I_2 &= \left(\int_0^1 \left(\rho^*\left((1-\varsigma)\tfrac{l+k}{2} + \varsigma k \right)^{\frac{1}{2}-(1-\varsigma)^{\alpha}} \right)^{d\varsigma} \right)^{\frac{k-l}{4}} \\
&= \left(\int_0^1 \left(\rho^*\left((1-\varsigma)\tfrac{l+k}{2} + \varsigma k \right)^{\frac{k-l}{2}\left(\frac{1}{2}-\frac{1}{2}(1-\varsigma)^{\alpha}\right)} \right)^{d\varsigma} \right) \\
&= \frac{(\rho(k))^{\frac{1}{4}}}{\left(\rho\left(\frac{l+k}{2}\right)\right)^{-\frac{1}{4}}} \cdot \frac{1}{\int_0^1 \left(\rho\left((1-\varsigma)\frac{l+k}{2} + \varsigma k \right)^{\frac{\alpha}{2}(1-\varsigma)^{\alpha-1}} \right)^{d\varsigma}} \\
&= \rho\left(\frac{l+k}{2}\right)^{\frac{1}{4}} \rho(k)^{\frac{1}{4}} \cdot \frac{1}{\exp\left\{ \frac{\alpha}{2} \int_0^1 (1-\varsigma)^{\alpha-1} \ln \rho\left((1-\varsigma)\frac{l+k}{2} + \varsigma k \right) d\varsigma \right\}} \\
&= \left(\rho\left(\frac{l+k}{2}\right) \right)^{\frac{1}{4}} (\rho(k))^{\frac{1}{4}} \cdot \frac{1}{\exp\left\{ \frac{2^{\alpha-1}}{(k-l)^{\alpha}} \alpha \int_{\frac{l+k}{2}}^{k} (k-u)^{\alpha-1} \ln \rho(u) du \right\}} \\
&= \left(\rho\left(\frac{l+k}{2}\right) \right)^{\frac{n}{2(n+2)}} (\rho(k))^{\frac{1}{n+2}} \cdot \frac{1}{\exp\left\{ \frac{2^{\alpha-1}\Gamma(\alpha+1)}{(k-l)^{\alpha}} \left(\frac{1}{\Gamma(\alpha)} \int_{\frac{l+k}{2}}^{k} (k-u)^{\alpha-1} \ln f(u) du \right) \right\}} \\
&= \frac{\rho\left(\frac{l+k}{2}\right)^{\frac{1}{4}} \rho(k)^{\frac{1}{4}}}{\left(\exp\left\{ \left(\frac{1}{\Gamma(\alpha)} \int_{\frac{l+k}{2}}^{k} (k-u)^{\alpha-1} \ln \rho(u) du \right) \right\} \right)^{\frac{2^{\alpha-1}\Gamma(\alpha+1)}{(k-l)^{\alpha}}}} \\
&= \left(\rho\left(\frac{l+k}{2}\right) \right)^{\frac{1}{4}} (\rho(k))^{\frac{1}{4}} \cdot \left(\left({}_*I^{\alpha}_{\frac{l+k}{2}} \rho \right)(k) \right)^{-\frac{2^{\alpha-1}\Gamma(\alpha+1)}{(k-l)^{\alpha}}}.
\end{aligned}
$$

Multiplying above equalities, we obtain

$$
\begin{aligned}
I_1 \times I_2 &= (\rho(l))^{\frac{1}{4}} \left(\rho\left(\frac{l+k}{2}\right) \right)^{\frac{1}{4}} \left(\left({}_l I^{\alpha}_* \rho\right)\left(\frac{l+k}{2}\right) \right)^{-\frac{2^{\alpha-1}\Gamma(\alpha+1)}{(k-l)^{\alpha}}} \\
&\times \left(\rho\left(\frac{l+k}{2}\right) \right)^{\frac{1}{4}} (\rho(k))^{\frac{1}{4}} \cdot \left(\left({}_*I^{\alpha}_{\frac{l+k}{2}} \rho \right)(k) \right)^{-\frac{2^{\alpha-1}\Gamma(\alpha+1)}{(k-l)^{\alpha}}} \\
&= \left((\rho(l)) \left(\rho\left(\frac{l+k}{2}\right) \right)^2 (\rho(k)) \right)^{\frac{1}{4}} \left(\left({}_l I^{\alpha}_* \rho\right)\left(\frac{l+k}{2}\right) \left({}_*I^{\alpha}_{\frac{l+k}{2}} \rho \right)(k) \right)^{-\frac{2^{\alpha-1}\Gamma(\alpha+1)}{(k-l)^{\alpha}}},
\end{aligned}
$$

which is the result. The proof is completed. □

Theorem 4. *Let $\rho : [l,k] \to \mathbb{R}^+$ be a multiplicatively differentiable mapping on $[l,k]$ with $l < k$. If $|\ln \rho^*| \leq \ln \mathcal{M}$ on $[l,k]$, then we have*

$$
\begin{aligned}
&\left| \left((\rho(l)) \left(\rho\left(\frac{l+k}{2}\right) \right)^2 (\rho(k)) \right)^{\frac{1}{4}} \left(\left({}_l I^{\alpha}_* \rho\right)\left(\frac{l+k}{2}\right) \left({}_*I^{\alpha}_{\frac{l+k}{2}} \rho \right)(k) \right)^{-\frac{2^{\alpha-1}\Gamma(\alpha+1)}{(k-l)^{\alpha}}} \right| \\
&\leq \mathcal{M}^{\frac{k-l}{4}\left(1+\frac{\alpha}{\alpha+1}\left(\frac{1}{2}\right)^{\frac{1}{\alpha}-1}\right)}.
\end{aligned}
$$

Proof. From Lemma 2, properties of multiplicative integral and using the fact that $|\ln f^*| \leq \ln \mathcal{M}$, we have

$$
\left|\left((\rho(l))\left(\rho\left(\tfrac{l+k}{2}\right)\right)^{2}(\rho(k))\right)^{\frac{1}{4}}\left(\left({}_{l}I_{*}^{\alpha}\rho\right)\left(\tfrac{l+k}{2}\right)\left({}_{*}I_{\frac{l+k}{2}}^{\alpha}\rho\right)(k)\right)^{-\frac{2^{\alpha-1}\Gamma(\alpha+1)}{(k-l)^{\alpha}}}\right|
$$

$$
=\left|\left(\int_{0}^{1}\left(\rho^{*}\left((1-\varsigma)l+\varsigma\tfrac{l+k}{2}\right)^{\varsigma^{\alpha}-\frac{1}{2}}\right)^{d\varsigma}\right)^{\frac{k-l}{4}}\right|\left|\left(\int_{0}^{1}\left(\rho^{*}\left((1-\varsigma)\tfrac{l+k}{2}+\varsigma k\right)^{\frac{1}{2}-(1-\varsigma)^{\alpha}}\right)^{d\varsigma}\right)^{\frac{k-l}{4}}\right|
$$

$$
=\left|\left(\int_{0}^{1}\left(\rho^{*}\left((1-\varsigma)l+\varsigma\tfrac{l+k}{2}\right)^{\frac{k-l}{4}\left(\varsigma^{\alpha}-\frac{1}{2}\right)}\right)^{dt}\right)\right|\left|\left(\int_{0}^{1}\left(\rho^{*}\left((1-\varsigma)\tfrac{l+k}{2}+\varsigma k\right)^{\frac{k-l}{4}\left(\frac{1}{2}-(1-\varsigma)^{\alpha}\right)}\right)^{d\varsigma}\right)\right|
$$

$$
\leq\left(\exp\left\{\int_{0}^{1}\left|\tfrac{k-l}{4}\left(\varsigma^{\alpha}-\tfrac{1}{2}\right)\ln\left(\rho^{*}\left((1-\varsigma)l+\varsigma\tfrac{l+k}{2}\right)\right)\right|d\varsigma\right\}\right)
$$

$$
\times\left(\exp\left\{\int_{0}^{1}\left|\tfrac{k-l}{4}\left(\tfrac{1}{2}-(1-\varsigma)^{\alpha}\right)\ln\left(\rho^{*}\left((1-\varsigma)\tfrac{l+k}{2}+\varsigma k\right)\right)\right|d\varsigma\right\}\right)
$$

$$
=\left(\exp\left\{\tfrac{k-l}{4}\int_{0}^{1}\left|\varsigma^{\alpha}-\tfrac{1}{2}\right|\left|\ln\left(\rho^{*}\left((1-\varsigma)l+\varsigma\tfrac{l+k}{2}\right)\right)\right|d\varsigma\right\}\right)
$$

$$
\times\left(\exp\left\{\tfrac{k-l}{4}\int_{0}^{1}\left|\tfrac{1}{2}-(1-\varsigma)^{\alpha}\right|\left|\ln\left(\rho^{*}\left((1-\varsigma)\tfrac{l+k}{2}+\varsigma k\right)\right)\right|d\varsigma\right\}\right)
$$

$$
\leq\left(\exp\left\{\tfrac{k-l}{4}\ln\mathcal{M}\int_{0}^{1}\left|\varsigma^{\alpha}-\tfrac{1}{2}\right|d\varsigma\right\}\right)
$$

$$
\times\left(\exp\left\{\tfrac{k-l}{4}\ln\mathcal{M}\int_{0}^{1}\left|\tfrac{1}{2}-(1-\varsigma)^{\alpha}\right|d\varsigma\right\}\right)
$$

$$
=\left(\exp\left\{\tfrac{k-l}{4}\ln\mathcal{M}\left(\int_{0}^{\left(\frac{1}{2}\right)^{\frac{1}{\alpha}}}\left(\tfrac{1}{2}-\varsigma^{\alpha}\right)d\varsigma+\int_{\left(\frac{1}{2}\right)^{\frac{1}{\alpha}}}^{1}\left(\varsigma^{\alpha}-\tfrac{1}{2}\right)d\varsigma\right)\right\}\right)
$$

$$
\times\left(\exp\left\{\tfrac{k-l}{4}\ln\mathcal{M}\left(\int_{0}^{1-\left(\frac{1}{2}\right)^{\frac{1}{\alpha}}}\left((1-\varsigma)^{\alpha}-\tfrac{1}{2}\right)d\varsigma+\int_{1-\left(\frac{1}{2}\right)^{\frac{1}{\alpha}}}^{1}\left(\tfrac{1}{2}-(1-\varsigma)^{\alpha}\right)d\varsigma\right)\right\}\right)
$$

$$
=\left(\exp\left\{\tfrac{k-l}{4}\left(\tfrac{2+2\alpha}{4(\alpha+1)}+\tfrac{2\alpha}{\alpha+1}\left(\tfrac{1}{2}\right)^{\frac{1}{\alpha}+1}\right)\ln\mathcal{M}\right\}\right)
$$

$$
\times\left(\exp\left\{\tfrac{k-l}{4}\left(\tfrac{2+2\alpha}{4(\alpha+1)}+\tfrac{2\alpha}{\alpha+1}\left(\tfrac{1}{2}\right)^{1+\frac{1}{\alpha}}\right)\ln\mathcal{M}\right\}\right)
$$

$$
=\mathcal{M}^{\frac{k-l}{4}\left(1+\frac{\alpha}{\alpha+1}\left(\frac{1}{2}\right)^{\frac{1}{\alpha}-1}\right)}.
$$

The proof is completed. □

Corollary 1. *In Theorem 4, if we take $\alpha = 1$, then we obtain*

$$\left| \left((\rho(l)) \left(\rho\left(\frac{l+k}{2}\right)\right)^2 (\rho(k)) \right)^{\frac{1}{4}} \left(\int_l^k \rho(u)^{du} \right)^{\frac{1}{l-k}} \right| \leq \mathcal{M}^{\frac{3}{8}(k-l)}.$$

Theorem 5. *Let $\rho : [l,k] \to \mathbb{R}^+$ be a multiplicative differentiable mapping on $[l,k]$ with $l < k$. If ρ^* is multiplicatively convex function on $[l,k]$, then we have*

$$\left| \left((\rho(l)) \left(\rho\left(\frac{l+k}{2}\right)\right)^2 (\rho(k)) \right)^{\frac{1}{4}} \left(\left({}_l I_*^\alpha \rho\right)\left(\frac{l+k}{2}\right) \left({}_* I_{\frac{l+k}{2}}^\alpha \rho\right)(k) \right)^{-\frac{2^{\alpha-1}\Gamma(\alpha+1)}{(k-l)^\alpha}} \right|$$
$$\leq [(\rho^*(l))(f^*(k))]^{\frac{k-l}{2}\left(\frac{2-\alpha^2-3\alpha}{8(\alpha+1)(\alpha+2)} + \frac{\alpha}{\alpha+1}\left(\frac{1}{2}\right)^{1+\frac{1}{\alpha}} - \frac{\alpha}{2(\alpha+2)}\left(\frac{1}{2}\right)^{1+\frac{2}{\alpha}} \right)}$$
$$\times \left(f^*\left(\frac{l+k}{2}\right)\right)^{\frac{k-l}{2}\left(\frac{2-\alpha}{4(\alpha+2)} + \frac{\alpha}{\alpha+2}\left(\frac{1}{2}\right)^{1+\frac{2}{\alpha}} \right)}.$$

Proof. From Lemma 2, the properties of the multiplicative integral and the multiplicative convexity of ρ^*, we have

$$\left| \left((\rho(l)) \left(\rho\left(\frac{l+k}{2}\right)\right)^2 (\rho(k)) \right)^{\frac{1}{4}} \left(\left({}_l I_*^\alpha \rho\right)\left(\frac{l+k}{2}\right) \left({}_* I_{\frac{l+k}{2}}^\alpha \rho\right)(k) \right)^{-\frac{2^{\alpha-1}\Gamma(\alpha+1)}{(k-l)^\alpha}} \right|$$
$$= \left| \left(\int_0^1 \left(\rho^*\left((1-\varsigma)l + \varsigma\frac{l+k}{2} \right)^{\varsigma^\alpha - \frac{1}{2}} \right)^{d\varsigma} \right)^{\frac{k-l}{4}} \right|$$
$$\times \left| \left(\int_0^1 \left(\rho^*\left((1-\varsigma)\frac{l+k}{2} + \varsigma k \right)^{\frac{1}{2} - (1-\varsigma)^\alpha} \right)^{d\varsigma} \right)^{\frac{k-l}{4}} \right|$$
$$= \int_0^1 \left| \rho^*\left((1-\varsigma)l + \varsigma\frac{l+k}{2} \right)^{\frac{k-l}{2}\left(\frac{1}{2}\varsigma^\alpha - \frac{1}{4}\right)} \right|^{d\varsigma}$$
$$\times \int_0^1 \left| \rho^*\left((1-\varsigma)\frac{l+k}{2} + \varsigma k \right)^{\frac{k-l}{2}\left(\frac{1}{4} - \frac{1}{2}(1-\varsigma)^\alpha\right)} \right|^{d\varsigma}$$
$$\leq \left(\exp\left\{ \frac{k-l}{2} \int_0^1 \left| \left(\frac{1}{2}\varsigma^\alpha - \frac{1}{4}\right) \right| \left| \ln \rho^*\left((1-\varsigma)l + \varsigma\frac{l+k}{2} \right) \right| d\varsigma \right\} \right)$$
$$\times \left(\exp\left\{ \frac{k-l}{2} \int_0^1 \left| \left(\frac{1}{4} - \frac{1}{2}(1-\varsigma)^\alpha\right) \right| \left| \ln \rho^*\left((1-\varsigma)\frac{l+k}{2} + \varsigma k \right) \right| d\varsigma \right\} \right)$$
$$\leq \left(\exp\left\{ \frac{k-l}{2} \int_0^1 \left| \left(\frac{1}{2}\varsigma^\alpha - \frac{1}{4}\right) \right| \left| \ln(\rho^*(l))^{(1-\varsigma)} \left(f^*\left(\frac{l+k}{2}\right)\right)^{\varsigma} \right| d\varsigma \right\} \right)$$
$$\times \left(\exp\left\{ \frac{k-l}{2} \int_0^1 \left| \left(\frac{1}{4} - \frac{1}{2}(1-\varsigma)^\alpha\right) \right| \left| \ln\left(\rho^*\left(\frac{l+k}{2}\right)\right)^{(1-\varsigma)} (f^*(k))^{\varsigma} \right| d\varsigma \right\} \right)$$
$$= \exp\left\{ \frac{k-l}{2} \left(\int_0^{\left(\frac{1}{2}\right)^{\frac{1}{\alpha}}} \left(\frac{1}{4} - \frac{1}{2}\varsigma^\alpha\right) \left| \ln(\rho^*(l))^{(1-\varsigma)} \left(f^*\left(\frac{l+k}{2}\right)\right)^{\varsigma} \right| d\varsigma \right. \right.$$

$$+\int_{\left(\frac{1}{2}\right)^{\frac{1}{\alpha}}}^{1}\left(\frac{1}{2}\varsigma^{\alpha}-\frac{1}{4}\right)\left|\ln(\rho^{*}(l))^{(1-\varsigma)}\left(f^{*}\left(\frac{l+k}{2}\right)\right)^{\varsigma}\right|d\varsigma\Bigg)\Bigg\}$$

$$\times\exp\left\{\frac{k-l}{2}\left(\int_{0}^{1-\left(\frac{1}{2}\right)^{\frac{1}{\alpha}}}\left(\frac{1}{2}(1-\varsigma)^{\alpha}-\frac{1}{4}\right)\left|\ln\left(\rho^{*}\left(\frac{l+k}{2}\right)\right)^{(1-\varsigma)}(f^{*}(k))^{\varsigma}\right|d\varsigma\right.\right.$$

$$\left.\left.+\int_{1-\left(\frac{1}{2}\right)^{\frac{1}{\alpha}}}^{1}\left(\frac{1}{4}-\frac{1}{2}(1-\varsigma)^{\alpha}\right)\left|\ln\left(\rho^{*}\left(\frac{l+k}{2}\right)\right)^{(1-\varsigma)}(f^{*}(k))^{\varsigma}\right|d\varsigma\right)\right\}$$

$$=\exp\left\{\frac{k-l}{2}\left(\int_{0}^{\left(\frac{1}{2}\right)^{\frac{1}{\alpha}}}\left(\frac{1}{4}-\frac{1}{2}\varsigma^{\alpha}\right)\left((1-\varsigma)\ln(\rho^{*}(l))+\varsigma\ln\left(f^{*}\left(\frac{l+k}{2}\right)\right)\right)d\varsigma\right.\right.$$

$$\left.\left.+\int_{\left(\frac{1}{2}\right)^{\frac{1}{\alpha}}}^{1}\left(\frac{1}{2}\varsigma^{\alpha}-\frac{1}{4}\right)\left((1-\varsigma)\ln(\rho^{*}(l))+\varsigma\ln\left(f^{*}\left(\frac{l+k}{2}\right)\right)\right)d\varsigma\right)\right\}$$

$$\times\exp\left\{\frac{k-l}{2}\left(\int_{0}^{1-\left(\frac{1}{2}\right)^{\frac{1}{\alpha}}}\left(\frac{1}{2}(1-\varsigma)^{\alpha}-\frac{1}{4}\right)\left((1-\varsigma)\ln\left(\rho^{*}\left(\frac{l+k}{2}\right)\right)+\varsigma\ln(f^{*}(k))\right)d\varsigma\right.\right.$$

$$\left.\left.+\int_{1-\left(\frac{1}{2}\right)^{\frac{1}{\alpha}}}^{1}\left(\frac{1}{4}-\frac{1}{2}(1-\varsigma)^{\alpha}\right)\left((1-\varsigma)\ln\left(\rho^{*}\left(\frac{l+k}{2}\right)\right)+\varsigma\ln(f^{*}(k))\right)d\varsigma\right)\right\}$$

$$=\exp\left\{\frac{k-l}{2}\left(\ln(\rho^{*}(l))\int_{0}^{\left(\frac{1}{2}\right)^{\frac{1}{\alpha}}}\left(\frac{1}{4}-\frac{1}{2}\varsigma^{\alpha}\right)(1-\varsigma)d\varsigma\right.\right.$$

$$+\ln\left(f^{*}\left(\frac{l+k}{2}\right)\right)\int_{0}^{\left(\frac{1}{2}\right)^{\frac{1}{\alpha}}}\left(\frac{1}{4}-\frac{1}{2}\varsigma^{\alpha}\right)\varsigma d\varsigma+\ln(\rho^{*}(l))\int_{\left(\frac{1}{2}\right)^{\frac{1}{\alpha}}}^{1}\left(\frac{1}{2}\varsigma^{\alpha}-\frac{1}{4}\right)(1-\varsigma)d\varsigma$$

$$\left.\left.+\ln\left(f^{*}\left(\frac{l+k}{2}\right)\right)\int_{\left(\frac{1}{2}\right)^{\frac{1}{\alpha}}}^{1}\left(\frac{1}{2}\varsigma^{\alpha}-\frac{1}{4}\right)\varsigma d\varsigma\right)\right\}$$

$$\times\exp\left\{\frac{k-l}{2}\left(\ln\left(\rho^{*}\left(\frac{l+k}{2}\right)\right)\int_{0}^{1-\left(\frac{1}{2}\right)^{\frac{1}{\alpha}}}\left(\frac{1}{2}(1-\varsigma)^{\alpha}-\frac{1}{4}\right)(1-\varsigma)d\varsigma\right.\right.$$

$$+\ln(f^{*}(k))\int_{0}^{1-\left(\frac{1}{2}\right)^{\frac{1}{\alpha}}}\left(\frac{1}{2}(1-\varsigma)^{\alpha}-\frac{1}{4}\right)\varsigma d\varsigma+\ln\left(\rho^{*}\left(\frac{l+k}{2}\right)\right)\int_{1-\left(\frac{1}{2}\right)^{\frac{1}{\alpha}}}^{1}\left(\frac{1}{4}-\frac{1}{2}(1-\varsigma)^{\alpha}\right)(1-\varsigma)d\varsigma$$

$$\left.\left.+\ln(f^{*}(k))\int_{1-\left(\frac{1}{2}\right)^{\frac{1}{\alpha}}}^{1}\left(\frac{1}{4}-\frac{1}{2}(1-\varsigma)^{\alpha}\right)\varsigma d\varsigma\right)\right\}$$

$$=\exp\left\{\frac{k-l}{2}\left(\left(\frac{\alpha}{4(\alpha+1)}\left(\frac{1}{2}\right)^{\frac{1}{\alpha}}-\frac{\alpha}{8(\alpha+2)8}\left(\frac{1}{2}\right)^{\frac{2}{\alpha}}\right)\ln(\rho^{*}(l))\right.\right.$$

$$
\begin{aligned}
&+\tfrac{\alpha}{8(\alpha+2)}\left(\tfrac{1}{2}\right)^{\frac{2}{\alpha}}\ln\left(f^*\left(\tfrac{l+k}{2}\right)\right)+\left(\tfrac{2-\alpha^2-3\alpha}{8(\alpha+1)(\alpha+2)}+\tfrac{\alpha}{4(\alpha+1)}\left(\tfrac{1}{2}\right)^{\frac{1}{\alpha}}-\tfrac{\alpha}{8(\alpha+2)}\left(\tfrac{1}{2}\right)^{\frac{2}{\alpha}}\right)\ln(\rho^*(l))\\
&+\left(\tfrac{2-\alpha}{8(\alpha+2)}+\tfrac{\alpha}{8(\alpha+2)}\left(\tfrac{1}{2}\right)^{\frac{2}{\alpha}}\right)\ln\left(f^*\left(\tfrac{l+k}{2}\right)\right)\Bigg)\Bigg\}\\
&\times\exp\Bigg\{\tfrac{k-l}{2}\Bigg(\left(\tfrac{2-\alpha}{8(\alpha+2)}+\tfrac{\alpha}{8(\alpha+2)}\left(\tfrac{1}{2}\right)^{\frac{2}{\alpha}}\right)\ln\left(\rho^*\left(\tfrac{l+k}{2}\right)\right)\\
&+\left(\tfrac{2-\alpha^2-3\alpha}{8(\alpha+1)(\alpha+2)}+\tfrac{\alpha}{4(\alpha+1)}\left(\tfrac{1}{2}\right)^{\frac{1}{\alpha}}-\tfrac{\alpha}{8(\alpha+2)}\left(\tfrac{1}{2}\right)^{\frac{2}{\alpha}}\right)\ln(f^*(k))\\
&+\tfrac{\alpha}{8(\alpha+2)}\left(\tfrac{1}{2}\right)^{\frac{2}{\alpha}}\ln\left(\rho^*\left(\tfrac{l+k}{2}\right)\right)+\left(\tfrac{\alpha}{4(\alpha+1)}\left(\tfrac{1}{2}\right)^{\frac{1}{\alpha}}-\tfrac{\alpha}{8(\alpha+2)}\left(\tfrac{1}{2}\right)^{\frac{2}{\alpha}}\right)\ln(f^*(k))\Bigg)\Bigg\}\\
&=\exp\Bigg\{\tfrac{k-l}{2}\Bigg(\ln(\rho^*(l))^{\left(\frac{2-\alpha^2-3\alpha}{8(\alpha+1)(\alpha+2)}+\frac{\alpha}{\alpha+1}\left(\frac{1}{2}\right)^{1+\frac{1}{\alpha}}-\frac{\alpha}{2(\alpha+2)}\left(\frac{1}{2}\right)^{1+\frac{2}{\alpha}}\right)}\\
&+\ln\left(f^*\left(\tfrac{l+k}{2}\right)\right)^{\frac{1}{2}\left(\frac{2-\alpha}{4(\alpha+2)}+\frac{\alpha}{\alpha+2}\left(\frac{1}{2}\right)^{1+\frac{2}{\alpha}}\right)}\Bigg)\Bigg\}\exp\Bigg\{\tfrac{k-l}{2}\Bigg(\ln\left(\rho^*\left(\tfrac{l+k}{2}\right)\right)^{\frac{1}{2}\left(\frac{2-\alpha}{4(\alpha+2)}+\frac{\alpha}{\alpha+2}\left(\frac{1}{2}\right)^{1+\frac{2}{\alpha}}\right)}\\
&+\ln(f^*(k))^{\left(\frac{2-\alpha^2-3\alpha}{8(\alpha+1)(\alpha+2)}+\frac{\alpha}{\alpha+1}\left(\frac{1}{2}\right)^{1+\frac{1}{\alpha}}-\frac{\alpha}{2(\alpha+2)}\left(\frac{1}{2}\right)^{1+\frac{2}{\alpha}}\right)}\Bigg)\Bigg\}\\
&=[(\rho^*(l))(f^*(k))]^{\frac{k-l}{2}\left(\frac{2-\alpha^2-3\alpha}{8(\alpha+1)(\alpha+2)}+\frac{\alpha}{\alpha+1}\left(\frac{1}{2}\right)^{1+\frac{1}{\alpha}}-\frac{\alpha}{2(\alpha+2)}\left(\frac{1}{2}\right)^{1+\frac{2}{\alpha}}\right)}\left(f^*\left(\tfrac{l+k}{2}\right)\right)^{\frac{k-l}{2}\left(\frac{2-\alpha}{4(\alpha+2)}+\frac{\alpha}{\alpha+2}\left(\frac{1}{2}\right)^{1+\frac{2}{\alpha}}\right)},
\end{aligned}
$$

where we have used

$$
\begin{aligned}
\int_0^{\left(\frac{1}{2}\right)^{\frac{1}{\alpha}}}\left(\tfrac{1}{4}-\tfrac{1}{2}\varsigma^{\alpha}\right)(1-\varsigma)d\varsigma&=\int_{1-\left(\frac{1}{2}\right)^{\frac{1}{\alpha}}}^{1}\left(\tfrac{1}{4}-\tfrac{1}{2}(1-\varsigma)^{\alpha}\right)\varsigma d\varsigma\\
&=\tfrac{\alpha}{4(\alpha+1)}\left(\tfrac{1}{2}\right)^{\frac{1}{\alpha}}-\tfrac{\alpha}{8(\alpha+2)}\left(\tfrac{1}{2}\right)^{\frac{2}{\alpha}},
\end{aligned}
\tag{2}
$$

$$
\begin{aligned}
\int_0^{\left(\frac{1}{2}\right)^{\frac{1}{\alpha}}}\left(\tfrac{1}{4}-\tfrac{1}{2}\varsigma^{\alpha}\right)\varsigma d\varsigma&=\int_{1-\left(\frac{2}{n+2}\right)^{\frac{1}{\alpha}}}^{1}\left(\tfrac{1}{4}-\tfrac{1}{2}(1-\varsigma)^{\alpha}\right)(1-\varsigma)d\varsigma\\
&=\tfrac{\alpha}{8(\alpha+2)}\left(\tfrac{1}{2}\right)^{\frac{2}{\alpha}},
\end{aligned}
\tag{3}
$$

$$
\begin{aligned}
\int_{\left(\frac{1}{2}\right)^{\frac{1}{\alpha}}}^{1}\left(\tfrac{1}{2}\varsigma^{\alpha}-\tfrac{1}{4}\right)(1-\varsigma)d\varsigma&=\int_0^{1-\left(\frac{1}{2}\right)^{\frac{1}{\alpha}}}\left(\tfrac{1}{2}(1-\varsigma)^{\alpha}-\tfrac{1}{4}\right)\varsigma d\varsigma\\
&=\tfrac{2-\alpha^2-3\alpha}{8(\alpha+1)(\alpha+2)}+\tfrac{\alpha}{4(\alpha+1)}\left(\tfrac{1}{2}\right)^{\frac{1}{\alpha}}-\tfrac{\alpha}{8(\alpha+2)}\left(\tfrac{1}{2}\right)^{\frac{2}{\alpha}},
\end{aligned}
\tag{4}
$$

$$
\begin{aligned}
\int_{\left(\frac{1}{2}\right)^{\frac{1}{\alpha}}}^{1}\left(\tfrac{1}{2}\varsigma^{\alpha}-\tfrac{1}{4}\right)\varsigma d\varsigma&=\int_0^{1-\left(\frac{1}{2}\right)^{\frac{1}{\alpha}}}\left(\tfrac{1}{2}(1-\varsigma)^{\alpha}-\tfrac{1}{4}\right)(1-\varsigma)d\varsigma\\
&=\tfrac{2-\alpha}{8(\alpha+2)}+\tfrac{\alpha}{8(\alpha+2)}\left(\tfrac{1}{2}\right)^{\frac{2}{\alpha}}.
\end{aligned}
\tag{5}
$$

The proof is completed. □

Corollary 2. *In Theorem 5, using the multiplicative convexity of* ρ^* *i.e.,* $f^*\left(\frac{l+k}{2}\right) \leq \sqrt{\rho^*(l)\rho^*(k)}$, *we obtain*

$$\left|\left((\rho(l))\left(\rho\left(\tfrac{l+k}{2}\right)\right)^2(\rho(k))\right)^{\frac{1}{4}}\left(\left({}_lI_*^\alpha\rho\right)\left(\tfrac{l+k}{2}\right)\left({}_*I_{\frac{l+k}{2}}^\alpha\rho\right)(k)\right)^{-\frac{2^{\alpha-1}\Gamma(\alpha+1)}{(k-l)^\alpha}}\right|$$

$$\leq[(\rho^*(l))(f^*(k))]^{\frac{k-l}{2}\left(\frac{1-\alpha}{4(\alpha+1)}+\frac{\alpha}{\alpha+1}\left(\frac{1}{2}\right)^{1+\frac{1}{\alpha}}\right)}.$$

Corollary 3. *In Theorem 5, if we take* $\alpha = 1$, *then we obtain*

$$\left|\left((\rho(l))\left(\rho\left(\tfrac{l+k}{2}\right)\right)^2(\rho(k))\right)^{\frac{1}{4}}\left(\int_l^k \rho(u)^{du}\right)^{\frac{1}{l-k}}\right|$$

$$\leq\left[(\rho^*(l))\left(f^*\left(\tfrac{l+k}{2}\right)\right)^2(f^*(k))\right]^{\frac{k-l}{32}}.$$

Corollary 4. *In Corollary 3, using the multiplicative convexity of* f^*, *we obtain*

$$\left|\left((\rho(l))\left(\rho\left(\tfrac{l+k}{2}\right)\right)^2(\rho(k))\right)^{\frac{1}{4}}\left(\int_l^k \rho(u)^{du}\right)^{\frac{1}{l-k}}\right| \leq [(\rho^*(l))(f^*(k))]^{\frac{k-l}{16}}.$$

3. Applications to Special Means

We shall consider the means for arbitrary real numbers l, k.
The Arithmetic mean: $A(l,k) = \frac{l+k}{2}$.
The Harmonic mean: $H(l,k) = \frac{2lk}{l+k}$
The logarithmic means: $L(l,k) = \frac{k-l}{\ln k - \ln l}$, $l,k > 0$ and $l \neq k$.
The p-Logarithmic mean: $L_p(l,k) = \left(\frac{k^{p+1}-l^{p+1}}{(p+1)(k-l)}\right)^{\frac{1}{p}}$, $l,k > 0, l \neq k$ and $p \in \mathbb{R}\setminus\{-1,0\}$.

Proposition 2. *Let* $l,k \in \mathbb{R}$ *with* $0 < l < k$. *Then, we have*

$$\left|e^{\frac{1}{4}\left(2H^{-1}(l,k)-A^2(l,k)\right)-L^{-1}(l,k)}\right| \leq e^{-\frac{3(k-l)}{8l^2}}.$$

Proof. The assertion follows from Corollary 1 applied to the function $\rho(\varsigma) = e^{\frac{1}{\varsigma}}$ whose $\rho^*(\varsigma) = e^{-\frac{1}{\varsigma^2}}$, $\mathcal{M} = e^{-\frac{1}{l^2}}$ and $\left(\int_l^k \rho(u)^{du}\right)^{\frac{1}{l-k}} = \exp\{-L^{-1}(l,k)\}$. □

Proposition 3. *Let* $l,k \in \mathbb{R}$ *with* $0 < l < k$. *Then, we have*

$$\left|e^{\frac{1}{4}\left(2A(l^p,k^p)+A^{2p}(l,k)\right)-L_p^p(l,k)}\right| \leq e^{p\frac{(k-l)\left(l^{p-1}+k^{p-1}\right)}{16}}.$$

Proof. The assertion follows from Corollary 3, applied to the function $\rho(\varsigma) = e^{\varsigma^p}$ with $p \geq 2$ whose $\rho^*(\varsigma) = e^{p\varsigma^{p-1}}$ and $\left(\int_l^k \rho(u)^{du}\right)^{\frac{1}{l-k}} = \exp\left\{-L_p^p(l,k)\right\}$. □

4. Conclusions

In this study, we have considered the fractional multiplicative Bullen-type integral inequalities, whose main results can be summarized as follows:

1. A new fractional identity for multiplicatively integrals is proved.
2. Some new fractional multiplicative Bullen-type inequalities for functions whose first multiplicative derivatives are multiplicative convex are established.
3. Some special cases are derived.
4. Applications of our findings are provided.

Author Contributions: Conceptualization, H.B., B.M. and A.M.; writing—original draft preparation, H.B., B.M. and A.M.; writing—review and editing, R.S., H.S., T.A. and E.E.A. All authors have read and agreed to the published version of the manuscript.

Funding: This research received no external funding.

Data Availability Statement: Not applicable.

Acknowledgments: This research has been funded by Scientific Research Deanship at University of Ha'il, Saudi Arabia through project number RG-21021.

Conflicts of Interest: The authors declare no conflict of interest.

References

1. Djenaoui, M.; Meftah, B. Milne type inequalities for differentiable *s*-convex functions. *Honam Math. J.* **2022**, *44*, 325–338.
2. Dragomir, S.S.; Agarwal, R.P. Two inequalities for differentiable mappings and applications to special means of real numbers and to trapezoidal formula. *Appl. Math. Lett.* **1998**, *11*, 91–95. [CrossRef]
3. Dragomir, S.S. Hermite-Hadamard type inequalities for *MN*-convex functions. *Aust. J. Math. Anal. Appl.* **2021**, *18*, 123.
4. Meftah, B. Ostrowski's inequality for functions whose first derivatives are *s*-preinvex in the second sense. *Khayyam J. Math.* **2017**, *3*, 61–80. [CrossRef]
5. Meftah, B. Fractional Hermite-Hadamard type integral inequalities for functions whose modulus of derivatives are co-ordinated log-preinvex. *Punjab Univ. J. Math. (Lahore)* **2019**, *51*, 21–37.
6. Meftah, B.; Merad, M.; Ouanas, N.; Souahi, A. Some new Hermite-Hadamard type inequalities for functions whose *n*th derivatives are convex. *Acta Comment. Univ. Tartu. Math.* **2019**, *23*, 163–178. [CrossRef]
7. Dahmani, Z. New classes of integral inequalities of fractional order. *Matematiche* **2014**, *69*, 237–247. [CrossRef]
8. Dragomir, S.S. Hermite-Hadamard type inequalities for generalized Riemann-Liouville fractional integrals of *h*-convex functions. *Math. Methods Appl. Sci.* **2021**, *44*, 2364–2380. [CrossRef]
9. Meftah, B.; Benssaad, M.; Kaidouchi, W.; Ghomrani, S. Conformable fractional Hermite-Hadamard type inequalities for product of two harmonic *s*-convex functions. *Proc. Amer. Math. Soc.* **2021**, *149*, 1495–1506. [CrossRef]
10. Set, E.; Butt, S.I.; Akdemir, A.O.; Karaoğlan, A.; Abdeljawad, T. New integral inequalities for differentiable convex functions via Atangana-Baleanu fractional integral operators. *Chaos Solitons Fractals* **2021**, *143*, 110554. . [CrossRef]
11. Ali, M.A.; Abbas, M.; Zhang, Z.; Sial, I.B.; Arif, R. On integral inequalities for product and quotient of two multiplicatively convex functions. *Asian Res. J. Math.* **2019**, *12*, 1–11. [CrossRef]
12. Ali, M.A.; Abbas, M.; Zafar, A.A. On some Hermite-Hadamard integral inequalities in multiplicative calculus. *J. Inequal. Spec. Funct.* **2019**, *10*, 111–122.
13. Budak, H.; Tunç, T.; Sarikaya, M.Z. Fractional Hermite-Hadamard-type inequalities for interval-valued functions. *Proc. Amer. Math. Soc.* **2020**, *148*, 705–718. [CrossRef]
14. Özcan, S. Some integral inequalities of Hermite-Hadamard type for multiplicatively preinvex functions. *AIMS Math.* **2020**, *5*, 1505–1518. [CrossRef]
15. Özcan, S. Hermite-Hadamard type inequalities for multiplicatively *h*-convex functions. *Konuralp J. Math.* **2020**, *8*, 158–164. [CrossRef]
16. Özcan, S. Hermite–Hadamard-type Inequalities for Multiplicatively h-Preinvex Functions. *Turkish J. Anal. Number Theory* **2021**, *9*, 65–70. [CrossRef]
17. Abdeljawad, T.; Grossman, M. On geometric fractional calculus. *J. Semigroup Theory Appl.* **2016**, *2016*, 2.
18. Budak, H.; Özçelik, K. On Hermite-Hadamard type inequalities for multiplicative fractional integrals. *Miskolc Math. Notes* **2020**, *21*, 91–99. [CrossRef]
19. Boruah, K.; Hazarika, B. Application of geometric calculus in numerical analysis and difference sequence spaces. *J. Math. Anal. Appl.* **2017**, *449*, 1265–1285. [CrossRef]
20. Çakır, Z. Spaces of continuous and bounded functions over the field of geometric complex numbers. *J. Inequal. Appl.* **2013**, *2013*, 363. [CrossRef]
21. Çakmak, A.; Başar, F. On the classical sequence spaces and non-Newtonian calculus. *J. Inequal. Appl* **2012**, 1–17.
22. Çakmak, A.F.; Başar, F. Certain spaces of functions over the field of non-Newtonian complex numbers. *Abstr. Appl. Anal.* **2014**, *2014*, 236124. [CrossRef]

23. Çakmak, A.F.; Başar, F. On line and double integrals in the non-Newtonian sense. In *Proceedings of the AIP Conference Proceedings*; American Institute of Physics: New York, NY, USA, 2014; Volume 1611, pp. 415–423.
24. Çakmak, A.F.; Başar, F. Some sequence spaces and matrix transformations in multiplicative sense. *TWMS J. Pure Appl. Math.* **2015**, *6*, 27–37.
25. Tekin, S.; Başar, F. Certain sequence spaces over the non-Newtonian complex field. *Abstr. Appl. Anal.* **2013**, *2013*, 739319. [CrossRef]
26. Türkmen, C.; Başar, F. Some basic results on the sets of sequences with geometric calculus. In Proceedings of the AIP Conference Proceedings. American Institute of Physics, Ft. Worth, TX, USA, 5–10 August 2012; Volume 1470, pp. 95–98.
27. Uzer, A. Multiplicative type complex calculus as an alternative to the classical calculus. *Comput. Math. Appl.* **2010**, *60*, 2725–2737. [CrossRef]
28. Uzer, A. Exact solution of conducting half plane problems in terms of a rapidly convergent series and an application of the multiplicative calculus. *Turk J. Elec. Eng. Comp. Sci.* **2015**, *23*, 1294–1311. [CrossRef]
29. Grossman, M.; Katz, R. *Non-Newtonian Calculus*; Lee Press: Rockport, MA, USA, 1972; p. viii+94.
30. Bashirov, A.E.; Kurpı nar, E.M.s.r.; Özyapıcı, A. Multiplicative calculus and its applications. *J. Math. Anal. Appl.* **2008**, *337*, 36–48. [CrossRef]
31. Başar, F. *Summability Theory and Its Applications*, 2nd ed.; CRC Press/Taylor & Francis Group: Boca Raton, FL, USA, 2022.
32. Mursaleen, M.; Başar, F. *Sequence Spaces: Topics in Modern Summability Theory*; CRC Press: Boca Raton, FL, USA, 2020.
33. Ali, M.A.; Budak, H.; Sarikaya, M.Z.; Zhang, Z. Ostrowski and Simpson type inequalities for multiplicative integrals. *Proyecciones* **2021**, *40*, 743–763. [CrossRef]

symmetry

Article

A Novel Three-Step Numerical Solver for Physical Models under Fractal Behavior

Muath Awadalla [1,*], Sania Qureshi [2,3,*], Amanullah Soomro [2] and Kinda Abuasbeh [1]

1 Department of Mathematics and Statistics, College of Science, King Faisal University, Hafuf 31982, Al Ahsa, Saudi Arabia; kabuasbeh@kfu.edu.sa
2 Department of Basic Sciences and Related Studies, Mehran University of Engineering & Technology, Jamshoro 6062, Pakistan; amanullah.soomro@faculty.muet.edu.pk
3 Department of Mathematics, Near East University TRNC, 99138 Mersin, Turkey
* Correspondence: mawadalla@kfu.edu.sa (M.A.); sania.qureshi@faculty.muet.edu.pk (S.Q.)

Abstract: In this paper, we suggest an iterative method for solving nonlinear equations that can be used in the physical sciences. This response is broken down into three parts. Our methodology is inspired by both the standard Taylor's method and an earlier Halley's method. Three evaluations of the given function and two evaluations of its first derivative are all that are needed for each iteration with this method. Because of this, the unique methodology can complete its goal far more quickly than many of the other methods currently in use. We looked at several additional practical research models, including population growth, blood rheology, and neurophysiology. Polynomiographs can be used to show the convergence zones of certain polynomials with complex values. Polynomiographs are produced as a byproduct, and these end up having an appealing look and being artistically engaging. The twisting of polynomiographs is symmetric when the parameters are all real and asymmetric when some of the parameters are imaginary.

Keywords: convergence analysis; fractals; efficiency index; symmetric twisting of polynomiographs; Newton's method

Citation: Awadalla, M.; Qureshi, S.; Soomro, A.; Abuasbeh, K. A Novel Three-Step Numerical Solver for Physical Models under Fractal Behavior. *Symmetry* **2023**, *15*, 330. https://doi.org/10.3390/sym15020330

Academic Editors: Hassen Fourati, Abdellatif Ben Makhlouf and Omar Naifar

Received: 3 January 2023
Revised: 16 January 2023
Accepted: 19 January 2023
Published: 24 January 2023

1. Introduction

Nonlinear equations of the form

$$\Phi(x) = 0,\ x \in \mathbb{R}, \tag{1}$$

are commonplace in many subfields of science and engineering. The current era of computer research, in which one must acquire maximal results in the shortest amount of time [1], necessitates the development of innovative and effective iterative approaches for the resolution of nonlinear equations and systems. The new approaches are anticipated to be higher-order convergent; however, the efficiency of time consumption and the reduction in the amount of computing information required are the primary concerns. In the field of computational sciences, one of the most crucial and topical challenges is to find a solution to the nonlinear equations that regulates the natural events that arise in real-world problems. There are a great number of non-linear equations for which it is extremely difficult to obtain exact solutions. When dealing with these kinds of problems, it is important to come up with plans for getting close to a solution.

The investigation of productive approaches to the solution of nonlinear equations and systems appears to be one of the most significant challenges facing the fields of mathematics and engineering sciences. The solution of nonlinear equations and systems is not only a distinct subfield of mathematical research, but it also has an impact on the progression of mathematical knowledge in other subfields. For instance, the standard discretization processes for nonlinear differential and integral equations [2,3] result in systems of nonlinear equations that need to be solved by iterative nonlinear solvers. These systems of equations can then be analyzed and interpreted. Numerous studies have focused their attention on nonlinear equation systems that demonstrate real-world applications. For instance, there are issues with blood flow and rheology in [4,5]. In [6,7], a multitude of difficult and well-known application issues of the system of nonlinear equations have been addressed. The systems of nonlinear ordinary and partial differential equations [8–12], when taken in steady-state, are converted to nonlinear algebraic equations and thereby require numerical solvers such as the one proposed herein. These problems involve chemical equilibrium, neurophysiology, combustion, economic modeling, and kinematics. There are some nonlinear equations and systems that do not have exact solutions. These equations and systems arise from the mathematical modeling of physical systems.

For this reason, mathematicians have concentrated their efforts on developing nonlinear methods that are robust. Researchers have focused their attention on developing strategies that involve an improvement in the order of convergence, the utilization of a smaller number of operations, and a reduction in the number of function and higher-order derivative evaluations per iteration to create reliable modifications of conventional methods. The Taylor's expansion, which was utilized for the Newton method, the Adomian decomposition, the Homotopy perturbation approach, the quadrature rules, and the variational iteration method are all examples of the many methods that can be employed to create novel nonlinear solvers [13–18]. The quadratic convergence of the second-order classical Newton method has led to it being given considerable weight. This is an old approach that can be used to solve nonlinear equations. Each repetition of the open-type Newton technique requires two evaluations: a functional evaluation and an evaluation of the first-order derivative to approximate the root. According to the hypothesis put forward by Kung and Traub [19], the order of convergence for the best iterative approach is $2^{\alpha-1}$, where α refers to the number of evaluations performed during each iteration. In this regard, the Newton technique might also be considered an ideal approach. Although the objective of current research studies has been to suggest improvements to the Newton method and its existing versions that are also optimal, it should be noted that approaches with a higher degree of convergence are also of significant practical value. Since the Kung and Traub argument is only a hypothesis, many studies have focused on improving the order in which techniques converge rather than on finding the optimal order. When ranking the different approaches, the efficiency index (ρ) is another factor that must be considered. When figuring out a technique's efficiency index, the number of evaluations that happen during each iteration (α) and the order (ω) in which the results converge are both taken into account. It may be noted that the efficiency index is computed as $\rho = \omega^{1/\alpha}$.

The following outline constitutes the framework of this study. In the next Section 2, you can find information on several existing schemes. After that comes the formulation of the suggested method (Section 3), followed by the determination of its order of convergence and the asymptotic error terms for both scalar and vector equations in Section 4. Some theoretical aspects are discussed, along with the suggested scheme's stability analysis and basins of attraction in Section 5. In Section 6, there is a presentation of some numerical experiments that involve applied problems. Section 7, which talks about the most important findings and where future research should go, is where the work comes to a close.

2. Existing Iterative Methods

In this section, we will conduct a quick overview of a few well-known numerical schemes that are widely used to identify approximate solutions to nonlinear models. These schemes can be found in a variety of mathematical fields. There is absolutely no analytical method that can produce correct findings when it comes to the solution of such nonlinear models. As a result, the utilization of numerical strategies is required of us.

When someone thinks of solving a nonlinear equation with a numerical scheme, the first scheme that comes to mind is the traditional Newton–Raphson, which has optimal second-order convergence. This is because the Newton–Raphson scheme has been around for a long time. In a nutshell, we denoted this method with the symbol CNM2 since it employs two function evaluations every iteration: one function evaluation and one first-order derivative evaluation. The outline of the plan is as follows:

$$x_{n+1} = x_n - \frac{\Phi(x_n)}{\Phi'(x_n)}, \quad n = 0,1,2,\ldots, \tag{2}$$

where $\Phi'(x_n) \neq 0$. In 2021, the authors of [20] proposed a new eight-order method with five function evaluations for solving non-linear equations. The method is shown below and abbreviated as VNM8:

$$\begin{aligned} y_n &= x_n - \frac{\Phi(x_n)}{\Phi'(x_n)}, \\ z_n &= y_n - \frac{\Phi(x_n)^2\Phi(y_n)}{\Phi(x_n)^2\Phi'(x_n) - 2\Phi(x_n)\Phi'(x_n)\Phi(y_n) + \Phi'(x_n)\Phi(y_n)^2}, \\ x_{n+1} &= z_n - \frac{\Phi(z_n)}{\Phi'(z_n)}, \quad n = 0,1,\ldots \end{aligned} \tag{3}$$

In 2010, Xia Wang and Liping Liu [21] presented a new eight-order iterative method that required four function evaluations per iteration for solving nonlinear equations. The method is shown below and abbreviated as PNM8:

$$\begin{aligned} y_n &= x_n - \frac{\Phi(x_n)}{\Phi'(x_n)}, \\ z_n &= x_n - \frac{\Phi(x_n)}{\Phi'(x_n)} \frac{4\Phi(x_n)^2 - 5\Phi(x_n)\Phi(y_n) - \Phi(y_n)^2}{4\Phi(x_n)^2 - 9\Phi(x_n)\Phi(y_n)}, \\ x_{n+1} &= z_n - \frac{\Phi(z_n)}{\Phi'(x_n)}\left[1 + 4\frac{\Phi(z_n)}{\Phi(x_n)}\right]\left[1 + \frac{8\Phi(y_n)}{4\Phi(x_n) - 11\Phi(y_n)} + \frac{\Phi(z_n)}{\Phi(y_n)}\right]. \end{aligned} \quad n = 0,1,\ldots \tag{4}$$

In 2020, Naseem, A. and et al. [22] presented a ninth-order iterative method that required six function evaluations per iteration for solving nonlinear equations. The method is shown below and abbreviated as PNM9:

$$\begin{aligned} y_n &= x_n - \frac{\Phi(x_n)}{\Phi'(x_n)} - \frac{\Phi^2(x_n)\Phi''(x_n)}{2\Phi'^3(x_n)}, \\ z_n &= y_n - \frac{\Phi(y_n)}{\Phi'(y_n)}, \\ x_{n+1} &= z_n - \frac{\Phi(z_n)}{\Phi'(y_n) - \beta\Phi(y_n)}, \quad n = 0,1,\ldots, \end{aligned} \tag{5}$$

where $\beta = 1$.

In 2011, Hu et al. [23] presented a three-step iterative method of order nine that required five function evaluations for solving nonlinear equations. The method is shown below and abbreviated as PNR9:

$$\begin{aligned} y_n &= x_n - \frac{\Phi(x_n)}{\Phi'(x_n)}, \\ z_n &= y_n - \left(1 + \left(\frac{\Phi(y_n)}{\Phi(x_n)}\right)^2\right)\left(\frac{\Phi(y_n)}{\Phi'(y_n)}\right), \\ x_{n+1} &= z_n - \left(1 + 2\left(\frac{\Phi(y_n)}{\Phi(x_n)}\right)^2 + 2\left(\frac{\Phi(z_n)}{\Phi(y_n)}\right)\right)\left(\frac{\Phi(z_n)}{\Phi'(y_n)}\right), \quad n = 0,1,\ldots \end{aligned} \tag{6}$$

In 2020, Cordero, A. et al. [17] presented some one-step variants of Halley's method with memory. One of such variants of order four that requires four function evaluations per iteration for solving nonlinear equations is shown below:

$$x_{n+1} = x_n - \frac{6\Phi(x_n)\Phi'(x_n)^2 - 3\Phi(x_n)^2\Phi''(x_n)}{6\Phi'(x_n)^3 - 6\Phi(x_n)\Phi'(x_n)\Phi''(x_n) + \Phi(x_n)^2\Phi'''(x_n)}, \quad n = 0, 1, \ldots \tag{7}$$

3. Proposed Iterative Technique

In this section, we have attempted to derive a nonlinear iterative method to solve nonlinear mathematical models of the type $\Phi(x) = 0$, which is supposed to be a differentiable real-valued function. Let us further assume that $\gamma \in D \subset \mathbb{R}$ is a simple zero of $\Phi(x) = 0$. Moreover, we assume that x_n be an initial estimate which is close enough to the exact root γ. After being motivated by a recent research study carried out in [24], the cubic approximation of $\Phi(x)$ via Taylor's expansion about the point x_n can be written as:

$$\Phi(x) = \Phi(x_n) + (x - x_n)\Phi'(x_n) + \frac{(x - x_n)^2}{2!}\Phi''(x_n) + \frac{(x - x_n)^3}{3!}\Phi'''(x_n). \tag{8}$$

Neglecting the quadratic term in (8) and assuming $\Phi(x_{n+1}) = 0$, we obtain the following relation:

$$\Phi(x_n) + (x_{n+1} - x_n)\Phi'(x_n) + \frac{(x_{n+1} - x_n)^3}{6}\Phi'''(x_n) = 0. \tag{9}$$

Solving the above equation for x_{n+1} only in the linear part, we get

$$x_{n+1} = x_n - \frac{\Phi(x_n)}{\Phi'(x_n)} - \frac{\Phi'''(x_n)}{6\Phi'(x_n)}(x_{n+1} - x_n)^3. \tag{10}$$

Substituting the variant of the Halley's method given in (7) for x_{n+1} only on the right hand side of (10), we obtain

$$x_{n+1} = x_n - \frac{\Phi(x_n)}{\Phi'(x_n)} - \frac{1}{48}\left[\frac{\Phi'''(x_n)\Phi(x_n)^3\Big(2\Phi'(x_n)^2 - \Phi(x_n)\Phi''(x_n)\Big)^3}{\Phi'(x_n)\Big(\Phi'(x_n)^3 - \Phi(x_n)\Phi'(x_n)\Phi''(x_n) + \frac{1}{6}\Phi(x_n)^2\Phi'''(x_n)\Big)^3}\right]. \tag{11}$$

To get rid of the third-order derivative in (11), we use the following identity taken from [24] as:

$$\Phi'''(x_n) = \frac{6\Phi(x_n)\Phi'(x_n)^3 - 3\Phi(x_n)^2\Phi'(x_n)\Phi''(x_n)}{2\Phi(x_n)^3}. \tag{12}$$

Substituting (12) into (11), we get

$$x_{n+1} = x_n - \frac{\Phi(x_n)}{\Phi'(x_n)} -$$

$$\left[\frac{4\Phi(x_n)^3\Big(\Phi(x_n)\Phi''(x_n) - 2\Phi(x_n)^2\Big)^3\Big(-\frac{1}{2}\Phi(x_n)^2\Phi'(x_n)\Phi''(x_n) + \Phi(x_n)\Phi'(x_n)^3\Big)}{\Phi'(x_n)\Big(-5\Phi(x_n)^2\Phi'(x_n)\Phi''(x_n) + 4\Phi'(x_n)^3\Phi(x_n) + 2\Phi(x_n) + 2\Phi(x_n)\Phi'(x_n)^3\Big)^3}\right]. \tag{13}$$

Using the classical Newton's method $z_n = x_n - \frac{\Phi(x_n)}{\Phi'(x_n)}$, the iterative method given in [25], and the proposed one-step iterative method given in (13), we obtain the final form of the proposed three-step method as follows:

$$z_n = x_n - \frac{\Phi(x_n)}{\Phi'(x_n)},$$
$$y_n = z_n - \left(1 + \frac{2\Phi(z_n)}{\Phi(x_n) - 2\Phi(z_n)}\right)\left(\frac{\Phi(z_n)}{\Phi'(x_n)}\right),$$
$$x_{n+1} = y_n - \frac{\Phi(y_n)}{\Phi'(y_n)} - \left[\frac{2\Phi(y_n)^3\left(\Phi(x_n)S - 2\Phi(x_n)^2\right)^3\left(\Phi(y_n)^2\Phi'(y_n)S - 2\Phi(y_n)\Phi'(y_n)^3\right)}{\Phi'(y_n)\left(5\Phi(x_n)^2\Phi'(x_n)S + 4\Phi'(x_n)^3\Phi(x_n) - 2\Phi(x_n)\Phi'(x_n)^3\right)^3}\right]. \tag{14}$$

$n = 0, 1, \ldots$

It may also be noted that the letter S in the third step of the above equations stands for the finite-difference approximation as $\frac{\Phi'(y_n) - \Phi'(x_n)}{y_n - x_n}$, which has been utilized for removing the second-order derivative $\Phi''(x_n)$. In addition, the method in (14) is abbreviated as PTNM, which stands for Proposed Taylor's expansion-based Numerical Method. The flowchart of the above eighth-order proposed three-step iterative method is shown in Figure 1. Moreover, the convergence order, the number of function evaluations per iteration, and the efficiency index of the proposed method are computed as 8, 5, and 1.5157, respectively. A comparative analysis of some methods under consideration based on these parameters is depicted in Figure 2.

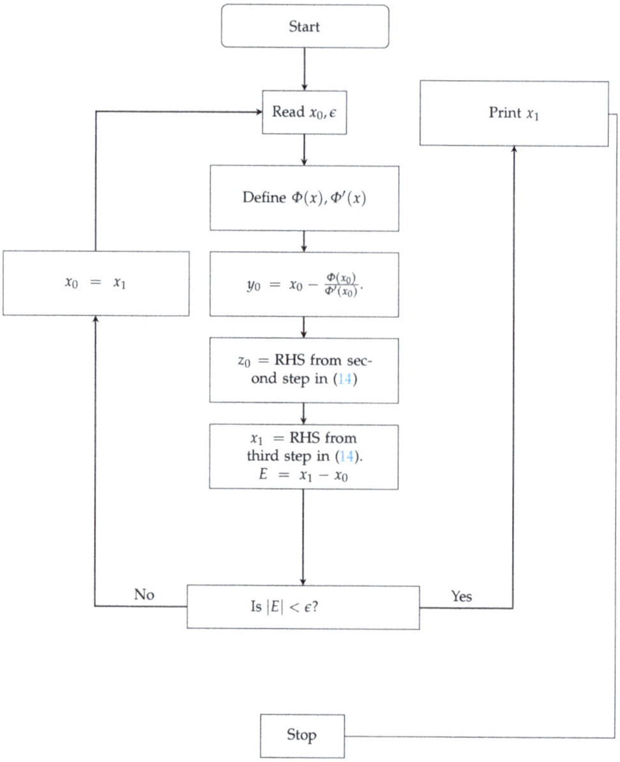

Figure 1. Flow chart of three-step eighth-order proposed method given in (14).

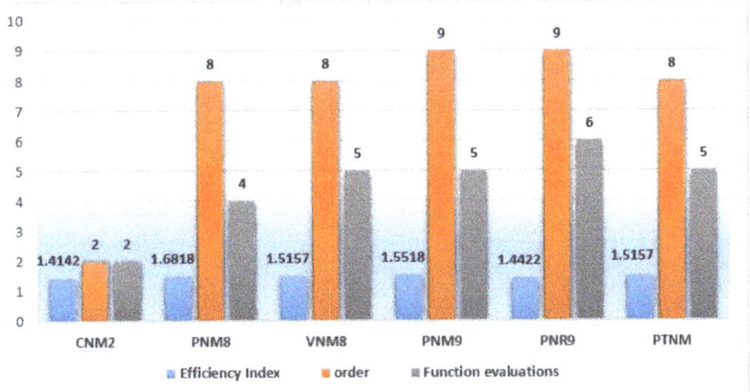

Figure 2. Comparison of the methods under consideration on the basis of efficiency index, order of convergence, and the number of function evaluations.

4. Convergence Analysis

When a convergence theorem for an iterative method claims convergence while presuming the existence of a solution x^* and a suitably chosen initial approximation close enough to x^*, it is referred to as a local convergence theorem. In contrast, a convergence theorem [26] pp. 575–600, does not presuppose the existence of any solution a prior but instead presupposes that specific criteria are true at the beginning point. A semilocal convergence theorem is what it is termed.

This section has been devoted to proving the convergence analysis based on the assumption of the existence of at least eighth-order derivatives of $\Phi(x) = 0$. The necessary order of convergence has been obtained through the application of Taylor's series expansion with a single variable. It is important to note that the convergence analysis is approached in a manner that is comparable to that of a large number of other previously published publications and that the primary interest in the creation of higher-order methods is of an intellectual nature. Even if higher-order algorithms are more difficult to understand, their efficiency can be assessed; this is why we have included the CPU time, which can be found in Section 6 of the article.

Theorem 1. *Suppose that $\gamma \in P$ is the exact root of a differentiable function $\Phi : P \subset \mathbb{R} \to \mathbb{R}$ for an open interval P. Then, the three-step proposed method given in* (14) *has eighth-order convergence and the asymptotic error term is determined to be:*

$$e_{n+1} = c_2^3(c_2^2 - c_3)e_n^8 + \mathcal{O}(e_n^9), \tag{15}$$

where $e_n = x_n - \gamma$, *and* $c_r = \dfrac{\Phi^{(r)}(\gamma)}{r!}$, $r = 1, 2, 3, \ldots$.

Expanding $\Phi(x_n)$ via series of Taylor about γ, we obtain

$$\Phi(x_n) = c_1 e_n + c_2 e_n^2 + c_3 e_n^3 + \mathcal{O}(e_n^4). \tag{16}$$

Expanding $\Phi'(x_n)$ via series of Taylor about γ, we obtain

$$\Phi'(x_n) = c_1 + 2c_2 e_n + 3c_3 e_n^2 + \mathcal{O}(e_n^4). \tag{17}$$

Applying Taylor series for function $\dfrac{1}{\Phi'(x_n)}$ about γ, we have

$$\frac{1}{\Phi'(x_n)} = \frac{-3\,c_1 c_3 e_n^2 + 4\,c_2^2 e_n^2 - 2\,c_1 c_2 e_n + c_1^2}{c_1^3} + \mathcal{O}(e_n^3). \tag{18}$$

Multiplying (16) and (18), we obtain:

$$\frac{\Phi(x_n)}{\Phi'(x_n)} = \frac{e_n(c_2e_n + c_1)(-3\,c_1c_3e_n^2 + 4\,c_2^2e_n^2 - 2\,c_1c_2e_n + c_1^2)}{c_1^3}. \tag{19}$$

Substituting (19) in the first-step of (14), we obtain

$$\hat{e}_n = \frac{e_n^2(3\,c_1c_2c_3e_n^2 - 4\,c_2^3e_n^2 + 3\,c_1^2c_3e_n - 2\,c_1c_2^2e_n + c_2c_1^2)}{c_1^3}, \tag{20}$$

where $\hat{e}_n = y_n - \gamma$. Using the Taylor's series for $\Phi(y_n)$ around γ, we obtain:

$$\Phi(y_n) = c_1\hat{e}_n + c_2\hat{e}_n^2 + \mathcal{O}(\hat{e}_n^3). \tag{21}$$

Expanding $\Phi'(y_n)$ via series of Taylor about γ, we obtain

$$\Phi'(y_n) = c_1 + 2c_2\hat{e}_n + 3c_3^2\hat{e}_n + \mathcal{O}(\hat{e}_n^4). \tag{22}$$

Applying Taylor series for function $\dfrac{1}{\Phi'(y_n)}$ about γ, we have

$$\frac{1}{\Phi'(y_n)} = \frac{-3\,c_1c_3\hat{e}_n^2 + 4\,c_2^2\hat{e}_n^2 - 2\,c_1c_2\hat{e}_n + c_1^2}{c_1^3} + \mathcal{O}(\hat{e}_n^3). \tag{23}$$

Multiplying (21) and (23), we obtain:

$$\frac{\Phi(y_n)}{\Phi'(y_n)} = \frac{\hat{e}_n(c_2\hat{e}_n + c_1)(-3\,c_1c_3\hat{e}_n^2 + 4\,c_2^2\hat{e}_n^2 - 2\,c_1c_2\hat{e}_n + c_1^2)}{c_1^3}, \tag{24}$$

where $\tilde{e}_n = z_n - \gamma$. Using the Taylor's series for $\Phi(z_n)$ around γ, we obtain

$$\Phi(z_n) = c_1\tilde{e}_n + c_2\tilde{e}_n^2 + \mathcal{O}(\tilde{e}_n^3). \tag{25}$$

Expanding the Taylor series using Equations (17) and (22), we obtain the expansion for the finite-difference quotient S as follows:

$$\begin{aligned} S &= 2c_2 + 3c_3e_n + (-2c_2(c_2^3 + c_2c_3) - 2c_2(-c_2^3 - c_2(4c_2^2 - 3c_3) - 2c_2(-4c_2^2 + 2c_3) \\ &+ 2c_2(2c_2^2 + 2c_3) - 2c_2(-c_2^2 + 2c_3)e_n^3 + \mathcal{O}(e_n^4). \end{aligned} \tag{26}$$

Using the Equations (16), (18) and (25) in the second step of the proposed method (14), we obtain

$$\hat{e} = (-c_2^3 - c_2(4c_2^2 - c_3) - 2c_2(-4c_2^2 + 2c_3) + 2c_2(-2c_2^2 + 2c_3) - 2c_2(-c_2^2 + 2c_3)e_n^4 + \mathcal{O}(e_n^5). \tag{27}$$

Using the Equations (16)–(18), (21)–(23) and (26) in the third step of the proposed method (14), we obtain

$$e_{n+1} = c_2^3(c_2^2 - c_3)e_n^8 + \mathcal{O}(e_n^9). \tag{28}$$

The aforementioned equation demonstrates that the suggested approach (14) converges to the eighth order.

5. Polynomiography: Fractal and Non-Fractal Images

Creative design and pattern development are two of the trickiest challenges in CAD. The process of creating patterns includes many different steps, such as analysis, creativity, and development. A designer must address all of these factors to create an engaging pattern that can be used in jewelry design, carpet design, tapestry design, etc. That is why it is so inspiring and practical to find novel ways to generate a wide range of fascinating patterns. Mathematical theory is one potential source for such procedures. As a type of mathematical object, polynomials have the potential to produce a wide range of interesting and lovely patterns. Polynomiography is commonly used to create patterns using polynomials.

Polynomiography is a method that combines mathematics with art to develop a new kind of visual art. The visuals that are produced are the outcome of an algorithmic visualization of repeated attempts to solve a polynomial problem. At the turn of the 21st century, Dr. Bahman Kalantari was the one who first articulated the meaning of this phrase [27]. Dr. Bahman Kalantari's research on polynomial root-finding served as the impetus for the development of the concepts of polynomiography. Polynomial root-finding is an age-old and time-honored field of study, but it never ceases to produce new insights with the advent of new generations of mathematicians and scientists. The term "polynomiography", which is a combination of the words "polynomial" and the suffix "graphy", was initially developed by Dr. Kalantari. A picture that was generated independently as a consequence of polynomiography is referred to as a "polynomiograph". "An iterative process for constructing two-dimensional colored drawings (polynomiographs) that represent polynomials", is how its definition reads.

Fractals are connected to polynomials via an area of mathematics known as polynomiography. Polynomiography is described as "the art and science of visualizing the zeros of complex polynomials utilizing fractal and non-fractal pictures formed using the mathematical convergence qualities of iteration functions. Instead of being a fractal image, a polynomiograph is a visual depiction of a polynomial's roots. Finding the roots of small to intermediate degree polynomials has received a lot of research, while big polynomials have received less attention since they are less frequently encountered in mathematical studies. The fractal patterns that were created were different and could be used in many different ways, such as in the textile and ceramics industries.

To generate polynomiographs over the complex plane $\mathbb{C}$ utilizing the computer program, we made use of a rectangle R along with the dimensions $[-2,2] \times [-2,2]$, and the maximum number of iterations of $N = 50$ with accuracy $\epsilon = 0.001$. This was done by taking some complex polynomials as shown in Equation (29). The areas of the image where the algorithm did not successfully converge have been assigned the color black. The pixel density of the produced visual representations is defined by the dividing of R; for example, if we partition the rectangle R into a grid of 2000, the plotting polynomiographs would have a higher resolution as a result. We used the following four complex polynomials including their roots (both real and complex) to show graphic elements in the complex plane:

$$
\begin{aligned}
&\Phi_1(z) = z^3 - 1,\ z_{1,2,3} = 1, -0.5 \pm 0.8660i,\\
&\Phi_2(z) = z^4 - 1,\ z_{1,\dots,4} = \pm 1, \pm i,\\
&\Phi_3(z) = z^5 + z,\ z_{1,\dots,5} = 0, 0.7071 \pm 0.7071i, -0.7071 \pm 0.7071i,\\
&\Phi_4(z) = 45z^{15} + 45z^8 - 1,\\
&z_{1,\dots,15} = 0.6187, -0.6243, -0.9967, 0.4367 \pm 0.4393i, -0.4423 \pm 0.4393i, -0.0028 \pm 0.6212i,\\
&\qquad 0.2257 \pm 0.975i, -0.6203 \pm 0.7819i, 0.9041 \pm 0.4339i.
\end{aligned}
\tag{29}
$$

The images obtained are shown in Figures 3–6 for the complex-valued polynomials given in Equation (29), respectively while considering the iterative techniques as follows:

(a) Classical Newton Method of second order convergence in (2).
(b) A method with eighth-order convergence in (3).
(c) A method with eighth-order convergence in (4).
(d) A method with ninth-order convergence in (5).
(e) A method with ninth-order convergence in (6).
(f) The proposed method with eighth-order convergence in (14).

It is worth to be noted that in each Figure, plot (a) shows the fractal behaviour of the classical Newton Method of second-order convergence, plot (b) shows the fractal behaviour of the eighth-order method given in (3), plot (c) shows the fractal behaviour of the eighth-order method given in (4), plot (d) shows the fractal behaviour of the ninth-order method given in (5), plot (e) shows the fractal behaviour of the ninth-order method given in (6), and plot (f) shows the fractal behaviour of the proposed eighth-order method given in (14). Darker regions in each plot indicate divergence regions that do not appear in fractal pictures generated using the suggested eighth-order approach. It demonstrates how, with a good first approximation, the approach can converge more quickly.

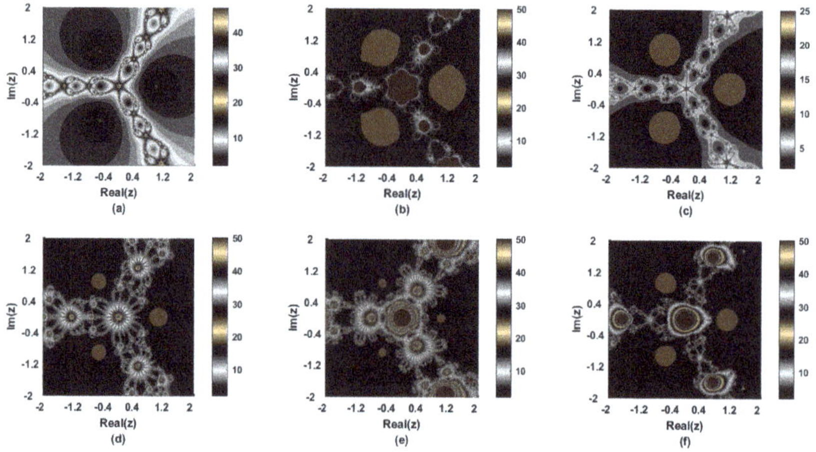

Figure 3. Polynomiographs for the complex function $\Phi_1(z) = z^3 - 1$ drawn with methods in (**a**) (2), (**b**) (3), (**c**) (4), (**d**) (5), (**e**) (6), and (**f**) (14).

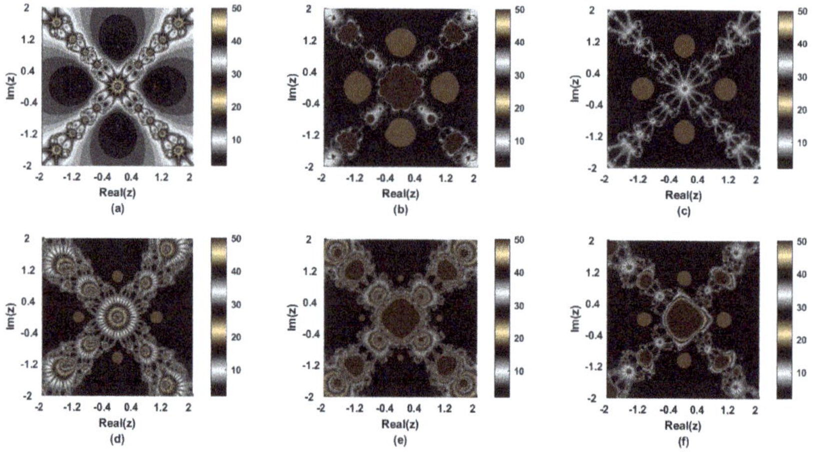

Figure 4. Polynomiographs for the complex function $\Phi_2(z) = z^4 - 1$ with methods in (**a**) (2), (**b**) (3), (**c**) (4), (**d**) (5), (**e**) (6), and (**f**) (14).

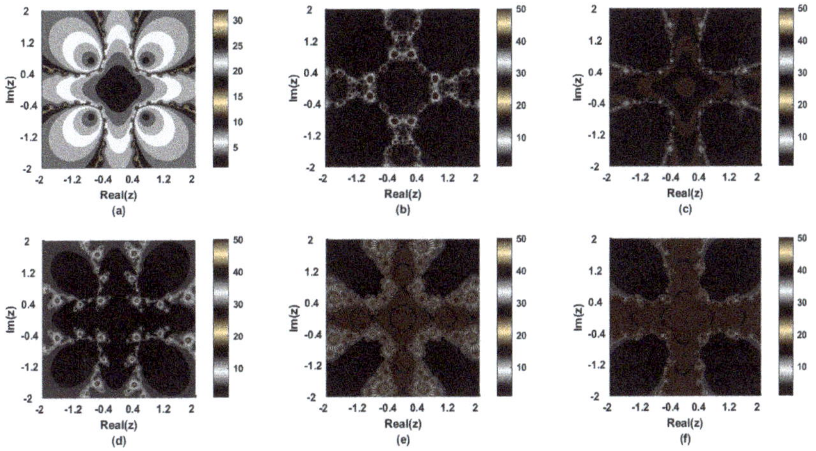

Figure 5. Polynomiographs for the complex function $\Phi_3(z) = z^5 + z$ with methods in (**a**) (2), (**b**) (3), (**c**) (4), (**d**) (5), (**e**) (6), and (**f**) (14).

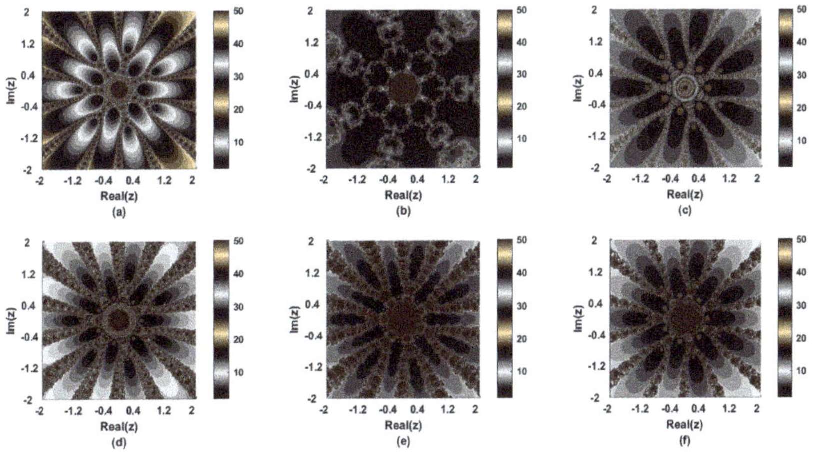

Figure 6. Polynomiographs for the complex function $\Phi_4(z) = 45z^{15} + 45z^8 - 1$ with methods in (**a**) (2), (**b**) (3), (**c**) (4), (**d**) (5), (**e**) (6), and (**f**) (14).

It may also be noted that the pseudo-code for the polynomiography via the proposed three-step method (14) is given in Algorithm 1. It has been explained how the different coloring is assigned in some regions and how the colormap works in case of different colors and shadings within the phase planes of several complex polynomials under consideration. Pseudo-code offers a way to find polynomiographs. The proposed three-step procedure is iterated in the algorithm for each point in the region $R \subset \mathbb{C}$ under consideration. We assume the resulting sequence converges to a root of p and stops iterating if the modulus of the difference between two successive points in the iteration process is less than the provided precision (ϵ). If the maximum number of cycles (N) is reached, then the generated sequence is assumed to not converge to a root of p. At the very end, we assigned a color to the location that was being considered by utilizing the colormap that was presented to us together with the iteration number when we exited the while loop.

Algorithm 1: Pseudo code for the polynomiograpghy with the proposed three-step method (14).

Input: $p \in \mathbb{C}[Z]$, $\deg(p) \geq 2$-polynomial, $R \subset \mathbb{C}$-area , N-the maximum number of iterations, ϵ-accuracy, colors$[0..N]$-colormap.
Output: Polynomiography for the polynomial p within the area R.

```
for z_0 ∈ R do
    n = 0
    while n ≤ N do
        z_{n+1} = proposed three-step method given in (14)
        if |z_{n+1} − z_n| < ϵ then
            break
        n = n + 1
    Show z_0 with colormap[n] color
```

6. Physical Models for Numerical Simulations

In this section, we will conduct some numerical simulations to highlight the performance of the suggested iterative technique with eighth-order convergence, which is given in the equation. There are many distinct kinds of nonlinear functions that are taken into account. Only applicable nonlinear models, such as those used in medical science, healthcare, population dynamics, and blood flow, are discussed in this article in order to provide the findings with more support and credibility. We utilize the stopping criterion $|\Phi(x_N)| \leq \varepsilon$ to determine when to end the number of iterations, where the tolerance is set to $\varepsilon = 10^{-300}$, and the needed accuracy is specified to be as high as 4000.

The following tabular representations of numerical results obtained from nonlinear practical models have been created, with each table containing an initial guess, a total number of function evaluations to achieve the tolerance, absolute error, the absolute value of the underlying function at the final approximated solution, and the amount of CPU time consumed by each approach, measured in seconds. The required numerical results were accomplished by using the program Mathematica 12.1 while operating under the Windows 10 operating system. The computer has an Intel(R) Core(TM) i7-1065G7 CPU running at a speed of 1.30 GHz. The installed memory was 24.0 GB.

Numerical Results and Discussions

Tables 1–3 show that the absolute error at the final iteration after simulating the chosen real models with the proposed method is the smallest of all the errors produced by other existing methods, as is the absolute functional value while consuming a reasonable amount of machine time measured in seconds. The number of function evaluations required by PTNM is appropriate for the first assumptions and, in some cases, it outperforms higher-order approaches. In addition, it is important to highlight that the suggested technique does not contain any aspects of divergence, in contrast to certain current methods, which do have such elements, as shown in Table 3. In conclusion, it has been demonstrated that the procedure described in (14) is applicable in a variety of real-life and physical circumstances where one must interact with a nonlinear phenomenon.

Problem 1. *We have taken a blood rheology nonlinear model from [4] as shown below:*

$$\Phi_1(x) = \frac{x^8}{441} - \frac{8x^5}{63} - 0.05714285714x^4 + \frac{16x^2}{9} - 3.624489796x + 0.36, \tag{30}$$

where x shows the plug flow of Caisson fluid flow. Caisson fluid is used to represent blood despite the fact that it is a non-Newtonian fluid. The Caisson fluid model hypothesizes that a simple fluid like water or blood will move through a tube in such a way that its central core will move as a plug with very little distortion and that a velocity gradient will develop along the tube's walls. It may be *noted that the blood comes under the category of Caisson fluid. The numerical simulations for the model* (30) *are presented in Table 1.*

Table 1. Comparison of several methods with the proposed method for the initial guess $x_0 = 5.5$ for the blood rheology model given in (30) having an approximate solution to be $x = 3.8200$.

Method	FE	$\varepsilon = \lvert x_N - x_e \rvert$	$\lvert \Phi_1(x_N) \rvert$	Time
CNM2	28	1.48×10^{-443}	2.70×10^{-884}	1.4100×10^{-1}
PNM8	20	1.49×10^{-492}	1.93×10^{-3933}	2.8200×10^{-1}
VNM8	30	1.46×10^{-1527}	1.00×10^{-3998}	1.8700×10^{-1}
PNM9	30	1.16×10^{-1895}	1.00×10^{-3998}	2.0400×10^{-1}
PNR9	30	4.34×10^{-316}	9.26×10^{-2835}	1.2500×10^{-1}
PTNM	30	3.00×10^{-2328}	1.00×10^{-3998}	3.1200×10^{-1}

Problem 2. *Law of Blood Flow* [5]*:*

$$\Phi_2(x) = \frac{P}{\eta l}\left(R^2 - x^2\right), \tag{31}$$

where $P = 4000, \eta = 0.027, R = 0.008,$ *and* $l = 2$ *are chosen for the simulations with* $x \in [0, R]$ *being the distance to be determined. With these parameters, the above model turns out to be*

$$R_f x^3 - 20p(1-x)^2 = 0, \tag{32}$$

where R_f stands for the radius of the fiber, p shows the specific hydraulic permeability, and $x \in [0, 1]$ is the porosity of the medium. If we assume $R_f = 100 \times 10^{-9}$ and $p = 0.4655$, we obtain the following third-degree polynomial:

$$\Phi_2(x) = -100 \times 10^{-9}x^3 + 9.3100x^2 - 18.6200x + 9.3100. \tag{33}$$

The numerical simulations for the model (33) are presented in Table 2.

Table 2. Comparison of several methods with the proposed method with the initial guess $x_0 = 2$ for the blood rheology model given in (33) having an approximate solution to be $x = 1$.

Method	FE	$\varepsilon = \lvert x_N - x_e \rvert$	$\lvert \Phi_2(x_N) \rvert$	Time
CNM2	46	5.56×10^{-382}	2.88×10^{-762}	1.0900×10^{-1}
PNM8	36	6.41×10^{-882}	3.00×10^{-3999}	1.2500×10^{-1}
VNM8	45	7.42×10^{-857}	7.00×10^{-3999}	7.8000×10^{-2}
PNM9	45	4.04×10^{-845}	2.00×10^{-3999}	7.8000×10^{-2}
PNR9	54	2.39×10^{-1231}	6.00×10^{-3999}	6.2000×10^{-2}
PTNM	45	1.09×10^{-1514}	7.00×10^{-3999}	1.4100×10^{-1}

Problem 3. *In the study of population dynamics, one of the models that is utilized most commonly is the mathematical representation of population growth, referred to as the population growth (PG) model. Using a first-order ordinary differential equation, the following expression can be used to describe the model:*

$$PG'(t) = \kappa PG(t) + \nu, \tag{34}$$

where $PG(t)$ *stands for the population growth at time* t, κ *shows the constant birth rate while* ν *is for constant immigration rate. The above linear ordinary differential equation has the following closed-form solution:*

$$PG(t) = PG_0 \exp(\kappa t) + \frac{\nu}{\kappa}\left(\exp(\kappa t) - 1\right), \tag{35}$$

where PG_0 is the population at $t = 0$ (initial population). In one particular piece of research, the problem is stated as follows: Let us say that a particular community had a starting population of 1,000,000 people, that 435,000 people immigrated into the community in the first year, and that the town had a total population of 1,564,000 people by the conclusion of the first year. Determine the rate of births (κ) in this population. Using the initial condition and values of the other parameters given as stated, the birth rate κ can be determined with the help of the following nonlinear equation which is the closed-form solution of the model (34) *after applying the stated situation:*

$$\Phi_3(x) = 1564 - 10^3 \exp(x) - \frac{435}{x}\Big(\exp(x) - 1\Big) = 0, \tag{36}$$

where $x = \kappa$ is the required birth rate. The numerical simulations for the model (36) *are presented in Table 3.*

Table 3. Comparison of several methods with the proposed method with the initial guess $x_0 = 5.5$ for the population growth model given in (36) having an approximate solution to be $x = 1.01 \times 10^{-1}$.

Method	FE	$\varepsilon = \lvert x_N - x_e \rvert$	$\lvert \Phi_3(x_N) \rvert$	Time
CNM2	32	4.29×10^{551}	1.16×10^{1098}	2.0300×10^1
PNM8	diverge	-	-	-
VNM8	30	5.37×10^{480}	8.23×10^{3834}	2.5000×10^1
PNM9	30	1.90×10^{508}	3.10×10^{3996}	1.5600×10^1
PNR9	diverge	-	-	-
PTNM	30	2.82×10^{995}	6.00×10^{3997}	2.0300×10^1

7. Concluding Remarks and Future Directions

The success of this investigation hinges on the development of a brand-new iterative strategy that converges at the eighth-order level after three iterations. The projected computational order of convergence is consistent with the theoretical demonstration of convergence provided by Taylor's series expansion for nonlinear equations. Thus, the PTNM method can be applied to problems with either a single nonlinear equation or a system of such equations. In addition, dynamical aspects of PTNM can be investigated using basins of attraction, which, when applied to complex-valued functions, yield aesthetically pleasing phase plane diagrams. This demonstrates the method's validity for making first estimates that are statistically very close to the underlying nonlinear model. We also get polynomiographs that are both aesthetically pleasing and intellectually stimulating. The real values of parameters have a symmetrical effect, but the imaginary values of parameters distort polynomials. In the end, some medically-relevant nonlinear equations were applied to PTNM and other well-known optimum and non-optimal techniques in the sense of King–Traub. It has been found that PTNM yields better results than other methods in the vast majority of cases. This is notably the case concerning the N-th iteration threshold for achieving the target precision, error, and functional value. It is also worth noting that the proposed method will always converge, regardless of how close to or far from the starting guess the approximate solution is. Remembering this is essential. The PTNM algorithm converges to the eighth order and is an iterative method that can compete with other algorithms. It can be used to find solutions to nonlinear systems and equations.

As far as we can tell, high-order approaches are solely of interest in the academic community since very precise approximations to answers are not needed in most real-world contexts. However, these methods are rather complex and do not significantly increase productivity relative to simpler alternatives. The method proposed here is also one of the memory-free techniques discussed in the article. In the case of nonlinear systems, it also requires the evaluation of additional Jacobian matrices, which increases the computing burden. To reduce the computational complexity of the current method, we plan to make a change in future research by proposing a finite-difference approximation for the first-order derivative. We will also look more closely at the proposed method to see if it has semilocal convergence and better visualization with a variety of convergence tests including distance and non-distance conditions over different types of metrics. In addition, the three-step numerical solver that was proposed can be extended to the concept of fractional calculus [28], in which the traditional derivative is replaced by the fractional Riemann–Liouville or Caputo derivatives. This allows the solver to be used to solve problems involving fractional calculus.

Author Contributions: The authors confirm their contribution to the paper as follows: M.A.: Conceptualization, Formal Analysis, Funding acquisition, and Writing—original draft; S.Q.: Writing-original draft, Investigation, Methodology, and Software; A.S.: Formal analysis, Software, Validation, and Visualization; K.A.: Supervision, Writing—review and editing. All authors have read and agreed to the published version of the manuscript.

Funding: This work was supported by the Deanship of Scientific Research, Vice Presidency for Graduate Studies and Scientific Research, King Faisal University, Saudi Arabia [Grant No. 2381].

Data Availability Statement: Not applicable.

Conflicts of Interest: The authors declare no conflict of interest.

References

1. Abro, H.A.; Shaikh, M.M. A new time-efficient and convergent nonlinear solver. *Appl. Math. Comput.* **2019**, *355*, 516–536. [CrossRef]
2. Cordero, A.; Gómez, E.; Torregrosa, J.R. Efficient high-order iterative methods for solving nonlinear systems and their application on heat conduction problems. *Complexity* **2017**, *2017*, 6457532. [CrossRef]
3. Babajee, D.K.R. On the kung-traub conjecture for iterative methods for solving quadratic equations. *Algorithms* **2015**, *9*, 1. [CrossRef]
4. Shams, M.; Rafiq, N.; Kausar, N.; Mir, N.A.; Alalyani, A. Computer Oriented Numerical Scheme for Solving Engineering Problems. *Comput. Syst. Sci. Eng.* **2022**, *42*, 689–701. [CrossRef]
5. Sutera, S.P.; Skalak, R. The history of Poiseuille's law. *Annu. Rev. Fluid Mech.* **1993**, *25*, 1–20. [CrossRef]
6. Grosan, C.; Abraham, A. A new approach for solving nonlinear equations systems. *IEEE Trans. Syst. Man -Cybern.-Part Syst. Humans* **2008**, *38*, 698–714. [CrossRef]
7. Tassaddiq, A.; Qureshi, S.; Soomro, A.; Hincal, E.; Baleanu, D.; Shaikh, A.A. A New Three-Step Root-Finding Numerical Method and Its Fractal Global Behavior. *Fractal Fract.* **2021**, *5*, 204. [CrossRef]
8. Villaverde, A.F. Symmetries in Dynamic Models of Biological Systems: Mathematical Foundations and Implications. *Symmetry* **2022**, *14*, 467. [CrossRef]
9. Shokri, A. The symmetric two-step P-stable nonlinear predictor-corrector methods for the numerical solution of second order initial value problems. *Bull. Iran. Math. Soc.* **2015**, *41*, 201–215.
10. Pankov, P.S.; Zheentaeva, Z.K.; Shirinov, T. Asymptotic Reduction of Solution Space Dimension For Dynamical Systems. *TWMS J. Pure Appl. Math.* **2021**, *12*, 243–253.
11. Shokri, A. The multistep multiderivative methods for the numerical solution of first order initial value problems. *TWMS J. Pure Appl. Math.* **2016**, *7*, 88–97.
12. Musaev, H.K. The Cauchy problem for degenerate parabolic convolution equation. *TWMS J. Pure Appl. Math.* **2021**, *12*, 278–288.
13. Ramos, H.; Monteiro, M.T.T. A new approach based on the Newton's method to solve systems of nonlinear equations. *J. Comput. Appl. Math.* **2017**, *318*, 3–13. [CrossRef]
14. Noor, M.A. Some iterative methods for solving nonlinear equations using homotopy perturbation method. *Int. J. Comput. Math.* **2010**, *87*, 141–149. [CrossRef]
15. Ramos, H.; Vigo-Aguiar, J. The application of Newton's method in vector form for solving nonlinear scalar equations where the classical Newton method fails. *J. Comput. Appl. Math.* **2015**, *275*, 228–237. [CrossRef]
16. Sana, G.; Noor, M.A.; Noor, K.I. Some multistep iterative methods for nonlinear equation using quadrature rule. *Int. J. Anal. Appl.* **2020**, *18*, 920–938.
17. Cordero, A.; Ramos, H.; Torregrosa, J.R. Some variants of Halley's method with memory and their applications for solving several chemical problems. *J. Math. Chem.* **2020**, *58*, 751–774. [CrossRef]
18. Muhammad, A.N.; Farooq, A.S.; Khalida, I.N.; Eisa, A.S. Variational iteration technique for finding multiple roots of nonlinear equations. *Sci. Res. Essays* **2011**, *6*, 1344–1350.
19. Kung, H.T.; Traub, J.F. Optimal order of one-point and multipoint iteration. *J. ACM (JACM)* **1974**, *21*, 643–651. [CrossRef]
20. Kong-ied, B. Two new eighth and twelfth order iterative methods for solving nonlinear equations. *Int. J. Math. Comput. Sci.* **2021**, *16*, 333–344.
21. Wang, X.; Liu, L. New eighth-order iterative methods for solving nonlinear equations. *J. Comput. Appl. Math.* **2010**, *234*, 1611–1620. [CrossRef]

22. Naseem, A.; Rehman, M.A.; Abdeljawad, T. Higher-order root-finding algorithms and their basins of attraction. *J. Math.* **2020**, *2020*, 5070363. [CrossRef]
23. Hu, Z.; Guocai, L.; Tian, L. An iterative method with ninth-order convergence for solving nonlinear equations. *Int. J. Contemp. Math. Sci.* **2011**, *6*, 17–23.
24. Sharma, E.; Panday, S. Efficient sixth order iterative method free from higher derivatives for nonlinear equations. *J. Math. Comput. Sci.* **2022**, *12*, 46.
25. Kou, J.; Li, Y.; Wang, X. Some variants of Ostrowski's method with seventh-order convergence. *J. Comput. Appl. Math.* **2007**, *209*, 153–159. [CrossRef]
26. Yamamoto, T. Historical developments in convergence analysis for Newton's and Newton-like methods. *J. Comput. Appl. Math.* **2000**, *124*, 1–23. [CrossRef]
27. Kalantari, B. Polynomiography: From the fundamental theorem of Algebra to art. *Leonardo* **2005**, *38*, 233–238. [CrossRef]
28. Gdawiec, K.; Kotarski, W.; Lisowska, A. Visual analysis of the Newton's method with fractional order derivatives. *Symmetry* **2019**, *11*, 1143. [CrossRef]

MDPI
St. Alban-Anlage 66
4052 Basel
Switzerland
www.mdpi.com

Symmetry Editorial Office
E-mail: symmetry@mdpi.com
www.mdpi.com/journal/symmetry

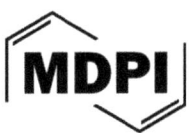

www.ingramcontent.com/pod-product-compliance
Lightning Source LLC
LaVergne TN
LVHW070420100526
838202LV00014B/1496
* 9 7 8 3 7 2 5 8 0 8 2 0 5 *